ACCA

Strategic Business Leader (SBL)

Practice & Revision Kit

For exams in September 2021, December 2021, March 2022 and June 2022

Fourth edition 2021

ISBN 9781 5097 3814 4
(previous ISBN 9781 5097 8394 6)
e-ISBN 9781 5097 3901 1

British Library Cataloguing-in-Publication Data
A catalogue record for this book
is available from the British Library

Published by

BPP Learning Media Ltd
BPP House, Aldine Place
142–144 Uxbridge Road
London W12 8AA

www.bpp.com/learningmedia

Printed in the United Kingdom

Your learning materials, published by BPP
Learning Media Ltd, are printed on paper
obtained from traceable, sustainable sources.

We are grateful to the Association of Chartered
Certified Accountants for permission to
reproduce past examination questions. The
suggested solutions in the Practice & Revision Kit
have been prepared by BPP Learning Media Ltd,
except where otherwise stated.

Contents

Review form

BPP LEARNING MEDIA

Finding questions

Question index

The headings in this checklist/index indicate the main question topic, but questions often cover several different topics.

The Strategic Business Leader examination was introduced in September 2018. There are four exam sittings per year, but ACCA only publish two exams' worth of questions per year. These releases are compiled from questions selected from the preceding sessions. These compilation exams are included as Mock Exam 3 and Mock Exam 4 in the index below.

Questions have been arranged in different sections to allow for a gradual build up towards exam readiness. Section 1 encourages knowledge development, with questions covering specific syllabus areas. Section 2 ensures that the professional skills relevant to the Strategic Business Leader examination are developed. Section 3 builds exam success skills and acts as a bridge to the mock examinations which reflect the style and structure of the real examination.

		Marks	Approximate time allocation (Mins)	Page number	
				Question	Answer

Section 4: Mock exams

Mock exam 1

Mock exam 2 (ACCA Specimen exam 2)

Mock exam 3 (ACCA March 2020 exam)

Mock exam 4 (ACCA September/December 2020 exam)

Mock exam 5

Topic index

Listed below are key SBL syllabus topics and the numbers of the questions in this Kit covering those topics. We have also included a reference to the relevant Chapter of the BPP SBL Workbook, the companion to the BPP SBL Practice and Revision Kit, in case you wish to revise the information on the topic you have covered. Questions from Mock Exams are indicated with the prefix 'ME...'; so, for example, ME2(1) signifies task 1 in Mock Exam 2.

If you need to concentrate your practice and revision on certain topics, you will find this index useful.

Syllabus topic	Question numbers	Workbook chapter
Agency (agency relationships)	6, 50(3), ME2(1a)	2
Artificial Intelligence	23	11
Audit committee	4(b), 26(b)	3
Auditor independence	25	8
Big data and data analytics	ME1(2b)	11
Board structures	10(a), ME2(1b), ME3(3c)	3
Budgeting (importance of budgeting)	38	10
Business cases	33, 48, ME5(2a), ME2(5)	15
Competitive strategies (generic strategies)	13(b), ME5(1b)	6
Corporate citizenship; corporate social responsibility	8(a), 39, 51(2), 52(1b), ME1(4b)	2
Corporate governance	7,9(a), 10, ME3(3c)	3
Cyber security	23, ME5(2b)	11
Disruptive technology	49(3b)	12
E-marketing	21, ME3(2b)	12
Environmental analysis (PEST analysis)	12, 13(a), 50(1a), 51(1a)	4
Ethical decisions	ME1(4a)	9
Ethics	4(a), 5, 45, ME3(1c) ME5(4)	9
Financial analysis	42, 52(a)	10
Financial decision making	27, 43, 47, 51(3)	10
Implementing change (POPIT: four view model)	30(b), ME5(3b)	13
Industry analysis (Porter's five forces)	12, 13(a), 14, 50(1b)	4
Internal audit	26(a)	8
Internal control problems; deficiencies	40, 49(4), ME2(2b)	8
Internal control systems	22, 24, ME3(1c)	8

BPP
LEARNING
MEDIA

Syllabus topic	Question numbers	Workbook chapter
Integrated reporting (<IR>)	8(b), 35, 52(1c), ME5(5),	2
Investment appraisal	ME3(2a)	10
Leadership	1, 37, ME3(1a)	1
Organisational change; strategic change	30, 31, 41, ME3(1a)	14
Organisational culture	2	1
Outsourcing	29, 52(3)	10
National competitive advantage (Porter's 'diamond')	36	4
Performance excellence (Baldrige model)	50(4)	13
Performance management	28, 49(1), ME1(1a), ME2(2a)	10
Portfolio management	17, ME1(1a)	6
Public sector governance	11, ME2(1b)	3
Process redesign	32	14
Project management	33, 48, ME5(2a), ME2(5b)	15
Responsible leadership	3(a)	9
Risk assessment; risk management	18, 19, 20, 34, 44, 49(3a), 51(1c), 52(2), ME5(3a), ME2(4), ME3(1a)	7
Stakeholder analysis; stakeholder management	3, 46, 51(1b), ME5(3a), ME1(3)	2
Strategic management process	1(a)	1
Strategic options	17, 49(2), 50(2), ME1(1b), ME3(1c)	6
SWOT analysis	16, ME5(a)	5
Systems security and control (IT controls)	22	11
Talent management (human resource management)	ME2(3)	13
Value chain	15	5

The exam

Computer-based exams

With effect from the March 2020 sitting, ACCA commenced the launch of computer-based exams (CBEs) for this exam with the aim of rolling out into all markets internationally over a short period. BPP materials have been designed to support you, whichever exam format you are studying towards. For more information on these changes, when they will be implemented and to access Specimen Exams in the Strategic Professional CBE software, please visit the ACCA website. Please note that the Strategic Professional CBE software has more functionality than you will have seen in the Applied Skills exams.

www.accaglobal.com/gb/en/student/exam-support-resources/strategic-professional-specimen-exams-cbe.html

Approach to examining the syllabus

Strategic Business Leader is ACCA's **case study examination** and is examined as a **closed book exam** of four hours, including reading, planning and reflection time which can be used flexibly within the examination. There is no pre-seen information and all exam-related materials, including case information, exhibits and questions, are available within the examination. The pass mark is **50%**.

Strategic Business Leader is an exam based on one main business scenario which involves candidates completing a **series of tasks** many of which will integrate syllabus areas in a single requirement.

All questions are compulsory and each examination will contain a total of **80 technical marks** and **20 professional skills** marks. Each exam will therefore assess both technical skills and the professional skills. Whilst marks will be awarded for the relevant technical points that candidates make, up to 20% of the total marks within each exam will be allocated to these professional skills, as determined by the task requirements.

The broad structure of each case will give candidates information about an organisation from a range of sources, such as the following:

- Interviews with staff
- Survey results
- Board or organisation reports
- Press articles/website extracts
- Organisation reports and <IR> extracts
- Emails
- Memos
- Spreadsheets
- Pictures
- Figures
- Tables

The Strategic Business Leader exam will **contain several task requirements** relating to the same scenario information. The number of task requirements can vary in each exam. The questions will usually assess and link a range of subject areas across the syllabus. The exam will require students to demonstrate high-level capabilities to understand the complexities of the case and evaluate, relate and apply the information in the case study to the task requirements. The examining team have stressed the importance of reading the case in detail, taking notes as appropriate and getting a feel for what the issues are. The exam will have a **global focus** and the scenarios will not name real countries or geographical regions.

Format of the exam

1 compulsory case scenario, containing a number of tasks
Application of syllabus (technical) knowledge marks   80
ACCA professional skills marks   20
                                                                                           100

Time allowed: 4 hours.

The **pass mark** is 50%.

Analysis of past exams

The table below shows when each element of the syllabus has been examined in respect of the most recent exams. We have also included a reference to the relevant Chapter of the BPP SBL Workbook, the companion to the BPP SBL Practice and Revision Kit, in case you wish to revise the information on the topic covered.

Workbook chapter		Specimen exam 2	Sept 2018	Dec 2018	Mar/Jun 2019	Sept/Dec 2019	Mar 2020
1	Agency (agency relationships)	Q1(a)					
12	Big data and data analytics		Q4		Q4(a)		
3	Board structures	Q1(b)					Q3(c)
15	Business cases	Q5(a)					
13	Change management						Q3(b)
3	Corporate governance		Q3(c)				Q3(c)
11	Cybersecurity			Q3(b)			
12	Disruptive technology			Q3(a)			
4	Environmental analysis (PEST analysis)				Q1(a)		
9	Ethics		Q3(a)		Q2(b)		Q1(c)
12	E-marketing						Q2(b)
10	Financial analysis			Q1			Q2(a)
10	Financial decision making				Q4(b)		
2	Integrated reporting			Q2(b)	Q5(a)(b)		
8	Internal control problems and deficiencies	Q2(b)	Q3(b)		Q3		
1	Leadership						Q3(a)
4	National competitive advantage (Porter's diamond)			Q1(a)	Q2(a)		

Workbook chapter		Specimen exam 2	Sept 2018	Dec 2018	Mar/Jun 2019	Sept/Dec 2019	Mar 2020
10	Performance management	Q2(a)					
15	Project management	Q5(b)	Q2				
7	Risk assessment and risk management	Q4			Q1(b)		Q1(a)
2	Stakeholder analysis and stakeholder management			Q2(a)			
6	Strategic options			Q1(b)	Q2(b)		Q1(b)
13	Talent management	Q3					

IMPORTANT!

The table above gives a broad idea of how frequently major topics in the syllabus are examined. It should **not be used to question spot** and predict, for example, that a certain topic will not be examined because it has been examined in the last two sittings. The examining team's reports indicate that they are well aware that some students try to question spot. The examining team avoid predictable patterns and may, for example, examine the same topic two sittings in a row. Equally, just because a topic has not been examined for a long time, this does not necessarily mean it will be examined in the next exam!

Syllabus and Study Guide

The complete SBL syllabus and study guide can be found by visiting the exam resource finder on the ACCA website.

Helping you with your revision

BPP Learning Media – ACCA Approved Content Provider

As an ACCA **Approved Content Provider**, BPP Learning Media gives you the **opportunity** to use revision materials reviewed by the ACCA examining team. By incorporating the examining team's comments and suggestions regarding the depth and breadth of syllabus coverage, the BPP Learning Media Practice & Revision Kit provides excellent, **ACCA-approved** support for your revision.

These materials are reviewed by the ACCA examining team. The objective of the review is to ensure that the material properly covers the syllabus and study guide outcomes, used by the examining team in setting the exams, in the appropriate breadth and depth. The review does not ensure that every eventuality, combination or application of examinable topics is addressed by the ACCA Approved Content. Nor does the review comprise a detailed technical check of the content as the Approved Content Provider has its own quality assurance processes in place in this respect.

BPP Learning Media do everything possible to ensure the material is accurate and up to date when sending to print. In the event that any errors are found after the print date, they are uploaded to the following website: www.bpp.com/learningmedia/Errata.

The structure of this Practice & Revision Kit

As we explain in the next section ('Essential skill areas to be successful in the Strategic Business Leader exam'), this exam requires you to demonstrate your competence in three key areas:

- Technical knowledge
- Professional skills
- Exam technique

The structure of this Kit reflects these areas.

The questions in Section 1 focus on testing your technical knowledge of topics from across the syllabus.

Section 2 focuses on professional skills.

Sections 3 and 4 then give you the chance to apply your knowledge and professional skills to the type of case study materials you will face in the exam. The questions in Section 3 are worth 50 marks, and so give you the chance to develop your exam technique, before tackling the five full-length (100 mark) mock exams in Section 4.

Question practice

Question practice under timed conditions is absolutely vital. We strongly advise you to create a revision study plan which focuses on question practice. This is so that you can get used to the pressures of answering exam questions in limited time, develop proficiency in the specific SBL skills and the Exam success skills. Ideally, you should aim to cover all questions in this Kit, and very importantly, all five mock exams.

Selecting questions

To help you plan your revision, we have provided a full **topic index** which maps the questions to topics in the syllabus (see page vii).

Making the most of question practice

At BPP Learning Media we realise that you need more than just questions and model answers to get the most from your question practice.

- Our **Top tips** included for certain questions provide essential advice on tackling questions, presenting answers and the key points that answers need to include.

- We include **marking guides** to show you what the examining team rewards (including professional skills as well as **technical knowledge**).

- We include **comments from the examining team** to show you where students struggled or performed well in the actual exam.

- We include some **annotated solutions** showing the difference between 'good' and 'bad' answers.

- We include short **debriefs** at the end of the Section 3 questions, to encourage you to identify areas where you can improve your performance.

Attempting mock exams

There are five mock exams to provide multiple opportunities for question practice. These will develop your knowledge, ACCA professional skills and exam success skills further, and they use case overviews and exhibits which simulate the Strategic Business Leader exam. Practising mock exams will help with coping with the pressures of the exam day.

Please note, Mock Exam 2 is the ACCA specimen 2 Strategic Business Leader exam; this was written and provided by the ACCA Strategic Business Leader examining team to give students an understanding of the format, content and structure of the exam, and to provide a clear expectation of types of scenarios and questions which will arise. Mock exam 3 and 4 are the real March 2020 and September/December 2020 exams respectively.

We recommend that you attempt all the mock exams in this Kit with at least three of these being attempted under timed exam conditions so you can assess how you are using your time and, if necessary, you can take action to improve your time management before the exam day.

A word about question timings

When attempting the Strategic Business Leader exam, ACCA recommends that candidates should be looking to spend at least 40 minutes reading, planning and interpreting the exhibit information and task requirements.

When taking the 40 minutes reading time into account, candidates should spend approximately 2.5 minutes attempting each mark. The 2.5 minutes per mark is based on the fact that the total exam is 240 minutes (4 hours) in duration, which when the 40 minutes reading/planning time is deducted gives 200 minutes. As candidates can earn the 20 professional skills marks by the virtue of attempting the 80 technical marks in the exam, the remaining 200 minutes can be divided by the 80 technical marks to give 2.5 minutes per mark.

It is important to remember however that the 40 minutes reading and planning time is only a guide and should be interpreted as such. Regardless of how their time is used, candidates still have 4 hours to attempt the exam.

The approximate timings given in the Question index in this Kit in respect of Sections 1 and 2 are based on 2 minutes per mark. The reason for this is that the question scenarios and exhibits are not as detailed as they would be in a full SBL exam, and therefore require less reading and planning. The approximate timings in respect of the questions in Section 3 have been based on half the length of the full SBL exam, ie 120 minutes as these mini mocks are worth 50 marks each.

Essential skill areas

There are five essential skills areas which students must develop to be successful in the ACCA Strategic Business Leader exam. ACCA is clear that students cannot expect to be successful in this exam without demonstrating competence in **all** three areas.

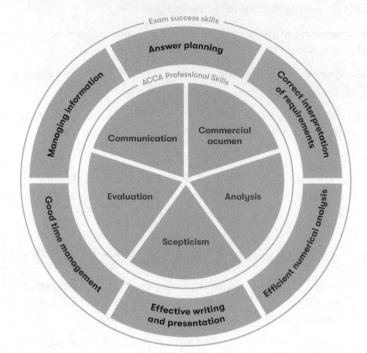

Technical knowledge

The syllabus for Strategic Business Leader is extensive and provides a vital foundation for students to demonstrate their abilities as accountants, strategic advisers and business leaders. Eighty marks are assigned to application of syllabus knowledge to specific business scenarios. Knowledge is developed through reading or listening to your tutor, reading the business press and, importantly, by practising new cases and completing question tasks as a principal focus of your studies.

Use of theories of models in the Strategic Business Leader Exam

Strategic Business Leader exam set by the ACCA Examining Team is a practical exam and unlike other exams will not test individual theories or models in isolation or require for these theories or models to be quoted in answers to exam questions. However, understanding the technical theories, models and knowledge is essential as these provide a framework for students to help them approach the practical tasks that they will need to complete in the Strategic Business Leader exam.

The use of models in the exam will be a judgement made by students and is part of the ACCA Professional Skills for analysis and evaluation. Students are advised to use models which they judge to be relevant for a particular task or scenario to generate the scope of their answer. There is not a prescriptive list of theories and models, however, the BPP Workbook focuses on the most relevant models which it considers to be most relevant to the syllabus and to aid students in being successful in Strategic Business Leader.

ACCA professional skills

Following consultation with employers, ACCA has identified that qualified accountants need to possess a range of key professional skills. In the Strategic Business Leader exam, 20 marks are assigned to the demonstration of ACCA professional skills. ACCA has defined five main 'professional' skills which will be assessed in the Strategic Business Leader exam and all five will be assessed at each exam sitting. Each ACCA professional skill has been clearly defined by ACCA, along with three further defined aspects, as follows:

ACCA professional skill: Definition	Three aspects of each ACCA professional skill
1. Communication To express yourself clearly and convincingly through an appropriate medium, while being sensitive to the needs of the intended audience.	Inform Persuade Clarify
2. Commercial acumen To show awareness of the wider business and external factors affecting business, and use commercially sound judgement and insight to resolve issues and exploit opportunities.	Demonstrate awareness Use judgement Show insight
3. Analysis To thoroughly investigate and research information from a variety of sources, and logically process it with a view to considering it for recommending appropriate action.	Investigate Enquire Consider
4. Scepticism To probe, question and challenge information and views presented to you, to fully understand business issues and to establish facts objectively, based on ethical and professional values.	Probe Question Challenge
5. Evaluation To assess situations, proposals and arguments in a balanced way, using professional and ethical judgement to predict future outcomes and consequences as a basis for sound decision making.	Assess Estimate Appraise

Throughout the BPP Practice & Revision Kit for the Strategic Business Leader exam, you will find a range of activities and questions which will help to develop your ACCA professional skills alongside your technical knowledge.

But what do the skills mean, and what do you have to do to demonstrate them?

The following section includes the defined aspects of each of the five ACCA professional skills and then makes suggestions to help you demonstrate them in your Strategic Business Leader studies.

Communication

Communication means to express yourself clearly and convincingly through the appropriate medium while being sensitive to the needs of the intended audience, and understanding both the context and situation. In the exam, this means to present written and numerical work in the required format with a professional tone and use of language and avoiding ambiguity, unnecessary explanations and repetition. **Communication** is assessed over three aspects: inform, persuade and clarify.

Inform concisely, objectively and unambiguously, while being sensitive to cultural differences, using appropriate media and technology.

Advice on demonstrating 'inform':

- Think about who you are addressing in your answer: eg if you are writing an extract for a board report, you need to focus on strategic issues, without going into lots of operational details

- Adopt an appropriate tone to suit your audience: eg formal vs informal; use language they will understand; will they understand jargon and technical terms, or should you avoid them?

- Use an appropriate style of communication: eg written vs graphic; slides; diagrams

- If the task requirement asks you to use a specific format, eg bullet point slides, you **must** present your answer in that format

Persuade using compelling and logical arguments demonstrating the ability to counter-argue when appropriate.

Advice on demonstrating 'persuade':

- Support your arguments with facts
- Explain why you think a course of action is suitable/unsuitable
- Use 'justifying' words, such as 'because': 'I recommend you do this **because**...'

Clarify and simplify complex issues to convey relevant information in a way that adopts an appropriate tone and is easily understood by the intended audience.

Advice on demonstrating 'clarify':

- Focus on key points, and avoid unnecessary detail
- Use succinct sentences
- Use headings to break down information into clearly identifiable sections
- Present your arguments in a logical order

Commercial acumen

Commercial acumen means showing awareness of the wider business and external factors affecting business, using commercially sound judgement and insight to resolve issues and exploit opportunities. In the exam, this includes considering the change in revenue, cost or profit as an important driver in decision making and avoid suggesting solutions which will have a negative financial impact, unless it is to address a wider sustainability issue, such as ethics and governance. **Commercial acumen** is assessed over three aspects: demonstrate awareness, use judgement and show insight, as follows.

Demonstrate awareness of organisational and wider external factors affecting the work of an individual or a team in contributing to the wider organisational objectives.

Advice on demonstrating awareness:

- Think about the specific context of a scenario and identify how this affects a decision

- Make sure recommendations are appropriate – and practical – to the context of the scenario

> **Use judgement** to identify key issues in determining how to address or resolve problems and in proposing and recommending the solutions to be implemented.

Advice on demonstrating judgement:

- Prioritise key points

- Only make points which are relevant to the scenario and which help to address/resolve the issue at hand

- Make sure recommendations resolve issues and/or exploit opportunities

- Avoid making points which are not supported by facts; recommendations need to be justified

> **Show insight** and perception in understanding work-related and organisational issues, including the management of conflict, demonstrating acumen in arriving at appropriate solutions or outcomes.

Advice on demonstrating insight:

- Make sure recommendations are appropriate and practical in the context of the scenario, eg are they feasible? Will they be acceptable to key stakeholders?

- Make sure recommendations address key issues identified in the scenario

- Make sure decisions and strategies are appropriate for an organisation, rather than just making generic points

- Ask yourself: will the points you are making help the organisation make a decision which successfully addresses the issues it is facing?

Analysis

Analysis means to thoroughly investigate and research information from a variety of sources and logically process it with a view to considering it for recommending appropriate action. In the exam, this means to produce relevant analysis from the information provided in the case overview and exhibits which creates new evidence in response to the task requirement and a basis for action you are recommending an organisation should take. **Analysis** is assessed over three aspects: investigate, enquire and consider, as follows.

> **Investigate** relevant information from a wide range of sources, using a variety of analytical techniques to establish the reasons and causes of problems, or to identify opportunities or solutions.

Advice on demonstrating 'investigation':

- Don't simply repeat points from the scenario; explain why they are significant and/or what their implications are

- Identify relevant data from different places within a scenario, rather than only including the most obvious (or most easily accessible) points

- Give reasons **why** a problem has happened, rather than simply stating the problem

> **Enquire** of individuals or analyse appropriate data sources to obtain suitable evidence to corroborate or dispute existing beliefs or opinions and come to appropriate conclusions.

Advice on demonstrating 'enquire':

- The reference to suitable evidence is key here: data and evidence must be relevant to the points you are making

- Does data in the scenario support arguments made elsewhere; for example, are revenue figures or profit margins consistent with how well someone says an organisation is performing?

> **Consider** information, evidence and findings carefully, reflecting on their implications and how they can be used in the interests of the department and wider organisational goals.

Advice on demonstrating 'consider':

- Make use of the information in the scenario in order to recommend appropriate actions
- How does the evidence in the scenario affect the suitability of a potential course of action?

Scepticism

Scepticism means to probe, question and challenge information and views presented, to fully understand business issues and to establish facts objectively, based on ethical and professional values. In the exam this means to be aware of the quality, scope, source and age of the information provided, as well as the purpose for which the information was produced and by whom; where necessary suggest information used for analysis, evaluation and decision making is updated, improved or extended through questioning or appropriate challenge. This is so the best possible information is applied before a final decision is made. **Scepticism** is assessed over three aspects: probe, question and challenge, as follows.

> **Probe** deeply into the underlying reasons for issues and problems, beyond what is immediately apparent from the usual sources and opinions available.

Advice on demonstrating 'probe':

- Don't automatically accept that the initial reason given to explain an issue is correct. (Is the explanation somebody gives you consistent with other evidence? Does the explanation properly explain the issue or problem you are addressing?) For example, if a management accountant is offering an explanation of a variance between actual figures and budget, are you satisfied their explanation properly explains the variance?

- Draw together information from different sources, rather than just including the most obvious (or most easily accessible) points. Does information from one source support, or contradict information from another source?

> **Question** facts, opinions and assertions, by seeking justifications and obtaining sufficient evidence for their support and acceptance.

Advice on demonstrating 'question':

- Scrutinise any assumptions being made: are they reasonable; can they be supported by the evidence available? (Don't simply accept everything you are told.)

- Question the motive or rationale behind facts or statements. For example, does the person making a statement have a vested interest in one decision being taken in preference to another? If so, how reliable, or objective, is their evidence likely to be?

- Identify additional information or evidence which may be required to corroborate facts or assertions being made

> **Challenge** information presented or decisions made, where this is clearly justified, in a professional and courteous manner; in the wider professional, ethical, organisational, or public interest.

Advice on demonstrating 'challenge':

- Highlight the weaknesses of, or problems with, information presented or potential decisions

- Use evidence to support your challenge, and justify challenges you make, perhaps by demonstrating evidence of wider reading

- Identify potential alternative interpretations of information or alternative courses of action, to reinforce your challenge

- Your 'challenge' should focus specifically on the problems with a decision, rather than trying to evaluate problems against benefits

Evaluation

Evaluation means to carefully assess situations, proposals and arguments in a balanced way, using professional and ethical judgement to predict future outcomes and consequences as a basis for sound decision making. In the exam this means ensuring possible courses of action are examined from different perspectives and, where relevant, clearly stating reasonable assumptions and including points both for and against. Conclusions and recommendations made should be consistent with the most persuasive factors presented which provide logical argument for the course of action suggested. **Evaluation** is assessed over three aspects: assess, estimate and appraise, as follows.

> **Assess** and use professional judgement when considering organisational issues, problems, or when making decisions, taking into account the implications of such decisions on the organisation and those affected.

Advice on demonstrating 'assessment':

- Consider the potential importance and urgency of a problem when deciding a suitable response to the problem

- Determine the potential advantages and disadvantages associated with a decision

- Determine the potential impact of a decision on key stakeholders, and how they are likely to react to it

> **Estimate** trends or make reasoned forecasts of the implications of external and internal factors on the organisation, or of the outcomes of decisions available to the organisation.

Advice on demonstrating 'estimate':

- Present sensible, justified estimates and forecasts; for example, in assessing the impact which a change in the business environment could have on an organisation's performance

- Identify the possible impact that different decisions could have on an organisation's performance

> **Appraise** facts, opinions and findings objectively, with a view to balancing the costs, risks, benefits and opportunities, before making or recommending solutions or decisions.

Advice on demonstrating 'appraise':

- Present the arguments for and against a proposed strategy, so that an informed decision can be made about whether or not to pursue that strategy

- Make decisions, or recommend solutions, which are appropriate to the circumstances, on the basis of a balanced appraisal of advantages and disadvantages. For example, do the potential benefits from a strategy justify the costs involved?

In summary

Overall, remember that technical knowledge is not intended to be learned for the purpose of being either described or explained as part of these skills – it is designed to be demonstrated appropriately as part of these skills through synthesis and application.

Exam success skills

Being successful in Strategic Business Leader and passing the examination requires more than applying syllabus knowledge and demonstrating the ACCA professional skills areas; it also requires the development of excellent exam technique through significant question practice and responding to feedback from practice assessments and mock exams.

Below are definitions for the **six** key skill areas which BPP considers vital for Strategic Business Leader exam success.

Exam success skill 1

Case scenario: Managing Information

This requires swift understanding of the case overview and exhibits, as well as the identification, prioritisation and assimilation of key facts, events, information and data (which is both unstructured and non-sequential) and to comprehend its usefulness, relevance and importance in responding to task requirements.

Advice on developing this skill

Using the scenario is essential to answer the task requirement and to pass the question. Most of what you write should relate directly to the scenario provided and be guided by the information given, with the remainder being based on the skills and experience you bring into the exam. The skill is using your judgement to determine what information is important to best answer each task requirement. If there is a lot of information and detail given on a specific issue then it is likely to play a big part in at least one of the tasks.

The ACCA Strategic Business Leader examining team advise that at least 40 minutes is spent during the exam on reading, highlighting and interpreting the information provided in the case overview and exhibits and considering each task requirement. The advised 40-minute reading time is a useful benchmark to check you are committing sufficient time to managing the information provided.

Computer-based exam

In a computer-based exam (CBE) the **highlighter tool** provided in the toolbar at the top of the screen offers a range of colours:

This allows you to choose **different colours to answer different aspects of a question**. For example, if a question asked you to evaluate the pros and cons of an issue then you could choose a different colour for highlighting pros and cons within the relevant section of the exhibits.

The **strikethrough function** allows you to delete areas of a question that you have dealt with - this can be useful in managing information if you are dealing with numerical questions because it can allow you to ensure that all numerical elements have been accounted for in your answer (although this is of limited use in the SBL exam).

The CBE also allows you to **resize windows** by clicking on the bottom right-hand corner of the window as highlighted in the following section:

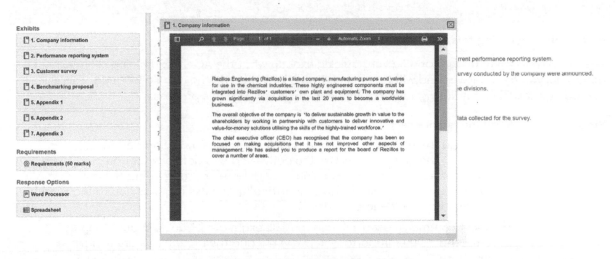

This functionality allows you to **display a number of windows at the same time**, so this could allow you to review:

- the question requirements and the exhibit relating to that requirement at the same time, or

- the window containing your answer (whether a word processing or spreadsheet document) and the exhibit relating to that requirement at the same time.

Exam success skill 2

Correct Interpretation of the Requirements

The active verb used often dictates the approach that written answers should take (eg 'explain', 'discuss', 'evaluate'). It is important you identify and use the verb to define your approach. The **Correct Interpretation of the Requirements** skill is correctly producing only what is being asked for by a task requirement. Anything not required will not earn marks.

Advice on developing this skill

There is a real skill to understanding very quickly exactly what the ACCA examining team expect you to deliver in an answer and within the time frame indicated by the mark allocation. This skill can be developed by analysing task requirements and applying this process:

Step 1	Read the requirement
	Firstly, read the task requirement a couple of times slowly and carefully, highlighting the active verbs. Use the active verbs to define what you plan to do. For example, **discuss** means consider and debate or argue about the pros and cons of an issue (remember also that **critically discuss** requires you to focus on the key points that you need to criticise).

The most commonly used verbs in the SBL exam are Discuss, Evaluate and Recommend. Other important active verbs and their meanings are explained below:

Verb	Meaning
Advise	This requires you to provide someone with useful information, or to **tell them what you think they should do** based on a consideration of the issues presented in a scenario.
Analyse	This requires you to **break an issue into separate parts** and discuss, examine, or interpret each part. This may require you to **give reasons for** the current situation or what has happened.
Assess	This requires you to **judge the importance** or estimate the nature, quality or significance of an issue. To do this, consider the strengths and weaknesses or significance of the issue under discussion.
Discuss	This will require you to consider and debate/argue about the **pros and cons** of an issue.
Evaluate	This will require you to present a **'balanced' discussion** of an issue looking both the positive and negative issues. Where numbers feature in a question, an evaluation will require you to use the numbers provided to create a value from which **a judgement** can be made.
Explain	This involves making an idea clear and could require you to, for example, show logically how a concept is developed or to **give the reason for** an event.
Recommend	If you are asked to **'recommend'** then you are expected to **use details presented in the exhibits** to create a logical and **justified** course of action.

Step 2   Read the scenario

By reading the task requirement first, you will have an idea of what you are looking out for as you read through the case overview and exhibits. This is a great time saver and means you don't end up having to read the whole question in full twice – it also allows you to identify which elements of the exhibit materials are most relevant for each task. As you go through the scenario you should be using the highlighting function in a CBE, or annotating key information on your question paper, which you think will play a key role in answering the specific task requirements.

Step 3   Read the requirement again

Read the task requirement again to remind yourself of the exact wording before starting your written answer. This will capture any misinterpretation of the task requirements or any missed tasks entirely. This should become a habit in your approach and, with repeated practice, you will find the focus, relevance and depth of your answer plan will improve.

Exam success skill 3

Answer planning: Priorities, Structure and Logic

This skill requires the drafting of the key aspects of an answer which accurately and completely responds to the task requirement in the format specified **before** calculations and a written answer are attempted. A good answer plan is one which prioritises what can be covered in the time available, is in a logical order and focuses on points that are likely to score the best marks in the exam.

Advice on developing this skill

This skill can be developed by applying the following process:

Step 1 **Identify key words and mark allocation**

The answer plan should directly relate to the key words in the task requirement and the mark allocation. Use the active verb to start your answer plan and use the mark allocation to determine the time available to complete the answer and guide the number of points to discuss.

Step 2 **Plan any calculations**

The creation of numerical analysis must be essential to completing the task requirement, otherwise it should not be included. Plan the scope of numerical work to avoid unnecessary complexity and to ensure analysis is relevant to the task.

In a **computer-based exam** you can begin to **input data needed for your calculations onto a spreadsheet**, allowing the spreadsheet functionality to perform computations for you.

Step 3 **Take time to plan in sufficient detail**

The plan should go into sufficient detail to enable you to move smoothly into writing out a good answer without having to stop too often and rethink. To do this requires creative thinking up front, but beware of writing too much at the planning stage; the plan is essential for a good answer, but is not an answer in itself.

Good answer planning has been shown as a valuable contributor to good time management and efficient answer writing – using the marks on offer can help with this time allocation as well.

In a **computer-based exam** you can use the copy and paste functions to **copy the task requirements to the beginning of your answer**. This will ensure that your answer plan addresses all parts of the task requirements.

You can also **copy the task requirements to the main body of your answer.** This will allow you to create sub-headings for your answer, again ensuring that your answer addresses all parts of the task requirements.

Copying and pasting simply involves highlighting the relevant information and either right clicking to access the copy and paste functions, or alternatively using Ctrl+C to copy and Ctrl+V to paste.

Exam success skill 4

Efficient Numerical Analysis

This skill is to maximise the marks awarded by making the process of arriving at the answer clear to the marker. This is achieved by laying out an answer in such a way that still scores well, even if a few errors occur along the way, with explanations of key figures or assumptions. It is vital that you do not lose marks purely because the marker cannot follow what you have done.

Advice on developing this skill

This skill can be developed by applying the following process:

Step 1   Use a standard proforma working where relevant

If answers can be laid out in a standard proforma or table then always plan to do so. This will help the marker to understand your working and locate the marks easily. It will also help you to work through the figures in a methodical and time-efficient way. In a **computer-based exam** you can use the spreadsheet functionality to present proformas and workings.

Step 2   Show your workings

Keep your workings as clear and simple as possible and ensure they are cross-referenced to the main part of your answer. Where it helps, provide brief narrative explanations to help the marker understand the steps in the calculation. This means that if a mistake is made then you do not lose any subsequent marks for follow-on calculations.

Step 3   Keep moving!

It is important to remember that, in an exam situation, it is difficult to get every number 100% correct. The key is therefore ensuring you do not spend too long on any single calculation. If you are struggling with a solution then make a sensible assumption, state it and move on.

Efficient numerical analysis means providing sufficient numerical evidence to support your written arguments, evaluations, conclusions and recommendations, so the creation of numerical work must not replace effective writing and presentation.

In a **computer-based exam** it is important to show the marker where numbers have come from ie it is not sensible to perform the calculations on a calculator and then manually transfer the result to the spreadsheet. For example, in the following spreadsheet the marker can see that the highlighted calculation in cell G14 is calculated as (D14-E14/E14) because this is what is recorded in the spreadsheet cell (as shown in the first row).

| G14 | ▼ | : | × ✓ ƒx | =(D14-E14)/E14 | | | | |

	A	B	C	D	E	F	G	H
1	Analysis of current performance							
2								
3	Zilber's financial performance in 20X7 compared to 20X6 can be summarised as follows							
4								
5				20X7	20X7			
6				Actual	Budget	Variance		
7				$'000	$'000	$'000	%	
8								
9			Revenue from rooms	131,072	129,347	1,725	1.3%	
10			Discounts	(24,904)	(19,402)	(5,502)	-28.4%	
11			Other revenue	34,079	33,630	449	1.3%	
12			Total revenue	140,247	143,575	(3,328)	-2.3%	
13			Operating costs	(117,964)	(115,764)	(2,200)	1.9%	
14			Operating profit	22,282	27,811	(5,529)	-19.9%	
15								
16								
17								

If the workings are visible in the cell as shown here then there is **less need to show detailed workings.** It will still sometimes be helpful to produce workings because they can reduce the likelihood of errors being made (if calculations are complex).

In a **computer-based exam** you can also use useful spreadsheet short-cuts to improve the efficiency of numerical analysis. For SBL useful short-cuts include the ability to calculate totals and averages and also to calculate NPV, IRR and MIRR.

Further details are given in the following table.

Function	Guidance & examples
Sum	=SUM(A1:A10) adds all the numbers in spreadsheet cells A1 to A10.
Average	=AVERAGE(A1:A10) averages the numbers in spreadsheet cells A1 to A10.
NPV	Net present value is based on future cash flows, assuming that the first cash flow is in one year's time. For example, if the future cash flows from a project arise over 5 years and need to be discounted at 10% then the formula could be as follows: =NPV(0.1, B10:F10) This would give the present value of cash flows from time period 1-5. The cash outflow in time 0 would then need to be deducted to calculate the net present value.
IRR	Internal rate of return is based on future cash flows, looking at cash outflows and inflows in each year of a project, from time 0 onwards. For example, to identify the internal rate of return of the future cash flows from a project arising over 5 years then the formula could be as follows: =IRR(A10:F10)

To help the marker locate your numerical analysis you should clearly label your workings. Any commentary should be provided in a word processing document with a **reference to calculations provided within the spreadsheet.**

Exam success skill 5

Effective Writing and Presentation

Written answers should be presented so that the marker can clearly see the different points you are making, presented in the format specified by the task requirement. The skill is to provide efficient written answers with sufficient breadth of points that actually answer the task set and provide necessary depth of explanation in the time available.

Advice on developing this skill

This skill can be developed by applying the following features to your written work.

Step 1 **Identify the appropriate format for your written work**

The SBL exam will ask you to present your answers In a variety of formats, including reports, briefing notes, emails and presentation slides/speaker notes. Review past exam questions to understand the differences in these format types so that you know how to replicate them in the exam. SBL is the only strategic professional exam where you may be asked to produce presentation slides. Be sure to keep slide content simple and uncluttered, developing your points in accompanying speaker notes. In a computer-based exam presentation slide software is provided for this purpose.

Step 2 **Use subheadings**

Using the subheadings taken from your answer plan will give you structure, order and logic. This will ensure your answer links back to the task requirement and is clearly signposted, making it easier for the marker to understand the different points you are making and award marks accordingly.

Step 3 **Write your answer in short, punchy sentences**

Use short, punchy sentences when presenting written answers with the aim that every written sentence should say something different and generate marks.

Step 4 **Extend your points with depth**

You should not leave the marker in a position asking why, or so what. A useful technique is to use short sentences to explain what you mean in one sentence and then to explain why it matters in the next. If further depth is required, consider how the consequences of inaction or making a decision will impact on the organisation in the future.

Computer-based exam

The ACCA examining team advises candidates to **keep formatting simple**. Use bold font for sub-headings avoiding the use of underlining or italics. There is no auto-correct or spell check functionality but **do not waste time on detailed spelling and grammar checks** of your work.

Exam success skill 6

Good Time Management

This skill means planning your time across all the task requirements so that all tasks have been attempted at the end of the four hours available and actively checking on time during your progress through the exam. This is so that, if necessary, you can flex your approach and prioritise tasks which, in your judgement, will generate the maximum marks in the available time remaining.

Advice on developing Good Time Management

This skill can be developed by applying the following process:

Step 1   **Stick to mark and time allocations**

At the beginning of a question, work out the amount of time you should be spending on each task requirement. The ACCA examining team advise spending at least 40 minutes on reading, which leaves 200 minutes to complete your answer planning and calculations and write up your answer.

Step 2   **Follow your answer plan**

It is not uncommon to spend five minutes creating a good plan then not use it when writing up the answer. This means explanations of good points which had been identified are missed or the time allocation is ignored. The key is using the answer plan to limit how much is written and how much time is used.

Step 3   **Keep an eye on the clock**

Aim to attempt all tasks, but be ready to be ruthless and move on if your answer is not going as planned. The challenge for many is sticking to planned timings. Be aware this is difficult to achieve in the early stages of your studies and be ready to let this skill develop over time.

The good time management skill means actively planning for exam success as your written answers cover more of the available marks.

If you find yourself running short on time and know that a full answer is not possible in the time you have, consider recreating your plan in overview form and then add key terms and details as time allows. Remember, some key marks may still be available, for example, simply stating a conclusion which you don't have time to justify in full.

Computer-based exam

When planning your answer, type your ideas into the word processor to create sub-headings, which can be developed further when you type up your full answer. Doing this will make the best use of your planning time, giving your final answer a professional structure and format.

The importance of question practice in your studies

The best study approach to improve your knowledge of the ACCA professional skills and exam success skills is to focus on question practice as a core part of learning new topic areas, ensuring you focus on improving the Exam Success Skills – personal to your needs – by obtaining feedback or through a process of self-assessment.

If sitting this exam as a computer-based exam, practising as many exam-style questions as possible in the ACCA CBE practice platform will be key to passing this exam. You should attempt questions under **timed conditions** and ensure you produce full answers to the discussion parts as well as doing any numerical analysis. Also ensure that you attempt all mock exams under exam conditions.

ACCA provides a free on-demand resource designed to mirror the live exam experience helping you to become more familiar with the exam format. You can access the platform via the Study Support Resources section of the ACCA website navigating to the CBE question practice section and logging in with your myACCA credentials.

How questions in this Kit will help you develop and improve your knowledge and skills

Section in this Kit	Question type	How are they useful?
Section 1	Questions which develop knowledge	These questions are aimed at developing the application of syllabus knowledge.
Section 2	Questions which develop knowledge and ACCA professional skills	Questions now include ACCA professional skills marks and suggested answers provide advice on improving your ACCA professional skills.
Section 3	Questions which develop knowledge, ACCA professional skills and exam success skills	These questions are mini-scenarios designed to replicate the Strategic Business Leader exam format. Answers provide advice on improving ACCA professional skills marks and advice on improving exam success skills.
Section 4	Mock exam questions which develop knowledge, ACCA professional skills and exam success skills	This is a bank of full mock exams which replicate the style, format and challenge of the Strategic Business Leader exam to support you in your final exam preparations. The mock exams illustrate how knowledge and ACCA professional skills marks are assessed.

Passing the Strategic Business Leader exam

Displaying the right knowledge, skills and qualities

The Strategic Business Leader examining team will expect you to display the following knowledge, skills and qualities.

Qualities required	Explanation
Applying your syllabus knowledge to the scenario	You need to identify the appropriate model or framework to use in relation to a particular scenario or task requirement. However, you then also need to apply the relevant theoretical models to the information presented in the scenario in order to answer the task.
	Theoretical frameworks and models are tools to help you answer the task. They are not the answer in themselves.
	You need to employ two different skills here:
	• Use relevant theory to provide a **framework** or model to plan what you will cover in your answer
	• Use the **scenario** to answer the task
	In case study exams, markers frequently comment that students fail to use the information in the scenarios properly. Answers that are too general or lack appropriate context as provided by the scenario will not score well.
Demonstrating ACCA professional skills: 1 Communication 2 Commercial acumen 3 Analysis 4 Scepticism 5 Evaluation	You must use your **technical knowledge and business awareness** to identify the key features of the scenario. This means that when you are asked to show higher level skills such as **analysis, evaluation** and **scepticism**, you will only score well if you demonstrate them. Merely describing something when you are asked to evaluate it will not earn you the marks you need.
	The measures you recommend must be **appropriate** for the organisation; you may need to discuss their strengths and weaknesses as there may be costs of adopting them. In doing this, you can gain marks for the quality and logical flow of your arguments. Ultimately, your business solutions must be **commercial** and improve the organisation; for example, by improving revenue and profit, managing cost and risk or improving the long-term sustainability of an organisation by recommending strategic change, innovation, investment in infrastructure, information technology or product development. The recommendations should clearly state what has to be done and **communicated** in a professional tone and format.

Qualities required	Explanation
Demonstrating exam success skills: 1 Case scenario: Managing information 2 Correct interpretation of the requirements 3 Answer planning: Priorities, structure and logic 4 Efficient numerical analysis 5 Effective writing and presentation 6 Good time management	To pass Strategic Business Leader will require a proactive approach in managing **time**, managing high volumes of **information**, correctly **interpreting the task requirements**, **planning** the scope of answers and presenting **numerical** and **written** work in an effective, efficient and professional way. For example, you may be expected to discuss both sides of a case, or present an argument in favour of or against something. The skill is explaining a sufficient breadth of relevant points in the time available. Making rapid judgements in the exam on your planned coverage and allocation of available time is a critical skill to ensure you **manage your time** and attempt all aspects of the exam to maximise earning sufficient marks to pass. These skills can only be developed with significant question practice, so this should be central to your self-study plans.

Avoiding weaknesses

Our experience enables us to predict a number of weaknesses that are likely to occur in many students' answers. You will enhance your chances significantly if you ensure you avoid these mistakes:

- **Failing to interpret the task requirements correctly and provide what the question verbs require** (discussion, evaluation, recommendation) or to write about the topics specified in the task requirements. It is vital that you read the task requirement very carefully so that you understand exactly what you are being asked to do.

- **Repeating the same material** and making similar points in different parts of answers.

- **Stating theories and concepts** rather than applying them. In Strategic Business Leader you are not required to explain a theory or model used. You are expected to select an appropriate model for the scenario and use it to plan and structure your answer.

- **Quoting chunks of detail** from the question that don't add any value. Your solution should focus on answering the task set and be 'future focused' so you are explaining what the company could be and the benefits of business change, rather than what the company currently is.

- **Forcing irrelevancies into answers**, for example irrelevant definitions or theories, or examples that don't relate to the scenario, as these will **not** score knowledge and professional marks.

- **Giving long lists or writing down all that's known** about a broad subject area, and not caring whether it's relevant or not. Here, the ACCA examining team will question your ability to prioritise and filter relevant information.

- **Focusing too narrowly on one area**, for example only covering financial risks when other risks are also important. The Strategic Business Leader exam is about demonstrating breadth to create a balanced view of many different factors, creating persuasive evidence supporting your evaluations and recommendations.

- **Letting your personal views prevent you from answering the question** – the task may require you to construct an argument with which you personally don't agree. In your role as an ACCA accountant you are expected be independent when formulating your views and providing analysis. If this is a particular challenge, it is helpful to view situations from different stakeholder perspectives as well as commercial and ethical viewpoints.

- **Unrealistic or impractical recommendations** means you are not demonstrating commercial acumen which is one of the ACCA professional skills. Your recommendations should be suitable for the size and nature of the business in the scenario and the financial and operational capacity of the organisation you are advising.

- **Vague recommendations** – instead of just saying improve risk management procedures, you should discuss precisely **why** the recommendation is required, **what** problem it will solve and **how** you would improve them.

- **Failing to answer sufficient questions**, or all parts of a task, because of poor time management. This simply limits the available marks to you, making it harder to pass the exam. Improving your exam success skills so you can attempt all task requirements must be a central goal in your learning which is why question practice, **and more question practice**, is such an important element of your studies for Strategic Business Leader.

Choosing which task to answer first

We recommend that you spend time at the beginning of your exam carefully reading through all of the tasks in the exam, and each of their requirements. Once you feel familiar with your exam we then recommend that you attempt the tasks in order, starting at Task 1. Although some of the task requirements could be independent, there could also be a 'story line' running through them (which is why we advise you to answer them in order).

The ACCA examining team suggest, as a guide, that at least 40 minutes is spent initially on reading the case scenario, the exhibits and the task requirements. This leaves 200 minutes to attempt the tasks set.

Comments from the examination teams of other syllabuses that have similar exam formats suggest that students appear less time pressured if they follow the predetermined task order as it removes a further decision of what parts of the examination to attempt first.

Remember also that small overruns of time can add up to leave you very short of time towards the end, which is why developing good time management skills and actively controlling time spent on reading and planning are major contributors to the ability to finish all tasks in the four hours available.

Tackling the tasks

You'll improve your chances by following a step-by-step approach to the case study along the following lines.

Step 1   Read the background

The first couple of paragraphs will provide some brief background scenario for the case. The majority of the detailed information you need to answer the task requirements comes in the exhibits. This brief background scenario provides the context for all of the rest of the information.

Step 2   Read the task requirements

There is no point reading the detailed information in the question until you know what it is going to be used for. Don't panic if some of the task requirements look challenging – identify the elements you are able to do and look for links between task requirements, as well as possible indications of the syllabus areas the question is covering.

Step 3   Identify the action verbs

These convey the level of skill you need to exhibit and also the structure your answer should have. A lower level verb such as 'define' will require a more descriptive answer; a higher level verb such as 'evaluate' will require a more applied, critical answer. It should be stressed that higher level task requirements and verbs are likely to be most significant in this exam.

Action verbs that are likely to be frequently used in this exam are listed below, together with their intellectual levels and guidance on their meaning.

Intellectual level		
1	Define	Give the meaning of
1	Explain	Make clear
1	Identify	Recognise or select
1	Describe	Give the key features
2	Distinguish	Define two different terms, viewpoints or concepts on the basis of the differences between them
2	Compare and contrast	Explain the similarities and differences between two different terms, viewpoints or concepts
2	Contrast	Explain the differences between two (or more) different terms, viewpoints or concepts
2	Analyse	Give reasons for the current situation or what has happened
3	Assess	Determine the strengths/weaknesses/ importance/significance/ability to contribute
3	Examine	Critically review in detail
3	Discuss	Examine by using arguments for and against
3	Explore	Examine or discuss in a wide-ranging manner
3	Criticise	Present the weaknesses of/problems with the actions taken or viewpoint expressed, supported by evidence
3	Evaluate/critically evaluate	Determine the value of in the light of the arguments for and against (critically evaluate means weighting the answer towards criticisms/arguments against)
3	Construct the case	Present the arguments in favour of or against, supported by evidence
3	Recommend	Advise the appropriate actions to pursue in terms the recipient will understand

Also make sure you identify all the action verbs; some tasks may have more than one.

Step 4   **Identify what each part of the task requires**

Think about what frameworks or theories you could choose if the task doesn't specify which one to use.

When planning, you will need to make sure that you aren't reproducing the same material in more than one part of the task.

Also, you're likely to come across part tasks with two requirements that may be at different levels; a part question may, for example, ask you to explain X and discuss Y.

You must ensure that you **fulfil both task requirements** and that your discussion of Y shows greater depth than your explanation of X (for example by identifying problems with Y or putting the case for and against Y).

Step 5   **Check the mark allocation to each part**

This shows you the depth anticipated and helps allocate time.

Step 6   **Read the whole case study through, including all the exhibits, highlighting key data**

Put points under headings related to task requirements. We call this 'reading with purpose'. With an understanding of the task requirements, you are able to read each exhibit and determine what information and data is important and relevant.

Step 7   **Consider the consequences of the points you've identified**

Remember that you will often have to provide recommendations based on the information you've been given. However, it is important that these recommendations are practical and appropriate to the context in the case study. For example, will the recommended course of action help an organisation to solve a problem it is facing? Does the organisation have the resources and capabilities to implement the course of action? Will the proposed course of action be acceptable to key stakeholders?

You might also have to criticise courses of action suggested by other people in the exhibits. Again, this may require you to consider the consequences of the actions, the interests of different stakeholders, and wider issues or viewpoints.

Step 8   **Write a brief plan for each task**

Your plans should contain sufficient detail of the scope of your planned numerical analysis, the headings and points you plan to include in your written answer. This process is critical to good time management and should always be included in your approach to answering tasks, so this is done automatically and efficiently during the exam itself.

Make sure you identify all the task requirements of the question in your plan – each task requirement may have sub-requirements that must also be addressed. If there are professional marks available, highlight in your plan where these may be gained (such as preparing a report).

Step 9   **Complete numerical analysis**

The results from your numerical analysis is likely to impact or change what you plan to write, so it is important this is completed first. If you struggle to complete the analysis, all is not lost, as you can use your judgement and estimate a reasonable outcome which you can explain and use this as a basis for your written answer.

Step 10   **Write the answer in the prescribed format**

Make every effort to present your answer clearly and in the format required by the Strategic Business Leader examining team in the task requirement, such as an email, memo, report extract, presentation or meeting notes. The Strategic Business Leader sample exams indicate that the ACCA examining team will be looking for you to make a number of clear points. The best way to demonstrate what you're doing is to put points into separate paragraphs with clear headers and aim to address the fundamental questions of **what, why, so what, what next** and **how**.

Adding depth to discussions

The **depth of discussion** will be important. Discussions will often consist of paragraphs containing two to three sentences. Each paragraph should:

- **Make a point**

- **Explain the point** (you must demonstrate why the point is important) and **illustrate the point** with evidence from scenario exhibits or from your own analysis

- Where relevant, **explain the impact or consequences** of inaction or taking a particular course of action

In this exam a number of task requirement verbs will expect you to express a viewpoint or opinion, for example explain, construct an argument, discuss, criticise and evaluate. When expressing an opinion, you need to provide:

- **What the task wants** – for instance, if you are asked to criticise something, don't spend time discussing its advantages. In addition, if a scenario provides a lot of information about a situation, and you are (say) asked to assess that situation in the light of good practice, your assessment is unlikely to be favourable.

- **Evidence** from theory or the scenario – again we stress that the majority of marks in most tasks will be given for applying your knowledge to the scenario.

Gaining the ACCA professional skills marks

As well as the marks available for demonstrating your technical knowledge, in the Strategic Business Leader exam there will also be **20 professional skills marks** available. Some of these should be easy to obtain, by following the instructions in the task requirement and presenting your answer in a professional and clear way. The ACCA examining team has stated that some marks will be available for presenting your answer in the form of formal business letters, briefing notes, memos, presentations, press releases, narratives in an annual report and so on. You may also be able to obtain marks for the format, effective use of professional language, layout, logical flow and persuasiveness of your answer.

What you write should always sound professional, and you will be awarded marks for good introductions and conclusions. You must use the format the task requires. You must also lay your answer out so that somebody could actually read it and take actions based on your evaluation and advice. The creativity and quality of your points is also part of being an ACCA professional accountant so by aiming to add as much value as possible to the organisation in the case scenario will help to earn the commercial acumen professional marks available.

How you make the document persuasive will depend on who you are and who the recipients are. If you are writing to management, you should consider how much information you need to provide. If you are trying to convince the reader that a decision is right, you should focus on the benefits.

As we have stated previously, the key to gaining the ACCA professional skills marks is question practice and **more question practice**.

Useful websites

The websites below provide additional sources of information of relevance to your studies for Strategic Business Leader.

- www.accaglobal.com

  ACCA's website. The students' section of the website is invaluable for detailed information about the qualification, past issues of *Student Accountant* (including technical articles) and a free downloadable Student Planner App.

  ACCA have created a microsite specifically for Strategic Business Leader, which includes articles from the examining team. You are strongly advised to visit the microsite as part of your preparation for the exam, and to read the articles provided on it.

- www.bpp.com

  Our website provides information about BPP products and services, with a link to ACCA's website.

- www.ft.com

  This website provides information about current international business. You can search for information and articles on specific industry groups as well as individual companies.

- www.economist.com

  Here you can search for business information on a week-by-week basis, search articles by business subject and use the resources of the Economist Intelligence Unit to research sectors, companies or countries.

- www.investmentweek.co.uk

  This site carries business news and articles on markets from Investment Week and International Investment.

- www.cfo.com

  This is a good website for financial officers.

- www.bbc.co.uk

  This website of the BBC carries general business information as well as programme-related content.

- www.strategy-business.com

  This is the website for Strategy + business, a business publication which focuses on corporate strategy and management issues.

Questions

Section 1 – Knowledge development

> **Important note:**
>
> The questions in this section are designed to test your understanding of topics across the syllabus. However, the focus of this section is technical knowledge, and so these questions do not replicate the style or format of the case study requirements in the Strategic Business Leader exam.
>
> Once you have developed your technical knowledge, in Section 2 of the Kit you will then have the chance to develop your professional skills, alongside applying your technical knowledge.
>
> Then in Sections 3 and 4 you will have the chance to apply your knowledge and your professional skills to scenarios which are more representative of the ones you will face in the Strategic Business Leader exam.

Leadership

Questions 1 to 5 focus on 'Leadership' – Section A of the Strategic Business Leader syllabus.

1 Rameses International   15 marks

Jeanette Singh was recently appointed Chief Executive of Rameses International, which is a long-established, family-run export house specialising in buying manufactured goods from Western Europe and the USA for re-sale in Africa and in the Middle East. Jeanette Singh was previously Marketing Director of one of Rameses International's biggest suppliers. She is the first CEO appointed from outside the family.

Rameses International had been very successful for many years, but has begun to suffer from increasing competition in its chosen markets, particularly from strong manufacturing companies expanding downstream to capture more of the value in the supply chain.

Rameses has introduced a number of initiatives over the last three years in order to try to respond to the challenges it has faced. These initiatives have included: seeking a wider range of products to re-sell from a broader supply base (more suppliers); attempting to have closer collaborative agreements with major suppliers to minimise any potential conflict; and attempting to operate in more markets.

However, none of these initiatives has been particularly successful, and turnover has stagnated.

Jeanette has said that one of the problems which is affecting Rameses' competitive position is that the underlying logic behind the initiatives appears to be finding ways of improving performance whilst maintaining the company's existing business model and culture. However, Jeanette has argued that in order to respond to the changing environment, Rameses needs to consider making some more fundamental changes to vision and strategy.

Jeanette has arranged a board meeting to discuss Rameses' future strategies and its strategic management process. The meeting was positive and constructive, although Jeanette has added the following note of caution: 'We need to remember that senior management teams within companies can often be good at analysing their company's position, and identifying potential strategic options available to it. However, they are often much less successful in actually implementing the chosen strategies.'

Required

(a) Explain, with reference to Johnson, Scholes and Whittington's model, the importance of strategic implementation in the strategic management process. **(5 marks)**

(b) With reference to Rameses, and the approaches to leadership used by its senior management team, evaluate the importance of leadership in achieving strategic success.

(10 marks)

(Total = 15 marks)

2 Frigate   15 marks

Introduction

Frigate Limited is based in the country of Egdon. It imports electrical components from other countries and distributes them throughout the domestic market. The company was formed 20 years ago by Ron Frew, who now owns 80% of the shares. A further 10% of the company is owned by his wife and 5% each by his two daughters.

Although he has never been in the navy, Ron is obsessed by ships, sailing and naval history. He is known to everyone as 'The Commander' and this is how he expects his employees to address him. He increasingly spends time on his own boat, an expensive motor cruiser, which is moored in the local harbour 20 minutes' drive away. When he is not on holiday, Ron is always at work at 8.00am in the morning to make sure that employees arrive on time and he is also there at 5.30pm to ensure that they do not leave early. However, he spends large parts of the working day on his boat, although he can be contacted by mobile telephone. Employees who arrive late for work have to immediately explain the circumstances to Ron. If he feels that the explanation is unacceptable then he makes an appropriate deduction from their wages. Wages, like all costs in the company, are closely monitored by Ron.

Employees, customers and suppliers

Frigate currently has 25 employees primarily undertaking sales, warehousing, accounts and administration. Although employees are nominally allocated to one role, they are required to work anywhere in the company as required by Ron. They are also expected to help Ron in personal tasks, such as booking holidays for his family, filling in his personal tax returns and organising social events.

Egdon has laws concerning minimum wages and holidays. All employees at Frigate Ltd are only given the minimum holiday allocation. They have to use this allocation not only for holidays but also for events such as visiting the doctor, attending funerals and dealing with domestic problems and emergencies. Ron is particularly inflexible about holidays and work hours. He has even turned down requests for unpaid leave. In contrast, Ron is often away from work for long periods, sailing in various parts of the world.

Ron is increasingly critical of suppliers ('trying to sell me inferior quality goods for higher prices'), customers ('moaning about prices and paying later and later') and society in general ('a period working in the navy would do everyone good'). He has also been in dispute with the tax authority who he accused of squandering his 'hard-earned' money. An investigation by the tax authority led to him being fined for not disclosing the fact that significant family expenditure (such as a holiday for his daughters overseas) had been declared as company expenditure.

This action by the tax authority has prompted Ron to appoint Ann Li as company accountant. Ann had previously worked as an accountant in a number of public sector organisations, which had formal controls and systems. She recommended to Ron that similar, formal processes be installed at Frigate but Ron resisted them, and within six months Ann resigned and left the company.

Required

Analyse the culture of Frigate Ltd using the cultural web.   **(15 marks)**

3 RDC

25 marks

Railway Development Co (RDC) was considering two options ('Route A' and 'Route B') for a new railway line connecting two towns in the country of Zeeland.

Route A involved cutting a channel through an area designated as being of special scientific importance because it was one of a very few suitable feeding grounds for a colony of endangered birds. The birds were considered to be an important part of the local environment with some potential influences on local ecosystems. As a result of the extra work involved in preserving as much of the bird's habitat as possible, Route A will take 25% more time to construct than Route B. In order to meet the government's construction targets in time, RDC will offer higher wages in exchange for employees waiving their right to a limit of 35 hours per working week. It is anticipated that employees will need to work a six-day week to complete the project on time.

The alternative was Route B which would involve the compulsory purchase and destruction of Eddie Krul's farm. Mr Krul was a vocal opponent of the Route B plan. He said that he had a right to stay on the land which had been owned by his family for four generations and which he had developed into a profitable farm. The farm employed a number of local people whose jobs would be lost if Route B went through the house and land. Mr Krul threatened legal action against RDC if Route B was chosen.

An independent legal authority has determined that the compulsory purchase price of Mr Krul's farm would be $1 million if Route B was chosen. RDC considered this a material cost, over and above other land costs, because the projected net present value (NPV) of cash flows over a ten-year period would be $5 million if Route A were chosen. The NPV would be reduced to $4 million if Route B were chosen.

The local government authority had given both routes provisional planning permission and offered no opinion of which it preferred. It supported infrastructure projects such as the new railway line, believing that either route would attract new income and prosperity to the region. It took the view that as an experienced railway builder, RDC would know best which to choose and how to evaluate the two options. Because it was very keen to attract the investment, it left the decision entirely to RDC. After discussing the company's values and taking into consideration various stakeholder viewpoints, the board of RDC selected Route A as the route to build the new line.

A local environmental pressure group, 'Save the Birds', was outraged at the decision to choose Route A. It criticised RDC and also the local authority for ignoring the sustainability implications of the decision. It accused the company of profiting at the expense of the environment and threatened to use 'direct action' to disrupt the building of the line through the birds' feeding ground if Route A went ahead.

Required

(a)   Assess the extent to which the Board of RDC demonstrated responsible leadership in its decision to choose Route A.
(10 marks)

(b)   Discuss the importance to RDC of recognising all of the stakeholders in a decision such as choosing between Route A and Route B.
(8 marks)

(c)   Explain what a stakeholder 'claim' is, and critically assess the stakeholder claims of Eddie Krul, the local government authority and the colony of endangered birds.
(7 marks)

(Total = 25 marks)

4 Hum and Hoo

17 marks

Hum and Hoo is an established audit practice in Deetown and has a large share of the audit services market among local businesses. Because Deetown is a relatively isolated area, many clients rely on Hum and Hoo for accounting and technical advice over and above the annual audit. This has meant that, over time, Hum and Hoo has also developed expertise in compliance advice, tax, strategy consulting and other professional services.

Because non-audit work is important to Hum and Hoo, staff have 'business growth' criteria strongly linked with bonuses and promotion. This means that many of the professional accountants in the firm actively seek to increase sales of non-audit services to businesses in the Deetown area, including from audit clients. The culture of the firm is such that everybody is expected to help out with any project which needs to be done, and this sometimes means that staff help out on a range of both audit and non-audit tasks. The lines between audit and non-audit services are sometimes blurred and staff may work on either, as workload needs demand. Managing partner Cherry Hoo told staff that the
non-audit revenue is now so important to the firm that staff should not do anything to threaten that source of income.

Cherry Hoo said that she was thinking of beginning to offer a number of other services including advice on environmental reporting and the provision of environmental auditing services. She said she had spoken to local companies which were looking to demonstrate their environmental sustainability and she believed that environmental reporting and auditing might be ways to help with this.

Required

(a)   Explain 'ethical threat' and 'ethical safeguard' in the context of external auditing, and discuss the benefits of effective ethical safeguards for Hum and Hoo.   **(8 marks)**

Some corporate governance codes prohibit audit firms such as Hum and Hoo from providing some non-audit services to audit clients without the prior approval of the client's audit committee. This is because it is sometimes believed to be against the public interest.

Required

(b)   Explain 'public interest' in the context of accounting services and why a client's audit committee is a suitable body to advise on the purchase of non-audit services from Hum and Hoo.   **(9 marks)**

(Total = 17 marks)

5 Esse   12 marks

Esse Co (Esse) is an international company based in Europe which trades principally in Asia and Europe. In its published Code of Ethics, Esse has committed itself to 'being a company that will trade fairly and sustainably'.

Esse has been pursuing an expansion strategy, which has led to the following three situations occurring:

Situation 1

At a recent presentation to investment analysts and financial journalists, Esse's Chief Executive Officer (CEO) gave a very optimistic forecast for the company's future, suggesting that revenue would double over the next three years and profits and dividends would increase by 50%.

However, the CEO had prepared his forecast in a hurry, and had not had it confirmed by anybody else within Esse. He did not mention that Esse's home government was considering legal action against the company for underpayment of import duties and had made a claim for damages. If successful, this claim would materially affect Esse's profit in the next year (20X3).

Situation 2

In connection with the legal case in Situation 1, Esse's home government had obtained a court order that all documents relating to Esse's export trade should be made available to the government's lawyers.

However, many of the documents covered by the court order were the subject of confidentiality agreements between Esse and various entrepreneurs. These documents included details of patents and processes with a high commercial value and if knowledge of them became public it would destroy some of Esse's competitive advantage.

Situation 3

This situation is unconnected to the other two.

Esse has a joint venture agreement with Pharm Co (Pharm). Under the terms of the joint venture agreement, each company has to make regular returns of financial performance to the other. Pharm is always late in making its returns, which are usually incomplete and contain many errors. Pharm's accounting staff are very reluctant to co-operate with Esse's accounting staff and the working relationship between the two companies is poor.

Esse's financial controller has been involved in a review of the joint venture with Pharm. Due to the many problems that Pharm has caused him and his staff, he has advised discontinuing the joint venture.

Required

Advise, giving your reasons, whether each of the three situations is in conflict with the principles of a code of ethics for a professional accountant, such as ACCA's Code of Ethics and Conduct.

(12 marks)

Governance

Questions 6 to 11 focus on 'Governance' – Section B of the Strategic Business Leader syllabus.

6 Sentosa House   17 marks

Sonia Tan, a fund manager at institutional investor Sentosa House, was reviewing the annual report of Eastern Products (Eastern), one of the major companies in her portfolio. Sentosa House, like Eastern's other major institutional investors, have become increasingly concerned about the company's management team.

The problems which have prompted the institutional investors' lack of confidence in Eastern's management started two years ago when a new Chair, Thomas Hoo, started to pursue what the investors regarded as very risky strategies, whilst at the same time failing to comply with a stock market requirement on the required number of non-executive directors on the board.

After reviewing Eastern's annual report, Sonia rang the company's investor relations department to ask why it still was not in compliance with the requirements relating to non-executive directors. She was told that, because Eastern was listed in a principles-based jurisdiction, the requirement was not compulsory. It was simply that Eastern chose not to comply with that particular requirement. When Sonia asked how its board committees could be made up with an insufficient number of non-executive directors, the investor relations manager said he didn't know and that Sonia should contact the Chair directly. She was also told that there was no longer a risk committee because the Chair saw no need for one.

Sonia then telephoned Thomas Hoo, the Chair of Eastern Products. She began by reminding him that Sentosa House was one of Eastern's main shareholders and currently owned 13% of the company. She went on to explain that she had concerns over the governance of Eastern Products and that she would like Thomas to explain his non-compliance with some of the stock market's requirements and also why he was continuing to pursue strategies viewed by many investors as very risky. Thomas reminded Sonia that Eastern had outperformed its sector in terms of earnings per share in both years since he had become Chair and that rather than question him, she should trust him to run the company as he saw fit. He thanked Sentosa House for its support and hung up the phone.

Required

(a)   Explain what an 'agency cost' is and discuss the problems that might increase agency costs for Sentosa House in the case of Eastern Products.   **(7 marks)**

(b)   Describe, with reference to the case, the conditions under which it might be appropriate for an institutional investor to intervene in a company whose shares it holds.   **(10 marks)**

(Total = 17 marks)

7 West vs Leroi   13 marks

At an academic conference, a debate took place on the implementation of corporate governance practices in developing countries. Professor James West from North America argued that one of the key needs for developing countries was to implement rigorous systems of corporate governance to underpin investor confidence in businesses in those countries. If they did not, he warned, there would be no lasting economic growth as potential foreign inward investors would be discouraged from investing.

In reply, Professor Amy Leroi, herself from a developing country, reported that many developing countries are discussing these issues at governmental level. One issue, she said, was about whether to adopt a rules-based or a principles-based approach. She pointed to evidence highlighting a reduced number of small and medium-sized initial public offerings in New York compared to significant growth in London. She suggested that this change could be attributed to the costs of complying with Sarbanes-Oxley legislation in the United States and that over-regulation would be the last thing that a developing country would need. She concluded that a principles-based approach, such as in the United Kingdom, was preferable for developing countries.

Professor Leroi drew attention to an important section of the Sarbanes-Oxley Act to illustrate her point. The key requirement of that section was to externally report on – and have verified – internal controls. This was, she argued, far too ambitious for the small and medium-sized companies that tended to dominate the economies of developing countries.

Professor West countered by saying that whilst Sarbanes-Oxley may have had some problems, it remained the case that it regulated corporate governance in the 'largest and most successful economy in the world'. He said that rules will sometimes be hard to follow but that is no reason to abandon them in favour of what he referred to as 'softer' approaches.

Required

There are arguments for both rules- and principles-based approaches to corporate governance.

(a) Describe the essential features of a rules-based approach to corporate governance.

(3 marks)

(b) Construct the argument against Professor West's opinion, and in favour of Professor Leroi's opinion that a principles-based approach would be preferable in developing countries. Your answer should consider the particular situations of developing countries. (10 marks)

(Total = 13 marks)

8 Plantex   19 marks

Plantex is a large international pharmaceutical company which has been at the forefront of research into developing cures for many tropical diseases. The nature of its business means that continuous and significant financial investment is required for research and development activities, for which its shareholders expect sizeable returns.

At a recent meeting of the board of Plantex, the Finance Director, Rachel Tang, submitted a paper on integrated reporting (<IR>) for discussion and consideration. She advised the board that Plantex had only ever disclosed the minimum information which it was required to by law, but recent developments in the International Integrated Reporting Framework have made a very strong case for broadening the amount of published corporate information.

The primary objective of <IR> is to demonstrate the clear link between a firm's competitive strategy, governance systems and financial performance, alongside the social, environmental and economic context within which the firm operates. Rachel Tang claimed that by integrating these different areas, the board of Plantex would be in a far better position to allocate its valuable resources more effectively and thereby make more environmental and socially sustainable decisions.

The Chair was highly supportive of the proposal as he had been trying to encourage a corporate citizenship agenda at recent board meetings. He suggested that <IR> would demonstrate that Plantex took corporate social responsibility seriously by being more transparent, accountable and responsive to its stakeholders' demands.

Rachel Tang further asserted that <IR> would have the effect of simplifying published financial information, with excessive detail being removed and critical information being highlighted. If Plantex voluntarily adopted <IR>, its shareholders, and other stakeholders, would better understand how the firm was really performing and so be able to make a meaningful assessment of the firm's long-term strategy. This openness could encourage further investment and strengthen the firm's competitive position.

The Chief Executive, Stanley Broadway, suggested that this all sounded very good in theory, but he found it hard to justify the extra expense without any recognisable return to shareholders. He said it was 'just another costly management fad that distracted the company from its real purpose – making money for its shareholders!'

Required

(a) Explain the concept of corporate citizenship, and assess the rights and responsibilities of Plantex as a corporate citizen. **(7 marks)**

(b) (i) Describe the advantages to Plantex and its stakeholders of adopting <IR>. **(6 marks)**

    (ii) Explain how using an <IR> approach will provide information about the six capitals including the resources and relationships on which Plantex depends. **(6 marks)**

(Total = 19 marks)

9 Geeland

25 marks

There has been a debate in the country of Geeland for some years about the most appropriate way to regulate corporate governance. Several years ago, there were a number of major corporate failures and 'scandals' caused in part by a number of single powerful individuals dominating their boards. Business leaders and policy-makers were sceptical about a rules-based approach, and this led the Geeland stock exchange to issue guidance in the 'Geeland Code' as follows.

'Good corporate governance is not just a matter of prescribing particular corporate structures and complying with a number of rules. There is a need for broad principles. All stakeholders should then apply these flexibly to the varying circumstances of individual companies.'

Given the causes of the Geeland corporate governance failures, there was a debate about whether the separation of the roles of Chair and Chief Executive should be made a legal requirement. This resulted in the stock exchange issuing guidance that whilst a rules-based or 'box ticking' approach would specify that 'the roles of Chair and Chief Executive officer should never be combined … We do not think that there are universally valid answers on such points.'

One company to take advantage of the flexibility in Geeland's principles-based approach was Anson Co. In July 20X0, Anson Co announced that it had combined its roles of Chair and Chief Executive in a single role carried out by one individual. In accordance with the Geeland listing rules, it made the following 'comply or explain' statement in its 20X1 annual report.

'Throughout the year the company complied with all Geeland Code provisions with the exception that from 1 July 20X0 the roles of Chair and Chief Executive have been exercised by the same individual, William Klunker. We recognise that this has been out of line with best practice. We understand the concerns of shareholders but believe that we have maintained robust governance while at the same time benefiting from having Mr Klunker in control. On 31 July 20X2 Mr Klunker will step down as executive Chair, remaining as Chair until we conclude our search for a non-executive Chair to succeed him, no later than March 20X3.'

Required

(a) Briefly distinguish between rules- and principles-based approaches to corporate governance. Critically evaluate the Geeland stock exchange's guidance that 'all stakeholders should then apply these flexibly to the varying circumstances of individual companies.' **(12 marks)**

(b) Explain why a separation of the roles of Chair and Chief Executive is considered best practice in most jurisdictions. **(8 marks)**

(c) Assess the 'comply or explain' statement made by Anson Co in its 20X1 annual report. **(5 marks)**

(Total = 25 marks)

10 Lum   25 marks

Lum Co is a family business that has been wholly owned and controlled by the Lum family since it was founded almost 100 years ago. The current Chief Executive, Mr Gustav Lum, is the great grandson of the company's founder and has himself been in post as CEO for the last 14 years. Because the Lum family wanted to maintain a high degree of control, they operated a two-tier board structure: four members of the Lum family comprised the supervisory board and the other eight non-family directors comprised the operating board.

Despite being quite a large company with 5,000 employees, Lum Co never had any non-executive directors because these were not required in privately owned companies in the country in which Lum Co was situated.

The four members of the Lum family valued the control of the supervisory board to ensure that the Lum family's wishes (being the only shareholders) were carried out. This also enabled decisions to be made quickly, without the need to take everything before a meeting of the full board.

Four years ago, the two tiers of the board met in joint sessions to discuss a flotation (issuing public shares on the stock market) of 80% of the company. The issue of the family losing control was raised by the CEO's brother, Mr Crispin Lum. He said that if the company became listed, the Lum family would lose the freedom to manage the company as they wished, including supporting their own
long-held values and beliefs. These values, he said, included managing for the long term and adopting a paternalistic management style. Other directors said that the new listing rules that would apply to the board, including compliance with the stock market's corporate governance codes of practice, would be expensive and difficult to introduce.

The flotation went ahead last year. In order to comply with the new listing rules, Lum Co took on a number of non-executive directors (NEDs) and formed a unitary board. A number of problems arose around this time with NEDs feeling frustrated at the culture and management style in Lum Co, whilst the Lum family members found it difficult to make the transition to managing a public company with a unitary board. Gustav Lum said that it was very different from managing the company when it was privately owned by the Lum family. The human resources manager said that an effective induction programme for NEDs and some relevant continuing professional development (CPD) for existing executives might help to address the problems.

Required

(a)   Compare the typical governance arrangements between a family business and a listed company, and assess Crispin's view that the Lum family will 'lose the freedom to manage the company as they wish' after the flotation.   **(10 marks)**

(b)   Assess the benefits of introducing an induction programme for the new NEDs, and requiring continual professional development (CPD) for the existing executives at Lum Co after its flotation.   **(8 marks)**

(c)   Distinguish between unitary and two-tier boards, and discuss the difficulties that the Lum family might encounter when introducing a unitary board.   **(7 marks)**

(Total = 25 marks)

11 Chambon school   25 marks

The independent board of governors of the state-funded Chambon school for 11- to 16-year-old children met to consider its most recent set of public examination results. (The board of governors is an independent oversight body, comprised of local residents, parents and other concerned citizens.)

One of the key responsibilities placed upon the school's governors is the delivery, to its local government authority, of a report on exam performance in a full and timely manner. A report on both the exam results and the reasons for any improvement or deterioration over previous years are required from the governors each year. Accordingly, the annual meeting on exam performance was always considered to be very important. Although the school taught the national curriculum (a standard syllabus taught in all schools in the country) as required of it, the exam results at Chambon had deteriorated in recent years and on this particular occasion, they were very poor indeed.

In order to address the weaknesses in the school, Chambon's budget had increased in recent years and a number of new teachers had been employed to help improve results. Despite this, exam performance continued to fall. A recent overspend against budget was funded through the closure of part of the school library and the sale of a sports field.

One member of the board of governors was Sally Murol. She believed that the local government authority might attempt to close Chambon school if these exam results were reported with no convincing explanation. One solution to avoid this threat, she said, was to either send the report in late or to select only the best results and submit a partial report so the school's performance looked better than it actually was. There is no central computerised exam results service in the country in which Chambon is located by which the local authority could establish the exam performance at Chambon school.

A general feeling at the governors' meeting was that the school needed some new leadership, and it might be time to remove the existing headteacher. Mr Besse had been in the role for many years and his management style was thought to be ineffective. He was widely liked by staff in the school because he believed that each teacher knew best how to manage their teaching, and so he tried not to intervene wherever possible. Mr Besse had sometimes disagreed with the governors when they suggested changes which could be made to improve exam performance, preferring to rely on what he believed were tried and tested ways of managing his teaching staff. He was thought to be very loyal to long-standing colleagues and had a dislike of confrontation.

Required

(a)   Explain, using evidence from the case, the characteristics which identify Chambon school as a public sector organisation and assess how its objectives as a public sector organisation have not been met.   **(10 marks)**

(b)   Explain the roles of a board of governors in the governance of Chambon school, and discuss, in the context of Sally Murol's suggestion, the importance of transparency in the board of governors' dealings with the local government authority.   **(9 marks)**

(c)   Discuss the potential advantages to Chambon school of replacing the headteacher as part of the process of addressing its problems.   **(6 marks)**

(Total = 25 marks)

Concepts of strategy

Questions 12 to 17 focus on 'Concepts of Strategy' – Section C of the Strategic Business Leader syllabus.

12 EcoCar   20 marks

The EcoCar company was formed six years ago to commercially exploit the pioneering work of Professor Jacques of Midshire University, a university in the country of Erewhon. Over a number of years, he had patented processes that allowed him to use lithium-ion batteries to power an electric car, which could travel up to 160 km before it needed recharging. Together with two colleagues from the university, he set up EcoCar to put the car into commercial production.

Coincidentally, an area in the south of Midshire was suffering from major industrial decline. This area was centred on the former Lags Lane factory of Leopard Cars, which had recently been shut down by its parent company, bringing to an end 60 years of continuous vehicle manufacture on that site. Many skilled car production workers had been made redundant in an area that already suffered significant unemployment. Grants from the regional council and interest-free loans from the government allowed EcoCar to purchase and refurbish part of the Lags Lane site, and take on 100 of the skilled workers made redundant by Leopard Cars.

The company now manufactures three car models: the original Eco, the EcoPlus, and the EcoLite. The EcoPlus is a luxury version of the Eco and shares 95% of the same components. The EcoLite is a cheaper town car and uses only 70% of the components used in the Eco. The rest of the components are unique to the EcoLite. A comparison of an Eco with a similar petrol-fuelled car (Kyutia 215) is given in Table 1. This table also gives a comparison with a hybrid car (Xdos-Hybrid C) where the petrol engine is supplemented by power from an electric motor. Hybrids are a popular way of reducing emissions and fuel consumption. Petrol currently costs $5 per litre in Erewhon. There are also experimental cars, not yet in production, which are fuelled by other low-emission alternatives to petrol such as hydrogen.

Table 1: Comparison of the Eco with comparable conventional and hybrid cars

Model	Eco	Kyutia 215	Xdos-HybridC
Power source	Lithium-ion batteries, electric motor	Petrol	Petrol with assistance from an electric motor
Price	$9,999	$7,999	$9,500
Emissions (CO_2)	Zero	180 g/km	95 g/km
Economy	Approximately $1 per 20 km (electricity charge)	8 litres/100km	5 litres/100km
Performance	0–100 kph: 18 seconds Max speed: 120 kph	0–100 kph: 10 seconds Max speed: 180 kph	0–100 kph: 12 seconds Max speed: 170 kph
Range	160 km until the battery needs recharging	550 km on a tank full of petrol	1,200 km on a tank full of petrol

The Eco model range can be re-charged from a domestic electricity supply. However, to supplement this, the government has recently funded the development of 130 charging stations for electric cars spread throughout the country. It has also given business tax incentives to switch to electric cars and is heavily taxing cars with high CO_2 emissions because of the detrimental effect of excess CO_2 on the environment. It has also enacted a number of laws on car safety which EcoCar has to comply with. Erewhon itself remains a prosperous, developed country with a well-educated population. The government is committed to tackling social and economic problems in areas such as South Midshire. EcoCar still receives significant government grants to help keep the company financially viable.

The EcoCar model range is largely bought by 'green' consumers in Erewhon, who are prepared to pay a price premium for such a car. They are also popular in the Midshire region, where the residents are proud of their car-making tradition and grateful to Professor Jacques and the government for ensuring its survival, albeit at a reduced level. Only 5% of EcoCar's production is exported.

Universal Motors

One year ago, EcoCar was bought by Universal Motors, the second largest car manufacturer in the world. Professor Jacques and his two colleagues remain as senior managers and board members of the company. Production of electric cars is still very low, but Universal Motors believes that demand for electric cars will be very significant in the future and purchased EcoCar as a way of entering this market. They believe that lithium-ion batteries (the power source for the EcoCar range) will eventually become lighter, cheaper and give better performance and range.

Although EcoCar was established in an area where there already existed a pool of skilled car workers, the subsequent retirement of many of these workers has left a skills gap. Although unemployment remains high in the area, applicants for jobs appear to lack the skills and motivation of the older workers. EcoCar is finding it difficult to recruit skilled labour and this shortage is being reflected in increased wages and staff costs at the Lags Lane site. The urban location of the Lags Lane site also causes a problem. Inbound logistics are made expensive by the relative inaccessibility of the site and the general congestion on Midshire's main roads. Finally, there is insufficient production capacity at the Lags Lane site to meet the current demand for EcoCar's products. EcoCar attempts to produce the most profitable combination of its products within this constraint. However, it is unable to completely satisfy market demand.

To address the problem it is facing in recruiting skilled labour within Erewhon, Universal Motors is considering outsourcing the manufacture of the EcoLite model to an overseas company.

Required

Making use of appropriate models, analyse the external macro-environment in which EcoCar is operating, and the marketplace (industry) in which it is competing. **(20 marks)**

13 Dormit   20 marks

You have just started a new job as a management accountant at the Dormit hotel (Dormit). The Dormit has not opened for business yet, but it intends to generate profit from its rooms and its restaurants. Other hotels in the local area generate a large amount of business by providing wedding packages. A wedding package includes the provision of a venue for the wedding ceremony, a meal for the wedding guests, entertainment after the wedding and overnight accommodation for the bride and groom.

Dormit's general manager is keen for the hotel to develop a wedding package, in addition to the standard bookings it will offer for its rooms and its restaurants. He has asked you to work on a planning team with him and the restaurants manager, to help formulate the hotel's strategy for its wedding package, and to ensure that the strategy fits with the competitive environment in which the Dormit will operate.

The competitor hotels market their weddings in a number of different ways. One hotel, the 'De Luxe', situated in a castle in a beautiful, rural setting, charges a minimum price of $50,000 for its wedding package which includes a meal for 100 guests and rooms for a bridal party of 10 guests for one night. The De Luxe has won many international awards for its food and for the high standard of its facilities and bedrooms.

In contrast, another competitor hotel, the 'Royal Albert' offers its wedding package for 100 guests for a total cost of $1,000, with no overnight accommodation provided in the basic price. The Royal Albert is a budget hotel situated next to a busy transport interchange in the nearby town.

There are another five hotels which the Dormit regards as competitors: these other hotels charge between $35 and $50 for each guest attending a wedding at their hotel.

Required

(a) Identify two models which the planning team could use to analyse the external environment, and explain how the team could use the models in formulating a wedding package strategy for the Dormit hotel. **(10 marks)**

(b) Explain how an understanding of different generic competitive strategies could help the team develop a successful wedding package for the Dormit hotel. **(10 marks)**

(Total = 20 marks)

14 NESTA   15 marks

NESTA is a large chain of fixed-price discount stores based in the country of Eyanke. Its stores offer ambient goods (goods that require no cold storage and can be kept at room temperature, such as cleaning products, stationery, biscuits and canned goods) at a fixed price of one dollar. Everything in the store retails at this price. Fixed-price discount chains focus on unbranded commodity goods which they buy from a number of small suppliers, for which these dollar shops are the most significant customers. Profit margins on the products they sell are low and overheads are kept to a minimum. The target price is fixed. The products tend to be functional, standardised and undifferentiated.

NESTA has observed the long-term economic decline in the neighbouring country of Eurobia, where a prolonged economic recession has led to the growth of these 'dollar shops'.

Three significant dollar shop chains have developed: ItzaDollar, DAIAD and DollaFellas (see Table 1). The shops of these three chains are usually found on the high streets of towns and cities where there is significant financial hardship. Many of these towns and cities have empty stores which are relatively cheap to rent. Landlords who once required high rents and long leases are increasingly willing to rent these stores for a relatively short fixed-term lease. The fixed-price dollar shop chains in Eurobia advertise extensively and continually stress their expansion plans. Few weeks go by without one of the chains announcing plans for a number of new shops somewhere in the country.

NESTA has recognised the growth of fixed-price discount retailers in Eurobia and is considering entering this market.

NESTA recently commissioned a brand awareness survey in Eurobia. The survey results showed that NESTA was relatively well known to respondents who work in the consumer goods retail market. Most of these respondents correctly identified the company as a discount fixed-price company with a significant presence in Eyanke. However, amongst general consumers, only 5% of the respondents had heard of NESTA. In contrast, the three current fixed-price dollar shop discounters in Eurobia were recognised by more than 90% of the respondents.

NESTA itself has revenue of $120,000m. It has cash reserves which could allow it to lease a significant number of shops in Eurobia and establish a credible market presence. It has recognised competencies in effective supplier selection and management, supported by effective procurement systems. Its logistics systems and methods are core strengths of the company.

There are also many conventional supermarket chains operating in Eurobia. The largest of these has annual revenue of $42,500m. Supermarkets in Eurobia tend to increasingly favour out-of-town sites which allow the stores to stock a wide range and quantity of products. Customer car parking is plentiful and it is relatively easy for supplying vehicles to access such sites. As well as stocking non-ambient goods, most supermarkets do also stock a very wide range of ambient goods, often with competing brands on offer. However, prices for such goods vary, and no supermarkets have yet adopted the discount fixed-price sales approach. In general, the large supermarket chains largely compete with each other and pay little attention to the fixed-price dollar shop discounters. Many supermarkets also have internet-based home ordering systems, offering (usually for a fee of $10) deliveries to customers who are unable or unwilling to visit the supermarket.

Table 1 shows the relative revenue of the three main discount fixed-price chains in Eurobia.

Table 1: Revenue of three main discount fixed-price chains in Eurobia

	20X2	20X1	20X0
	$m	$m	$m
ItzaDollar	330	300	275
DAIAD*	310	290	250
DollaFellas	290	235	200
Total	930	825	725

*Don't Ask, It's A Dollar

Required

Use Porter's five forces framework to assess the attractiveness, to NESTA, of entering the discount fixed-price retail market in Eurobia. **(15 marks)**

> **Tutorial note:** When you attempt your real SBL exam you are unlikely to be told which theoretical model/framework to use. The reference to Porter's five forces model has been included here to provide you with an opportunity to apply your technical knowledge to a question scenario.

15 Independent Living   25 marks

Introduction

Independent Living (IL) is a charity that provides living aids to help elderly and disabled people live independently in their own home. These aids include walkers, wheelchairs, walking frames, crutches, mobility scooters, bath lifts and bathroom and bedroom accessories.

IL aims to employ people who would find it difficult or impossible to work in a conventional office or factory. IL's charitable aim is to provide the opportunity for disabled people to 'work with dignity and achieve financial independence'. IL currently employs 200 disabled people and 25 able-bodied people at its premises on an old disused airfield site. The former aircraft hangars have been turned into either production or storage facilities, all of which have been adapted for disabled people.

Smaller items (such as walking frames and crutches) are manufactured here. These are relatively unsophisticated products, manufactured from scrap metal bought from local scrap metal dealers and stored on-site. These products require no testing or training to use and they are packaged and stored after manufacture. IL uses its own lorry to make collections of scrap metal but the lorry is old, unreliable and will soon need replacing.

Larger and more complex items (such as mobility scooters and bath lifts) are bought in bulk from suppliers and stored in the hangars. Delivery of these items to IL is organised by their manufacturers. These products are stored until they are ordered. When an order is received for such products, the product is unpacked and tested. An IL logo is then applied and the product is re-packaged in the original packing material with an IL label attached. It is then dispatched to the customer. Some products are never ordered and last year IL had to write off a significant amount of obsolete inventory.

All goods are sold at cost plus a margin to cover wages and administrative costs. Prices charged are the same whether goods are ordered online or by telephone. Customers can also make a further voluntary donation to help support IL if they wish to. About 30% of customers do make such a donation.

Ordering and marketing

IL markets its products by placing single-sided promotional leaflets in hospitals, doctors' surgeries and local social welfare departments. This leaflet provides information about IL and gives a direct phone number and a web address. Customers may purchase products by ringing IL directly or by ordering via its website. The website provides product information and photos of the products which are supplied by IL. It also has a secure payment facility. However, customers who ring IL directly have to discuss product requirements and potential purchases with sales staff over the phone. Each sales discussion takes, on average, ten minutes and only one in two contacts results in a sale. Twenty per cent of sales are through their website (up from 15% last year), but many of their customers are unfamiliar with the internet and do not have access to it.

Goods are delivered to customers by a national courier service. Service and support for the bought-in products (such as mobility scooters, and bath lifts) are supplied by the original manufacturer.

Commercial competitors

IL is finding it increasingly difficult to compete with commercial firms offering independent living aids. Last year, the charity made a deficit of $160,000, and it had to sell some of its airfield land to cover this. Many of the commercial firms it is competing with have sophisticated sales and marketing operations and then arrange delivery to customers directly from manufacturers based in low labour cost countries.

Required

IL fears for its future and has decided to review its value chain to see how It can achieve competitive advantage.

(a)   Analyse the primary activities of the value chain for the product range at IL.   **(10 marks)**

(b)   Evaluate what changes IL might consider to the primary activities in the value chain to improve their competitiveness, whilst continuing to meet their charitable objectives.

(15 marks)

(Total = 25 marks)

Tutorial note: When you attempt your real SBL exam you are unlikely to be told which theoretical model/framework to use. The reference to Porter's value chain model has been included here to provide you with an opportunity to apply your technical knowledge to a question scenario.

---

16 Reink Co   20 marks

Eland – the country

Eland is an industrial country with a relatively high standard of living. Most commercial and domestic consumers have computers and printers. However, the economic performance of the country has declined for the last seven years and there are large areas of unemployment and poverty. The economic problems of the country have led to a significant decline in tax revenues and so the government has asked its own departments (and the public sector as a whole) to demonstrate
value-for-money in their purchases. The government is also considering privatising some of its departments to save money. The Department of Revenue Collections (DoRC), which is responsible for collecting tax payments in the country, has been identified as a possible candidate for future privatisation.

The people of Eland are enthusiastic about the principles of reuse and recycling. There has been a notable rise in the number of green consumers. Mindful of this, and aware of the economic benefits it delivers, the government is also encouraging its departments (and the economy as a whole) to recycle and reuse products.

The printer consumables market

There is a significant computer printer market in Eland, dominated by original equipment manufacturers (OEMs). Many of these are household names such as Landy, IPD and Bell-Tech. OEMs also dominate the printer consumables market, which is worth about $200m per year. However, there are also independent companies who only supply the printer consumables (printer cartridges and toner cartridges) market, offering prices which significantly undercut the OEMs. The printer and printer consumables markets are both technology driven, with companies constantly looking for innovations which make printing better and cheaper.

It is relatively easy to enter the independent printer consumables market and so companies tend to compete on price. There is little brand loyalty amongst consumers, who regularly change their choice of brand. The independent companies constantly focus on finding technologies which make the print cartridges cheaper to buy and are of better quality. Used print cartridges can be reused for their material alone (recycled) or reused by being refilled with ink. However, there are still printing products on the market which can only be used once or are expensive to recycle.

The emergence of independent printer consumables suppliers has not been welcomed by the OEMs. They have brought legal actions against the independents in an attempt to make refilling their branded products illegal. However, they have not succeeded. The government in Eland has ruled this to be anti-competitive. However, the OEMs continue to promote their case with political parties, claiming that they need the revenues from printer consumables to fund innovations and advances in printer technology. They also regularly issue statements which worry consumers, claiming that printers may be harmed by using ink which is not from the OEM. Landy has been particularly aggressive in this regard. It continues to pursue legal claims against the independents and has also issued a statement which makes clear that if one of their printers is found to be faulty whilst using non-Landy ink, then the printer's warranty will be void.

ReInk Co

ReInk Co (ReInk) was formed five years ago by Dexter Black, a technology entrepreneur with expertise in printer technologies. He still remains the only shareholder. He set up ReInk to produce and market his designs for reusable ink systems. ReInk is focused primarily on the reuse of printer cartridges by using a process to refill them with ink. Key technical elements of ReInk's innovative process for refilling cartridges have been patented, but in Eland, such patents only last for eight years. The current patent has a further six years to run.

The company was established in a declining industrial town in Eland with high unemployment. Government grants were available for two years to help support hi-tech industry, and purpose-built factories were cheap, readily available and, initially, rent free. Although the company now pays rent for its factory and offices, the annual rent is relatively low. The area has a good supply of people suitable for administrative and factory jobs in the company. ReInk's location is also close to an attractive area of countryside, which Dexter felt would appeal to the technology experts needed to help him exploit and develop his printer technology ideas. It would help provide a good standard of living and relatively cheap property and so he could attract good staff for modest salaries. His assumption proved correct. He has been able to attract an expert team of technologists who have helped him develop a unique approach to printer cartridge reuse. As one of them commented, 'I took a pay cut to come here. But now I can afford a bigger house and my children can breathe fresh country air.'

ReInk is an attractive company to work for and the team of technologists are enthusiastic about working with such an acknowledged industry expert, where technical innovation is recognised and rewarded. Both his staff and competitors acknowledge Dexter's technical expertise, but his commercial expertise is less well regarded. Dexter recognised this as a weakness and it was the prime driver behind his decision to recruit two new directors to the company.

To fund the development of the printer refilling technology, ReInk has needed significant bank loans and a substantial overdraft. Although the company has made a small operating profit for the last three years, interest repayments have meant that it has recorded a loss every year. It currently has revenues of $6m per year, 20% of which are derived from a long-term contract with the DoRC. ReInk is not one of the independent companies currently being sued by Landy.

To help him address these continuing financial losses, Dexter recently recruited a sales director to attempt to increase revenue through improved sales and marketing, and a human resources (HR) director to review and improve staffing practices. Together with the financial director and Dexter himself, they make up the board of Relnk.

Although both of these recently appointed directors had the commercial expertise which Dexter lacked, neither has been a success. The technologists within the company are particularly scathing about the two new appointments. They claim that the sales director has never really made the effort to understand the market and that 'he does not really understand the product we are selling'. There has been no evidence so far that he has been able to generate more sales revenue. The HR director upset the whole company by introducing indiscriminate cost cutting and attempting to regrade staff to reduce staff costs. The technologists believe that the HR director 'clearly has no experience of dealing with professional staff'.

Despite the appointment of the new sales director, Relnk is still not recognised by the majority of the consumers who were surveyed in a recent brand awareness survey. No significant marketing is undertaken outside of the development and promotion of Relnk's website. In search results, it often appears alongside companies which appear to offer similar services and usually have very similar trading names.

Relnk continues to struggle financially, and its bank, Firmsure, in response to its own financial difficulties, has recently reduced Relnk's overdraft facility, creating a cash flow crisis which threatens the company's very existence. At present, it does not have enough cash to meet next month's payroll payments.

The employees of the company are well aware of the company's financial position and although they are proud of the company's technical achievements, they believe that the company may soon go into administration and many are actively looking for other jobs in the industry or in the area. A combination of poor management (particularly from the new directors) and the company's uncertain financial position has demotivated many of the employees, particularly the technologists who created the company's vital technical edge over its competitors.

Vi Ventures

Vi Ventures (VV) are venture capitalists who inject money and management expertise into struggling companies, in exchange for a certain degree of control, ownership and dividend reward. They have acknowledged financial and management competencies which they have used in a variety of commercial environments. They are experienced change managers.

VV have been introduced to Relnk by Firmsure and they are considering some form of involvement. Actual arrangements are still under consideration and will only be discussed after they have made their standard assessment of Relnk's strategic position. The first stage of this standard assessment report is preparing a SWOT analysis.

Required

Prepare a SWOT analysis of Relnk Co. **(20 marks)**

> **Tutorial note:** When you attempt your real SBL exam you are unlikely to be told which theoretical model/framework to use. The reference to SWOT analysis has been included here to provide you with an opportunity to apply your technical knowledge to a question scenario.

17 MMI   25 marks

Assume it is now the end of 20X8.

In 20X2 the board of MMI had met to discuss the strategic direction of the company. Established 50 years ago, MMI specialised in mineral quarrying and mining, and in 20X2 it owned 15 quarries and mines throughout the country. However, three of these quarries were closed and two others were nearing exhaustion. Increased costs and falling reserves meant that there was little chance of finding new sites in the country which were economically viable. Furthermore, there were significant security costs associated with keeping the closed quarries safe and secure.

Consequently, the Chief Executive Officer (CEO) of MMI suggested that the company should pursue a corporate-level strategy of diversification, building up a portfolio of acquisitions that would 'maintain returns to shareholders over the next 50 years'. In October 20X2, using cash generated from their quarrying operations, MMI acquired First Leisure, a company that owned five leisure parks throughout the country. These leisure parks provided a range of accommodation where guests could stay while they enjoyed sports and leisure activities. The parks were all in relatively isolated country areas and provided a safe, car-free environment for guests.

The acquisition was initially criticised by certain financial analysts who questioned what a quarrying company could possibly contribute to a profitable leisure group. For two years MMI left First Leisure managers alone, letting them get on with running the company. However, in 20X4 a First Leisure manager commented on the difficulty of developing new leisure parks due to increasingly restrictive government planning legislation. This gave the CEO of MMI an inspired idea and over the next three years the five quarries which were either closed or near exhaustion were transferred to First Leisure and developed as new leisure parks. Because these were developments of 'brown field' sites, they were exempted from the government's planning legislation. The development of these new parks has helped First Leisure to expand considerably (see Table 1). The company is still run by the managers who were in place when MMI acquired the company in 20X2, and MMI plays very little role in the day-to-day running of the company.

In 20X4 MMI acquired two of its smaller mining and quarrying competitors, bringing a further five mines or quarries into the group. MMI introduced its own managers into these companies which resulted in a spectacular rise in revenues and profits that caused the CEO of MMI to claim that 'corporate management capabilities' were now an important asset of MMI.

In 20X6 MMI acquired Boatland, a specialist boat maker constructing river and canal boats. The primary rationale behind the acquisition was the potential synergies with First Leisure. First Leisure had experienced difficulties in obtaining and maintaining boats for its leisure parks and it was expected that Boatland would take on the construction and maintenance of these boats. Cost savings for First Leisure were also expected and it was felt that income from the First Leisure contract would also allow Boatland to expand its production of boats for other customers. MMI perceived that Boatland was underperforming and it replaced the current management team with its own managers. However, by 20X8 Boatland was reporting poorer results (see Table 1). The work force had been used to producing expensive, high-quality boats for discerning customers who looked after their valued boats. In contrast, the boats required by First Leisure were for the casual use of holiday makers who often ill-treated them and certainly had no long-term investment in their ownership. Managers at First Leisure complained that the new boats were 'too delicate' for their intended purpose and unreliability had led to high maintenance costs. This increase in maintenance also put Boatland under strain, and its other customers complained about poor quality workmanship and delays in completing work. These delays were compounded by managers at Boatland declaring First Leisure as a preferred customer, requiring that work for First Leisure should take precedence over that for other customers. Since the company was acquired almost half of the skilled boat builders employed by the company have left to take up jobs elsewhere in the industry.

An information technology solutions company, InfoTech, recently approached MMI with a proposal for MMI to acquire it. The failure of certain contracts has led to falling revenues and profits, and the company needs new investment. The Managing Director (MD) of InfoTech has proposed that MMI should acquire InfoTech for a nominal sum and then substantially invest in the company so that it can regain its previous profitability and revenue levels. However, after its experience with Boatland, the CEO of MMI is cautious about any further diversification of the MMI group.

Table 1: Financial and market data for selected companies (all figures in $m)

MMI quarrying and mining	20X8	20X6	20X4	20X2
Revenue	1,680	1,675	1,250	1,275
Gross profit	305	295	205	220
Net profit	110	105	40	45
Estimated market revenue	6,015	6,050	6,200	6,300
First Leisure	20X8	20X6	20X4	20X2
Revenue	200	160	110	100
Gross profit	42	34	23	21
Net profit	21	17	10	9
Estimated market revenue	950	850	770	750
Boatland	20X8	20X6	20X4	20X2
Revenue	2.10	2.40	2.40	2.30
Gross profit	0.30	0.50	0.50	0.60
Net profit	0.09	0.25	0.30	0.30
Estimated market revenue	201	201	199	198
InfoTech	20X8	20X6	20X4	20X2
Revenue	21	24	26	25
Gross profit	0.9	3	4	4
Net profit	(0.2)	2	3	3
Estimated market revenue	560	540	475	450

Required

(a)   In the context of MMI's corporate-level strategy, explain the rationale for MMI acquiring First Leisure and Boatland and assess the subsequent performance of the two companies.

(15 marks)

(b)   Assess the extent to which the proposed acquisition of InfoTech represents an appropriate addition to the MMI portfolio.

(10 marks)

(Total = 25 marks)

Risk

Questions 18 to 20 focus on 'Risk' – Section D of the Strategic Business Leader syllabus.

18 Branscombe   25 marks

Branscombe Co has been supplying and fitting premium bathrooms and kitchens in hotel chains throughout Effland for the past 20 years. The company started as a small family concern, but because of the rapid growth it experienced and an associated need for additional capital, it was recently listed on the national stock exchange via an initial public offering.

To remain fully compliant with the Effland corporate governance code, the board established audit, remuneration and nomination committees which were solely populated by independent non-executive directors. However, it did not consider it necessary to create a separate risk committee because the board believed that the remit of the audit committee included all aspects of risk management policy. This explanation was formally submitted to the shareholders at Branscombe Co's first general meeting, and the shareholders agreed with the board's proposal.

As part of its expansion strategy, the board of Branscombe Co decided it needed to enter overseas markets, and in particular the developing country of Geeland. The reason that Geeland was selected as a suitable market was because it had experienced rapid economic growth and domestic prosperity following the discovery of rich, offshore mineral deposits. Unfortunately, this small island nation has never enjoyed stable democratic government and is notorious for corrupt business practices, with customs officials regularly demanding bribes from both importers and exporters. As a result, Geeland has a poor international credit rating. In order to attract both domestic and foreign inward investment, the government of Geeland operates with very low levels of indirect tax, which has stimulated the island's tourist industry and led in turn to a significant increase in hotel building.

Following a successful tendering exercise, Branscombe Co was awarded the contract to supply all of the bathroom equipment for a 200-room hotel, currently under construction in a remote area of the island. The total value of the supply contract amounted to 1,800,000 Geeland dollars and it was to be paid in three equal instalments as the bathrooms were delivered to the hotel. The contract assigns responsibility for shipping the goods the 3,000 km from Effland to the island solely with Branscombe Co, and no payment will be made until an agreed volume of goods clears Geeland customs. A further problem is that the Geeland dollar is quite volatile, but recently it has been weakening against the Effland dollar. As all contract payments are to be made in Geeland currency, Branscombe Co is exposed to foreign exchange risks.

The many contract-related issues amount to significant risks to Branscombe Co, requiring effective management if the supply contract is to be a success and contribute to the company's ambitious growth targets.

Required

(a)   Explain the function and roles of a risk committee within an effective corporate governance framework, and discuss the advantages which a risk committee could add to the governance of Branscombe Co.   (10 marks)

(b)   Explain the term risk appetite, and assess how the risk appetite of Branscombe Co has influenced both its corporate strategy and the risks it has chosen to bear.   (7 marks)

(c)   Explain how Branscombe Co could effectively control the strategic and operational risks which arise from the Geeland supply contract.   (8 marks)

(Total = 25 marks)

The board of YGT discussed its need for timely risk information. The consensus of the meeting was that risk consultants should be engaged to review the risks facing the company. One director, Raz Dutta, said that she felt that this would be a waste of money as the company needed to concentrate its resources on improving organisational efficiency rather than on gathering risk information. She said that many risks 'didn't change much' and 'hardly ever materialised' and so can mostly be ignored. The rest of the board, however, believed that a number of risks had recently emerged whilst others had become less important and so the board wanted a current assessment as it believed previous assessments might now be outdated.

The team of risk consultants completed the risk audit. They identified and assessed six potential risks (A, B, C, D, E and F) and the following information was discussed when the findings were presented to the YGT board:

Risk A was assessed as unlikely and low impact whilst Risk B was assessed as highly likely to occur and with a high impact. The activities giving rise to both A and B, however, are seen as marginal in that, whilst the activities do have value and are capable of making good returns, neither is strategically vital.

Risk C was assessed as low probability but with a high potential impact and also arises from an activity that must not be discontinued, although alternative arrangements for bearing the risks are possible. The activity giving rise to Risk C was recently introduced by YGT as a result of a new product launch.

Risk D was assessed as highly likely but with a low potential impact, and arose as a result of a recent change in legislation. It cannot be insured against nor can it be outsourced. It is strategically important that YGT continues to engage in the activity that gives rise to Risk D, although not necessarily at the same level as is currently the case.

In addition, Risks E and F were identified. Risk E was an environmental risk and Risk F was classed as a reputation risk. The risk consultants said that risks E and F could be related risks. In the formal feedback to the board of YGT, the consultants said that the company had to develop a culture of risk awareness and that this should permeate all levels of the company.

Required

(a)   Criticise Raz Dutta's beliefs about the need for risk assessment. Explain why risks are dynamic and therefore need to be assessed regularly.   **(8 marks)**

(b)   Using the TARA framework, select and explain the appropriate strategy for managing each of risks A, B, C and D. Justify your selection in each case.   **(6 marks)**

(c)   Explain what 'related risks' are and describe how Risks E and F might be positively correlated.

(5 marks)

(Total = 19 marks)

> **Tutorial note:** When you attempt your real SBL exam you are unlikely to be told which theoretical model/framework to use. The reference to the TARA framework has been included here to provide you with an opportunity to apply your technical knowledge to a question scenario.

20 H&Z   25 marks

John Pentanol was appointed as risk manager at H&Z Co a year ago and he decided that his first task was to examine the risks that faced the company. He concluded that the company faced three major risks, which he assessed by examining the impact that would occur if each risk were to materialise. He assessed Risk 1 as being of low potential impact as even if it materialised it would have little effect on the company's strategy. Risk 2 was assessed as being of medium potential impact whilst a third risk, Risk 3, was assessed as being of very high potential impact.

When John realised the potential impact of Risk 3 materialising, he issued urgent advice to the board to withdraw from the activity that gave rise to Risk 3 being incurred. In the advice he said that the impact of Risk 3 was potentially enormous and it would be irresponsible for H&Z Co to continue to bear that risk.

The company commercial director, Jane Xylene, said that John Pentanol and his job at H&Z Co were unnecessary and that risk management was 'very expensive for the benefits achieved'. She said that all risk managers do is to tell people what can't be done, and that they are pessimists by nature. She said she wanted to see entrepreneurial risk takers in H&Z Co and not risk managers who, she believed, tended to discourage enterprise.

John replied that it was his job to eliminate all of the highest risks at H&Z Co. He said that 'all risk was bad and needed to be eliminated if possible. If it couldn't be eliminated, then it should be minimised.' He also added that 'the risk manager has an important role to play in an organisation's risk management.'

Required

(a) (i)   Describe the roles of a risk manager.   **(4 marks)**

     (ii) Assess John Pentanol's understanding of his role.   **(4 marks)**

(b) With reference to a risk assessment framework as appropriate, criticise John's advice that H&Z should withdraw from the activity that incurs Risk 3.   **(6 marks)**

Jane Xylene expressed a particular view about the value of risk management in H&Z Co. She also said that she wanted to see 'entrepreneurial risk takers'.

Required

(c) (i)   Define 'entrepreneurial risk' and explain why it is important to accept entrepreneurial risk in business organisations.   **(4 marks)**

     (ii) Critically evaluate Jane Xylene's view of risk management.   **(7 marks)**

                                                                (Total = 25 marks)

Technology and data analytics

Questions 21 to 23 focus on 'Technology and data analytics' – Section E of the Strategic Business Leader syllabus.

21 Cronin Auto Retail   **25 marks**

Cronin Auto Retail (CAR) is a car dealer that sells used cars bought at auctions by its experienced team of buyers. Every car for sale is less than two years old and has a full service history. The company concentrates on small family cars and, at any one time, there are about 120 on display at its purpose-built premises. The premises were acquired five years ago on a 25-year lease and they include a workshop, a small café and a children's playroom. All vehicles are selected by one of five experienced buyers who attend auctions throughout the country. Each attendance costs CAR about $500 per day in staff and travelling costs and usually leads to the purchase of five cars. On average, each car costs CAR $10,000 and is sold to the customer for $12,000. The company has a good sales and profitability record, although a recent economic recession has led the managing director to question 'whether we are selling the right type of cars. Recently, I wonder if we have been buying cars that our team of buyers would like to drive, not what our customers want to buy?' However, the personal selection of quality cars has been an important part of CAR's business model and it is stressed in their marketing literature and website.

Sales records show that 90% of all sales are to customers who live within two hours' drive of CAR's base. This is to be expected as there are many competitors and most customers want to buy from a garage that they can easily return the car to if it needs inspection, a service or repair. Consequently, CAR concentrates on display advertising in newspapers in this geographical area. It also has a customer database containing the records of people who have bought cars in the last three years. All customers receive a regular mail-shot, listing the cars for sale and highlighting any special offers or promotions. The company has a website where all the cars are listed with a series of photographs showing each car from a variety of angles. The website also contains general information about the company, special offers and promotions, and information about its vehicle maintenance and repair services.

CAR is keen to expand the service and mechanical repair side of its business. It would particularly like customers who have purchased cars from them to bring them back for servicing or for any mechanical repairs that are subsequently required. However, although CAR holds basic spare parts in inventory, it has to order many parts from specialist parts companies (called motor factors) or from the manufacturers directly. Mechanics have to raise paper requisitions which are passed to the procurement manager for reviewing, agreeing and sourcing. Most parts are ordered from regular suppliers, but there is an increasing backlog and this can cause a particular problem if the customer's car is in the garage waiting for the part to arrive. Customers are increasingly frustrated and annoyed by repairs taking much longer than they were led to expect. Another source of frustration is that the procurement manager only works from 10.00am to 4.00pm. The mechanics work on shifts and so the garage is staffed from 7.00am to 6.00pm. Urgent requisitions cannot be processed when the procurement manager is not at work. The backlog of requisitions is placing increased strain on the procurement manager who has recently made a number of clerical mistakes when raising a purchase order.

Requests for stationery and other office supplies also go through the same requisitioning process, with orders placed with the office supplier who is offering the best current deal. Finding this deal can be time consuming and so employees are increasingly submitting requisitions earlier so that they can be sure that new supplies will be received in time.

The managing director is aware of the problems of the requisitioning system but is reluctant to appoint a second procurement manager because he is trying to keep staff overheads down during a difficult trading period. He is keen to address 'more fundamental issues in the marketing and procurement processes'. He is particularly interested in how the 'interactivity, intelligence, individualisation and independence of location offered by e-marketing media can help us at CAR'.

Required

(a)   Evaluate how the principles of interactivity, intelligence, individualisation and independence of location might be applied in the e-marketing of the products and services of CAR.

(16 marks)

(b)   Explain the principles of e-procurement and evaluate its potential application to CAR.

(9 marks)

(Total = 25 marks)

22 BeauCo   25 marks

BeauCo is a medium-sized manufacturer of specialist computer components. The market has become particularly competitive in recent years, with component manufacturers vying to sell products to large technology companies. BeauCo's operations are heavily dependent on IT. Production materials are purchased through the company's state-of-the-art online procurement and inventory management systems, and all sales are made via the company's website. A back-up of all information stored across BeauCo's IT systems is taken every three months.

Component parts department

BeauCo pays engineers working in the component parts department a generous salary. This is due to the specialist nature of the work undertaken and long hours worked. Engineers are frequently required to work overtime in order to meet customer orders. During the company's most recent board meeting, BeauCo's Managing Director, Thomas Gethings, revealed a fraud that had been uncovered by the assistant head of human resources.

Fraud

The fraud was carried out by two employees. Alice Perkin, the payroll officer, had recently been left in charge of the payroll department as the payroll supervisor was on maternity leave. The payroll supervisor always reviewed and signed off the payroll data produced by Alice prior to finance releasing payments. Due to the supervisor's absence, Alice had taken over both roles.

Adam Thomas, operations manager of the component parts department was responsible for producing and authorising the overtime worked by the engineers each month. He would send Alice the approved monthly overtime figures to enter onto the payroll system.

BeauCo's human resources department maintains standing data on all employees. The standing data is updated when an employee joins or leaves the organisation. This data contains each employee's personal bank details used by the finance department in paying the monthly staff salaries. The assistant head of human resources was designated to update the standing data stored on her computer. Late one evening, Alice was able to access the data where she added three fictitious engineers with the same bank account details. The human resources department had disabled the required security settings on all computers as many in the department regarded the need to continually update their passwords as too cumbersome.

In a bid to improve security on site all internal doors leading to areas containing confidential information, including finance and human resources, had been fitted with a pass code entry system. To gain access, authorised staff were required to enter a four-digit code to unlock the doors. Due to early glitches with the system, all internal entrances had been left unlocked.

Adam submitted false overtime claims to the payroll department in respect of the fictitious employees. Using the company's payroll processing system Alice was able to put through significant monthly payments for each fictitious employee.

Company policy requires that significant deviations in staff costs should be discussed with the head of production, prior to payments being made. Initially, a member of the finance department queried the sudden rise in overtime payments with Adam, who downplayed the concern, saying that 'the overtime had been needed to meet a shortage of staff'. No further action was taken.

Alice and Adam were able to amass a significant amount of additional pay, which was received into a new bank account operated by the fraudsters. The fraud was uncovered five months later when the assistant head of HR conducted a review of the standing data and noticed the three fictitious employees all had the same bank account details.

IT review

In response, Thomas Gethings ordered a full review of the company's IT and information systems to ensure that a similar event could not occur again. To support the board an external IT consultancy firm has been approached to recommend improvements to help safeguard BeauCo's IT systems and processes. During one meeting with the BeauCo board one consultant made reference to the importance of continuity planning and disaster recovery.

Required

(a) Analyse the adequacy of BeauCo's internal control processes. (You should give particular consideration to the IT controls and payroll processes in place at the company and suggest practical recommendations on how these could be improved.) **(16 marks)**

(b) The board of BeauCo would like to gain a better understanding of the terms continuity planning and disaster recovery. Advise the board as to why both continuity planning and disaster recovery activities are likely to be important for BeauCo. You should refer to the use of cloud computing in your answer. **(9 marks)**

(Total = 25 marks)

23 Flamingo   25 marks

Flamingo is an online fashion retail business targeting men and women in the 18-40 age range. It was established four years ago by two fashion and design graduates who were disappointed by the lack of clothing choice available online. The business has grown rapidly since its inception and is now the most recognised online clothing company among its target demographic. The fashion industry is fast paced and customers have low switching costs, buying from whichever retailer has the best deals or the most up-to-date styles. Barriers to entry are low with new online fashion businesses using social media to build a customer base.

Sales strategy

Customers are incentivised to order several items of clothing at a time with an offer of free delivery if they spend over $100. Once received, if the clothes don't fit Flamingo offers free returns. Flamingo finds that this policy drives higher sales revenues because many customers simply keep the clothing sent to them. A national newspaper has recently published insights from an undercover reporter, revealing how returned clothes are either sent to landfill or burnt rather than being resold. This has sparked heavy criticism of Flamingo and there has been a resulting fall in sales revenue.

Use of Artificial Intelligence at Flamingo

Flamingo already uses predictive analytics allowing it to predict the likelihood of a sale using historical customer purchase data. This helps Flamingo with demand planning and inventory management. However, Flamingo would like to develop their Artificial Intelligence capability to increase sales. The board is investigating the use of a new AI powered app called PerfectFit. The app asks customers to upload a photo of themselves as well as answering a series of questions about height, weight, age, and their size in popular brands. The app combines this information with data already held about the customer (previous purchases and style information) to filter the clothes customers see on the website. If a customer clicks on an item of clothing they are interested in, the app uses the photo and size measurements to show the customer how the item would appear on them.

Cyber security

Flamingo has over 6 million online customers. The company stores customer data, including personal and payment details, in a cloud-based database. A competitor online fashion company has recently been the victim of a cyber-attack so in light of the intended app launch Flamingo is keen to understand the risks this could pose for them as well as the controls that should be put in place.

Required

(a) Evaluate the benefits and risks of using the proposed AI technology to improve the service Flamingo offers. **(15 marks)**

(b) Identify the problems that could arise as a result of a cyber-attack and recommend controls that could be put in place to minimise the risk. **(10 marks)**

(Total = 25 marks)

Organisational control and audit

Questions 24 to 26 focus on 'Organisational control and audit' – Section F of the Strategic Business Leader syllabus.

24 Yaya   25 marks

In Yaya Co, Operations Director Ben Janoon recently realised there had been an increase in products failing the final quality checks. These checks were carried out in the quality control (QC) laboratory, which tested finished goods before their release for sale. The product failure rate had risen from 1% of items two years ago to 4% now, and this meant an increase of hundreds of items of output a month which were not sold on to Yaya's customers. The failed products had no value to the company once they had failed QC, as the rework costs were not economic. Because the increase was gradual, it took a while for Mr Janoon to realise that the failure rate had risen.

A thorough review of the main production operation revealed nothing that might explain the increased failure and so attention was focused instead on the QC laboratory. For some years, the QC laboratory at Yaya, managed by Jane Goo, had been marginalised in the company, with its two staff working in a remote laboratory well away from other employees. Ben Janoon, who designed the internal control systems in Yaya, rarely visited the QC lab because of its remote location. He never asked for information on product failure rates to be reported to him, and did not understand the science involved in the QC process. He relied on the two QC staff, Jane Goo and her assistant John Zong, both of whom had relevant scientific qualifications.

The two QC staff considered themselves low paid. Whilst in theory they reported to Mr Janoon, in practice, they conducted their work with little contact with colleagues. The work was routine and involved testing products against a set of compliance standards. A single signature on a product compliance report was required to pass or fail products in QC and the compliance reports were then filed away with no-one else seeing them.

It was eventually established that Jane Goo had found a local buyer to pay her directly for any of Yaya's products which had failed the QC tests. The increased failure rate had resulted from her signing products as having 'failed QC' when, in fact, they had passed. She kept the proceeds from the sales for herself, and also paid her assistant, John Zong, a proportion of the proceeds from the sale of the failed products.

Required

(a) Explain typical reasons why an internal control system might be ineffective.   (5 marks)

(b) Explain the internal control deficiencies that led to the increased product failures at Yaya Co.

(10 marks)

(c) Discuss the general qualities of useful information, stating clearly how they would be of benefit to Mr Janoon, and recommend specific measures which would improve information flow from the QC lab to Mr Janoon.   (10 marks)

(Total = 25 marks)

25 Anne Hayes   19 marks

It was the final day of a two-week-long audit of Van Buren Co, a long-standing client of Fillmore Pierce Auditors. In the afternoon, Anne Hayes, a recently qualified accountant and member of the audit team, was following an audit trail on some cash payments when she discovered what she described to the audit partner, Zachary Lincoln, as an 'irregularity'. A large and material cash payment had been recorded with no recipient named. The corresponding invoice was handwritten on a scrap of paper and the signature was illegible.

Zachary, the audit partner, was under pressure to finish the audit that afternoon. He advised Anne to seek an explanation from Frank Monroe, the client's Finance Director. Zachary told her that Van Buren was a long-standing client of Fillmore Pierce and he would be surprised if there was anything unethical or illegal about the payment. He said that he had personally been involved in the Van Buren audit for the last eight years and that it had always been without incident. He also said that Frank Monroe was an old friend of his from university days and that he was certain that he wouldn't approve anything unethical or illegal. Zachary said that Fillmore Pierce had also done some consultancy for Van Buren so it was a very important client that he didn't want Anne to upset with unwelcome and uncomfortable questioning.

When Anne sought an explanation from Mr Monroe, she was told that nobody could remember what the payment was for but that she had to recognise that 'real' audits were sometimes a bit messy and that not all audit trails would end as she might like them to. He also reminded her that it was the final day and both he and the audit firm were under time pressure to conclude business and get the audit signed off.

When Anne told Zachary what Frank had said, Zachary agreed not to sign off the audit while Anne was still investigating the irregularity, but warned her that she should be very certain that the irregularity was worth delaying the sign-off for. It was therefore now Anne's decision whether to extend the audit or have it signed off by the end of Friday afternoon.

Required

(a)   Explain why 'auditor independence' is necessary in auditor-client relationships and describe **three** threats to auditor independence in the case.   **(9 marks)**

Anne is experiencing some ethical tensions due to the conflict between her duties and responsibilities as an employee of Fillmore Pierce and as a qualified professional accountant.

Required

(b)   (i)   Compare and contrast Anne's duties and responsibilities in the two roles of employee and professional accountant.   **(6 marks)**

      (ii) Explain the ethical tensions between these roles that Anne is now experiencing.
                                                                                   (4 marks)

                                                                      (Total = 19 marks)

26 Blup
25 marks

When Blup Co (a listed company involved in water supply) decided to establish an internal audit function, in line with new listing rules, the board approached Karen Huyer, an external consultant. She explained that internal audit is especially important in highly regulated industries but that it could also offer benefits to companies regardless of the industry context.

Karen was particularly keen to talk to John Xu, the head of the audit committee. John explained that because Blup Co was a water supply company and was thus highly regulated, he considered it important that all of the members of the audit committee were professional water engineers so that they fully understood the industry and its technical challenges. All three members of the audit committee were non-executive directors and all were recently retired members of the Blup executive board. When Karen asked about the relationship with external auditors, John said that they had an 'excellent' relationship, saying that this was because the external audit practice was run by the Chair's son-in-law.

Karen said that one of the essential functions of internal audit is to provide assurance that the internal controls which underpinned financial reporting are effective. She said that effective internal controls are necessary for maintaining the integrity of financial reporting and that the new internal audit function could help with that.

Required

(a)   Discuss the importance of internal audit in a highly regulated industry such as the water industry in which Blup Co operates.   **(7 marks)**

(b)   (i)   Assess the ways in which Blup Co's audit committee has failed to meet best practice.
                                                                                        (6 marks)

        (II)   Explain why the audit committee is responsible for overseeing the internal audit function.   **(6 marks)**

(c)   Discuss how effective internal controls can provide assurance on the integrity of financial reporting.   **(6 marks)**

                                                                    (Total = 25 marks)

Finance in planning and decision making

Questions 27 and 28 focus on 'Finance in planning and decision-making' – Section G of the Strategic Business Leader syllabus.

27 World Engines   15 marks

World Engines (WE) is one of the largest producers of aircraft and ship engines in the world. It has assets in excess of $600bn. It is currently considering improvements to its marine engine production facilities. These improvements include the introduction of specialist hardware and software engine testing technology. Two companies have been shortlisted for supplying this technology.

Amethyst is a well-established company whose product provides sophisticated testing facilities and costs $7m. The software that supports the product is written in a conventional programming language. The solution is widely used, but it is relatively inflexible and it has an out-of-date user interface. Amethyst has been trading profitably for 20 years and currently has an annual turnover of $960m.

Topaz is a relatively new company (formed three years ago) whose product is more expensive ($8m) but it offers significant advantages in high-volume performance and stress testing. It has a modular software design that allows it to be easily maintained and upgraded. It is written in a relatively new powerful programming language and it also has an attractive and contemporary user interface. Topaz currently has a turnover of $24m per year. Some WE executives are concerned about purchasing from such a young, relatively small company, although externally commissioned credit reports show that Topaz is a profitable, liquid and lightly geared company.

Unfortunately, the financial specialist who had been leading the evaluation project has been taken ill, and will be off work for the foreseeable future. One of the divisional directors of WE has been asked to run the testing technology evaluation project in the specialist's absence.

The director has found the following table (Table 1) produced by the financial specialist. The divisional director recalls that these returns were based on 'tangible benefits resulting from the two options. The returns reflect the characteristics of the two products. Topaz produces better returns if demand for testing is high, but is less effective in low demand circumstances. This is a reflection of the fact that the two solutions differ slightly in terms of their functional scope and power.'

Table 1: Expected returns for three demand and supplier combinations

Option	Supplier	IF high demand	IF low demand
A	Amethyst	$3m per annum	$0.5m per annum
B	Topaz	$4m per annum	$0.1m per annum

The divisional director also recalls a workshop convened to consider future market demand.

'Demand in the marine industry is currently affected by global economic uncertainty and it is increasingly difficult to predict demand. I remember that we were also asked to estimate demand for our marine products for the next six years. We eventually came up with the following figures, although it was relatively hard to get everyone to agree and debate at the workshop became a little heated.'

- High demand for six years: probability p = 0.4
- Low demand for six years: probability p = 0.4
- High demand for three years, followed by low demand for three years: probability p = 0.2

These figures are confirmed by a document in the financial specialist's files. 'As I recall', said the divisional director, 'the financial specialist intended to develop a decision tree to help us evaluate the Amethyst and Topaz alternatives. However, there is no evidence that he ever constructed it, which is a shame because we could have taken the procurement decision on the basis of that decision tree.'

Required

(a)   Develop a decision tree from the information given in the scenario and discuss its implications and shortcomings.

Ignore the time value of money in your analysis.   **(9 marks)**

(b)   The divisional director suggests that the procurement decision could have been taken on the evidence of the decision tree.

Discuss what other factors (not considered by the decision tree analysis) should also be taken into consideration when deciding which option to select.   **(6 marks)**

(Total = 15 marks)

28 Mantis & Gear   **25 marks**

Introduction

Mantis & Gear (M&G) was formed over 50 years ago to manufacture branded electrical and electronic goods for other companies. These goods are made to the specification required by these companies, whose own brand logos are attached to the products during the production process. M&G currently manufactures hundreds of products, although some are very similar in specification, with slight differences due to the requirements of each customer. M&G does not sell its own products to individual domestic consumers. Sales teams therefore focus on high volume sales to large companies. Since its founding M&G has always operated a traditional finance function, which undertakes a range of tasks including: processing accounting transactions, maintaining records, preparing month end reports and reporting on key financial performance measures. Members of the finance function report to M&G's Finance Director, Gary Belham.

The electrical and electronic goods market is increasingly competitive, with overseas companies entering the market. M&G's customers have responded to this by demanding lower prices and better quality products from M&G. As the electrical and electronic goods market is technologically innovative, there is also a requirement to continually develop new products or enhance existing ones.

The sales manager, James Slater, has revealed his sales team figures for the last year (20X4) and is excited to announce that the team has exceeded sales volume targets. However, his enthusiasm is not shared by the business controller, Furzana Khan, who has written a report to the Chief Executive Officer (CEO) suggesting that there are fundamental performance problems in the company. An extract of her report is given below:

Business performance

'In a period of increased competition and growing product ranges, we are failing to keep control of the profitability of our business. Table 1 presents a summary of our performance for 20X4, showing problems with our pricing and/or our cost control. This has affected profitability.

Table 1: Budgeted versus actual performance for 20X4

	Budget units	Actual units
Sales volume	243,000	270,000
	Budget	Actual
	$'000	$'000
Sales revenue	36,450	36,450
Direct materials	(15,795)	(18,630)
Direct labour	(3,402)	(4,725)
Fixed overheads	(8,250)	(11,450)
Operating profit	9,003	1,645

I recommend that we move from our traditional absorption costing system to that of activity-based costing (ABC) in order to better understand our costs and to introduce an appropriate strategy to turn around our business performance. Specifically, we should ensure that we incorporate both product and customer costing into our ABC analysis to determine our profitable and unprofitable products and customers.'

BPP
LEARNING
MEDIA

James Slater has seen the report and has angrily confronted Furzana. 'We are in a period of increased competition and have successfully managed to grow our sales in difficult times. We even managed to fulfil some special orders with very short lead times. We should be celebrating these successes, not treating them as poor performance. We should expect some fall in profitability as our customers are able to shop around, so we have to make our products and our prices more attractive to them.'

Required

It is clear that the business controller and the sales manager have different opinions about the current performance of the company.

(a)   Analyse the data shown in Table 1, suggesting possible reasons why performance may not be as positive as the sales manager portrays it.   **(15 marks)**

Gary Belham, M&G'S Finance Director, recently read an article titled *The changing role of the finance function*, which focused on the rise of the business partner model. Gary Belham would like to gain a better understanding of the business partner model.

(b)   Briefly explain the meaning of the 'finance function as a business partner' and outline the potential benefits to M&G of establishing its own finance function a business partner.

(10 marks)

(Total = 25 marks)

Innovation, performance excellence and change management

Questions 29 to 33 focus on 'Innovation, performance excellence and change management' –
Section H of the Strategic Business Leader syllabus.

29 Country Car Club   25 marks

Introduction

The Country Car Club (3C) was established 50 years ago to offer breakdown assistance to
motorists. In return for an annual membership fee, members of 3C are able to phone for
immediate assistance if their vehicle breaks down anywhere in the country. Assistance is provided
by 'service patrol engineers' who are located throughout the country and who are specialists in
vehicle repair and maintenance. If they cannot fix the problem immediately then the vehicle (and
its occupants) are transported by a 3C recovery vehicle back to the member's home address free
of charge.

Over the last 15 years, 3C has rapidly expanded its services. It now offers vehicle insurance,
vehicle history checks (to check for previous accident damage or theft) as well as offering a
comprehensive advice centre where trained staff answer a wide range of vehicle-related queries.
It also provides route maps, endorses hotels by giving them a 3C starred rating, and lobbies the
government on issues such as taxation, vehicle emissions and toll road charging. All of these
services are provided by permanent 3C employees and all growth has been organic culminating
in a listing on the country's stock exchange three years ago.

However, since its stock market listing, the company has posted disappointing results and a
falling share price has spurred managers to review internal processes and functions. A business
architecture committee (BAC) made up of senior managers has been charged with reviewing the
scope of the company's business activities and the way they are structured. The BAC has been
asked to examine the importance of certain activities and to make recommendations on the
sourcing of these activities (in-house or outsourced). The BAC has also been asked to identify
technological implications or opportunities for the activities that they recommend should remain
in-house.

First review

The BAC's first review included an assessment of the supply and maintenance of 3C's company
vehicles. 3C has traditionally purchased its own fleet of vehicles and maintained them in a central
garage. When a vehicle needed servicing or maintenance it was returned to this central garage.
Last year, 3C had 700 vehicles (breakdown recovery vehicles, service patrol engineer vans,
company cars for senior staff etc) maintained by 30 staff permanently employed in this garage.
A further three permanent employees were employed at the garage site with responsibility for the
purchasing and disposal of vehicles. The garage was in a residential area of a major town, with
major parking problems and no room for expansion.

The BAC concluded that the garage was of low strategic importance to the company and,
although most of the processes it involved were straightforward, its remoteness from the home
base of some vehicles made undertaking such processes unnecessarily complicated.
Consequently, it recommended outsourcing vehicle acquisition, disposal and maintenance to a
specialist company. Two months ago, 3C's existing vehicle fleet was acquired by AutoDirect, a
company with service and repair centres nationwide, which currently supplies 45,000 vehicles to
companies throughout the country. It now leases vehicles back to 3C for a monthly payment.
Over the next ten years (the duration of the contract) all vehicles will be leased from AutoDirect on
a full maintenance basis that includes the replacement of tyres and exhausts. 3C's garage is now
surplus to requirements and all the employees that worked there have been made redundant,
except for one employee who has been retained to manage the relationship with AutoDirect.

Second review

The BAC has now been asked to look at the following activities and their supporting processes. All of these are currently performed in-house by permanent 3C employees.

- **Attendance of repair staff at breakdowns** – currently undertaken by permanent 'service patrol engineers' employed at locations throughout the country from where they attend local breakdowns.

- **Membership renewal** – members must renew every year. Currently renewals are sent out by staff using a bespoke computer system. Receipts are processed when members confirm that they will be renewing for a further year.

- **Vehicle insurance services** providing accident insurance which every motorist legally requires.

- **Membership queries** handled by a call centre. Members can use the service for a wide range of vehicle-related problems and issues.

- **Vehicle history checks.** These are primarily used to provide 'peace of mind' to a potential purchaser of a vehicle. The vehicle is checked to see if it has ever been in an accident or if it has been stolen. The check also makes sure that the car is not currently part of a loan agreement.

Required

(a)   The BAC has been asked to make recommendations on the sourcing of activities (in-house or outsourced). The BAC has also been asked to identify technological implications or opportunities for the activities that they recommend should remain in-house.

Suggest and justify recommendations to the BAC for each of the following major process areas:

(i)   Attendance of repair staff at breakdowns

(ii)   Membership renewal

(iii)   Vehicle insurance services

(iv)   Membership queries

(v)   Vehicle history checks   **(15 marks)**

(b)   Analyse the advantages that 3C will gain from the decision to outsource the purchase and maintenance of their own vehicles.   **(10 marks)**

(Total = 25 marks)

30 Finch Co   25 marks

The company

Finch Co is a national grocery retailer, consisting of 230 stores throughout the country. The company has a strong reputation for selling quality food and drink products, supported by excellent standards of customer service. The company is regarded as a relatively small player in the market. However, Finch Co has a loyal customer and staff base, and many employees have worked for the company for a number of years.

Historically, the company has limited its use of IT in its operations. The company does have a small IT team based at head office. The current information system allows for weekly sales reports to be generated per store. All inventory ordering for stores is done manually at head office. Six years ago, Finch Co developed its first website. The site offered basic information such as opening times and store locations.

Trading conditions

In recent years Finch Co has suffered from a drop in profits and seen its market share fall. The Chief Executive Officer (CEO), Brendon Finch, identified rising store costs, as well as technological developments by competitors as being the two main causes behind the company's dip in performance. In response, he recommended that Finch needed to introduce new processes and services to improve its performance, and he established a project team to generate proposals to address the company's declining performance. The project was overseen by a project committee consisting of the CEO, Operations Director and the Customer Service Director – none of whom had been involved in any similar projects in the past.

Project proposals

The project committee agreed to the implementation of two new systems without delay.

New checkout system

The first new system saw Finch Co replace staffed checkouts (tills) in all of its stores with 'state-of-the- art' scanner systems. As a result, a significant number of the company's checkout operators have been made redundant. The scanner system works by allowing shoppers to scan product barcodes using a hand-held scanning device as they pass around the store. Once scanned these items can then be placed in the shopper's trolley. At the checkout, the customer then attaches the device to a small docking port which downloads the scanned items, removing the need to physically move items from the trolley to conveyor belt. The customer then pays for their items using a self-service payment function.

To reduce the scope for product theft, where items are put in a trolley without being scanned, some of the former checkout operators have been assigned to assisting customers download their scanned items at the checkouts. Brendon Finch believes this should help deter customers from leaving the store without paying for all of the items in the trolley as staff should be able to clearly identify such disparities between the downloaded data and the physical items in the trolley or basket.

The project committee were particularly attracted by the hardware supplier's promise that the new system would cut the amount of time customers spend queuing at the checkout, on average, from 5 minutes to 2 minutes. Brendon Finch decided to limit the amount of training all store staff would receive regarding the usage of the scanner system before it went live, insisting that 'staff learn best by simply getting stuck in and learning as they go'.

The new system can generate 'real time' sales reports per store and has been integrated into the company's inventory ordering system to remove the need for manual ordering.

'Click and collect'

The second development introduced was based upon systems which are already used by Finch Co's competitors. A 'click and collect' feature was added to Finch Co's existing website. The system allowed shoppers to order goods online to be collected from their nearest store arranged at a convenient time for them. All stores have been fitted with a new customer service counter where customers collect their orders at the designated time slot. Prior to the implementation of the service, the Operations Director anticipated online orders to be in the region of 3,000 orders each month per store.

Unveiling the developments to Finch Co's store staff, Brendon Finch stated that 'the new systems represent a bold move for our company. For too long we have believed that the key to our success was only selling good quality products. The world has moved on and we need to evolve if we are to remain a competitive player. Customers now expect more from us, convenience is what people want. If we don't adapt, our customers will shop with our rivals. I hope you will all get behind these changes and support each other through this time.'

Post-implementation

Since the introduction of the new systems, things have not gone smoothly. Finch Co has seen a dramatic increase in the number of customer complaints it receives.

A significant number of complaints relate to customers not understanding how the in-store scanner system operates. This has caused delays at the checkouts, with many customers queuing up the aisles to pay for their goods. Store managers have complained that some loyal shoppers have started to walk out of the store when noticing the growing queues. One comment left on an online shopping forum claimed that 'customers were struggling to connect the scanners to the checkout. When I asked a member of staff for help he just looked at me blankly and said I'm not too sure, I only had 10 minutes training this morning.'

Actual orders through the 'click and collect' service have been much higher than anticipated. On average 8,000 orders each month per store have been received since the system went live. This has resulted in numerous cases of online orders not being ready when due for collection. One shop worker complained that 'no one knows what they are doing. I am not sure if I am supposed to be stocking items on the shop floor or preparing click and collect orders for collection or helping customers with the scanners. It's a mess.'

Required

(a) Assess the extent to which new processes and systems are necessary to help Finch Co remain competitive. **(7 marks)**

(b) Evaluate the extent to which the different aspects of organisational change highlighted in the four-view model have contributed to the failure of the new systems. **(18 marks)**

(Total = 25 marks)

> **Tutorial note:** When you attempt your real SBL exam you are unlikely to be told which theoretical model/framework to use. The reference to the four-view model has been included here to provide you with an opportunity to apply your technical knowledge to a question scenario.

31 Pharmacy Systems International   25 marks

Introduction

Retail pharmacies supply branded medicinal products, such as headache and cold remedies, as well as medicines prescribed by doctors. Customers expect both types of product to be immediately available and so this demands efficient purchasing and inventory control in each pharmacy. The retail pharmacy industry is increasingly concentrated in a small number of nationwide pharmacy chains, although independent pharmacies continue to survive. The pharmacy chains are increasingly encouraging their customers to order medicinal products online and the doctors are being encouraged to electronically send their prescriptions to the pharmacy so that they can be prepared ready for the patient to collect.

Pharmacy Systems International

Pharmacy Systems International (PSI) is a privately owned software company which has successfully developed and sold a specialised software package meeting the specific needs of retail pharmacies. PSI's stated objective is to be a 'highly skilled professional company providing quality software services to the retail pharmacy industry'. Over the last three years PSI has experienced gradual growth in turnover, profitability and market share (see Table 1).

Table 1: PSI financial information

	20X7	20X6	20X5
Turnover ($'000)	11,700	10,760	10,350
Profits ($'000) (pre-tax)	975	945	875
Estimated market share	26%	24%	23%
Number of employees	120	117	115

PSI has three directors, each of whom has a significant ownership stake in the business. The Chief Executive is a natural entrepreneur with a past record of identifying opportunities and taking the necessary risks to exploit them. In the last three years he has curbed his natural enthusiasm for growth as PSI has consolidated its position in the market place. However, he now feels the time is right to expand the business to a size and profitability that makes PSI an attractive acquisition target and enables the directors to realise their investment in the company. He has a natural ally in the Sales and Marketing Director and both feel that PSI needs to find new national and international markets to fuel its growth. The Software Development Director, however, does not share the Chief Executive's enthusiasm for this expansion.

The Chief Executive has proposed that growth can best be achieved by developing a generic software package which can be used by the wider, general retail industry. His plan is for the company to take the current software package and take out any specific references to the pharmaceutical industry. This generic package could then be extended and configured for other retail sectors. The pharmaceutical package would be retained but it would be perceived and marketed as a specialised implementation of the new generic package.

This proposed change in strategic direction is strongly resisted by the Software Development Director. He and his team of software developers are under constant pressure to meet the demands of the existing retail pharmacy customers. Online ordering of medicinal products and electronic despatch of prescriptions are just two examples of the constant pressure PSI is under from retail customers. PSI must continuously update its software package to enable the pharmacies to implement technical innovations that improve customer service.

Ideally, the Software Development Director would like to acquire further resources to develop a more standardised software package for their current customers. He is particularly annoyed by PSI's salesmen continually committing the company to producing a customised software solution for each customer and promising delivery dates that the software delivery team struggle to meet. Frequently, the software contains faults that require expensive and time-consuming maintenance. Consequently, PSI is being increasingly criticised by customers. A recent user group conference expressed considerable dissatisfaction with the quality of the PSI package and doubted the company's ability to meet the published deadline for a new release of the software.

Required

(a)   The proposal to develop and sell a software package for the retail industry represents a major change in strategy for PSI.

Analyse the nature, scope and type of this proposed strategic change for PSI.   **(10 marks)**

(b)   The success of any attempt at managing change will be dependent on the context in which that change takes place.

Identify and analyse, using an appropriate model, the internal contextual features that could influence the success or failure of the Chief Executive's proposed strategic change for PSI.   **(15 marks)**

(Total = 25 marks)

32 Institute of Analytical Accountants   15 marks

The Institute of Analytical Accountants (IAA) offers three certification programmes which are assessed through examinations using multiple choice questions. These questions are maintained in a computerised question bank. The handling process for these questions is documented in Figure 1 and described in detail below.

The IAA is currently analysing all its processes, seeking possible business process redesign opportunities. It is considering commissioning a bespoke computer system to support any agreed redesign of the business process. The IAA is keen to implement a new solution fairly quickly because competitors are threatening to move into their established market.

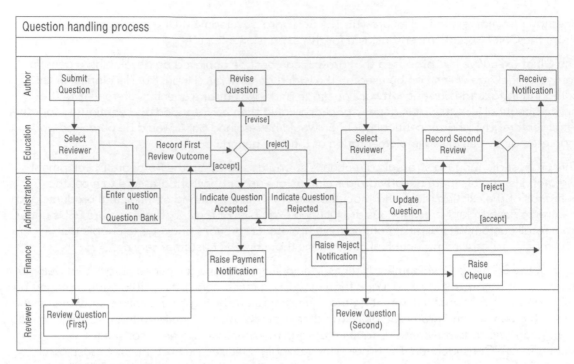

Figure 1: Question handling process at IAA

The author (the question originator) submits the question to the IAA as a password-protected document attached to an email. The education department of the IAA (which is staffed by subject matter experts) selects an appropriate reviewer and forwards the email to them. At no point in the process does the author know the identity of the reviewer. A copy of the email is sent to the administration department, where administrators enter the question in a standard format into a computerised question bank. These administrators are not subject matter experts and sometimes make mistakes when entering the questions and answers. A recent spot-check identified that one in ten questions contained an error. Furthermore, there is a significant delay in entering questions. Although five administrators are assigned to this task, they also have other duties to perform and so a backlog of questions has built up. Administrators are paid less than education staff.

The reviewer decides whether the question should be accepted as it is, rejected completely, or returned to the author for amendment. This first review outcome is recorded by the education department before the administration department updates the database with whether the question was accepted or rejected. On some occasions it is not possible to find the question which needs to be updated because it is still in the backlog of questions waiting to be entered into the system. This causes further delay and frustration.

Any amended questions are returned by the author to the education department, who forward them on to the reviewer. Copies are sent to the administration department so that they can amend the questions held on the database.

On the second review, the question is either accepted or rejected.

The finance department is notified of all accepted questions, and a payment notification is raised which eventually leads to a cheque being issued and sent to the author.

Rejected questions (irrespective of when they are rejected) are notified to the finance department who raise a reject notification and send it back to the author.

Required

The IAA would like to consider a number of redesign options, ranging from very simple improvements to radical solutions.

Identify a range of redesign options the IAA could consider for improving their question handling process. Evaluate the benefits of each option.   **(15 marks)**

33 Brighttown

The town of Brighttown in Euraria has a mayor (elected every five years by the people in the town) who is responsible for, amongst other things, the transport policy of the town.

A year ago, the mayor (acting as project sponsor) instigated a 'traffic lite' project to reduce traffic congestion at traffic lights in the town. Rather than relying on fixed timings, he suggested that a system should be implemented which made the traffic lights sensitive to traffic flow. So, if a queue built up, then the lights would automatically change to green (go). The mayor suggested that this would have a number of benefits. Firstly, it would reduce harmful emissions at the areas near traffic lights and, secondly, it would improve the journey times for all vehicles, leading to drivers 'being less stressed'. He also cited evidence from cities overseas, where predictable journey times had been attractive to flexible companies who could set themselves up anywhere in the country. He felt that the new system would attract such companies to the town.

The Eurarian government has a transport regulation agency called OfRoad. Part of OfRoad's responsibilities is to monitor transport investments and it was originally critical of the Brighttown 'traffic lite' project because the project's benefits were intangible and lacked credibility. The business case did not include a quantitative cost/benefit analysis. OfRoad has itself published a benefits management process which classifies benefits in the following way.

Financial: A financial benefit can be confidently allocated in advance of the project. Thus, if the investment will save $90,000 per year in staff costs then this is a financial benefit.

Quantifiable: A quantifiable benefit is a benefit where there is sufficient credible evidence to suggest, in advance, how much benefit will result from the project. This benefit may be financial or non-financial. For example, energy savings from a new building might be credibly predicted in advance. However, the exact amount of savings cannot be accurately forecast.

Measurable benefit: A measurable benefit is a benefit which can only be confidently assessed post-implementation, and so cannot be reliably predicted in advance. Increase in sales from a particular initiative is an example of a measurable benefit. Measurable benefits may either be financial or non-financial.

Observable benefit: An observable benefit is a benefit which a specific individual or group will decide, using agreed criteria, has been realised or not. Such benefits are usually non-financial. Improved staff morale might be an example of an observable benefit.

One month ago, the mayoral elections saw the election of a new mayor with a completely distinct transport policy with different objectives. She wishes to address traffic congestion by attracting commuters away from their cars and onto public transport. Part of her policy is a traffic light system which gives priority to buses. The town council owns the buses which operate in the town, and they have invested heavily in buses which are comfortable and have significantly lower emissions than the conventional cars used by most people in the town. The new mayor wishes to improve the frequency, punctuality and convenience of these buses, so that they tempt people away from using their cars. This will require more buses and more bus crews, a requirement which the mayor presents as 'being good for the unemployment rate in this town'. It will also help the bus service meet the punctuality service level which it published three years ago, but has never yet met. 'A reduction in cars and an increase in buses will help us meet our target', the mayor claims.

The mayor has also suggested a number of initiatives to discourage people from taking their cars into the town. She intends to sell two car parks for housing land (raising $325,000) and this will reduce car park capacity from 1,000 to 800 car spaces per day. She also intends to raise the daily parking fee from $3 to $4. Car park occupancy currently stands at 95% (it is difficult to achieve 100% for technical reasons) and the same occupancy rate is expected when the car park capacity is reduced.

The new mayor believes that her policy signals the fact that Brighttown is serious about its green credentials. 'This', she says, 'will attract environmentally aware people to come and live in our town and "green" companies to set up here. These companies and consumers will bring great benefit to our community.' To emphasise this, she has set up a 'Go Green' team to encourage green initiatives in the town.

The 'traffic lite' project to tackle congestion proposed by the former mayor is still in the development stage. The new mayor believes that this project can be modified to deliver her vision and still be ready on the date promised by her predecessor.

Required

(a)   A 'terms of reference' document (project initiation document; or project charter) was developed for the 'traffic lite' project to reduce traffic congestion.

Discuss what changes will have to be made to the 'terms of reference' to reflect the new mayor's vision of the project.   **(5 marks)**

(b)   The new mayor wishes to redefine the business case for the project, using the benefits categorisation suggested by OfRoad.

Identify costs and benefits for the revised project, classifying each benefit using the guidance provided by OfRoad.   **(15 marks)**

(Total = 20 marks)

Important note:

You have now reached the end of the Section 1 of this Kit.

Please remember the focus of this section has been on testing your **technical knowledge** of topics across the syllabus. However, the Strategic Business Leader (SBL) exam requires you to combine technical knowledge and professional skills, and the next section of the kit focuses on these **professional skills**.

Also, remember that the questions in the SBL exam will be set within the context of an integrated case study scenario. Sections 3 and 4 later in the Kit will give you the chance to apply your knowledge and professional skills to the type of case study material you will face in the exam.

Section 2 – Professional skills development

Important note:

In this section of questions, the level of challenge increases as we focus not only on syllabus knowledge but also introduce specific ACCA professional skills marks into the requirements. This section therefore replicates the expected requirement format in Strategic Business Leader but utilises short or condensed case scenarios to allow you to focus on applying syllabus knowledge and demonstrating the ACCA professional skills of communication, commercial acumen, analysis, scepticism and evaluation for the first time and developing your skills in these areas. The level of challenge has remained moderate, so the quantity and complexity of information provided in the case scenarios is manageable in these earlier stages of your learning and skills development.

We recommend these questions are completed during the later stages of the learning phase and before you start your revision phase.

34 P&J   10 marks

For the past 60 years, P&J has been Emmland's largest importer and processor of, among others, a product named X32 which is a compound used in a wide variety of applications. The rapid growth of X32 use has made P&J a very successful company.

X32 is mined in developing countries where local communities depend on it for their livelihoods. Income from the mining activities is used to support community development. The X32 is processed in dedicated P&J facilities near the mining communities, supporting many more jobs. It is then exported to Emmland for final manufacture into finished products and distribution.

In Emmland, P&J is the major employer in several towns. In Aytown, for example, P&J employs 45% of the workforce and in Betown, P&J employs 3,000 people and also supports a number of local causes including a community centre, football club and adult education classes. In total, the company employs 15,000 people in Emmland and another 30,000 people in various parts of the supply chain (mining and processing) in developing countries. Unlike in Emmland, where health and safety regulations are strong, there are no such regulations in most of the developing countries in which P&J operates.

Recently, research by Professor Harry Kroll discovered that X32 was very harmful to human health, particularly in the processing stages, causing a wide range of fatal respiratory diseases, including some that remain inactive in the body for many decades. The discovery caused a great deal of distress at P&J, and also in the industries which used X32.

Given that 60% of P&J's business was concerned with X32, Professor Kroll's findings could not be ignored. Although demand for X32 remained unaffected by Kroll's findings in the short to medium term, the company had to consider a new legal risk from a stream of potential litigation actions against the company from workers in many areas. These potential claims are currently unquantified, but even the best-case scenario is likely to result in huge liabilities.

Chief Executive Officer, Laszlo Ho, commissioned a report which found that it would be very difficult to reduce the risk posed by X32 in the supply chain unless facilities were redesigned and rebuilt. Finance Director (FD) Hannah Yin calculated that a full refit of all of the company's mines, processing and manufacturing plants (which Mr Ho called 'Plan A') was not affordable given the current market price of X32 and costs of production. Laszlo Ho then proposed the idea of a partial refit of the Aytown and Betown plants because they were more visible to investors and most other stakeholders.

Mr Ho reasoned that this partial refit ('Plan B') would enable the company to claim it was making progress on improving internal controls whilst managing current costs and 'waiting to see' how the market for X32 fared in the longer term. Under Plan B, no changes would be made to limit exposure to X32 in the company's operations in developing countries.

Mr Ho offered to substantially increase the FD Hannah Lin's share options if she played down the risks from litigation when talking to shareholders, and highlighted Plan B as evidence of the company's social responsibility. She agreed, and when she met with shareholders she also confirmed that P&J was aware of Professor Kroll's research but that the findings were not conclusive and therefore not a serious risk to the company's activities.

A financial journalist has now discovered the whole story and feels that the public, and P&J's shareholders in particular, should know about these events and the decisions that have been taken in P&J.

Required

Writing as the journalist who discovered the story, draft a short article for the specialist magazine *Investors in Companies*. Your article should distinguish between strategic and operational risk and explain why Professor Kroll's findings are a strategic risk to P&J.   (8 marks)

Professional skills marks are available for demonstrating **communication** skills in distinguishing between strategic and operational risks and explaining why the findings are a strategic risk to P&J.

(2 marks)

(Total = 10 marks)

35 Alpha Software   12 marks

Gemma Murphy has recently been appointed as the CEO of Alpha Software plc. The company develops specialist software for use by accountancy professionals. The specialist software market is particularly dynamic and fast changing, and it is common for competitors to drop out of the market. The most successful companies have been particularly focused on enhancing their offering to customers through creating innovative products and investing heavily in training and development for their employees.

Turbulent times

Alpha has been through a turbulent time over the last three years. During this time there have been significant senior management changes which resulted in confusion among shareholders and employees as to the strategic direction of the company. One investor complained that the annual accounts made it hard to know where the company was headed.

The last CEO introduced an aggressive cost-cutting programme aimed at improving profitability. At the beginning of the financial year the annual staff training and development budget was significantly reduced and has not been reviewed since the change in management.

Future direction

In response to the confusion surrounding the company's strategic direction, Gemma and the board published a new mission, the primary focus of which centres on making Alpha the market leader. Gemma was appointed as the CEO having undertaken a similar role at a competitor. The board were keen on her appointment as she is renowned in the industry for her creativity and willingness to introduce 'fresh ideas'. In her previous role Gemma oversaw the introduction of an integrated approach to reporting performance. This is something she is particularly keen to introduce at Alpha.

Gemma has been dismayed by the Finance Director's reaction to her proposal to introduce integrated reporting at Alpha Software. He has made it clear that he is not convinced of the need for such a change, arguing that 'this talk of integrated reporting in the business press is just a fad, requiring a lot more work, simply to report on things people do not care about. Shareholders are only interested in the bottom line.'

Gemma has asked you to help her strengthen her proposal to introduce integrated reporting, as she intends to take it up at the next board meeting.

Required

Prepare a briefing note for the Finance Director that addresses his concerns, and explains how integrated reporting may help Alpha Software to communicate its strategy to stakeholders and improve its strategic performance.   (10 marks)

Professional skills marks are available for demonstrating **communication** skills in persuading the Finance Director of the merits of integrated reporting for Alpha Software.   (2 marks)

(Total = 12 marks)

36 MachineShop   **12 marks**

Arboria is a prosperous industrial country with an established consumer culture that is distinguished by demanding and assertive consumers. Many companies find it difficult to compete successfully in the country but MachineShop is a notable exception. MachineShop sells small electrical machines and tools to both trade (people who use the machines/tools in their work) and domestic customers (people who use the machines/tools at home). For example, it sells a range of paint strippers retailing from $100 to $3,500. These paint strippers are bought by both tradesmen and ordinary domestic customers who use them to maintain their own home. It is estimated that 65% of sales are to domestic customers. MachineShop currently has 50 brightly decorated stores throughout Arboria. On average, a further two stores are opened every month. The company has no direct competitors. Most firms offering similar machines only sell them to tradesmen. In many respects MachineShop has defined a new market and it is the only company which, at present, seems to understand the dynamics of this market.

MachineShop is a private company still wholly owned by its directors. The board is headed by Dave Deen, a dynamic entrepreneur who enjoys a high national media profile. He likes the excitement of business and is determined to grow MachineShop – an ambition shared by his fellow directors. In 20X4, on a turnover of $50m, MachineShop recorded a gross profit margin of 28% and an operating margin of 17%. It delivered a return on capital employed (ROCE) of 17.5%. It currently has a gearing ratio (defined as long-term loans/capital employed) of 15% and an interest cover ratio of 3.5.

Dave Deen has ambitious growth plans, which he intends to achieve through internal growth, and undertaking business combinations such as acquisitions. Dave Deen is also keen to explore the establishment of external partnering arrangements with third parties in the form of strategic alliances. The opening of further stores in Arboria is providing internal (organic) growth. Much of this drive for growth is fuelled by a desire to exploit MachineShop's unique competencies before the idea is copied, both within Arboria and elsewhere in the world. However, the company is having difficulty finding companies to acquire, as there are few equivalent companies to target, either in Arboria or elsewhere in the world. Although MachineShop has never traded outside Arboria, the search for acquisitions is worldwide, with Dave Deen particularly keen to explore international markets in his desire to build a worldwide brand. He has specifically identified the developing country of Ceeland as a potential target, because macroeconomic trends suggest that a consumer society is emerging there, which is similar to the one in Arboria.

Ceeland

The government of Ceeland has spent the last decade building an effective road transport system, supported by low fuel and road taxes which make it cheap to use. The government has also installed a fast digital communication network, providing broadband internet access to all of the population. This is important to MachineShop because internet order placement (either for collection or delivery) is an important part of their business model. The government has also lifted certain restrictions which had been in place under its predecessor. For example, it has removed the need for companies trading in the country to be registered in Ceeland and to have at least one Ceeland citizen on the board. Until recently, there were restrictions on what machines could be used by domestic customers. However, these restrictions have also been removed, as part of a government initiative to encourage the development of light manufacturing in the country. Indeed, one brand of products already stocked by MachineShop is made by a company based in Ceeland.

Dave Deen recently read about Porter's 'diamond' but he cannot remember the details. He wants a concise explanation of its principles, relevance and application for MachineShop for inclusion in a presentation that he is giving to the board at their next strategy meeting.

Required

Prepare THREE slides, with supporting notes, to be presented to Dave Deen that explain the principles of Porter's 'diamond', and use those principles to describe the relative attractiveness of Ceeland and Arboria as environments in which MachineShop's growth ambitions could be achieved.

(10 marks)

Professional skills marks are available for demonstrating **communication** skills in clarifying the principles of Porter's diamond and applying this in relation to MachineShop's growth ambitions.

(2 marks)

(Total = 12 marks)

37 Rock Bottom

14 marks

This scenario summarises the development of a company called Rock Bottom through three phases, from its founding in 1975 to 2018 when it ceased trading.

Phase 1 (1975–1998)

In 1975 Rick Hein established his first shop specialising in the sale of imported electrical audio products, which were smaller, more reliable and more sophisticated than the domestic products found in larger department stores. Such a specialist shop was a new departure, and Rick Hein quickly established a chain of them, staffed by young people who understood the capabilities of the products they were selling. He invested in national press advertising, branding his shops as 'Rock Bottom', a name which specifically referred to his cheap prices, but also alluded to the importance of rock music and its influence on product sales.

Hein developed a high public profile and enjoyed being unconventional. He encouraged the managers of his stores to be the same, and rewarded individuality with high salaries, generous bonus schemes and autonomy.

However, by the late 1990s the profitability of the Rock Bottom shops had begun to decline significantly. Direct competitors using a similar approach had emerged, including specialist sections in the large general stores. Hein himself became less flamboyant in order to satisfy the banks who provided his finance.

Phase 2 (1999–2012)

In 1999 Hein floated the company on the country's stock exchange. He used some of the capital raised to expand the business, and sold shares to help him throw the 'party of a lifetime' and to purchase expensive goods and gifts for his family. Hein became Chair and Chief Executive Officer (CEO) of the newly quoted company, but over the next 13 years his relationship with his board and shareholders became increasingly difficult. New financial controls and reporting systems were put in place. Most of the established managers left as controls became more centralised and formal. The company's performance was solid but unspectacular. The company was legally required to publish directors' salaries in its annual report and the generous salary package enjoyed by the Chair and CEO increasingly became an issue and dominated the 2012 Annual General Meeting.

Phase 3 (2013–2018)

In 2013 Hein found substantial private equity investment and took Rock Bottom private again. He also used all of his personal fortune to help re-acquire the company from the shareholders, and held a huge and expensive celebration party. However, most of the new generation of store managers found Hein's style to be too loose and unfocused. Furthermore, changes in products and how they were purchased meant that fewer people bought audio products from specialist shops. The reliability of these products now meant that they were replaced relatively infrequently. Hein, belatedly, started to consider selling via an internet site, but he was reluctant to make the investment that was required. Turnover and profitability plummeted. In 2017 Hein considered franchising the company, but in early 2018 the company ceased trading and Hein himself filed for personal bankruptcy.

Required

Prepare extracts for a briefing paper which evaluates how Rick Hein's leadership style contributed to the success or failure of each of the three phases identified in the scenario. **(12 marks)**

Professional skills marks are available for demonstrating **commercial acumen** in displaying awareness of leadership styles and other factors that affected the achievement of organisational objectives at Rock Bottom. **(2 marks)**

(Total = 14 marks)

38 ATD

ATD is a medium-sized engineering company providing specialist components for the marine engineering market. The sales manager is currently under pressure from the other departmental managers to explain why his sales revenue forecasts are becoming increasingly unreliable. Errors in his forecasts are having consequential effects on production, inventory control, raw materials purchasing and, ultimately, on the profitability of the company itself. He uses a 'combination of experience, intuition and guesswork' to produce his sales forecast, but even he accepts that his forecasts are increasingly inaccurate.

The recent failure of the company to meet its sales targets for quarters 1 and 2 has prompted the Chief Executive Officer (CEO) to put into place a broad cost-cutting policy. He has banned business travel, cancelled a number of marketing initiatives and introduced a complete freeze on recruiting for posts which become vacant on the resignation of the current post holder. He claims that 'our failure to meet sales targets means we must ruthlessly cut costs'. However, many of the departmental managers are critical of such an indiscriminate approach and believe that the measures might be counter-productive.

This cost cutting has particularly demotivated the production manager and the inventory manager, who both blame the Sales Director for setting unrealistic targets. The production manager has commented that, 'I am working tirelessly to keep costs down, but the result is that I cannot replace one of my best purchasing administrators who left last month'. In general, departmental managers at the company feel 'powerless and undervalued'.

The company currently does not have a formal budgeting process in place. The production manager is sure that such a process, particularly if senior managers were involved in the budget-setting process, would help address the issues that ATD is facing.

Required

Prepare extracts for a briefing paper which explain how introducing a formal budgeting process would address the problems at ATD. **(10 marks)**

Professional skills marks are available for demonstrating **commercial acumen** in using judgement to identify the key problems at ATD, and ways in which a budgeting process could help to address them. **(2 marks)**

(Total = 12 marks)

39 Pulpo

Pulpo is a local pulp and paper factory. As a subsidiary of a major international company, Pulpo has not produced a social and environmental report for itself, but instead provided data which was fed into the parent company's group report. There was some discussion about Pulpo having an environmental report on its own website but no resources were provided for its development, so no separate report has ever been produced.

Mary Wong was the manager at Pulpo whose responsibility was to monitor and report on environmental emissions. It was her responsibility to monitor emissions and to feed data into the company's internal control systems on resource consumption (energy and water) and waste. It was a job she enjoyed because it enabled her to express her personal concern for the environment in her work. When she took over her role two years ago, she was told that the company had very ambitious voluntary emissions targets and that these would eventually be reduced to make the company even more environmentally responsible over time. Mary found this exciting and it was on this basis that she agreed to accept the appointment. Because of the sensitive nature of some of the data she managed, her employment terms and conditions included a confidentiality clause in which she agreed never to publicly disclose the environmental targets or the company's performance against them.

When investment in new manufacturing capital was delayed because of a deteriorating profit performance, Mary was informed that the emissions target would be temporarily increased because the ageing equipment would not be able to maintain the low level of emissions. Dismayed by this change, she complained to the company Chief Executive but was told that she had to accept the higher emissions until the company could afford its factory investment, which could be several years in the future.

Mary decided to tell the local press about the higher level of emissions, and there was an angry reaction from long-standing critics of the factory and its impact on the environment. When the board of the company discovered her actions, she was dismissed for breach of her terms and conditions in publically disclosing the confidential information.

Required

Prepare extracts for a briefing paper which explain the arguments in favour of Pulpo now publishing an environmental report on its own website, in addition to that provided by the parent company.

(8 marks)

Professional skills marks are available for demonstrating **commercial acumen** in identifying the reasons why Pulpo should publish an environmental report and the benefits that it could derive from doing so.

(2 marks)

(Total = 10 marks)

40 Mary Jane   12 marks

The Mary Jane was a large passenger and vehicle ferry operating across a busy section of ocean known as the 'Northport route'. Prior to this, the Mary Jane had operated for many years in the much calmer waters of the 'Southsea route' but she had been transferred to the Northport route because she could carry more passengers and vehicles per journey. The Mary Jane belonged to Sea Ships Co, a long-established international company with a fleet of ships. The Mary Jane had large doors at both the front and rear. Vehicles would drive in through the rear doors and when she arrived in Northport, the Mary Jane would dock the other way round so that the vehicles could drive straight out using the forward doors. There were two doors at each end, upper and lower, and it was important that all four doors were securely closed before setting out to sea.

The safety procedures aboard the Mary Jane were subject to regulation, but her design left one weakness. From the main control bridge of the ship, it was not possible to see the front or rear doors, which meant that it was not possible to check from the main control bridge that they were closed. On the night of 7 November, the Mary Jane was crossing to Northport at night in stormy weather. When she was only a few kilometres out to sea, water entered the car decks through the upper rear doors that had been left open. The Mary Jane began to lean before completely falling over onto her side. The speed of the event meant that escape was not possible and the Mary Jane sank with the loss of many lives.

Among the survivors was first officer Ned Prop. Mr Prop later told how a recent change to staff reporting procedures meant that responsibility for checking that the rear doors were closed before sailing had changed. Under the new system two people were responsible for safety on the car deck, but each person assumed that the other had checked that the upper rear doors had been closed. A reporting system in which each department head on the ship separately reported readiness for sea to the captain at the beginning of each journey had been abandoned because it took too long to operate. Mr Prop said that the normal procedure was that if they didn't hear anything to the contrary by the departure time, he and the captain assumed that all was well and the ship could sail.

Mr Prop told how procedures on board ship often relied on 'human teamwork' rather than 'following paperwork systems'. It also emerged that, on the day of the disaster, a mistake in loading vehicles onto the wrong decks had delayed the ship's departure and created pressure to leave as soon as possible. Mr Prop said that this may have been a contributory factor to the confusion over who should have checked that the rear doors were closed.

Sea Ships Co, the Mary Jane's owner, was one of the longest established and most respected companies listed on the stock exchange. It was considered by investment analysts to be a 'steady and reliable' investment and the company Chief Executive, Wim Bock, had often said that Sea Ships Co employed 'the highest standards of corporate ethics'. It valued its reputation as a well-run company and believed that the company's value was primarily due to its reputation for 'outstanding customer care'.

When Sea Ships' board met to discuss how to proceed after the disaster, Wim Bock said that the company could expect to receive substantial claims from victims' relatives. He also reported that, because of a regrettable oversight in the company's legal department, only a proportion of that liability would be covered by the company's insurance. There would also be punitive fines from the courts, the size of which would, a legal adviser said, reflect the scale of Sea Ships' negligence in contributing to the disaster. The Finance Director, Jill Wha, reported that if the company met the expected uninsured liabilities in full, even if reduced on appeal, it would severely threaten future cash flows as it would most likely have to sell non-current assets to settle the claims. If large punitive fines were also imposed after the legal process, Mr Bock said that the company may not survive.

The government ordered an enquiry. In her conclusions, enquiry chair Caroline Chan found that in addition to human error in not ensuring that the upper rear doors had been closed, the Mary Jane had been travelling above the local shipping speed limit. The excess speed had caused increased turbulence in the water and this was made much worse by the storm. Mrs Chan said that contrary to the board's perception of itself as a well-run company, there was a 'culture of carelessness' at Sea Ships and the internal control systems were inadequate. She reserved particular criticism for the board of Sea Ships, saying that it was unbalanced, lacking both independent scrutiny and, because none of the directors had ever served on board a ship, any representation from technically qualified officers.

After the enquiry was concluded, but before the level of claims and punitive damages had been set by the courts, a document emerged within the company showing that independent advice had been received from an external consultant. Because the Northport route is a much rougher area of sea, the advice concerned structural changes to the Mary Jane that would make her safer. Had the advice been followed, the Mary Jane would have had additional doors fitted inside the car deck to act as a second internal bulkhead to prevent flooding. The report was not passed on to appropriate staff members and as a result the company had not acted on its advice.

Required

Prepare extracts for a briefing paper which analyses the internal control failures at Sea Ships Co and on the Mary Jane, and the reasons for them. **(10 marks)**

Professional skills marks are available for demonstrating **analysis** skills in identifying the internal control problems and the reasons for them. **(2 marks)**

(Total = 12 marks)

41 The BA Times   12 marks

Victor is the editor of the *BA Times*, a subscription magazine, published once a month, which provides news and articles preparing engineering students for the examinations of industry associations, such as the Associate of Chartered Engineers (ACE) and the Institute of Engineering and Construction (IEC). The magazine is edited and printed in offices and an adjoining factory in Ambosium. The offices and factory are leased and the magazine currently employs 20 people, all of whom live close to the offices. It is the only independent magazine in the sector. Each association has its own magazine and website, but relatively tight control is maintained over their editorial policies. Victor was the editor of the magazine *Engineering Today* for 16 years before establishing the *BA Times* nine years ago. Because of its independence, the *BA Times* can be a little more controversial and provocative than its rivals and it is popular with students and well respected by the engineering profession.

However, despite such recognition, the magazine is currently unprofitable due to increased production, distribution and office costs, falling subscriptions and reduced advertising. Changing reading habits in Umboria, particularly amongst the young, has led to less reading of printed media and a new focus on online content. All of the traditional media providers are experiencing financial problems. The sales of printed magazines and the profits of publishers are both falling dramatically throughout Umboria.

Furthermore, evidence has shown that advertisers are increasingly unconvinced about the effectiveness of advertising in printed magazines and so advertising revenues are also falling.

The *BA Times* currently has a website but its role is to convince the visitor to order the printed magazine. The website offers extracts of news and articles which may only be read in full in the printed magazine.

Recent survey

A recent survey of people who had decided not to renew their *BA Times* subscription revealed the following comments:

'In-depth articles on the latest IEC exam sittings are of no interest to me. I quite enjoy reading the news parts, but I do wonder why I cannot do this online.'

ACE student

'I have reached the final stage of my examinations and don't want to read articles about the stages I have already passed. I reckon only about 15% of *BA Times* is relevant to me now.'

ACE Final Stage student

'Some of the readers' letters are really irritating or just plain wrong, but the editor seldom makes a comment!'

IEC Student

'I became an engineer to get a job, not just to sit examinations and read about exam topics.'

IEC Student

The examinations are getting more demanding and Victor is under pressure to increase the number of technical articles in the magazine, despite the fact that this will make the magazine longer and increase its print and distribution costs.

Victor is aware that new technology and new media offer opportunities for changing the business model and the financial performance of the *BA Times*. However, he likes the feel of printed magazines and he feels that subscribers do as well. He does not believe that harnessing new technology will make him money, particularly if it leads to decreasing sales of the printed magazine.

He is also concerned about how his subscribers and advertisers will react to change. He worries that some subscribers will not have access to online technology and that many advertisers would prefer to continue with display advertisements in a printed magazine.

Required

Prepare extracts for a briefing paper in relation to Victor's concerns, which analyses the effect of any potential technology or media change on his subscribers, his advertisers and the financial viability of his company. **(10 marks)**

Professional skills marks are available for demonstrating **analysis** skills in relation to Victor's concerns regarding changes in technology and media and the impact of this on subscribers, advertisers and the financial viability of the *BA Times*. **(2 marks)**

(Total = 12 marks)

42 Graffoff   **10 marks**

Emile Gonzalez is an industrial chemist who worked for the government of Pablos for more than 20 years. In his spare time, he continually experimented with formulating a product that could remove graffiti from all surfaces. After many years of experimentation, Emile developed a product that can be produced economically and applied safely and effectively without the need for protective clothing.

Three years ago, Emile left his job to focus on refining the product and bringing it to market. He formed a limited liability company, Graffoff, with initial share capital funded by savings and a legacy from a wealthy relative. He is the sole shareholder in the company. The company has filed two years of results (see Table 1 for extracted information from the second year), and it is expected to return similar net profit figures in its third trading year. Emile takes a significant dividend out of the company each year and he wishes that to continue. He also wishes to remain the sole owner of the company.

Four years ago, Emile was granted a patent for the formula on which his product is based and a further patent on the process used to produce the product. In Pablos, patents are protected for ten years and so Emile has six years before his formula becomes available to his competitors. Consequently, he wants to rapidly expand the company and plans to lease premises to create 30 new graffiti removal depots in Pablos, each of which will supply graffiti removing services. He needs $500,000 to finance this.

Emile has mixed feelings about his expansion plan. Despite the apparent success of his company, he prefers working in the laboratory to managing people. He is aware that he lacks business experience and, despite the technical excellence of the product, he has failed to build a highly visible brand. He also has particular problems in the accounts receivables department. He dislikes conflict with customers and often offers them extended payment terms, to the dismay of the accounts receivables staff who feel that their effectiveness is undermined by his concessions. In contrast, Graffoff pays bills very promptly, due to a zealous administrator in accounts payable.

In Pablos, all goods are supplied to customers on 30 days' credit. However, the average settlement period for payables is 40 days. One supplier commented that 'Graffoff is unique in its punctuality of payment'.

Table 1: Extracted financial data for Graffoff's second year of trading, reported at 31 December 20X1

Extract from the statement of financial position as at 31 December 20X1

	$'000
Assets	
Non-current assets	
Property, plant and equipment	1,385
Intangible assets	100
Total non-current assets	1,485
Current assets	
Inventories	100
Trade receivables	260
Cash and cash equivalents	30
Total current assets	390
Totals assets	**1,875**
Equity and liabilities	
Share capital	1,500
Retained earnings	30
Total equity	1,530
Non-current liabilities	
Long-term borrowings	250
Total non-current liabilities	250
Current liabilities	
Trade and other payables	75
Current tax payable	20
Total current liabilities	95
Total liabilities	345
Total equity and liabilities	**1,875**

Extract from the statement of profit or loss as at 31 December 20X1

	$'000
Revenue	1,600
Cost of sales	(1,375)
Gross profit	225
Administrative expenses	(100)
Finance costs	(15)
Profit before tax	110
Income tax expense	(20)
Profit for the period	90

Required

A consultant has claimed that Graffoff should be able to completely fund its proposed organic expansion (at a cost of $500,000) through internally generated sources of finance. Prepare a briefing paper which analyses whether this claim is valid. **(8 marks)**

Professional skills marks are available for demonstrating **analysis** skills in relation to assessing the consultant's claim. **(2 marks)**

(Total = 10 marks)

43 Yvern Trinkets   12 marks

Yvern is a large region in the country of Gaulle. It is ethnically and culturally distinct from the rest of the country and it has aspirations for independence. The desire for this independence is reflected by consumers in Yvern preferring to buy products which have been produced in the region.

Yvern Trinkets Regional (YTR) is a manufacturer of giftware products aimed at the Yvern market. Its products are bought primarily by residents of Yvern and visitors to the Yvern region. It is the third largest company of its type in the region, and the 50th largest producer of giftware in Gaulle. Its marketing message stresses the regional identity of the company and its employment of local skills and labour. It currently manufactures four products, A, B, C and D. The company does not sub-contract or outsource any element of production and it has never done so. Data concerning products A, B, C and D are given in Table 1.

Table 1: Production and marginal cost data for the YTR product range

	A	B	C	D
Monthly production (in units)	2,000	5,500	4,000	3,000
Direct materials cost ($ per unit)	3	5	2	4
Direct labour cost ($ per unit)	9	6	9	6
Variable production overheads ($ per unit)	2	3	1	2

YTR recently appointed a new managing director, born outside the region. He has been tasked with improving the profitability of the company.

After a short period of consultation, the new managing director produced a proposal for the board. Here is an extract of his proposal.

'First of all, we need to be clear about our generic strategy. Strategists have suggested that we have four alternatives. I have reproduced them in this slide (shown here as Table 2).

Table 2: Generic strategies

Cost Leadership	Differentiation
Cost Focus	Differentiation Focus

'My vision for YTR is that we should pursue a cost leadership strategy. I have already established that our products can be produced by an established company in the distant country of Tinglia at the following prices (see Table 3). These costs include the delivery of products to our warehouse here in Yvern.

Table 3: Contract prices per unit from the external supplier in Tinglia

	A	B	C	D
Buy-in price ($ per unit)	11.50	16.50	12.50	13.50

'Our Financial Director of YTR has also estimated that we have company-wide fixed overheads of $75,000 per month. He assures me that $16,000 per month of these is directly attributable to the production of products A, B, C and D, evenly split across the four products, each having $4,000 of fixed overheads. So, we could save overheads of $16,000 per month by outsourcing all of our products to the Tinglia supplier.

'I realise that this leaves us with $59,000 per month fixed overheads, but I will be looking for savings there also. The information technology of YTR is outdated and inefficient. Productivity benefits will follow from harnessing the power of modern technology.

'However, returning to my main concern: production costs. My view is that increased profitability can only be achieved if we take advantage of the cheaper production costs now available to us. All four products can be produced more cheaply by the supplier in Tinglia. So, this strategy of outsourcing is the one we should pursue to achieve our cost leadership strategy.'

Required

Prepare extracts for a briefing paper which evaluates the claim of the Managing Director that 'all four products can be produced more cheaply by the supplier in Tinglia' and discuss the issues raised by outsourcing the production of YTR's products to Tinglia. **(10 marks)**

Professional skills marks are available for demonstrating **scepticism** skills in evaluating the claims of the Managing Director. **(2 marks)**

(Total = 12 marks)

44 Coastal Oil   12 marks

Coastal Oil is one of the world's largest petrochemical companies. It is based in Deeland and employs 120,000 people in many countries. It has an especially strong presence in Effland because of Effland's very large consumption of oil and gas products and its large oil reserves. Coastal Oil is organised into three vertically integrated business units: the exploration and extraction division; the processing and refining division; and the distribution and retailing division.

Because of the risks and the capital investment demands, Coastal Oil has joint venture (JV) agreements in place for many of its extraction operations, especially those in the deep-water seas. A joint venture is a shared equity arrangement for a particular project where control is shared between the JV partners. In each of its JVs, Coastal Oil is the largest partner, although operations on each rig are divided between the JV member companies and the benefits are distributed according to the share of the JV.

Coastal Oil has long prided itself on its safety record and its ethical reputation. It believes both to be essential in supporting shareholder value. Its corporate code of ethics pledges its commitment to the 'highest standards' of ethical performance in the following areas: full compliance with regulation in all jurisdictions; safety and care of employees; transparency and communication with stakeholders; social contribution; and environmental responsibility. In addition, Coastal Oil has usually provided a lot of voluntary disclosure in its annual report and on its website.

One of the consequences of dividing up the different responsibilities and operations on an oil or gas rig is that Coastal Oil does not have direct influence over some important operational controls. The contractual arrangements on any given oil rig can be very complex. Given that Coastal Oil has JV interests in hundreds of deep-water oil and gas rigs all over the world, some observers have said that this could be a problem should an accident ever occur.

This issue was tragically highlighted when one of its deep-water rigs, the Effland Coastal Deep Rig, had an explosion earlier this year. It was caused by the failure of a valve at the 'well-head' on the sea floor. The valve was the responsibility of Well Services, a minor partner in the JV. Eight workers were killed on the rig from the high pressure released after the valve failure, and oil gushed into the sea from the well-head. It was soon established that Well Services' staff failed to inspect the valve before placing it at the well-head. In addition, the valve was attached to a connecting part that did not meet the required technical specification for the water depth at which it was operating.

Reports in the media on the following day said that the accident had happened on a rig 'belonging to Coastal Oil' when, in fact, Coastal Oil was technically only a major partner in the joint venture. Furthermore, there was no mention that the accident had been caused by a part belonging to Well Services. A journalist did discover, however, that both companies had operated a more lax safety culture on the deep-water rigs than was the case at facilities on land. He said there was a culture of 'out of sight, out of mind' on some offshore facilities. It was the responsibility of management on each rig to enforce internal controls and head office would only be informed of a problem if it was judged to be 'an exceptional risk'.

The accident triggered a lengthy argument between Coastal Oil and Well Services about liability. Lawyers on both sides pointed out that liability was contractually ambiguous because the documentation was complex and unclear. In the absence of any official statement from Coastal Oil while the argument dragged on, the media strongly criticised Coastal Oil. Oil from the ruptured valve continued to spill directly into the sea off the Effland coast. With no contingency plan in place, the ruptured valve took several months to repair, meaning that many thousands of tonnes of crude oil polluted the sea off Effland. Images of seabirds covered in crude oil were broadcast and thousands of businesses on the coast reported that the polluted water would disrupt their business. Public statements from Coastal Oil that it was not responsible for the ruptured valve only inflamed the situation.

A review by the Coastal Oil board highlighted several areas where risk management systems might be tightened to reduce the possibility of a similar accident happening again. Finance Director, Tanya Tun, suggested that the company should disclose this new information to shareholders. In particular, she said that a far more detailed voluntary statement on environmental risk would be material to the shareholders. The annual report would, she believed, be a suitable vehicle for this disclosure.

Because of the high media profile of the event, politicians from Effland involved themselves. Senator Jones's constituency on the coast nearest the rig was badly affected by the oil spill and many of his constituents suffered economic loss. He claimed in a newspaper interview that Coastal Oil's CEO, Susan Ahmed, 'should have known this was going to happen', such was the poor state of some of the internal controls on the Effland Coastal Deep Rig.

Mrs Ahmed was summoned to appear before a special committee of the Effland national legislature. The Coastal Oil board agreed that this would be a good opportunity for her to address a number of issues in detail and repair some of the company's damaged reputation. The board agreed that Mrs Ahmed should provide as full a statement as possible on the internal control failures to the special committee.

In preparing to appear before the special committee, CEO Mrs Ahmed has been informed that she will be asked to explain the causes of the accident and to give assurances that an accident of this type will not re-occur.

Required

Prepare a statement for Mrs Ahmed that argues against Senator Jones's view that Mrs Ahmed 'should have known this was going to happen', and explains why Coastal Oil cannot guarantee the prevention of further health and safety failures, referring to the ALARP (as low as reasonably practicable) principle. **(10 marks)**

Professional skills marks are available for showing **scepticism** skills in questioning the opinions expressed by Senator Jones, and Coastal Oil's ability to guarantee that any further accidents can be prevented.

(2 marks)

(Total = 12 marks)

45 Jones Co   10 marks

You are a student accountant at Miller Dundas, a medium-sized firm of auditors. John Yang is your training manager, overseeing the progress of the firm's student accountants.

You recently sent John an email describing a situation on the audit of Jones Co, a medium-sized, family-run business and long-standing client of Miller Dundas. You were checking non-current asset purchases when you noticed an entry of $100,000 for a security system for an address in a well-known holiday resort with no obvious link to the company. On questioning this with Ellen Tan, the financial controller, you were told that the system was for Mr Martin Jones's holiday cottage (Martin Jones is Managing Director and a minority shareholder in Jones Co). You were told that Martin Jones often takes confidential company documents with him to his holiday home, and so needs the security system on the property to protect them. It is because of this, Ellen said, that it is reasonable to charge the security system to the company.

Ellen Tan expressed surprise at your concerns, and said that auditors had not previously been concerned about the company being charged for non-current assets and operational expenses for Mr Jones's personal properties.

You told the engagement partner, Potto Sinter, what you had found and Potto simply said that the charge was not a cause for concern. He did say that he would ask for a formal explanation from Martin Jones before he signed off the audit. You were not at the final clearance meeting but later read the following in the meeting notes: 'discussed other matter with client, happy with explanation'. When you discussed the matter with Potto afterwards you were told that the matter was closed.

BPP LEARNING MEDIA

John Yang has now read your email about what happened, and spoken to you. He realises that there is an ethical dilemma. Not only should there be disclosure of Mr Jones's transaction, but the situation is complicated by the fact that Potto Sinter is senior to John Yang in Miller Dundas and also by the fact that Potto Sinter and Mr Jones are good friends. He is thinking about what to do next, and has asked for your thoughts.

Required

Prepare extracts for a briefing paper which criticise Potto Sinter's ethical and professional behaviour in this case. **(8 marks)**

Professional skills marks are available for demonstrating *scepticism skills* in challenging the behaviour of Potto Sinter in respect of the audit of Jones Co. **(2 marks)**

(Total = 10 marks)

46 Rosey and Atkins

10 marks

Rosey and Atkins (R&A) is one of the largest institutional investors in the country. Its investment strategy has traditionally been to own a minor shareholding in each of the top 200 companies on the stock exchange. The R&A shareholding is typically between 2% and 10% of each company and it manages funds for over two million clients (people and businesses who buy into share funds managed by R&A).

Established over 200 years ago, R&A has always believed itself to be socially responsible. As part of its CSR strategy, R&A recently purchased 100% of the shares in a national housebuilder, Natcon, which it owns as a direct holding and does not include in its managed funds. Natcon, in turn, owns a large amount of land suitable for future low-cost housing development. The R&A website reported that the reason for this purchase was to address the board's concerns over a shortage of affordable housing in the country which R&A feels they can help to address by having outright ownership of Natcon. R&A reported that there is a large social need for affordable homes, and it hopes to create many hundreds of new low-cost homes each year.

Natcon wants to build a large estate of new homes in the town of Housteads, and the local government authority is considering whether to grant the required building permission. The nearby University of Housteads strongly opposes it, because it believes that the new houses will ruin what is considered to be a panoramic view from the university campus which helps it to recruit staff and students to the university. Both the Housteads local government authority and the University of Housteads have money invested as clients with R&A, but the university has a substantially smaller investment in the fund than the local government authority. The local government authority also owns shares in R&A, meaning that it is both an investor in funds and an R&A shareholder.

Required

Prepare extracts for a briefing paper which:

(a)   Explains how stakeholder claims are sometimes in conflict; and **(2 marks)**

(b)   Using a suitable stakeholder analysis framework, assess the competing claims of the local government authority and the University of Housteads in the proposed housing development. **(6 marks)**

Professional skills marks are available for demonstrating **evaluation** skills in assessing the implications of the housing project, and the competing claims of the stakeholders identified. **(2 marks)**

(Total = 10 marks)

47 iTTrain

12 marks

For 11 years, Marco was a senior salesman at AQT, a company specialising in IT certification courses. During that time, AQT became the most successful training provider in the market.

Marco has now left AQT and established his own training company, iTTrain, aimed at the same IT certification market. He wishes to offer premium-quality courses in a high-quality environment with high-quality teaching. He has selected a number of self-employed lecturers and he has agreed a daily lecturing fee of $450 per day. He has also selected the prestigious CityCentre training centre as his course venue. It has a number of training rooms which hold up to nine delegates. Each training room costs $250 per day to hire. There is also a $10 per day per delegate charge for lunch and other refreshments. Printing costs mean that there is also a $20 cost for the course manual which is given to every delegate.

Marco has scheduled 40 courses next year, as he is limited by the availability of lecturers. Each course will have a maximum of nine delegates (determined by the room size) and a minimum of three delegates. Each course will be three days long.

iTTrain has been set up with $70,000 of Marco's own money. He currently estimates that fixed annual costs will be $65,000 (which includes his own salary) and he would like the company to return a modest profit in its first year of operation as it establishes itself.

Marco is currently considering the price he wishes to charge for his courses. AQT charges $900 per delegate for a three-day course, but he knows that it discounts this by up to 10% and a similar discount is also offered to intermediaries who advertise AQT courses on their websites. Some of these intermediaries have already been in touch with Marco to ask if he would be prepared to offer them similar discounts in return for iTTrain courses being advertised on their websites. There are also a number of cheaper training providers who offer the same courses for as little as $550 per delegate. However, these tend to focus on self-financing candidates for whom price is an issue. These courses are often given in poor-quality training premises by poorly motivated lecturers. Marco is not really interested in this market. He wants to target the corporate business market, where quality is as important as price and the course fee is paid by the delegate's employer. He is currently considering a price of $750 per delegate.

Required

Prepare extracts for a briefing paper which evaluate Marco's suggested price of $750 per delegate, including estimates of the level of contribution that he could expect next year.

(6 marks)

In the light of your evaluation, describe possible options for Marco in pricing iTTrain's courses.

(4 marks)

Professional skills marks are available for demonstrating **evaluation** skills in relation to the implications of the suggested pricing strategy and generation of possible options. (2 marks)

(Total = 12 marks)

48 Tillo Community Centre   14 marks

Introduction

The country of Mahem is in a long and deep economic recession, with unemployment at its highest since the country became an independent nation. In an attempt to stimulate the economy the government has launched a Private/Public investment initiative, where the government invests in capital projects with the aim of stimulating the involvement of private sector firms. The building of a new community centre in the industrial city of Tillo is an example of such a project. Community centres are central to the culture of Mahem. They are places where people can socialise, local organisations can hold conferences and meetings and farmers can sell their produce. The current community centre in Tillo is in an old building that is relatively energy inefficient, rented (at $12,000 per month) from a local landowner.

In 20X0 a business case was put forward to build a new centre on local authority owned land on the outskirts of Tillo. The costs and benefits set out in the business case are shown in Table 1. As required by the Private/Public investment initiative, the project showed payback during Year 4 of the investment.

Table 1: Costs and benefits of the business case for the community centre at Tillo

	Year 1 $	Year 2 $	Year 3 $	Year 4 $	Year 5 $
Costs: Initial	600,000				
Costs: Recurring	60,000	60,000	60,000	60,000	60,000
Benefits: Rental savings	144,000	144,000	144,000	144,000	144,000
Benefits: Energy savings	30,000	30,000	30,000	30,000	30,000
Benefits: Increased income	20,000	20,000	70,000	90,000	90,000
Benefits: Better staff morale	25,000	25,000	25,000	25,000	25,000
Cumulative net benefits	(441,000)	(282,000)	(73,000)	156,000	385,000

New buildings built under the Private/Public initiative must attain energy level targets and this is the basis for the estimate of the energy savings. It was expected that the new centre would attract more customers who would pay for the centre's use, as well as increasing the use of facilities such as the cafeteria, shop and business centre. These benefits were estimated, in Table 1, under increased income. Finally, it was felt that staff would be happier in the new building and their motivation would improve. The centre employed 20 staff, 16 of whom had been with the centre for more than five years. All employees would be transferred from the old to the new centre. These benefits are shown as 'better staff morale' in Table 1.

Unfortunately, when the new centre opened, it was not as successful as had been predicted, and did not deliver the benefits the local authority expected.

The local authority has commissioned the Project Audit Agency (PAA) to look into the way the project was managed. The PAA believes that the four sets of benefits identified in the original business case (rental savings, energy savings, increased income, and better staff morale) should have been justified more explicitly.

Required

Draft an analysis on behalf of the PAA that formally categorises and critically evaluates each of the four sets of proposed benefits defined in the original business case.   **(12 marks)**

Professional skills marks are available for **evaluation** skills in assessing the validity of the benefits outlined in the business case and for undertaking an objective appraisal of each benefit specified.
(2 marks)

(Total = 14 marks)

Section 3 – Exam success skills development

Important note:

This section contains four mini-scenarios of 50 marks, so each scenario represents approximately half a Strategic Business Leader exam. The mini-scenarios replicate the expected question format in Strategic Business Leader, although they use shorter scenarios so you can efficiently study across many syllabus topics. The level of challenge reflects the standard expected in the real exam in terms of the tasks with Case Scenarios having significant detail and complexity to allow you to develop further your syllabus knowledge and ACCA professional skills of communication, commercial acumen, analysis, scepticism and evaluation.

In the tutorial notes presented after each model answer, we focus on the six exam success skills: 1. Case scenario: Managing information; 2. Correct interpretation of requirements; 3. Answer planning: Priorities, structure and logic; 4. Efficient numerical analysis; 5. Effective writing and presentation; and 6. Good time management. Each suggested answer provides explanation and advice on developing your abilities for each of the six exam success skills. Once you have completed a mini-scenario we will ask you to consider for yourself which of the exam success skills in particular you need to focus on in order to improve through a process of self-review.

We recommend these questions are completed during your revision phase and are completed before you begin your final exam preparations.

49 Zilber Hotels

You have recently started work as a management accountant at Zilber Hotels, reporting to the financial controller.

Draft management accounts have been prepared for the year just finished, and the financial controller has told you that one of your first jobs will be helping her to analyse the results in order to produce the board report. However, she has warned you to expect a wide variety of tasks, because the year end is always a very busy time.

The financial controller has given you some information to help you familiarise yourself with the company and the issues it is facing (Exhibits 1–3) and you have also collected some further information yourself (Exhibits 4 and 5):

Exhibit 1: Company overview, prepared by the financial controller

Exhibit 2: Summary management accounts

Exhibit 3: Email from Chief Executive Officer (CEO), showing a potential strategic opportunity for the company

Exhibit 4: Notes from meeting with the Head of Internal Audit

Exhibit 5: Internal memo from the Head of Internal Audit

The task requirements are included in the tasks shown below:

1   Required

Using the information provided, draft an extract for the board report which analyses Zilber Hotels' performance in 20X7, including both financial and non-financial aspects of performance. (14 marks)

Professional skills marks are available for demonstrating **analysis** skills relating to Zilber Hotels' performance. (2 marks)

(Total = 16 marks)

2   The Finance Director (FD) has forwarded you the CEO's email about a potential strategic opportunity for Zilber, and asked for your thoughts about it.

Required

Draft a briefing paper for the FD which evaluates the appropriateness of the proposed acquisition. (8 marks)

Professional skills marks are available for demonstrating evaluation skills in assessing the appropriateness of the acquisition. (2 marks)

(Total = 10 marks)

3   The FD tells you that one of Zilber's non-executive directors has raised some concerns about the balance of strategic and operational risks included on the company's risk register.

The FD asks you to follow up this issue, by speaking to the Head of Internal Audit about the register.

(a)   Required

Prepare briefing notes which assess the risks currently included in Zilber's risk register in the light of the non-executive director's concerns, and your meeting with the head of internal audit. (6 marks)

Professional skills marks are available for demonstrating **scepticism** skills in questioning the range of risks covered in the register. (2 marks)

(b)   The FD also mentions that an additional issue to consider in relation to the risk register is the potential impact that disruptive technology could have on the hotel industry.

However, the FD is concerned that some of the directors may not yet be familiar with the concept of 'disruptive technology'.

Required

Prepare a slide to be presented to the board, including relevant bullet points and supporting notes, explaining what 'disruptive technology' is and highlighting its potential impact on Zilber.   (6 marks)

Professional skills marks are available for demonstrating **communication** skills in highlighting the key points to include in the slide, with clear supporting notes.   (2 marks)

(Total = 16 marks)

4   Shortly after your meeting, the Head of Internal Audit sends you a memo about a recent incident which he felt you should be aware of, in case the external auditors ask you about it.

However, the Head of Internal Audit is now on leave, and the FD has asked for your thoughts about how the internal control deficiency exposed in the fraud could be addressed.

Required

Prepare a memo to the Finance Director which recommends how the specific internal control deficiency exposed by the fraud could be addressed.   (6 marks)

Professional skills marks are available for demonstrating **commercial acumen** in judging how to address the deficiency and recommending an appropriate response.   (2 marks)

(Total = 8 marks)

Exhibit 1: Company overview

Zilber Co operates a chain of 35 hotels across the country of Teeland. The hotels are all of a similar size, and on average each hotel has 90 rooms.

The majority of Zilber's hotels are located in major cities, and the company's target market has primarily been business customers. In recent years, however, demand from business customers has started to decline, due to tough economic conditions.

The company's policy is to set standard prices for the rooms in each hotel, with that price reflecting the hotel's location and taking account of competitors' prices. However, hotel managers have the authority to offer discounts selectively in order to obtain bookings – for example, by reducing the room rate for regular customers, or lowering prices at times when occupancy rates are expected to be low.

Each hotel manager has the authority to offer a discount of up to 25% off the standard room rate.

The average standard price per night (across all 35 hotels) was $150 in 20X7, compared to $145 in 20X6. All of Zilber's hotels are open 365 days per year.

All the hotel rooms have the same facilities and specification, so that business customers staying in any Zilber hotel across the country will know in advance what to expect from their stay. Hotels in Teeland are rated on a 'star' system, with 5* hotels being the most luxurious. Zilber's hotels all have 4* ratings.

In addition to room bookings, the hotels also generate revenue from additional activities, such as restaurants and bars. No discounts are offered on any of these additional revenue streams.

At the end of their stay, all customers are invited to complete a short survey identifying the reasons they chose to stay in a Zilber hotel and how satisfied they were with their stay.

Feedback from these surveys shows that the comfort of Zilber's rooms, the convenience of the hotels' locations, and the quality and efficiency of customer service are key factors in customers' choice of hotel. The quality of the guest's experience, and their level of satisfaction, influences not only the likelihood of them making repeat bookings but also the likelihood of them recommending Zilber Hotels to friends or colleagues.

As such, the board have identified customer satisfaction scores as a key performance indicator. Other key indicators the board monitor are occupancy rates (% of rooms occupied) and operating profit margin.

Exhibit 2: Summary management accounts

	Year ended 30 June 20X7 Actual $'000	Year ended 30 June 20X7 Budget $'000	Year ended 30 June 20X6 Actual $'000
Revenue – rooms at standard price per night	131,072	129,347	121,701
Room discounts or rate reductions	(24,904)	(19,402)	(18,255)
Other revenue (food, drink)	34,079	33,630	32,251
Total revenue	140,247	143,575	135,697
Operating costs	(117,964)	(115,764)	(111,965)
Operating profit	22,283	27,811	23,732

Other performance information

	20X7 – Actual	20X7 – Budget	20X6 – Actual
Operating profit %	15.9%	19.4%	17.5%
Capital employed	$52.1m	$54.7m	$49.1m
Return on capital employed (*)	42.8%	50.8%	48.3%
Occupancy rates	76%	75%	73%
Customer satisfaction scores (**)	8.5	n/a	8.9

Notes:

*: Capital employed is calculated using the depreciated cost of non-current assets at all of the hotels plus net working capital.

**: Customer satisfaction scores are graded on a scale of 1–10, where '10' represents 'Excellent'. On average, in any given location, the top 10% of hotels earn scores of 9 or above. The top 25% of hotels earn scores of 8.5 or above.

Three themes have become increasingly frequent in the comments customers give alongside their scores:

- Customers resent having to wait to check in to their rooms, and several have asked whether Zilber could implement an automated check-in process.

- Customers who have stayed in Zilber Hotels before have commented that the standard of service in recent visits has not been as good as in earlier visits.

- The rooms would benefit from re-decorating, and some of the fixtures and fittings need replacing (for example, the beds would benefit from new mattresses to improve the level of comfort they provide to guests).

Zilber had originally planned a two-year refurbishment programme beginning in 20X7, in which all of its hotel rooms would be refurbished. However, this programme has been delayed, due to the current economic conditions and the need to reduce expenditure.

Exhibit 3: Email from CEO

From: CEO

To: Directors of Zilber

Re: Potential acquisition

Dear All,

Our strategic review earlier this year identified 'profitable expansion' as one of Zilber's key objectives, and our shareholders are becoming increasingly vocal about their desire for the business to grow.

To date, Zilber has grown organically, and we have identified a list of desirable locations where we would like to open new hotels, but there are currently no suitable properties available in those locations.

However, I have learned that a small privately owned chain of hotels – Havis Co – is coming up for sale, because the majority owners are looking to retire.

Havis owns ten hotels. Four of these are in-town, while the other six are rural hotels. Havis' hotels all have 4* ratings, like Zilber's own hotels.

The majority of Havis' guests are leisure travellers, and many of them choose to say in Havis hotels because they have a charm and character which is not found in more contemporary hotel designs. However, due to a lack of capital expenditure from the current owners, some of the hotels are in relatively poor condition internally and externally.

I would be keen to get your thoughts about this potential acquisition.

Exhibit 4: Notes from meeting with the Head of Internal Audit

Zilber – Risk management policy

Overview of Zilber's internal controls and risk management system

The company's internal controls and risk management system are designed to help us achieve our business objectives and protect our business.

This relates not only to ensuring the safety and security of physical assets, people, systems and processes, but also to Zilber's brand, reputation and business model more generally, and our ability to respond effectively to changes in the market place.

Key risks

It is vitally important that Zilber provides a safe and secure environment for all of our guests as well as our staff working in our hotels. As such, we need to maintain high standards of health and safety across all of our hotels, and to ensure we have appropriate information and systems in place to identify and address any health and safety concerns.

We regularly consult with our hotel managers to ensure that risks are identified, and prioritised, and improvement actions are identified as necessary.

Risk register

We summarise the key risks facing our business in our risk register. The register describes the key risks we face, and identifies the controls in place to mitigate them. I can let you have a look at the register in detail later if you want, but the risk areas covered in the register are:

Guest safety	There is a constant need to protect the safety and security of our hotels, our guests staying in them. This underpins our whole risk management programme.
Security	Includes the physical security of the hotel buildings overall, as well as the individual rooms.
Staff safety	Safety doesn't only relate to guests. We also need to ensure the health and safety of our staff working in them.
Staff retention	As a service business, we need to recruit and retain the right people to ensure we can deliver the quality of service our customers expect. Failure to do this is likely to damage our financial performance and our longer-term growth.
Technology	Technology has increased the information available to customers (for example through comparison websites and social media reviews) as well as changing booking channels (with online bookings). Booking is an important part of the guest experience so we need to ensure that our booking processes are as efficient as possible. A number of our smaller competitors in the Teeland hotel sector have very recently started to accept cryptocurrency payments for accommodation bookings made via their online booking systems. Zilber does not currently operate the IT infrastructure necessary to accept cryptocurrency payments. The need to continue to invest in our IT systems is crucial.
Information security	We need to ensure that information – particularly about customers' details and payment cards – is held securely.

Exhibit 5: Notes on internal control issue

A fraud has recently been discovered in one of our hotels. The hotel manager had been encouraging customers to pay in cash by offering them small discounts of around 5% to 10% for doing so. However, he was then recording the discount at the maximum 25% and retaining the difference for himself.

The manager's wife worked on the front desk of the hotel, and so received the money from the customers and she provided false invoices to them.

The manager and his wife have both been dismissed now, although we have not yet worked out how much they stole.

More importantly, though, we will be reviewing our internal controls to try to prevent similar frauds happening again.

50 Ling Co

You are a management consultant, working for WZZ, a consultancy firm based in Wyeland.

Your firm has been commissioned by Ling Co. You are part of the team working on the Ling assignment, and you have been asked to prepare a consultancy report for the client on the strategic issues facing them, as well as advising them on other issues.

Assume that it is now the end of 20X6.

You have collected and analysed the following information to help you prepare the consultancy report:

Exhibit 1: Background information on Ling Co

Exhibit 2: Profile of conditions in Zedland

Exhibit 3: Background on the Zedland electric light bulb industry

Exhibit 4: Notes from a telephone conversation between Man Lal and your manager at WZZ

Using this information, you are now starting to prepare the consultancy report and associated tasks for Ling.

The task requirements are included in the tasks shown below:

1   **From the information that you have collected, draft a section of the consultancy report for the directors of Ling to include the following:**

   (a)   **An analysis of the macro-environmental factors affecting the Zedland light bulb industry. Your analysis should reflect the fact that Ling might enter this industry directly by setting up a distribution company for its products, or through the acquisition of Flick.** **(6 marks)**

   Professional skills marks are available for demonstrating **analysis** skills in assessing the macro-environmental factors affecting the Zedland light bulb industry.

(2 marks)

   (b)   **An evaluation of the attractiveness of the Zedland light bulb industry.**

(15 marks)

   Professional skills marks are available for demonstrating **evaluation** skills relating to the attractiveness of the light bulb industry in Zedland for Ling Co.   **(2 marks)**

(Total = 25 marks)

2   The Finance Director of Ling is concerned that Ling has no expertise in acquiring foreign companies and he is advocating a strategic alliance with Flick instead, and has asked for your advice.

   Required

   Prepare a briefing paper which discusses the appropriateness of such an approach to facilitating Ling's proposed entry into the Zedland light bulb market.   **(6 marks)**

   Professional skills marks are available for demonstrating **commercial acumen** in assessing the suitability of a strategic alliance.   **(2 marks)**

(Total = 8 marks)

3   Man Lal has sought your advice regarding the issues raised by the letter from 'Watching Business'. He says to you: 'I get really frustrated whenever anybody gets in the way of our most important relationship, that is, the one with our shareholders! Overall, I do think that Higgs Investments are right and 'Watching Business' can be safely ignored. However, I want your help in explaining my position to the rest of the board.'

Required

Prepare briefing notes for Man Lal which explain the agency relationship between the board of Ling Co and Higgs Investments, and provide advice on how the demands from Watching Business (WB) should be considered.

(7 marks)

Professional skills marks are available for demonstrating **scepticism** skills in challenging Man Lal's views about WB.

(2 marks)

(Total = 9 marks)

4   Man Lal has been reading about the Baldrige model of performance excellence, whose underlying purpose is to help organisations achieve excellence via performance improvements. He feels Ling Co could use the Baldrige model to improve its performance, and would like to make a presentation on the model to the board of directors of Ling Co.

Required

Prepare THREE slides for a presentation to the board of directors of Ling Co that explains the Baldrige model, and how it might be used to help Ling Co achieve continuing corporate success.

(6 marks)

Professional skills marks are available for demonstrating **communication** skills in highlighting the key points to include in the slides.

(2 marks)

(Total = 8 marks)

Exhibit 1: Background information on Ling Co

Ling is a large and successful light bulb manufacturing company, with global revenues of $750m. From its factories in Wyeland it supplies a worldwide market for LED (light emitting diode) light bulbs. Its workforce is skilled and motivated, and the company enjoys good relations with its employees.

The company's founder and CEO, Man Lal, spotted the potential of LED light bulbs and entered large-scale production whilst rivals were still producing candescent and halogen bulbs. LED light bulbs provide a cheaper, more energy efficient and greener solution than any alternative. Consumers in Wyeland strongly approve of Ling Co's green and environmentally ethical credentials. In fact, many countries have now passed legislation requiring domestic and business consumers to replace candescent light bulbs with greener equivalents.

Man Lal is now planning to visit Zedland, a country which has recently passed efficient lighting legislation which, from 20X7, bans the use of candescent bulbs in commercial premises and outlaws their production and importation after that date. Domestic consumers are expected to replace their candescent bulbs with newer technology. Man Lal confidently expects that LED will be the technology of choice.

While in Zedland, Man Lal will visit Flick Co, a light bulb producer which Ling is interested in acquiring. This would represent a new growth method for Ling. Up until now, its worldwide expansion has been achieved by establishing wholly owned distribution companies in each targeted country. All production has remained in Wyeland. However, Ling is now considering entering the Zedland market via acquisition of Flick, a light bulb manufacturer based in Zedland.

Man Lal intends to fund the updating of production facilities at Flick to allow the production of LED lights, alongside the continued production of candescent and halogen light bulbs. He wants to achieve this before domestic competitors in Zedland gear up their own LED light bulb production. He believes that Ling's competencies in LED manufacture will give Flick a head start. Initial discussions with Flick suggest that the company is open to acquisition and a bid price has been agreed which is acceptable to both parties.

To help fund global expansion, Man Lal has sold 49% of Ling to institutional investors. These institutional investors require growth and high dividends, and Ling is having difficulty meeting their demands. There is now very little growth in the domestic Wyeland market, and the distribution approach used to expand into foreign countries to date is taking a long time to mature. The investors are demanding quicker growth and acquisitions appear to promise this. Despite paying high dividends over the last few years, Ling Co still has significant retained profits and this is another issue for the institutional shareholders. They feel that this money should be used to promote growth and have agreed to a $400m acquisition fund. However, Man Lal still feels more comfortable with the idea of organic growth through setting up distribution companies. Ling Co has made acquisitions in Wyeland, but has never bought a foreign company before.

Exhibit 2: Profile of conditions in Zedland

In recent years, the Zedland nationalist movement had become increasingly popular. In the words of one politician, 'Most people are fed up with Zedland being pushed around by other countries. We want prosperity and jobs for our people.'

Nicholas Perch, the newly elected nationalist leader of the Zedland government, recently outlined his plans for the future. 'We are committed to a return to prosperity', he said. 'To achieve this, we have to make some short-term adjustments which may be unpopular with our trading partners. We are currently considering the imposition of import taxes as a way of protecting our home industry. We wish to create a commercial environment here in Zedland in which our companies can prosper.

'We must also ask our citizens to continue with their energy-saving measures to help us manage the energy supply and try to reduce the number of power failures, which sadly have become a regular feature of life in Zedland. As you know, the government has agreed that all street lighting will be turned off from 23:00 hours to 05:00 hours. I have also decreed that all government offices must proactively embrace energy-saving lighting and heating. In the same way, I expect our citizens to look at ways of saving money and energy.

'The government also recognises that the country continues to be in a recession, and that disposable income is falling for all people. However, I cannot condone the recent demonstrations against foreign goods. We must rebuild our country peacefully and legally.'

Exhibit 3: Background on the Zedland electric light bulb industry

All electric light bulbs are largely made out of glass and metal. In Zedland, 90% of glass is produced by three companies. However, for each of these companies, light bulb manufacturers are not important customers. Most glass manufacture goes to the construction industry, and light bulb manufacturers take less than 0.5% of the country's glass production. Metal manufacture in Zedland is dominated by one company, OmniMetal. Most metal is sold to the automobile industry, with light bulb manufacturers taking less than 0.1% of OmniMetal's production. However, the quality of glass and metal required by the light bulb manufacturers is standard, so switching between suppliers is, in theory, relatively easy. Light bulb manufacture takes place in factories which require substantial initial investment and have no obvious alternative use.

In Zedland, light bulbs are low-cost commodity products. Some businesses have recently switched all their bulbs to light emitting diode (LED) to save energy, reduce costs in the long term and reflect their aspirations as 'green businesses'. There is very little brand awareness in the light bulb market, and all light bulbs have to fit the standard sockets used in the country.

Electric light bulb manufacture in Zedland is dominated by the five companies listed in Table 1. Two years ago, a large American light bulb manufacturer, Krysal, attempted to enter the market. The five dominant companies in the industry reacted to this by cutting prices, running marketing campaigns which emphasised the benefits to the country of home-based production and lobbying supermarket groups not to stock products produced by the new entrant. Krysal withdrew from the market after six months. When not focused on fighting new entrants, the five main competitors are regularly involved in price cutting, disruption of competitors' distribution channels and aggressive marketing.

Table 1: Zedland-based light bulb manufacturers

Company	Revenue (20X5) $m	Revenue (20X0) $m
Voltface	85	80
LiteWorld	80	80
Flick	70	65
ABC	65	60
L2L	60	60
Other companies	140	145
Total	500	490

The products produced by the Zedland light bulb industry are largely sold through supermarket groups (50%), home improvement superstores (30%) and large electrical chains (10%). The rest of the production is sold through small shops, except for a small percentage of production (less than 1%) which is sold directly to large organisations, such as government departments. However, light bulbs do not constitute a large sales item for any of these distribution channels. In fact, in a recent report, light bulb sales were one of the products which contributed less than 0.1% of a major supermarket's revenue.

The light bulb companies in Zedland have largely focused on candescent (60% of production) and halogen (30% of production) technologies.

Exhibit 4: Notes from a telephone conversation between Man Lal and WZZ manager

Man Lal opened the conversation:

'Thanks for calling. I'd like to talk to you about some issues which have arisen in relation to our proposed acquisition of Flick. Last year, Flick was widely criticised over operations at one of its factories in Zedland, when investigative journalists produced material showing poor conditions for the largely migrant workforce, and dangerous pollution in an important local waterway, caused by discarded glass and metal fragments. They also suggested that Flick had paid bribes to local officials in order to avoid having the factory shut down, but did not produce any real evidence for this. After the episode, Flick replaced the management team at the factory concerned, but they have become very sensitive to any criticism, and rather secretive about their business.

'When I discussed my planned visit with them last week, they said that they are confident that the problems are now behind them. A recent press statement promised that Flick will strive to uphold the highest standards of integrity, workers' rights and environmental protection in Zedland in the future, but it seems that some parties remain sceptical.'

In response, the WZZ manager said that Ling's interest in Flick has now been covered in the business press.

Man Lal continued:

'Yes it has, and just today I received two letters. The first was from a prominent environmental lobbying organisation that you may have heard of, called 'Watching Business' (WB). In the letter, the lobbying group said that because of its 'unfortunate record' in Zedland, Flick continues to be carefully monitored. WB said its interest in Flick's activities has increased since it saw the news about the possible takeover by Ling, and strongly recommended that we do not make the investment because of Flick's past activities and potential for recurring problems in the future.

'I am inclined to dismiss threats from groups of this type, but I know that WB has a lot of support among senior politicians and legislators both in Wyeland and abroad, and that some of our shareholders are likely to be influenced by the opinions of WB and will be worried about the proposed acquisition. WB is also respected as an environmental research organisation, and its advice is often sought by politicians both here and overseas.

'The second letter I received is from the head of Higgs Investments, Ling Co's biggest institutional shareholder. The letter points out that the Ling board is employed by its shareholders, and that I should be determined and resolute in maximising shareholder returns above all other considerations. The letter encourages the board not to be diverted by any "misinformed outsiders concerned with things that are actually none of their business, and which happened a while ago".'

51 Cheapkit

You have recently joined Cheapkit as a senior finance manager, reporting to the Finance Director.

Cheapkit is a large clothes retailer, based in Essland, a major developed country, whose currency is the $. Cheapkit sells a wide range of products, but its underlying aim is to sell fashionable clothes at the lowest possible prices.

Cheapkit obtains most of its clothes from suppliers in developing countries. A factory belonging to one of Cheapkit's suppliers – Cornflower – collapsed recently, killing or injuring a large number of people.

The Finance Director has warned you that working at Cheapkit will be busy, and he will need you to help him with a number of different tasks. However, he arranged induction meetings for you with key members of staff, as well as giving you a file with some useful information.

Exhibit 1: Press report: 'Cheapkit – Company analysis' (From a reputable business newspaper in Essland)

Exhibit 2: Briefing note given to you by Cheapkit's Procurement Director during your induction meeting

Exhibit 3: Press article following the accident at Cornflower's factory

Exhibit 4: Blog posting by Jess Lui

Exhibit 5: Memo from the Sales Director of Cheapkit about a new business opportunity

The task requirements are included in the tasks shown below:

1   (a)   The directors are going to discuss Cheapkit's strategic plans at the next meeting, and the Finance Director thinks it will be useful to have an analysis of the business environment to provide some context for their discussions.

Required

From the information you have gathered during your time at Cheapkit, prepare a memo to the Finance Director evaluating the business environment in which Cheapkit operates.

(8 marks)

Professional skills marks are available for demonstrating **evaluation** skills in assessing the business environment. (2 marks)

(b)   Another topic for discussion in the board meeting is Cheapkit's relationship with its stakeholders and how this could influence the company's strategy. The Finance Director has asked for some input from you here as well.

Required

Prepare a briefing note for the Finance Director which analyses the stakeholder claims of Cheapkit's customers, suppliers, and pressure groups (such as PWR) and how these claims may be in conflict.

(8 marks)

Professional skills marks are available for demonstrating **analysis** skills in considering the claims of different stakeholders. (2 marks)

BPP
LEARNING
MEDIA

(c) As the Procurement Director mentioned in your induction meeting, Cheapkit's board has identified three areas of risk which they believe are particularly important: exchange rate risk; supply chain risk; and international political risk.

The Finance Director has asked for your thoughts on these risk areas, and why they are important for Cheapkit's shareholders.

Required

Prepare a briefing note for the Finance Director which explains these risks and how each of them may be significant for Cheapkit's shareholders.

(8 marks)

Professional skills marks are available for demonstrating **commercial acumen** in identifying the significance of the risks for Cheapkit's shareholders. (2 marks)

(Total = 30 marks)

2 The board feels that Cheapkit's reputation has been damaged following the publication of Jess Lui's letter and her blog, which have received a lot of supportive comments in the media. Therefore, the board has decided to make a public response to her comments, and the Finance Director has asked you to draft a press statement.

Required

Draft a press statement from the board of Cheapkit explaining its role as a 'corporate citizen' given its international supply chain. (6 marks)

Professional skills marks are available for demonstrating **communication** skills for the tone of the statement and for responding diplomatically to the comments made against Cheapkit. (2 marks)

(Total = 8 marks)

3 Although the Sales Director seems enthusiastic about the potential contract from Yummy, some of the other directors are less keen on it, and the Finance Director has asked for your thoughts.

Required

Prepare a report which advises whether or not Cheapkit should accept the contract from Yummy, taking into account the risks and strategic implications as well as the expected financial returns. (10 marks)

Professional skills marks are available for demonstrating **scepticism** skills in highlighting issues which could affect the suitability of the proposed contract for Cheapkit. (2 marks)

(Total = 12 marks)

Exhibit 1: Press report: 'Cheapkit – Company analysis'

For most fashion retailers, e-commerce plays a key role in fulfilling customer demands. However, Cheapkit has achieved its success despite not having an online store.

The lack of an online store does not mean that Cheapkit does not have an online presence. Cheapkit has generated an active online following, in which customers share photos and images of their recent purchases via social media.

Cheapkit recently announced that it is opening five new stores, and the Finance Director said 'Despite the fact that the economy in Essland is still relatively weak, customers recognise the value for money which Cheapkit offers, and we expect to see like-for-like sales continuing to increase over the next year.'

However, the company warned that the rising costs of key raw materials – such as cotton – and the relatively weak value of Essland's currency, could reduce profit margins, as could the increase in the minimum wage in Essland which the government is expected to announce in its next budget. Many of the retail assistants who work in Cheapkit's stores are paid the minimum wage.

The company would not comment on whether its prices would increase during the coming year, but most analysts think this is likely. As one analyst noted, 'Ensuring product ranges remain fashionable will be vital for retaining sales, because the cost increases are likely to affect all retailers, putting pressure on their margins.'

Changing consumer attitudes to fashion could also be significant. Although some still want to be able to buy new fashion lines as quickly and cheaply as possible, others are becoming more critical of this so-called 'fast fashion' on the basis that it encourages a 'throw-away' culture (where clothes might only be worn once before being discarded).

Critics of 'fast fashion' argue that it is not socially responsible – either in terms of the impact the throw-away culture has on resource usage, or in terms of its supply chain. Companies like Cheapkit rely on suppliers in developing countries to supply them with low-cost products, but there is a human cost involved in terms of the low wages and poor working conditions experienced in the factories. However, there is increasing global pressure to introduce tougher health and safety regulations and to improve working conditions for factory workers in these countries.

Exhibit 2: Briefing note given to you by Cheapkit's Procurement Director during your induction meeting

Our business strategy is based around cost leadership, and we pride ourselves on selling fashionable garments for men, women and children at very low prices compared to our main rivals.

For many years, we have been able to maintain our low prices by carefully sourcing our garments from suppliers in developing countries where labour is cheaper than in Essland. Also, we typically earn a gross margin of between 10% and 13% on our products, whereas most clothing retailers look at margins in the region of 20%.

As Cheapkit is a company with a complex international supply chain, the board regularly reviews the company's risks. The board has identified that three risks are of particular concern to the Cheapkit shareholders: exchange rate risk; supply chain risk; and international political risk. Each one of these risks is carefully monitored and the board receives regular briefings on each, because the board thinks that any of these risks could be a potential source of substantial loss to our shareholders.

For the past decade or so, Cheapkit has bought in a substantial proportion of its supplies from Athland, a relatively poor developing country known for its low labour costs and weak regulatory controls. Last year, 65% of Cheapkit's supplies came from this one country. As it does with all suppliers from foreign countries, Cheapkit pays Athland suppliers in their own currency.

Although Athland has a reputation for corruption – including among government officials – its workforce is hard-working and reliable.

Most employees in Athland's garment industry are employed on 'zero hours' contracts, meaning that they are employed by the hour as they are needed and released with no pay when demand from customers, like Cheapkit, is lower.

Exhibit 3: Press article following the accident at Cornflower's factory

In the aftermath of the tragedy at Cornflower's factory, our reporter has been looking into the factors which contributed to the collapse, and has uncovered some very worrying findings.

After only two years of normal operation, the new Cornflower building collapsed with the loss of over 1,000 lives. Collapsing slowly at first, the number of people killed or injured was made much worse by the shortage of escape exits and the large number of people in the building. As news of the tragedy was broadcast around the world, commentators reported that the weakness in the building was due to the West's 'obsession with cheap clothes'.

Cornflower is a significant, and long-standing supplier to the clothes retailer Cheapkit. Around half of Cheapkit's purchases from Athland are from Cornflower.

Owned by the Fusilli brothers, Cornflower outgrew its previous factory and wished to build a new manufacturing facility in Athland for which permission from the local government authority was required.

In order to gain the best location for the new factory, and to hasten the planning process, it appears the Fusilli brothers paid a substantial bribe to local government officials. When we asked Cornflower about this, the company's response was that the Fusilli brothers had felt under great pressure from Cheapkit to keep their prices low and so they sought to reduce overall expenditure, including capital investments.

Because the enforcement of building regulations is weak in Athland, the officials responsible for building quality enforcement were bribed to provide a weak level of inspection when construction began, thereby allowing the brothers to avoid the normal Athland building regulations.

In order to save costs, inferior building materials were used which would result in a lower total capital outlay, as well as a faster completion time. In order to maximise usable floor space, the brothers were also able to have the new building completed without the necessary number of escape doors or staff facilities. In each case, bribes were paid to officials to achieve the outcomes the Fusilli brothers wanted.

Once manufacturing began in the new building, high demand from Cheapkit meant that Cornflower was able to increase employment in the facility. Although, according to Athland building regulations, the floor area could legally accommodate a maximum of 500 employees, over 1,500 were often working in the building in order to fulfil orders from foreign customers, Cheapkit.

We asked Cheapkit for a comment, but the company would only state that it had entered into legal contracts with Cornflower in order to provide its customers with exceptional value for money. Cheapkit said that it was appalled and disgusted that Cornflower had acted corruptly and that the Cheapkit board was completely unaware of the weaknesses and safety breaches in the collapsed building.

Exhibit 4: Blog posting by Jess Lui

One person who escaped the Cornflower building as it collapsed was Jess Lui, although she witnessed a number of people who had been killed or injured during the collapse.

Jess is also the leader of the national pressure group 'Protect workers' rights' (PWR) which has been lobbying the Athland government to improve working conditions and health and safety practices for workers in the country.

After the accident, Jess posted a blog on PWR's account in which she wrote:

'Although the Athland government must do more to enforce health and safety legislation, much of the blame for the accident lies with Cheapkit, and the pressure it continually placed on Cornflower to keep prices low.

'Is it acceptable for multinational companies, such as Cheapkit, to exert so much pressure on companies based in developing countries?

'You are supplying a market in your home country, which is obsessed with cheap clothes. Nobody at Cheapkit cares about how the clothes are produced. All you care about is how many clothes you sell – and keeping the price cheap helps you sell more clothes.

'The constant pressure on prices has created a culture of 'exploitative wages' – not only at Cornflower but at many similar suppliers.

'However, it is time that large international companies, such as Cheapkit, recognise their responsibilities to other groups beyond their shareholders, and their duty to act in the public interest.

'In my opinion, the defective Cornflower factory in Athland would not have existed without demand from Cheapkit, so Cheapkit needs to acknowledge its responsibilities to its supply chain, and its accountability for this tragedy.'

Exhibit 5: Memo from the Sales Director of Cheapkit about a new business opportunity

All,

I have been approached by the national fast food chain, Yummy, with a proposal for us to supply them with staff uniforms at all of their restaurants across Essland.

As far as I know, this is the first time Cheapkit has been approached with a view to supplying a bulk order for another firm.

However, the volume of uniforms that Yummy are looking to buy could provide us with some significant additional revenue.

I've summarised details of the proposal below:

Yummy are looking for a supplier to supply all the shirts and trousers for its staff uniforms (which are very similar for male and female employees).

Volume would be a minimum of 125,000 short-sleeve shirts and 125,000 pairs of trousers per year for two years, at a price of $5.80 per shirt and $9.70 per pair of trousers.

This price is slightly lower than the price at which we sell similar garments in our stores, but this reflects the size and standardised nature of the order, plus the fact that we will not incur any of the retail costs associated with stocking and selling the shirts and trousers in our stores.

The estimated cost of producing the garments (converted to $ at the current exchange rate) will be:

	Shirts	Trousers
Manufacturing – Year 1	$5.40	$8.95
Manufacturing – Year 2 (allowing for wage increases and increases in raw material costs (eg price of cotton)	$5.45	$9.05
Logistics and distribution (both years)	$0.20	$0.25

If we accept the contract, it is estimated that we will also incur additional fixed costs, linked to the contract, of $25,000 in each of the two years.

52 Domusco

Assume it is now 1 November 20X5.

You are a qualified accountant and have recently joined the construction company Domusco as a group finance manager. You report to the group Finance Director, and will be expected to help him on a number of strategic matters.

You have collected the following information to help you with your work:

Exhibit 1: Overview of the Domusco Group – Notes you have made from induction meetings with your colleagues

Exhibit 2: Extracts from the October 20X5 board meeting

Exhibit 3: Press clipping from *Zeeland Times* about reaction to the proposed development at Metsa

Exhibit 4: Transcript of a meeting you held with Peter Boskov, Director of Major Construction Projects, discussing the motorway construction project in Wye

Exhibit 5: Initial feedback from staff survey; memo prepared by the Group HR Director

The task requirements are included in the tasks shown below:

1   Martyn Lite, the Finance Director, has asked you to help him review the Metsa development.

He has asked you to use a discount rate of 12% for evaluating the construction project, to allow for the risk involved; and he told you to assume that all the cash flow figures discussed in the board meeting are pre-tax figures that occur at the end of the year to which they relate.

Required

(a)   **Prepare a briefing paper which analyses the financial attractiveness, for Domusco, of the potential development at Metsa.**   **(10 marks)**

Professional skills marks are available for demonstrating **scepticism** skills in questioning the reliability of the figures and their implications for the attractiveness of the project.   **(2 marks)**

(b)   The board have emphasised on a number of occasions the need to consider corporate social responsibility issues as well as financial considerations when evaluating a project.

Required

Prepare a report that analyses the potential corporate social responsibility issues Domusco needs to consider when deciding whether or not to bid for the Metsa contract.   **(8 marks)**

Professional skills marks are available for demonstrating **analysis** skills in identifying the key issues to be considered.   **(2 marks)**

(c)   Martyn has mentioned to you several times that, given Domusco's commitment to social responsibility and sustainability, he thinks it would be useful for the group to adopt the integrated reporting <IR> framework in order to demonstrate this commitment more clearly. The majority of Domusco's published corporate information currently focuses on its financial performance.

Martyn raised this issue at the last board meeting, but a number of the directors said they wanted more information about <IR> before discussing the proposal any further. Martyn has asked you to help him prepare some information in advance of the next meeting.

Required

Prepare information for a presentation slide, plus briefing notes, for Martyn to present at the next board meeting, highlighting the key features of integrated reporting and how it differs from traditional financial reporting. (6 marks)

Professional skills marks are available for demonstrating **communication** skills in highlighting the key features of integrated reporting and how it differs from traditional financial reporting. (2 marks)

(Total = 30 marks)

2   One of Domusco's major ongoing projects includes the construction of a new motorway in Wye, but this is running behind schedule.

Martyn thinks this is partly due to shortcomings in Domusco's risk analysis and management processes, and he has asked you to discuss the issues with Peter Boskov.

Required

Prepare briefing notes which discuss how shortcomings in Domusco's risk analysis and risk management processes could have contributed to the group's failure to treat the risks associated with the motorway construction project adequately. (8 marks)

Professional skills marks are available for demonstrating **commercial acumen** in recognising the weaknesses in the risk analysis and risk management processes. (2 marks)

(Total = 10 marks)

3   In the light of the initial findings from the employee survey, the HR Director has recommended that Domusco reconsiders the extent to which it uses sub-contractors on major construction projects.

Required

Prepare a briefing paper for the board which assesses the issues the directors should consider when deciding whether to continue using sub-contracted staff or to recruit additional construction staff.

(8 marks)

Professional skills marks are available for demonstrating **evaluation** skills in assessing the potential advantages and disadvantages of the two approaches. (2 marks)

(Total = 10 marks)

Exhibit 1: Overview of the Domusco Group

Domusco was formed 45 years ago, and became a listed company 30 years ago, in its home country of Zeeland. (Zeeland is a relatively prosperous, developed nation.)

The Domusco group structure comprises three wholly owned subsidiary companies operating in different construction business segments:

- Major construction projects
- Office building construction
- House building

Although many of the projects Domusco undertakes are within Zeeland, it also undertakes projects in foreign countries. Domusco's major construction projects are usually undertaken on behalf of government authorities, for example building new road or rail links.

Domusco has established a favourable reputation for the high quality of its work, and as a socially responsible company.

Sustainability

Domusco acknowledges the importance of sustainability and social responsibility in relation to four key areas:

- Communities – helping to establish and maintain thriving and sustainable communities

- Environment – minimising its environmental footprint by improving operating practices at its developments and throughout its supply chain

- People – promoting a culture that encourages employees to develop their talents and skills

- Health and safety – protecting employees, contractors and all other stakeholders affected by its activities.

Current major construction projects

The Major Construction Projects subsidiary had five main contracts in progress during 20X4/5:

- The construction of a sports stadium in the Middle East (in a country where it has undertaken many projects before), which is due for completion in February 20X7. The total profitability on this project is forecast to be $78 million over four years.

- The construction of a motorway in a different country in the Middle East, which is due for completion in early 20X6. The overall updated forecast profitability on this project is $280 million.

- The construction of motorways and bridges in the neighbouring European country of Wye.

- Road and motorway construction and road improvements in Zeeland. The project spans two years, is due to be completed by mid-20X6 and its forecast profitability is $220 million.

- Construction work on a new marina in Zeeland. Work commenced in August 20X4 and is due for completion in November 20X6. The total project profitability is forecast to be $170 million.

Key staff

Bill Umm, the Chief Executive, has seen the group's revenue grow at over 10% per annum for most of the last ten years. He has personally been the driving force behind many of the large construction projects that Domusco has been awarded over the last few years.

Bill Umm has good government connections and has always found time to deal with many personnel matters. He is considered to be fair in his business dealings, and has been able to maintain Domusco's reputation as being scrupulously fair in its contract negotiations. He is also in touch with his workforce, and is well liked and respected by most of the Domusco board as well.

However, Bill's relationship with the Finance Director, Martyn Lite, is less good. This is primarily because Martyn often argues that Bill wants to pursue projects that may not be in the shareholders' interests. On several occasions, Martyn has stated that a project that appears to be profitable can be too risky, or that Domusco is taking on too much construction work and has insufficient management resources. On most occasions, Bill has over-ruled Martyn. Although Bill respects Martyn, he considers him to be too conservative.

Staffing levels and sub-contractors

Most companies operating in the construction industry use a mix of their own employees and sub-contractors. The mix varies by country and also by construction segment. In the house-building segment, Domusco employs its own staff for site surveying and site management, as well as for a proportion of the house-building construction work. Specialised sub-contractors undertake the rest of the house-building construction work. Domusco also directly employs all of the sales and marketing teams and administrative support for Domusco's house-building subsidiary companies. The majority of the sub-contractors that Domusco uses have worked closely with Domusco for several years.

In major construction projects, particularly motorway construction, specialised sub-contractors undertake the majority of the construction work. The location and the level of staffing required varies enormously with each major project and Domusco does not wish to employ large numbers of staff that may be located in the wrong area or with unsuitable skills. The use of sub-contractors gives Domusco flexibility.

Domusco's operational management has, however, experienced problems with the use of some sub-contractors. Although Domusco has repeatedly used the same sub-contracting companies as on previous occasions, the make-up of the teams used on projects that undertake the work change far too often. Despite supervision by the sub-contractors' management and subsequent inspections by Domusco's project management, there are large numbers of unskilled workers who are not capable of completing certain stages of construction to the required standard, which causes delays while the extent of the faulty work is identified and rectified. Additionally, as sub-contractors are paid a fixed fee for various stages of construction, they want to complete the job in the least possible time, so that their employees can move on to the next job. This leads to jobs being rushed and not thoroughly or professionally completed.

Domusco always uses its own staff for project management and surveys and inspections.

Exhibit 2: Extract from minutes of board meeting held in October 20X5

Potential development at Metsa

The Zeeland government has announced proposals for a major new development at Metsa. The Zeeland government is pleased with the way that Domusco is managing its existing projects in Zeeland, and has encouraged Domusco to bid to be the lead contractor on the new development. Alongside the major construction work required to develop the infrastructure for the new development (eg road and rail access), the project will also involve the construction of new houses and office buildings.

Peter Boskov (Director of Major Construction Projects) highlighted that it is difficult to estimate construction costs with any accuracy until detailed survey work has been undertaken. The site for the new development is quite rugged, so initial land preparation could be difficult and expensive.

However, as a guide for discussion Peter presented high-level estimates of costs and revenues:

Cash outflows for Metsa construction project

	Year 1 $m	Year 2 $m	Year 3 $m	Year 4 $m	Total $m
High-cost scenario	275	350	375	350	1,350
Low-cost scenario	130	160	340	380	1,010

Revenue (cash inflows) from Mesta project

	Year 1 $m	Year 2 $m	Year 3 $m	Year 4 $m	Total $m
Sales of housing	80	510	790	880	2,260
Sales of office buildings	30	50	60	50	190
	110	560	850	930	2,450

The final cost scenario (high cost; low cost) will depend on the degree of problems Domusco encounters during construction. Peter stressed that, at this stage, he doesn't know how likely the high-cost scenario is compared to the low-cost scenario.

Domusco will need to take out an additional loan in the region of $600m to fund the project. The loan will need to be drawn down at the start of the project to fund the construction costs before any sales are made. Based on preliminary enquiries with Domusco's bank, it seems likely they would be prepared to lend the additional amount required.

Using a discount factor of 12% (which is considered appropriate for the potential level of risk in the project) the net present value of the project under the high-cost scenario is $127 million, increasing to $414 million under the low-cost scenario.

The Sales and Marketing Director and Bill Umm both think the revenue (cash inflow) figures are reasonable, but Martyn Lite thinks they are too optimistic. Because the Metsa region is one of the less developed regions in Zeeland, house prices tend to be lower there than in many parts of the country. As such, Martyn suggested that Peter's figures for housing revenue are overstated by 10%.

Martyn produced the following total revenue projections which he recommended should be used for an initial high-level evaluation of the project:

	Year 1 $m	20X7 $m	20X8 $m	20X9 $m	Total $m
Total revenue	102	509	771	842	2,224

Exhibit 3: Newspaper article – *Zeeland Times*

Environmental concerns about proposed development at Metsa

Plans for a major new development at Metsa have been met with horror and anger by environmental groups.

The Metsa area is home to several rare plant species, and contains a number of sites of archaeological interest which will be destroyed by the development. Local opposition groups have already started campaigning against the development, and several hundred campaigners held a peaceful demonstration at the site today during a visit by a government minister. An online petition, set up by the leading environmental charity – Zeeland Trust – calling for the government to re-consider the development, has so far been signed by over 20,000 people.

The national government has publicly stated that development of the Metsa area is vital to promote economic growth in Zeeland.

Exhibit 4: Transcript from interview you held with Peter Boskov, Director of Major Construction Projects, discussing the motorway construction project in Wye

You: Thank you for sparing the time to talk to me.

First of all, could you briefly describe the background to the project and the problems it is currently facing?

Peter: Domusco was selected from a shortlist of four international companies for this construction project, which involves crossing some very difficult terrain. The motorway project commenced in Spring 20X4 and was due for completion by the end of 20X6.

Unfortunately, the project is currently running behind schedule, as a result of unforeseen extra construction work that will be required because of heavy rainfall this summer (Summer 20X5). The heavy rain caused some of the completed sections of the motorway, and some of the foundations for other sections, to be partially washed away. Some areas of the motorway will require totally new, stronger foundations to be constructed.

You: I can see how that could result in the project running behind schedule. Have you got an estimate of the impact of the extra construction work?

Peter: I have been trying to renegotiate our contract with the Wye government to reflect the extra work.

I have estimated that the extra work required will take about 14 weeks, and I have presented a case to Wye's government that they should pay the cost of the 14 weeks' additional work, plus the associated construction costs, out of their road building budget. The heavy rains were not foreseen when we agreed to undertake the project for them, and no allowance for them had been included in the contract price.

However, Wye's government minister for transport has publicly stated that the agreed budget cannot be exceeded and that we should have ensured that the quality of the foundations were stronger, given the environment and the terrain.

Even though all of the completed foundations had been fully inspected and approved by Wye's government department prior to the heavy rainfalls, the government is refusing to pay any compensation for the delays or any rebuilding work.

You: Presumably that will have a significant impact on the profitability of the project?

Peter: Yes indeed. However, as I reported to the board at the last board meeting, we need to be careful not to damage our relationship with the Wye government at the moment. There are some other major construction projects in Wye forthcoming in the next few years which Domusco is planning to bid for.

The original business case for the motorway project showed it had an expected value profitability of $105 million. The project was approved on that basis. However, it is now forecast to make an overall loss of $35 million, unless the Wye government changes its mind on any compensation payments.

At the last board meeting, Martyn Lite said that we should not let the possibility of future projects affect our negotiations with the Wye government in relation to the delays and rebuilding costs on the motorway project. However Bill Umm disagreed, and said that this way the first of many projects in Wye and that long-term profitability was more important than one single project.

Exhibit 5: Memo: Feedback from the most recent employee survey

From: HR Director

To: Senior management team

Re: Staff survey

Domusco has recently undertaken the annual employee survey, and we are now analysing the detailed results.

However, there are several key findings which I wanted to share with you now, in advance of this more detailed analysis.

Perhaps the most important issue arising from the survey is the extent to which Domusco employees are unhappy about the quality of the work undertaken by sub-contractors.

The employees are also aware that some sub-contractors are paid a larger daily fee than their own salaries, and feel that they are undervalued.

Domusco's employees have commented that an increasing number of the sub-contract firms are employing workers with insufficient training or inadequate experience. Zeeland is experiencing something of a construction boom at the moment, and inexperienced people are seeking work in the construction industry.

Domusco's employees are concerned that some of these inexperienced contract workers demonstrate a lack of awareness of the importance of safety. Some Domusco employees have even refused to work at one site where there have been a number of accidents caused by sub-contractors.

Answers to questions

Answers to Section 1 questions – Knowledge development

1 Rameses International

Marking scheme

		Marks
(a)	1 mark for each relevant point up to a maximum of 5 marks	5
	Valid points could include: a definition of strategic implementation; explanation	
	that the three elements of the model are equally valid; the importance of	
	interdependence between the elements; implementation is crucial in order	
	for strategic plans to be delivered	
(b)	1 mark for each relevant point up to a maximum of 10 marks	10
		15

Part (a)

Johnson *et al*'s (2017) model characterises the strategic management process as having three inter-related elements: strategic position (or strategic analysis); strategic choice; and strategic implementation.

The focus of strategic analysis is on understanding the current strategic position of an organisation. Strategic choice involves evaluating and choosing between the alternative strategies the organisation can pursue, while strategic implementation looks at how these strategies are actually put into practice.

Strategic implementation is the conversion of the strategy into detailed plans or objectives for operating units. Therefore, it is a vital part of the strategic management process, because a strategy can only start delivering benefits to an organisation once it has been put into practice. In order to be beneficial to an organisation, a strategy must be able to be implemented. The

BPP
LEARNING
MEDIA

strategic implementation element of the process highlights key issues such as resource availability and organisational structure, as well as the potential need for change within an organisation in order to implement the strategy successfully.

Johnson *et al's* (2017) model also emphasises that the strategic management process should not be seen as a linear model, in the way that the traditional rational planning model, for example, portrays it. Rather, strategic implementation is interlinked with both strategic analysis and strategic choice. For example, in the process of implementing a strategy, an organisation might discover features of its resources and structure which will lead to it to re-evaluate its assessment of strategic position and strategic choices. Similarly, when evaluating a strategy, an organisation needs to consider whether it has the necessary resources to implement the strategy successfully, and whether strategy fits with the organisation's structure and culture.

Part (b)

Leadership is required for strategic success in any organisation, and strategic leadership can be one of the key drivers of effective strategy implementation.

Strategic leaders need to have a clear vision for where an organisation needs to go, and to communicate this vision in order to motivate and inspire others to achieve the vision.

Transformational vs transactional leadership

Johnson *et al* (2017) suggest that two general styles of leadership exist: transactional and transformational leadership.

Transactional leadership focuses on systems and controls, and the existing processes and activities within an organisation, and it tries to achieve efficiencies within the current environment. In general, transactional leaders seek improvement rather than change. Transactional leadership can be important for the implementation of existing strategic plans; however, transactional leadership alone is often not sufficient to achieve strategic success.

Transformational leadership. Where changes to an organisation's culture, mindset or values are required – in order to help the organisation respond effectively to changes in the environment – transformational leadership is required. Unlike transactional leaders (who focus primarily on maintaining the status quo within an organisation), transformational leaders recognise the need for change, and develop an alternative vision for the future which can be used to enable their organisation to achieve strategic success. As such, transformational leadership is typically more appropriate than transactional leadership for achieving strategic success.

It appears that Rameses is facing some significant changes in its competitive environment, which are having an adverse effect on its performance. Therefore, transformational leadership is likely to be needed, to develop a new vision and strategy which can help to restore Rameses' competitive success.

In recent years, before Jeanette's appointment, Rameses' senior management appear to have adopted a transactional approach, and have focused on initiatives which try to respond to market changes whilst preserving the company's existing business models, rather than developing bolder new strategies which will allow it to take advantage of new opportunities. As such, under its previous leadership, Rameses appears to have been in danger of strategic drift, and appointing Jeanette (as the first CEO from outside the family) could be seen as an attempt by the family to bring in a leader with the necessary creativity and vision to restore the company's fortunes.

Change management. We have noted above that transformational leaders recognise the need for change, but creating an environment for change could be a major challenge for Jeanette. Jeanette will need to communicate her vision for the future, and to overcome any resistance to change – which could be a particular challenge in a business which is not used to having to make major strategic changes.

Again, the contrast between transformational and transactional leadership could be important here. Over the past three years, Rameses' senior management team has recognised the need for change in what they do, but – in keeping with a transactional approach – have proposed solutions which don't really alter Rameses' business model. Although they have tried a range of slightly different initiatives, none of these has been particularly successful. This suggests that more fundamental, **visionary and innovative changes** may be required to restore Rameses' competitive position.

In order to implement any new strategies successfully, Jeanette Singh will also need to **empower** others, and to provide **clarity of purpose** and direction to Rameses' management and staff. These again are important characteristics of transformational leaders.

Importance of management as well as leadership. While leadership is crucial in identifying vision and strategy for an organisation, achieving strategic success – and successfully implementing strategies – requires management as well as leadership. Managers will play a key role in ensuring commitment to change among Rameses' staff, and providing advice on practical requirements for change and potential obstacles to it.

Similarly, managers will play a vital role in implementation and control, and helping to translate overall changes of strategy into specific operational contexts – for example, in terms of the relationships with suppliers and customers.

2 Frigate

Top tips. The scenario provides lots of details which can be applied to the different facets of the cultural web, so a sensible approach to this question would be to treat each element of the web as a heading in your answer and then relate the relevant points in the scenario to that heading.

It is important to link the points you make back to the model, rather than simply repeating points from the scenario without going on to explain their significance in relation to the culture at Frigate.

It is also important that your answer focuses specifically on the culture at Frigate, and you do not waste time describing – or drawing – the cultural web itself in general terms.

Marking scheme

	Marks
1 mark for each relevant point up to a maximum of 4 marks for any single aspect of the web	
Up to a maximum of 15 marks in total	15

The cultural web created by Johnson (1992) illustrates the combination of assumptions that make up the **paradigm**, together with the **physical manifestation** of culture. It is applied to Frigate below.

Symbols

Organisations are represented by symbols such as logos, offices, dress, language and titles. Symbols at Frigate that indicate how the Managing Director wishes the company to be perceived and run include:

- Ron's nickname 'The Commander'
- Ron's use of naval terminology
- The naval-inspired name of the company

Ron's motor cruiser is a symbol of his success.

Power structures

Power structures look at who holds the real power within an organisation. At Frigate the power comes from one person, Ron, whose leadership style is based on his strong opinions and beliefs.

Organisational structures

The structure of the organisation often reflects the power structure. There is little formal structure at Frigate, and the attempt to install a formal organisational structure failed.

Control systems

Organisations are controlled through a number of systems including financial systems, quality systems and rewards. The areas that are controlled closest indicate the priorities of the organisation. The focus in Frigate is on cost control and the emphasis is on punishment (such as wage deductions for being late) rather than reward.

There are few formal process controls at Frigate, and the attempt – by Ann – to install such controls was heavily resisted by Ron, to the extent that Ann left the company.

Routines and rituals

The daily behaviour and actions of staff signal what the organisation considers to be 'acceptable' expectations and management values. At Frigate, there is one rule for the Managing Director (flexible hours, extended holidays etc) and another for everyone else (minimum holiday, no flexibility, wage deductions for arriving late).

Stories

The people and past events talked about in an organisation can illustrate the values of the organisation and the behaviour it encourages. Stories at Frigate relate to the Managing Director as 'The Commander'. He is the hero of the organisation who constantly has to deal with numerous villains – lazy staff, poor quality suppliers, customers who delay paying, the tax authority and society in general (who he believes all need to do a stint in the navy).

Paradigm

The paradigm signifies the basic assumptions and beliefs that an organisation's decision makers hold in common and take for granted. It summarises and reinforces the rest of the cultural web. The paradigm at Frigate shows a company run for the personal gratification of the Managing Director and his family. Ron believes that his lifestyle and benefits are the reward for taking risks in a hostile environment.

3 RDC

> **Top tips.** The discussion in part (a) on responsible leadership requires you to assess whether the decision to choose Route A considered the views of different stakeholder groups and was a sustainable long-term option.
>
> As in real life there may be no one solution that is 'right' and you have to consider different viewpoints; for example, considering a company's responsibility to generate value for its shareholders, as opposed to its social responsibility. The discussion on sustainability brings out the conflict between environmentally sustainable and socially sustainable.
>
> Note, also, that you weren't simply asked to describe responsible leadership, you were asked to 'assess the extent to which the board of RDC demonstrated responsible leadership' in choosing Route A. This involves examining the scenario to identify areas where responsible leadership was and was not demonstrated, before concluding whether the RDC board succeeded overall in showing responsible leadership.
>
> Part (b) is about analysing stakeholders in order to identify which stakeholders have (or should have) influence over RDC's actions. Each of the first three points relates to an important category of stakeholder, power to approve (primary), desire to take action (active) and most affected by the organisation's strategy (narrow). Dealing with conflict in this part is seen in terms of identifying and minimising disagreements, possibly therefore trying as hard as possible to avoid having to decide between conflicting claims.
>
> In part (c), stakeholder claims are used to enforce outcomes that stakeholders desire or to avoid undesirable outcomes. In order to assess the claims, you need to consider on what basis the claims are legitimate and also whether the stakeholders are likely to be able to enforce them.

Marks

(a) Up to 2 marks for a discussion of each point, but capped at ½
    mark per point for identification only (rather than discussion)   Max 10
    2 marks for balanced summary   Max 2
    Up to a maximum for part (a) of 10   10

(b) Up to 2 marks for each relevant point discussed, but capped at
    ½ mark per point for identification only (rather than discussion)
    Up to a maximum for part (b) of 8   8

(c) 2 marks for explanation of stakeholder claim   Max 2
    2 marks for assessment of each claim   Max 6
    Up to a maximum for part (c) of 7   7
                                      25

(a) Responsible leadership requires leaders to work *with* different stakeholders, considering their needs and viewpoints when making decisions. A responsible leader considers the wider societal and environmental impacts of business decisions whilst also protecting shareholder interests.

Maximising shareholder wealth

Route A delivers a higher net present value and the board of RDC have a duty to act in the best interests of shareholders. Projections demonstrate that its NPV is positive $5 million, $1 million more than if Route B was chosen.

Legal requirements

The local government authority has given planning permission for Route A, so RDC seems to have fulfilled government planning requirements. RDC does not appear to face the threat of legal action with Route A that it could have faced if it had chosen Route B.

Protection of jobs

RDC has made a decision to protect the jobs of local farm workers as well as preserving the livelihood of Eddie Krul, demonstrating a desire on behalf of RDC's leaders to work collaboratively with the local community when making decisions. Alternatively, the decision may have been taken to avoid legal action, as threatened by Eddie Krul, rather than as an effort to act responsibly and ethically.

Employee rights

Although workers on Route A are being offered higher wages, they will have to forego their right to a limit on their working hours. It is not clear whether employees have been consulted on this change - they may feel pressured into the decision in order to keep their jobs. Longer working weeks may also impact on the health and safety of construction workers on Route A. Such a decision suggests that the board are more focused on meeting targets than on the welfare of employees.

Sustainability

The decision to choose Route A appears to be the **less environmentally sustainable decision**. It could **threaten the existence of an endangered species** and **disrupt the local ecosystems,** with possible unforeseen consequences. However, had RDC chosen Route B there would have been implications for social sustainability, with loss of jobs at the farm and adverse impacts on the local community.

Summary

Whichever decision RDC made would have had **negative implications** for some stakeholders. Responsible leadership is not about keeping all stakeholders happy but rather about weighing up the business's overall impact on and contribution to society at

BPP
LEARNING
MEDIA

large. On balance, it appears that the board at RDC have demonstrated responsible leadership in considering the sustainability of the rail route. Although the project is not environmentally sustainable in the short term, efforts are being made to preserve the birds' habitat as much as possible. In the long term, the choice of Route A is a sustainable investment since it preserves local jobs and should ultimately reduce the number of cars on the roads.

(b) **Conflict between different stakeholders**

In a situation where there are a number of possible stakeholder claims, it is important to recognise and analyse the importance of all stakeholder groups for the following reasons.

Stakeholder approval

RDC needs to recognise first which stakeholders have the **power** to **approve the decision** before it can start work on the project and how much **interest** in the project those stakeholders will show. Here the stakeholder with the **power** is the local government authority, which has the responsibility of granting planning permission. RDC would have had to **fulfil any requirements laid down by the local government authority** before it could go ahead.

Stakeholder action

RDC needs to identify which stakeholders are likely to **take action** that will have a **major impact upon the success** of the investment. This means here in particular the risk of the pressure group being **able to disrupt the project** and how great **the adverse consequences of disruption would be**. RDC also has to weigh up how much disruption the pressure group could cause against the delays possibly imposed by legal action by Eddie Krul.

Reputation issues

From an ethical and reputation viewpoint, RDC not only needs to consider the amount of influence each stakeholder has but also the **impact upon each group**. There may be disapproval from society if the **adverse impact on vulnerable stakeholders appears particularly great**, and RDC may face protests or political pressure. It is therefore also important to identify stakeholders such as the Save the Birds pressure group who hope to use this threat to reputation to pressurise RDC.

Conflicting stakeholder claims

It is important to be aware of all stakeholders when, as here, the claims of influential stakeholders are likely to come into **conflict**. In order to have a clear rationale for deciding between stakeholder claims, RDC needs to assess the **relative influence** of each stakeholder upon the project and where disagreements are likely to occur. It can then try to minimise the threat of disruption from stakeholders by trying to **resolve the disagreements** between them.

(c) **Stakeholder claim**

A stakeholder is any person who **affects** or is **affected** by the activities of an organisation. A claim is the **outcome** that the **stakeholder seeks** or the outcome which would **benefit the stakeholder most or harm it least**. This therefore brings in claims by stakeholders who do not understand or cannot voice the claims that they have, for example here the rare birds.

Eddie Krul

Eddie Krul's claim is that RDC should avoid his farm. The **legitimacy** of his claim is based on the **fairness** argument that his farm has been **owned by his family** for four generations and the **economic argument** that he provides local employment opportunities. Since he **understands his claim** and is able to **voice his concerns**, he is clearly able to enforce his claim.

Local government authority

The **legitimacy** of the local government authority's claim is based on its being given the power by law to **grant or deny planning permission**. Its decision on whether to use its claim appears to have been determined by the **economic benefits** that would accrue to the region. Since the local government authority has the power to influence how the investment is undertaken, arguably it has **not made good use of its claim** in that it has not expressed an opinion and not required RDC to implement effective safeguards to protect the bird colony.

Bird colony

The legitimacy of the bird colony's claim is based on the threat to its existence. However, there may be concerns that RDC will fail to recognise this claim because the birds lack the ability to understand their claim and cannot vocalise it themselves, although the pressure group can advocate it for them.

4 Hum and Hoo

Top tips. Beware of producing bare lists where these are not called for, and make sure that any examples chosen are actually relevant to the situation in the question.

The case in this question was about a small audit firm and the ethical threats relating to the provision of non-audit services.

Part (a) asked about these ethical threats and the importance of ethical safeguards to address those threats. However, note that there are three different elements of the requirement (worth 8 marks in total). Therefore, you only needed to give a brief explanation of what an ethical threat is; not to list each of the five threats (self-interest; self-review etc) and explain each one in turn.

When discussing the benefits of ethical safeguards for Hum and Hoo, it was necessary to analyse the case to understand the particular situation that Hum and Hoo were in.

Part (b) also starts by asking for an explanation – this time of what 'public interest' is. Again, though, you shouldn't spend too long on the explanation, because the second part of the requirement is more substantial – explaining why a company's audit committee is a suitable body to advise on non-audit service purchase from Hum and Hoo. This task requires you to think about the role of an audit committee in a listed company, and particularly its role in ensuring the independence of external auditors.

Marking scheme

			Marks
(a)	Up to 2 marks for explanation of ethical threat	Max 2	
	Up to 2 marks for explanation of ethical safeguard	Max 2	
	Up to 2 marks for each benefit identified and discussed (up to a maximum of 6)	Max 6	
	Up to a maximum (for part (a)) of 8		8
(b)	Up to 3 marks for explanation of public interest in the context of accountancy services	Max 3	
	Up to 2 marks for each relevant point on audit committee (up to a maximum of 6)	Max 6	
	Up to a maximum (for part (b)) of 9		9
			17

(a) Ethical threat

Any factor which may reduce the effectiveness of a professional person's ability to act in the public interest without threatening independence can be counted as an ethical threat.

Both the ACCA (2018) and IESBA Codes of Ethics (2018) identify five ethical threats: self-interest; self-review; advocacy; familiarity; and intimidation. Since external auditors conduct their work on behalf of shareholders and provide them with an independent auditor's report, it is particularly important that auditors are free from ethical threats.

Ethical safeguard

Any measure put in place to prevent the occurrence of an ethical threat is an ethical safeguard. Safeguards can be either wide-ranging, imposed on the profession as a whole by legislation or regulation, or they can be devised by individual firms.

Benefits of ethical safeguards

Hum and Hoo are facing a number of ethical threats with regard to the provision of non-audit services, not least of which is the threat to independence. They need to put in place effective safeguards to protect the firm and its staff and these safeguards need to be transparent.

Having safeguards in place will enhance the trust placed by the shareholders in the audit firm and will demonstrate that independence remains undiminished. Without their reputation for independence, the role of accountants and auditors can be called into question.

Finally, having safeguards in place will enable the firm to deliver both audit and non-audit services without facing the difficulties imposed by ethical threats.

(b) **Public interest**

To act in the public interest means to act for the collective wellbeing of society as a whole. Accountants should serve the interest of their own clients, shareholders, governments and other stakeholders. Accountants need to be aware that, when conducting an audit, they need to be impartial and unbiased because they are employed by shareholders to act on their behalf. It is important for the public at large that accounts are true and fair and that auditors express an independent view that is professional and unbiased.

Approval by audit committee

Some codes of corporate governance, such as Sarbanes-Oxley (2002), specify that some non-audit services can be provided by the external audit firm but only with the express consent of the client's audit committee. There is similar provision in other codes regarding the acceptability of external auditors taking on non-audit work for their audit clients.

Suitability of audit committee

- The audit committee is responsible for the independence of the external audit and is in a position to make a judgement as to whether non-audit work could jeopardise that independence

- The presence of non-executive directors (NEDs) on the audit committee will improve impartiality as they have no vested financial interest in the company

- It is the responsibility of the audit committee to represent the interest of the shareholders in the face of any vested interest executive directors might have in the short-term performance of the company

The audit firm itself is responsible for determining whether providing non-audit services would constitute a threat to independence.

5 Esse

> **Top tips.** A useful approach to this question would be to try to identify which ethical principle is at risk in each of the situations described in the scenario. For each situation, you should try to identify which of the fundamental principles (Professional competence and due care; Integrity; Professional behaviour; Confidentiality; and Objectivity) **could** be threatened by the issues identified, and then explain how the situation **could** lead to a conflict with the principle in question.
>
> Then you should assess whether the situation **actually** represents a conflict with that principle. This assessment should form the basis of your advice.

Note that you have been asked to 'advise' whether (or not) each of the situations is in conflict with ethical principles so you must reach a clear conclusion in each section of your answer, and state whether there is a conflict or not.

Marking scheme

Marks

For each situation:

For identifying the ethical principles relevant to the situation – 1 mark

For explaining the principle – 1 mark

For explaining why the situation does (or does not) represent a conflict with the
    principle – up to 2 marks

For clear advice about each situation – 1 mark

Up to a total of 4 marks for each situation

Up to a maximum (for the three situations in total) of 12   12

Ethical threat

Situation 1

Integrity. This situation could be in conflict with the fundamental principle of integrity.

Professional codes of ethics (such as ACCA's Code of Ethics and Conduct, 2018) highlight that the principle of integrity requires accountants to be 'straightforward and honest' in all business relationships. The principle of integrity also implies that business professionals should not be associated with any information which they believe contains a materially false or misleading statement, or which is misleading by omissions.

Contain a materially false or misleading statement. The CEO has presented a very optimistic forecast for Esse's profits, and this could be misleading if the government's claim for damages against the company is successful.

Omits information where such omission would be misleading. Although the government's claim for damages would 'materially affect' Esse's profit for 20X3 if it were successful, the CEO did not mention the claim in his presentation to the analysts and journalists. This omission is therefore misleading, because it prevents his audience from being aware that Esse's profit for 20X3 might be materially lower than the figure given in the forecast.

> **Tutorial note:** The principle of integrity also requires professional accountants to disassociate themselves from statements or information which have been 'furnished recklessly'.
>
> **Contain statements or information furnished recklessly.** The CEO prepared his forecast in a hurry, and did not check the figures with anyone else in the company. Given that Esse is an international company, the CEO could be seen as reckless for presenting a forecast without asking anybody else in the company to confirm it. Such actions suggest the CEO has perfect knowledge of the company and its prospects, but that seems very unlikely.

Advice:

The CEO's forecast and presentation demonstrate the characteristics of communications which conflict with the principle of integrity. The CEO has not been honest in his dealings with the analysts and the journalists, and therefore **Situation 1 represents a conflict with the principle of integrity**.

Situation 2

Confidentiality. The principle which could be jeopardised here is confidentiality. Professional codes of ethics require accountants and firms to refrain from disclosing, outside their own firm, confidential information which has been acquired as a result of business relationships with that firm.

Many of the documents which the government's lawyers have requested contain confidential information, which suggests there could be a conflict with the principle of confidentiality if they are handed over.

Exception: Legal proceedings. However, codes of ethics make an exception to the principle of confidentiality in the context of legal proceedings. In other words, the principle of confidentiality is not breached if confidential information is disclosed when it is required in the course of legal proceedings.

This is the case in Situation 2. Esse has been required to produce the documents as a result of the court order obtained by the government.

Advice:

Although the documents contain confidential information, **Situation 2 does not represent a conflict** with the principles of a Code of Professional Ethics.

Situation 3

Objectivity. The principle which could be at stake in this situation is objectivity.

The principle of objectivity requires accountants not to allow bias, conflict of interest, or the undue influence of others to override their professional or business judgements.

Reasons for financial controller's decision. The financial controller's advice about discontinuing the joint venture appears to have been driven by the poor working relationship between the accounting staff in the two companies, and the problems which Pharm has caused him and his staff.

The financial controller does not appear to have considered the profitability of the joint venture, or the commercial benefits to Esse of continuing with it.

Conflict. In this respect, it appears that the financial controller's decision has been biased as a result of the problems which he and his staff have encountered in working with Pharm.

Advice:

This situation **represents a conflict with the ethical principles**, and specifically with the principle of objectivity.

6 Sentosa House

Top tips. Part (a): Although the requirement asks for an explanation of agency costs, simply knowing the definition will not be enough to pass part (a). The majority of the marks are available for relating agency costs to the scenario and for discussing the issues that might increase those costs. (The key elements that incur agency costs are means of obtaining information and controls established over the agent.)

In (b) you need to think about threats to value and the various problems associated with a cavalier attitude towards control – including, potentially, risks to the investor's own reputation for being associated with it.

Marks

(a)   Up to 2 marks for definition of agency costs   2

        1 mark for each problem identified and briefly discussed   5

        Up to a maximum (for part (a)) of 7 marks   7

(b)   1 mark for each relevant point identified, and briefly

        described, on   Max 7

          conditions for intervention, up to 7 marks

        1 mark for each relevant point made in relation to the Eastern

          Products case, up to a maximum of 4 marks   Max 4

        Up to a maximum (for part (b)) of 10 marks   10

                                                      17

(a) Definition of agency costs

Agency costs arise from the need of **principals** (here shareholders) to monitor the activities of agents (here the board, particularly the Chair). This means that principals need to **find out what the agent is doing**, which may be difficult because they may not have as much information about what is going on as the agent does. Principals also need to **introduce mechanisms to control the agent** over and above normal analysis. Both finding out and introducing mechanisms will incur costs that can be viewed in terms of money spent, resources consumed or time taken.

Problems with agency costs in Eastern Products

Attitudes to risk

The first reason for increased agency costs is that the company's attitude to risk is a major area of concern. Thomas Hoo appears to be pursuing strategies which Sentosa (and other institutional) investors consider to be very risky, and therefore Sentosa wants to understand more about the strategies and Eastern's risk appetite.

Unwillingness of Chair to be monitored

Agency costs will certainly increase because Thomas Hoo is **unwilling to supply any information about the reasons for his policies**, certainly indicating arrogance and also a **lack of willingness to accept accountability**. This means that Sentosa will have to **find out from other sources**, for example any non-executive directors who are on the board. Alternatively, they may contact other investors and take steps to put more pressure on Thomas Hoo, for example by threatening to requisition an extraordinary general meeting.

Inadequacy of existing mechanisms

Agency costs will also increase because existing mechanisms for communicating concerns appear to be **inadequate**. There are **insufficient non-executive directors** on the board to exert pressure on Thomas Hoo. There is **no risk management committee** to monitor risks. The investor relations department is **insufficiently informed and unhelpful**. Thomas Hoo has abruptly dismissed the phone call. Because of the seriousness of the concerns, ideally there should be **regular meetings** between Thomas Hoo and the major shareholders, **requiring preparation** from both parties and increasing agency costs.

Combining shareholder concerns

Thomas Hoo may be able to ignore shareholder concerns, because of the **shareholding patterns**. Although institutional shareholders are concerned, those who want to take action may not together hold a sufficiently large shareholding to enforce their views. Building a shareholder alliance will also increase agency costs.

(b) **Active intervention**

Active intervention by an institutional shareholder by making an attempt, for example, to change the board is regarded as a serious step, and may result in a **significant increase in agency costs**. However, there are a number of reasons why it might happen.

Threats to value of shareholding

Institutional shareholders may intervene if they perceive that management's policies could lead to a fall in the value of the company and hence the **value of their shares**. There could be concerns over strategic decisions over products, markets or investments or over **operational performance**. Although they can in theory sell their shares, in practice it may be difficult to offload a significant shareholding without its value falling. Here, although Eastern Products is currently making high returns, Sentosa may judge that the **risk of a major strategy** going wrong is **too high**.

Lack of confidence in management integrity

Institutional investors may intervene because they feel management cannot be trusted. At worst they may fear **management fraud**; this could be a worry in this scenario given that Thomas Hoo has removed a key component of the control system (the risk committee) without good reason.

Failure to control management

Institutional investors may take steps if they feel that there is **insufficient influence** being **exercised by non-executive directors** over executive management. The disappearance of the risk committee is also a symptom of this problem.

Lack of control systems

Intervention would be justified if there were **serious concerns about control systems**. Thomas Hoo's actions may indicate a fundamental flaw in control arrangements with management able to bypass whatever systems are in place.

Failure to address shareholder concerns

Even if there is no question of dishonesty, there may be intervention if institutional investors feel that management is **failing to address their legitimate viewpoints**. Institutional investors' own investors may exert pressure on them **not to invest in high-risk companies, or companies with a poor ethical reputation**. Thomas Hoo is solely focused on returns whilst **failing to address the issue of risk**.

Failure to comply with stock market requirements

Eastern Products' failure to comply with corporate governance concerns appear to be quite blatant. The institutional investors may be concerned that they will **suffer criticism** if they are perceived as being party to these breaches because they have not taken action to address them. It may also **threaten the value of their shareholding** if the stock market turns against Eastern Products.

7 West vs Leroi

Marking scheme

		Marks
(a)	1 mark for each essential feature of a rules-based approach, briefly described	
	Up to a maximum (for part (a)) of 3 marks	3
(b)	1 mark for each relevant point made on the advantages of principles-based approach to governance, up to a maximum of 4	4
	Up to 2 marks for each relevant point about the suitability of a principles-based approach for developing countries, up to a maximum of 6	6
	Up to a maximum (for part (b)) of 10 marks	10
		13

(a) **Rules-based approaches**

Lack of flexibility

Rules-based approaches allow **no leeway**; the key issue is whether you have complied with the rules.

Visibility

It should be easy to **assess** whether or not a company has complied with the rules.

Aspects of governance emphasised

Rules-based approaches emphasise aspects of governance that can be verified easily, such as whether there is an **audit committee**. They place less emphasis on areas such as organisational culture that cannot be governed by clear rules.

(b) **Overall compliance**

A principles-based approach emphasises to businesses the need to comply with the **overall spirit of governance codes**. It thus is more likely to encourage the **continuous improvement** that is particularly important in developing countries. Adopting a rules-based approach means that the focus is on conformance with a (possibly limited) set of rules.

Lack of local resources

A rules-based approach will only be effective if companies can draw on **sufficient local resources** to fulfil those rules. This may not be the case in developing countries. For example, requiring all companies to set up an audit committee including non-executive directors with financial knowledge will be ineffective if there is an insufficient pool of individuals within the country who are willing to serve on audit committees.

Varying circumstances

Companies in developing countries are likely to develop their governance structures at different speeds as their businesses develop. Requiring all companies to meet the standards that are necessary for the **largest, most developed companies** will not be **cost-effective.**

Local legislation

Professor Leroi highlighted the discussions going on at government level. A **rules-based approach to corporate governance** may only be effective if it is backed by government legislation; governments may not be willing to introduce this legislation because of the cost to the taxpayer and corporate sector.

International appeal

If companies in developing countries follow a recognised international principles-based code, for example the **OECD code**, this may inspire more confidence in investors than if they follow a local, rules-based code. Investors will be judging against an internationally recognised benchmark. Also, the emphasis in international codes on comply or explain encourages **transparency** by companies. This should also increase confidence because the accounts should explain clearly the company's current state of corporate governance.

8 Plantex

> **Top tips.** Note that, in effect, there are two parts (a): first, explaining what corporate citizenship is, in general terms; then, assessing Plantex's rights and responsibilities as a corporate citizen.
>
> Similarly, note that (b) (i) doesn't only ask you to describe the advantages to Plantex of adopting <IR>, but also the advantages to its stakeholders.
>
> Importantly, your answer should focus on the advantages of adopting <IR>, and you shouldn't spend time, for example, simply describing what <IR> is.
>
> A similar argument also applies to (b) (ii), where your focus should be on the information which <IR> could provide about the six capitals, rather than simply explaining what the six capitals are in general terms.

Marking scheme

				Marks
(a)	Up to 2 marks for an explanation of the concept of corporate citizenship		Max 2	
	Up to 3 marks for assessing Plantex's rights as a corporate citizen		Max 3	
	Up to 3 marks for assessing Plantex's responsibilities as a corporate citizen		Max 3	
	Up to a maximum (for part (a)) of 7 marks			7
(b)	(i)	1 mark for each <IR> advantage to Plantex described, up to a maximum of 4 marks	Max 4	
		1 mark for each <IR> advantage to Plantex's stakeholders, up to a maximum of 4 marks	Max 4	
		Up to a maximum (for b(i)) of 6 marks		6
	(ii)	Up to 6 marks for explaining the importance of the capitals used in <IR> (Answers capped at ½ mark per capital for simply explaining what the capital is, but not relating it to Plantex)		6
				19

(a) Corporate citizenship is an approach which can be adopted by any business with the aim of shaping its core values, so that they more closely align the decisions made each day by its directors, managers and employees with the needs of the society in which the business operates.

There are three principles which lie behind successful corporate citizenship:

(i) Minimising any harm caused to society by the decisions and actions of a business, which could include avoiding harm to the natural environment as well as the social infrastructure. The very nature of Plantex's business operations means that it is promoting health and wellbeing among wider society through the development of life-enhancing pharmaceuticals.

(ii) Maximising any benefit created for society as a consequence of normal business activity. Any successful business will stimulate local economic activity and increase employment, but a good corporate citizen will do this with greater sensitivity to its environmental and social impacts.

(iii) Remaining clearly accountable and responsive to a wide range of its stakeholders, thereby combining business self-interest with a greater sense of responsibility towards society at large.

By embracing the corporate citizenship agenda, Plantex is able to recognise its fundamental rights and acknowledge that it has responsibilities towards the wider community.

Rights

Plantex has the right to exist as a separate legal entity and carry out its lawful business within a society. By further extending these fundamental rights to a corporate citizen, Plantex is able to enjoy the full protection of the law as long as it acts within the law. In effect, society grants Plantex the necessary protection under the law to enable it to develop, expand and succeed as a business.

Responsibilities

Responsibilities are the duties which are owed to society by the corporate citizen as a consequence of it belonging to that society, and thereby enjoying the rights and privileges afforded it. In order to enjoy this level of protection, Plantex must comply with all laws that affect it, and conduct its business in accordance with society's behavioural norms.

Plantex's shareholders and management would normally determine the extent to which it is socially responsible for meeting their legal, ethical and economic responsibilities. However, corporate citizenship goes further by ensuring a better quality of life in the communities in which the business operates, while still preserving profitability and wealth creation for shareholders.

(b) (i) **Integrated reporting**

Through an understanding of the connections between a business's operations and the environments in which it operates, Plantex's management is able to take more environmentally and socially sustainable decisions and allocate its scarce non-renewable resources more effectively. Consequently, the information contained within <IR> (International Integrated Reporting Council, 2018) enables investors and other stakeholders to better understand how a firm is holistically performing.

The following are recognised advantages to Plantex of adopting <IR>:

Decision-making. The connections made through <IR> enable investors to better evaluate the combined impact of the diverse factors, or 'capitals', affecting the business. This in turn should result in better investment decisions by the shareholders, and more effective capital allocation by the firm.

Reputation. The greater transparency and disclosure of <IR> should result in a decrease in reputation risk, which in turn should result in a lower cost of, and easier access to, sources of finance.

Harmonisation. <IR> provides a platform for standard setters and decision makers to develop and harmonise business reporting. This in turn should reduce the need for costly bureaucracy imposed by central authorities.

<IR> also provides the following advantages to Plantex stakeholders:

Communications. The additional information would help to strengthen communication links between Plantex and its key stakeholders. This would enable the alignment of interests between the firm and its stakeholders to be assessed and improved as necessary.

Relationships. The information will lead to a higher level of trust from, and engagement with, a wide range of stakeholders. This emphasis on stakeholder engagement should lead to greater consultation with stakeholder groups and enable the company to handle their concerns more effectively.

Accountability. Due to the broader perspective required by <IR>, both in terms of the resources and relationships which it takes into account and the longer time frame over which value creation is considered, it makes Plantex more accountable as stewards of society's common resources, in particular human, natural and social capital.

(ii) **Capitals**

<IR> simplifies accounting information, as it dispenses with unnecessary levels of detail and focuses attention on more critical information. <IR> (International Integrated Reporting Council, 2018) aims to make visible the 'capitals', resources and relationships on which Plantex depends. It also illustrates how Plantex utilises and impacts on those 'capitals' and effectively transforms them.

There are six 'capitals' described in the <IR> framework:

1   **Financial capital.** This comprises the pool of funds available to Plantex, which includes both debt and equity finance. This description of financial capital focuses on the source of funds, rather than its application (for example in funding production of drugs or the purchase of equipment). However, Plantex needs financial capital to enable it to develop other capitals, in particular manufactured capital.

2   **Manufactured capital.** This is the human-created, production-oriented equipment and tools used in production or service provision, such as buildings, equipment and infrastructure. This would include the specialist equipment used by Plantex for the development of new drugs. Manufactured capital draws a distinction is between inventory (as a short-term asset) and plant and equipment (tangible capital).

3   **Intellectual capital.** This is a key element in an organisation's future earning potential, with a close link between investment in R&D, innovation, human resources and external relationships, as these can determine the organisation's competitive advantage. Plantex depends heavily on intellectual capital as it is key to its ongoing success, as developed pharmaceuticals become patented products which ultimately derive value to the firm and its shareholders.

4   **Human capital.** Is understood to consist of the knowledge, skills and experience of the company's employees and managers, as they are relevant to improving operational performance. Pharmaceutical companies like Plantex are knowledge-intensive businesses which rely heavily on the innovation and creativity of the talented scientists who work within it.

5   **Natural capital.** This is any stock of natural resources or environmental assets which provide a flow of useful goods or services, now and in the future. Plantex will require access to refined, pure chemicals in order to create its pharmaceutical solutions.

6   **Social and relationships capital.** Comprises the relationships within an organisation, as well as those between an organisation and its external stakeholders, depending on where social boundaries are drawn. These relationships should enhance both social and collective wellbeing.

9 Geeland

Top tips. The first part of (a) should be a relatively simple test of knowledge, but the second part requires you to evaluate the guidance specifically reported in the scenario. However, note the verb requirement is to 'critically evaluate' so your answer needs to identify the benefits/advantages of the guidance as well as problems/disadvantages with it. Cost vs consistency, and lack of clarity are issues that have to be weighed up. Note also flexibility can be seen as a point for and against a principles-based approach.

(b) and (c) cover a central part of the corporate governance debate, which sometimes features in the news – separation (or lack of separation) of the roles of Chair and Chief Executive. Hopefully you are familiar with the practical and ethical arguments in (b), but note also the point about compliance with governance guidelines. Comply or explain is only satisfactory if the shareholders accept the explanations. They are less likely to do so if companies do not explain why non-compliance has occurred (a significant issue in (c)). In some cases, though, the best way to keep shareholders happy is to assure them that non-compliance is temporary, as has happened here.

Note that for part (c) you need to comment specifically on the statement provided by Anson Co, not to explain – in general terms – what 'comply or explain' means.

Marking scheme

			Marks
(a)	Distinguishing between rules-and principles-based approaches, up to 4 marks	Max 4	
	Up to 2 marks for each argument in favour of, or against, the guidance	Max <u>10</u>	
	Up to a maximum for part (a) of 12 marks		12
(b)	Up to 2 marks for each point of explanation (capped at ½ mark each for identifying reasons why separation is considered best practice, but not explaining them)		
	Up to a maximum (for part (b)) of 8 marks		8
(c)	Up to 2 marks for each relevant point of assessment (capped ½ mark for identification only)		
	Up to a maximum (for part (c)) of 5 marks		<u>5</u>
			<u>25</u>

(a) **Rules-based approach**

A rules-based approach requires companies to comply with regulations. There are **no exceptions** apart from those allowed for in the regulations. A rules-based approach is generally underpinned by law. Companies which do not comply will face **legal sanctions**.

Principles-based approach

A principles-based approach is likely to be underpinned by some company law, but the principles will also cover areas not included in legislation. Principles-based approaches emphasise the **objectives of governance**, rather than good governance being achieved by taking a number of prescribed actions. Companies operating under a principles-based code cannot, however, just ignore it. The code will often be incorporated into listing rules. They have to state that they have complied in their accounts or identify and explain the areas where they have not complied. Investors will then decide whether they accept the company's justification for non-compliance and may take action that impacts upon share price.

Geeland's approach

The guidance in the Geeland code clearly identifies that the code is **principles-based**, as it states that there is more to governance than complying with rules. Good governance requires broad principles which should be applied flexibly to individual companies.

Arguments in favour

Areas of application

A principles-based approach can **extend more widely** than a rules-based approach and can focus on areas where it would be unrealistic to apply rules. For example, a principles-based approach can require directors to undertake professional development to extend their knowledge and skills without laying down how many courses they should go on each year. A principles-based approach can require boards to maintain good relations with major (institutional) shareholders without laying down how much contact there should be each year.

Cost to companies

A principles-based approach is also less costly in terms of time and expenditure.

Companies in a rules-based jurisdiction may have to invest considerable time and monies in developing information and reporting systems that evidence compliance. There is evidence that companies have turned away from US stock markets, where they would be under the rules-based, Sarbanes-Oxley (2002) regime on the grounds of cost of compliance. To be effective, a rules-based regime also has to have bodies to **monitor and enforce compliance**. The costs of maintaining these bodies are often passed on to companies in the form of listing costs.

Flexibility of approach

A principles-based approach can require companies to maintain adequate structures, for example effective risk management systems, but allow what is adequate to vary by company or industry. For example, in some industries companies will avoid hazardous activities and will not therefore require **elaborate health and safety control systems**. Other industries, for example extractive industries, inevitably involve hazardous activities and so require complex risk management systems, to ensure that risks are reduced to levels that are as low as reasonably practicable.

Flexibility in application

Principles-based codes can allow for flexibility in application of provisions in circumstances where non-compliance can be justified. Companies may have to deal with a period of transition, for example where a Chair leaves the board suddenly and it takes time to recruit a permanent successor. In these circumstances having the same person act as Chair and Chief Executive on a temporary basis may be felt to be the most **practical solution**. Provided the non-compliance is explained clearly, investors may accept the justification.

Arguments against

Consistency of approach

A rules-based approach means all companies are **complying with the same standards**. It should be easy for investors to see that **compliance** has been **achieved**. Comparison between companies should be **straightforward**. Some investors may have **more confidence in a rules-based approach** as a result. It is also therefore easier to enforce a rules-based approach on companies.

Broad principles

The principles in a principles-based code may be so broad as to mean that companies have excessive leeway in following the code. Some companies may therefore try to do as little as possible to comply with the code, and therefore gain **cost and competitive advantage** over other companies that have been more conscientious.

Compulsory requirements

Where principles-based codes include specific recommendations, for example that the role of **Chair and Chief Executive be split**, there may be confusion over whether these recommendations are compulsory or not. Recommendations that are underpinned by company law requirements will be compulsory, but the status of recommendations that are not underpinned may be unclear. In some countries, the adoption of governance codes by stock exchanges means that specific recommendations in codes have been seen as **listing rules requiring compliance**. Companies that lack compliance expertise may find it difficult to judge whether and how they should comply.

Explanations

Explanations for non-compliance may not be adequate for shareholders. Shareholders **may not understand** the **reasons for, and consequences of, non-compliance**. Accounts may provide unclear explanations, with directors knowing that, even if some shareholders are unhappy, their positions are guaranteed by having the support of sufficient large shareholders.

(b) **Power**

Having the same person in both roles means that **power is concentrated** in one person. A common feature of governance scandals that have prompted the development of guidance has been an individual exercising excessive power. The board may be **ineffective in controlling the Chief Executive** if it is led by the Chief Executive. For example, the Chair is responsible for providing information that the other directors require to manage the company. If the Chair is also Chief Executive, the directors cannot be sure that the information they are getting is **sufficient and accurate**. Separation of the role also means that the board can **express its concerns more effectively** by providing a point of reporting for the non-executive directors.

Accountability

The board cannot make the Chief Executive **truly accountable** for management if it is chaired and led by the Chief Executive. The Chair carries the **authority of the board** and the Chief Executive carries **authority delegated by the board**. Separating the roles emphasises the Chief Executive's accountability to the board's leader, the Chair, and also the shareholders whose interests the Chair represents. Separation should **reduce the risk of conflicts of interest** where the Chair/Chief Executive focuses on his own self-interest.

Demands of roles

Splitting the posts between different people reflects the reality that both jobs are **demanding roles** and no-one person will have the **skills and the time** to do both jobs well. The Chief Executive can concentrate on running the company's operations, developing business and risk management strategy, reviewing investment policy and managing the executive team. The Chair can concentrate on running the board effectively and ensuring that directors develop an understanding of the views of major investors.

Under governance best practice, the Chair should be an independent non-executive director, and hence well placed to adopt a **supervisory and monitoring role**.

Governance requirements

Splitting the roles **ensures compliance with governance requirements and reassures shareholders**. Investor confidence is important in maintaining company value and being seen to comply with governance best practice should contribute to investor confidence about the way a company is being run.

(c) **Comply or explain**

Compliance with governance requirements

Anson Co has fulfilled the requirements of the listing rules to identify areas of non-compliance. The statement **clearly highlights the area** where Anson Co has not complied. It unambiguously states that it is not in accordance with governance best practice. It specifies as well that Mr Klunker is the individual concerned. This may be significant for shareholders who may be less concerned about the breach because they have confidence in Mr Klunker.

Why it has happened

However, the statement does not state clearly why Anson Co has not complied. It does not explain the reasons for the company benefiting from having Mr Klunker in control. The statement that the company has maintained robust corporate governance is also vague. Stating the company understands the concerns of shareholders is not the same as saying that the company has responded to them.

Time limit to non-compliance

However, shareholders will be reassured by the fact that Anson Co is planning to **comply with governance requirements in future**. Anson has made a clear commitment to separate the roles and has set a time limit on this.

10 Lum

> **Top tips.** The scenario provides a number of clues of issues to discuss in (a), particularly the lack of formal requirements, such as the appointment of non-executive directors and the focus on the long-term. Note that as a listed company, the views of other stakeholders and society as a whole may become more important, as well as the requirements of external stakeholders.
>
> To score well in (b), you need to mention, where possible, the problems that Lum has found in operating as a limited company, in order to show why induction and CPD are required. Note that, in effect, there are two parts to requirement (b): firstly, the benefits of introducing an induction programme for new directors; secondly, the benefits of CPD for existing directors, so you should have structured your answer into two parts accordingly.
>
> Note also, that the requirement asks specifically about the 'benefits' of an induction programme; not, for example, what the contents of an induction programme should be.
>
> In (c), there are different ways in which multi-tier boards can work, but the scenario makes clear that the supervisory board was in overall control of strategy. A key issue here, though, is how introducing a unitary board might affect the control the Lum family might have over the company after flotation, and the implications of this for the family.

Marking scheme

			Marks
(a)	Up to 4 marks for contrasting governance arrangements in family businesses compared to listed companies	Max 4	
	Up to 2 marks for each relevant point of assessment relating to Crispin's view (about the impact of the flotation)	Max <u>6</u>	
	Up to a maximum for part (a) of 10 marks		10
(b)	1 mark for each benefit of having an induction programme	Max 4	
	1 mark for each benefit of requiring continual CPD	Max <u>4</u>	
	Up to a maximum for part (b) of 8 marks		8
(c)	Up to 4 marks for distinguishing between the two types of board (2 marks for the key characteristics of each type)	Max 4	
	1 mark for each difficulty discussed	Max <u>6</u>	
	Up to a maximum for part (c) of 7 marks		<u>7</u>
			<u><u>25</u></u>

(a) **Comparison between family business and listed company**

Legal formalities

In most jurisdictions, family companies are only subject to limited legal requirements affecting their governance. Listed companies face **greater statutory requirements and also**

are subject to listing rules. These are designed to give investors assurance about the way listed companies are governed and hence increase their confidence in their investment.

Formality

Family company boards are likely to be run informally because they are **not accountable** to **external shareholders outside the small family group.** Governance arrangements for listed companies have to be much more formal, in order to ensure their accountability to external shareholders who are not involved in the company. Hence, for example, listed companies are subject to regulations that require them to report information about the board of directors, such as the number of meetings each year and the work of board committees.

Composition and structure

Many family companies will have **no non-executive directors.** Many governance codes require listed company boards to be **balanced between executive directors and non-executive directors.** For example, the UK Corporate Governance Code requires at least half of the board to be independent non-executive directors. Family companies may not need to operate any board committees as they have enough time to discuss all important issues. Listed companies are required to have a **number of committees,** partly to monitor the activities of executive directors and ensure their remuneration is fair.

Objectives

The boards of family companies will need to take account of the wishes of the few major shareholders. Often this group will want the company to **invest for the long term.** The board of a listed company will have to address **varying requirements of different shareholder groups and other stakeholders.** Some may want **longer-term capital gains but others will require strong short-term profits and dividends.**

Impact of flotation

Long-term values and beliefs

Whether the board will still be able to manage in accordance with its beliefs will depend on how shareholders view these beliefs. Shareholders, for example, may believe that the board is **excessively focused on the long term** and instead needs to focus more each year on **achieving a target profit.** This may mean that the board is forced to take action on a business segment that investors perceive has **underperformed one year,** rather than accepting that the segment be allowed to build up resources for longer-term success.

Impact of institutional investors

A significant proportion of Lum's shares may well be held by financial institutions. They will require **regular information from Lum, including briefings on financial results,** and explanations from Lum if its financial performance or behaviour does not meet their expectations.

Meeting expectations

Lum will have to demonstrate it meets the expectations of the stock market. Because a listed company's activities are **more visible in society,** it also becomes increasingly **subject to society's expectations.** This may mean that it has to change the way it acts and is organised in a number of areas, to fulfil the requirements of society and key stakeholder groups.

Paternalistic management style

Crispin Lum emphasised the paternalistic management style of Lum prior to the flotation. The directors may **not be able to manage in this way** if the company becomes listed. Investors may require a **stricter approach** to dealing with employees and Lum to focus more on **controlling labour costs.** Employees may expect better-defined management procedures, with **more formal human resource structures and policies** being introduced.

(b)   **Benefits of induction:**

Better-informed NEDs

Non-executive directors (NEDs) need to be given information about Lum to enable them to develop an understanding of its **business and its markets,** and hence to be able to make informed contributions at board meetings. This includes information about Lum's business strategy and model, its products and markets, major competitors, major risks and performance indicators.

Management and culture of the business

Particularly as there have been problems with NEDs becoming frustrated, induction also needs to include guidance on how the company is managed, including how the board is **structured and exercises its responsibilities**. NEDs also need to develop an understanding of the company's **management style and culture**. This does not mean that they will necessarily accept all aspects of it, but it should give them a better understanding of what the executive directors are trying to achieve.

Establishing communication with personnel

Again because of the clashes with established members of the board, induction should enable the NEDs to establish strong links with the **company's personnel**. This includes meetings with board members outside the boardroom, meetings with other senior managers and visits to company sites other than headquarters.

Stakeholder relationships

Induction also should enable NEDs to build up **understanding of Lum's stakeholders**, including customers and suppliers. Most importantly, induction should enable NEDs to **build relationships** with stakeholders with whom they will be dealing, such as the external auditors, or whose interests they are representing, for example institutional investors.

Benefits of CPD:

Purpose of CPD

The main purpose of CPD is for directors to **extend their knowledge and skills on an ongoing basis**. This means that it should aim to **enhance areas of performance** where directors appear to be struggling or to brief directors on **developments in the business environment** and changes in the requirements that the company faces.

Compliance

As discussed, as a listed company, Lum became subject to a **significantly greater number of regulations.** Lum's directors should have been given training about the **differences in legal requirements** facing a listed company as opposed to a private company. They should also have been briefed on the **requirements of listing rules and corporate governance codes.**

Personal skills and leadership

The problems in establishing relationships with the NEDs suggest that board members should have training in personal skills, including dealing with people whose **perspectives and requirements do not coincide with theirs**. Also, as it seems that existing directors are struggling to manage the company, they need **training in different leadership styles** so that they can guide Lum more effectively, rather than relying on a paternalistic style that is no longer appropriate.

Investor requirements

Lum's board should also have had training in **managing relationships with the investors** who now have shares in Lum. This would include the **requirements of institutional investors** and how to enhance relationships with them. It also includes **methods of communication** with shareholders, particularly the management of general meetings, which may be more difficult occasions now that the number of shareholders is much larger.

(c) **Unitary board:**

Legal responsibility

All participants in a unitary board have **equal legal responsibility for management of the company and strategic performance**. This requires active involvement not just by executive directors, but also non-executive directors who are supervising and monitoring executives.

Involvement in decision making

All directors will be **members of a single board and attend the same board meetings**. They should all **participate in decision making and have equal access to information**.

Two-tier board:

Separation of duties

A two-tier board provides a clear **separation of duties** between the executive or operational board, which runs the operations of the company, and the supervisory board, which monitors the executive board. The supervisory board is also responsible for legal and regulatory compliance issues.

Responsibility for strategy

The supervisory board will be **responsible for developing business strategy**. The executive board will be **responsible for executing this strategy**.

Difficulties for the Lum family:

Different ways of operating

A unitary board means that **all directors will be entitled to participate in decision making** on all areas. Beforehand the supervisory board, which only consisted of Lum family members, exercised control of the company, but now the Lum family is having to get used to others participating in controlling the company. Governance requirements aim to prevent boards being controlled by a small group of directors and the Lum family may find this frustrating.

Slower decision making

With a unitary board, **notice of board meetings is required and the board often meets on fixed dates**. This may mean that **decision making is slower**, and it means that the directors can **respond less quickly to changing circumstances**, which again may annoy the Lum family.

Change in board culture

The Lum family has to get used to **working in a different way on a unitary board**. The Lums must consult with, and achieve the agreement of, non-family members and also justify their decisions and actions to the rest of the board.

11 Chambon school

> **Top tips.** In part (a), it should have been relatively easy to pick out (from the scenario) the characteristics which identify Chambon school as a public sector organisation. However, the requirement asks you to 'explain' the characteristics, not to 'list' them; so to score well in this question, each relevant point needs to be explained, not simply listed as a bullet point.
>
> Note that having explained the characteristics, you also assess how Chambon school has failed to meet its objectives. A useful framework to use here would be the 'three Es', and to assess how the school is failing to meet the criteria of economy, efficiency and effectiveness which are central to the performance of public sector organisations.
>
> In part (b) there are also two requirements. The first is to explain the role of a board of governors (for example, in facilitating the effective running of the organisation; and dealing with the funders, in this case, the local government authority). However, in any dealings with the funders, governors need to act with integrity and transparency – and this is the issue in the second part of the requirement. If the governors submitted a partial report, as Sally Murol suggested, they would have failed in their duty of transparency.
>
> In the first part of the requirement, if you were struggling to think about the role of governors, it might have been useful to think about possible parallels between the role of the board of governors in running a school and the role of the board of directors (especially non-executive directors) in running a company.

Part (c) concerned the possible replacement of the head teacher at Chambon school. The case highlighted several problems with Mr Besse, which were relevant to the discussion, so this part of the question should have been relatively straightforward if you had read through the scenario carefully. However, it is important to focus specifically on the potential advantages of replacing Mr Besse (and not, for example, to discuss any of the practical considerations around finding a replacement).

Marking scheme

		Marks
(a)	1 mark for each explanation of Chambon as a public sector organisation to a maximum of 4 marks (½ mark each for characteristics of public sector organisations, explaining how Chambon exhibits them)	Max 4
	Up to 2 marks for each relevant point of assessment as to how Chambon has failed to meet its objectives – up to a maximum of 6 marks	Max 6
	Up to a maximum for part (a) of 10 marks	10
(b)	1 mark for each role of governors, to a maximum of 4 marks	Max 4
	Up to 2 marks for each point on transparency, to a maximum of 4 marks	Max 4
	1 mark for evidence of understanding of transparency (anywhere in the answer)	1
	Up to a maximum for part (b) of 9 marks	9
(c)	Up to 2 marks for each advantage discussed	
	Up to a maximum for part (c) of 6 marks	6
		25

(a) **Characteristics of a public sector organisation**

The following information from the case identifies Chambon as a public sector organisation.

- Funding – the school is state-funded, which means that the money needed to run the school comes from taxation.

- Purposes and objectives – to provide education for 11- to 16-year-old children; there is no profit motive.

- Performance – the school is required to provide an annual report on exam performance to the local education authority (not to shareholders as in the private sector).

- Ownership – the school is subject to a national curriculum set by central government, and may be threatened with closure by the local authority if it fails to meet its exam performance targets.

- Stakeholders – the independent board of governors is comprised of local residents, parents and other concerned citizens.

How Chambon is meeting its objectives as a public sector organisation

Chambon's success in meeting its objectives can be assessed by using the public sector value for money, or 'three Es' model, to determine whether it is achieving economy, efficiency and effectiveness.

Economy is defined as obtaining inputs of the appropriate quality at the lowest price available. Chambon has had its budget increased in recent years so that it can improve the exam results. A number of new teachers were employed but despite this performance continued to deteriorate, so much so that a budget overspend led to the closure of part of the school library and the sale of a sports field. Chambon has not therefore been successful in achieving economy.

Efficiency means delivering the service to the appropriate standard at minimum cost, time and effort. Despite the fact that Chambon's budget was increased and more teachers were employed, exam performance continued to fall. In other words, inputs in the form of income and teaching staff have not been converted to an increase in outputs in the form of exam performance.

The third element of the 'three Es' model is **effectiveness**, which means achieving the desired objectives as stated in an entity's performance plan. Chambon school is state-funded, it teaches the national curriculum and is subject to national government and local authority scrutiny. Its primary responsibility is to provide education for 11- to 16-year-old children. Whether the achievement of this objective can be measured solely in exam results is debatable. We do, however, know that pupils have lost part of the library and a sports field, thereby reducing the effectiveness of the learning environment.

(b) **Roles of board of governors**

The main role of the board of governors is to provide independent oversight of the running of the school. There are several aspects to this role:

- Ensuring that the school complies with the local authority's requirement to report on exam performance. In order to do this the board must ensure that systems are in place to collect and collate this information in an appropriate format for both internal and external reporting.

- Reporting promptly, truthfully and without bias within the time frame set by the local authority.

- Being answerable to all interested parties on the topic of school performance and to provide explanations for the continued deterioration in exam results.

- Responsibility for how the school is run, including leadership and staffing, and the quality of education provided for its pupils.

- Appointing senior staff, including the headteacher, and monitoring their performance. The board should look into the criticisms of Mr Besse and decide on what action to take.

- Budget setting and monitoring, to ensure that the school has adequate resources and that expenditure is controlled.

The importance of transparency

Transparency means open and clear disclosure of relevant information to stakeholders, not concealing information, open discussion and adopting a default position of information provision rather than concealment.

The board of governors is obliged to report on exam performance in a full and timely manner, and should therefore reject Sally Murol's suggestion that the report be delayed or modified.

The school is state funded and must therefore inform its funding body how it has spent the money allocated to it and how it has performed. If successful it should be able to show that public funding has obtained value for money in the provision of education by the school.

As there is no central information-gathering system for exam results, the accuracy of the information provided to the local authority is crucial. It is likely that this information is used for future planning and funding decisions and could therefore have an impact on the country as a whole.

(c) **Replacement of headteacher**

The current headteacher, Mr Besse, has been in post for many years. He is said to be loyal and popular with staff as he does not believe in interfering with what teachers do, and he also dislikes confrontation. These qualities may be positive ones but could also point to an unwillingness to address poor performance amongst the teaching staff. Such a culture could lead to poor practices becoming embedded and difficult to challenge. A new leader would be forced to confront this culture and change it if it was having a negative effect on the performance of the school.

The appointment of a new head would signal a willingness on behalf of the school and the board to make a fresh start and bring in new ways of working in order to improve exam performance. Any members of staff underperforming would have targets put in place and monitored over time against key performance indicators.

A new headteacher, appointed by the board of governors, would be in a position to work together with all the stakeholders represented on the board in order to put the necessary changes in place. Mr Besse may have been acting in the school's best interest but may also have been unwilling to confront failure and to change long-standing behaviour.

12 EcoCar

> **Top tips.** The requirement asks you to analyse the environment at two different levels: the macro-environment and the marketplace (industry) environment.
>
> Although the requirement doesn't prescribe any specific models to use, PESTEL analysis and Porter's (1980) five forces were two frameworks you could have used to provide a structure for your answer. PESTEL should be used to evaluate the macro-environment, while Porter's (1980) five forces should help to analyse the competitive forces within an industry.
>
> Remember, however, that environmental analysis focuses only on the **external** environment (macro-environment; industry environment), so your answer should focus on factors which represent opportunities or threats to EcoCar, not its own strengths and weaknesses (which are internal factors).

Marking scheme

	Marks
1 mark for each relevant point of analysis about the macro-environment (eg PESTEL factors) – up to 10 marks	10
1 mark for each relevant point of analysis about the industry environment (eg Porter's (1980) five forces) – up to 10 marks	10
	20

PESTEL

The **macro-environmental analysis** will be carried out using the PESTEL model to consider the political, economic, social, technological, environmental and legal factors that affect EcoCar.

Political position

EcoCar has received significant support from the government in the form of tax incentives, grants and interest free loans. The government has also supported green technology by heavily taxing cars with high CO_2 emissions whilst funding the development of 130 charging centres nationwide where EcoCars can be recharged.

EcoCar must monitor the government's continued commitment to green technologies and environmental protection, as well as the policies of the political opposition.

Economic position

As EcoCar is both more expensive and has poorer acceleration and speed than its rivals, and sales are driven by the social factor of compassion for the environment. EcoCar must monitor the state of the economy and disposable income levels, as significant changes may mean that consumers are no longer prepared to pay a premium price for an environmentally friendly car that has poorer performance than conventional alternatives.

Social factors

EcoCar's customers are 'green' consumers who are concerned about the use of oil – a non-renewable energy source – in conventional cars and the effect of CO_2 emissions on the environment. These people have changed their buying approach based on their belief that their own choices really do make a difference to the future of the Earth, and EcoCar's future success is likely to depend on its cars continuing to be seen as an environmentally friendly alternative to traditional cars.

EcoCar's success will also depend on attitudes towards 'green' consumption. The general views of society also may change away from a green mindset towards a more immediate and self-centred buying approach. Such a trend would be a significant threat to the survival of EcoCar. Trends such as these must be monitored.

Technological factors

EcoCar is a technology-driven company and its success depends on its ability to innovate. It is therefore important that it monitors any advances in technology. Particularly, EcoCar should be aware of any improvements to lithium-ion batteries that may make them cheaper, lighter or more powerful as such developments will allow EcoCar to improve their product.

However, EcoCar should also be aware of any alternatives to lithium-ion batteries which could emerge (eg hydrogen) as such alternatives may create a threat to the viability of EcoCar.

Environmental factors

The key environmental factors are closely linked to the social factors we have considered earlier; namely:

* Continued scientific evidence that environmental damage is caused by CO_2 emissions

* Continued concern for the environment to prompt the existence and growth of 'green' customers

* Willingness of customers to continue to pay a premium for environmentally friendly cars

Legal factors

A number of general laws on car safety have been put in place by the government with further legislation expected. EcoCar must monitor this and ensure it complies with these laws.

This PESTEL analysis highlights a number of threats which EcoCar should consider and, via risk management processes, they must ensure suitable controls are put in place to reduce the risk surrounding these threats. The risks of alternative technology emerging or the number of 'green' consumers declining must also be considered and managed where possible.

Industry environment

The industry environment in which EcoCar operates can be analysed using Porter's (1980) five forces model. However, the level of competition in the industry will also depend on the scope of the industry. The 'industry' could be considered to be the car industry as a whole, the sector of the car industry that is focused on reducing emissions or the entire transport industry.

Porter's (1980) five forces

Threat of substitute products

There are a number of alternatives and hybrids are either under development or already available. EcoCar must monitor and keep up with changes occurring in the technological environment. The threat from substitutes is relatively high as there is no clear successor to conventional petrol or diesel cars.

In addition, it is possible that a car may not be needed at all, as other valid substitutes for such green transportation include cycling, walking and public transport.

Threat of new entrants

There is a constant threat of new entrants to the market as the successor to conventional cars has not yet become clear. However, there are significant barriers, in the form of high capital investment costs, which prevent others entering the environmentally friendly car market. EcoCar have overcome these barriers with the help of Universal Motors, who provided some capital investment, and grants and interest free-loans provided by the government.

This governmental assistance is unlikely to be available in all counties and regions as they specifically relate to reducing the high levels of unemployment in the area in which EcoCar operates. Funding on the scale of that provided by Universal Motors may also not be available to potential competitors.

Further barriers to entry are the lack of skilled labour with car-building expertise and the processes that Professor Jacques has patented.

Bargaining power of suppliers

The bargaining power of suppliers is unclear. It is likely that their power will be high in an industry with a specialised product of this nature, as switching between suppliers can be difficult. This is particularly true for smaller companies, such as EcoCar, which has little bargaining power. However, EcoCar is now owned by Universal Motors which may have more influence and hence use its power to help EcoCar negotiate favourable contracts with suppliers and reduce the bargaining power that those suppliers have over EcoCar.

Labour can also be considered to be a supplier, and there is an increasing shortage of skilled labour available. This has led to an increase in labour rates, causing EcoCar to consider outsourcing the production of one of their models.

Competitive rivalry

There is likely to be high competitive rivalry in the car industry as a whole due to the high fixed costs and cost of leaving the industry. However, EcoCar is part of a specialised segment of the market dealing with minimal environmental impact cars. This sector of the market is still immature and differentiated, and therefore the competitive rivalry within this sector is likely to be lower than in the car industry as a whole.

Regardless of the way in which EcoCar decides to define the industry in which it operates, it should identify the risks it faces from existing competitors and ensure they are dealt with via the company's risk management processes.

Bargaining power of customers

If the industry is considered to be the car industry as a whole, the switching costs for the consumer are relatively low as they can just purchase an alternative car; they are not locked in to a specific company. However, EcoCar is purchased by customers who are driven by the environmental credentials of the car, rather than the cost. This type of green customer may not be actively seeking a cheaper alternative and, despite knowing they exist, they will not purchase and compromise their 'green' beliefs.

13 Dormit

Top tips. Part (a). Part of the challenge here is to identify the models you need to select, but the reference to the competitor hotels should have indicated that Porter's (1980) five forces was one of them. Similarly, you should have recognised that the most appropriate framework for environmental analysis (and therefore the second model you should have chosen) was PESTEL analysis.

The structure of the question (Identify... explain....) should have helped you answer it. To begin with you should briefly explain the models in general terms, and then you need to apply them specifically to the scenario. For example, how could an understanding of economic and social (demographic) factors affect the wedding business' strategy?

Part (b). From reading the scenario, you should have identified that the 'De Luxe' hotel was following a differentiation strategy, while the 'Royal Albert' was pursuing a strategy of cost leadership. Understanding these strategic positions will be important for Dormit's planning team as they come to design their own wedding package strategy, for example, by suggesting that it may be most appropriate for the Dormit to follow some kind of focus strategy.

A sensible way to approach this part of the question would be to (briefly) explain each of the generic strategies, and then apply them to the scenario in order to show they could help the team develop a strategy for Dormit.

Marks

(a) For each model (PESTEL; Porter's (1980) five forces) identified and
        explained – up to 2 marks each   Max 4
      For explaining how PESTEL could be used to help formulate a
        wedding package strategy – 1 mark per relevant point –
        up to 4 marks   Max 4
      For explaining how Porter's (1980) five forces could be used to help
        formulate a wedding package strategy – up to 4 marks   Max 4
      Up to a maximum for part (a) of 10 marks   10

(b) For relevant points about how an understanding of generic strategies
        could help the team design a successful wedding package strategy
        – 1 mark per relevant point
      Up to a maximum for part (b) of 10 marks   10
                                                                                    20

(a) Two models that could be used to analyse the external environment are Porter's (1980) **five forces and PEST (or PESTEL) analysis).**

Porter's (1980) five forces looks at the competitive forces which determine the level of profits that can be sustained by an industry. The five competitive forces are:

(i)   The threat of new entrants to the Industry
(ii)   The bargaining power of customers
(iii) The bargaining power of suppliers
(iv)   The threat of substitute products
(v)   The competitive rivalry between the existing firms in the industry

PEST analysis helps to identify the external factors which constitute opportunities or threats to an organisation. The PEST acronym stands for:

Political factors – for example, any government regulation

Economic factors – for example, the rate of economic growth or recession

Social factors – for example, demographic trends among the population

Technological factors – for example, new inventions and new product development

Sometimes, these four factors are also supplemented by **E**nvironmental and **L**egal factors, such that PEST becomes PESTEL.

Porter's (1980) five forces model

Assessing profitability – The team could use the five forces model to assess the strength of the competition the Dormit is likely to face if it enters the market for wedding packages, and accordingly how profitable the market could be for the Dormit. If the competitive forces are too strong, it may not be profitable for the Dormit to enter the market at all.

Choosing position in the market – The competitive rivalry between the firms in an industry is one of the forces which determine profitability. It will be important for the Dormit to assess the strength of this rivalry because it has identified seven competitor hotels in the market. For example, if it seems that the competition is more intense at the lower cost end of the market, then it may be more profitable for the Dormit to target the higher price end of the market.

PEST analysis

Understanding demand – The external environment will play an important role in determining the level of demand for any packages the Dormit might offer. For example, social trends, such as changes in the number of people getting married each year, will affect the demand for wedding packages overall.

Equally, economic and social factors could influence demand for particular types of wedding. For example, in a recession or in times of higher unemployment, the amount people are willing and able to spend on their wedding may be reduced, which may encourage the team to offer less expensive wedding packages. Equally, people may look to have smaller weddings, so the team may decide to offer a package for fewer than 100 guests.

Congruence between the two models

It is important that the team considers the consistency of any findings from the two models. For example, if the analysis of competitive rivalry (in the five forces model) suggests that the Dormit may be better advised to target the higher cost end of the market, but PEST analysis suggests that the economic environment means that lower cost packages may be more popular, the team will have to decide which of the two influences is likely to have more impact on the success of any potential strategy.

Ongoing review of the environment

While the models could assist the team in formulating their initial package strategy for the hotel, the team should also continue to monitor the environment to ensure that their strategy remains appropriate. For example, if additional hotels start offering wedding packages, will the Dormit need to make any changes to its packages in response to this new threat?

(b)   Porter's (1980) three generic strategies suggest that, in order to compete successfully, the Dormit hotel should aim to pursue one of three strategies:

Cost leadership

Differentiation

Focus

Cost leadership

As a cost leader, the Dormit hotel should seek to have the lowest costs of any hotel in the market as a whole. To achieve this, the Dormit is likely to have to simplify and standardise its processes and its products (for example, its menu) so that is able to deliver a wedding package more cheaply than any of its competitors.

Sustainable competitive advantage – However, it is unlikely that this strategy will give the Dormit a sustainable competitive advantage, because it does not appear to give the hotel any distinctive competences its competitors cannot replicate.

Consequently, the team should not look to adopt a cost leadership strategy for the design of their wedding packages.

Differentiation

If it follows a differentiation strategy, then the Dormit hotel needs to offer a level of service or quality that none of its competitors can match, so that customers perceive the Dormit's packages as being unique, and accordingly they are prepared to pay a premium price to host their wedding at the hotel.

Competition with 'De Luxe' hotel – The 'De Luxe' appears to be following a differentiation strategy, using its physical position (a castle in a beautiful, rural setting) and the high quality of its food and facilities, to offer packages which customers perceive to be superior to any others on the market. This allows the 'De Luxe' to charge premium prices for its packages (starting at £500 per guest).

If the Dormit is going to pursue a differentiation strategy successfully, it will need to have some attributes or characteristics that distinguish it from all the other hotels (including the 'De Luxe') in the same way that the 'De Luxe' currently differentiates itself from the other six competitors. It is not clear from the scenario that the Dormit has any such differentiating characteristics, and if it does not, then a differentiation strategy is unlikely to be appropriate.

Focus

Given this context, it seems that the Dormit is most likely to be successful if it adopts a focus strategy.

Cost leadership focus – The difficulty that the Dormit faces is that the market for wedding packages is already a specific niche within the overall hotel market. Therefore, the Royal Albert's packages could be seen as following a cost leadership focus strategy, specifically targeting people who want to get married but who only have a very limited budget to spend on their weddings.

In this respect, it would appear that the Dormit should design a package using a differentiation focus strategy.

Differentiation focus – Given the De Luxe's position in the market, the Dormit may not simply be able to use the quality of its wedding catering or the standard of its rooms and facilities as its differentiating factors. Accordingly, the Dormit may need to highlight another aspect of its service which differentiates it from its competitors – for example, allowing customers to have flexibility in the number of guests they can invite (rather than standardising the package for 100 guests) or providing differentiation by hosting 'themed' wedding packages (for example, a Las Vegas-style package).

Stuck in the middle

An understanding of Porter's (1980) generic strategies should remind the team that the Dormit's packages are unlikely to be successful if they end up being 'stuck in the middle'. There are already five hotels which charge between $35 and $50 per guest, and there is a danger that these hotels could become 'stuck in the middle' since they are neither the cost leader (the Royal Albert) or differentiators (like the 'De Luxe'). Unless the Dormit can develop some underlying differentiating characteristics like those described above, then there is a danger that it too could get 'stuck in the middle,' which will restrict its profitability.

14 NESTA

Top tips. The requirement tells you which model to apply, and the scenario provides you with a number of points which relate to the different 'forces'.

Note, however, the question asks you about the attractiveness of Eurobia as a market for NESTA to enter; not simply about the strength of the competitive forces in Eurobia. So, in effect, you first need to identify the strength of the forces, and then consider what implications this has for the attractiveness of the industry.

As well as analysing the narrative information in the scenario, did you also make use of the financial data in Table 1? This data was important because it revealed two things: firstly, that the three companies in the industry were of a very similar size; and, secondly, that the market they were participating in was growing. Both of these factors could have important implications for the level of competitive rivalry in the industry (and therefore its potential attractiveness to NESTA).

Marks

1 mark for each relevant point, up to a maximum of 4 marks for any single 'force'
  within the framework (competitive rivalry; bargaining power of suppliers;
  bargaining power of customers; substitutes; threat of new entrants)
Up to a maximum of 15 marks   15

Porter's (1980) five forces model

Existing rivalry

There are three existing rivals in the market and competition would appear to be strong. It is likely these companies would resist a new entrant in this market, in particular a large, international rival such as NESTA. This would probably be achieved via rapid store expansion, increased marketing and the tightening of supplier contracts.

However, the information given in the scenario suggests that the dollar shop market sector is still growing, even though the economy is in recession. This would mean that competitors need only keep up with industry performance in order to improve their results. The market may even gain legitimacy and continue to grow as a result of NESTA entering the market, as more geographical areas can be exploited which are not yet fully served by the existing competitors.

Bargaining power of suppliers

NESTA's suppliers have low bargaining power. There are a number of small suppliers and the dollar shops are their main customers. The products are also undifferentiated and so the dollar shops can switch suppliers very easily. It is unlikely that any of these suppliers could become competitors of their current customers by applying forward integration.

In addition, NESTA has recognised competencies in effective supplier management, supported by effective procurement systems. These core strengths, combined with the low bargaining power of the suppliers, make this market in Eurobia very attractive to NESTA.

Landlords could also be considered to be suppliers in this case. The bargaining power of these suppliers is also low due to the number of empty properties and the low rents and short leases offered in order to fill them.

Bargaining power of customers

NESTA's customers have strong bargaining power. This is due to a number of factors:

- There is a low profit margin on the products which provides an attraction for customers seeking lower purchasing costs.

- NESTA sells unbranded commodity goods and so it would be easy for the buyer to switch to an alternative supplier. The switching costs are therefore low.

- Standard, undifferentiated products can be easily provided by other suppliers. Customers can therefore choose which supplier to use and can play the companies off against each other in order to obtain the best terms of supply.

- Customers are likely to be very price sensitive and so will invest a lot into trying to ensure the best terms of supply.

Threat of substitutes

The conventional supermarkets are potential substitutes for the dollar shops as they offer a wide range of ambient goods, often with competing brands on offer. However, the prices vary and no supermarkets have yet adopted the discount fixed-price sale approach, choosing instead to differentiate using known brands. Location is also a key differentiator as the supermarkets are located out of town with plentiful parking and vehicle access. However, NESTA is an established, large-scale player in the fixed-price market, and as such its arrival in Eurobia may lead supermarkets to reconsider their approach.

Conventional supermarkets also offer internet shopping and home delivery options. Ambient goods such as those offered by the dollar shops are well suited to this approach and so the internet could also be considered to be a substitute channel. However the $10 delivery charge might reduce this threat (given customers' price sensitivity).

Potential entrants and barriers to entry

A significant barrier to entry to this market is the high level of capital that is required in order to establish a credible presence. However, for NESTA this is unlikely to be a problem as it has the cash reserves available to allow it to lease a significant number of shops in Eurobia, and establish a credible market presence there.

Capital costs are also lowered by the reduced rental costs that are now available in Eurobia as many of the towns and cities now have empty stores which are relatively cheap to rent. In addition, landlords who once required high rents and long leases are increasingly willing to rent these stores for a relatively short fixed-term lease. This reduces the exit costs that are faced by this market.

One barrier to entry which may be a problem for NESTA is brand awareness. The existing competitors have very high levels of brand recognition (90%), whereas NESTA is only recognised by 5% of general consumers. NESTA may have to commit significant resources to a large-scale marketing campaign if it is to successfully break into this market.

15 Independent Living

Top tips. Both parts (a) and (b) deal with the primary activities of Porter's (1985) value chain only. Therefore, it was important that you focused specifically on these, and didn't digress into talking about the support activities or potential improvements to support activities. A useful starting point (for part (a) of this question) would be to identify what each of the activities is, and then to use each 'activity' as a heading for your answer. (You weren't asked to draw the value chain though, so you shouldn't have spent time doing that.)

Note that the requirement asked you to analyse the activities for the 'product range' at IL. However, the 'product range' means that, in effect, there are two different value chains at IL – one for simple, manufactured products; one for bought-in products. Did you analyse the value chain activities for both types of product?

Finally, think about how the two parts of the question link together. Part (a) asked you to analyse the current primary activities of the value chain for IL, while part (b) asked about potential changes which could be made to improve the charity's competitiveness. So, your analysis of the current activities (for part (a)) should help you to identify weaknesses or areas for improvement – which can then be addressed by the changes you consider in part (b). However, it is important that any changes you suggest are practical – and appropriate for the context of IL. (Remember that IL is a charity.)

Marking scheme

		Marks
(a)	1 mark for identifying each primary activity (for example, inbound logistics) and up to 2 marks for discussing its application to IL in both contexts (metal scrap collection, supplier delivery)	
	Up to a maximum for part (a) of 10 marks	10
(b)	1 mark for each relevant, significant point (for example, arrange bought-in products to be delivered directly to the customer from the manufacturer)	
	Up to a maximum for part (b) of 15 marks	15
		25

(a) **Porter's (1985) value chain applied to Independent Living**

Independent Living (IL) supplies two kinds of products: simple items manufactured in-house, such as walking frames and crutches, and larger bought-in items such as mobility scooters. The primary activities of the value chain for these two product sets are shown below:

Inbound logistics: Receiving, handling and storing the inputs

Manufactured products (MP): Collecting material from scrap merchants and storage of materials prior to use

Bought-in products (BiP): Inbound logistics handled by supplier. Products stored in warehouse prior to use

Operations: Converting resource inputs into the final product

MP: Production and packaging of the crutches/walking frames/other small products

BiP: Unpacking, testing and adding logo to products. Repacking and applying IL label to product

Outbound logistics: Storing the product and distributing to customers

MP and BiP: Storage of products, receipt of orders placed online and by telephone, and distribution of products to customers using national courier company

Marketing and sales: Informing the customer about the product, persuading and enabling them to buy it

MP and BiP: Promotional leaflets placed in hospitals, doctors' surgeries and local social welfare departments

Website and online ordering system, and product advice and telesales

Service: Installing, repairing and upgrading products, and other after-care services

MP: No details are provided about service for MP. The simple nature of the product means no training or after-care service is required. It is not clear if a repair service is available if a product breaks, or whether customers would have to buy a replacement.

BiP: Provided by original manufacturer

(b)

> **Top tip.** Remember that this is a **charity** and do make sure that your suggestions are relevant to the context. For example, one of the aims of the charity is to employ disabled people and so the operations cannot be changed too much.

IL could make the following changes to the primary activities in the value chain to improve their competitiveness:

Inbound logistics:

Manufactured products (MP):

- Request dealers store material until it is required. This would transfer the cost of storage to the dealer.

- Look into possibility of the dealers delivering the metal. This may be cheaper than IL maintaining their own vehicle.

Bought-in products (BiP):

- Use a specialist logistics company for inbound and outbound logistics, and possibly storage facilities. This would reduce costs due to economies of scale.

Operations:

MP:

- Difficult to change without compromising the core objective of providing work and income for the disabled. IL must retain this process to meet its objectives. This objective could be used as a source of differentiation for IL allowing customers to make an ethical choice.

BiP:

- Request manufacturers affix IL logo and test products, then IL can redeploy employees in other roles, for example order processing.

- Request manufacturers deliver directly to customers, reducing both delivery and inventory costs for IL.

Outbound logistics:

MP and BiP:

- Encourage use of the website (eg online discounts) to reduce costs and time involved in taking orders over the phone.

- Simplify the telephone ordering process by providing details of products to customers in advance (see marketing and sales).

Marketing and sales:

MP and BiP:

- A physical product catalogue could be produced.

- In addition to marketing leaflets, the product catalogue could be left in hospitals, doctor's surgeries etc.

- Advertise in newspapers/magazines including details of how to obtain a catalogue.

- Investigate possibility of installing customer relationship marketing (CRM) systems to manage donors, for instance by contacting the donors to try to ensure they will continue giving.

- Charitable status of IL and details of their work should be on all marketing literature to differentiate it from competitors.

- Website (and possibly tear-off slip in adverts) should allow for readers to 'become a regular donor' or 'make a one off donation', thus encouraging donations as well as sales and widening their target market.

- Provide an email update facility. People visiting the website could sign up to receive regular updates about the work of IL. These people could then also be targeted as potential donors or fundraisers for IL.

Service:

MP and BiP:

- Expand website to give general support on mobility and independent living.

16 ReInk Co

Top tips. The scenario for this question is quite long, but this also means that it provides you with lots of information about ReInk's strengths, weaknesses, opportunities and threats.

However, the key to answering this question well is to correctly identify which part of the 'SWOT' matrix different items relate to. Strengths and weaknesses relate to factors internal to ReInk Co, whereas opportunities and threats relate to factors in the external environment.

The classification of points is very important in SWOT analysis – without it, the 'analysis' becomes little more than an unstructured list.

Equally, it is important that you explain *why* the points you identify are strengths, weaknesses, opportunities or threats – rather than simply copying out extracts from the scenario. Even if the points are relevant, simply copying them out from the scenario, without classifying them, will score you very few marks.

Marks

1 mark for each relevant point, up to a maximum of 6 marks for each heading within the SWOT analysis (Strength, Weakness, Opportunity, Threat)

Up to a maximum 20 marks.

20

This analysis considers the internal strengths and weaknesses of ReInk and the external opportunities and threats the company is currently facing.

Strengths:

Expertise

ReInk is renowned for its technological expertise and innovation in the process of refilling printer cartridges. This strength has been largely driven by the enthusiasm and expertise of ReInk's founder, Dexter Black. Dexter Black's reputation helped to attract technology experts to join the company, with many regarding the prospect of working for a leading expert in the field as being highly appealing. The ability to attract a skilled team of technologists is particularly important given the need for constant innovation in the printer consumables market.

Patent

ReInk currently has six years remaining of an eight-year patent to protect its innovative process for refilling ink cartridges. This patent is a key strength as it prohibits competitors from developing copycat processes in the foreseeable future.

Department of Revenue Collections (DoRC) contract

ReInk has a long-term contract with Eland's Department of Revenue Collections (DoRC). The government's drive to promote recycling in Eland potentially places ReInk in a strong position to win future contracts with other government departments.

(Note, however, ReInk's dependence on the DoRC contract could also be seen as a weakness; 20% of ReInk's $6m revenue comes from the DoRC, so if ReInk were to lose the contract this could potentially have a serious financial impact.)

Location in Eland

ReInk has historically been able to exploit its chosen location to help the company grow. Dexter Black's decision to establish ReInk in a declining industrial town has enabled the company to access government grants aimed at attracting hi-tech entities to set up operations in the area. The low rental prices charged by local landlords have helped ReInk to establish offices and a factory.

ReInk's location near an attractive area of countryside has helped the company to attract expert technologists to work for the company. This has been further supported by the low prices of residential property in the town which has allowed ReInk to offer prospective employees lower salaries, while offering a better standard of living than might be available with competing firms. This is illustrated by the comment made by one of the expert technologists 'I took a pay cut to come here. But now I can afford a bigger house and my children can breathe fresh country air.'

Weaknesses:

Financial position

ReInk's financial position is a major weakness. Recent moves by ReInk's bank (Firmsure) to reduce the company's overdraft appear to have been in response to the continued reporting of annual losses. Although ReInk has been successful in generating operating profits over the last three years, the need to make large interest repayments on its 'substantial overdraft' have wiped these profits out. Firmsure's decision to reduce ReInk's overdraft facility has created a cashflow crisis which has left the company unable to meet the next month's payroll payments. Unless the current situation can be resolved it seems unlikely that Relnk will be able to continue in operation.

Directors

Dexter Black has recognised that his lack of commercial expertise represents a weakness to Relnk. In response he decided to appoint two new directors (a sales and human resources director). The aim had been to boost sales and to enhance staffing practices. However, the appointments have not achieved the results originally intended. The technologists argue that the sales director's arrival has failed to increase sales revenue, with some suggesting that 'he does not really understand the product we are selling'. Furthermore, the HR director's drive to cut staff costs has been poorly received, with some technologists commenting that the director 'clearly has no experience of dealing with professional staff'.

The current abilities of Relnk's management team can be regarded as representing a significant weakness.

Employee demotivation

The ongoing financial and management turbulence at Relnk is having a detrimental impact on employee motivation, particularly the technologists, with many seeking employment elsewhere. This represents a worrying development for Relnk as the company's technologists have been instrumental in creating its 'vital technical edge' over competing firms.

Promotion and marketing

Relnk currently lacks a strong, coherent marketing message. This is evident as the Relnk brand was not recognised by many of the consumer participants in the recent brand awareness survey. This can be explained in part by the company's narrow approach to marketing, which consists of promoting the Relnk brand through its website while excluding other channels of marketing. Furthermore, internet searches for the Relnk website are hard to distinguish from similar competitor services.

Opportunities:

Recycling

There has been a recent increase in the number of 'green' consumers in the country of Eland. This represents a significant opportunity for Relnk, especially as its own business model is built upon reusing printer cartridges and refilling them with ink. The Eland government's commitment to recycling suggests that this trend will continue into the foreseeable future, thereby increasing demand for Relnk's services.

Underperforming economy

The ailing state of the economy in Eland is likely to support an increase in demand for recycling ink cartridges and represents a real opportunity for Relnk. The majority of commercial and domestic consumers in Eland own printers, with a significant number of people looking to reduce their printing costs.

Government contracts

The government in Eland is suffering from a fall in tax revenues, and in a bid to reduce costs the government is now requiring all departments to demonstrate value-for-money in purchases made. This requirement presents Relnk with an ideal opportunity to build upon the long-term relationship it already has with the DoRC, as further government departments are likely to be interested in using Relnk's services.

Threats:

Legal challenges

Original equipment manufacturers (OEMs) have taken legal action against independent companies which provide cartridge refill services of OEM-branded printer consumables. Such action has so far failed, with the government ruling that to make such services illegal would be anti-competitive. However, there is a threat that the OEMs may succeed with future legal bids as these larger companies continue to promote their argument to political parties in Eland.

BPP
LEARNING
MEDIA

New innovations

The printer consumables market in Eland is heavily technology driven. Players in the market are focused on developing 'innovations which make printing better and cheaper'. This represents a significant threat as new printer cartridge refilling processes may be developed which make ReInk's own processes more expensive or unappealing to customers. Furthermore, the patent on ReInk's refill process only has another six years to run, after which time competitors would most likely be able to develop their own version of the same technology. This could prove to be a real threat to ReInk, unless the company is able to enhance or develop newer processes to replace its existing approach.

Competition

The printer consumables market in Eland is highly competitive, due to a number of factors. The OEMs dominate the market and consist of a number of well-known household brands. Coupled to these larger players there are a large number of independent companies supplying printer cartridges. It is easy for new independent suppliers to enter the market, meaning that companies predominantly compete on price and customers show little brand loyalty to any one supplier. To combat the threat of independent players, the large companies such as Landy have taken to invalidating warranties on any Landy-branded printers which are found to have used non-Landy ink.

Privatisation of the DoRC

The government in Eland is currently considering privatising the DoRC. This is potentially a significant threat to ReInk as the company currently derives 20% of its $6m revenue from the DoRC. An independently run DoRC may choose to switch its supplier of reusable ink.

17 MMI

Top tips. From the scenario you should have identified that MMI initially acquired First Leisure with a view to diversification, while the Boatland acquisition was intended to create synergies. However, the subsequent performance of First Leisure has been far better than Boatland's. Does this indicate anything about MMI's strategic rationale (and its ability in creating value from the group?)

Note that part (a) in effect contains two requirements: (i) explain the rationale for the acquisitions; then (ii) assess the subsequent performance of the companies acquired. Remember to use the financial information provided in Table 1 to support your answer; there are marks specifically available for interpreting this data.

Although the requirement does not specify any models to use, the BCG matrix (Henderson, 1970) would have helped you consider how the strategic business units (SBUs) fit into MMI's corporate portfolio.

Your analysis in part (a) should help your answer to part (b). In part (a) you should have identified MMI's strengths and weaknesses as a corporate parent, and you can use this to help assess how well it could manage the InfoTech acquisition. Does MMI have the competences required to make this acquisition successful?

An alternative way of approaching this question would be to look at the markets in which MMI and InfoTech are operating, and then consider the suitability of the proposal. (Suitability is one of the three key criteria used for judging strategic options: suitability; acceptability; feasibility.)

However, make sure you look at InfoTech's underlying performance in Table 1 – for example, it is a loss-making company. What will acquiring InfoTech contribute to MMI's portfolio? What value will InfoTech bring to the MMI group? And importantly, does MMI have any experience at turning around failing companies?

Marks

(a) **First Leisure**

Up to 5 marks for explaining the rationale for acquiring First Leisure   Max 5

Up to 4 marks for assessing the performance of First Leisure post acquisition   Max 4

Boatland

Up to 5 marks for explaining the rationale for acquiring Boatland   Max 5

Up to 5 marks for assessing the performance of Boatland post acquisition   Max 5

Up to a maximum of 15 marks for part (a)   15

(b) Up to 3 marks for interpreting the financial performance of MMI and summarising its acquisition strategy   Max 3

Up to 2 marks for recognising a 'hands-off' approach has been more successful when MMI has pursued unrelated diversification   Max 2

Up to 2 marks for recognising the difficulty of pursuing this approach at InfoTech   Max 2

Up to 2 marks for interpreting the financial and market data   Max 2

Up to 2 marks for overall assessment of the extent to which acquiring InfoTech is appropriate for MMI   Max 2

Up to a maximum of 10 marks for part (b)   10

25

(a) **Rationale for acquiring First Leisure**

Growing market – MMI's original business of quarrying and mining is a declining market, whose total revenue fell 4.5% between 20X2–X8. Increased costs and falling reserves meant that industry profitability is likely to continue declining, and moreover meant that there was little chance of MMI finding new sites in its existing market in which to invest. Therefore, **MMI was forced to look for new investment opportunities.**

In contrast to the quarrying and mining market, the leisure market was growing rapidly, and its total revenue increased by 26.7% from 20X2–X8. Within this market, First Leisure was a profitable company.

So the original rationale for MMI acquiring First Leisure was to enable it to **diversify out of a declining market into an expanding market.**

Unrelated diversification – However, when MMI acquired First Leisure, there didn't appear to be any synergies between the two companies, and so MMI's strategy appeared to be one of unrelated diversification. This lack of synergy initially prompted some finance analysts to question the wisdom of the acquisition.

Economies of scope – After the acquisition, certain synergies between MMI and First Leisure emerged, resulting from the fact that **disused or unprofitable quarry sites could be converted into leisure parks.** These synergies had not been foreseen at the time of acquisition.

Converting quarry sites into leisure parks had two benefits:

(i) MMI no longer had to incur the costs of running unprofitable mines or to maintain security and safety at disused sites.

(ii) First Leisure was able to acquire new sites easily and cheaply, in an environment where planning legislation was otherwise making it increasingly expensive and difficult to purchase new sites.

In this way, MMI was able to **benefit from economies of scope** – changing the use of under-utilised resources (from quarries into leisure parks) in a way which benefited the group overall.

Performance of First Leisure post acquisition

Rapid growth – First Leisure's turnover has doubled from $100m in 20X2 to $200m in 20X8, and its market share has increased from 13% to 21% over the same period. First Leisure's growth in an expanding market suggests that in terms of the BCG matrix it is a **star business unit** (Henderson, 1970), and so it is likely that **MMI will continue to encourage its growth.**

Stable profit margins – Gross profit margins have remained constant, suggesting that market conditions have allowed it to grow without having to offer any discounts. Furthermore, net profits have increased slightly, suggesting that First Leisure is **keeping its costs under control,** despite the recent reliability issues with the boats from Boatland, which are likely to have increased maintenance costs.

Rationale for acquiring Boatland

Expected synergy with First Leisure – The primary reason for MMI's acquisition of Boatland was the synergies it expected between Boatland and First Leisure. **First Leisure had experienced difficulties in obtaining and maintaining boats for its parks,** so acquiring a boat-making company was seen as a way of overcoming these difficulties.

Backward integration and cost savings – MMI also felt that bringing Boatland into the Group would **provide cost savings for First Leisure,** through backward integration. First Leisure would **no longer need to buy boats from an external supplier,** because they would be provided by another group company.

Underperforming company – MMI perceived that Boatland was underperforming, so MMI felt it could **apply its managerial competencies to drive extra value from Boatland.** MMI felt that Boatland's existing management team had no ambitions to expand, but producing boats for First Leisure would provide a steady income and cash flow which Boatland could then use to help it expand.

Synergies not realised

MMI's rationale in acquiring Boatland has not been justified though, and the synergies it foresaw have not been realised, because Boatland's specialist boats are not hard-wearing enough for the way they are used by First Leisure's customers. Unfortunately, this has meant that maintenance time and costs have increased, and because Boatland has had to spend more time repairing First Leisure's boats the quality of service it has been able to give its other customers has fallen.

Therefore, rather than providing an opportunity for it to expand, **the Boatland/First Leisure integration has actually damaged Boatland's business.**

Performance of Boatland post acquisition

Declining revenue and market share – Although the total market size has remained constant between 20X6–X8, at $201m, Boatland's revenues have declined from $2.4m to $2.1m, rather than expanding as MMI had hoped.

Decline in profit margins – Gross profit has fallen from $0.5m (20X6) to $0.3m (20X8), and net profit has similarly fallen from $0.25m (20X6) to $0.09m (20X8). This means that Boatland's net profit margin is now only 4.3%, down from 10.4% in 20X6.

Staff turnover – Alongside its poor financial performance, since the acquisition Boatland has also lost nearly half of its skilled boat builders. This suggests there is a problem of **cultural fit** with the acquisition. Boatland has historically made a small number of high-quality boats, for customers who look after them. After the acquisition, Boatland has had to produce a larger number of robust boats which can be used by holiday makers. To this extent, the synergies which MMI had envisaged were an illusion, because the two boat markets are quite distinct from one another.

Consequently, the benefit opportunities from acquiring Boatland were significantly less than MMI had initially realised.

In this context, and given Boatland's small share of a static market, MMI should consider **divesting the business**. However, divestment would mean that it has to find an alternative boat supplier for First Leisure, so it should look to find this replacement supplier before divesting of Boatland.

(b) **Composition of portfolio** – Although MMI's portfolio only contains three businesses, they are strategically quite diverse, and have met with varying degrees of success.

MMI has consolidated its position in the quarrying market by acquiring two of its smaller competitors, and its market share has increased from 20% (20X2) to 28% (20X8). MMI has also significantly increased its net profit margin, because it no longer has the costs of maintaining the redundant quarries and operating the unprofitable ones that it has redeployed as leisure resources for First Leisure.

First Leisure has turned out to be a very successful acquisition, due to the unexpected synergies between it and MMI.

However, the **Boatland** acquisition, which was expected to deliver synergies with First Leisure, has not been successful, and has actually destroyed value rather than created it.

Corporate management capabilities – Following the acquisition of the two smaller mining and quarrying companies in 20X4, MMI introduced its own managers to run the businesses, and this resulted in a spectacular rise in revenues. This success prompted MMI's CEO to claim that **corporate management capabilities are now an important strategic asset** for MMI.

However, the CEO's assessment is perhaps extravagant. MMI has successfully improved the performance of businesses in an industry it is familiar with. But, the post-acquisition performance of **Boatland has been much less successful**.

Because MMI did not really understand the boat industry, it did not appreciate the differences between Boatland and First Leisure, and **tried to create artificial synergies** between the two.

MMI's acquisition of First Leisure has been much more successful, but in this case MMI has left the day-to-day management of the business to First Leisure's own, experienced, managers.

So it appears MMI may **better adopt a hands-off approach to corporate management**, except for acquisitions directly related to its own core business (quarrying and mining).

InfoTech

Current financial position – Although the information technology solutions market has grown by nearly 25% between 20X2–X8, InfoTech's **revenues have actually fallen,** meaning it has suffered a significant decline its market share. InfoTech's low market share in a growing market means it is a **question mark** business unit using the terminology of the BCG matrix (Henderson, 1970).

Moreover, InfoTech has suffered a marked **decrease in both its gross and net profits,** especially over the two-year period from 20X6–X8. The decline in profitability means that InfoTech actually made a **net loss of $0.2m in 20X8**.

Corporate management – InfoTech's recent results suggest that the current management team may not be able to turn around its financial performance, and therefore if MMI acquired it, **MMI would have to introduce a new management team.**

Industry experience – However, MMI needs to appreciate that the **information technology solutions industry is very different to the quarrying and mining industry**. Therefore despite the CEO's comments about MMI's corporate management capabilities, it is unlikely that MMI can successfully make up this new management team from within its existing staff.

The relative failure of the Boatland acquisition should alert MMI to the need to install managers who are experienced in the information technology solutions industry, and understand its culture.

Financial risk – When MMI acquired First Leisure and Boatland they were both relatively successful, profitable companies in their own right. However, InfoTech is loss-making, and so is likely to need a considerable **cash investment to support it**. InfoTech's classification as a question mark (Henderson, 1970) also suggests it could require investment in order to try to increase its market share.

However, **MMI doesn't have any experience of acquiring a failing company and turning it round**. This suggests InfoTech is not an appropriate choice for acquisition, especially given MMI's lack of experience in the information technology industry.

18 Branscombe

> **Top tips.** Part (a): the first part of the requirement is a test of knowledge: explaining the function and roles of a risk committee. However, the second part of the requirement needs to be applied to the case: how could having a risk committee benefit Branscombe? (There are some clear indicators of risk in the scenario: the company is growing rapidly; it has recently been listed on the stock exchange; and it is planning to enter new markets – which in turn will increase the need for greater expertise.) An important point to recognise here is that the audit committee might not be in a good position to continue to manage all aspects of risk management, so having a separate committee will help the board ensure that adequate risk management systems are in place across the company.
>
> Part (b) also contains two tasks; firstly, explaining what 'risk appetite' is, then assessing how Branscombe's risk appetite has influenced its strategy and the risks it has chosen to bear. In the first part of the task, your explanation should have mentioned that the spectrum of risk appetite runs from risk adverse to risk seeking; and in turn, this should have helped you to identify that Branscombe is risk seeking (for example, the potential high returns from the economic growth and low indirect taxation in the new country attract it to expand there, despite the many risks in the country).
>
> In order to answer part (c) you need to identify (from the scenario) relevant strategic and operational risks which could arise from the supply contract. However, the focus of your answer should be on how Branscombe could **control** those risks – not simply identifying what the risks are. Equally, to score well, you need to relate the controls you recommend specifically to the case, rather than just mentioning general controls (for example, using the general headings of the 'TARA' framework).

		Marks
(a)	Up to 4 marks for explaining the function and roles of a risk committee	Max 4
	Up to 2 marks for each advantage of a risk committee to Branscombe, up to a maximum of 6 marks (Maximum of 1 mark for each advantage if it is not related to Branscombe)	Max <u>6</u>
	Up to a maximum of 10 marks for part (a)	10
(b)	Up to 2 marks for an explanation of risk appetite	Max 2
	Up to 2 marks for each relevant point of assessment about how risk appetite has influenced corporate strategy and the risks Branscombe has chosen to bear, up to a maximum of 6 marks	Max <u>6</u>
	Up to a maximum of 7 marks for part (b)	7
(c)	Up to 2 marks per well explained point on relevant risks and how to manage them (Maximum of 1 mark per point if not applied to the scenario)	
	Up to a maximum of 8 marks for part (c)	<u>8</u>
		<u>25</u>

(a)   The primary function of a risk committee is to recommend to the board a sound system of risk oversight, management and internal control.

Its roles include:

(i)   The recommendation to the board of a risk management strategy which identifies, assesses, manages and monitors all aspects of risk throughout the company

(ii)   Reviewing reports on key risks prepared by business operating units, management and the board, and then assessing the effectiveness of the company's internal control systems in dealing with them

(iii)   Advising the board on risk appetite and acceptable risk tolerances when setting the company's future strategic direction

(iv)   Advising the board on all high-level risk matters and monitoring overall exposure to risk and ensuring it remains within limits set by the board

(v)   Informing shareholders, and other key stakeholders, of any significant changes to the company's risk profile

Although not a prescribed requirement in corporate governance codes and legislation, a risk committee would ensure the robust oversight of the management of risk throughout the company. In its absence, its duties and responsibilities would be discharged by the mandatory audit committee.

The establishment of a risk committee could be advantageous to the governance of Branscombe Co in a number of ways:

1   **Formalise business practices**

Establishing a sub-committee at board level would ensure that risk is high on the company's agenda when devising strategy and making key business decisions. The recent successful Geeland tender may have been considered differently by the company if all of the inherent risks associated with the contract were identified and assessed from the outset.

A formal risk management process would have required Branscombe Co to evaluate its exposure to risk, including exchange rate risk, when considering any business opportunity, so that only those opportunities within the company's risk tolerances would be progressed.

2   **Focus attention**

Risk is the likelihood that business activities may not go according to plan. Sometimes the outcomes may exceed expectations but there is also a downside to risk which exposes the company to potential losses and financial distress. The establishment of a separate risk committee helps the board to ensure that adequate risk management systems are in place to meet every eventuality. A risk committee would take the lead in promoting awareness and driving through the required changes.

By agreeing to set up a risk committee, Branscombe Co will be clearly raising the profile of risk throughout the company, and helping to inculcate a more risk-aware culture amongst all staff. In turn, this should to lead to less dysfunctional decision making and improve overall business performance.

3   **Reduce control breaches**

Through the establishment of a formal reporting system, the risk committee monitors internal control compliance and considers any breach of the company's agreed risk appetite. Any resultant action plans designed to address significant breaches of the company's principal risk policies should reduce the likelihood and frequency of control breaches.

At Branscombe Co, it is unclear if it currently has any structured risk management procedures and internal control systems. However, its ambitious expansion plans necessitate robust procedures and practices to manage the vast array of different risks it faces; this includes a hedging strategy to manage its exposures to volatile foreign exchange rates, as this could reduce its profitability from the Geeland venture and put a strain on its cash flows and working capital.

4 **Improve communication**

An effective risk management framework integrates all business planning and management activities across the company, which in turn correctly aligns power and authority with responsibility and accountability lines. A risk committee, established at the apex of this framework, will set a tone of risk awareness at the top which then permeates down through the whole organisational structure. This flow of communication ensures that everyone is adequately informed of their responsibilities and so they are more likely to discharge their duties correctly.

The risk committee is required to formally report to shareholders annually on the effectiveness of the company's risk management strategy, and report any material control breaches which may have occurred, together with resultant actions taken to avoid a recurrence. Such communication adequately informs shareholders, and other stakeholders, as to how well risk is being managed by the company.

(b) **Risk appetite**

Risk appetite can be explained as the nature and strength of risks which an organisation is prepared to accept or seek. It comprises two key elements:

(i) The level of risk which the company's directors consider desirable; and

(ii) The capacity of the company to actually bear the level of risk.

A company which opts for riskier ventures to attain higher returns is said to be risk-seeking, whereas with a more cautious approach is risk averse.

At Branscombe Co, it is apparent that the company has adopted a risk-seeking approach to making strategy. The board has decided that the best way for the company to achieve ambitious levels of growth, and satisfy the demands of its shareholders, is to adopt a higher risk appetite. In effect, this means that the risk tolerance boundaries have been set so that most business opportunities would be viewed as acceptable under these criteria.

The selection of Geeland as a suitable country for expansion was driven by the opportunities presented from the boom in its economic fortunes and generous indirect tax incentives offered by the Geeland government, rather than the risks associated with operating in an unstable political system in which corruption is evident. Clearly the board of Branscombe Co, when weighing up the advantages and disadvantages of this venture, determined that the potential benefits outweighed the identified risks and so submitted a successful tender for the hotel contract. However, the resultant supply contract has placed a significant burden of risk on Branscombe Co in terms of logistics and the transportation of equipment, payment terms and foreign exchange exposure. Provided that sound internal control systems have been set up to manage all aspects of risk associated with this contract, then the risk-seeking policy adopted should deliver the expected return to the company.

(c) The Geeland supply contract presents a number of strategic and operational risks for Branscombe Co which could be controlled as follows:

Trading risk

International trade presents its own special risks due to the increased distances and times involved. The types of trading risk include:

1 Physical risk of goods being lost, stolen or damaged in transit, or the legal documents accompanying the goods going missing

2 The customer refusing to accept the goods on their delivery

3 Cancellation of an order whilst in transit

To overcome the trading risks described above, Branscombe Co could employ local agents in Geeland to liaise with the management and project team for the new hotel, and co-ordinate the shipment of goods to meet the precise requirements of the client. This means that only those items actually required will be despatched and they will be accepted on delivery. Additionally, it might be prudent to take out an insurance policy covering the value of goods which could be lost or damaged on the long journey to Geeland, as well as any liquidated damages which might be claimed by the customer for non-delivery.

Probity risk

There is a general risk of unethical behaviour by one or more persons involved in a business activity, and as Geeland has a bad reputation for corrupt business practices, the risk is high. It might be that corrupt officials require a 'facilitation payment' to be made to them to allow the goods to pass through import controls in Geeland. It would never be acceptable to make such a payment and indeed in many jurisdictions paying a bribe is illegal, so Branscombe Co must make this clear in its code of practice. To overcome this possible probity risk, the contract should be drafted to make it clear that the client should undertake the local administrative measures necessary for the importing of and acceptance of goods on their arrival at the island.

Political risk

The unstable legacy of political administrations in Geeland suggests a possible political risk. Should there be a change of government, the incentives which encouraged Branscombe Co to trade with Geeland could be withdrawn and the contract could become less attractive. It would be inappropriate to lobby, engage or ally the business with any foreign government or political party; by adopting a policy of political neutrality Branscombe Co would be less likely to be negatively affected by any change in the Geeland government.

Foreign currency risk

There is always the risk of a loss arising from exchange rate movements between the time of entering into an international trading transaction and the time of cash settlement. When Branscombe Co remits an invoice to its client in Geeland $, it will be exposed to foreign currency risk. If the Geeland $ continues to weaken against the Effland $ (as it has been recently) this will mean that, once converted into Effland $, the final amount receivable will be less than Branscombe originally anticipated when it raised the invoice.

If this risk is considered material, Branscombe Co may wish to hedge its exposure. There are a number of hedging methods designed to counter the effect of movements in exchange rates including forward contracts and money market hedges.

19 YGT

Top tips. Part (a): the first paragraph of the scenario quotes Raz as saying that risks 'didn't change much' and 'hardly ever materialised' with the result that they can mostly be ignored, and meaning that undertaking a risk assessment would be a waste of money for YGT. The contrast between these views and the notion of 'dynamic risk' should help you identify the basis on which Raz's beliefs can be criticised. Similarly, the scenario clearly states that Risks C and D have been affected by recent events – suggesting that not only have the risks changed, but also that understanding how they have changed could be useful to YGT.

In (b) the descriptions of the risks are worded carefully to make clear where each fit on the impact/likelihood risk assessment map. Therefore, you first need to identify where they fit on the map, and then select the appropriate strategy for managing them. Note, however, that you are asked to 'justify' your selection, so you shouldn't simply state the strategy you think is appropriate, but also explain why.

In (c) the key point was that in some cases, increased environmental losses can result in deterioration of a company's reputation (ie a rise in reputation risk). Because both risks rise and fall together, they can be said to be positively correlated. However, that does not mean their relationship is exact, because of the different consequences that they have.

Marks

(a) Up to 2 marks for each relevant criticism of Raz Dutta's beliefs   Max 4
Up to 2 marks for each point identifying, and explaining, the
dynamic nature of risks   Max 4
Up to a maximum of 8 marks for part (a)   8

(b) For each risk: ½ mark for selecting the correct strategy   Max 2
For each risk: 1 mark for explaining and justifying the strategy
chosen   Max 4
Up to a maximum of 6 marks for part (b)   6

(c) Up to 2 marks for explaining what related risks are   Max 2
Up to 2 marks for each relevant point describing how Risks
E and F might be positively correlated   Max 4
Up to a maximum of 5 marks for part (c)   5
     19

(a) **Raz Dutta's beliefs**

Both Raz Dutta's assertions are incorrect.

Risks don't change much

It is untrue to say that the risks YGT faces do not change much. The new product, for example, has given rise to Risk C and the change in legislation has given rise to Risk D. Risk assessment is needed to translate these events in the environment into an analysis of the **consequences for YGT and the likelihood** that these consequences will occur.

Risks hardly ever materialise

The risk assessment that the consultants carried out revealed that this assertion is **incorrect**, which justified the assessment being made. Risk B is assessed as **highly likely to occur and with a high impact**. The risk assessment should **prompt action to be taken quickly**, perhaps abandoning the activity.

The assessment has also revealed that Risk C will have a high potential impact if it materialises. The risk assessment should therefore **prompt the board to weigh up this assessment** against **the low probability** of the risk materialising and see whether it is worth taking the alternative actions mentioned.

Why risk assessment is dynamic:

Risk continuum

Most businesses **operate on a continuum** somewhere between highly static and highly dynamic. Few businesses operate very near the static end of the continuum, because of the **changing forces** in the outside world and the need for them to respond. These may include any or all of the PESTEL factors (political, economic, social, technological, environmental, legal). Risks may become more or less likely to materialise or have increased or decreased impact. Stricter legislation, for example, may increase the impact of the risk of non-compliance because it introduces tougher penalties for breaking the law.

Strategic decisions

The product launch, and the risks associated with that launch, will have arisen because YGT is seeking to gain a **competitive advantage**. Competitors are likely to take action in response to the product launch, resulting in further changes in risk levels.

Operational changes

The risks from the external environment will also prompt changes in the **organisation's activities and operations,** such as the introduction of procedures to comply with new legislation. Changes will carry their own risks, for example modifications in production processes when a new product is introduced may make machine breakdowns more likely.

(b) **Risk A**

Risk A should be **accepted**. Although the activity is marginal and could be abandoned, the **high returns** generated outweigh the low likelihood and impact and justify continuing with the activity.

Risk B

Risk B should **probably be avoided**. Although it generates high returns, it is not vital to YGT's continued existence. It is unlikely that the risk appetite determined by the directors should permit YGT to continue to be involved in an activity that is peripheral and which will probably generate large losses.

Risk C

Risk C should be **transferred**. Although it might have a high impact, it cannot be avoided. The scenario mentions alternative actions being taken. These could include insurance or outsourcing production, if the risk is associated with manufacture.

Risk D

Risk D should be **reduced**. Some action has to be taken to **avoid the business suffering frequent, small losses**. This action clearly cannot include transferring the risk. As the risk is associated with a change in legislation, the action could be whatever is necessary to comply with the new rules. The action could also include reducing the activity or carrying it out in a different way. The directors would need to weigh up the benefits of continuing to carry out the activity at the present level against the increased costs of doing so, and repeat this assessment at other levels or for other methods of performance.

(c) **Related risks**

A related risk is a risk that is **not independent of other risks**. Its level is linked to the level of the other risk, and its level will change as the level of the other risk changes. **Correlation** is an example of a relationship between risks.

Environmental risk links with reputation risk

Environmental risks are exposures to losses through the **impacts** the organisation makes on the environment or the **resources it consumes**. The organisation may suffer bad publicity, and hence a risk to its reputation, as a result of environmental risk arising. **Reputation risk** is thus likely to be **positively correlated** to environmental risk because they have a **common cause**, an impact or event that adversely affects the environment. Actions taken to reduce the likelihood of adverse environmental impacts or events occurring will also decrease the likelihood of reputation risk materialising.

Environmental risk distinction from reputation risk

The losses incurred from environmental risks materialising are separate from the losses resulting from damage to reputation. Environmental risk losses may include **clean-up costs or legal penalties**, reputation risk losses may include **lost sales** as customers boycott the business. The impact of reputation risk materialising is also not only dependent on the environmental impact or event that has occurred, but also on how people have **reacted to it**. If there is no reaction, then reputation risk has not materialised.

20 H&Z

Top tips. Part (a)(i) is a text of knowledge, but note the verb is 'describe' so you need to provide some detail about the roles, not simply a list of single line bullet points.

Just because somebody has been appointed to a role doesn't necessarily mean they understand that role properly. This is the key issue in (a)(ii). Having described the role of a risk manager (in (a)(i)) you now need to assess the extent to which John's understanding of the role fits – or doesn't fit – with the aspects you have described. For example, is John's assertion that 'it was his job to eliminate all of the highest risks at H&Z' valid (given the description of a risk manager's role)?

In (b), the most helpful risk assessment framework is the likelihood-consequences matrix, and this is the one you should have used in your answer. However, it is important to think carefully about the axis of the matrix – 'likelihood' and 'consequences' – and John's advice in the context of them. Crucially, although John has considered the potential impact of the risk ('consequences') he has not considered the 'likelihood' of it occurring. As such, how valid is his advice?

Part (c)(i) looks at the necessity of accepting risk as a part of a successful strategy. However, note that as well as defining 'entrepreneurial risk' you also have to explain why it is important for businesses to accept it.

Part (c)(ii) asks you to 'critically evaluate' Jane's view on risk management, and so you should have considered arguments in favour of it as well as against it. Importantly, though, your answer needs to 'evaluate' Jane's view, not simply repeat, or rephrase, her remarks from the scenario.

Marking scheme

				Marks
(a)	(i)	1 mark for each relevant role described (½ mark if role identified rather than described)		4
		Up to a maximum of 4 marks for part (a)(i)		
	(ii)	1 mark for each relevant point assessing John's understanding of the role		4
		Up to a maximum of 4 marks for part (a)(ii)		
(b)		Up to 2 marks for explaining a relevant risk assessment framework	Max 2	
		Up to 5 marks for criticising John's advice	Max 5	
		Up to a maximum of 6 marks for part (b)		6
(c)	(i)	Definition of entrepreneurial risk	2	
		Explanation of the importance	2	
		Up to a maximum of 4 marks for part (c)(i)		4
	(ii)	1 mark for each relevant point made in support of Jane Xylene's view	Max 4	
		1 mark for each relevant point made in opposition to Jane Xylene's view	Max 4	
		Up to a maximum of 7 marks for part (c) (ii)		7
				25

(a) (i) **Establishing a risk management framework**

The framework should **cover all aspects of risk** across the organisation, integrating enterprise risk management with other business planning and management activities and framing authority and accountability for enterprise risk management in business units. Development of policies includes the **quantification of management's risk appetite through specific risk limits, defining roles and responsibilities** and **participating in setting goals for implementation.**

Promoting enterprise risk management competence

This includes **training managers and staff** to help them develop risk management expertise and **helping managers align risk responses with the entity's risk tolerances.**

Dealing with insurance companies

The risk manager needs to deal carefully with insurers because of **increased premium costs, restrictions in the cover available** (will the risks be excluded from cover) and the **need for negotiations** if claims arise. If insurers require it, the risk manager needs to demonstrate that the organisation is actively taking steps to manage its risks.

Risk reporting

The risk manager is responsible for **implementing risk indicators and reports,** including losses and incidents, key risk exposures and early warning indicators. He should **facilitate reporting by operational managers**, including **quantitative and qualitative thresholds**, and **monitor** this reporting process.

(ii)   **Flaws in risk assessment**

It is understandable that John wanted to carry out one of the most important tasks quickly. However, by doing it as soon as he started at H&Z, it seems he didn't give himself sufficient time to understand the company's **background and strategic aims**. The fact also he had not had time to establish a risk management framework will have meant that his assessment of risk is based on inadequate information.

Form of advice

John's advice to the board is expressed too strongly. The board has responsibility for **taking key strategic decisions** and John is exceeding his remit by telling them so bluntly to stop the activity associated with Risk 3.

Support for advice

John's advice does not appear to be **backed by the supporting information** necessary for the board to take an informed decision on the risk.

Risk management

John is not responsible for **eliminating or minimising all the highest risks** facing the company. Some risks, for example the risks of operations being disrupted by natural disasters, are risks that John cannot influence much, it at all. John will also need to consider whether some high-impact risks **cannot be effectively lessened**, but could be **transferred**, for example to **H&Z's insurers**.

(b)   **Probability-impact/Likelihood-consequences matrix**

This matrix is used to group risks and assess their relative importance. As such, it is a useful tool when you are considering, as John is, the **impact of major risks**.

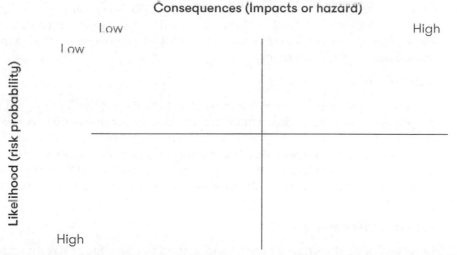

This diagram maps two continuums on which risks are plotted. The **nearer the risk is** towards the **bottom right-hand corner** (the high-high corner), the **more important** the risk will be. This profile can then be used to set priorities for risk mitigation.

Failure to consider probability

The most significant failure in John's approach to assessing risk is his failure to consider the **likelihood** that the risk will materialise. As Jane points out, in order for H&Z to continue in business, it will have to bear some **significant entrepreneurial risks**. However, the investments can be justified if the risks are **low**.

BPP
LEARNING
MEDIA

Risk and return

John has also failed to take into account what the directors have established as the company's **risk appetite**. The directors may believe that taking significant risks is justified by the possibility of achieving **high returns** from the associated activities. Risk elimination or minimisation may not always achieve high returns. Instead better returns may be achieved by **risk reduction or transfer**.

Uncertainties of assessment

John has also not taken into account inevitable **uncertainties in the data used** to make the likelihood-consequences assessment. His strongly expressed view fails to take into account the importance of the assumptions made, the likelihood of different scenarios and other issues surrounding the assessment.

(c)   (i)   **Entrepreneurial risks**

Entrepreneurial risks are the risks that arise from **carrying out business activities,** for example the risks of a major investment failing to deliver required returns or profits being lessened by a competitor's activities.

Acceptance of entrepreneurial risks

Few, if any, business activities are risk free. For example in all business situations other than a monopoly, the business will face **risks arising from competition**. Also **shareholders** will have invested in a business on the grounds that they wish to **achieve higher returns** than those offered by risk-free investments. A business can only earn these returns if it takes risks.

(ii)   **Benefits vs costs**

Jane correctly identifies the needs to balance the benefits of risk management against costs. **Expenditure on over-elaborate risk management systems** may not be warranted by the **losses they prevent** or the **disruption to operating activities** that they cause.

Opportunity costs

Jane also correctly identifies the problems with taking a completely pessimistic view of risk, treating all risks as pure risks with only negative consequences. **Speculative risks**, the risks relating to doing business, are risks from which **good or harm** may result. The upside of these risks needs to be taken into account when managers decide how to deal with them.

'Stop' errors

Jane also, correctly, wants to ensure that potential opportunities are not rejected simply because they involve a high level of risk. If an opportunity looks likely to produce returns that are higher than the costs of generating them, then that opportunity should be pursued. As Jane suggests, an unduly pessimistic approach could be a source of 'stop' errors – where projects are rejected on account of the risk involved even though they could have been beneficial to H&Z if they had been pursued.

Lack of understanding

However, Jane does not appear to understand the benefits of risk management and why corporate governance guidance insists that listed companies have appropriate risk management structures in place. Directors need to gain assurance that the decisions they take about **what risks** should be **borne**, and how the **risks borne** should be **managed**, are enforced. The risk management function helps to **give them this assurance**. The risk management function also **provides information** to the board to help decide on the risk implications of strategy, and also to operational managers so that they can recognise and deal with risks when they arise.

Risk-return relationship

Jane seems to be operating at the other extreme to John, and as such has an equally flawed view of the risk-return relationship. **Shareholder**s may require risks to be taken so that they can achieve an adequate return, but they will also judge some risks to be too high for the **potential returns from taking them**. Jane does not appear to recognise any limits to **H&Z's risk appetite**. John is right in saying that there are some risks that are too great for the company to bear, that will threaten its existence and cannot be justified whatever the return.

Risk management strategies

Jane incorrectly views risk avoidance and the forbidding of activities as the only strategies recommended by risk managers. Risk managers can **recommend risk reduction strategies** that will increase the chances of commercial success, for example piloting a new product to a small audience before it is launched.

21 Cronin Auto Retail

Top tips. Part (a): don't fall into the trap of listing generic points under each of the 'I' headings, as they may not always apply. For example, to what extent does 'independence of location' really apply to this organisation? Although, in theory, e-marketing can provide organisations with 'global reach' it is unlikely that this kind of reach could be achieved through using e-marketing at CAR, or would even be needed.

This highlights a very important point about answering scenario questions: always read the scenario carefully, and make sure you apply your knowledge in a way which is relevant to the specific situation described.

Part (b) has two elements, with the first being to 'Explain the principles of e-procurement'. This is a test of knowledge alone, and so doesn't require any application to the scenario.

The second part of the requirement – 'potential application to CAR' – does need to be linked to the scenario. However, the scenario highlights some pretty clear problems with CAR's current procurement process, which should have prompted you to consider the extent to which e-procurement could help to solve those problems.

Also note that there are two different elements to procurement in CAR: procuring parts for cars, and procuring general items such as stationery; so make sure you consider the potential impact that e-procurement could have on each of these.

Marking scheme

		Marks
(a)	Up to 1 mark for each point up to a maximum of 4 marks for each element (interactivity; intelligence; individualisation; and independence of location) Up to a maximum of 16 marks for part (a)	16
(b)	1 mark for each relevant point Up to a maximum of 9 marks for part (b)	9
		25

(a) Principles of e-marketing

The 6 I's of e-marketing were developed by McDonald and Wilson (2011). The answer below considers four of these (interactivity, intelligence, individualisation and independence of location) in relation to CAR.

Interactivity

Interactivity relates to the development of a two-way relationship between the customer and the supplier. CAR currently uses a traditional 'push' method of advertising consisting of adverts in local newspapers and customer mail-shots. Although CAR has a website, this is currently used as an 'online catalogue' and so also represents 'push' media.

CAR could immediately save money by replacing their mail-shots with emails. However, this still allows little consumer interaction and so remains a 'push' technique.

Moving to a 'pull' approach would increase the level of interactivity between CAR and the customers, and this could be done in a number of ways.

CAR could:

- Develop their website in such a way that allows customers to **book a test drive** or to **book their car in for a service/repair online**

- Set up a **discussion thread** on the website to encourage potential buyers to discuss and ask questions about cars that interest them. This both increases the information available to customers which may lead to them purchasing the car, and may encourage potential buyers to proceed quickly for fear for 'losing out' should someone else purchase the car first.

- Encourage customers to provide **feedback** on the website following completion of their purchase. This provides customers with useful information and strong testimonials provide future buyers with confidence, making it more likely they will go ahead with a planned purchase.

Intelligence

Intelligence is linked to market and marketing research. It involves identifying and understanding the needs of potential customers and how they wish to be communicated with. CAR does very little research about what its customers actually want. Instead, it relies on what their sales people **think** their customers want and a small database of historical data consisting only of people who have actually bought cars from CAR.

CAR could improve its interactivity by collecting email addresses through interactivity initiatives and promotions such as those described above. This would give CAR access to a wider pool of **potential customers** who then can be kept up to date via email.

Providing these potential customers with the ability to 'submit requests' either to the website or by email, or 'vote for your favourite car' would allow CAR to build up a better picture of what potential buyers are really interested in. This may support the concern that the buyers are making the wrong decisions at auctions and potentially lead to a change in buying policy.

Individualisation

In conventional media, such as that currently used by CAR, the same information tends to be sent to everyone. Individualisation relates to the tailoring of marketing information to each individual, and using personalisation to build up a relationship with the customer.

CAR could implement a **personalised** approach by selectively emailing individuals who have shown an interest in a certain model or type of car when a car that meets their requirements comes into inventory. This approach could also be used with existing CAR customers, for example by emailing them two or three years after purchase with opportunities to upgrade to a newer or improved model.

After-sales service can also be improved via individualisation. For example, if the correct details are kept, current customers can be emailed with an invitation to book in for a service when their MOT is due, and to send them updates on services for specific features relevant to their car (eg air-conditioning maintenance would only be suggested for customers who bought air-conditioned cars).

Individualisation can only be successful, however, if **sufficient details** have been collected. The methods discussed under intelligence and interactivity above will be central in providing this information.

Independence of location

Independence of location relates to the geographical location of the company. This is of benefit to many organisations as the use of electronic media means that no matter where the organisation is physically located, it can potentially serve markets anywhere in the world.

However, independence of location is unlikely to be particularly useful to CAR as it is stated that the majority of customers live within two hours' drive in order to benefit from local service and support. The type of cars sold by CAR are commodities with many competitors throughout the country selling similar models. Often these will also be garages that offer local service and support.

Independence of location would be more relevant to CAR were it to change focus and sell classic or rare and collectible cars as potential customers are more likely to travel a long distance for something they perceive to be a 'one-off'. However, the long lease on CAR's premises means that any opportunity to relocate to a cheaper location that would allow CAR to take advantage of independence of location could not be taken.

One factor in independence of location that would be relevant to CAR is the fact that electronic media is available at all hours (24/7), whenever the customer wishes to make use of it. Potential buyers can access information at a time convenient to them and, if the suggestions made under interactivity are implemented, they will be able to book a test drive or arrange a service at their convenience online, rather than having to arrange this during office hours.

(b) Procurement relates to organisational purchasing and involves locating items of the right **price**, that are available at the right **time**, of the right **quality**, in the right **quantity** and from the right **source**. E-procurement looks at the potential opportunities that can be gained from automating aspects of the procurement process.

CAR is involved in two very different procurement processes: production-related procurement (cars) and non-production procurement (office supplies etc).

Production-related procurement

The purchase of cars and parts is directly linked to the core activities of the organisation. CAR uses experienced buyers to purchase its cars in person at auctions at the cost of $500 per day. On average, five cars per day are purchased, and therefore the purchasing cost of each car is $100 representing 5% of the average profit margin on each car ($100/$2,000).

This cost could be eliminated if cars were instead purchased through **e-auctions**, where bids are made online. However, this could be risky as it is not possible to physically inspect the car prior to purchase. This risk could be minimised if the technique is only used to buy cars that are less than two years old with a full service history.

Non-production procurement

CAR currently orders parts needed for service and maintenance from motor factors or manufacturers. CAR has long-term relationships with a number of regular suppliers and employs a systematic sourcing method.

In the current process, all requisitions have to be passed through the procurement manager incurring cost, delay and customer frustration. A backlog of requisitions has built up, which creates particular problems when a customer's car is in the garage awaiting a part. Not only is the customer annoyed by the delay, but the garage space cannot be put to other, more profitable use.

This is made worse by the restricted working hours of the manager. Urgent requisitions can only be processed when he is at work and the growing backlog is placing him under increased strain, leading to increases in costly mistakes. This has also led to increased frustration among the mechanics who, despite working longer hours, can only make orders when the procurement manager is also at work.

E-procurement could help reduce these problems by providing a procurement system which gives mechanics the authorisation to order parts at any time, up to a pre-defined limit through agreed internet channels. This should speed up repairs and services, reduce cost and lead to an increase in customer goodwill.

CAR could also use e-procurement to facilitate the competitive bidding for the supply of parts over the internet. They would do this by publishing their requirements on their website and inviting suppliers to bid. This would mean that CAR could gain the lowest price for each part by using many different suppliers. If this is combined with just-in-time supply, the costs of holding inventory could be significantly reduced.

Stationery and office supplies are also ordered regularly by CAR and fall into the category of non-production procurement. E-procurement can be equally helpful here to help CAR to lower the costs of the purchasing cycle and so improve profitability without selling more products.

With cheap, standardised items such as stationery, the cost of procurement can exceed the cost of the goods. E-procurement should lead to the easier identification of cheap suppliers and allow spot sourcing to fulfil immediate needs.

Overall CAR can greatly benefit from e-procurement as it should reduce the burden on the procurement manager, allowing him to focus on more strategic aspects of the procurement process.

22 BeauCo

Top tips. Part (a). The fact that there has been a fraud should have raised concerns about the adequacy of BeauCo's control processes.

A good approach to use is to identify the different types of controls which should be in operation, and then to assess where the controls are weak. Once you have analysed the weaknesses, you then also need to suggest 'practical recommendations' to overcome them.

Adopting this kind of approach – analyse a weakness; identify recommendation to address that weakness – should help you to structure your answer.

Part (b). The board want to get a 'better understanding' of the terms, so you should begin your answer with a brief explanation of each term. Then you need to advise why the concepts are important for BeauCo – this should have been relatively clear, provided you identified the importance of IT to the company's operations (and therefore the potential impact that disruption to IT systems could have on BeauCo's business). As the requirement specifies that you include a reference to the use of cloud computing it is important that you relate this to the situation at BeauCo.

Marking scheme

		Marks
(a)	Up to 2 marks for a discussion of the different types of controls at BeauCo	Max 2
	Up to 2 marks for each control weakness identified at BeauCo	Max 8
	Up to 2 marks for each practical recommendation for improving the controls	Max 8
	Up to a maximum of 16 marks for part (a)		16
(b)	1 mark for an explanation of continuity planning and disaster recovery	Max 1
	Up to 3 marks for the significance of continuity planning at BeauCo	Max 3
	Up to 3 marks for the significance of disaster recovery to BeauCo	Max 3
	Up to 2 marks for a discussing cloud computing at BeauCo	Max 2
	Up to a maximum of 9 marks for part (b)		9
		25

(a) **Adequacy of BeauCo's internal controls**

A number of weaknesses in BeauCo's internal controls significantly contributed to the payroll system fraud.

Operational controls

Operational controls are aimed at ensuring that an organisation's day-to-day activities run effectively. Most organisations establish operational controls aimed at influencing an individual's behaviour. Strong internal company policies often stop situations arising which lead to one individual having too much power over a particular function. This is often achieved through ensuring a segregation of duties.

Until recently there appears to have been a segregation of duties in the payroll department with the payroll supervisor reviewing the work processed by the payroll officer. This arrangement worked adequately until the supervisor went off on maternity leave, thereby giving the payroll officer complete control over the payroll system.

To compound matters, the finance department failed to follow company policy when querying the rise in staff costs. Such deviations should have been brought to the attention of the head of production, not the operations manager of the component parts department. This failing represents a significant weakness in BeauCo's internal control environment which must be rectified to avoid similar instances arising in the future.

Recommendation

The board at BeauCo need to ensure that at all times two or more individuals are involved in the processing of key information such as the monthly payroll. During times of staff absence it is important that an appropriate individual is designated to fill in and conduct a review of any processing before payment is made.

As BeauCo is a medium-sized company there may be some difficulty in assigning an individual to this role, as there are less staff available to choose from than there might be if it was a large company. Ideally such a review should be carried out by an independent member of staff, but as this concerns pay it is likely that this task should be carried out by a member of senior management, such as the HR Director or the Finance Director.

Furthermore, the board should communicate the importance to the finance team of following company policy when it comes to approving deviations in expenses. This could be supplemented by providing a reminder of the management authority hierarchy.

Controls over physical access

Physical access controls are aimed at stopping unauthorised individuals from accessing an entity's assets, including its IT assets. Such measures are also directed at preventing physical damage to the IT infrastructure which may occur as a result of natural hazards, including fires and flooding.

It is evident that BeauCo have been proactive in enhancing its physical access controls as the company had recently moved to install a pass code entry system on its internal doors. However, the effectiveness of these controls has been undermined as the glitches in the system have not been addressed, meaning that doors to rooms containing systems with confidential information on them have been left unlocked.

Recommendation

BeauCo should move to correct the current situation by ensuring that the pass code system is fixed. All staff requiring access to these areas should then be provided with their own personal entry number. To supplement this it is recommended that a log of all employee door codes is maintained. When an employee leaves BeauCo it is important that the individual's pass code is deactivated to prevent potential unauthorised access in the future.

To reduce the likely impact on BeauCo's IT assets in the event of a natural disaster such as a fire, it is recommended that if a ceiling sprinkler system has not already been installed, one should be introduced. Other measures could include the installation of fire doors and air conditioned 'cold rooms' to help maintain IT servers in the event of a fire.

Control over logical access

Logical access controls are aimed at ensuring that only authorised users of IT systems are provided with access. Such measures are directed towards identifying and confirming the authenticity of the user. A common mechanism in protecting computerised data is through the use of passwords.

At BeauCo the ability to set passwords on the HR system was disabled as it was regarded as being too cumbersome. This played a significant part in the fraud as it allowed the payroll officer easy access to employees' standing data.

Recommendation

The password control mechanism was put in place to prevent unauthorised access to highly confidential information. The move to disable the security settings should not have been decided by the HR department (and should not have happened at all). Such decisions should only be determined by senior management. To overcome this issue it is recommended that passwords are used on all systems. It needs to become a matter of company policy that all employees are expected to use and regularly update their computer password. Breaches of policy should be treated as a disciplinary matter.

Controls over data input

Controls over data input are aimed at ensuring the quality of the system's output. The focus of such mechanisms is to ensure that only valid data is accepted by the system. Data validation is likely to centre upon ensuring that data entered into a system has been posted to the correct account codes, that only acceptable values are allowed and that input data is in a suitable format.

A key failure in the controls over BeauCo's payroll system was that the payroll officer was able to input new overtime entries significantly higher than the average monthly amounts without the system flagging this. It is evident that no higher level permission was required to post these entries to the payroll.

However, the payroll system's most prominent failing was that the software actually allowed the entry of three bogus employees each with the same bank account details. Most modern payroll and accounting systems are designed to detect and reject duplicate entries. This underlying failure with BeauCo's payroll software suggests that the system perhaps lacks functionality due to its age or was not properly configured when initially installed.

Recommendation

It is recommended that the payroll system has predetermined entry limits. Therefore, any entries input which exceed the processing limit will require a user with a higher level of authority to approve the posting. Furthermore, it is highly recommended that management investigate the weaknesses in the actual software to prevent further instances of duplicated entries occurring. This may require the purchase of a newer payroll application to replace the existing system.

(b) ### Continuity planning

Continuity planning is focused on ensuring the survival of an organisation and its operations in the face of short-term adversity. Many internal weaknesses and external threats exist which could have a severe impact on an organisation's ability to achieve its long-term objectives and ultimate survival. Events including natural disasters (eg fire and floods) and computer network failures (eg supply chain interruption) are likely to be highly detrimental to an organisation's operations.

Continuity planning is concerned with having in place courses of action directed towards combating and preventing the significant risks an organisation faces. Given the extensive use of computers in modern business, a strong focus of continuity planning is devoted to protecting IT assets (disaster recovery).

Most large organisations today produce business continuity plans which detail key parts of an organisation's operations to assist with operational recovery in the event of a risk materialising. Plans often include details about key personnel, customer and supplier contacts and related information about the entity's data back-ups.

Disaster recovery

Disaster recovery is part of continuity planning. It is predominantly concerned with the processes and procedures that an organisation uses to allow its IT systems to continue in operation in the event of a disaster occurring. In the event of critical functions being interrupted, a company's disaster recovery processes are directed at restoring the organisation's operations within an acceptable time frame.

Importance for BeauCo

Continuity planning and disaster recovery are important for BeauCo due to the company's reliance on IT. BeauCo's operations are dependent on its online procurement and inventory management systems to enable the completion of customer orders. Furthermore, the company makes all of its sales through its website.

Such reliance on IT and information systems increases the potential impact that technology failure, malicious attacks on the company's website and natural disasters may have on BeauCo's IT performance.

Trading conditions

The competitive nature of the computer components industry increases the likelihood that BeauCo could suffer significantly in the event of any risk materialising. Damage caused to BeauCo's website in the event of a malicious attack by a third party could potentially leave the company unable to take customer orders. The competitive nature of the market suggests that customers may choose to shop elsewhere should BeauCo's website be out of action for any significant amount of time. Any such problems with the company's website would need to be addressed as quickly as possible to avoid losing key customers.

BeauCo's disaster recovery plan could address such an issue by allowing orders to be taken over the phone while the IT team recovers the website.

Similar problems could also occur should there be a technology failure with the online procurement system. An inability to order materials to meet demand will likely lead to lost custom and potentially leave the manufacturing department unable to operate.

Back-ups

At the current time, BeauCo takes a back up of all information stored on its computer system every three months. Taking a copy of all information is best practice as it allows the company to continue its operations with limited disruption should there be a systems failure. To maximise the effectiveness of this measure, BeauCo should look to ensure that a system back-up is taken much more frequently than at present, for example on a daily basis. It has become common practice in most industries that back up information is stored offsite, or in the cloud, in the event that the site of the company's IT infrastructure is destroyed.

Cloud computing

The growing use of cloud computing in business is helping to drive down the associated costs of cloud-based data storage when compared to the costs involved in purchasing 'owned' hardware. As such cloud computing may form a key element of BeauCo's approach to disaster recovery. Cloud computing would enable workers at BeauCo to access the company's data anywhere in the world, and would help to overcome any disruption caused when attempting to access data in the event of a disaster event disabling the company's existing IT infrastructure.

This approach is not without its problems as the use of a third party cloud-based storage service would require BeauCo to give up control of its data which heightens the potential for it to be stolen, lost or corrupted. Careful consideration would also need to be given to any restrictions imposed by data protection regulations especially if BeauCo intends to store personal data on a third party cloud computing platform.

23 Flamingo

Marking scheme

			Marks
(a)	Up to 2 marks for a discussion of the benefits of using the app	Max 8	
	Up to 2 marks for a discussion of each risk of using the app	Max 8	
	Up to a maximum of 15 marks		15
(b)	Up to 2 marks for each problem identified	Max 6	
	Up to 2 marks for each control recommended	Max 6	
	Up to a maximum of 10 marks for part (b)		10
			25

(a) Benefits of using the AI app

Tailored service

Flamingo operates in a competitive fast-moving industry and needs to offer something different to customers if it wishes to continue to thrive. Using digital technology will move their service from a generic one to one that is tailored to the requirements of each individual shopper. The app acts like a personal shopper for the customer and removes the main flaw with online clothes shopping: determining the right size without first trying an item on.

Reduced cost

If the app proves effective customers will receive clothes that fit and suit them since they have had the opportunity to try the clothes on virtually. This will reduce the cost to Flamingo, in terms of postage, returns administration and also the costs associated with destroying or restocking the items.

Improved CSR

Use of AI via the app will serve to reduce the volume of clothing returns since customers are more likely to buy clothes that fit/suit them. Flamingo will be able to respond effectively to media claims that its sales strategy is wasteful. Instead Flamingo can use the app to demonstrate its commitment to CSR and improve the company's perception in the eyes of the customer.

Customer loyalty

The app is new technology, not yet in common usage in the retail sector. It therefore acts as a point of differentiation and renders the online shopping process as close to shopping in person as possible. The more the customer uses the service the more the AI functionality will learn about the customer, making it increasingly able to identify the right clothing for each shopper. This is likely to deliver higher customer satisfaction and increase loyalty to Flamingo.

Increased sales

As with any AI technology the more data that Flamingo captures about the customer the easier it will be to persuade customers to make a purchase. With the introduction of the app Flamingo can combine size and style knowledge with purchase history. The AI database can rapidly review a customer's individual data to make real-time suggestions as customers browse the website. This is likely to increase the chances of a customer placing an item in their basket and committing to the purchase.

Risks of using the AI app

Reliance on IT/IS

The new app relies on the technology and information systems functioning correctly which gives rise to some increased risks. It is not clear how much expertise Flamingo has in this area and to ensure a seamless service it may need to consider outsourcing the development and maintenance of the app to a specialist company.

Data protection

For the app to be effective a large amount of data has to be collected and stored. The data gathered by Flamingo will include personal customer data, including financial details and personal images, which could be at risk from a cyber attack like that experienced by competitors. Any loss of data would damage customer confidence and potentially result in fines from breaching data protection regulations.

Costs

The introduction of the new app will require high levels of investment in designing the app, purchasing the physical hardware and software and maintaining the system so that it can cope with the volume of traffic that Flamingo sees. As an emerging technology these costs are likely to be significant.

Lack of empathy

The app is designed to showcase which clothes fit and suit the customer. However, AI does not have the human ability to use tact and subtlety if an item is not the right style or shape for a customer's physique. If care is not taken when designing the chatbot, customers could be offended by the chatbot's comments with regard to an item of clothing not being the right fit. In turn this could damage customer relations with Flamingo.

Conclusion

The introduction of the AI app has the potential to significantly improve the service offered to Flamingo's customers, leading to increased customer sales and loyalty. However, the technology is not without risks. The costs of the system and the necessary security measures need to be considered in the light of the benefits that these will bring.

(b) **Problems arising from a cyber-attack**

Damaged reputation

A cyber-attack resulting in a breach of customers' personal data will damage trust with customers. Flamingo operates in a competitive environment and customers have low switching costs so any damage to confidence will lead to customers shopping elsewhere. Due to the number of new entrants and lack of loyalty in the industry Flamingo would then need to work very hard to rebuild customer confidence.

Fines - breach of data protection rules

Flamingo has a duty of care to protect customers' personal and financial data. Data protection regulations aim to ensure this and fines are levied to companies that fail to do so. Such fines can be expensive as well as contributing further to any negative publicity surrounding a cyber-attack.

Financial loss

A cyber-attack of any scale is likely to lead to financial loss for Flamingo. There may be theft of financial information or even of money. For example, a ransomware attack is a type of malware that requests a ransom before users can regain access to their system. There will certainly be disruption to normal trading from systems failing temporarily or from a need to shut down the website to investigate and resolve the problem. Reputation damage, as discussed above, will lead to a loss of sales as customers lose trust in Flamingo.

Controls to minimise risk

Risk management culture

It is important that the tone for risk management is set at board level so that Flamingo is encouraged to embed a culture of sound risk management across the business. It is good corporate governance to have effective risk management in place with cyber risk being a specific risk that the board should take responsibility for. A Non-Executive Director should be assigned responsibility to keep the main board informed of cyber threats and to ensure that risk management policies are in place.

Network security

Security around Flamingo's network needs to be reviewed and tightened where necessary. Firewalls must be updated regularly and employees asked to reset their passwords frequently. Restrictions should be placed on the use of mobile data storage such as USB memory drives and home-based employees should access Flamingo's network via a secure Virtual Private Network (VPN). Specialist advice may be required to assess whether the software and security controls used are fit for purpose.

Employee training

Employees need to be made aware of all the different types of cyber risk and what they can do to prevent them. Cyber risk is constantly evolving so training should not be a 'one-off' event. Flamingo could make use of online training as well as visual reminders (posters) placed around offices or on the company intranet.

Data back ups

In the event of a cyber-attack Flamingo needs to be able to resume operations as quickly as possible to minimise financial and reputational damage. Flamingo should therefore ensure that all data is securely backed up to allow the business to reduce any disruption or downtime caused by an attack.

Insurance

Whilst it is important to implement controls to reduce the chance and limit the impact of a cyber attack, Flamingo would be advised to take out insurance against any losses incurred in the event of an attack. In this way, shareholders are shielded as much as possible from financial loss.

24 Yaya

> **Top tips.** Part (a): the reference to 'typical reasons' indicates that this task is primarily a test of knowledge, and so you don't have to relate your answer to the scenario, although the scenario could help to remind you of some of the reasons (for example, collusion between staff). Note that (a) is only worth 5 marks though, so if you use points from the scenario, be careful to avoid making points in (a) that you then repeat in (b). Also, note that the verb is 'explain' (rather than 'identify' or 'list' for example, so to score well, you need to provide sufficient explanation of each reason you include.
>
> By contrast to (a), your answer to (b) does need to relate specifically to the scenario. A sensible approach to this task would be to identify the internal control deficiencies in the scenario, and then use each 'deficiency' as a heading in your answer, with a paragraph explaining the

implications (or significance) of the deficiency and how it contributed to increased product failure.

Part (c): although there was no requirement to use a specific framework here, it could have been helpful to use the 'ACCURATE' mnemonic to remind yourself of the qualities of good information. You don't need to bring in all the categories, although most are relevant here. Importantly, though, as well as discussing the qualities of good information in general terms, you also need to relate them specifically to the scenario in order to show how they would be of benefit to Mr Janoon.

Note also the final part of the task: to recommend 'specific measures' which would improve the information flow from the QC lab to Mr Janoon. Try to think about specific, practical improvements which are relevant to the scenario. For example, we know that Mr Janoon rarely visited the lab, so one way to improve information flows could be for him to visit the lab more often.

Marking scheme

		Marks
(a)	1 mark for each relevant point explaining why an internal control might be ineffective (Capped at ½ mark for each reason identified but not explained)	
	Up to a maximum for part (a) of 5 marks	5
(b)	Up to 2 marks for each relevant internal deficiency explained	
	Up to a maximum for part (b) of 10 marks	10
(c)	Up to 2 marks for each quality discussed in the context of the case (Capped at ½ mark for identifying general qualities of useful information, without stating how they would benefit Mr Janoon)	Max 6
	Up to 2 marks for each relevant measure recommended	Max 4
	Up to a maximum for part (c) of 10 marks	10
		25

(a)   **Reasons why an internal control system can be ineffective**

Mistakes or poor judgement

The successful operation of many controls depends on the **people operating them**. Staff may fail to operate controls because, for example, they are tired or **do not understand** what they have to do. They may **make errors** operating controls, for example incorrectly failing an item they have tested.

Collusion between staff

Segregation of different tasks is a key aspect of control systems, as is the **involvement of more than one staff member in activities** so that staff know that someone else will see what they are doing. Fraudulent collusion between staff, as here, undermines segregation and oversight. John Zong did not report Jane Goo's fraud because she involved him in it.

Management over-ride

Senior management may be able to insist that certain activities or transactions are not subject to controls that would normally operate. Staff operating the controls may **lack the authority or be unwilling to challenge** senior managers.

Coping with unusual situations

Control systems may be designed to cope with an organisation's **routine transactions**. If transactions occur that are out of the ordinary, it may be difficult to apply controls. Similarly if unforeseen circumstances arise, normal controls may become irrelevant.

Deterioration over time

Controls may be designed to cope with a set of circumstances and business environment that **changes over time**, making the controls less relevant. Staff also may become less conscientious about applying controls over time, particularly if they are dissatisfied with the organisation.

(b) **Internal control weaknesses**

No check on Jane's activities

No-one **reviewed the compliance work** that Jane had done to see if it was correct. There was **no need for a second signature. No one saw the quality control reports** after they had been filed. Jane was thus able to file fraudulent reports.

Failure to deal with products that had failed

Yaya relied on Jane Goo to **dispose of the products** that had failed. It did not insist that the goods were returned and disposed of independently. It thus gave Jane the **opportunity** to sell the products that she incorrectly claimed had failed.

Opportunity for collusion between Jane and John

There was collusion between Jane and John. Both considered themselves to be **poorly paid** and both **derived financial benefit** from the fraud. The **isolation of the QC facility** meant that for the fraud to be successful, only two people needed to be involved.

Identification of increased failure rate

There was **no automatic reporting** of the increase in the failure rate. An **acceptable failure rate** had **not been established**. Hence there was no trigger that the rate was excessive. Since the failure rate increased gradually, it did not become noticeable for quite some time.

Failure of supervision

Ben Janoon failed to carry out a **number of supervisory checks**. He did **not visit the site very often**, did **not insist on automatic reporting** and **failed for a long time to spot an increase in failure rates**. Possibly as he designed the systems, he had misplaced confidence that they would work properly.

(c) **Qualities of useful information**

Accurate

Information needs to be **accurate, complete, unbiased and reliable**. Ben Janoon needed to be able to trust the information that he was receiving. If Ben Janoon had had accurate information, he would have been able to assess whether there was a problem with products failing quality checks.

Cost-beneficial

The value of the information needs to **outweigh the costs of collecting it**. Clearly there would be costs involved in scrapping faulty products. Therefore feedback from the QC lab could enable Ben Janoon to see why products were failing and isolate where in the production process problems might be occurring.

User-targeted

Readers of the information need to be able to **understand it** and clearly **grasp the salient points**. This is particularly important when the user does not have the same level of knowledge as the preparer of the information. Although Ben Janoon did not have a science degree, the QC lab ought to be able to supply a summary of the results of its testing that he could **understand** and based on which he could **make decisions**.

Relevant

Information needs to be relevant to the user's requirements, with anything that is not useful excluded. This means that the QC lab should report anything that **impacts upon Ben Janoon's responsibility for operations**. This includes overall impressions of quality, as well as changes in failure rates.

Timely

Information needs to be **available when it is needed**. The user needs to have time to **process the information and use it for decision making**. If, for example, there had been a sudden large increase in the failure rate of products, Ben Janoon would need to be informed immediately due to the costs involved.

Specific measures

More frequent reports

Ben Janoon could require the QC lab to provide **regular reports**, weekly or monthly, of failure rates and other metrics. These would help identify upward trends requiring investigation at an earlier stage.

Greater detail

The information supplied could have been **much more detailed**, with a breakdown of why products had failed, ideally **measured against precise metrics**. This would have provided useful operational information for Ben Janoon and made it more difficult for Jane Goo to fake results, as she would have to have supplied reasons for each failure. The information also ought to be in a format specified by Ben Janoon to ensure that he, and not Jane Goo, controlled the information flow.

Physical contact

Ben Janoon could make **more frequent visits** to the QC lab to see what is going on there. One reason for the QC lab staff feeling that they could get away with the deception was that they were rarely visited and their work was not monitored in other ways. The QC lab needs to be seen as a more important function at Yaya. Moving it to a more central site may assist this.

25 Anne Hayes

> **Top tips.** Part (a): the scenario seems to be emphasising the long-standing relationship between Fillmore Pierce and Van Buren, and Van Buren's importance as a client. This should have highlighted the threat that 'familiarity' could reduce Fillmore's independence. However, when describing three threats you need to apply these specifically to the case, rather than simply describing 'familiarity' or 'self-interest', for example, in general terms.
>
> Thinking about this question in the context of professional ethics could also help you think about the overall reasons why auditor independence is important – particularly in relation to the accountancy profession's responsibility to act in the public interest.
>
> The dilemma highlighted in (b) is whether an accountant should uphold professional standards or let things go in order to have an easier life and promote their employer's interests. Note that the requirement is 'Compare and contrast' so it is important that you consider Anne's responsibilities as an employee of Fillmore Pierce, as well as considering her responsibilities as a professional accountant.

Marks

(a) 1 mark for each relevant point explaining the importance of auditor
      independence   Max 3
      1 mark for each relevant threat to auditor independence identified
        from the case   Max 3
      1 mark for each threat to auditor independence briefly described   Max <u>3</u>
      Up to a maximum for part (a) of 9 marks   9

(b) (i)   1 mark for each organisational duty identified and briefly
            described   Max 3
            1 mark for each professional duty identified and briefly   Max 3
            described
            1 mark for each potential point of conflict identified between the
              duties   Max <u>2</u>
      Up to a maximum of 6 marks for part (b) (i)   6
      (ii) 1 mark per relevant point explaining the ethical tensions Anne faces

            (between her role as an employee and as a professional
            accountant)
      Up to a maximum for part (b)(ii) of 4 marks   <u>4</u>
                                                                                          <u>19</u>

(a) **Necessity for independence**

Reliability of financial information

Corporate governance reports have highlighted **reliability of financial information** as a key aspect of corporate governance. Shareholders and other stakeholders need a trustworthy record of **directors' stewardship** to be able to take decisions about the company. Assurance provided by independent auditors is a key quality control on the reliability of information.

Credibility of financial information

An unqualified report by independent external auditors on the accounts should give them more **credibility**, enhancing the appeal of the company to investors. It should represent the views of independent experts, who are not motivated by personal interests to give a favourable opinion on the annual report.

Value for money of audit work

Audit fees should be set on the basis of charging for the work **necessary to gain sufficient audit assurance**. A lack of independence here seems to mean important audit work may not be done, and thus the shareholders are not receiving value for the audit fees.

Threats to professional standards

A lack of independence may lead to a failure to **fulfil professional requirements** to obtain enough evidence to form the basis of an audit opinion, here to obtain details of a questionable material item. Failure by auditors to do this **undermines the credibility of the accountancy profession** and the standards it enforces.

Threats to independence

Familiarity with client

Zachary Lincoln has been partner in charge of the audit for **longer than the period recommended by most governance reports** (between five and seven years). His familiarity appears to have influenced his judgement, leading him to make the dubious assumption that because there has been no problem on this audit in the past, there cannot be a problem now.

Personal friendship – self-interest

Zachary Lincoln appears to be **allowing his personal friendship** with Frank Monroe to **bias his judgement** on whether to investigate the questionable payment. There is a **self-interest threat** involved in Zachary's wish to maintain the friendship, and also a **lack of objectivity.**

Non-audit services – self-interest

Governance codes identify **provision of non-audit services** as a potentially significant threat to auditor independence. This scenario illustrates why; a **qualified opinion** on Van Buren's accounts may mean that the company stops using Fillmore Pierce to provide consultancy services. Thus it is clearly in Fillmore Pierce's **self-interest to give an unmodified audit opinion,** and therefore it seems doubtful that the firm is truly independent.

(b) (i) **Obedience**

As an employee Anne owes the duty of **obedience** to her **managers,** and should comply with reasonable orders provided they do not breach her professional duties.

As a professional accountant Anne should comply with the **technical and ethical standards established by her professional body,** even if these conflict with what she is being required to do in the workplace.

Interests of employer and profession

As an employee, Anne has a responsibility to **promote the interests of her employer.** These include the **commercial, fee-earning, interests,** making efforts to obtain new work and keep existing clients happy.

As a professional accountant, Anne has a responsibility to maintain the good name of her accountancy body. This includes acting **honestly and objectively,** and not allowing herself to be associated with misleading information or a misleading report.

Obligations of employment and membership

As an employee, Anne owes a general duty to **'fit in'**, be part of a team and behave in ways that are in accordance with the **organisational culture** of her employer.

As a member of a professional accounting body, Anne owes the duty to act in accordance with the **norms** of that body, including its stress on **professional behaviour.**

(ii) **Acting non-commercially**

The main tension between the roles that Anne is experiencing is that if she acts in accordance with professional standards, and pursues a full explanation for the payment, she will not be acting in her employer's **commercial interests**. The audit will go on longer than budgeted, meaning that the assignment is **less profitable**. She also risks upsetting the client and **putting future income at risk.**

Anne's own interests

There is also the issue of whether Anne should take into account her own interests and if so how she should do this. She may feel that in order to make her life **easier as an employee** of Fillmore Pierce, she should allow the report to be signed. Against this is the fact that, as a newly qualified accountant, she will want to uphold the ethical principles of competence and due care. If she allows the report to be signed (and in doing so, overlooks the irregularity) this would mean she has not upheld the **ethical principles of her profession**. This could be a particular concern if the irregularity subsequently turns out to be material, and therefore the audit report, in turn, is misleading.

BPP
LEARNING
MEDIA

26 Blup

Marking scheme

			Marks
(a)	Up to 2 marks for a general explanation of the role of internal audit	Max 2	
	Up to 2 marks for each relevant point discussing the importance of internal audit in a highly regulated industry	Max 6	
	Up to a maximum of 7 marks for part (a)		7
(b) (i)	Up to 2 marks for each relevant point assessing weaknesses or failings of Blup Co's audit committee		
	Up to a maximum of 6 marks for part (b)(i)		6
(ii)	Up to 2 marks for each relevant point explaining why the audit committee is responsible for overseeing the internal audit function		
	Up to a maximum of 6 marks for part (b)(ii)		6
(c)	Up to 2 marks for each relevant discussion point about how internal controls can provide assurance on the integrity of financial reporting		
	Up to a maximum of 6 marks for part (c)		6
			25

(a)   **Internal audit**

Internal audit is an **independent appraisal function** within an organisation that examines and evaluates its activities. It acts as a **service**, helping employees carry out their responsibilities. Its remit includes review of accounting systems, internal controls, risk management, compliance and value for money.

Internal audit in regulated industries

Compliance

Internal audit is particularly important for organisations in regulated industries because they need to comply with **stringent external requirements**. Non-compliance may result in very serious consequences, for example loss of a licence to operate or substantial fines. Internal auditors therefore need to focus on whether systems to ensure compliance are **appropriate** and **operate effectively**, and **investigate suspected incidents of non-compliance**. This monitoring and testing role is required to provide management with sufficient assurance that compliance is taking place.

Information provision

As well as compliance with technical regulations, organisations in regulated industries are required to produce information and reports for regulators. Regulators require **assurance** that the organisation's information systems are **capable of producing reliable information** and the **information produced is correct**. Appraisal of systems and examination of information by an internal audit function that is independent of those producing that information provides that assurance.

Reputation

Apart from legal penalties, a regulated organisation's reputation for **compliance and fair dealing** is also a **strategic asset**. Failure to comply may lead to pressure from government that may threaten the organisation's continued existence in its current form. Non compliance may also result in protests by consumers and pressures to compensate them if failure to meet regulations has damaged their interests.

(b)   (i)   **Lack of financial knowledge and experience**

Karen's comments about the importance of controls over financial reporting highlights the **lack of financial expertise** that the three non-executive directors have. All three may be qualified to advise on technical risks relating to the water industry, but the comfort they can give on financial reporting is limited. For example, the Sarbanes-Oxley (2002) legislation requires one member of the audit committee to be a **financial expert** and other jurisdictions have similar requirements.

Lack of independence

Most jurisdictions require audit committee members to be independent non-executive directors. However, none of the directors on Blup's audit committee would qualify as independent under generally accepted practice, since they have all **recently been executive directors**. Some jurisdictions impose a time limit before a retired executive director can become a non-executive. In any case there are obvious ethical issues. Early on, the non-executive directors may be considering the consequences of board decisions made when they were executive directors. Relationships built up with other executives may also impair their objectivity.

Independence of audit partner

One key function of the audit committee is to consider **threats to external auditor independence**. Blup's audit committee appears not to have done this. They have not identified a situation where a close personal relationship between the lead partner and Chair poses a problem of familiarity, which is identified as a threat to independence in professional codes.

(ii) **Objectives of internal audit**

The audit committee is responsible for setting the **objectives and terms of reference of internal audit**. As directors on the full board, audit committee members will also be involved in establishing Blup's strategic objectives. They thus should be able to ensure that internal audit work is **focused on areas that are important to the strategy of the company** and that audit work concentrates on **risks that threaten achievement** of strategic aims.

Compliance requirements

The audit committee should also be able to ensure that sufficient internal audit attention is given to reviewing **compliance with the regulations that the company faces**. Here certainly the industry knowledge that audit committee members have should ensure that internal audit work is directed into **the** right areas.

Independence

Reporting to the audit committee and being able to communicate with the audit committee without executives being present **helps maintain the independence of the internal audit function**. Audit committee members have no executive responsibilities, and so audit committee members will have **no self-interest** in diverting internal audit's attention away from their area of the business. This should mean that internal audit is not compromised by pressure from operational management.

Authority

Reporting to the audit committee means that internal audit has authority **delegated from the audit committee**. This should give internal audit the power it needs to enforce its demands and obtain the access it requires to people and documents.

(c) **Importance of financial reporting**

Shareholders rely on financial reporting as the **basis for making decisions about their investment** in the company. They therefore need to have confidence in this information. To provide shareholders with this assurance, most corporate governance codes require companies to report on controls over financial reporting.

Information systems

Effective internal controls should ensure that companies produce **timely, relevant and reliable information** that underpins accurate financial accounts and aids management decision making. Controls ensuring that assets and transactions are recorded completely and appropriately measured, accounting entries are recorded correctly and that cut-off has been applied properly should ensure that systems produce information that can be trusted and that uncertainties surrounding figures are minimised.

Personnel

Effective personnel controls can help give significant assurance about financial reporting. They can ensure that **accountability for key tasks** such as producing information is clearly defined. Controls can ensure that organisational structures have **segregation of duties built in as an important check on activities. They should also ensure that staff have sufficient knowledge and competence** for the tasks that they undertake, in particular that everyone is well briefed on current financial reporting requirements.

Audit trail

Financial reporting controls should also assist in providing a **detailed audit trail** that can be followed by internal or external auditors. This should make it easy for auditors to **analyse the reliability and correctness of the information** provided and means that their work can provide greater assurance. If auditors find errors, a detailed audit trail may make it easier to assess how the errors occurred and make correction of errors easier.

27 World Engines

> **Top tips.** Part (a): the scenario clearly identifies the expected returns at each level of demand, and the likelihood (probability) of each level of demand occurring. Therefore, if you work methodically through the information in the scenario, you should be able to construct the decision tree relatively easily. Remember that when calculating the expected value from each supplier's product you need to subtract the cost of the product, as well as calculating the expected returns.
>
> Also, note that part (a) doesn't only require you to do a calculation, you are also asked to discuss the 'implications and shortcomings' of the decision tree. For example, given the difficulty of predicting demand, how much reliance can actually be placed on the figures in the decision tree?
>
> Your discussion of the 'shortcomings' of the decision tree (in part (a)) should highlight the danger of basing the procurement decision on it alone. This then links into part (b) of the question which asks you to consider other factors which need to be considered.
>
> Importantly, note that part (b) asks about 'other factors', so you need to avoid repeating the same points you already made in part (a). Equally, you are not asked about other appraisal techniques which could be used to evaluate the projects. Instead, your primary focus in this part of the question should be on the non-financial factors which need to be considered in the investment decision – for example, the usability of the different products, or the relative levels of risk associated with each option.

Marking scheme

Marks

(a) Up to 5 marks for developing the decision tree

Typically this will include:

Diagram of the decision tree: 1 mark
Expected income from Amethyst: 1 mark

Expected value of Amethyst: 1 mark
Expected income from Topaz: 1 mark
Expected value of Topaz: 1 mark
Conclusion (Topaz): 1 mark   Max 5

Up to 4 marks for discussing the decision tree and its shortcomings
   (including subjective nature of probabilities, sensitivity analysis,
   and only being part of the procurement decision)   Max 4

Up to a maximum of 9 marks for part (a)   9

(b) 1 mark for each relevant point to be considered when deciding which
     option to select
     Up to a maximum of 6 marks for part (b)   6
                                                                                     ──
                                                                                     15

(a)

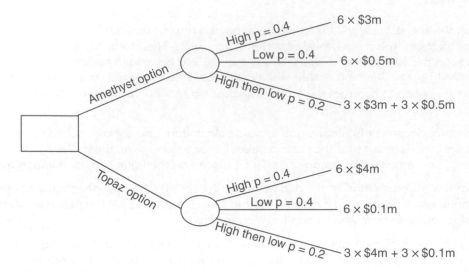

The expected value of Amethyst is:

($18m × 0.4) + ($3m × 0.4) + ($10.5m × 0.2)

= $10.5m **minus** cost of $7m

= **$3.5m**

The expected value of Topaz is:

($24m × 0.4) + ($0.6m × 0.4) + ($12.3m × 0.2)

= $12.3 **minus** cost of $8m

= **$4.3m**

The decision tree shows that Topaz has the higher expected value and therefore is the option that should be chosen.

However, there are limitations to making an investment decision based solely on the decision tree analysis as the analysis is only based on information that was available at this point in time.

The decision tree is based on probabilities that have been determined in the workshop rather than on actual past statistical data. There was debate and heated discussion in attempting to agree these figures, demonstrating the subjective nature of the data on which the analysis is based. WE should determine the sensitivity of the outcome to slight changes in the assessments of these probabilities.

The predicted returns may also be slightly inaccurate as the basis upon which these have been estimated is unclear. Again, a sensitivity analysis of the outcome to slight changes in the returns would be beneficial. The Topaz option in particular would benefit from this. The high demand predicted value of $4 represents around 78% (ie 9.6/12.3) of the total expected value of the option. If annual returns have been overestimated by, for example, 10% ($3.6m rather than $4m per annum), then Topaz would no longer have the higher expected return and as such would no longer be considered to be the best option.

There may be scope for negotiation with the potential software suppliers in regards to prices and structure. Any such possibilities may significantly affect the expected value of the two options.

The decision tree, therefore, should be only one of a range of factors and analyses on which the procurement decision is actually based.

(b)   In addition to the decision tree analysis, a number of other factors should be taken into account when making the purchasing decision. These include:

Intangible benefits

As well as the financial returns identified above the non-tangible benefits, such as the contemporary user interface offered by Topaz, should be considered. This is important as such an interface may be more user-friendly and provide a better user experience, which will increase the worth of the system to WE.

Intangible benefits of both Amethyst and Topaz should be identified and documented.

Risk assessment

A risk assessment of both options should be carried out and the findings documented. It is likely that, as an established supplier, Amethyst would be a much less risky choice than the smaller Topaz, a relative newcomer.

This risk, and any other risks that may be associated with each of the options should be documented in the business case so that it can be considered when the ultimate decision is taken.

Relative impact on the organisation

The two options operate very differently and the level of functionality and scope offered by the two products are unlikely to have the same implications for the company in terms of the degree of change they would inflict, and the effect they would have on organisational processes and responsibilities.

Effective selection procedure

All features associated with each solution should be weighted by importance so that all factors are taken into consideration. As well as financial viability, factors to consider should include the level of support available, process certification, user group effectiveness and so on. The extent to which the system is fit for purpose, its usability, flexibility and design will also have to be taken into consideration.

28 Mantis & Gear

Top tips. The verb in requirement (a) was 'analyse' which requires a combination of numerical work (to identify the key issues) and narrative work (to discuss the reasons for them).

Central to attempting this requirement was recognising the type of calculations needed. The scenario mentions concerns over pricing and cost control, and Table 1 shows that although M&G sold 27,000 more units than originally budgeted, actual sales revenue was exactly the same as the budgeted sales revenue. The difference between budgeted and actual sales volumes should have been a clue that a flexed budget would provide a more appropriate basis for assessing performance – rather than simply looking at variances between actual figures and the original budget.

To score well when attempting requirements like this, you need to explain any variances you identify. Simply stating, for example, that 'sales price variance is adverse' adds no value to the calculations you have already performed, and so will score no additional credit. However, given that we know (from the scenario) there is a competitive operating environment and the sales team focus on high volume sales to large companies, it might be reasonable to suggest that the sales team are offering discounts to secure sales – (and this could then explain the sales price variance).

Note. An alternative approach to flexing the budget might have been to compare the budgeted and actual figures per unit – and this would lead to an equivalent analysis.

When attempting requirement (b) it was important that you applied your knowledge of the business partner model to the scenario at Mantis & Gear, and avoided simply producing a list of generic benefits that this approach can bring.

Marks

(a) Up to 1 mark for each item of quantitative analysis, including variances and profitability ratios

Up to 1 mark for each appropriate qualitative point, specifically reasons for variances and how the variances contribute to the current situation

Up to 1 mark for all other qualitative points not related to variances but relevant to understanding, and/or managing, the company's performance

Up to a maximum of 15 marks for part (a)   15

(b) Up to 2 marks for explaining the meaning of the 'finance function as a business partner'

Up to 2 marks for each relevant benefit of the business partner model applied to M&G

Up to a maximum of 10 marks in total $\underline{10}$
$\underline{\underline{25}}$

(a) **Analysis of performance**

The sales manager is correct in that the sales volume has outperformed budgeted sales volume by 27,000 units, or 11.1% over budget. This is a positive sign in a situation where there is increased competition and more demanding customers.

However, profitability is much lower than budgeted, at 4.5% rather than the 24.7% budgeted, or the 27% expected if the budget was flexed to represent actual sales volume. This reduction in profitability could have a serious impact on the future sustainability of the business.

The flexed budget can be analysed to determine where performance has been worse than expected. Differences between expected and actual performance can then be investigated. The flexed budget and variances are as follows:

	Budget units	Actual units	Flexed budget	Variance to flexed budget
Sales volume	243,000	270,000	270,000	
	Budget	Actual		
	$'000	$'000	$'000	$'000
Sales revenue	36,450	36,450	40,500	4,050 Adverse
Direct materials	15,795	18,630	17,550	1,080 Adverse
Direct labour	3,402	4,725	3,780	945 Adverse
Fixed overheads	8,250	11,450	8,250	3,200 Adverse
Operating profit	9,003	1,645	10,920	

When actual performance is compared against the flexed budget, every area of performance shows an adverse variance. Although the actual sales revenue is the same as budgeted, this is from a much higher sales volume. The average selling price per unit was budgeted at $150, but the average actual selling price per unit was $135, a decrease of 10%. It may be that this was reduced in order for the sales team to hit targets, especially if their commission is based on sales volume rather than revenue. Alternatively, it could be that the price had to be reduced in order to maintain sales in the face of increased competition.

Direct materials should have cost $17.55m for the actual volume of units produced. However, they cost $18.63m, an adverse materials variance of $1.08m. This may either be due to the price or quality of materials used, but further information would be required to determine this. It is possible that price is an important factor, as the sales manager mentioned fulfilling orders with a short lead time. This may have meant that higher prices were paid if materials were sourced at short notice, or not using economic order techniques. Furthermore, it was stated that customers wanted 'more attractive' products, which may have led to more advanced component parts, thereby increasing costs. In addition, the industry is a dynamic one with rapidly developing technology; the cost of new technology may be higher than the standard costs budgeted for. This is one of the difficulties of using standard costing in an environment where products are frequently enhanced or new products developed.

Direct labour also shows an adverse variance of $945,000. This may be due to either the rate paid, or the hours worked on products. If orders were satisfied at short notice, this may have required overtime, which could have affected the labour rate variance – causing it to be higher because of enhanced overtime payments. In addition, new products or customer-specific orders may require longer working hours than well-established, standard products as they may not yet have benefited from the learning curve effect associated with standard, repeat orders.

Fixed overheads show a $3.2m adverse variance, which is 39% higher than budgeted. This is clearly a major problem and suggests that either the standard absorption rate of overheads is incorrect, or that overheads have not been monitored and controlled throughout the year. The focus on meeting increased orders may have distracted management attention from overhead control, thus leading to inefficiencies related to these costs. Overheads include those indirect elements of cost which are not specifically attributed to a product, such as cleaning materials, machine maintenance, supervisor salaries and factory rent and rates, heating and lighting. By treating them as fixed overheads, the suggestion is that they should not change with a variation in activity volumes. It is vital that the company analyses the overhead spend urgently, as this has had a major impact on profitability.

Overall, M&G should have made a budgeted profit of $10.92m on the actual sales, but instead made a profit of $1.645m, a difference of $9.275m.

One of the problems of using a standard costing system is that standard costs are based on historical information, and in a changing environment these are unlikely to remain accurate for long. It may be that the standards used in the budget are simply no longer realistic, and these need analysing before the blame is placed upon any particular department within the organisation. The suggestion of activity-based costing could certainly assist with this in terms of understanding the overheads, although it will have no impact on the labour or material standards used; these would need separate analysis.

(b) **The finance function as a business partner**

In recent times there has been a shift in the role of the modern finance function. Traditionally finance departments have only been responsible for reporting performance, and explaining deviations from budgets. An increasing number of organisations now expect the finance function to take on a more commercially-focused role than it has in the past. Today there is a greater focus on finance professionals being able to use sophisticated budgeting techniques, to have the skills to model data for decision-making purposes, and to get involved in costing up prospective strategic options. Finance professionals are now expected to participate as members of operational teams and to bring greater financial expertise to the management process.

Benefits to M&G

At present the finance function at the M&G fulfil the traditional role expected of finance professionals (processing accounting transactions and preparing month end reports). The concerns raised by Furzana Khan over M&G's approach to costing, and the need to identify unprofitable activities heightens the potential benefit for the company to adopt a business partner model.

Improved information for strategic decision-making

The increasingly competitive environment has led to M&G continually needing to develop new products or enhance its existing products. Product development is expensive and as alluded to by Furzana Khan, needs to be carefully planned to ensure that M&G does not develop unprofitable products or serve unprofitable customers. The finance function as a business partner could enhance the quality of information provided to the board when making strategic decisions relating to the types of customer served or products manufactured. The finance function operating as a business partner could combine internal financial information such as profit forecasts with external data relating to key movements in trends for electrical goods. Improved information for decision-making is also likely to lead to the setting of better quality strategic objectives.

Improved information for operational decision-making

The business partner model should enable members of the M&G finance function to provide financial expertise to operational managers. For example, helping managers like James Slater to produce more realistic sales budgets. This may help to avoid some of the issues currently being experienced with the adverse variances being reported.

Improved communication

The establishment of the finance function as a business partner may help M&G to better communicate with a broader range of internal and external stakeholders. Relevant financial and non-financial information could be prepared and interpreted for different users to suit their needs. The tasks currently undertaken by M&G's finance function solely focus on financial matters, with no apparent consideration given to non-financial issues. In light of M&G's performance it is likely that the company's directors may benefit from being provided with non-financial performance measures. Tasks such as this could be undertaken by M&G's finance team when operating as a business partner.

29 Country Car Club

Top tips. Part (a) required you to suggest and justify recommendations for outsourcing or improvement in five different process areas. There were 15 marks available, meaning three marks for each process area.

Although you did not need to mention it by name, Harmon's (2014) process-strategy matrix provides a useful framework for this question; and analysing each of the processes in terms of their strategic importance and process complexity should enable you to make sensible recommendations for all of them.

In questions like this – as is often the case with business decisions in real life – there is no definitive right answer here. Therefore, if your justification is logical and supports your recommendation you would score marks.

Part (b) focuses on the advantages of outsourcing. However, to score well, you need to make your points relevant to the scenario, rather than making general points about the advantages of outsourcing. And remember to think through the implications of any scenario fully – for example, by outsourcing its vehicle maintenance, 3C no longer needs its garage facilities meaning that it could sell them for development. The scenario told you the garage was in a residential area of the town.

Note. Part (b) relates to outsourcing of 3C's own fleet, not outsourcing the maintenance of members' cars. It is important to read the question requirement carefully to identify exactly what it is you are being asked to analyse.

Marks

(a) Up to 3 marks for the recommendation and its justification in
each of the process areas required by the question:

Attendance at breakdowns   Max 3
Membership renewal   Max 3
Vehicle insurance   Max 3
Membership queries   Max 3
Vehicle history checks   Max 3

Five process areas required, giving a maximum for part (a) of
15 marks   15

(b) Up to 2 marks for each appropriate advantage identified and
analysed

Up to a maximum for part (b) of 10 marks   10

  25

(a) When analysing 3C's processes, the BAC should consider the **complexity of the processes** and the value they add to the business – their **strategic importance**. Strategic importance and process complexity form the basis of Harmon's (2014) process-strategy matrix.

As a general rule, 3C should try to retain processes with **high strategic importance in-house**, and should consider **outsourcing processes of less strategic importance** or ones which fall **outside its core competences**.

Equally, where possible 3C should look to **automate straightforward processes** to improve efficiency, and concentrate its business process improvement efforts on its complex, dynamic processes.

(i) **Attendance at breakdowns**

Strategic importance – This is the most strategically important of all 3C's processes, and so should definitely be retained in-house.

Process complexity – Although some breakdowns may be easy to fix, others may be more complicated. The service patrol engineers need to be capable of dealing with the full range of breakdowns, as well as providing a good quality of service to customers. The range of possible situations engineers face makes this a complex process.

It appears that the speed with which engineers can attend breakdowns has already been addressed by having a range of locations across the country. However, 3C should ensure that the engineers' efficiency in solving breakdowns is maintained by ensuring they have up-to-date equipment for diagnosing and fixing faults. The engineers may also be given laptops with a database of previously observed faults for each make of car, and ways of fixing them, so that the engineers have an easily accessible reference point if they cannot immediately fix the problem themselves.

(ii) **Membership renewal**

Strategic importance – Although the membership renewal process is not strategically as important as attendance at breakdowns **it is still strategically important** for 3C because it supports 3C's core revenue stream. Therefore, it should continue to be managed in-house rather than outsourced.

Process complexity – Membership renewal should be a **relatively straightforward process,** so should be automated as far as possible to maximise efficiency.

3C already has a **bespoke computer system** for dealing with membership renewals, which indicates the process is already automated. However, the **design of the**

system could be changed to improve efficiency. Currently, members have to renew every year, and receipts are only processed when members confirm they will be renewing. A more efficient alternative would be to assume that members are continuing their membership unless they inform 3C they wish to cancel. In this way, all the routine membership renewals and receipts can be **processed automatically**, and the only transactions which require attention from staff are those where members wish to cancel their membership.

(iii) **Vehicle insurance services**

Strategic importance – Insurance is one of the new services 3C has added to its product portfolio over the last 15 years, rather than being a core product. Consequently, it is likely to have relatively low strategic importance.

Process complexity – Providing insurance services involves a number of potentially **complex processes**, most notably **assessing risks** in order to determine premiums. Providing insurance services also requires very **different skills** from those which 3C needs for its core business of breakdown assistance.

In addition, insurance business is subject to significant regulatory requirements. Consequently, 3C should look to **outsource the provision of vehicle insurance services** to a specialist insurance company. Insurance could still be offered in 3C's name, but the policies and risks would be administered and managed by the insurance company. An additional benefit of this is that the insurance company will benefit from **economies of scale** and **specialist knowledge** which 3C are unlikely to have.

(iv) **Membership queries**

Strategic importance – The quality of service which members receive is very important, because if members are not satisfied with the way their queries are handled this could lead them to cancel their membership. Phone calls about membership queries are therefore a very **important contact point between 3C and its customers,** and a fall in service levels could also affect revenues if customers do not renew their memberships. To this end, membership queries are strategically important, and therefore we would recommend the queries process should be **retained in-house.**

Nonetheless, 3C may wish to review the **location of the call centre,** because it may be able to move it to an area where property rents are lower and/or wages are cheaper than 3C is currently paying.

Process complexity – As with breakdown assistance itself, the complexity of queries is likely to vary – some will be easy, some much more complicated. Therefore, the process should be considered as **potentially complex**. Although 3C may consider having a **'Frequently Asked Questions'** section on a website customers can refer to, the main focus of the queries process needs to be on the staff working in the call centre. It will be important to ensure that **staffing levels** are sufficient to ensure customers to receive a prompt response to their queries. However, it will also be important to ensure that the call centre is not over-staffed leading to unnecessary costs.

Staff training is another key issue. 3C needs to ensure that staff are properly trained and briefed so that they can deal accurately and courteously with a wide range of queries.

(v) **Vehicle history checks**

Strategic importance – Vehicle history checks, like insurance services, **do not appear to be central to 3C's business,** and require **different competences** to the core business of breakdown assistance. Therefore they appear to have **relatively low strategic importance**.

Process complexity – The basic history check initially appears to be a relatively simple process, comparing registration details against a database of vehicle records. However, obtaining the vehicle history **may be more complicated than it first seems**, and may also have some **risks attached to it**. For example, if a vehicle has been damaged and 3C doesn't identify this, this may lead to someone buying a vehicle on the basis of inaccurate information. If the damage subsequently does come to light, the purchaser might be able to make a claim against 3C, particularly if the vehicle has been involved in an accident caused by the damage.

Consequently, 3C may be better advised to **outsource the history checks** to a specialist organisation in this field, who can operate the checks on their behalf.

(b)   3C will gain a number of advantages 3C from outsourcing the purchase and maintenance of their own vehicles. These are as follows:

Economies of scale – AutoDirect currently supplies 45,000 vehicles to companies throughout the country. This volume should allow them to negotiate discounts on the price, meaning they can buy the vehicles more cheaply than 3C could in their own name.

Also, AutoDirect may **replace vehicles more frequently** than 3C historically used to. This may have an added benefit for 3C because **fuel consumption** should be lower in the newer vehicles, thereby reducing 3C's fuel costs.

Quicker repairs and maintenance – Because 3C only had one garage from which to service its nationwide fleet of vehicles, any vehicle needing a repair had to be brought to the garage before it could be worked on. AutoDirect has nationwide repair centres, which should reduce the overall time for which 3C's vehicles are out of action while being repaired.

Easier to budget costs – The lease deal means that 3C pays a single lease payment to AutoDirect each month, and 3C knows in advance what the payment will be. When 3C maintained its own vehicles, costs could vary from one month to the next depending on the level of repairs and maintenance required. The new arrangement means that 3C can budget its costs and associated cash flows more accurately, which should assist with its working capital management.

Reduced capital requirements – Traditionally, 3C purchased its own vehicles. This is likely to have required significant levels of capital, invested in assets which only have short economic lives. Under the lease scheme with AutoDirect, 3C will be able to invest the capital elsewhere in the business.

Reduced overhead costs – 3C used to employ 30 staff in its garage to maintain its vehicle fleet, and a further three staff to purchase and dispose of vehicles. However, it no longer needs these staff, so the outsourcing deal should generate significant savings in wage costs over time (although, in the short term, 3C will have to make redundancy payments to its maintenance staff).

Profit on sale of garage – Similarly, 3C no longer needs its garage site. Given that the garage was in a residential area of a major town, 3C should seek to sell the garage site for residential development – thereby hopefully making a significant profit on the sale.

30 Finch Co

Top tips. Part (a): the scenario highlights that, although Finch Co has a loyal customer base, and currently provides excellent customer service, its performance is deteriorating. One of the reasons identified for this is that Finch has failed to match the technological developments of its competitors – and this is the context behind the question. Can Finch Co compete successfully if it doesn't develop new processes and services?

Part (b): the four views model developed by Paul et al (2010) helps organisations understand a wider range of areas that will require consideration when looking to improve a business system. Too often, senior management only concentrate on the IT aspects when enhancing a business system, so the model highlights the importance of also considering 'people', the 'organisation' and existing 'processes' within the organisation.

A sensible approach to this question would have been to use each 'view' as a heading in your answer, and then consider how the various problems identified in the scenario have been affected by that aspect of the model.

Marking scheme

			Marks
(a)	Up to 2 marks for a definition/explanation of strategic alignment	Max 2	
	Up to 2 marks for exploring real world changes in shopping behaviour	Max 2	
	Up to 3 marks for points made in support of the CEO's comment	Max 3	
	Up to a maximum of 7 marks for part (a)		7
(b)	Up to 2 marks per relevant point evaluating the extent to which aspects of organisational change highlighted in the four view model (people; processes; organisational context; technology) have contributed to the failure of the new system		
	Up to a maximum of 18 marks for part (b)		18
			25

(a)   Competitive position

Finch Co needs to ensure that it responds effectively to any opportunities or threats which could affect its performance. As such, it is important to monitor the external environment, and competitors' actions, to ensure that when any significant changes arise, Finch considers the implications of these for its own strategies. As such, responding to external change – including technological changes – is likely to be important in ensuring Finch's competitive success.

CEO's comments

Brendon Finch's comments about technological developments by Finch's competitors suggest that Finch's competitive position could be weakened if it does not introduce similar developments. Crucially, however, any new processes or services will only be beneficial to Finch if they provide value to its customers.

Changes in shopping behaviour

In recent decades, there have been significant changes in the way consumers choose to shop, and internet technologies have been a major facilitator of these developments. The demand for online shopping has seen most retailers develop e-commerce facilities; and many supermarkets provide customers with the ability to purchase goods online with either the option of home delivery or collection from store ('Click and collect').

Similarly, many retailers have introduced self-service tills, allowing customers to reduce the amount of time that they spend in store.

Competitors – Although we don't know the details of any initiatives they have introduced, it seems that Finch Co's competitors have successfully integrated technology into their operations – leading Brendon to think that Finch's failure to do the same is contributing to its declining profits.

Customer requirements – As Brendon acknowledges, customers value convenience, and offering good quality products is no longer sufficient to remain competitive, or to prevent customers defecting to rival supermarkets.

This therefore supports the argument that Finch needs to invest in new processes and services which make shopping more convenient for its customers. (The 'convenience' factor is probably the main benefit to customers of a 'click and collect' service.)

As such, the introduction of the 'click and collect' and new till systems, coupled to Finch Co offering higher quality products, should be seen as ways to help the company to remain competitive.

However, as Finch's experience demonstrates, new processes and systems will only help it remain competitive if they are appropriate for the company, and can be implemented successfully. Simply introducing new processes or systems does not, in itself, guarantee success.

(b) **Four views model (Paul et al, 2010)**

People

Lack of experience in project work

The project committee consisted of three directors, none of whom had prior experience in managing similar process improvement projects in the past. Although no details are given in the scenario, it would appear that the decision to introduce both systems at the same time was made with limited consideration of the potential implications that this may bring post-implementation. Market research and consultation with key stakeholder groups such as customers and staff may have helped to identify the potential issues before each system went live.

Furthermore, the IT department's level of experience in supporting such projects is unknown. Based on the limited use of IT in Finch Co historically this is likely to have been inadequate.

Lack of staff training

The committee also appear not to have understood the practical, operational implications of the projects for Finch's staff. For example, the need for in-store staff to receive full training on the new scanner system prior to it going live appears to have been overlooked. This sentiment was echoed by the shop worker who remarked of only having had 10 minutes' training on the system in the morning, after the system had gone live for use by store customers. The inability of staff to resolve the problems customers were experiencing with the system led to a significant increase in customer complaints and lost sales as customers walked out in frustration.

Lack of contingency

Brendon was strongly motivated to ensure that Finch Co reduces its store costs as a way of reversing the decline in profits of recent years. However, the decision to make the majority of the checkout staff redundant appears to have been rather short-sighted. A contingency plan, of retaining these workers and existing tills would have been advantageous, especially during the initial systems changeover. Such a move would have allowed customers to become familiar with the new scanners more gradually, whilst also providing an option for customers to pay for their shopping at a conventional till in the event of any problems. The apparent decision to go for a direct system changeover appears to have been a major contributing factor in the systems failure.

Lack of co-ordination

Demand for the new 'click and collect' service appears to have been poorly forecast with more orders having been placed online than originally anticipated. The Operation Director's forecast of demand appears to have been determined by guesswork, as actual online orders across all stores were 1,150,000 per month (5,000 orders × 230 stores) higher than predicted. There also appears to have been a lack of planning during the introduction of the 'click and collect' service. This is particularly evident as the staffing levels required to run the service do not seem to have been considered properly. The quantity of orders placed has put the store staff under more strain, resulting in a poor customer experience. Customers have been unable to collect orders at the allocated time as these have not been ready. This suggests a lack of store level co-ordination, as staff members do not appear to know what is expected of them.

Processes

Lack of communication

Finch Co appears not to have spent sufficient time communicating to its customers how the new till system should work. The significant increase in complaints from those customers made to queue in the aisles appears to have been particularly damaging to the Finch brand. Although some checkout operators were retained to help customers download their purchases at the tills, it would appear that not enough staff have been made available to assist shoppers. The impact of this has reduced the quality of the customer experience when shopping in store. The sight of customers leaving stores in disgust could also prompt other customers to do likewise.

This problem may have been largely avoided by having fully trained staff readily available to assist shoppers as they progressed through the store. Demonstrations of how the system works could have been provided on the company's website to support customers.

Limited use of expertise

Finch Co's historic lack of IT in its business operations would appear to have been detrimental to its decision to offer a 'click and collect' service. Although this is unclear from the scenario, it would appear that no external specialist advice was sought by the project committee regarding the website upgrade. However, given the size and complexity of the projects, and Finch's limited resources and experience, it would have seemed beneficial to get external input. For example, external consultants might have been able to help Finch Co forecast customer demand for the service.

It is worth noting that although Finch Co's approach to forecasting demand from its 'click and collect' service requires improvement, the company's upgraded website itself appears to have been a success. This is evident as the upgraded website has been capable of handling 1,840,000 online orders per month (8,000 orders × 230 stores). This is particularly promising for Finch Co as it suggests that the 'click and collect' service has the potential to generate a significant amount of revenue for the company in the future, provided the current, in-store issues are resolved.

Organisational context

Senior management support

The management at Finch Co clearly need the new systems to work, as the company has undertaken a significant capital investment in new technologies. Although, the CEO's message to the company was clear in stating that all staff need to support the changes, this appears to have been the extent of any encouragement in using the new systems. Brendon's misplaced optimism that shop workers would learn how the new till system works through simply getting 'stuck in' has proven detrimental to the success of the project.

Finch Co's lack of innovation in the past may mean that staff are not used to change or adapting to new technology, meaning that the staff did not learn how to use the new tills as quickly and easily as the CEO had assumed they would.

Confusion over responsibilities

The confusion in store over the role and responsibilities of the shop floor staff indicates a lack of planning by the project team. If a store is to work efficiently then jobs and responsibilities need to have been defined in advance and there need to be sufficient staff available to do the work required.

Assigning store management set tasks such as overseeing the management of the new checkout system and 'click and collect' desk could have helped avoid the confusion among shop floor staff.

Technology

The technology employed in developing the two new systems would appear to be the most positive development to come from the project. Although the scenario doesn't mention this specifically, it would appear that the actual hardware used in operating the new till system and 'click and collect' ordering mechanism is working effectively.

Once the new till system is fully embedded, Finch Co should benefit from the ability to generate individual store sales reports in 'real time'. This may allow stores to boost sales. On days when sales fall below the stores' intended target, managers may be in a better position to influence demand by running in-store promotions or changing store displays to attract customers.

The ability to take customer orders online may also help to attract new shoppers to use Finch Co on the basis of the convenience of the 'click and collect' service.

However, the success of both systems depends on Finch Co's ability to successfully address the people and process issues which the projects have created.

31 Pharmacy Systems International

> **Top tips.** Part (a) asked you to analyse the nature, scope and type of change which the proposed strategy at PSI will involve. The terminology in the question should have highlighted that the relevant model was Balogun and Hope Hailey's (2008) matrix, whose axes are nature and scope of change.
>
> However, to score well in this question you need to focus specifically on PSI and analyse the type of change it is facing, rather than explaining types of change, or the nature and scope of change, in general terms.
>
> The answer below takes each of the four quadrants of the Balogun and Hope Hailey's (2008) matrix and then assesses the situation at PSI to see which quadrant it fits best. As with many strategic issues, there isn't a definitive correct answer – is the change adaptation or is it evolution? – provided that your argument is sensible and you support it with evidence from the scenario you will score marks.
>
> Part (b). Although the requirement refers to 'an appropriate model' the subsequent reference to 'internal contextual features' should have been a very clear signpost that the model you were expected to use was Balogun and Hope Hailey's (2008) contextual features.
>
> A sensible approach to this question would be to use each of the contextual features as headings (time, scope, preservation, diversity, capability, capacity, readiness and power) and then use the clues from the scenario to assess how the different features could influence the success of the proposed change.
>
> Even if you couldn't remember all of the different features from the model, there were still plenty of clues in the scenario which could have provided the basis for an answer. However, to score well in this question it is vital to discuss how the features will affect the success of the proposed change, rather than just analysing different aspects of the culture within PSI.

(a) Types of change (Balogun and Hope Hailey, 2008)

PSI currently sells to a specialist **niche market** – the retail pharmacy market. Therefore the proposed strategic change – to sell to the **general retail market** – represents a **significant change to PSI's product and its market**. In this respect, it represents a **diversification strategy**.

Nature of change – The nature of a change describes whether it is incremental or a one-off 'Big Bang' change.

Incremental change builds on existing methods and approaches rather than challenging them. However, a **'Big Bang' change** involves a major change to existing methods, processes and cultures. Such an approach is usually required in times of crisis when rapid responses are required.

Scope of change – The scope of a change describes the extent to which an organisation's business activities or its business model need changing. In this respect, a change can either be a **realignment** of a firm's existing strategy, or it can be a **transformational change** in which radical changes are made to the existing business model.

Types of change

Bringing together these different components of change means we can identify four different types of change: adaptation; reconstruction; evolution; and revolution.

Scope of change

Nature of change		Realignment	Transformation
	Incremental	Adaptation	Evolution
	'Big bang'	Reconstruction	Revolution

Adaptation is a change where the existing model is retained, and the change only occurs incrementally. Because the proposed change at PSI represents a diversification of strategy, it is debatable whether the existing business model will remain valid.

The Chief Executive and the Sales and Marketing Director may see the move to selling to the general retail industry as an adaptation of the existing model, but the Software Director's resistance to the change might suggest that he believes the change will involve a more significant transformation.

Reconstruction requires a significant, and rapid, change in the operations and processes of an organisation often in response to crisis such as a long-term decline in performance. However, it does not involve any major change to the business model.

The proposed changes at PSI are borne out of a desire for growth, rather than in response to any critical problems facing the company. Therefore, they do not represent a reconstruction.

Evolution is an incremental process that leads to a new business model. Evolutionary change often arises as a result of business analysis, leading to a planned change.

This appears to be the case at PSI. The move into the generic retail market represents a **fundamental change in strategic direction** and it is likely that the company's processes and structure will have to change significantly to develop and sell the new packages successfully. However, the change has come about due to the Chief Executive's **desire to grow the business rather than in response to external financial pressures**. Therefore the changes are likely to be relatively incremental rather than a sudden reconstruction of the business.

Revolution is a rapid and wide-ranging response to extreme pressures for change. It is likely to require a fundamental shift in the business model, and in the way a company operates. Although the proposed changes at PSI represent a diversification, they are not radical enough to represent a revolution.

(b)

> **Tutorial note:** For tutorial purposes, the answer below includes all headings from the contextual features model because all of them are relevant here. However, the resulting answer is longer, and more comprehensive, than you would be expected to produce for 15 marks.

The context of change

The context of change is provided by the organisational setting; this has many aspects and can therefore be very complex. However, this complexity can be approached in a manageable way by considering it under eight general headings proposed by Balogun and Hope Hailey (2008), which we will analyse below.

Time

No need to rush – Many companies are forced into changes in response to difficulties they are facing in their business. However, PSI does not appear to be facing any financial problems so time is not pressing in that respect.

Development time – Given that the software development team already appears to be under pressure to deliver and upgrade the current software, it also seems unlikely that they will be able to develop the software package for the general market quickly. Therefore a longer time scale may be more realistic anyway.

Chief Executive's expectations – The Chief Executive wants to introduce the changes quickly to accelerate the growth of the company and make it an attractive acquisition target. So the timetable for change could become a source of conflict between the Chief Executive and the Software Director and his staff.

Scope of change

Evolution or adaptation – We have already suggested in (a) that the proposed changes represent an evolutionary change, because the change from serving a niche market to serving a general retail market represents a substantial change of focus.

Changes to marketing mix – Moreover, PSI will need to develop new marketing skills for selling to the general retail market rather than to the specific niche of the pharmacy retail market.

One possible threat to the success of the change is if the Chief Executive and the Sales and Marketing Director underestimate its scope.

Preservation

Software developers – The software development team are critical to the success of the proposed changes, and PSI's business more generally. Therefore it is vital that PSI retains as many of its key software staff as possible. However, the software developers are already under constant pressure to meet the demands of existing customers, and so if their workload is increased still further a number may decide to leave PSI.

If a number of key software developers leave PSI the whole change project could be jeopardised.

Software Development Director – Persuading the Software Development Director to support the changes will also be crucial to their success. Not only is a supportive director more likely to lead to support from the software developers themselves, but the director will also need to play a key role in the design of the new product.

Diversity

Diversity of experience – The change process is likely to be made easier in companies which have diversity of experience, and so have experienced different ways of doing things. However, it appears that PSI has very little diversity and has been following a single, specialist strategy for many years.

Therefore, it appears that the business' current experience does not support the Chief Executive's ambitious plans for expansion.

Diversity of expectations – The goals of the sales team and those of the software developers seem to conflicting. The sales team is making promises to customers that the developers are struggling to meet. As a result, quality standards are falling, leading to customer dissatisfaction.

As the business expands, this scope for differences between the sales team and the developers will increase, and this could hamper PSI's efforts to enter the new market successfully.

Capability

Capability to manage change – Although the Chief Executive and the Sales and Marketing Director are both keen on the proposed changes, the Software Development Director and his team are far less so. The Chief Executive will need to **convince the software team of the merits of the proposals** so that they support the changes. If the software team remain unconvinced and unenthusiastic, the changes are unlikely to be successful.

Past experience – We do not know anything about the **directors' past experiences of managing change**. PSI has been relatively settled over the last three years, so if the directors do not have any previous experience of managing change this could hinder the proposals. Equally, we do not know if any of the software team has experienced change processes before, such that their experience could be used to increase the chances of success.

Capacity

People – The Software Development Director already wants to acquire further resources to support the existing product, and the quality of PSI's package has recently been criticised at a user group conference. This suggests that PSI's software team is already working to capacity. Therefore, it is likely it will need to **recruit a significant number of suitably skilled new developers** to support the planned expansion. This will increase costs, but it will also take **time** – to recruit new staff, and to allow them to become familiar with PSI's systems.

This timetable may again be problematic for the Chief Executive if he wants to progress quickly, and PSI's product quality could suffer still further if developers have to start work on a product before they fully understand it.

Funding – We do not know the details of PSI's financial position, but it seems likely that it will have to increase its borrowings to fund the expansion. PSI is a private company, and so cannot raise capital through an issue of shares on the stock market. There may be scope for the directors to raise the funds for expansion by launching an Initial Coin Offering (ICO). ICO's tend to be used by smaller, unlisted companies (like PSI) which struggle to get access to traditional methods of finance to fund business projects. PSI would need to publish a 'whitepaper' detailing the aims of the proposal to develop the generic software package, and provide details as to the type of currency that investors could use to support the project, ie cryptocurrency or real currency. Prior to deciding on this approach the directors would need to give careful consideration to the suitability, acceptability and feasibility of obtaining funding via an ICO.

An alternative approach would be to look to the current shareholders for additional funding, but that means essentially looking to the directors. The Software Development Director is unlikely to fund changes he does not support, and the Chief Executive seems keener on getting money from a sale of the company rather than investing in it further. Consequently, PSI's plans could be constrained by the amount of additional loan funding they can raise from their banks.

Readiness for change

The software developers would prefer to improve the software package that they offer to existing customers rather than moving to this new generic package. Therefore it is likely that they will **resist the Chief Executive's proposed changes rather than support them**.

Moreover, since PSI has been **growing gradually** over the last three years, there is little evidence to suggest that it is ready for the significant changes proposed.

Power

The **Chief Executive appears to be the dominant power** at PSI, supported by the Sales and Marketing Director. However, in practical terms the success of the changes depends on the software team and the Software Development Director.

The Software Development Director appears justified in being cautious over the changes. However, there is a risk that the other directors will **force through the changes**, possibly even by buying out the Software Director's shares and replacing him with a new director.

32 Institute of Analytical Accountants

Top tips. The requirement asks you to identify a range of redesign options, and then to evaluate the benefits of each option.

However, before you can identify the redesign options you first need to identify the problems in the current process which the redesigned options need to overcome. In effect, your answer needs to include three elements:

- Problems with current process

- Consequences of the problem identified

- Potential redesign options to overcome those problems and the benefits from each redesign option

To illustrate the three different elements, we have presented our suggested solution in a three-column table. Although you did not need to use this format, you should try to follow a similar, clear logic in your answer: identifying the current problem; highlighting the consequences of the problem; identifying a solution to it and evaluating the benefit of that proposed solution.

When suggesting ways that the process can be redesigned, make sure you provide specific options in the context of the scenario. For example, making generic points such as 'reduce the number of hand offs' is insufficient and will earn you very few marks. Whilst the process does currently have too many hand offs, giving the IAA practical advice about the ways they can reduce the number of hand offs will be much more valuable to them than simply telling them that they need to reduce the amount of them.

Also note the instruction before the requirement: the IAA wants to consider 'radical solutions' as well as 'simple improvements.' In effect, this suggests you should consider ways the whole process could be re-engineered, as well as smaller scale improvements within the existing process (redesign).

Marking scheme

	Marks
1 mark for each relevant point up to a maximum of 15 marks	15

Relevant points could relate to:
- Problems with the existing process
- Implications of the problems with the existing process
- Potential solutions to the problem
- Benefits of the potential solution (and potential issues with the solution)

Redesign

The process could be redesigned in a number of ways to solve the various problems with the existing process.

Problem	Consequences	Potential solutions
Bottleneck in the entering of questions into the question bank; there are too many questions for the amount of time the administrators have available. This is compounded by the fact that administrators are also not technical experts and therefore unable to check the accuracy of the material they have input.	Questions received back from reviewer cannot be found on the database (because they have not been entered). Therefore they cannot be updated to reflect the outcome of the review. This leads to frustration and delay. Quality of data – 1 in 10 has an error and so is unfit for purpose.	**Employ more administrators** to enter the data; however, this would be costly and does not address the issues with quality. **Delay question entry until the question has been accepted.** This would mean time is not wasted inputting questions that go on to be rejected, and also prevents further errors that are made when updating questions with amendments following a review.
Too many hand offs between departments	Errors such as those mentioned above Delays and bottlenecks created	Reduce the number of departments involved in the process (ie the number of 'swim lanes' in the process diagram), perhaps by **moving the tasks performed by the administrative department to the education department.** This would reduce the number of errors as the education department has more technical expertise. However, this change is likely to be resisted by the education department, and also would mean reducing the number of administrators and employing more expensive employees in the education department. Alternatively, there may be scope to embrace the concepts of **internal partnering**, which advocates greater co-operation and collaboration between departments within the same organisation. This might involve Subject Matter Experts in the education department working more closely with the administrators when inputting questions into the computerised question bank. This should help to address the number of question errors that occur, particularly if the errors relate to the technical content of the question. Such misunderstandings could potentially be avoided if the administrators directed their queries to the education department before inputting into the question into the computerised bank. This may however, lead to resistance among the Subject Matter Experts if they perceive that this change will increase their current work load. **Changing the sequence**: select the reviewer before the questions are submitted so that all questions from one author are automatically sent to a specific reviewer.

Problem	Consequences	Potential solutions
		This would reduce the time spent forwarding questions, but it may remove the anonymity of the reviewer (if the author liaises directly with the reviewer) and so might not be acceptable to IAA.
		The task of **raising a reject notification** should be reallocated to either the administration or education department to remove the unnecessary involvement of the finance department.

Re-engineering

Re-engineering involves redesigning the process completely from scratch by focusing on the goals of the process. In this case the goal might be to have a bank of accurate, reviewed questions held in a computer system at minimal cost.

One way this could be achieved is to change the process so that the author enters the question directly into the computer system. This would both reduce the chances of mistakes (which should be picked up by the reviewer anyway should they occur) and transfer the input cost to the author, thereby removing the bottleneck and reducing administrative costs.

The reviewer would then be responsible for informing the author of the acceptability of the question. Accepted responses would automatically raise a payment notification to be sent to the finance department, and rejection would automatically generate a reject notification which is electronically sent to the author. Revision requests would also be automatically sent to the author so that the relevant amendments could be made and the question resubmitted for the second review process.

There may be some staffing implications with this re-engineered process, as there would be much less need for administrators and potentially also educational staff. The involvement of finance personnel is also significantly reduced. As a result, implementing such a process could lead to redundancies, making this solution unpopular among the staff and therefore potentially harder to implement successfully.

33 Brighttown

Top tips. Part (a): in order to discuss what changes will be required to the project initiation document (or the terms of reference document) you first need to think what the key elements within this document are. Typically, a project initiation document will contain information such as the project's purpose and objectives; the expected start and finish dates; the sponsor; and it may also include an outline of the project scope and summary budget information.

Once you identify these elements, you should be able to identify some clear pointers in the scenario about the potential changes which will be required.

Note, however, that the focus of your answer needs to be on the changes that will be required to the document (following the change of mayor), not simply listing the different elements of the document.

Part (b): although the requirement (and the scenario) emphasises the benefits classification provided by OfRoad, it is important that you includes costs as well as benefits in your answer.

The requirement tells you that the mayor wants to 're-define the business case' and so this will involve identifying any changes to the cost of the project (for example, from the increasing number of buses and bus crews) as well as to the potential benefits it could deliver.

Nonetheless, as the requirement specifically refers to the benefits guidance provided by OfRoad, you should make use of this in your answer. In effect, for each benefit you identify, you should be looking to write a short paragraph in which you: (briefly) describe the benefit, classify it (as financial, quantifiable, measurable or observable) and then explain the reason for your classification.

Marks

(a) 1 mark for each appropriate point about changes required to the
       'terms of reference' document
       Up to a maximum of 5 marks for part (a)   5

(b) Identifying costs:
       1 mark for each appropriate point relating to costs of the revised
          project   Max 4
       Identifying and classifying benefits:
       Up to 2 marks for identifying and explaining each benefit   Max10
       ½ mark for correctly classifying each benefit (financial; quantifiable;
          measurable; observable)   Max 3
       1 mark for correctly calculating values for each quantitative or
          financial benefit   Max 3
       Up to a maximum of 15 marks for part (b)   15
                                                                                 20

(a) **Objectives and scope**

From the perspective of the 'traffic lite' project, the change in mayor has led to an
immediate change in the objectives driving the project. This illustrates how public sector
projects are susceptible to sudden external environmental changes outside their control.
The project initially proposed to reduce traffic congestion by making traffic lights sensitive
to traffic flow. It was suggested that this would improve journey times for all vehicles using
the roads of Brighttown. However, the incoming mayor now wishes to reduce traffic
congestion by attracting car users onto public transport. Consequently she wants to
develop a traffic light system which will give priority to buses. This should ensure that buses
run on time. The project is no longer concerned with reducing journey times for all users.
Indeed, congestion for private cars may get worse and this could further encourage car
users to switch to public transport.

An important first step would be to confirm that the new mayor wishes to be the **project
sponsor** for the project, because the project has lost its sponsor, the former mayor.

The **project scope** also needs to be reviewed. The initial project was essentially a
self-contained technical project aimed at producing a system which reduced queuing
traffic. The revised proposal has much wider political scope and is concerned with
discouraging car use and improving public bus services. Thus there are also proposals to
increase car parking charges, to reduce the number of car park spaces (by selling off
certain car parks for housing development) and to increase the frequency, quality and
punctuality of buses. The project scope appears to have been widened considerably,
although this will have to be confirmed with the new project sponsor.

Only once the scope of the revised project has been agreed can revised **project objectives**
be agreed and a new **project plan** developed, allocating the resources available to the
project to the tasks required to complete the project. It is at this stage that the project
manager will be able to work out if the proposed delivery date (a **project constraint**) is still
manageable. If it is not, then some kind of agreement will have to be forged with the
project sponsor. This may include reducing the scope of the project, adding more
resources, or some combination of the two.

(b)   **Costs and benefits**

Benefits

The re-defined project will have much more tangible effects than its predecessor and these could be classified using the standard approach suggested in the scenario. Benefits would include:

- One-off financial benefit from selling certain car parks – this appears to be a predictable **financial benefit** of $325,000 which can be confidently included in a cost/benefit analysis.

- Increased income from public bus use – this appears to be a **measurable benefit**, in that it is an aspect of performance which can be measured (for example, bus fares collected per day), but it is not possible to estimate how much income will actually increase until the project is completed.

- Increased income from car parks – this appears to be a **quantifiable benefit** if the assumption is made that usage of the car parks will stay at 95%. There may indeed be sufficient confidence to define it as a **financial benefit**. Car park places will be reduced from 1,000 to 800, but the increase in fees will compensate for this reduction in capacity. Current expected daily income is 1,000 × $3 × 0.95 = $2,850. Future expected income will be 800 × $4 × 0.95 = $3,040.

- Improved punctuality of buses – this will again be a **measurable benefit**. It will be defined in terms of a Service Level promised to the residents of Brighttown. Improved punctuality might also help tempt a number of vehicle users to use public transport instead.

- Reduced emissions – buses are more energy efficient and emit less carbon dioxide than the conventional vehicles used by most of the inhabitants of Brighttown. This benefit should again be **measurable** (but non-financial) and should benefit the whole of the town, not just areas around traffic lights.

- Improved perception of the town – the incoming mayor believes that her policy will help attract environmentally sensitive consumers and 'green' companies to the town. Difficulties in classifying what is meant by these terms makes this likely to be an **observable benefit**, where a group, such as the Go Green team, established by the council itself, can decide (based on their judgement) whether the benefit has been realised or not.

Costs

The costs of implementing the project will also have to be re-assessed. These costs will now include:

- The cost of purchasing more buses to meet the increased demand and frequency of service

- The operational costs of running more buses, including salary costs of more bus drivers

- Costs associated with the disposal of the car parks

The technical implementation requirements of the project will also change and this is almost certain to have cost implications because a solution will have to be developed which allows buses to be prioritised. A feasibility study will have to be commissioned to examine whether such a solution is technically feasible and, if it is, the costs of the solution will have to be estimated and entered into the cost/benefit analysis.

BPP
LEARNING
MEDIA

Answers to Section 2 questions – Professional skills development

34 P&J

	Marks
Distinguishing between strategic and operational risk	2
2 marks for each reason why risk is strategic	6
	<u>8</u>

Professional skills may be rewarded as in the following rubric:

How well has the candidate demonstrated professional skills as follows:	No marks	Half marks	Full marks
Communication skills in distinguishing between strategic and operational risks and explaining why the findings are a strategic risk to P&J.	The candidate has failed to use the format of a short article and has not successfully communicated the key points on risk in the manner required.	The candidate has attempted a short article format, and there is explanation of operational and strategic risk, but the overall effect is not objective or persuasive enough.	The candidate has structured the answer well, appropriately and objectively selecting and prioritising the key points on strategic and operational risk, with a logical flow and in the appropriate article format.
	0	1	2

Three solutions in respect of the question P&J have been provided below. Each of the three solutions provides an indication of the different level of skills marks that could be earned.

NO PROFESSIONAL SKILLS MARKS

> Not set out as an article – no headline or introduction

Distinguishing between strategic and operational risks

> Basic explanation of strategic vs operational risk, not suitable for a specialist readership

P&J is facing a very serious situation indeed. There are several kinds of risk that any business faces. The risks that are troubling P&J the most are not operational risks, which are those risks arising from within the company and which affect internal business processes day-to-day. Operational risks relate to matters that can go wrong on a day-to-day basis while the organisation is carrying out its business.

The most worrying risks are strategic risks, which are the risks to future profits from the nature of P&J's business, and which affect the company as a whole and threaten its future profitability. Strategic risk can be defined as those risks that relate to the fundamental decisions that the directors take about the future of the organisation.

Kroll's findings

Text covers the points but they are not developed sufficiently, and they are not clearly laid out. Bullet points could help here. There is no end point or conclusion to the article.

The findings of Professor Kroll's report pose a strategic risk to P&J for a number of reasons. Firstly, his findings affect all the company. P&J has previously taken the decision to adopt vertical integration, which means that it undertakes all stages of the production process.

Secondly it is very difficult now for P&J to position itself so that it appeals to its key stakeholders. Banks will not be advancing further funds given the difficulties that the company is experiencing. Shareholders will be more likely to sell their shares than to make a further investment, because they believe that P&J has no future. Customers will be looking in the longer term for safe alternatives to X32 as it will be withdrawn from use. Current employees will leave for more secure opportunities. It is difficult to see how new employees can be attracted.

Thirdly, the most serious strategic issue facing P&J is whether it can survive at all. It is likely to face declining demand and a fall in revenues from X32. It may not have the cash surpluses to make changes to its business. It also faces legal costs and liabilities, which may wipe the company out.

HALF PROFESSIONAL SKILLS MARKS

Appropriate title and later sub-headings

P&J – the future?

No-one would envy the current position of P&J. The situation its directors currently face in relation to X32 is the most serious in the company's history. The board is more concerned with keeping up appearances than with doing all they can to deal with the issues.

Introduction captures attention, but may lack objectivity

Strategic and operational risks

Operational risks relate to matters that can go wrong on a day-to-day basis while the organisation is carrying out its business, but these are not the ones that are most directly threatening P&J at the moment.

Clearer explanation of strategic risk and operational risk in the context of P&J

The reality is that the difficulties P&J is facing will influence its whole direction in the future. Strategic risks are risks that relate to the fundamental decisions that P&J directors must take about the future of the organisation.

Kroll's findings

The findings of Professor Kroll highlight the risks to future profits that now arise from the nature of P&J's business and its use of X32. These risks affect the company as a whole. The directors need to decide whether they should continue using X32 or should switch to a different product.

No persuasive explanation of why the problems with X32 pose a strategic risk, particularly as regards stakeholders. Points are made but they are not backed up or developed further. Bullet points would help with presentation.

The findings of Professor Kroll's report pose a strategic risk to P&J for a number of reasons. Firstly, his findings clearly affect all the company. P&J has previously taken the decision to adopt vertical integration, which means that it undertakes all stages of the production process: mining, processing and manufacturing. Professor Kroll's findings impact on each stage.

Stakeholders

Secondly it is very difficult for P&J to position itself so that it appeals to its key stakeholders. Banks will not be advancing further funds given the difficulties that the company is experiencing. Shareholders will be more likely to offload their shares than make a further investment because they are worried about P&J's future. Customers will be looking in the longer term for safe alternatives to X32. Current employees will leave for more secure opportunities. It is difficult to see how new employees can be attracted.

Can it survive?

The most serious strategic issue facing P&J is whether it can survive at all. Over time it faces a dwindling in demand and a fall in revenues from X32. It may not have the cash to make changes to its production processes or products. As well as this, it faces legal costs and unquantified legal liabilities.

FULL PROFESSIONAL SKILLS MARKS

P&J – the future?

Appropriate title and introduction that sets out the issues confronting P&J

The situation faced by the directors of P&J is the most serious in the company's history. There are no easy answers to the problems, but sympathy begins to disappear when it appears that the board is more concerned with keeping up appearances than with doing all they can to deal with the issues presented by X32. Of course, P&J management needs to address issues of worker health. However, it also needs to consider how to take the company forward into a future without X32.

Strategic and operational risks

More persuasive explanation of strategic risk and operational risk in the context of P&J. Consideration of the future, and good use of illustrative example.

It is not just operational risks that are directly threatening P&J at the moment.

The reality is that the difficulties P&J is facing will influence its whole future direction. Strategic risks relate to the fundamental decisions that P&J directors must take. Can X32 be phased out, and an alternative found? It may be time for P&J to reduce its reliance on one compound. Of key importance here is the ability of P&J's processes to adapt and innovate.

If strategic risks materialise, they can cause individual companies, even whole industries, to disappear. As an example, consider the case of asbestos. Once a key building material, its use is now heavily restricted and even banned, and liability for its past use remains a concern for some companies.

The findings clearly affect the whole company. P&J has previously taken the decision to adopt vertical integration, undertaking all stages of the production process: mining; processing; and manufacturing. Professor Kroll's findings impact on each stage where X32 is used.

Stakeholders

Use of bullet points and clear explanation of the effects on various stakeholders

P&J also needs to consider the perspectives of key stakeholders:

- Banks may not be happy to advance further funds given the difficulties that the company is experiencing

- Shareholders may be more likely to sell their shares than make a further investment if they feel that the company has no future

- Customers will be looking for alternatives to X32 as it will need to be withdrawn from use soon

- Employees may leave for more secure opportunities, with replacements hard to find

Wiped out?

Development of a logical conclusion that draws upon points made earlier

All of this implies that the most serious strategic issue facing P&J is whether it can survive at all. Over time it is likely to face declining demand and a fall in revenues. It may not have the cash to make fundamental changes to its production processes or significantly reposition its products. Most worryingly of all, it faces legal costs and unquantified legal liabilities, which may turn out to be enough to wipe the company out.

35 Alpha Software

	Marks
1 mark for explaining the current stakeholder confusion at Alpha	1
Up to 3 marks for a discussion on how integrated reporting can help to communicate strategy	Max 3
Up to 2 marks for a discussion on how integrated reporting can improve Alpha's performance	Max 2
Up to 4 marks for a discussion of the Finance Director's comments	Max 4
Up to a maximum of 10 marks for technical skills	10

Professional skills may be rewarded as in the following rubric:

How well has the candidate demonstrated professional skills as follows:	No marks	Half marks	Full marks
Communication skills in persuading the Finance Director of the merits of integrated reporting for Alpha Software.	The candidate has failed to describe the features of integrated reporting as they could relate to Alpha Software. A compelling and logical argument has not been put forward for its use.	The candidate has made some attempt at a persuasive argument and there is explanation of the benefits of integrated reporting, but the answer is not sufficiently focused on the areas required and the overall effect is not persuasive enough to highlight its benefits.	The candidate has structured the answer well, selecting the key points on integrated reporting and its links with strategic performance, with a logical flow, sound arguments and in the appropriate tone.
	0	1	2

Briefing paper

FAO: Finance Director

Merits of integrated reporting at Alpha Software

Reduce confusion among stakeholders

As a result of the recent management changes at Alpha Software, the company has struggled to communicate its 'strategic direction' to key stakeholders. The company's annual accounts have made it hard for shareholders to understand Alpha's strategy, which has led to confusion. Uncertainty among shareholders and employees is likely to increase the risk of investors selling their shares and talented IT developers seeking employment with competitors.

Communicating strategy

The introduction of integrated reporting should help Alpha to overcome these issues as it places a strong focus on the organisation's future orientation. An integrated report should detail the company's mission and values, the nature of its operations and how it differentiates itself from its competitors.

Including Alpha's new mission to become the market leader in the specialist accountancy software industry would instantly convey what the organisation stands for.

Resource allocation – In line with best practice in integrated reporting, Alpha could supplement its mission with how the board intends to achieve this strategy. Such detail would focus on resource allocations over the short to medium term. For example, plans to improve the company's human capital through hiring innovative software developers would help to support the company's long-term mission. To assist users in appraising the company's performance, Alpha could provide details on how it will measure value creation in each 'capital'. 'Human capital' could also be measured by the level of investment in training and employee turnover rates.

Key performance indicators – A key feature of integrated reporting focuses on the need for organisations to use non-financial customer-oriented performance measures (KPIs) to help communicate the entity's strategy. The most successful companies in Alpha's industry are committed to enhancing their offering to customers through producing innovative products. Alpha could report through the use of KPIs how it is delivering on this objective, and measures could be set which, for example, measure the number of new software programs developed in the last two years.

Improving long-term performance

The introduction of integrated reporting should help Alpha to enhance its performance. Historically, the company has not given consideration to how decisions in one area have impacted on other areas. This is clearly indicated by the former CEO's cost-cutting programme which served to reduce the staff training budget. Although this move may have enhanced the company's short-term profitability, it has damaged long-term value creation if Alpha is unable to produce the innovative software that customers demand.

Finance Director's comments

<IR> as a 'fad' – It is important to understand how the company's activities and 'capitals' interact with each other in delivering value. To regard developments in integrated reporting as simply being a 'fad' contradicts the commitment of accounting bodies worldwide to promoting its introduction.

Shareholders – The assertion regarding shareholders is likely to some degree to be correct. However, many shareholders will be interested in how the board proposes to create value in the future. Ultimately, Alpha's focus will be on maximising shareholder value, the achievement of which requires the successful implementation of both short- and long-term strategies.

Stakeholders – Furthermore, integrated reports highlight the importance of considering a wider range of users. Key stakeholder groups such as Alpha's customers and suppliers are likely to be interested in assessing how the company has met or not met their needs beyond the 'bottom line'. Integrated reporting encourages companies to report performance measures which are closely aligned to the concepts of sustainability and corporate social responsibility.

Performance management – Ultimately, as integrated reporting provides senior management with a greater quantity of organisational performance data, this should help in identifying previously unrecognised areas which are in need of improvement. Focusing management's attention on the non-financial aspects of Alpha's performance as well as its purely financial performance should be expected to lead to performance improvements in those areas. For example, if innovation is highlighted as a key factor in sustaining Alpha's long-term value, a focus on innovation could help to encourage it within the company.

36 MachineShop

Marks

1 mark for each appropriate point up to a maximum of 5 marks for
general points made about the model within the slides   Max 5

1 mark for each appropriate point up to a maximum of 5 marks for
points specific to conditions in Arboria or Ceeland contained in the
slides   Max 5

Up to a maximum of 10 marks for technical skills   10

Professional skills may be rewarded as in the following rubric:

How well has the candidate demonstrated professional skills as follows:	No marks	Half marks	Full marks
Communication skills in clarifying the principles of Porter's diamond and applying this in relation to MachineShop's growth ambitions.	The answer is not presented in a slide format, with supporting notes. The candidate has failed to present a clear explanation of the principles of the diamond and no attempt has been made to link it with MachineShop's growth ambitions.	The answer is presented in a slide format, but the number of bullet points per slide is either too high or too low. Notes are provided but the links between these and the slides are not always clear. The candidate has set out the elements of the diamond, but the relevance of each one for MachineShop has not been clearly explained.	The answer is presented in a slide format, with an appropriate number of points per slide, and with the supporting notes clearly relating to the points on the slide. The candidate has clearly set out the elements of the diamond and applied them to MachineShop's circumstances.
	0	1	2

Slide 1: Porter's (1990) diamond model

- Purpose of the model

- Four elements of the 'diamond':
    - Factor conditions
    - Demand conditions
    - Related and supporting industries
    - Firm strategy, structure and rivalry

- Understanding national competitiveness

Notes:

Porter's (1990) diamond model was developed to explore national competitive advantage. The 'diamond' consists of four key elements which determine the attractiveness of different countries for different industries.

BPP
LEARNING
MEDIA

It can be a particularly useful tool in understanding why companies operating in certain nations appear better placed to compete.

Next slides look at the elements in more detail, and how they influence the relative attractiveness of Ceeland and Arboria for MachineShop.

Slide 2: Factor conditions

Bullet points:

- Basic factors
- Advanced factors
- Developments in Ceeland

Demand conditions

- Level of demand
- Consumer characteristics and product preferences
- Home market vs overseas market
- Demand conditions in Ceeland

Notes:

Factor conditions

Factor conditions can be classified as being either basic or advanced. Basic factor conditions include unskilled labour and the natural environment, whereas skilled labour and the transport infrastructure are regarded as being advanced factors as these offer sustained advantages.

Both types of conditions are deemed necessary if an organisation wishes to compete successfully in a particular industry.

In relation to Ceeland, the government has built up an effective road transport system which is cheap to use. The ability to easily distribute goods around the country is an attractive factor for MachineShop in considering whether to enter the market. MachineShop's interest has also been supported by the recent developments to Ceeland's digital communication network, since the ability to accept orders over the internet is a key part of its business model.

Demand conditions

Demand conditions are concerned with the level of demand by consumers for a particular product or service in a company's home market. The ability of an organisation to supply products and services to demanding discerning consumers in its home market may help when anticipating and satisfying buyer requirements in comparable overseas markets. This would appear to be a critical issue for MachineShop.

MachineShop has benefited in this regard by serving consumers in Arboria, where buyers are demanding and assertive. MachineShop would appear to be well positioned to exploit opportunities to expand into Ceeland, where consumers may be less demanding.

Dave Deen has suggested that a similar consumer society to Arboria is emerging in Ceeland. The decision by the government of Ceeland to lift restrictions on the type of machines permitted for use by citizens is likely to increase the demand for such machinery, thereby strengthening demand conditions. Prior to any venture into Ceeland MachineShop would need to conduct full market research to ensure that the predicted social trends do occur. If sufficient demand is found to exist then careful consideration would also need to be given as to whether market entry via a business combination approach (ie acquiring an existing Ceeland business) would be appropriate.

Slide 3:

Related and supporting industries

- Competitive success in one industry is linked to success in related industries
- Co-operation and co-ordination
- Already using a Ceeland supplier

Firm strategy, structure and rivalry

- Rivalry encourages market participants to continually develop
- Few competitors in Arboria
- Ceeland market still developing

Notes:

Related and supporting industries

Related and supporting industries within a country are those which help to underpin the performance of other organisations, by co-operating with each other and co-ordinating their activities to achieve joint success.

MachineShop currently stocks products made by a supplier in Ceeland. The ability for a foreign entity such as MachineShop to source products of sufficient quality for sale in Arboria serves to make Ceeland even more appealing. This heightens the scope for MachineShop to potentially realise Dave Deen's plans to enter into external partnering arrangements with third parties. The establishment of a strategic alliance with the Ceeland supplier, could lead to the development of further products which could appeal to customers in both Arboria and Ceeland.

Firm strategy, structure and rivalry

The final component of the 'diamond' model concerns firm strategy, structure and rivalry. Porter (1990) identified that significant rivalry in a given market encourages competitors to continually develop their own products and services in order to maintain competitive advantage.

MachineShop's success to date in Arboria has not been influenced by this factor due to a lack of competitors. As Ceeland's economy is still developing, domestic rivalry will also be lacking. (This is seen as a disadvantage in the 'diamond', because the lack of rivalry means companies don't have to continually develop products to remain competitive.)

Tutorial note:

Additional element you could have included:

Government

Bullet points:

- Not included in Porter's (1990) original model
- Government activity potentially a very important factor
- Examples provided by the Ceeland government

Notes. Although Porter's (1990) original model did not include governments as a factor which influenced national competitiveness, the diamond has now been extended to reflect the potential importance of governments; in this case, the extent to which Ceeland's government can increase the attractiveness of Ceeland to outside companies. Ceeland's government has invested heavily in its transportation infrastructure and information technology systems and has lifted restrictions on the type of machinery that can be used by domestic customers.

---

37 Rock Bottom

Marks

Up to 1 mark for each relevant point up to a maximum of 4 marks for each phase
Three phases required, giving a maximum of 12 marks for technical skills

12

Professional skills may be rewarded as in the following rubric:

How well has the candidate demonstrated professional skills as follows:	No marks	Half marks	Full marks
Commercial acumen in displaying awareness of the leadership styles and other factors that affected the achievement of organisational objectives at Rock Bottom	The candidate has not demonstrated awareness, by failing to analyse the commercial situation in each phase properly, or to make appropriate links between leadership style and its influence on the commercial fortunes of the company.	The candidate has demonstrated some limited understanding that Rick Hein's leadership style has had an influence on the company, but aspects of his leadership style have not always been directly related to the commercial realities of each phase, as required by the question.	The candidate has produced a good answer that clearly illustrates how leadership style has influenced the company, and has clearly linked the effects of leadership style to each phase of Rock Bottom's commercial development.
	0	1	2

Three solutions in respect of the question Rock Bottom have been provided below. Each of the three solutions provides an indication of the different level of skills marks that could be earned.

NO PROFESSIONAL SKILLS MARKS

> Failure to identify the phases of the industry life cycle and to clearly relate them to leadership style.

In 1975 Rick Hein established his first shop specialising in imported electrical audio products, which were more sophisticated than the domestic products found in larger department stores. When Rock Bottom first opened it therefore offered a significant contrast to the department stores. The imported goods were smaller and more reliable than domestic equivalents. It was able to distinguish itself from competitors.

Rick's leadership style contributed to the success in Phase I. He was a charismatic leader and entrepreneur.

Rick was also very good at marketing and selling. He appointed staff who were young and understood the products they were selling, and he rewarded them well.

> Answer tends to repeat material from the scenario, rather than analysing it from a commercial standpoint.

By the late 1990s, a number of competitors had entered the market, and Rock Bottom was not doing so well as a result. Sales and profits declined.

Rick's approach was to float the company on the stock exchange and expand the business. He did use some of the capital raised to expand the business, but he also sold shares so that he could throw a large party and buy expensive gifts. His relationship with his board and shareholders became increasingly difficult. Most of the established managers left as controls became more formal.

This decision to float the company on the stock exchange therefore created several problems for the company because it was now a public company and it had shareholders to keep happy. New financial controls and reporting systems were put in place. The company's performance was solid but unspectacular.

Rick changed the organisational structure and style. There was less freedom and flexibility for managers and they were not as well paid. His personal image and lifestyle were damaging the company and he found it difficult to abide by the rules and not be able to do as he liked with the company.

In 2013 Hein took Rock Bottom private again, but most of the new store managers found Hein too unfocused at a time when changes in the products and how they were purchased meant that fewer people bought from specialist shops. Rock Bottom continued to operate as a 'bricks and mortar' retailer, without developing an online capability which would have helped him to increase sales.

In early 2018 the company ceased trading and Hein himself filed for personal bankruptcy.

HALF PROFESSIONAL SKILLS MARKS

Phase I – introduction and growth

When Rock Bottom first opened it offered a significant contrast to the department stores. The imported goods that it offered in its specialist outlets were more sophisticated and more reliable than the domestic equivalents that were mainly found in general department stores.

Rock Bottom marketed its goods in an innovative way. Along with Hein's high public profile, the company stood out from the competition and attracted large numbers of customers as it represented a new and exciting offering in the market.

In addition, Rick was a charismatic leader and he encouraged his staff by rewarding them well.

Rick was also a motivator. He appointed staff who were young and understood the products that they were selling. Rick appreciated that the skills and knowledge of his staff were important in communicating enthusiasm for the products to the customer, thereby promoting sales growth.

Phase II – maturity

By the late 1990s, a number of competitors had entered the market, and Rock Bottom's advantage in products and services approach had been eroded. Sales and profits began to decline as customers were shared between an increasing number of competitors in a more mature market.

Rick floated the company on the stock exchange and used the capital raised to expand the business, but he was still not properly focused on the business or disciplined in its management in the way that important stakeholders such as the banks required. There were problems for the company as it was now under pressure to provide returns to shareholders and disclose information about directors' remuneration, which proved damaging.

There was less freedom and flexibility for managers. Rick's personal image and lifestyle were damaging the company.

Phase III - decline

Rock Bottom's product range had never changed to reflect new products and new ways of selling them in its market, and the demand for old models has fallen.

Rock Bottom continued to operate as a 'bricks and mortar' retailer, without developing an online capability. The operating costs associated with a branch network, as opposed to online, are higher, but the initial investment that would have been required for online selling dissuaded Hein.

As with Phases 1 and 2, Rick's leadership style affected Rock Bottom in Phase 3 and damaged its prospects.

FULL PROFESSIONAL SKILLS MARKS

Phase I – introduction and growth

Good analysis of the commercial realities of each phase, including the relating of each one to the product life cycle

At first, Rock Bottom offered a contrast to the department stores. Its imported goods were more sophisticated and reliable than domestic equivalents. The products were in the introduction and growth phases of their product life cycles, as was the store format.

The innovative way that Rock Bottom marketed its goods, along with Hein's high public profile, also distinguished it.

Leadership style – The success described above came partly from the market and environment, but Rick's leadership also contributed to success. He was a charismatic leader and entrepreneur, building a vision for the organisation, and then encouraging staff. He appreciated that the skills and knowledge of his staff were important to success, and staff were well rewarded.

Phase II – maturity

By the late 1990s, a number of competitors had entered the market, and Rock Bottom's advantage in product and service had been eroded. Sales and profits declined as customers were shared between an increasing number of competitors in a mature market.

Appropriate leadership was needed for the maturity phase. Rick floated the company on the stock exchange and used the capital for expansion (as well as parties and gifts).

As a public company, however, Rock Bottom was now under pressure to provide acceptable returns to shareholders, with dividends and share price growth, and it had to disclose information about its directors' remuneration, which proved damaging.

Specific sub-headings that explicitly relate to leadership style, and explaining how the style influenced commercial performance

In an attempt to establish the company so that it could deliver value to its shareholders, Rick changed its organisational structure and style. There was less freedom and flexibility for managers. In addition, the reward packages were more tightly controlled. The managers were not impressed with the changes, and many left.

Leadership style – Ultimately, Rick failed to adapt to a maturing marketplace. His personal image and lifestyle damaged the company and he found it difficult to abide by rules and governance principles, including having to take account of stakeholders and shareholders rather than doing what he wanted.

Phase III – decline

Whereas in Phase I, Rock Bottom was offering new and exciting products, music is now increasingly played from downloaded computer files or through MP3 players. Rock Bottom's product range never changed to reflect this. Even where people still use traditional hi-fi systems, these are much more reliable and durable. Consequently, people replace their equipment less frequently.

Explanation of recent commercial environment, eg product developments and their effect on the market.

Rock Bottom continued to operate as a 'bricks and mortar' retailer, without developing an online capability. The operating costs associated with a branch network, as opposed to online, meant that Rock Bottom had no cost advantage over any competitors who did have an online presence. The internet makes pricing more transparent, allowing consumers to compare retailers and products before deciding what and where to buy.

Leadership style – as was the case in Phases 1 and 2, Rick's leadership style affected Rock Bottom in Phase 3. He alienated his managers with his approach, and reacted to the freedom gained from no longer being a public company by spending a large amount of money on a celebration party rather than focusing on commercial changes and investment that were needed by the business. This is likely to have aggravated the damage that had already been done, and the business could not adapt to the changed environment with such a leader.

38 ATD

Marking scheme

Marks

Analysis of benefits of budgeting in terms of improved accountability, flexed budget preparation and better understanding of costs
1 mark for each relevant point, up to a maximum of 10 for technical skills | 10

Professional skills may be rewarded as in the following rubric:

How well has the candidate demonstrated professional skills as follows:	No marks	Half marks	Full marks
Commercial acumen in using judgement to identify the key problems at ATD, and ways in which a budgeting process could help to address them.	The candidate has demonstrated no appreciable commercial acumen or understanding as to how the problems at ATD could be addressed through a formal budgeting process.	The candidate has demonstrated some commercial acumen in that they have identified some of the key benefits of the formal budgeting process in addressing the problems at ATD, showing some limited level of judgement and understanding.	The candidate has demonstrated excellent commercial acumen and judgement, making clear links between the budgeting process and problem resolution at ATD.
	0	1	2

A budget can be viewed as an internal tool used by an organisation to assist in the achievement of its long-term objectives. Budgets are commonly used in the short term to allow managers to take action regarding the resources within their functional areas of responsibility. Historically, ATD's approach to forecasting its sales revenue has been determined by the sales manager through a combination of 'experience, intuition and guesswork'. This has resulted in increasingly inaccurate forecasts being produced.

However, an accurate sales budget is critical to the preparation of all other budgets. The level of anticipated sales will drive the organisation's requirements in terms of raw material levels and production staffing levels.

Accountability

A well-prepared budget will help an organisation to set realistic targets across all departments. This would support ATD in improving its approach to forecasting. Realistic targets place a degree of accountability on functional management for their departments. As an example, the head of the production division can monitor the monthly spending on raw materials against the departmental budget. This is beneficial as it allows the manager to take corrective action should costs rise beyond the intended level.

Where managers are provided with clear targets related solely to their area of responsibility this may serve to boost their morale, motivating them to work harder as their own performance can be closely measured against the budgets set. Central to improving motivation is to ensure that all targets set are robust and achievable, otherwise there is an increased risk that demotivation may occur.

Flexed budgets

In the event that sales targets are missed, it would help to assess divisional performance if divisional budgets were flexed accordingly. When sales targets are not met this will have a direct impact on the level of purchases needed to satisfy customer orders. In such instances the purchases budget should be flexed to reduce the level of materials needed. This should lead to a more accurate indication of the production manager's performance.

For example, ATD may miss its sales targets for a quarter, but the production manager may still have been able to significantly reduce the target cost of raw material purchases. It would therefore clearly be wrong to ignore this factor when appraising the performance of the production manager.

The current approach adopted by the CEO at ATD appears to penalise departmental managers when sales targets are missed even though department managers cannot influence sales figures. This is illustrated by the comment made by the production manager, 'I am working tirelessly to keep costs down, but my only reward is that I cannot replace one of my best purchasing administrators who left in the last month'.

Motivation amongst the departmental managers may be further improved if they were able to participate in the budget-setting process. Departmental managers at ATD claim the current approach leaves them feeling 'powerless and undervalued'. However, allowing the departmental managers to be more involved in target setting would help to illustrate that their experiences and opinions are valued.

ATD may benefit from increased goal congruence as senior management can convey what is expected of departmental heads while also improving the understanding of target setting and co-ordination between departments.

Cost cutting at ATD

The CEO at ATD has been very bold in introducing the cost-cutting measures in response to the missed sales targets. The decision to cut costs without formalising these in a budget means that the CEO has no way of knowing whether the cost savings are being achieved.

Moreover, the decision to 'ruthlessly cut costs' may actually prove to be detrimental to ATD's performance. The freeze on the recruitment of new staff may lead to a situation where departments are not able to operate effectively if they are under-staffed. The same is also true of the decision to cut back on the marketing initiatives. Reduced marketing is likely to result in fewer sales being achieved. To evaluate the effectiveness of the cost-cutting measures the CEO should have specified cost-reduction targets which could have been monitored through the use of variance analysis. This illustrates the need for a formal budgeting process at ATD.

39 Pulpo

Marks

Up to 2 marks for each relevant argument made and developed
Up to a maximum of 8 marks for technical skills

8

Professional skills may be rewarded as in the following rubric:

How well has the candidate demonstrated professional skills as follows:	No marks	Half marks	Full marks
Commercial acumen in identifying the reasons why Pulpo should publish an environmental report and the benefits that it could derive from doing so.	The candidate has demonstrated no appreciable commercial acumen or insight into the benefits of an environmental report for Pulpo in managing its local relationships. The answer is limited to restating the problems outlined in the scenario and talking about environmental reporting in general terms.	The candidate has demonstrated some commercial acumen in that they have demonstrated a limited level of insight into the specific benefits of environmental reporting for Pulpo because of its local stakeholders. The candidate has therefore shown some appreciation of the factors involved.	The candidate has demonstrated excellent commercial acumen, constructing a case as to why Pulpo should produce its own environmental report because of its own challenges as described in the question scenario, showing strong commercial understanding of the effect of stakeholder interests and also the practicalities behind report preparation.
	0	1	2

Arguments in favour of Pulpo publishing an environmental report

> **Tutorial note:** When attempting this requirement it was important that you only focused on the arguments in favour of Pulpo publishing an environmental report. Discussing the arguments against would only serve to waste your time and earn you no marks.

Given the recent problems which Pulpo has been having, there is a strong case for increased environmental disclosure directly relating to Pulpo.

The first point to make is that the company already gathers data on environmental matters to supply to the parent company for its own group environmental report. This means that the systems must therefore be in place to produce environmental data and so the marginal costs will be relatively modest. Extra effort will mainly centre on the drafting of information pages and having them published on the website.

It will increase the appearance of transparency at Pulpo, and help to repair the damaged relationships with the residents' association and the newspaper. Mary Wong's honest disclosures clearly angered these groups, and so a lack of trust is likely to exist towards Pulpo as a result.

Measures capable of restoring trust and legitimacy include increased disclosure and efforts to increase the transparency of the company, especially to those who have been historically critical of it.

An environmental report framed in terms of explaining the inputs, processes and outputs, including waste, would help Pulpo to explain its business model and possibly provide information to address the environmental challenges. These might include helping to offset criticisms about the smell and the water pollution which are perceived to be a problem by local residents.

If, for example, the company provides a full explanation of why fumes are generated and what those fumes are, whilst perhaps not fully satisfying residents, they may at last understand why they are necessary.

The publication of environmental information may help to improve the local reputation of Pulpo, which appears to have had some recent problems. If it wishes to continue to enjoy the support of the local community, from which it presumably draws a lot of its labour, its reputation will be important.

If a company such as Pulpo loses the implicit or explicit support of the local community, it may suffer, not only in its ability to recruit employees but in the wider issues of local support when, for example, building planning permission is needed for similar developments which may have an impact on the local environment.

40 Mary Jane

	Marks
1 mark for identification of each control failing 1 mark for analysis of each failing Up to a maximum of 10 marks for technical skills	10

Professional skills may be rewarded as in the following rubric:

How well has the candidate demonstrated professional skills as follows:	No marks	Half marks	Full marks
Analysis skills in identifying the internal control problems and the reasons for them.	The candidate has demonstrated limited analysis skills, and has failed to consider and reflect on the information given in the question scenario in order to be able to identify internal control failures and the reasons for them.	The candidate has demonstrated some analysis skills in selecting from the lengthy scenario a range of points to discuss in regard to internal control failures. Some attempt has been made to expand on the reasons for the problems.	The candidate has produced a good answer that has taken the relevant points from throughout the scenario, and clearly analysed the internal control failures as required by the question. The answer clearly demonstrates that the candidate has considered why problems have occurred, and the reasons for this.
	0	1	2

Three solutions in respect of the question Mary Jane have been provided below. Each of the three solutions provides an indication of the different level of skills marks that could be earned.

NO PROFESSIONAL SKILLS MARKS

Very few analysis skills are demonstrated, and assumptions are made that are not supported by evidence

Although the board of Sea Ships Co believed that it was a well-run company and boasted about its reputation, it was not. The major failing was that a design fault was highlighted in the consultant's report, but the consultant's report was not acted on and seems to have been ignored by the company for reasons of cost. This has resulted in a major accident that is likely to cost Sea Ships Co much more, both in financial terms and also in damage to its reputation. The Mary Jane should never have been allowed to sail on the Northport route and it was unethical to allow it to do so.

Failure to clearly specify that there are issues around internal controls

The way that the ship was operated prior to departure was inadequate as it allowed vehicles to be loaded wrongly onto ships, putting pressure on the schedule as more time was needed to sort the problems out before sailing.

The accident was caused by the failure to secure the doors, and the checks over door security were also inadequate. No review would take place from the deck of the ship, and reliance was placed on someone else carrying out the check.

In addition, the ship's reporting system relied upon assuming that all was well to set sail unless the bridge heard otherwise. This was not an effective system, because it led to mistakes being made. When communications are faulty, problems will not be reported. The previous system of reporting by each department should not have been abandoned.

Answer gives the overall impression that the scenario has not been fully analysed with reference to the question requirements

With schedules under time pressure, captains could always give speed of departure and sailing priority over compliance with the law. There was no way to prevent ships breaking the speed limit and this failing led directly to the accident.

The legal department appears to have been poorly run, with the result that the ship was not properly insured. The legal department should have reviewed insurance arrangements to check that they were adequate.

HALF PROFESSIONAL SKILLS MARKS

Shows an understanding of the presence of internal control failures

As part of a long-established company which valued its reputation and operated a fleet of ships, it might be expected that a robust system of internal controls would have been in operation on the Mary Jane. There were, however, several failings as set out below.

Design fault

A suitable range of internal control failures has been selected from the scenario

There was a major failing when the design fault, highlighted in the consultant's report, was not acted on because it seems to have been ignored by the company. This suggests a serious failure within the company to understand its safety responsibilities, which is not to be expected of a long-established and respected company.

Problems with loading

Control systems prior to departure were inadequate as they allowed vehicles to be loaded wrongly onto ships. These problems contributed to time pressure.

Failure to secure doors

The accident was caused by the failure to secure the doors, and the control checks over door security were inadequate. There was no formal requirement for acknowledgement that the doors had been checked. Instead, reliance was placed on someone else carrying out the check.

Reporting system

The ship's reporting system relied on reporting by exception – assuming all was well to sail unless the bridge heard otherwise. However, if communications were faulty, problems may not have been reported to the bridge. The previous system of positive reporting by each department head being required should have been retained.

Emphasis on speed

Some points are not properly developed in terms of why they caused problems

The systems were ineffective in allowing captains to give speed of departure and sailing priority over compliance with the law. There were no control systems on board to prevent the ships breaking local speed limits.

Failure to insure

The liability of Sea Ships Co was not properly insured. The legal department should have annually reviewed the insurance arrangements to ensure adequate coverage.

FULL PROFESSIONAL SKILLS MARKS

Relating internal controls to business operations

As part of a long-established company which valued its reputation it might be expected that a robust system of internal controls would have been in operation on the Mary Jane, ensuring operational effectiveness, reliable systems and compliance both with external laws and regulations and Sea Ships Co's own internal policies. There were, however, several failings to be identified and their effects are set out below.

Design fault

Internal control failings are clearly identified and analysed

There was a major failing of information provision and compliance with standards when the design fault, highlighted in the consultant's report, was not acted on because of internal communication breakdown. This suggests both a serious failure within the company to understand its safety responsibilities and a failure in information provision within the company, as information should have been passed on to those who could assess its importance.

Problems with loading

Control systems prior to departure also were inadequate as they allowed vehicles to be loaded wrongly onto ships. Well-trained staff or physical controls such as better signing would have prevented this happening. These problems contributed to the time pressure that led to the disaster.

Failure to secure doors

The accident was caused by the failure to secure the doors, and the checks over door security were inadequate. A design flaw meant that no review could take place from the deck of the ship. There was no formal requirement for acknowledgement that the doors had been checked. Instead, reliance was placed on someone else carrying out the check and the confusion over responsibilities meant that the control was not carried out.

Reporting system

Good use of evidence from the scenario, with suggestions made

The ship's reporting system relied on reporting by exception – assuming all was well to sail unless the bridge heard otherwise. However, if communications were faulty, problems may not have been reported to the bridge. The previous system of positive reporting by each department head being required should not have been abandoned just because it was time-consuming to operate.

Emphasis on speed

The internal control systems were also ineffective as they allowed captains to give speed of departure and sailing priority over compliance with the law. There were no control systems on board to prevent the ships breaking local speed limits.

Failure to insure

Controls also failed to operate in Sea Ships' legal department, with the result that the liability was not properly insured. The legal department should have annually reviewed the insurance arrangements to check that they covered all liabilities and recommended major changes in cover or terms if this proved necessary.

41 The BA Times

Marks

1 mark for each relevant point up to a maximum of 10 marks for technical skills

10

Professional skills may be rewarded as in the following rubric:

How well has the candidate demonstrated professional skills as follows:	No marks	Half marks	Full marks
Analysis skills in relation Victor's concerns regarding changes in technology and media and the impact of this on the subscribers, advertisers and the financial viability of the *BA Times*.	The candidate has demonstrated limited analysis skills and has failed to fully appreciate the effects of technological change on the business model of the *BA Times*. No attempt has been made to address the beliefs of Victor regarding the impact of technology.	The candidate has demonstrated some analysis skills in presenting a range of factors to discuss in regard to the impact of technology on magazine publishing. Some attempt has been made to address Victor's particular concerns and dispute some of his beliefs.	The candidate has demonstrated comprehensive analysis skills using most of the information from the scenario. This has been used to dispute the concerns raised by Victor and present a case for greater investment in technology to overcome the problems that the magazine is currently facing.
	0	1	2

Drivers and barriers to the introduction of new technologies and media

Drivers for change

BA Times is operating in a highly challenging climate. The magazine is currently experiencing increasing production and distribution costs in its home market. Conditions are also worsening in part due to changes in reading habits, especially amongst younger readers who no longer want hard copies. These drivers for change indicate that new technologies could offer *BA Times* the ability to address the threats it currently faces.

Barriers to change

Victor's somewhat old-fashioned attitude towards the introduction of new technology and media is a barrier to embracing new processes at *BA Times*. Victor likes the feel of printed magazines. He is concerned that existing subscribers and advertisers will not react positively to any technological change. This indicates that business decisions at *BA Times* are predominantly based on Victor's personal preferences as opposed to commercial realities. The company's current position makes overcoming this reluctance even more important.

Impact of change on key stakeholders

Subscribers

An improved website should attract potential subscribers to the magazine. The ability to tailor online content is likely to be attractive to existing and prospective subscribers. Free articles focusing on forthcoming examinations could be posted. These may entice users to subscribe to relevant online news content or to purchase the physical magazine (if it continues to be published).

The business would need to investigate Victor's concerns regarding the number of subscribers without internet access. These may be fewer in number than Victor believes. Based on changing reading habits it appears likely that a move online would be well received by subscribers.

A stronger online presence should help *BA Times* to maintain its respected status among subscribers. This may act as a draw for new subscribers too, if they believe they are paying for content that is not available elsewhere.

Advertisers

The evidence indicates that advertisers are increasingly unconvinced about the effectiveness of advertising in printed magazines, which has led to falling magazine advertising revenues. Victor is likely to be incorrect in his view that many advertisers would prefer to continue with display advertisements in a printed magazine. As fewer young people are choosing to purchase print media and traditional print advertising is reducing, it is increasingly likely that advertisers will need to adapt their methods of reaching their intended target market. Developing the magazine's website to allow advertisers to reach subscribers seems a move that most advertisers will support.

Online advertising may also allow advertisers greater scope to individualise and tailor their marketing message, thereby increasing the likelihood that the message is received. Based on these factors it seems unlikely that Victor's concerns regarding the advertiser's reaction to technological changes are justified.

BA Times – financial viability

Introducing new technology could help *BA Times* reduce its print production costs. The development of an enhanced website with more features would allow *BA Times* to extend its offering to its subscribers. This may serve to reduce the demand for the printed product thereby reducing the associated costs of production.

As the founder of *BA Times*, any such changes would require Victor to 'buy in' to the developments. This may prove to be particularly difficult given his current concerns. Victor needs to be convinced that the business will benefit financially from any such move. Introducing new technology could offer up new opportunities for revenue generation. For example, recruitment agencies could take out banner adverts on the website, advertising their services directly to the magazine's subscribers. The fees *BA Times* receives from the advertisers will increase the revenue generated.

As illustrated by the survey, one of the respondents not choosing to renew his subscription to the magazine claims that he wanted to become an engineer in order to get a job, not just sit examinations and read about exam topics. *BA Times* could therefore look to exploit the use of an enhanced website to offer a greater range of services.

42 Graffoff

Marks

Consideration of the claim may include analysis of:

Tighter credit control	Max 2
Delayed payments	Max 2
Debt factoring	Max 2
Conclusion	1
Appropriate calculations in support	1
Up to a maximum of 8 marks for technical skills	<u>8</u>

Professional skills may be rewarded as in the following rubric:

How well has the candidate demonstrated professional skills as follows:	No marks	Half marks	Full marks
Analysis skills in relation to assessing the consultant's claim.	The candidate demonstrated limited analysis skill and has failed to include enough consideration of the available evidence to be able to draw a conclusion on the consultant's claims.	The candidate has demonstrated some analysis skill by considering the evidence in the scenario and performing supporting calculations. The implications of the findings from this analysis are not clearly expressed and no real conclusion is drawn.	The candidate has demonstrated comprehensive analysis skill by using the data and evidence from the scenario. These, along with wider issues, have been used to consider the consultant's suggestion. A clear conclusion has been arrived at that can be used to advise Emile as he considers his options.
	0	1	2

Emile is committed to paying high dividends, therefore the possible sources of internal finance open to him are tighter credit control and delayed payment to suppliers.

Tighter credit control

Customers are given a 30-day payment term, however, the average time taken for them to pay their debts is 59 days [(260/1,600) × 365 = 59.31].

If credit control is tightened up and the average is brought down to 30 days approximately $128,500 could be released for funding.

Reducing the average to 40 days – the industry standard – would release approximately $84,500.

Emile dislikes conflict with customers. This is why he has allowed the extended payment terms to occur. A change to enforcing the 30-day payment terms could create difficulties and put a strain on relationships with customers. If this is to be done, Emile will have to stop undermining the accounts receivable department with offers of such generous terms.

Delayed payment to suppliers

On average, Graffoff takes only 20 days to pay its suppliers [(75/1,375) × 365 = 19.91]. This is far quicker than the industry standard of 40 days. If the company were to delay its payments so that they were only made after 40 days, approximately $75,500 could be released for investment.

There is no reason why this change could not be put in place as the fast payment appears to be simply due to the 'zealous administrator in accounts payable who likes to reduce creditors'. It is also noted that Graffoff is 'unique in its punctuality of payments'.

Even if payments are only delayed to 30 days (the normal credit terms for the country), $38,000 would still be realised.

So, if changes were made to both tighten credit control to 30 days, and delay payments to suppliers to the industry standard of 40 days, a total of $204,000 ($128,500 + $75,500) could be raised, resulting in a short-term, one-off acceleration of cash inflow.

Debt factoring

This would involve a third party taking over Graffoff's debt collection. Factoring companies will generally pay 80% of approved trade receivables in advance, which would translate to an immediate cash input of $208,000. Given the existing problems with credit control, this could be an attractive alternative. It could potentially also address the motivation and staffing problems in the accounts receivable section.

Conclusion

However, regardless of the option chosen, it is not possible for internal finance resources to raise the full $500,000 that would be needed for the organic growth plan. The consultant's claim is therefore incorrect and some external funding would also be needed.

However, it would seem that internally raised finance could be sufficient to finance either franchising, or an opportunistic alliance with The Equipment Emporium.

43 Yvern Trinkets

Marking scheme

		Marks
1 mark for each appropriate point, which could include:		
Analysis of quantitative data	Max 5	
Analysis of qualitative factors	Max 3	
Summary/conclusion	Max 2	
Up to a maximum of 10 marks for technical skills		10

Professional skills may be rewarded as in the following rubric:

How well has the candidate demonstrated professional skills as follows:	No marks	Half marks	Full marks
Scepticism skills in evaluating the claims of the Managing Director.	The candidate has failed to demonstrate any scepticism of the Managing Director's claim. There is no evidence of questioning the claim or undertaking deeper analysis of the data to enable reflection on its implications.	The candidate has demonstrated some scepticism skills in probing the claim of the Managing Director and has provided some analysis of the data. However, the analysis is not fully developed which limits the ability to fully consider the implications and really probe the claim in depth.	The candidate has demonstrated strong professional scepticism regarding the claim of the Managing Director, with good data analysis and understanding of the issues surrounding outsourcing combining to allow the candidate to challenge the claim.
	0	1	2

Three solutions in respect of the question Yvern Trinkets have been provided below. Each of the three solutions provides an indication of the different level of skills marks that could be earned.

NO PROFESSIONAL SKILLS MARKS

Quantitative factors

Here is a monthly analysis of the data given in the scenario.

Product	A	B	C	D	Total
Production (units)	2,000	5,500	4,000	3,000	
Unit marginal costs	$	$	$	$	$
Direct materials	3	5	2	4	
Direct labour	9	6	9	6	
Variable production overheads	2	3	1	2	
Variable cost per unit	14	14	12	12	
Total monthly variable cost	28,000	77,000	48,000	36,000	
Fixed monthly overheads	4,000	4,000	4,000	4,000	
Total in-house monthly cost	32,000	81,000	52,000	40,000	205,000
Buying costs per unit	11.5	16.5	12.5	13.5	
Total monthly buy in cost	23,000	90,750	50,000	40,500	204,250

No probing of the results of the analysis

The data suggest that only products A and C can be sourced more cheaply through outsourcing. Products B and D can be produced more cheaply in-house, but overall it is cheaper to outsource everything ($204,250 compared with $205,000).

If just products A and C are sub-contracted, as they can be sourced more cheaply than the other products, the company would then have spare capacity for further production for B and D, which is a powerful argument for outsourcing anyway.

It can be seen that the variable production cost of C is less than the buy-in cost ($48,000 compared with $50,000), but the addition of the fixed overhead makes the outsourcing option cheaper.

Qualitative factors

The company has no experience in managing an outsourced supplier. Contractual terms will have to be established. The management of the outsource supplier will itself incur costs.

The company has always advertised itself as producing locally in the region but outsourcing might destroy this message.

The reaction of the company's workforce also has to be taken into consideration. Redundancies may be required if demand for labour is reduced.

Summary

The company has considerable experience in making the products and the location they are produced in appears to be important to customers. In contrast, the company has no experience in outsourcing and managing outsourced providers. However, the new Managing Director's assertion that 'all four products can be produced more cheaply by the supplier in Tinglia' is correct. Cost data would need to be confirmed, and other costs associated with outsourcing investigated.

HALF PROFESSIONAL SKILLS MARKS

Quantitative factors

Here is a monthly analysis of the data given in the scenario.

Product	A	B	C	D	Total
Production (units)	2,000	5,500	4,000	3,000	
Unit marginal costs	$	$	$	$	$
Direct materials	3	5	2	4	
Direct labour	9	6	9	6	
Variable production overheads	2	3	1	2	
Variable cost per unit	14	14	12	12	
Total monthly variable cost	28,000	77,000	48,000	36,000	
Fixed monthly overheads	4,000	4,000	4,000	4,000	
Total in-house monthly cost	32,000	81,000	52,000	40,000	205,000
Buying costs per unit	11.5	16.5	12.5	13.5	
Total monthly buy in cost	23,000	90,750	50,000	40,500	204,250

The data suggest that only products A and C can be sourced more cheaply through outsourcing. Products B and D can be produced more cheaply in-house.

If products A and C are sub-contracted, the company would then have spare capacity. Investigation might show that Yvern could utilise this to produce more of B and D. If this is the case, that is another argument for just outsourcing A and C.

The justification for outsourcing product C in particular is made on the saving of fixed costs attributable to its manufacture. The variable production cost of C is less than the buy-in cost ($48,000 compared with $50,000), but the addition of the fixed overhead makes the outsourcing option cheaper. The reliability of this estimate of fixed costs and the likelihood of these savings needs to be investigated to be able to fully support the Managing Director's view.

If the outsourcing prices offered depend on outsourcing the whole of production to Tinglia, then the outsourcing option is indeed cheaper ($204,250 compared with $205,000).

Qualitative factors

The company has no experience in managing an outsourced supplier. Contractual terms will have to be established for specifying the terms of supply quality and other factors. The management of the outsource supplier will require one-off and continuing costs which do not appear to have been factored into the proposal.

Deeper analysis of qualitative factors

The company has always advertised itself as producing locally in the region, but sourcing the products through outsourcers could invalidate this message.

The reaction of the company's workforce also has to be taken into consideration, as redundancies may be required. Evidence also suggests that products A and C require more labour-intensive processes. So, even if spare capacity can be used in the production of B and D, demand for labour would reduce.

Summary

Recognition that it might not just be a cost decision

The decision to make or buy certain products should not be taken on cost savings alone. The company has considerable experience in making the products and the location they are produced in appears to be important to both the company and its customers. In contrast, the company has no experience in outsourcing and managing outsourced providers. In addition, the new Managing Director's assertion that 'all four products can be produced more cheaply by the supplier in Tinglia' is not entirely correct. The products can be made more cheaply in Tinglia if all of the products are outsourced, although data on overhead costs would need to be confirmed, and other costs associated with outsourcing investigated. It is not the case that each of the products can individually be produced more cheaply in Tinglia.

More scepticism as to Managing Director's view, but not fully developed

FULL PROFESSIONAL SKILLS MARKS

Quantitative factors

Here is a monthly analysis of the data given in the scenario.

Product	A	B	C	D	Total
Production (units)	2,000	5,500	4,000	3,000	
Unit marginal costs	$	$	$	$	
Direct materials	3	5	2	4	
Direct labour	9	6	9	6	
Variable production overheads	2	3	1	2	
Variable cost per unit	14	14	12	12	
Total monthly variable cost	28,000	77,000	40,000	36,000	
Fixed monthly overheads	4,000	4,000	4,000	4,000	
Total in-house monthly cost	32,000	81,000	52,000	40,000	205,000
Buying costs per unit	11.5	16.5	12.5	13.5	
Total monthly buy in cost	23,000	90,750	50,000	40,500	204,250

The data suggest that only products A and C can be sourced more cheaply through outsourcing. Products B and D can be produced more cheaply in-house.

Evidence of deeper questioning of the analysis

If products A and C are sub-contracted, the company would then have spare capacity. There is no evidence from the scenario that there is any demand for further production for B and D. More research has to be conducted to see if, in fact, production capacity is a limiting factor at the company and can be effectively utilised to produce more of B and D. If this is the case, then there would be a powerful argument for outsourcing A and C.

The justification for outsourcing product C in particular is purely made on the saving of fixed costs attributable to its manufacture. The variable production cost of C is less than the buy-in cost ($48,000 compared with $50,000), but the addition of the fixed overhead makes the outsourcing option cheaper. There are two important considerations here: the reliability of this estimate of fixed costs and the likelihood that these savings can be delivered by management when the production of the product is outsourced. It seems unlikely that all four products will have exactly the same direct effect on fixed costs; it looks more like an arbitrary figure. Furthermore, on many occasions, fixed costs savings do not actually materialise.

> *Emphasis upon the effect of fixed costs and expression of scepticism*

If the outsourcing prices offered depend on outsourcing the whole of production to Tinglia, then the outsourcing option is very slightly cheaper ($204,250 compared with $205,000). This again depends on the reliability of the fixed overhead data and the ability of management to save these fixed costs once production is outsourced.

> *Recognition that the difference is marginal*

Qualitative factors

The company has no experience in managing an outsourced supplier and ensuring that supplied products are of the required quality. Contractual terms will have to be established for specifying the terms of supply quality and other factors. The management of the outsource supplier will require one-off and continuing costs which do not appear to have been factored into the proposal.

> *Fuller analysis of qualitative factors*

The company has always advertised itself as producing locally in the region. It is part of their marketing campaign and an attraction to local customers. Sourcing the products through geographically remote outsourcers invalidates this marketing message.

The reaction of the company's workforce also has to be taken into consideration. If production of B and D cannot be expanded to take up the spare capacity, then redundancies may be required which will be costly. Evidence also suggests that products A and C require more labour-intensive processes. So, even if spare capacity can be used in the production of B and D, demand for labour would reduce.

Summary

> *Recognition that not just a cost decision*

The decision to make or buy certain products should not be taken on cost savings alone. The company has considerable experience in making the products and the location they are produced in appears to be important to both the company (for its marketing message) and its customers. In contrast, the company has no experience in outsourcing and managing outsourced providers.

In addition, the new Managing Director's assertion that 'all four products can be produced more cheaply by the supplier in Tinglia' is ambiguous. If he means that the products can be made more cheaply in Tinglia if all four products are outsourced, then he is just about correct, although the results are marginal and so data on overhead costs would need to be confirmed, along with an investigation of any other costs associated with outsourcing. However, if he means that all products can individually be produced more cheaply in Tinglia, then he is incorrect. Products B and D can be produced more cheaply in-house. Partial outsourcing may lead to spare labour and machine capacity issues in the factory in Yvern.

> *Evidence of sceptical treatment of the Managing Director's views, with comments to justify scepticism.*

44 Coastal Oil

	Marks
Distinguishing between objective and subjective risk	1
1 mark for explanation of each and/or evidence of understanding	Max 2
2 marks for each argument developed against the senator's statement	Max 4
Evidence of understanding of ALARP	1
Explanation of why health and safety risks cannot be completely eliminated under ALARP	Max 2
Up to a maximum of 10 marks for technical skills	10

Professional skills may be rewarded as in the following rubric:

How well has the candidate demonstrated professional skills as follows:	No marks	Half marks	Full marks
Scepticism skills in questioning the opinions expressed by Senator Jones, and Coastal Oil's ability to guarantee that any further accidents can be prevented.	The candidate has failed to demonstrate any questioning of claims made by the senator and has not provided a strong argument as to why Coastal Oil cannot guarantee that problems will not arise again. Answer does not constitute an acceptable statement for the CEO to present.	The candidate has questioned the claims of the senator but this is not backed up by enough convincing argument about risk assessment and the realities of joint venture arrangements. The overall statement does not provide a robust challenge to the senator's views, or provide justification for Coastal's position in not being able to provide any guarantees.	The candidate has demonstrated strong professional scepticism regarding the claim of the senator, with technical analysis of risk assessment allowing the candidate to question and ultimately deny the claim in an authoritative and professional manner.
	0	1	2

Statement to special committee

Although Coastal Oil accepts its share of responsibility for problems with controls, I would highlight that we were acting as a major partner in a joint venture and did not have complete control over what happened on the rig. Other partners had responsibilities for maintaining controls over operations and safety. However, discussions after the accident have highlighted a lack of clarity in the responsibilities of ourselves and our joint venture partner. Because we must place some reliance on the controls maintained by our partner, we acknowledge the need for clearer agreements in future.

In direct response to Senator Jones's comment that we must have known that an accident would happen, this must be questioned because it is important to realise that risk assessment is a complex process, involving the assessment of both the likelihood of a risk materialising and the impact if it does materialise.

One important distinction in risk assessment is between objective and subjective risk assessment. Objective risk assessment involves measuring the likelihood and impact of risks precisely or at least to a high degree of accuracy. Subjective risk assessment means using judgement to assess risk levels that cannot be determined using objective criteria.

Argument against Senator Jones's view

I must respond to Senator Jones's comment that I, as the company's Chief Executive, 'should have known that the accident was going to happen'. I accept that the Senator is very angry because of the impact of the disaster on the area he represents. However, I do disagree with his comments because it fails to take into account the complexities of risk management.

Subjective assessment of accident

The probability of a workplace accident occurring is not something that can be assessed with precision. It has to be assessed subjectively and I could therefore never be certain that an accident would happen. Subjective assessment of the probability and impact of a risk occurring is also very difficult. Coastal Oil operates hundreds of rigs worldwide and does so in conjunction with a number of joint venture partners. The nature of the processes are such that it is very difficult to predict the probability that an accident will happen on any rig, and even more so that an accident will occur on a specific rig such as the Effland Coastal Deep Rig. Similarly, it is virtually impossible to predict the scale of the impact if an accident occurs.

Lack of information

Assessment of the risk of accidents was also made more difficult by the information systems we have had in place. As I have already explained, the rig's management informed us of problems by exception. They failed to report internal control failures on their rigs to land-side management and hence the board was unaware of these failings. In future we expect that the information that the board receive from the rigs will be enhanced. They will include reports by management on the operation of controls, even if there have been no incidents caused by lapses in control.

Impossibility of eliminating risk

I share the committee's desire for an accident like this not to happen again. However, I cannot guarantee that the risk can be reduced to zero. It is impossible for us to avoid undertaking hazardous activities. The controls that we have in place cannot eliminate the risks associated with these activities, since, for example, the company may face extreme circumstances or errors may be made by staff operating controls. Governance best practice acknowledges that sound control systems can reduce, but not eliminate, risks and that the costs of operating elaborate controls may outweigh their benefits.

ALARP

Our risk management procedures are instead based on the ALARP (as low as reasonably practicable) principle. This is based on the idea that the higher the level of the risk, the less acceptable it is. Nonetheless, it is important to balance this against the commercial realities and recognise that the process of drilling for oil is inevitably high risk. Adopting the ALARP approach allows us to identify where practicable those risks judged as being high risk, and to then put in place effective control measures to reduce their likelihood and impact. We can, for example, reduce the likelihood of a risk to health and safety materialising by training staff so that they are aware of threats and less likely to make mistakes that will jeopardise safety. We can reduce the impact of a health and safety risk materialising by taking measures to protect staff, for example by insisting that they wear safety clothing.

Judgement

However, as I have already explained, the assessment of the risks that we face is a subjective process. It therefore follows that judgements about the controls necessary to reduce risks are also a matter of judgement. This means that I cannot guarantee that the probability of health and safety risks materialising is zero, but it would emphasise that we intend to maintain vigilance in order to keep risk levels as low as reasonably practicable.

45 Jones Co

			Marks
1 mark for each criticism identified in the context of the case		Max 5	
1 mark for the development of the criticism with reference to practice or application		Max 5	
Up to a maximum of 8 marks for technical skills			8

Professional skills may be rewarded as in the following rubric:

How well has the candidate demonstrated professional skills as follows:	No marks	Half marks	Full marks
Scepticism skills in challenging the behaviour of Potto Sinter in respect of the audit of Jones Co.	The candidate has failed to demonstrate any scepticism regarding the behaviour of Potto Sinter, and has therefore failed to identify any ethical or professional issues.	Although the candidate has displayed some scepticism and knowledge of ethical issues, there is a failure to structure the answer properly or to provide enough detail related to the scenario, suggesting a limited ability to apply knowledge and challenge behaviour against business and professional ethical codes.	The candidate has demonstrated an excellent level of scepticism regarding Potto Sinter's behaviour, challenging it in all relevant aspects and making appropriate commentary on the specific situation in the scenario.
	0	1	2

Thinking about the stakeholders involved in corporate governance and the auditors' duty to them is helpful when considering the behaviour of Potto Sinter. There are five clear ethical and professional issues in the case attributed to Mr Sinter which are described below.

Agreeing to corruption

It appears that Potto could be implicated in a misappropriation of company funds for Martin Jones's personal use. He has either agreed to this or accepted a weak explanation, raising issues about his integrity and/or his professional competence.

Duty to shareholders

Potto seems to have allowed his relationship with Martin to override his duty to the rest of the shareholders. Potto is reporting to the shareholders that the financial statements are true and fair. He should therefore have taken an objective view of Martin's conduct and he has failed to do this.

Duty to tax authorities

As well as a duty to shareholders, Potto has a duty to stakeholders who have a legal or other right to rely on the reliability and completeness of information in the accounts. This particularly applies to the tax authorities in any regime, and in many regimes Potto could be charged with colluding in tax evasion.

Duty to professional colleagues

Potto has let down his partners and staff in a number of ways. Querying the transaction was justified, and Potto's initial response would have given the impression that he was not taking the concern seriously. Potto then accepted what appeared to be an inadequate explanation, and did not provide any reason for his decision. Not only was this poor conduct of professional relationships, it was setting a poor example.

Failure to fulfil accounting and auditing standards

Potto has breached auditing standards by allowing an unmodified report to be issued on accounts with a breach of accounting standards. All related party transactions should be disclosed, regardless of value.

46 Rosey and Atkins

	Marks
2 marks for explanation of stakeholder claims in conflict	Max 2
2 marks for evidence of understanding of an appropriate stakeholder analysis framework	Max 2
2 marks for assessment of each of the two stakeholders – up to 4 in total (2 × 2)	Max 4
Up to a maximum of 8 marks for technical skills	8

Professional skills may be rewarded as in the following rubric:

How well has the candidate demonstrated professional skills as follows:	No marks	Half marks	Full marks
Evaluation skills in assessing the implications of the housing project, and the competing claims of the stakeholders identified.	The candidate was not able to effectively assess the competing claims of the two groups of stakeholders and provided no assessment of the implications.	The candidate was able to explain the implications of the project and demonstrated some skill in assessing the stakeholders competing claims, but did not use their findings to extend their answer further, ie to make suggestions on how the relationships could be managed.	The candidate has shown excellent evaluation skills in assessing the implications of the project. The candidate clearly explained the claims of the two stakeholder groups and explained how they are in competition. The candidate extended their answer by clearly explaining how the groups could be managed.
	0	1	2

Three solutions in respect of the question Rosey and Atkins have been provided below. Each of the three solutions provides an indication of the different level of skills marks that could be earned.

NO PROFESSIONAL MARKS

The subject of its stakeholders is central to any understanding of a business. Any group or individual who can affect or be affected by an organisation can be referred to as a stakeholder. The range of stakeholders relevant to an organisation will depend on that organisation's size and on its activities. Some stakeholders want to influence what the organisation does, while others are more concerned with the way that they are affected by the organisation and may want to change the way that the activities of the organisation affect them.

Stakeholder 'claims' are the results sought in a given situation by a specific stakeholder. Stakeholder claims are often in conflict. The university in the case does not want new housing to be built, because it wants to protect a view, whilst R&A and the local government authority are both in favour of the development for valid economic and social reasons.

In any stakeholder situation, the levels of influence that different ones have need to be ascertained.

The local government authority can grant or withhold planning consent. It is also a shareholder of R&A, and an investor in R&A's funds. As it is interested in the construction of low-cost housing because it is both a client and a shareholder of R&A, there might be some conflict issues here to be overcome.

The university cannot influence the planning decision and it is not a shareholder in R&A. It also has a lesser investment in R&A's funds than the local authority as an R&A client. It may find that its views therefore are ignored.

The local government authority must balance the claims of a number of stakeholders when taking decisions of this type, including the economic interests of R&A. The university is of the opinion that the new houses will reduce the view over countryside currently enjoyed. The weight given to the value of the view, against the social value of the new housing development to the local government authority and the local community, is likely to be decided in favour of the development, and this seems to be appropriate.

HALF PROFESSIONAL MARKS

Some stakeholders want to influence what the organisation does, while others are more concerned with the way that they are affected by the organisation and may want to change the way that the activities of the organisation affect them.

Stakeholder claims are the outcomes sought in a given situation by a specific stakeholder. If a stakeholder (such as a university or a local government authority) has a voice, then the outcome that is being sought can be put forward. Stakeholder claims are often in conflict, meaning that stakeholders want different outcomes in a certain situation. The university in the case does not want new housing to be built, whilst R&A and the local government authority are both in favour of the development.

In any stakeholder situation, including those which are in conflict, the influence can be ascertained by using Mendelow's (1991) matrix. This is one way of mapping the influence of stakeholders. Identified stakeholders are assessed according to their relative power and interest. Those stakeholders with the highest combination of these variables are those with the most influence over outcomes.

The local government authority has more power than the university because of its ability to grant or withhold planning consent. It also has power as a shareholder of R&A, and influence as an investor in R&A's funds. There are considerable conflict issues, however. It has a social obligation to see the development approved, but this is in conflict with concern for the profitability of the R&A company.

Margin annotations (left column):

- Definition of 'stakeholder' is not required by the question
- Basic evaluation of each stakeholder claim, with conflict not fully explained
- No use of models, and appears to be pre-judging
- Conclusion appears subjective and is not properly supported
- Some explanation of conflicting claims, but nothing as to why they might arise in this case
- Reference made to appropriate model
- Evaluation of power and interest of each stakeholder is clearly set out, along with the potential for conflict

The university has no power over the planning decision, is not a shareholder in R&A and has a lesser investment in R&A's funds than the local authority as an R&A client. It is likely, though, that the views of such an important local institution would be taken into account.

Competing claims are not thoroughly assessed and no recommendation on how to manage them

The local government authority must balance the claims of a number of stakeholders when taking decisions of this type. The university is of the opinion that the new houses will reduce the view over countryside currently enjoyed. The local community may also have an opinion on this. The weight given to the value of the view, against the social value of the new housing development to the local government authority and the local community, will therefore also have ethical and environmental dimensions and the final decision will be subject to many factors.

FULL PROFESSIONAL MARKS

Good application of relevant model, with recognition of its limitations

Some stakeholders want to influence what the organisation does, while others are more concerned with the way that they are affected by the organisation and may want to change the way that the activities of the organisation affect them.

Good explanation of why there is conflict in this particular case

Stakeholder claims are the outcomes sought in a given situation by a specific stakeholder. If a stakeholder (such as a university or a local government authority) has a voice, then the outcome that is being sought can be put forward. Stakeholder claims are often in conflict, meaning that two stakeholders want different outcomes in a certain situation. The university in the case does not want new housing to be built, whilst R&A and the local government authority are both in favour of the development, because each organisation has different and competing objectives on a range of both social and economic issues.

In any stakeholder situation, including those which are in conflict, the influence that each stakeholder has over an organisation's objectives or strategy can be ascertained by Mendelow's (1991) matrix. Identified stakeholders are assessed according to their relative power (how much they can influence objectives) and interest (how much they actually want to). Those stakeholders with the highest combination of these variables are those with the most influence. This is one way of mapping the influence of stakeholders and it is often used, although it can be difficult to measure an individual stakeholder's power and interest, and changing events can mean that stakeholders move around the matrix.

Clear explanation of the claims and the conflicts using evidence from the case

In this example, the local government authority has a higher power than the university because of its ability to grant or withhold planning consent. This is a power devolved from central government, although it is usually required that local consultation be entered into before final approval is granted. It also has more limited power as a shareholder of R&A, and possibly some influence as an investor in R&A's funds. As an external stakeholder, being an authority interested in the construction of low-cost housing and both a client and a shareholder of R&A, there are considerable conflict issues. It has a social obligation to see the development approved, as this will allow lower-cost housing to be built, but this is potentially in conflict with concern for the profitability of the R&A company in which it holds shares.

The university has less power over the planning decision because it has no statutory power, is not a shareholder in R&A directly and has a lesser investment in R&A's funds than the local authority. It is likely that the views of such an important local institution would be taken into account, however, because a successful university is important in the development of the town.

Recognition of potential for complexity in such decisions

The local government authority must balance the claims of a number of stakeholders when taking decisions of this type, including, but not limited to, the economic interests of R&A. The university is of the opinion that the new houses will reduce the views over countryside that are currently enjoyed. Whether or not it is true that the view helps to recruit students and staff to the university, the local community is also likely to have an opinion on its value. The weight given to the value of the view, against the social value of the new housing development to the local government authority and the local community, will therefore also have ethical and environmental dimensions and the final decision will be subject to many factors.

47 iTTrain

	Marks
Evaluation of $750 price:	
Marketing objectives of iTTrain	Max 2
Estimate of forecast contribution levels	Max 4
Options:	
Increase price	1
Use of intermediaries to promote services	Max 2
Decrease costs	1
Up to a maximum of 10 marks for technical skills	10

Professional skills may be rewarded as in the following rubric:

How well has the candidate demonstrated professional skills as follows:	No marks	Half marks	Full marks
Evaluation skills in relation to the implications of the suggested pricing strategy and generating possible options.	The candidate's answer has failed to make use of the information in the scenario to be able to make an evaluation of the proposed pricing strategy, and no consideration has been given to the possible options for Marco.	The candidate has demonstrated evaluation skills in making some use of the information in the scenario. The evaluation does not give sufficient attention to the implications of the suggested pricing strategy. Valid suggestions for options have not been made.	The candidate has shown strong evaluation skills by making good use of the information in the scenario which has included the implications of the suggested pricing strategy. This has been followed by an evaluation of available options.
	0	1	2

Evaluation of suggested price

Marketing objectives

The price that an organisation charges customers for its products or services is likely to form a key part of its strategy. Customer perception forms an important element in determining an appropriate selling price as the value a customer derives from using a particular service needs to be sufficiently attractive in light of the price demanded. Marco intends to position iTTrain as a quality provider of IT certification training.

Based on his understanding of prices charged by competing firms, and his wish to generate a 'modest' profit in his first year, Marco has proposed a price of $750. This appears to represent a reasonable price given the high-quality customer experience iTTrain is hoping to provide. Cheaper training providers offer courses for $550, but such courses represent a 'no frills' offering with attendees being those 'for whom price is an issue'.

AQT, the dominant provider, offers similar courses for $900 for a three-day programme, but this price is often discounted to $810. It appears that price alone is not the only consideration for some customers when choosing where to study. At a price of $750 per delegate, Marco is offering a high- quality customer experience at a lower and more competitive price.

Marco's desire to offer a premium service at a higher price which principally targets the corporate market may prove successful, especially if these customers are prepared to pay more for their delegates to receive higher quality training.

Financial evaluation

The following financial evaluation is based on the information provided. The income figures are calculated based on Marco's proposed price of $750.

Workings

Table 1: Contribution generated per course

Number of delegates per course (based on AQT)	Number of courses run (based on AQT)	Lecturer costs per day ($450 x 3 days)	Training room costs per day ($250 x 3 days)	Course manual costs ($20 per manual per delegate)	Lunch cost per delegate ($10 per delegate per day)	Total cost	Income ($750 per number of delegates)	Contribution
3	150	$1,350	$750	$60	$90	$2,250	$2,250	$0
4	210	$1,350	$750	$80	$120	$2,300	$3,000	$700
5	250	$1,350	$750	$100	$150	$2,350	$3,750	$1,400
6	190	$1,350	$750	$120	$180	$2,400	$4,500	$2,100
7	70	$1,350	$750	$140	$210	$2,450	$5,250	$2,800
8	80	$1,350	$750	$160	$240	$2,500	$6,000	$3,500
9	50	$1,350	$750	$180	$270	$2,550	$6,750	$4,200

Table 2: Operating profit or loss based on number of delegates attending

Number of delegates based on AQT	Contribution (contribution per course calculated in Table 1 x 40 courses per annum)	Fixed costs per annum	Operating profit or (loss)
3	$0	($65,000)	($65,000)
4	$28,000	($65,000)	($37,000)
5	$56,000	($65,000)	($9,000)
6	$84,000	($65,000)	$19,000
7	$112,000	($65,000)	$47,000
8	$140,000	($65,000)	$75,000
9	$168,000	($65,000)	$103,000

Table 2 illustrates that, based on a selling price of $750 and the contribution calculated per course in Table 1, iTTrain will need to ensure that, on average, at least six delegates are on each of the 40 courses offered in order for it to generate a profit after taking into account annual fixed costs.

From the financial analysis conducted, it appears that Marco's proposed fee of $750 may be too low to guarantee a profit in the coming year if his class sizes are smaller than six attendees, or if all 40 courses do not run as scheduled.

Marco will need to give careful consideration to any associated costs that iTTrain may incur, should scheduled courses have to be cancelled due to low numbers. Self-employed lecturers and the training venue may require iTTrain to make penalty payments if there is insufficient notice of cancellation.

Options

Increase prices

In light of the above analysis, Marco may wish to consider amending the proposed price of $750. An increase in the price charged to, say, $800 per delegate would bring iTTrain's fees nearer to the discounted fees charged by AQT. This option would allow iTTrain to preserve its competitive pricing approach and help Marco to attract customers and achieve the profit he is seeking in Year 1.

Use of intermediaries

A feature of the market is the role that intermediaries play in the supply chain, advertising courses on their websites in exchange for discounted prices. This has implications for the prices that Marco is attempting to determine. Some intermediaries have already asked about the possibility of iTTrain offering similar discounts to those received from AQT.

In the event that Marco did offer a 10% discount on iTTrain's courses, this would reduce the price per delegate from $750 to $675. Such a move would have to be fully considered prior to being accepted, to assess its impact on contribution and profitability. It may be more appropriate for iTTrain to offer 'early bird' schemes, where customers receive a discount in exchange for early payment. This approach is particularly effective at improving cash flows. Again, establishing a price of $800 per delegate may be more suitable if discounts are going to be offered. A higher selling price would help to offset the effects of discounting.

Decrease costs

Marco could explore the possibility of lowering the costs of running the courses. The costs of hiring the self-employed lecturers and renting the training centre rooms are set as standard prices. There may be scope to realise discounted rates on bookings if these are made in bulk. Lower costs would help to improve the contribution and profits generated.

48 Tillo Community Centre

Marking scheme

		Marks
1 mark for correctly categorising each set of benefits	Max 4	
Up to 3 marks for evaluating each set of benefits	Max 10	
Up to a maximum of 12 marks for technical skills		12

Professional skills may be rewarded as in the following rubric:

How well has the candidate demonstrated professional skills as follows:	No marks	Half marks	Full marks
Evaluation skills in assessing the validity of the benefits outlined in the business case and for undertaking an objective appraisal of each benefit specified.	The candidate has failed to evaluate the benefits as set out in the business case, so there is no meaningful assessment of their validity as a basis for the building project.	The candidate has demonstrated some evaluation skills in assessing the relevant aspects of the business case as required by the question, and has developed the evaluation by drawing upon the circumstances in the scenario, but conclusions as to their validity have not been clearly stated.	The candidate has clearly evaluated the benefits outlined in the business case, and has carried out a full appraisal of each benefit. The candidate made good use of the information contained in the scenario which has enabled a firm conclusion on the validity of each of the benefits to be drawn.
	0	1	2

Observable benefits

The realisation of observable benefits, such as increased staff morale, can only be determined by the judgement or experience of someone who is qualified to make such an assessment. Staff morale could perhaps be assessed via an independent survey carried out both before and after the community centre was up and running, but the results of this could only be assessed once the project was completed and the building had been in use for some time.

The impact of benefits like this should never be devalued or underestimated, as increased motivation could well lead to reduced staffing costs as a result of lower staff turnover, and improved customer service could lead to the use of more facilities or more repeat visits. However, such observable benefits should not be included in the business case.

If a satisfaction survey did indicate an improvement in staff morale and motivation, there would be no way of knowing if the move to the new centre was actually responsible for this shift, as each employee would be affected by their own personal factors.

The business case included a benefit of $25k per year under staff morale, which presumably related to increased customer usage and reduced staff turnover. However, if there was an increase in customer use, it would be impossible to determine how much of this was attributable to increased motivation of staff rather than factors such as improved facilities. Staff turnover savings were unlikely to be particularly high as the centre only employs 20 staff, 16 of them having been there for over five years. Combined with the ongoing deep recession faced by the country, it would seem that staff retention was not a problem.

Measurable benefits

Measurable benefits, such as increased income, is an area of the business where performance could be measured, but the impact of the improvement is difficult to quantify. Current income can be measured now, and again in the future, but it is not known with certainty how much income will be increased.

The basis on which the figures included in the business case were calculated needs to be established, and more information is needed to back up the large increases anticipated in Years 3 and 4. It also seems unlikely that this benefit would be seen before the centre had a chance to build up its reputation. Recurring costs would be unlikely to remain the same each year if revenue was increasing.

Quantifiable benefits

Quantifiable benefits, such as energy savings, differ from measurable benefits because it is possible to quantify the degree of improvement before the change is actually made. Buildings constructed under the Private/Public initiative need to have met specific target energy levels, and so the design of the building and the construction methods employed should have ensured that these targets were met. The likely energy savings could be predicted fairly reliably by comparing the new targets to the energy usage of the current building. Actual savings, however, could only be known once the building was operational.

Financial benefits

A quantifiable benefit can be converted to a financial benefit by applying a financial formula (such as cost or price) to that benefit. Assuming that the new building meets the minimum target energy levels, it might be possible to re-classify energy savings as a financial benefit. However, this would still be based on assumptions (for example, the new building may exceed the minimum levels required) and real energy savings could only be assessed once the building has been in use for some time.

A true financial benefit would be rental savings, as the amount paid for both properties is known in advance. This is recorded correctly in the projected payback.

Overall, while measurable benefits are important and should be included within the business case, it is only appropriate to include financial and quantifiable benefits in the payback calculation.

Where measurable benefits are included in the business case, they should be supported with details of the underlying assumptions used so as to be able to quantify them, along with information relating to the likely probability of such benefits.

Answers to Section 3 questions – Exam success skills development

49 Zilber Hotels

Marking scheme

		Marks
1	Up to 10 marks for analysis of aspects of financial performance, including any relevant calculations (Calculations capped at ½ mark each)	Max 10
	Up to 8 marks for analysis of aspect of non-financial performance, and their interrelationship with financial performance.	Max <u>8</u>
	Up to a maximum of 14 marks in total for task 1	14
2	One mark per relevant point for potential benefits/advantages of the acquisition – up to 4 marks	Max 4
	One mark per relevant point for pote ntial problems/drawbacks to the acquisition – up to 6 marks	Max <u>6</u>
	Up to a maximum of 8 marks in total for task 2	8
3 (a)	One mark per relevant point about the range of risks covered in the register – up to 4 marks	Max 4
	One mark per relevant point about the mix of strategic and operational risks in Zilber's risk register – up to 4 marks	Max <u>4</u>
	Up to a maximum of 6 marks in total for task 3(a)	6
(b)	One mark for defining/explaining the concept of disruptive technology	1
	One mark per relevant point for identifying the impact of technology on Zilber, including ways Zilber could respond to it – up to 6 marks	Max <u>6</u>
	Up to a maximum of 6 marks in total for task 3(b)	6
4	One mark per relevant point for identifying the factors which contributed to the fraud – up to 4 marks	Max 4
	One mark per relevant control or action which could be taken to reduce the risk of similar frauds occurring – up to 4 marks	Max <u>4</u>
	Up to a maximum of 6 marks in total for task 4	6

Professional skills may be rewarded as in the following rubric:

1

How well has the candidate demonstrated professional skills as follows:	Not at all	Not so well	Quite well	Very well
1 – Analysis skills relating to Zilber Hotels' performance.	The candidate has demonstrated very limited analysis skills, and has failed to select appropriate metrics for assessing performance. The candidates has failed to evaluate, or reflect on, any calculations performed.	The candidate demonstrated some analysis skills in selecting appropriate metrics for assessing Zilber's performance. However, the candidate's comments on the calculations are primarily descriptive and there is only limited evaluation or reflection on the calculations performed.	The candidate has demonstrated analysis skills by selecting a range of relevant performance calculations from the information provided. The candidate has made a reasonable attempt to comment and reflect on the calculations.	The candidate has demonstrated excellent skills in presenting a wide range of relevant performance calculations. The candidate has reflected on the calculations and considered their implications for Zilber's performance.
	0	0.5	1	2

2

How well has the candidate demonstrated professional skills as follows:	Not at all	Not so well	Quite well	Very well
2 – Evaluation skills in assessing the appropriateness of the acquisition.	The candidate has not demonstrated any evaluation skills in assessing the relative advantages and drawbacks of the proposal, and therefore whether or not it is appropriate for Zilber.	The candidate has demonstrated some evaluation skills in assessing the potential advantages and drawbacks of the proposal. However, the candidates has used little professional judgement in evaluating the impact these have on the overall appropriateness of the proposal.	The candidate has demonstrated some sound evaluation skills in assessing the advantages and drawbacks of the proposal. The candidate has made a reasonable attempt to assess the impact these have on the overall appropriateness of the proposal.	The candidate has demonstrated excellent evaluation skills in assessing the relative advantages of the proposal compared to its drawbacks. The answer focuses clearly on whether or not the acquisition is appropriate or not for Zilber.
	0	0.5	1	2

ANSWERS

3(a)

How well has the candidate demonstrated professional skills as follows:	Not at all	Not so well	Quite well	Very well
3(a) – Scepticism skills in questioning the range of risks covered in the register.	The candidate has failed to demonstrate any scepticism around the range of risks included in the register or the mix between strategic and operational risks and has therefore failed to identify any problems with the register.	The candidate has demonstrated some limited scepticism in identifying the types of risks and questioning the mix (between strategic and operational). However, the candidate hasn't shown any further scepticism in questioning the overall range of risks included in the register (and whether any key risks have been omitted).	The candidate has demonstrated scepticism by questioning whether the mix between strategic and operational risks in the register is appropriate. The candidate has also raised some concerns about the overall range of risks included the register.	The candidate has demonstrated deep scepticism by questioning the mix of risks included in the register and the implications of this for effective risk management. The candidate has also identified the key concerns with the overall range of risks included in the register, and highlighted some of the key risks which have been omitted from the register.
	0	0.5	1	2

3(b)

How well has the candidate demonstrated professional skills as follows:	Not at all	Not so well	Quite well	Very well
3(b) – Communication skills in highlighting the key points to include in the slide, with clear supporting notes.	The candidate has failed to use a slide format to communicate the impact of disruptive technology.	The candidate has only loosely used a slide presentation format, but has too many or too few points, and has failed to explain what disruptive technology is, as well as its impact on the hotel industry. The candidate has produced some notes but they do not adequately explain the points on the slide effectively.	The candidate has used a slide and bullet points, and has explained what disruptive technology is as well as its impact, but there are either too many points on the slide or they have not been expressed succinctly enough. The candidate has supplied notes, but they only loosely explain the bullet points selected.	The candidate has used a slide to present clear and succinct bullet points about what disruptive technology is, and its impact on the industry. The candidate has also produced clear supporting notes which relate closely to the points selected on the slide.
	0	0.5	1	2

4

How well has the candidate demonstrated professional skills as follows:	Not at all	Not so well	Quite well	Very well
4 – Commercial acumen in judging how to address the deficiency and recommending an appropriate response.	The candidate has failed to understand the deficiency and has made generic recommendations rather than ones which are appropriate to the context.	The candidate has demonstrated little commercial acumen in considering the nature/impact of the fraud, meaning that the recommendations the candidate suggested had limited value in this context.	The candidate has demonstrated some understanding of the context and nature of the fraud, but has not fully considered the implications of this when making their recommendations.	The candidate has demonstrated a clear understanding of the context of the fraud, and displayed incisive commercial acumen in recommending responses whose cost will be proportionate to their potential benefit.
	0	0.5	1	2

Suggested solutions

Note. It is not always possible to publish suggested answers which comprehensively cover all the valid points which candidates might make. Credit will be given to candidates for points not included in the suggested answers, but which, nevertheless, are relevant to the task requirements.

In addition, in this integrated case study examination points made in one question may be re-introduced or fully developed in other question(s) as long as these are made in the specific context of the task requirements of the part of the question being answered.

The suggested answers presented below may give much more detail than would be expected from most candidates under examination conditions; they may also have used a particular approach or model which should not be taken as the only approach or model which could have been used. Different approaches and structuring of the answers are expected and full credit will be given for relevant and appropriate solutions to the tasks given. The answers provided here are intended to support revision and tuition for future examinations.

Finally, it should be noted that candidates will not get full professional skills marks in a task requirement if they have not presented their answers according to the format asked for. For example, if a task is to be completed using a report and evaluation skills are tested, even if the answer has met the specifically stated evaluation criteria, candidates will not be able to earn all the professional skills marks available if they have not used the report format.

Strategic Business Leader – Mini-Mocks – Good answer

Task 1

Extract for the board report

Analysis of current performance

Gross room revenue – The increase in 'gross' room revenue (based on standard room rates before any discounts) compared to the prior year reflects the higher occupancy rates (76% vs 73%) and the increase in standard room rates ($150 vs $145 per night).

> Good demonstration of analysis skills – reflecting on the results and implications of them.

However, looking at 'gross' revenue gives a potentially misleading impression of how well the hotels have performed in the current year, because it appears that occupancy rates have only been achieved as a result of offering significantly more discounts.

Revenue after discounts – Revenue from room sales, adjusted for discounts or rate reductions offered, is only 2.6% higher than last year, and is actually 3.4% below budget.

In the light of the tough market conditions, the decision to increase the standard room rate for 20X7 (from $145 to $150) appears quite ambitious. Similarly, it is perhaps not surprising that the actual results for 20X7 are adverse to budget.

Despite the increase in the standard room rate, the actual average rate per 'room night' booked has fallen from $123.25 in 20X6 to $121.50 in 20X7.

This means that, on average, in 20X7, rooms were sold at a 19% discount to the standard price ($150 – $121.50/$150). Given that the maximum reduction managers can apply is 25%, the level of discounts required to maintain occupancy levels appears to be a cause for concern.

> Increase in discounts offered is one of the key factors affecting performance.
>
> This solution scores well here because it calculates performance measures which reflect the impact of the discounts, and it then goes on to analyse the implications of these.
>
> This solution has used the information in the scenario to identify additional performance measures, rather than simply calculating variances for the information provided in the scenario.

		20X7 Actual $'000	20X7 Budget $'000	20X6 Actual $'000	% variance vs budget	% variance vs prior year
Revenue at standard rate		131,072	129,347	121,701	1.33%	7.70%
Discounts offered		24,904	19,402	18,255	28.36%	36.42%
Revenue net of discounts	(A)	106,168	109,945	103,446	−3.44%	2.63%
Total 'room nights' available (W1)		1,149,750	1,149,750	1,149,750		
Occupancy (%)		76	75	73		
Room nights' booked	(B)	873,810	862,313	839,318	1.33%	4.11%
Revenue per night ($)	(A)/(B)	121.50	127.50	123.25	−4.71%	−1.42%

W1: 35 hotels × 90 rooms × 365 nights per year

It appears that, faced with tough economic conditions, and a declining number of business customers, managers have decided to offer lower room rates in order to try to retain as many of their business customers as possible, and thereby preserve occupancy rates. (Occupancy rates are one of the key indicators monitored by the board.)

Good explanation of the commercial implications of different revenue streams.

Additional revenue – As the discounts offered increase, then additional revenues potentially become a more important income stream (not least, because no discounts are offered on food and drink sales). Even if guests are paying less per room per night, some of this shortfall could be recouped through additional food and drink sales.

This point demonstrates that the writer has thought about the commercial context; providing insight into the factors which have shaped the hotels' performance.

Zilber appears to have been reasonably successful in increasing food and drink sales, because additional revenues have increased by over 5% compared to last year, and have exceeded budget. Hotel managers and staff should be encouraged to promote spending in this area, and we could possibly consider some kind of incentive scheme to reward hotels who perform particularly well here.

Total revenue – In total, although revenues are below budget they are still 3.4% higher than last year ($140.2m vs $135.7m). Given the tough competitive environment, we could potentially see any increase in revenues as positive.

Moreover, provided the revenue rate achieved per room is greater than the variable cost of the room, then increasing occupancy rates should increase the hotels' contribution to profit.

Operating profit – Despite the increase in revenues, operating profits have fallen by 6% compared to prior year, and are substantially (19.9%) below budget. Here again, the 20X7 results are influenced by the level of discounts given, but they also reflect increasing costs.

Example of drawing out valid commercial implications from the context of the scenario.

In an increasingly competitive market, cost control is likely to be very important. However, despite the budget for operating costs in 20X7 being $3.8 million higher than in 20X6, actual operating costs were still $2.2 million higher than budget. This means 20X7 operating costs were $6 million higher than in 20X6, representing an increase of 5.4%.

However, although cost control is important, when looking to reduce costs, it will be very important to do so in a way which does not compromise customer satisfaction. For example, Zilber needs to avoid cutting expenditure in areas which will have a detrimental impact on customer satisfaction ratings (for example, not replacing mattresses even though they are becoming uncomfortable to sleep on).

Linking together different points from the scenario. Although cost control is important, Exhibit 2 has also highlighted the importance of customer satisfaction.

Operating profit margin – The increase in costs, coupled with the increased discounts, has also led to a fall in operating profit margin from 17.5% (20X6) to 15.9% (20X7).

However, the revenue figure used to calculate margin has already had discounts deducted from it. It is perhaps more instructive to treat discounts as an additional cost, and to calculate margin percentages based on standard room rates. This will help to highlight the impact that discounts are having. When operating profit margin is based on 'gross' revenue (and discounts are treated as a cost), operating profit margin has decreased from 15.4% (20X6) to 13.5% (20X7), and is significantly below budget of 17.1%.

Another good example of the way this answer digs below the surface of the scenario, and identifies the challenges the company is facing.

Operating profit margin and occupancy rates are two of Zilber's key performance indicators, and the relationship between them provides a good illustration of the problems Zilber appears to be facing. Although hotel managers have so far been able to maintain occupancy rates, they have only been able to do so by reducing room rates.

ROCE – This reduced profitability is also reflected in the company's return on capital employed (ROCE), which has fallen from 48.3% to 42.8%.

This decline here could be a particular concern given the relative lack of capital investment in the hotels recently. Because Zilber's capital employed figure is based on the depreciated cost of non-current assets at all of the hotels, if the renovation programme is undertaken, this could mean that ROCE falls further, because the programme will result in the cost of the assets increasing.

Customer satisfaction scores

> When analysing the hotels' performance, it is important to consider the full range of indicators given in the scenario. In particular, it is important to analyse the non-financial indicators, as well as the financial ones.

Customer satisfaction scores are another of Zilber's key performance indicators; and, although the reduction in profitability should be a concern, the reduction in customer satisfaction scores should potentially be seen as a greater cause for concern.

The scores suggest that, in the space of one year, Zilber hotels have gone from being just outside the top 10% of hotels to only just making the top 25%. This is a significant decline in one year, and one which Zilber cannot afford to continue, particularly given the competitiveness in the market place, and Zilber's focus on trying to attract business customers.

The factors commented on by customers – such as the comfort of the hotel rooms and the quality of service – are key factors which people consider when deciding whether or not to stay in a Zilber hotel. Falling customer satisfaction levels are likely to mean that fewer existing customers will stay at a Zilber hotel in future, or recommend Zilber to their friends or colleagues – thereby threatening occupancy rates, and prices, in future.

> Clear analysis of the implications of the performance indicators given in the scenario.

Moreover, the scores suggest that the decision to defer the refurbishment programme could be short-termist. Although it might reduce expenditure in the short term, the lack of investment is likely to be detrimental to longer-term performance.

This problem is exacerbated by Zilber's business model and the fact that rooms have the same facilities and specifications. As such, if the quality and comfort of any one hotel is unsatisfactory, a customer will justifiably be concerned that this will also be the case in Zilber's other hotels – thereby deterring them from making any further bookings.

A similar argument (about the experience customers receive in one hotel influencing their attitude towards staying in others) could also apply to customer service and the efficiency of the check-in process; which suggests that Zilber should look for ways of improving performance in both of these areas – for example, by improving the customer service training given to staff.

> Considering 'Suitability', 'Feasibility' (and 'Acceptability') can be a useful way to evaluate a strategic option – although, in this case, the scenario doesn't provide much information about 'acceptability', so the answer is structured around 'Suitability' and 'Feasibility' only.

Task 2 – Potential acquisition

Briefing paper

FAO: Finance Director of Zilber

Evaluation of proposed acquisition

Suitability

The opportunity to acquire the Havis hotels might initially seem a beneficial one for Zilber, because it could provide a source of the growth which we, and our shareholders, are looking for. Moreover, the standard of Havis' hotels – with 4* ratings – appears to be broadly similar to ours.

However, there are some important differences between the two companies and their current strategies which could affect the logic of the acquisition.

> Words like 'However...' are very important in an evaluation. Evaluation needs to consider both the advantages and the disadvantages/ drawbacks of a proposal.

Although Havis' hotels are a similar standard to Zilber's, they appear to have a different target market. Zilber's main focus is on business travellers who value the convenience of our hotels and the consistency in their style and facilities, regardless of which hotel they are staying at. By contrast, Havis' market appear to be leisure customers who value the character and individuality of its hotels.

Similarly, six out of the ten hotels are in rural locations.

Purpose of acquisition

An important issue here is the purpose of the acquisition.

It appears that Zilber is considering an acquisition because it hasn't been able to find any suitable buildings or land to enable it to grow organically. This suggests that the main driver behind the acquisition is obtaining additional capacity to facilitate growth, rather than acquiring the Havis brand as such.

In this respect, the strategic logic of acquiring Havis appears relatively weak, given its focus on different market segments.

Alternatively, the acquisition could provide Zilber with an opportunity to diversify as a group.

We have noted that demand from business customers in Zilber's existing hotels has been falling, so acquiring Havis would allow us to reduce our dependence on the business market.

In particular, one potential approach might be to maintain the Havis hotels as a separate brand post acquisition, rather than integrating them into the existing Zilber brand.

> Good range of commercially relevant factors to be considered

A further consideration is that it seems that the Havis hotels will require significant capital expenditure, due to the under-investment by its current owners. Therefore, it might be possible to convert the four in-town hotels to the Zilber brand as part of the process of refurbishing and renovating them, leaving the six rural hotels as a separate Havis brand.

The counter argument, however, is that if there remains significant market demand from leisure travellers for in-town hotels which retain period charm, Zilber might be better advised to retain all of the Havis hotels as a distinct brand.

Feasibility

Finance – Another important factor which will influence the attractiveness of the acquisition is the purchase price, and whether Zilber has sufficient funds available to make the acquisition and then to undertake the capital investment needed in the hotels. (We have deferred the refurbishment programme in our hotels to 'reduce expenditure'. If there is an ongoing need for this, then raising additional finance for an acquisition, and servicing any new debt, could prove problematic.)

> This point demonstrates good use of scenario as a whole. Although the refurbishment programme was mentioned in Exhibit 1, and in relation to Task 1, issues around Zilber's cash flow and finances could be equally relevant to a potential acquisition.

> This answer correctly recognises that the acquisition marks a change from Zilber's previous strategy of organic growth. Therefore, a consideration of 'management capabilities' needs to focus on management's ability to make an acquisition, not just their ability to run a hotel business.

The CEO has not given any indication as to a guide price for the acquisition, but we really need to know this in order to decide whether the acquisition is worth considering any further or not.

Management capabilities and risk appetite – To date, Zilber has expanded organically, and so has no experience of making acquisitions.

Growth via acquisition inherently involves a higher level of risk than organic growth, but the level of risk Zilber faces will be increased further by the fact that this deal will be its first acquisition.

Therefore, another factor to consider is the level of risk that the board – and Zilber's shareholders – are prepared to accept, alongside the potential returns which could be achieved as a result of making the acquisition.

Task 3(a)

Briefing notes

Risk register and mix of strategic and operational risks

Strategic risks relate to the fundamental long-term decisions Zilber takes, for example in relation to its business model, its business strategy and its ability to survive in the long term. The external environment in which Zilber operates (and, for example, changes to political, economic or technological factors) can influence strategic risk in relation to Zilber's ability to continue to offer hotel facilities which meets customers' needs.

By contrast, **operational risks** relate to the day-to-day risks involved in dealing with guests or ensuring that processes run smoothly. Risks relating to the safety and security of hotels, guests and staff are operational risks.

> Although the primary focus of the question is on the range of risks covered, and the mix between strategic and operational, it is useful to begin by clarifying (briefly) what strategic and operational risks are. Note, though, that this initial section is kept brief, and is kept relevant to Zilber.

Operational risks should typically be mitigated through internal controls and business processes. However, strategic risks should be a key feature of the board's agenda – because their 'strategic' nature means they cannot effectively be mitigated through internal controls or business processes.

> The answer is now moving from talking about strategic vs operational risks in general terms to considering more specifically the potential mix which might be expected on the register.

As the head of internal audit has identified, Zilber's **brand and reputation**, as well as its ability to respond effectively to changes in the market place, are all important in achieving the company's objectives and protecting the business. Reputation and brand protection could therefore be seen as a potential strategic risk, but it is not currently included in the risk register.

Similarly, responding effectively to **changes in the market place** would also appear to be an important element of strategic risk. However, although the register identifies the importance of responding to technological change eg the rise of cryptocurrencies, it does not include changes in the market place more generally – such as the falling demand from business travellers which is currently affecting the market.

> This point and the one in the paragraph below use information provided in Exhibit 4 to clearly demonstrate scepticism by identifying important risks which are not currently on the register.

Risk register

As such, the focus of the risk register does appear to be more on operational risks rather than strategic risks, and therefore the non-executive director's concerns appear to be justified.

> This is a clear demonstration of scepticism, linked back to the initial concerns raised in the task requirement.

The risks included in the register are all significant risks for Zilber, and therefore it is appropriate that they have been identified on the register. However, the concern is that there are other, potentially even more important risks, which have not been included. As well as the strategic risks around brand and reputation, and changing market conditions, the register also does not include any financial risks. For example, our ability to grow via acquisition is likely to depend on having sufficient capital to make the acquisition. Therefore, as well as considering the balance between strategic and operational risks on the register, the board might also consider whether they should include any financial risks.

> Another clear demonstration of scepticism, linked back to (and supported by) the information provided in Exhibit 4.

Task 3(b)

The slide focuses on a small number of key points only; with supporting detail then being given in the notes.

It is important to avoid having too much text on the slide itself.

Disruptive technology

Slide:

Disruptive technology

– Technology helping to create new business models

Impact on the hotel industry

– Entry of new competitors
– Importance of technology, as well as people, in the hotel industry

Impact on Zilber

– Potential threat to occupancy levels

– Importance of price

Need to develop initiatives to defend our strategic position

- Focus on the things customers value
- Role of technology

Supporting notes:

The sequence of the notes is clearly mapped back to the points on the slide.

1. **What is disruptive technology?**

   A **disruptive technology** is one that leads to the emergence of new business models within an industry, or – in some cases – even creates a completely new industry. By creating new business models, disruptive technology can present a threat to existing firms in an industry.

2. Impact of disruptive technology on the hotel industry

The Exhibits don't provide much detail about disruptive technology beyond the mention of cryptocurrencies, so using relevant, real world examples can help to provide context.

   New competitors – Disrupters (such as Airbnb) are new entrants to the market, capturing market share from existing competitors (hotels).

   The challenge to existing hotel companies is to keep their customers satisfied so that they remain loyal. If hotels do not satisfy their customers, this potentially makes it easier for 'disrupters' to gain market share.

   Importance of technology – Aside from disruptive technology, technology more generally has become increasingly important in the hotel industry; for example, through (potential) customers using search engines to find potential places to stay; looking at review and ranking sites (for example, TripAdvisor); making and managing bookings online; and paying for accommodation using cryptocurrencies. Services (such as Wi-Fi) which might previously have helped to distinguish a hotel from its competitors are now considered as standard.

   Although we often focus on the importance of people (staff) in relation to customer service and customer experience, we also need to recognise the importance of technology (for example, in supporting bookings ie developing the ability to accept cryptocurrency payments, and reservation systems).

3. Potential impact of disruptive technology on Zilber

   Occupancy rates – The emergence of new competitors poses a threat to occupancy levels.

   Price – Disruptive technologies often seek to establish themselves in a market by offering lower prices than existing players. Given the tough economic conditions in Teeland at the moment, price could become increasingly important in determining where people choose to stay. So we need to ensure that our hotels provide good value for money for our customers.

BPP
LEARNING
MEDIA

ANSWERS

Zilber needs to recognise the potential threat in order that we can defend our position and develop appropriate strategies.

To do this, we need to understand:

– What do our customers want?

– Are we offering these things?

– Are we offering things customers do not value, which could be eliminated to reduce cost?

Role of technology – Technology could help us offer what customers want. For example, customers have commented about the check-in process being slow. Could we speed up this process (for example, by sending a key code to a customer's smartphone which they can use to unlock their room, instead of needing a key card)?

The fact that smaller competitors in the Teeland hotel sector have very recently started to accept cryptocurrency payments indicates that this functionality is something which customers increasingly expect. In time it is likely that feedback from customers may reflect growing demand for such functionality when purchasing accommodation from Zilber. Therefore, developing the necessary IT infrastructure is something which Zilber will need to address.

> Using the information provided about cryptocurrencies in the Exhibit, and then explaining its potential impact on Zilber was important.

Digital technologies are not restricted to disrupters. So Zilber, like other existing hotels, can use technology to improve business processes. However, we also still need to focus on factors which are important to customers (for example, customer service).

Task 4

MEMORANDUM

To:	**Finance Director**
From:	**Management Accountant**
Date:	XX/XX/XXXX
Subject:	**Internal control deficiency**

Fraud and segregation of duties

The fraud committed related to controls over cash at the point of sale. This is a particular risk in a service business, such as a hotel, as there are no goods to be exchanged, and so, for example, there aren't any inventory records which can be monitored in relation to sales.

> It is necessary to understand the specific circumstances of the fraud before making recommendations for how to address it.

This particular fraud involved collusion between the manager (who authorised the discount, and therefore had control over the accounting record) and his wife (who collected the cash, and therefore had control of the asset).

Normal segregation of duty controls are designed to prevent one individual controlling both assets and revenue, but in this case the pair managed to circumvent these controls because, in effect, they were acting as an individual.

> The answer focuses on the specific circumstances of the fraud in question, rather than talking about generic control issues.

Internal control systems do not normally focus specifically on controls over collusion, but would instead expect to rely on a robust segregation of duties. In a case like this, where a husband and wife are working together, it may be unwise to rely too heavily on segregation of duties.

Importantly, though, the number of customers who pay for their rooms in cash (rather than using a debit/credit card, or paying on a company account) should be low, particularly amongst business customers. This has two significant implications:

– First, the scope for this type of fraud should be quite limited, and therefore the cost of any procedures implemented to reduce it must reflect the fact that benefits may be limited

– Second, monitoring the proportion of cash sales (vs card sales) in each hotel could be an effective analytical procedure for identifying unusual sales patterns

Similarly, the fact that internal audit have highlighted that we do not know how long the fraud had been occurring indicates the need for controls which can 'detect' fraud, in addition to ones designed to 'prevent' it.

The following are actions which could be taken to reduce the risk of similar frauds occurring, and of them not being detected:

The task requirement asks for a 'recommendation' as to how the deficiency could be addressed, and this list offers a range of practical, recommended actions.

- Separate system of recording and reporting of cash transactions

- Segregation of duties to be rotated periodically

- Internal audit to review cash transactions

- Segregation of duties to avoid close personal relationships

- Analytical procedures on cash transactions to identify high incidence in particular hotels

- Analytical procedures on high incidence of discounts or their association with cash transactions

- The introduction of blockchain technology which records transactions between parties on an incorruptible distributed ledger would increase transparency. Blockchain records payments and receipts made over the internet. This would be appropriate as it would help to reduce Zilber's need to accept cash, and would also develop Zilber's IT infrastructure to keep pace with technological change.

Strategic Business Leader – Mini-Mocks – Poor answer

Task 1

Analysis of current performance

Zilber's financial performance in 20X7 compared to 20X6 can be summarised as follows:

	20X7 Actual	20X7 Budget	Variance		20X6 Actual	Variance	
	$'000	$'000	$'000	%	$'000	$'000	%
Revenue from rooms	131,072	129,347	1,725	1.3%	121,701	9,371	7.7%
Discounts	(24,904)	(19,402)	(5,502)	−28.4%	(18,255)	(6,649)	−36.4%
Other revenue	34,079	33,630	449	1.3%	32,251	1,828	5.7%
Total revenue	140,247	143,575	(3,328)	−2.3%	135,697	4,550	3.4%
Operating costs	(117,964)	(115,764)	(2,200)	1.9%	(111,965)	(5,999)	5.4%
Operating profit	22,282	27,811	(5,529)	−19.9%	23,732	(1,450)	−6.1%

Revenue – Room revenue in 20X7 was $131.1 million which is $9.4m (7.7%) higher than the equivalent revenue in 20X6, and $1.7m (1.3%) higher than budgeted. This suggests the hotels have performed quite well during the year, despite the tough economic conditions currently affecting the hotel industry in Teeland, which might have been expected to lead to a fall in revenue. In this context, the fact that Zilber's occupancy rates were higher in 20X7 than in 20X6 is perhaps unexpected, and this could be contributing to the increase in revenue.

The increase in room rates (from $145 to $150 per night) is also likely to have contributed to the increase in revenues.

Discounts – The level of discounts offered to customers in 20X7 was $24.9 million, which is $6.6 million (36.4%) higher than in 20X6, and $5.5 million (28.4%) higher than budgeted. This means that the amount of discounts managers have offered to customers has increased, significantly, even though managers only have the authority to offer discounts of up to 25% below standard prices.

It seems likely that the managers have been using discounts to try to attract customers at times when occupancy rates might otherwise have been low. This has helped to maintain the occupancy rates in 20X7, and occupancy rates are one of the key performance indicators for the hotels.

Additional revenue – Other revenues are $1.8 million (5.7%) higher than last year, and are slightly (1.3%) higher than budget.

Interestingly, food and drink sales performance against budget (+1.3%) is the same as the revenue from rooms, so there appears to be a correlation between the number of people staying in the hotel and the amount of revenue generated through food and drink sales.

Total revenue – Although total revenues for 20X7 are $4.6 million (3.4%) higher than those for 20X6, they are $3.3 million (2.3%) below budget for the year. This appears to be largely due to the level of discounts offered in 20X7, although the tough economic conditions in Teeland might also have affected the hotels' performance during the year.

Margin annotations:

Although calculating the variances will score some marks, this answer doesn't consider whether any additional measures to those already given might provide greater insight into Zilber's performance (eg revenue per room after discounts have been applied).

The 'analysis' supporting the calculations provides little, if any, value in understanding performance. Revenue figures based on standard room rates have little relevance if significant discounts are given (as has been the case in 20X7).

This answer fails to consider the wider issues around the discounts offered, and their impact on 'actual' revenue per room.

This answer needs to bring in more points like this from the scenario, and then to assess how they might be affecting Zilber's performance.

Given that the figures have been calculated in the 'table' at the start of the answer, writing them out again doesn't add any value to the report and won't gain any marks.

This answer only repeats facts from the scenario, without providing any insight into the implications of offering the discounts.

In particular, no attempt is made to calculate revenue net of discounts offered, or the actual room rates achieved per night.

Operating costs – Zilber's operating costs are $2.2 million (1.9%) above budget for 20X7, and are $6.0 million (5.4%) higher than they were in 20X6. This increase is a worry for Zilber because if its costs are increasing more than revenues, then profits will fall. Given the tough economic conditions in Teeland, Zilber should be looking at ways to make significant cost savings, in order to help it preserve its profits.

Operating profit – Operating profits have fallen $1.5 million (6.1%) compared to 20X6, and are significantly (19.9%) below budget. The variance to budget is due to the combination of actual revenue being below budget, while operating costs are above budget. This reinforces the point, noted above, that Zilber needs to make significant cost savings in order to help it preserve its profits.

Operating profit margin – Operating profit margin has also fallen from 17.5% (20X6) to 15.9% (20X7), meaning that operating profit for the year is significantly below the budget target of 19.4%.

Operating profit margin is one of Zilber's key performance indicators, so these figures are a cause for concern, and so the company should look for ways to improve profit margins.

ROCE – Return on capital employed has fallen from 48.3% in 20X6 to 42.8% in 20X7. This again reflects the fall in the company's operating profits, and means that the value Zilber is generating from its assets is falling.

The fact that Zilber's capital employed figure is based on the depreciated cost of non-current assets at all of the hotels means that ROCE could fall further if the renovation programme is undertaken, because that programme will mean that the cost of the assets in the hotels will increase.

Occupancy rates – As we have already mentioned, the hotel managers have managed to maintain occupancy rates during the year, and occupancy rates have actually been slightly higher than budget (76% vs 75%). However, in the future it might be appropriate for Zilber to consider a more flexible pricing scheme, whereby the prices in a hotel change automatically according to forecast occupancy rates for a given period, rather than the hotel managers manually having to apply discounts to a standard price.

Customer satisfaction scores

The average customer satisfaction score has fallen from 8.9 in 20X6 to 8.5 in 20X7, and customers have commented that the standard of service in recent visits has not been as good as in previous visits. Zilber's average rating for 20X7 means that it is only just in the top 25% of hotels in Teeland.

Customer satisfaction scores are another of Zilber's key performance indicators, and this seems sensible because ensuring the satisfaction of hotel guests is likely to be crucial for the company's ongoing success, because unsatisfied guests will be less likely than satisfied ones to stay with Zilber again in future.

It is important that cost savings focus on areas where cutting costs does not jeopardise customer satisfaction.

These are the sorts of 'commercial' implications which this answer fails to mention, but which will be crucial to Zilber's board.

This is a good point. However, it could be developed further to link in to the customer feedback pointing to the need for renovations in the hotels.

This point is a repeat of facts from the scenario and so doesn't provide any insight or analysis. For example, what are the likely consequences of declining customer satisfaction levels?

This point doesn't provide any analysis for the board (possibly also linked to the fact that the answer has failed to consider the impact of discounts on 'actual' revenue; and also the inter-relationship between the profit margin and the other KPI: occupancy rates).

Although this is a reasonable suggestion, the focus of the task requirement here should be Zilber's actual performance in 20X7 – in particular, the level of discounts which were required in order to maintain the occupancy rates (something this answer doesn't analyse at all).

This is the key point. In contrast to many of the earlier points in this answer, the 'because' in this sentence explains why the point being made here is important.

However, the customer feedback has highlighted three main areas which are contributing to falling satisfaction levels. One is the standard of service (as noted above); one is inefficiencies in the checking-in process; and the third is that guests are unhappy with the standard of decoration and the comfort of their rooms. This third issue should be resolved when the refurbishment programme takes place; but it is also important to see if there are any measures which can be taken to improve customer service or to improve the efficiency of the check-in process.

This point would be improved by acknowledging the current uncertainty over the refurbishment programme (ie thinking about how the different issues in the scenario inter-relate).

Task 2

Evaluation of the acquisition

The proposed acquisition can be evaluated using the three criteria which organisations can use to guide their strategic choices: suitability; feasibility; and acceptability.

The CEO wants practical advice about the potential acquisition; so there is no need describe the 'Suitability, Acceptability, Feasibility' model here (and there will be few, if any, marks available for doing so).

Suitability – Suitability relates to the strategic logic of the strategy, and whether it fits with a company's current strategic position. For example, whether the strategy helps a company exploit its strengths, address its weaknesses, take advantage of opportunities and address threats.

The underlying logic is valid here. But the answer should be focusing specifically on the acquisition of Havis, not the suitability of growth via acquisition in general terms.

One of Zilber's key objectives is to grow. However, there are currently no suitable properties available, in desirable locations, which we could buy in order to grow organically. Therefore, it appears that making an acquisition will be a suitable way for us to grow.

In addition, Havis' hotels all have 4-star ratings, like Zilber's hotels, so they should be a similar standard to our existing hotels, meaning that the acquisition will fit with our current generic strategy.

Moreover, Havis's hotels attract leisure travellers, so acquiring the hotels will help Zilber diversify into the leisure market, rather than being so dependent on the business travel market as we currently are.

The answer here has identified some relevant points from the scenario, but has failed to properly 'evaluate' the implications of them. In particular, the answer has only focused on advantages, rather than highlighting any potential problems with the acquisition.

Feasibility – Feasibility relates to whether a strategy can be implemented, and so in this case relates to whether Zilber has the strategic capability to acquire Havis and then run the hotels post-integration.

There are a number of aspects we can consider when evaluating the feasibility of the acquisition:

The points below are all generic points relating to a consideration of 'feasibility'; but they don't provide any specific insight into the feasibility of the acquisition proposed in the scenario.

– Management: Does Zilber's management team have the skills required to deliver the strategy?

– Make-up: Is Zilber's organisational structure and culture appropriate to support the acquisition?

– Materials: Does Zilber have access to sufficient materials required to deliver the strategy successfully (for example, by renovating Havis' hotels where they have suffered from a lack of capital expenditure)?

– Manpower: Will the acquisition require Zilber to take on extra staff?

– Money: Does Zilber have sufficient funds available to purchase Havis, or – if not – can it raise the finance that will be required to make the acquisition?

Zilber is already experienced at operating and managing 4-star hotels, which suggests that we have the skills and capabilities to manage Havis' hotels as well if we acquire them.

> This is the only part of the answer specifically about the proposal. However, it fails to consider the key issue that managing the acquisition will require a different set of skills to managing the hotels. (Zilber has always grown organically in the past).

Acceptability – The acceptability of a strategy depends on expected performance outcomes and the extent to which these are acceptable to key stakeholders.

> This is one of the few points in the answer which are specifically linked to the scenario.

One of Zilber's key objectives is 'profitable expansion' and Zilber's shareholders have become increasingly vocal about their desire for the business to grow.

The acquisition of Havis hotels should provide Zilber with a source of profitable growth, which will help the company achieve its objectives and satisfy its shareholders.

> Although these are potential considerations within 'acceptability', there is nothing in the scenario about them. This answer would be better to focus on the issues specifically raised in the scenario.

As mentioned in relation to feasibility, Zilber may need to raise additional funds to pay for the acquisition. If we decide to take out additional bank loans, then our plans will need to be acceptable to our bank as well.

Finally, we may also need to consider Havis' customers, and whether they will continue to stay in the hotels if we acquire them. If we don't make any major changes to the way Havis hotels are run, then the acquisition should have little impact on the hotels' customers. In fact, if we invest in the hotels which are currently in relatively poor condition this could make them more attractive to potential customers.

Overall, therefore, the proposal is likely to be acceptable.

> Although this answer has offered a conclusion, it is not based on a thorough evaluation of the facts in the scenario. For example, at no point does the answer consider the potential disadvantages with the acquisition.

In summary, the proposal appears suitable, feasible and acceptable, and therefore it would seem appropriate for Zilber to acquire Havis Hotels.

Task 3(a)

Briefing notes

Risk register and mix of strategic and operational risks

Strategic risks are risks that relate to the fundamental decisions that directors take about the future of their business, for example about its strategy, or its business model, and the impact those decisions have on the business' profitability. Factors which can determine the level of strategic risk in a business include: the type of market in which it operates; the state of the economy; and the actions of competitors.

> As with the good answer, this answer starts with a brief description of strategic and operational risks, but these opening points should have included some references to Zilber or the context of the hotel industry.

By contrast, **operational risks** relate to the day-to-day risks which are incurred while an organisation is carrying out its business. Operational risks could include: IT failures; fraud; or staff failing to comply with regulations or internal procedures.

Having identified the two main types of risk mentioned by the non-executive director, we can classify the risks included on Zilber's risk register according to whether they are strategic or operational:

Guest safety – Ensuring the safety of Zilber's guests is a key consideration within all of the hotels' day-to-day activities. As such it is an operational risk.

Security – Again, ensuring the security of our hotels – to protect the hotels' assets as well as those of our guests – is another key issue within our day-to-day activities. As such, this is also an operational risk.

Staff safety – This is another operational risk, because it relates to the ongoing activities of the business.

Staff retention – The loss of individual members is another operational risk, because it will affect the day-to-day running of the hotels. However, if staff losses mean that we can no longer deliver the quality of service our customer expect, and our financial performance suffers as a result, this could become a strategic risk.

Technology – The risk of problems with IT systems disrupting the booking process is an operational risk. However, if we fail to invest in technology eg developing the ability to accept cryptocurrency payments, our systems become obsolete, and damage our ability to compete with our rivals; here again technology could become a strategic risk.

Information security – Here again, the risk of security problems leading to a loss of information is an ongoing, operational risk; but the impact of a major security breach could have a significant impact on our reputation and on future bookings, meaning it would also become a strategic risk.

Balance of risks – Overall, there are more operational risks than strategic risks on the register, and therefore the non-executive director does appear justified in questioning the balance. However, the risks included in the register are all important risks facing Zilber.

> This point is relevant and valid, but this is the only part of the answer which displays any 'scepticism' (as opposed to simply categorising the risks).

> The task requirement has not asked for a categorisation of the different risks, and so – even though the categorisations here may be correct – this part of the answer will score very few marks.
>
> What was required in this task was an overall assessment of the mix between strategic vs operational risks in the register, not a line-by-line categorisation.

Task 3(b)

Disruptive technology

Disruptive technology leads to the emergence of **new business models** within an industry.

Technological developments and technological change occur across the business environment, but many of these changes are **sustaining technologies** – incremental improvements to established technologies – rather than disruptive ones.

Impact of disruptive technology

New competitors – Disrupters (such as Airbnb) have entered the market capturing market share from existing hotels.

One of the main dangers for existing businesses is that they fail to recognise the threat posed by disrupters, or dismiss that threat, only to find that the disrupters are capturing their market share.

The challenge to existing hotel companies is to keep their customers satisfied so that they remain loyal. If hotels do not satisfy their customers, this potentially makes it easier for 'disrupters' to gain market share.

Importance of technology – Technology as a whole is becoming increasingly important in the hotel industry; for example, through (potential) customers using search engines to find potential places to stay; looking at review and ranking sites (for example, TripAdvisor); making and managing bookings on line; and paying for accommodation using

> Virtually all of the 'technical' content in this answer is similar to that in the good answer; and in a couple of places even includes a bit more detail.
>
> However, this answer is not presented in the format required (ie bullet point slide with supporting notes).
>
> Therefore it will not earn any professional skills marks.
>
> So, the maximum this answer can score is 6; whereas the 'good' answer can score 8 (6 technical skills + 2 professional skills).

cryptocurrencies. Services (such as Wi-Fi) which might previously have helped to distinguish a hotel from its competitors are now considered as standard.

Although we often focus on the importance of people (staff) in relation to customer service and customer experience, we also need to recognise the importance of technology (for example, in supporting booking and reservation systems).

Impact of disruptive technology on Zilber

Occupancy rates – The emergence of new competitors poses a threat to occupancy levels, because they increase the choice customers have about where to stay.

Price – Disruptive technologies often seek to establish themselves in a market by offering lower prices than existing players. Given the tough economic conditions in Teeland at the moment, price could become increasingly important in determining where people choose to stay. So we need to ensure that our hotels provide good value for money for our customers.

However, given Zilber's target market (business customers) the impact of disruptive technologies may be less significant than on existing hotels at the lower cost end of the market.

Potential threat to strategic position – Zilber needs to recognise the potential threat of disruptive technologies in order that we can defend our position and develop appropriate strategies. To do this, we need to understand:

– What do our customers want?
– Are we offering these things?
– Are we offering things customers do not value, which could be eliminated to reduce cost?

Role of technology – Technology could help us offer what customers want. For example, customers have commented about the check-in process being slow. Could we speed up this process (for example, by sending a key code to a customer's smartphone which they can use to unlock their room, instead of needing a key card)?

The fact that smaller competitors in the Teeland hotel sector have very recently started to accept cryptocurrency payments indicates that this functionality is something which customers increasingly expect. In time it is likely that feedback from customers may reflect growing demand for such functionality when purchasing accommodation from Zilber. Therefore, developing the necessary IT infrastructure is something which Zilber will need to address.

Digital technologies are not restricted to disrupters. So Zilber, like other existing hotels, can use technology to improve business processes. However, we also still need to focus on factors which are important to customers (for example, customer service).

Task 4

Memo

FAQ: FD at Zilber

Internal control deficiency

Ultimately, responsibility for managing the risks and controls within Zilber rests with the board of directors, and so the board needs to ensure that Zilber has adequate controls in place to prevent frauds such as this recurring, and to safeguard the company's assets. The board also needs to monitor and assess the internal controls in the business on a regular basis.

Internal audit

Internal audit can play an important part in this work, and internal auditors' work typically includes:

– Identifying controls at an entity and operational level

– Reviewing the completeness of documentation around those controls

ANSWERS

- Testing the controls
- Advising management on the effectiveness of the control system and disclosing any material weaknesses

The head of internal audit has already identified the need for Zilber to review its internal controls to try to prevent any similar frauds happening again.

At the moment, we do not know the extent of the fraud, but it is important that the cost of any new controls is not greater than their benefits, so we need to try to work out how much was stolen before deciding how many additional controls are required.

The issue of the cost/impact of the fraud vs the potential benefits of additional controls needs to be explored in more detail to score the professional marks available for commercial acumen

Limits of control systems

However, control systems can only ever reduce – rather than eliminate – the possibility of risks materialising, due to the potential for human error, or control processes being deliberately circumvented. The actions of the hotel manager and his wife were clearly designed to enable them to work together to steal from the company, and internal control systems cannot prevent collusion such as this.

Given their actions, it is entirely appropriate that the manager and his wife have both been dismissed.

This is a generic suggestion. (But it would not prevent fraud through collusion, as was the case in this scenario.)

Again, 'authorisation and approval' is a generic suggestion.

But is it practical for managers to get approval for every discount offered?

Prevent and detect controls

More generally, we need to ensure that we have suitable controls in place to prevent and detect fraud. Possible measures to prevent fraud include segregation of duties, and checking references when staff are recruited. Another potential control is that transactions required authorisation or approval by an appropriate responsible person. So possibly we could require the hotel managers to get discounts approved by their own managers in advance of them being offered to customers.

The information from information systems can provide a 'detect' control to highlight unusual transactions or trends that may be signs of fraud. In this case, it is likely that the level of cash payments in the hotel where the fraud was taking place level was higher than in other hotels, and so the reason for this should have been investigated.

By contrast to the other controls mentioned, this one is appropriate to the context.

However, it is not presented as a 'recommendation' – although that is what had been asked for in this task.

Zilber – Mini-Mock Exam 1

Tutorial notes to help you improve your exam success skills performance

Skill	Examples of the skills
Case scenario: Managing information	The company overview in Exhibit 1 provides a number of important details which you need to keep in mind across the whole scenario – for example, it tells us about the company's target market; its pricing policy; the features of the hotels (4* rating; standard facilities) and the importance of customer satisfaction.
	This context is important when analysing Zilber's performance (task requirement 1) For example, how might its revenues be influenced by changing market conditions?
	Equally, when considering the potential acquisition (task requirement 2) it is important to consider how the target company's strategy might 'fit' with Zilber's (for example, from the information in Exhibit 3, how do the characteristics of Havis' hotels, and its target market, compare with Zilber's?
Correct interpretation of requirements	Task requirement 3a asks you to assess, critically, the risks included in Zilber's register, in the light of the NED's concerns and your meeting with the head of internal audit (Exhibit 4).
	'Assess' means to judge the worth or importance of something or to evaluate its nature, quality or significance.
	A useful tip when 'assessing' something is to try to determine its strengths or weaknesses, or its importance/significance. So, in the context of this task requirement, where Exhibit 4 identifies the risk areas currently included in the register, you should be asking:
	— How useful is the risk register (in helping the board to manage the key risks Zilber faces)?
	— Does the register actually include the key risks (or are there risks which are not covered)?
	— Is the balance between strategic and operational risks appropriate (or is there too much focus on one type of risk at the expense of the other)?
Answer planning: Priorities, structure and logic	Task requirement 2 asks you to evaluate the appropriateness of the proposed acquisition.
	The 'Suitability, acceptability, feasibility' approach can often provide a useful framework for evaluating strategic choices. The scenario in this question doesn't provide much information about 'acceptability', but using 'suitability' and 'feasibility' as headings can still provide a useful structure for your answer, as follows:
	Suitability
	— Havis hotels appear similar quality to Zilber's (4* rating): +ve
	— But different target market (leisure vs business): −ve
	— Difference in style of hotel (character and individuality vs standardised): −ve
	— Could moving into a new market segment (diversifying) be a good thing though?: +ve/−ve

Skill	Examples of the skills
	Feasibility
	– Capital investment required (in tough economic conditions)? –ve
	– Management capabilities: Zilber has no experience of making acquisitions: –ve
	– Risks involved in acquisition vs organic growth: –ve
	(**Note.** As you are asked to 'evaluate' the proposal, you need to think about whether the points you identify are benefits (+ve) or drawbacks (–ve) of it.)
Efficient numerical analysis	The management account information in Exhibit 2 is central to your analysis of Zilber's performance (task requirement 1).
	You should be able to score some relatively easy marks by calculating ratios (or movements between years) and then commenting on them.
	However, the fact that the management accounts show revenue at standard rate, and then discounts given, should have been a clue about the significance and impact of discounts. (In effect, managers have had to offer greater discounts in order to maintain occupancy rates.)
	Although Exhibit 1 tells us the standard room rate, a more useful metric for understanding Zilber's performance is the 'actual revenue per night'. Therefore calculating this will demonstrate to the examining team that you are thinking about the business context of the information provided, rather than simply calculating ratios.
Effective writing and presentation	The time constraints of the exam also mean that you cannot afford to be writing lengthy paragraphs to explain a single point.
	Therefore you need to find a balance. As a guide, aim to write 1 or 2 sentences to explain each point. Look at the following extract from the solution to Task 3(a) (critically assessing the risk register):
	'…Responding effectively to changes in the market place would also appear to be an important element of strategic risk. However, although the register identifies the importance of responding to technological change, eg the rise of cryptocurrencies, it does not include changes in the market place more generally – such as the falling demand from business travellers which is currently affecting the market.'
	The short paragraph identifies an important strategic risk; and then goes on to identify that it is not included in the register – so this 'omission' helps to critically assess the register.
	As in this paragraph, the use of words such as 'because', 'therefore' or 'however' are vital in helping to explain the significance of the points you make.
	Ask yourself: Why is something important? What are the implications of it? Review your answer and highlight areas where explanation is missing and then update your answer.
Good time management	As a guide, you should aim to spend 20 minutes reading and analysing the overall scenario, which then leaves you with 100 minutes to plan and write your answers (ie 2 minutes per mark).
	Applying the rule of 2 minutes per mark, the time available for each task requirement in this question is:
	Task requirement 1: 16 marks (14 technical + 2 professional skills): 32 minutes
	Task requirement 2: 10 marks: 20 minutes
	Task requirement 3(a): 8 marks: 16 minutes
	Task requirement 3(b): 8 marks: 16 minutes
	Task requirement 4: 8 marks: 16 minutes

Skill	Examples of the skills
	However, if you spend too long on task requirements 1 or 2, for example, this will increase the risk of you running out of time on the later tasks.
	Did you follow this timing, or spend too much or too little time for certain task requirements?
	There are potentially a very large number of points you could make for task requirement 1, so it is important you prioritise here, and that you don't run over on time.

Diagnostic

Did you apply these skills when reading, planning and writing up your answer? Identity the exam success skills where you think you need to improve and capture your thoughts here of what you want to achieve when attempting questions in future.

50 Ling Co

Marks

1 (a) 1 mark for discussion of each relevant point made in respect
of the macro-environmental factors
Up to a maximum of 6 marks in total for task 1(a)   6

(b) Up to 2 marks per relevant point made in respect of the
issues affecting the attractiveness of the light bulb industry
in Zedland
Up to a maximum of 15 marks in total for task 1(b)   15

2   Definition of strategic alliance   1
Basis for an alliance between Ling and Flick   Max 2
Different types of alliance (joint venture, licensing) Max 2
Conclusion as to suitability   1
Up to a maximum of 6 marks in total for task 2   6

3   Analysis of relevant stakeholder relationships   1
Agency relationship with Higgs Investments   Max 3
Analysis of the demands of World Business   Max 3
Up to a maximum of 7 marks in total for task 3   7

4   1 mark per relevant point about the Baldridge model and how it
can be used to achieve corporate success.
Up to a maximum of 6 marks in total for task 4   6

Professional skills may be rewarded as in the following rubric:

1(a)

How well has the candidate demonstrated professional skills as follows:	Not at all	Not so well	Quite well	Very well
1(a) – Analysis skills in assessing the macro-environmental factors affecting the Zedland light bulb industry.	The candidate demonstrated very few analysis skills, and has therefore failed to assess and reflect upon any of the factors identified.	The candidate demonstrated some analysis skills in analysing the factors in the macro-environment. However, the approach is descriptive rather than being properly applied to the scenario.	The candidate demonstrated analysis skills by selecting a range of relevant factors from the information provided. The candidate has made a reasonable attempt to comment and reflect on the factors identified.	The candidate demonstrated excellent analysis skills in identifying most of the key facts presented in the case and reflected on the impact the environmental factors have on the light bulb industry in Zedland.
	0	0.5	1	2

1(b)

How well has the candidate demonstrated professional skills as follows:	Not at all	Not so well	Quite well	Very well
1(b) – Evaluation skills relating to the attractiveness of the light bulb industry in Zedland for Ling Co.	The candidate has failed to assess how attractive the industry is.	The candidate has identified some of the relevant factors which will affect the attractiveness of the industry. However, there is little evidence of professional judgement in the evaluation, or an assessment of the overall attractiveness of the industry.	The candidate has demonstrated some sound evaluation skills in assessing the attractiveness of the industry. The candidate has made a reasonable attempt to assess the impact that different factors will have on the potential attractiveness of the industry.	The candidate has demonstrated excellent evaluation skills by assessing how the key characteristics of the light bulb Industry affect its attractiveness. The candidate has included substantially all of the major, relevant factors identified in the case, and assessed them accordingly.
	0	0.5	1	2

2

How well has the candidate demonstrated professional skills as follows:	Not at all	Not so well	Quite well	Very well
2 – Commercial acumen in assessing the suitability of a strategic alliance.	The candidate has failed to understand the factors that determine the suitability of a strategic alliance and has made a generic comments rather than ones which are appropriate to the context.	The candidate has demonstrated little commercial acumen in considering the suitability of a strategic alliance, meaning that the points made by the candidate have limited value in this context.	The candidate has demonstrated some understanding of the context and nature of a strategic alliance, but has not fully related the points made to the question scenario.	The candidate has demonstrated a clear understanding of strategic alliances, and displayed strong commercial acumen in making suitable and relevant points.
	0	0.5	1	2

How well has the candidate demonstrated professional skills as follows:	Not at all	Not so well	Quite well	Very well
3 – Scepticism skills in challenging Man Lal's views about WB.	The candidate has failed to demonstrate any scepticism towards the views of the CEO, and has therefore failed to identify the key issues or any problems with the suitability of the views on the stakeholders for presenting to the board.	The candidate has demonstrated some limited scepticism in questioning the views of the CEO in general terms, but has not identified or explained the key issues relevant to this scenario and so has not questioned the views in any depth.	The candidate has demonstrated scepticism by questioning whether the views on the stakeholder relationships, as expressed by the CEO, are valid. The candidate has made some reference to issues relevant to this scenario.	The candidate has demonstrated deep scepticism by identifying problems in the views expressed by the CEO. The candidate has clearly identified the key relevant issues and used them to recommend how the stakeholders should be managed.
	0	0.5	1	2

How well has the candidate demonstrated professional skills as follows:	Not at all	Not so well	Quite well	Very well
4 – Communication skills in highlighting the key points to include in the slides.	The candidate has failed to use a slide format to communicate the key features of the Baldrige model.	The candidate has loosely used a slide presentation format, but has failed to use bullet points and/or to recognise the importance of the audience being able to interpret the slide clearly. The candidate has produced some notes but they do not adequately explain the points on the slide effectively.	The candidate has used slides and bullet points to cover relevant points clearly and succinctly. The candidate has supplied notes, but although these support the slide they could be explained more clearly.	The candidate has used slides to present clear and succinct points in a logical order. The candidate has also produced clear supporting notes which relate closely to the points selected on the slide.
	0	0.5	1	2

Suggested solution

1   (a)   **To:**   The board of Ling Co

                 From: Management consultant

                 Date: [today's date]

                 Subject: Macro-environmental factors and attractiveness of Zedland

The first part of this report uses the PESTEL framework as a basis for analysing the macro-environmental factors affecting the light bulb industry in Zedland. The relevance of these factors for Ling may depend upon whether Ling decides to enter the light bulb market directly or to enter it by acquiring a Zedland-based company. In some instances, the factor affects the industry wherever it is based, though.

Political

The government is considering the imposition of import taxes. This would be a threat if Ling decides to enter the market place using the distribution company approach, and retain manufacturing in Wyeland. However, it presents an opportunity if Ling decides to acquire Flick and continue to run it as a Zedland-based company. The imposition of import taxes would lead to an expectation that the number of imports would fall, meaning that sales of Zedland-produced bulbs would increase.

Economic

Although the country of Zedland is in recession and consumer disposable income is falling, it seems unlikely that a low-cost commodity product like light bulbs will be greatly affected. This is an industry which is unlikely to be touched by changes in economic prosperity. The only minor issue may be the effect of switching off street lights. This may lengthen the lifespan of the bulb. However, overall, this is likely to have very little effect on total light bulb demand.

Sociocultural

There is a growing nationalist movement in Zedland who are keen to keep jobs within the country. There have been instances, in other industries, where imported goods have been boycotted. It seems unlikely that a backlash against foreign goods would affect the market for light bulbs, but it is possible, and any potential consumer backlash can be avoided by buying a Zedland-based company and manufacturing light bulbs locally.

Technical

Ling has so far benefited from technological innovations which have put it ahead of competitors who chose to focus on candescent and halogen bulbs. However, Ling needs to make sure that it continues to monitor all future developments in lighting technology. This monitoring is required whether Ling enters the Zedland market directly or acquires a company such as Flick.

Legal

The 'efficient lighting' legislation due to become law in Zedland in 20X7 is an opportunity for Ling to enter the market with its innovative LED products. This is an opportunity whether the company enters the market directly or buys a local company such as Flick.

Environmental

Businesses and consumers in Zedland are increasingly aware of energy issues. This is partly due to increasing energy prices as well as more frequent breaks in the electricity supply. The LED bulbs offered by Ling are greener and more efficient than candescent and halogen bulbs, which are still widely made in the home industry. In the case of businesses, many are quickly moving to LED light bulbs to reduce running costs and boost their environmental credentials. The environmental attractions of its products are important to Ling, but again this is independent of whether they are made by a company based in Zedland or one based abroad.

(b)   The second part of this report analyses the attractiveness of the light bulb industry in Zedland, using Porter's (1980) five forces model as a framework.

Bargaining power of customers

The main customers of the industry's products are large supermarket groups, home improvement superstores and large electrical chains. These customers, particularly the supermarket groups, purchase a large volume of the industry's products (90%) and so, on the face of it, they can demand favourable prices. However, the products the buyer purchases from the industry represents a relatively insignificant fraction of the buyer's costs or purchases. A recent report suggested that light bulb sales contributed less than 0.1% of a supermarket's revenue. Light bulbs are much less important to supermarket groups than food and drink. When the product sold by the industry is a small fraction of the customers' total costs, then customers are less price sensitive. They are more likely to bargain with food suppliers than light bulb suppliers.

Customers' bargaining power in the light bulb industry is strengthened by the product being undifferentiated, with low customer switching costs. However, the customers are extremely unlikely to move backwards in the supply chain to manufacture their own light bulbs and so this potentially limits their bargaining power. Again, their focus is likely to be elsewhere.

Some of the factors which concern these customers also relate to the end consumer of the bulbs as well. To the end consumer, light bulbs are undifferentiated and there are no switching costs. Light bulbs are an insignificant fraction of their total spend and so they are unlikely to shop around to get the lowest price.

Bargaining power of suppliers

A supplier group is more powerful if it is dominated by a few companies and is more concentrated than the industry it sells to. This appears to be the case in Zedland, where 90% of glass production is accounted for by three companies and metal production is largely concentrated in the hands of one very large company, OmniMetal. The customers (such as Flick) are large but they are more fragmented than the suppliers. Furthermore, the supplier group is, by and large, not obliged to contend with other substitute products for sale to the industry. Light bulbs are largely made of glass and metal and it seems unlikely that this will change in the near future. This lack of substitutes increases the power of the supplier.

The light bulb industry is not an important customer for the supplier group. Most glass is sold to the construction industry. Most metal is sold to the automobile industry. The light bulb manufacturers use less than 0.5% of the country's glass production and less than 0.1% of its metal production. The relative unimportance of light bulb manufacturers as customers increases the supplier group's power, because suppliers' fortunes are not closely tied to the industry and they will not need to protect it through reasonable pricing.

Another factor increasing suppliers' power is that the products (glass and metal) are a vital part of the customers' light bulb business.

On the other hand, the supplier group's products are largely undifferentiated and switching costs between suppliers appears to be reasonably low. Finally, it seems unlikely that the supplier group poses a credible threat of forward integration into light bulb manufacture and this will be a factor which reduces supplier bargaining power.

Threat of new entrants

Ling is considering entering this market and so the barriers to entry and the potential reaction of current suppliers is important to consider here. The main barriers to entry appear to be:

Economies of scale: The five large dominant companies in the industry should be enjoying economies of scale which force any potential new entrant to come into the market with large-scale production, which carries with it a high risk of failure. This is not an issue for Ling which also currently enjoys economies of scale in its manufacture. However, it will deter many other entrants.

Capital requirements: The manufacture of light bulbs requires new entrants to invest large financial resources into production plants. Although capital may be available, the risk associated with large-scale entry may lead to high premiums on borrowed capital.

Access to distribution channels: This may be very significant, as the distribution channels are very specific (supermarket groups, home improvement superstores and major electrical chains). The new entrant will have to persuade these channels to accept its products, perhaps through offering price discounts. It seems unlikely that the new entrant can create a completely new channel. Selling directly to the consumer seems unlikely in this industry where individual purchases are both infrequent and low value.

The reaction to new entrants of existing firms in the industry is likely to be relatively forceful as they have a history of vigorous retaliation to prospective entrants. The upsurge of nationalism in the country will also give them a powerful card to play in this retaliation.

Threat of substitute products

Substitute products are products which can perform the same function as the product of the industry under consideration. It is hard to envisage any potential substitute for light bulbs except for candles which, in the long term, are likely to be much more expensive. Another possible substitute is to do without lighting altogether. This is the approach taken by Zedland government policy on street lighting. It is turned off from 23:00 hrs to 05:00 hrs. However, it seems unlikely that consumers will choose to sit in the dark. In the short term, the threat of substitute products seems very low. However, in the long term, newer technologies may emerge.

Competitive rivalry in the industry

Equally balanced competitors: When an industry is dominated by a small number of firms and these firms are relatively well balanced in terms of size, it creates potential instability because they may be prone to fight each other. This appears to be the case in Zedland where five fairly similar sized firms produce 72% (20X5) of the light bulbs sold in the country and wage short-term price-cutting wars, disrupt competitors' supply lines and react aggressively to potential new entrants.

Slow industry growth: There is little market growth. Between 20X0 and 20X5 the market grew by just over 2% (from total revenues of $490m to $500m). In mature markets with little scope for overall growth, the only way a firm can increase market share is to take it from its competitors. Consequently, slow industry growth increases competitive rivalry.

Lack of differentiation or switching costs: Competitive rivalry is increased where the product is perceived as a commodity, as is the case for light bulbs. In such circumstances the buyer's decision is largely based on price, and pressures for intense price competition result.

High exit barriers: Exit costs are high because of the investment required in plant and the fact that light bulb factories have no obvious alternative use. When exit costs are high, companies will remain in the industry and may resort to extreme tactics which weaken the profitability of the industry as a whole.

2   **Briefing paper**

FAO: FD at Ling Co

Strategic alliance with Flick

There are many documented cases where acquisitions have been unsuccessful and so the Financial Director's caution is understandable. Strategic alliances appear to offer a less risky way of entering a market.

A strategic alliance is where two or more organisations share resources and activities to pursue a strategy. The basis for an alliance between Ling and Flick would be co-specialisation, allowing each partner to focus on their core capabilities, with Ling being able to use Flick's local knowledge and expertise in distribution, marketing and customer support. In such an alliance, Ling could exploit a new market, retain all production in its own country and save itself the costs of acquisition and due diligence. In return, Flick would gain new energy-efficient products for its home market which would allow it to fulfil the requirements of impending legislation. The profit of the alliance would have to be split, on some agreed basis, between the two companies.

There are different types of strategic partnership. In a joint venture, a new organisation is created which is jointly owned. The parent companies remain independent trading companies. This is unlikely to be attractive in the Ling/Flick situation. It seems more likely that Flick would wish to sell the product as its own, and not confuse the market with an offering from a related company. A joint venture is probably more appropriate where the participating companies are entering into a different market.

Different levels of formality of the alliance lead to different characteristics. For example, if speed to market is important, then a more informal alliance would be preferred to a joint venture. Indeed the terms of a joint venture might even take longer to agree and legally establish than the completion of an acquisition.

The form of the strategic alliance can be shaped to take into account the environmental factors which affect the industry and the different capabilities of the participants. It can also be made responsive to cultural differences. However, in the Ling/Flick situation, it is difficult to see how a strategic alliance will address the needs of the institutional stakeholders for growth. Furthermore, there may be concerns about the long-term viability of any such alliance. It seems likely that Ling would be reluctant to license a product which could be easily imitated by the licensee. Furthermore, just as Ling has limited expertise in acquisitions, there is no evidence in the scenario that Ling has experience of strategic alliances. Success requires expertise in setting up and monitoring clear goals, governance, financial arrangements and other organisational issues.

3   **Briefing notes**

Introduction

The letters from Higgs Investments and 'Watching Business' (WB) highlight the importance of the relationship between Ling and its shareholders, as well as the potential significance of other stakeholders. Whilst a range of stakeholders have the power to require explanations from Ling, the shareholders are arguably the most significant. They own the company, and their rights are enforceable under company law.

Agency relationship between Ling's board and Higgs Investments

The directors of Ling are employed as agents by the company's shareholders, who own the company. As owners, the shareholders have the right to comment upon, and influence, the company's objectives. The directors are responsible for managing the company in accordance with the shareholders' views. The main objective is normally assumed to be maximisation of returns to shareholders, subject to any constraints imposed by laws and society's values. Higgs Investments has thus correctly reminded the board of its responsibilities towards shareholders and appears to be supportive of the investment in Flick.

Demands of WB

Despite the assertions of Higgs Investments that WB are 'misinformed outsiders concerned with things ... which happened a while ago', it is actually the case that WB will have some power, because of its influence in society, and so it cannot be dismissed so easily. The problems at Flick only occurred a year ago, and it could be that other problems could come to light. Because of Flick's recent record, about which it remains sceptical, WB has advised Ling not to invest in Flick, even though this is a strategy that may yield high returns for shareholders.

WB's significance for Ling derives from its influence over legislators and the wider public in several countries. Its high levels of support by politicians cannot be ignored. It is a well-known organisation that could use its influence to promote a boycott of a company and its products. Consequently, its influence cannot be 'safely ignored' as you have suggested it could.

Because of this high influence, Ling has to consider its claims seriously, despite the fact that it is, in Higgs Investments' words, an 'outsider'. Stakeholders do not have to be internal to Ling, or directly connected, to be relevant. The following issues are particularly significant.

Strategic interests

Ling's longer-term strategic interests may be harmed by WB's lobbying. Ling may face greater regulations and pressures from policymakers not to ignore potential environmental concerns. Ling has benefited from being associated with high 'green' and environmentally ethical standards in Wyeland, but it could lose this advantage if WB's claims are valid and problems with Flick's activities persist post acquisition that take time to be resolved.

Reputation risk

Any adverse coverage in the future may result in consumers boycotting Ling's products, because they do not wish to be associated with a company that is seen as misrepresenting its environmental credentials.

Conclusion

The concerns of WB cannot be ignored, but ought to be taken into account when the investment decision is made. If Ling does decide to invest, it must carefully manage any threats to its reputation by emphasising the positive reasons for investing in Flick and Zedland. Although this may not satisfy WB, other interested parties such as politicians may take a more positive view.

4 Slide: 1

The Baldrige model of performance excellence (National Institute of Standards and Technology, n.d)

What does it aim to do?

- Provide a framework for assessing performance
- Help organisations to achieve excellence

How does it do this?

- Helps an organisation to identify its strengths
- Highlights areas for improvement

(see supporting notes)

Slide: 2

What are the criteria that are used to assess an organisation?

The National Institute of Standards and Technology (n.d) highlight that six key criteria shape an organisation's ability to perform, and help to achieve the seventh criteria.

1   Leadership
2   Strategy
3   Customers
4   Measurement, analysis and knowledge management
5   Workforce
6   Operations

Leading to ...

7   Results

(see supporting notes)

Slide: 3

How are the criteria evaluated and applied?

The National Institute of Standards and Technology (n.d) highlight that **criteria 1–6** are evaluated in relation to four dimensions:

- Approach
- Deployment
- Learning
- Integration

Results (Criterion 7) are evaluated against four (different) dimensions:

- Levels
- Trends
- Comparisons
- Integration

(see supporting notes)

Supporting notes for Slide 1:

The National Institute of Standards and Technology (n.d) highlight that the underlying purpose of the Baldrige model is to help organisations improve, and to achieve performance excellence

The model doesn't prescribe how an organisation should operate. Rather, it is based on the idea that there are certain beliefs and behaviours that are found in all high-performing organisations, and which underpin corporate success. By evaluating beliefs and behaviours within Ling against these benchmarks, we could identify our current strengths, but equally importantly identify areas for improvement.

The beliefs and behaviours are:

– Visionary leadership

– A focus on success

– Ethics and transparency

– Societal responsibility

– Organisational learning and agility

– Valuing people

– Customer-focused excellence

- Delivering value and results
- Management by fact: an emphasis on feedback, and a fact-based, knowledge-driven system for improving performance and competitiveness

Supporting notes for Slide 2:

Areas for assessment within each of the criteria are as follows:

Leadership – Assessment of the senior leadership team, and governance and social responsibilities

Strategy – The development and definition of the goals for the company, and the implementation of the strategy

Customers – Assessing how well the company listens to its customers, how well it engages with them and meets their needs

Measurement, analysis and knowledge management – Assessing how well the company uses these to improve organisational performance, with appropriate feedback systems and use of information technology

Workforce – Assessment of the working environment and the skills and motivation of staff

Operations – Assessing the efficiency and effectiveness of the company's work processes

Results – An assessment against other organisations, over time, of its products and processes, customers, workforce, leadership and governance standards, and how they have contributed towards its financial results and market position

Supporting notes for Slide 3:

Approach	How does Ling accomplish its work? How effective are its key approaches?
Deployment	How consistently are key processes used in relevant parts of the organisation?
Learning	How well has the organisation evaluated and improved its key approaches? How well have improvements been shared? What is the potential for innovation in the future?
Integration	How well are the organisation's approaches aligned to its current and future needs? How well are processes and operations, and any associated targets and performance measures, harmonised across the organisation?

Levels	What is the organisation's current performance level?
Trends	Are results improving, staying the same or getting worse?
Comparisons	How does the Ling's performance compare with that of other organisations, or against benchmarks/targets?
Integration	Does Ling track the results, also considering the expectations of key stakeholders? Does the organisation use these results in decision making?

Ling Co – Mini-Mock Exam 2

Tutorial notes to help you improve your exam success skills performance

Skill	Examples of the skills
Case scenario: Managing information	Exhibit 1 provides you with critical context, which you can then use as you analyse and respond to all the task requirements. Man Lal has built Ling into a highly successful company by spotting and taking advantage of trends in the marketplace, particularly energy efficiency. The operational model is kept simple, with all manufacturing for export markets in Wyeland.
	However, faced with market saturation and impatient shareholders, Man Lal is considering changing this approach and making an overseas acquisition which includes manufacturing capability. This is new and uncharted territory, carrying significant risks. This should inform the way you read all the information.
Correct interpretation of requirements	You need to read the task requirements carefully to pick up where they are directing you. Task requirement 1(b) of this question asks for:
	'An evaluation of the attractiveness of the Zedland light bulb industry.'
	Notice that you are analysing 'attractiveness' – is the industry where Ling is looking to make an acquisition likely to be profitable and so worth their investment? Secondly, you are being asked to analyse the 'industry', not Zedland as a physical location.
	Considering these points should lead you to realise that the most suitable framework in the syllabus is Porter's (1980) five forces, which deals with exactly these issues. You may prefer to not use a model at all when attempting this task. Provided the points that you make are valid and applied to the scenario you would receive credit.
Answer planning: Priorities, structure and logic	Task requirement 3 is quite tricky and requires careful thought before you start writing:
	'Man Lal has sought your advice regarding the issues raised by the letter from "Watching Business". He says to you: "I get really frustrated whenever anybody gets in the way of our most important relationship, that is, the one with our shareholders! Overall, I do think that Higgs Investments are right and 'Watching Business' can be safely ignored. However, I want your help in explaining my position to the rest of the board."
	Required
	Prepare briefing notes for Man Lal which explain the agency relationship between the board of Ling Co and Higgs Investments, and provide advice on how the demands from Watching Business should be considered. **(7 marks)**
	Professional skills marks are available for demonstrating scepticism skills in challenging Man Lal's views about WB. **(2 marks)**
	(Total = 9 marks)
	Man Lal has been contacted by a lobbying organisation and by its biggest institutional shareholder and needs to consider how to respond. You are directed to analyse this in the context of agency theory. So a good starting point is to discuss what that means, ie the responsibility the directors of Ling have to their shareholders. However, you are also directed to use professional scepticism, so we need to question Man Lal's immediate reaction to dismiss 'Watching Business'. They are a legitimate stakeholder and if the situation is managed badly, Ling could face political pressure or even a consumer boycott. So you need to think carefully about how to balance the competing interests and also use tact if you need to explain to Man Lal that his initial reaction may need revising.

Skill	Examples of the skills
Efficient numerical analysis	This question has less numerical content than some others, but the data about each company can be used to make a number of points: • The five biggest companies are roughly equal in size. This will tend to increase competitive rivalry. • The market as a whole is very slow-growing – 2% in five years. This suggests it is very mature and the only way to grow the business will be to win market share from others, which will add to the level of competition. • Flick's market share has risen very slightly, from 13% to 14%. This also implies a high level of competition in the industry, reducing opportunities for profit.
Effective writing and presentation	This question requires you to communicate in a number of different forms – a section of a consultancy report, response to the Finance Director, a briefing paper, briefing notes and a presentation. You will need to take account of this in your solution and will gain credit for varying your style accordingly. You will be expected to maintain an appropriate business style, whatever format you are using. Make sure you picked up on this, particularly part 4, where you were required to provide presentation slides and notes. If you are asked to prepare slides, it is important to keep the points on the slides brief, and not to include too much detail on the slides. The supporting detail should be included on the notes which accompany the slides, not on the slides themselves. Remember slides are likely to be presented to an audience, so make sure the slides have titles or headings, and that the points on them will be easy for an audience to read. (This reinforces the point about not including too much detail on the slides.)
Good time management	As a guide, you should aim to spend 20 minutes reading and analysing the overall scenario, which then leaves you with 100 minutes to plan and write your answers (ie 2 minutes per mark). Applying the rule of 2 minutes per mark, the time available for each task requirement in this question is approximately: Task requirement 1(a): 8 (6 technical + 2 professional skills): 16 minutes Task requirement 1(b): 17 (15 technical + 2 professional skills): 34 minutes Task requirement 2: 8 marks (6 technical + 2 professional skills): 16 minutes Task requirement 3: 9 marks (7 technical + 2 professional skills): 18 minutes Task requirement 4: 8 marks (6 technical + 2 professional skills): 16 minutes Part 1(b) has the highest number of marks by some margin, so you should have spent the most time on this task. Having said that, there would be a temptation to spend too long on this, leaving you running out of time in the final task.

Diagnostic

Did you apply these skills when reading, planning and writing up your answer? Identity the exam success skills where you think you need to improve and capture your thoughts here of what you want to achieve when attempting questions in future.

51 Cheapkit

				Marks
1	(a)	One mark per relevant point relating to relevant environmental factors		
		Up to a maximum of 8 marks in total for task 1(a)		8
	(b)	Up to 2 marks for examining the claims of each stakeholder – up to 6 marks	Max 6	
		Up to 3 marks for discussing the conflict between claims of different stakeholders – up to 3 marks	Max <u>3</u>	
		Note. Answers must relate to Cheapkit's stakeholders, not Cornflower's		
		Up to a maximum of 8 marks in total for task 1(b)		8
	(c)	For each risk: one mark for definition – up to 3 marks	Max 3	
		For each risk: up to 2 marks for explaining their significance for Cheapkit's shareholders – up to 6 marks	Max <u>6</u>	
		Up to a maximum of 8 marks in total for task 1(c)		8
2		Up to 2 marks for explaining the concept of corporate citizenship	Max 2	
		One mark per relevant point for explaining aspects of citizenship (ie rights and responsibilities) in the context of the case – up to 6 marks	Max <u>6</u>	
		Up to a maximum of 6 marks in total for task 2		6
3		Up to 4 marks for calculating the profitability of the contract	Max 4	
		One mark per relevant point in relation to potential advantages/ disadvantages of the contract or issues arising from it – up to 6 marks	Max 6	
		For reasoned advice about whether or not Cheapkit should accept the contract – up to 2 marks	Max <u>2</u>	
		Up to a maximum of 10 marks in total for task 3		10

Professional skills may be rewarded as in the following rubric:

1(a)

How well has the candidate demonstrated professional skills as follows:	Not at all	Not so well	Quite well	Very well
1(a) – Evaluation skills in assessing the business environment.	The candidate has failed to assess the external environment and has simply listed factors from the case study, and has therefore failed to assess their relevance to Cheapkit's strategic position or strategy.	The candidate has assessed the external environment, but has made only a limited assessment of how the factors identified could affect Cheapkit.	The candidate has identified a good range of relevant environmental factors, and has used some evaluation skills to assess how these could affect Cheapkit's strategy and/or performance.	The candidate has comprehensively identified a range of environmental factors from the case. The candidate has then assessed the potential significance of these factors for Cheapkit, and how they could influence its strategy and/or performance.
	0	0.5	1	2

1(b)

How well has the candidate demonstrated professional skills as follows:	Not at all	Not so well	Quite well	Very well
1(b) – Analysis skills in considering the claims of different stakeholders.	The candidate has failed to consider the nature of the different stakeholders' relationships with Cheapkit, and has therefore failed to identify their expectations of or claims on Cheapkit.	The candidate has shown some basic analysis skill in identifying the stakeholders' claims on Cheapkit, but has failed to consider how the claims of the different stakeholders may be in conflict.	The candidate has demonstrated good analysis skills by considering the nature of the stakeholders' relationships with Cheapkit, and has made a reasonable attempt to reflect on how the claims of the different stakeholders may be in conflict.	The candidate has demonstrated excellent analysis skills by clearly considering the nature of each stakeholder group's interests in Cheapkit. The candidate has reflected on the claims of each of the different stakeholder groups and, as a result, has identified the key areas in which the stakeholders' claims may be in conflict.
	0	0.5	1	2

1(c)

How well has the candidate demonstrated professional skills as follows:	Not at all	Not so well	Quite well	Very well
1(c) – Commercial acumen in identifying the significance of the risks for Cheapkit's shareholders.	The candidate has failed to understand the significance of the risks, and how they can affect Cheapkit's performance, thereby making them important for Cheapkit's shareholders.	The candidate has explained the significance of the risks in general terms, but has failed to explain their potential impact on Cheapkit's performance and therefore why they are significant for Cheapkit's shareholders.	The candidate has demonstrated some commercial acumen in identifying the significance of the risks, and has identified some of the implications of these which make them significant for Cheapkit's shareholders.	The candidate has demonstrated excellent commercial awareness by identifying most, if not all, of the implications of the risks which make the risks significant for Cheapkit's shareholders.
	0	0.5	1	2

How well has the candidate demonstrated professional skills as follows:	Not at all	Not so well	Quite well	Very well
2 – Communication skills for the tone of the statement and for responding diplomatically to the comments made against Cheapkit.	The candidate has demonstrated poor communication skills. They have failed to adopt an appropriate tone for their press statement, and have failed to defend Cheapkit's actions in response to the claims made against it.	The candidate has demonstrated some basic communication skills in presenting their answer as a press statement. Some relevant information is included in the statement, although the statement doesn't respond clearly to the comments made against Cheapkit.	The candidate has demonstrated good communication skills in selecting an appropriate tone for the press statement, and has addressed most of the relevant issues in the statement in a way which defends Cheapkit from the comments made against it.	The candidate has demonstrated excellent communication skills. The press statement demonstrates appropriate sympathy for the people who suffered in the tragedy but also clearly defines Cheapkit's roles and responsibilities and defends its position in relation to the allegations that have been made about it.
	0	0.5	1	2

How well has the candidate demonstrated professional skills as follows:	Not at all	Not so well	Quite well	Very well
3 – Scepticism skills in highlighting issues which could affect the suitability of the proposed contract for Cheapkit.	The candidate has accepted the Sales Director's optimism about the proposal, and has failed to demonstrate any scepticism skills in questioning whether it will actually be appropriate or beneficial for Cheapkit.	The candidate has demonstrated some limited scepticism in questioning how appropriate or beneficial the proposal is for Cheapkit. However, the candidate has missed the key issues which affect the appropriateness of the proposal.	The candidate has demonstrated some scepticism in recognising some of the most important issues with the proposal, and has highlighted why these affect the suitability of the proposed contact.	The candidate has demonstrated excellent scepticism skills by identifying substantially all of the key issues which could reduce the apparent attractiveness of the proposal. Accordingly, the candidate presented justified advice against the proposal, despite the Sales Director's support for it, and it potentially making a positive contribution to profit.
	0	0.5	1	2

Suggested solution

1   MEMORANDUM

To: Finance Director

From: Senior Finance Manager

Date: XX/XX/XXXX

Subject: An evaluation of Cheapkit's business environment

(a)   We can analyse the business environment in which Cheapkit operates using the PESTEL framework.

Political

The government of Essland is expected to increase the minimum wage in its next budget. This will be a threat to Cheapkit because it will increase wage costs. Given Cheapkit's low-cost business model, it pays many of its retail staff the minimum wage, so the impact of the minimum wage increase could be more significant for Cheapkit than for other retailers whose rates of pay are already above the minimum wage.

Economic

Although the economy in Essland is relatively weak, this could benefit Cheapkit, rather than being a threat. If Cheapkit is perceived as offering value-for-money clothes, customers may switch to it away from more expensive alternatives – hence enabling the like-for-like sales increase which the Finance Director anticipates over the next year.

Rising commodity prices and a weakening currency will both increase Cheapkit's costs, which again could be a particular problem given its low-cost business model. Cheapkit will be faced with a dilemma about how far to pass on cost increases to customers (through higher prices), or to absorb them itself through lower margins.

Sociocultural

Cheapkit has so far benefited from customers' desire to buy fashion lines as quickly and cheaply as possible. However, it seems that customer attitudes toward 'fast fashion' are beginning to become more critical now, which could pose a threat to retailers like Cheapkit. (There is also an **environmental** aspect to changing attitudes here – in relation to the sustainability of 'fast fashion' and its throw-away attitude to resource usage.)

More generally, the notion that fast fashion is not socially responsible could be a threat if it begins to influence customers' purchasing decisions. However, in practice, if Cheapkit continues to offer customers value-for-money, fashionable products, it is perhaps debatable how many will stop buying them on grounds of social responsibility.

Technological

Cheapkit has been able to succeed so far without having an e-commerce platform, which suggests the impact of e-commerce in low-cost retail is less significant than in other sectors (perhaps because of the size of delivery charges compared to the cost of garments purchased online).

It will be important for Cheapkit to monitor the extent to which its competitors sell online, and how successful they are, to ensure that Cheapkit does not lose market share as a result of not selling online.

As Cheapkit has already recognised, social media provides a marketing opportunity. However, while social media can help to promote Cheapkit's products and brand, any negative feedback via social media could damage the company's brand and reputation.

Legal

If governments in developing countries introduce new regulations around health and safety and working conditions, this could increase the costs faced by Cheapkit's suppliers. In turn, this is likely to increase Cheapkit's costs, because – if it wants to be seen as a responsible corporate citizen – Cheapkit will need to increase the price it pays its suppliers.

(b) **Briefing notes**

Stakeholder claims

Stakeholders can affect, or be affected by, the achievements of an organisation's objectives. A stakeholder relationship is two-way, and each stakeholder group has different expectations and has different claims upon an organisation.

Customers

Cheapkit's customers want fashionable items at low prices. Cheapkit's ability to offer garments at lower prices than its main rivals is likely to be critical in ensuring that it meets customers' expectations.

Cheapkit will need to offer clothes in styles which customers want to buy, and of reasonable quality (despite the low price). In addition, continuity of supply – and availability of the products they want to buy at any given time – will be important for customers. This is likely to be particularly important in a fast-paced industry such as fashion retailing.

Suppliers

Cheapkit is likely to be a major customer for suppliers (like Cornflower) and therefore the suppliers' primary interest will be in retaining their contracts with Cheapkit, and the revenue this brings them.

However, the balance of power in the relationship lies with Cheapkit rather than the suppliers, and it is likely that if a particular supplier fails to meet Cheapkit's requirements (for cost or quality), it will move to another supplier.

Pressure groups

The pressure groups are concerned with the working conditions in the suppliers' factories and in improved health and safety legislation. Their immediate concern – in the aftermath of the tragedy at Cornflower's factory – is for safer working conditions, although more generally they are likely to want improved pay and secure contracts for workers.

Conflict between claims

Cheapkit's low cost strategy (and customers' desire for low-priced clothes) is likely to conflict with attempts to improve the pay and working conditions of workers in supplier factories, as this will result in higher production costs.

The suppliers' primary focus appears to be on keeping costs low to ensure they retain their contracts. However, the pressure groups are likely to be more aggressive in challenging the current position (because they do not have any contracts or direct relationships with Cheapkit).

Nonetheless, if costs in Athland start increasing (as a result of changes to health and safety legislation and wage legislation), Cheapkit may move look for an alternative supplier. As such, instead of improving conditions in the garment industry in Athland, the pressure groups' campaigns could potentially result in job losses.

(c)   Briefing notes

Risks

Exchange rate risk

When a company trades with a foreign supplier or customer, it will expose itself to exchange rate or currency risk unless both countries share the same currency (as in the eurozone for example). Movements in foreign exchange rates create risk in that the final amount payable or receivable will be uncertain.

Cheapkit pays Cornflower and its other Athland suppliers in the currency of Athland; if the exchange rate for this currency increases in relation to Cheapkit's own currency then Cheapkit's costs of buying from Athland will increase. Last year 65% of Cheapkit's supplies came from Athland, so an adverse movement in exchange rates could have a significant impact on profit, which will be of concern to shareholders.

Supply risk

This is the risk that Cheapkit will fail to procure the necessary supplies to meet demand from its customers. Cheapkit relies heavily on imports from Athland, and the collapse of the building means that Cornflower will not be able to deliver its orders, at least in the short term. Cornflower produces a third* of Cheapkit's products, so this loss is significant.

Cheapkit's business strategy is based on providing a range of fashion items at cheap prices. The tragedy in Athland will mean a reduction in the items available in the stores, increased prices or possibly both. This could have an impact on Cheapkit's revenue and competitiveness in the market and thus on shareholder value.

In addition to specific risks around disruption of Cheapkit's supply chain, there could also be more general risks that if suppliers act unethically, or illegally (as Cornflower did), this could damage Cheapkit's reputation through their association with the suppliers.

> *: Around 65% of Cheapkit's supplies come from Athland (Exhibit 2), and around half of the supplies from Athand come from Cornflower (Exhibit 3). This suggests Cornflower produces around 32.5% of Cheapkit's products.

International political risk

Political risk is the risk that political action will affect the position and value of an organisation. It is connected with country risk, the risk associated with undertaking transactions with a particular country. Political changes can be favourable or unfavourable.

In Athland, the state failed to implement and enforce building and health and safety regulations, and this was a contributory factor in the disaster at the Cornflower factory.

For Cheapkit's shareholders, the weakness of the state means that a significant part of the supply chain is unreliable – again, potentially jeopardising Cheapkit's revenue and competitiveness in the market.

Another key risk in dealing with suppliers in Athland is the apparent prevalence of bribery and corruption, which could lead to repercussions for Cheapkit personnel if there is UK-style anti-corruption legislation in place. There could also be damage to reputation as a result of dealing with a country where corrupt practices are perceived by consumers to be common.

2   PRESS STATEMENT

Issued by the board of Cheapkit in response to recent events in Athland

The board of Cheapkit wish to issue the following statement in response to comments received following the recent tragic events in the Cornflower factory in Athland.

The Cornflower factory is one of Cheapkit's major suppliers, and we wish to express our condolences and sympathy to all those affected.

We should like to reassure our shareholders and the general public that we are working closely with our contacts in Athland in order to establish why the factory collapsed, and to help ensure that such a disaster never happens again.

This statement will address the Cheapkit's role as a corporate citizen, which has been questioned in the aftermath of the tragedy.

Cheapkit's role as corporate citizen

Corporate citizenship is the contribution an organisation makes to society through its activities and the choices made each day by its executives, managers and employees as they engage with society.

Three core principles define the essence of corporate citizenship, and every company should apply them in a manner appropriate to its distinct needs: minimising harm; maximising benefit; and being accountable and responsive to its stakeholders. The general concepts of rights and responsibilities are fundamental to the definition of corporate citizenship.

Cheapkit has the right to conduct business with suppliers and customers within the confines of the law in each country in which it operates. We have at all times acted lawfully with respect to our suppliers, customers, employees and shareholders. The tragic events in Athland occurred because of illegal practices in that jurisdiction, and as such were beyond our control. Although we expect our suppliers to take responsibility for their own actions, we will be reviewing whether there are steps we can take to prevent them from acting illegally.

We recognise our responsibilities as a corporate citizen in our fair dealings with all our stakeholders. Cheapkit has always strived to maximise shareholder wealth by providing value for money for our customers, whilst at the same time acknowledging our duty to secure good working conditions for our employees, and to pay a fair price for goods purchased from our suppliers.

3   **Report**

To:	**FD at Cheapkit**
From:	**Senior Finance Manager**
Date:	**XX/XX/XXXX**
Subject:	**Contract: acceptance, risk, implications and returns**

Terms of reference

This report will assess whether Cheapkit should accept the Yummy contract. The report will examine the expected financial returns as well as the risks and strategic implications of the contract.

Yummy contract

In simple financial terms, the new contract creates an overall positive contribution of $106,250 over the two years, as follows:

Year 1		$
Sales	(125,000 × $5.80) + (125,000 × $9.70)	1,937,500
Manufacturing costs	(125,000 × $5.40) + (125,000 × $8.95)	1,793,750
Logistics costs	(125,000 × $0.20) + (125,000 × $0.25)	56,250
Fixed costs		25,000
Contribution		62,500

Year 2		$
Sales	(125,000 × $5.80) + (125,000 × $9.70)	1,937,500
Manufacturing costs	(125,000 × $5.45) + (125,000 × $9.05)	1,812,500
Logistics costs	(125,000 × $0.20) + (125,000 × $0.25)	56,250
Fixed costs		25,000
Contribution		43,750

The contract generates a positive contribution over the two years, which might initially suggest that Cheapkit should accept it.

Moreover, the order quantities of 125,000 units per year are minimum figures, so the actual quantities ordered may be higher than this, meaning the contribution could also be higher (assuming no incremental fixed costs are incurred at the higher volumes). Similarly, the contract may be renewed on more favourable terms at the end of two years, providing Cheapkit with a greater contribution to profit in the future.

In addition, the principle of producing standardised designs in large quantities fits with the low-cost business model which Cheapkit operates.

Fixed price – However, there are several major issues with the proposal, including the fact that the contract is based on a fixed price over two years. Costs are unlikely to remain fixed over the two years, as the estimated figures illustrate. Therefore, Cheapkit faces a risk that volatility in raw material costs, or foreign exchange rates, could affect the profitability of the contract. Cheapkit will be committed to supplying at least 125,000 units each of shirts and trousers per year, regardless of changes in costs.

Although the contract currently appears profitable, the relatively low level of the profit ($106,250 over two years; or 2.7% net margin) suggests that it could be relatively sensitive to increases in costs.

Change in business model – Another concern is that the proposal represents a change in our business model. Currently, Cheapkit sells to individual consumers via its stores. However, the proposal is for a 'business to business' arrangement in which Cheapkit sells to Yummy as a single corporate customer. Cheapkit will, in effect, become the lead supplier for Yummy, rather than being a retailer in its own right.

Under this arrangement, Yummy will have a greater bargaining power over Cheapkit than individual customers currently do. (This could already be reflected in the demand for a fixed price contract over two years.)

Conclusion

Cheapkit appears to already be growing successfully (with five more shop openings planned for the coming year) so it is debatable whether there is any need to take on this new contract. Moreover, there already appears to be pressure on suppliers to meet demand, so taking on a bulk contract like this will only add to that pressure.

Given the relatively low profit margin the contract is expected to generate, Cheapkit would be advised not to accept the contract, and to focus instead on its existing retail business.

Cheapkit – Mini-Mock Exam 3

Tutorial notes to help you improve your exam success skills performance

Skill	Examples of the skills
Case scenario: Managing information	As you read through the scenario and exhibits initially, think about the aspects of the organisation's strategy and business model. In this case, the opening paragraph to the introduction tells us Cheapkit's 'underlying aim is to sell fashionable clothes at the lowest possible prices.'
	An important point to consider throughout the scenario is how this aim could influence Cheapkit's relationships with its customers and suppliers. Some of the Exhibits are suggesting that Cheapkit's focus on low costs mean it cannot be a responsible corporate citizen, but are such suggestions justified?
Correct interpretation of requirements	A single task can sometimes require you to consider more than one point.
	Task requirement 3 illustrates this:
	'Prepare a report which advises whether or not Cheapkit should accept the contract from Yummy, taking into account the risk and strategic implications as well as the financial returns.'
	In effect, within this single task you need to do four things:
	• Advise whether or not Cheapkit should accept the contract
	• Consider the risk involved in the contract
	• Consider the strategic implications of the contract
	• Consider the financial returns from the contract
	In practice, your advice will need to come after you have considered the other points, but a key point at the end of your answer will be to make a recommendation to Cheapkit as to whether or not it should accept the contract.
Answer planning: Priorities, structure and logic	Task 1(b) is another question which contains more than one sub-requirement: (i) analyse the claims of three different stakeholder groups (customers; suppliers; and pressure groups); and (ii) how these claims may be in conflict.
	A sensible approach to a question like this is to use each of the stakeholder groups as headings (in order to analyse their individual claims), and your analysis of the individual claims should help to identify the areas where they may be in conflict. In effect, the structure of the task requirement should help you to answer it.
	Importantly, though, the verb 'analyse' means break into separate parts and discuss or examine these parts. A key point when 'analysing' something is to give reasons for it.
	So in this question, analysing the stakeholder claims does not simply mean stating whether they have high interest or high power. A more useful approach to this question is to consider what the interests of each of the stakeholders are, because it is these interests which give rise to the potential conflicts (for example, between customers wishes for low prices, and a desire to improve the pay and working conditions in suppliers' factories).

BPP
LEARNING
MEDIA

Skill	Examples of the skills
Efficient numerical analysis	The potential financial returns Cheapkit could achieve from the Yummy contract are one of the key factors which will determine whether or not it should accept the contract.
	Exhibit 5 tells you that the proposed contract is for two years, and gives details of the volume, sale price and cost of the different garments.
	The figures for the two years are different, so you need to produce separate workings for each year. Nonetheless, the calculations should be relatively straightforward, meaning you can produce a contribution statement (showing revenue less costs) for each year.
Effective writing and presentation	Task requirement 1 asks you to evaluate the business environment in which Cheapkit operates.
	An appropriate framework that you may consider using here is PESTEL, because you are asked to evaluate the general business environment, rather than, for example, the industry environment.
	You can use the headings from the framework (Political, Economic etc) which should also help you to structure your answer. You may prefer to not use a model at all when attempting this task requirement. Provided the points that you make are valid and applied to the scenario you would receive credit. Importantly, however, your answer should not just be a list of environment factors picked from the scenario.
	To add value to your briefing note, you also need to consider how these factors will affect Cheapkit, as the following excerpt from the suggested solution illustrates:
	'Political
	The government of Essland is expected to increase the minimum wage in its next budget. This will be a threat to Cheapkit because it will increase wage costs. Given Cheapkit's low-cost business model, it pays many of its retail staff the minimum wage, so the impact of the minimum wage increase could be more significant for Cheapkit than for other retailers whose rates of pay are already above the minimum wage.'
	The opening sentence identifies the environmental factor; the second sentence then identifies why it is relevant to Cheapkit, and its potential impact; the third sentence then explains why the factor is important.
	Review your answers and consider whether you have properly explained the points you have made.
Good time management	As a guide, you should aim to spend 20 minutes reading and analysing the overall scenario, which then leaves you with 100 minutes to plan and write your answers (ie 2 minutes per mark).
	Applying the rule of 2 minutes per mark, the time available for each task requirement in this question is:
	Task requirement 1(a): 10 (8 technical + 2 professional skills): 20 minutes
	Task requirement 1(b): 10 marks: 20 minutes
	Task requirement 1(c): 10 marks: 20 minutes
	Task requirement 2: 8 marks: 16 minutes
	Task requirement 3: 12 marks: 24 minutes
	Did you notice that task requirements 1(a), 1(b) and 1(c) were all worth the same number of marks, and therefore you should have allocated the same amount of time to each of them?
	Similarly, did you notice that task 3 was worth the highest number of marks, so it was very important that you didn't spend too long on 1(a) or 1(b) (for example) with the result that you didn't then have sufficient time to answer task 3 properly.

Diagnostic

Did you apply these skills when reading, planning and writing up your answer? Identify the exam success skills where you think you need to improve and capture your thoughts here of what you want to achieve when attempting questions in future.

52 Domusco

				Marks
1	(a)	Up to 3 marks for each NPV calculation (low revenue, low cost; and low revenue, high cost) – up to 6 marks	Max 6	
		One mark per relevant point for issues relating to financial attractiveness of the contracts, including discussion of uncertainty around the figures – up to 6 marks.	Max <u>6</u>	
		Up to a maximum of 10 marks in total for task 1(a)		10
	(b)	Up to 2 marks for general discussion of aspects of corporate social responsibility (CSR)	Max 2	
		One mark per relevant point for CSR issues to consider in relation to the Metsa contract – up to 8 marks	Max <u>8</u>	
		Up to a maximum of 8 marks in total for task 1(b)		8
	(c)	One mark per relevant point for highlighting key feature of integrated reporting <IR> (International Integrated Reporting Council, 2018) – up to 4 marks	Max 4	
		One mark per relevant point for highlighting differences between <IR> and traditional financial reporting – up to 4 marks	Max <u>4</u>	
		Up to a maximum of 6 marks in total for task 1(c)		6
2		One mark per relevant point for discussing how shortcomings in risk analysis and risk management processes contributed to inadequate treatment of risks associated with the project		
		Up to a maximum of 8 marks in total for task 2		8
3		One mark per relevant point for assessing issues which influence the decision of whether to use sub-contractors or retain work in-house		
		Up to a maximum of 8 marks in total for task 3		8

Professional skills may be rewarded as in the following rubric:

1(a)

How well has the candidate demonstrated professional skills as follows:	Not at all	Not so well	Quite well	Very well
1(a) – Scepticism skills in questioning the reliability of the figures and their implications for the attractiveness of the project validity.	The candidate has failed to demonstrate any scepticism around Domusco's ability to achieve the higher revenue figures and has therefore failed to identify the fact that the project might potentially make a loss.	The candidate has demonstrated some limited scepticism in questioning the figures used to forecast the profitability of the project, but hasn't calculated a revised forecast using the lower estimates nor shown any further scepticism in questioning the overall level of uncertainty in the figures and the difficulty in assessing the attractiveness of the project.	The candidate has demonstrated some scepticism by questioning whether the higher revenue figures are achievable, calculating a revised forecast based on the lower figures and considering the implications of this scenario for the project. However, the candidate hasn't really questioned the overall level of uncertainty in the figures and the resulting difficulty in assessing the project.	The candidate has demonstrated significant scepticism by questioning the original revenue figures, calculating a revised forecast based on the lower figures and considering the implications of this scenario for the project. The candidate has also raised some valid concerns about the overall level of uncertainty in the figures and the resulting difficulty of assessing the attractiveness of the project.
	0	0.5	1	2

1(b)

How well has the candidate demonstrated professional skills as follows:	Not at all	Not so well	Quite well	Very well
1(b) – Analysis skills in identifying the key issues to be considered.	The candidate has demonstrated no appreciable understanding of the concept of corporate social responsibility and has therefore failed to analyse any relevant CSR issues.	The candidate demonstrated some analysis skills in considering the aspects of corporate social responsibility. However, there is little consideration of CSR issues in the specific context of the Metsa contract, and Domusco's decision making in relation to that contract.	The candidate has demonstrated good analysis skills by considering how corporate social responsibility issues can affect business decisions. The candidate has also related some relevant CSR issues to the specific context of the Metsa contract, and their impact on Domusco's decision making.	The candidate has demonstrated excellent analysis skills in considering how corporate social responsibility issues can affect business decisions. The candidate has also identified many of the CSR issues which Domusco needs to consider when deciding whether or not to bid for the contract.
	0	0.5	1	2

1(c)

How well has the candidate demonstrated professional skills as follows:	Not at all	Not so well	Quite well	Very well
1(c) – Communication skills in highlighting the key features of integrated reporting and how it differs from traditional financial reporting.	The candidate has failed to use a slide format to communicate the key features of integrated reporting.	The candidate has only loosely used a slide presentation format, but has used either to many or too few points so that the slide does not convey the key features of <IR> clearly to the reader. The candidate has produced some notes but it is difficult to see how these relate to the points on the slide.	The candidate has used a slide and bullet points to cover relevant points clearly and succinctly. The candidate has supplied notes which relate closely to the points on the slide; however, the notes could be explained more clearly.	The candidate has used a slide which clearly and succinctly highlights the key features of <IR> and how it differs from traditional financial reporting. The candidate has also produced clear supporting notes which relate closely to the points selected on the slide, and clearly explain the points on the slide.
	0	0.5	1	2

How well has the candidate demonstrated professional skills as follows:	Not at all	Not so well	Quite well	Very well
2 – Commercial acumen in recognising the weaknesses in the risk analysis and risk management processes.	The candidate has failed to understand the significance of risk analysis and risk management, and how shortcomings in these areas have contributed to the problems Domusco is now facing with the project.	The candidate has demonstrated some commercial acumen in identifying the shortcomings in Domusco's risk analysis and risk management processes, and the potential business implications of these. However, the candidate has failed to identify how the key problems relate to its failure to treat risks adequately.	The candidate has demonstrated commercial acumen in identifying the business implications of the shortcomings in Domusco's risk analysis and risk management processes, and has shown some awareness of how these shortcomings have contributed to the problems being experienced on the project.	The candidate has demonstrated incisive commercial acumen in identifying how many of the problems being experienced on the project relate to Domusco's failure to treat the risks associated with it adequately; with this failure, in turn, resulting from shortcomings in Domusco's risk analysis and risk management processes.
	0	0.5	1	2

3

How well has the candidate demonstrated professional skills as follows:	Not at all	Not so well	Quite well	Very well
3 – Evaluation skills in assessing the potential advantages and disadvantages of the two approaches.	The candidate has not demonstrated any evaluation skills in assessing the issues at stake or the relative advantages and drawbacks of the two approaches. The candidate has therefore failed to provide the directors with any useful insight which could help them decide which staffing model to use.	The candidate has demonstrated some evaluation skills in considering some of the issues at stake and the potential implications of the two approaches. However, the candidate has used little judgement in considering the advantages and disadvantages of the two approaches.	The candidate has demonstrated some sound evaluation skills in assessing the potential implications of the two approaches. The candidate has used some judgement to assess some of the most obvious advantages and disadvantages of the two approaches.	The candidate has demonstrated excellent evaluation skills in assessing the potential implications of the two approaches. The candidate has demonstrated considerable judgement in assessing the most important advantages and disadvantages of the two approaches.
	0	0.5	1	2

Suggested solution

1   (a)   **Briefing paper**

FAO: Board of Directors

Potential development at Metsa and CSR issues

Peter's figures suggest the forecast net present value of the project ranges from $127 million (under the high-cost scenario) to $414 million (under the low-cost scenario). Positive net present values like these would initially suggest that accepting the project will help to generate value for our shareholders, and therefore we should bid for the contract.

Levels of uncertainty involved – However, as the range of outcomes from Peter's estimates show, it is difficult for Domusco to assess the likely profitability of the development due to the levels of uncertainty in the figures.

The extent of this uncertainty increases even further if we include the potential uncertainty over the revenue figures as well as the cost figures.

If there is a risk that housing revenues for this project might be lower than for similar projects in Zeeland, then this also needs to be considered when looking at potential outcomes for the project.

Using the lower revenue figures (suggested by Martyn), the potential net present values of the project would be:

BPP
LEARNING
MEDIA

High cost, low revenue scenario

	Year 0 Z$m	Year 1 Z$m	Year 2 Z$m	Year 3 Z$m	Year 4 Z$m	Total Z$m
Project costs	0	(275)	(350)	(375)	(350)	(1,350)
Loan (at start – Year 0)	(600)					(600)
Cash inflows	0	102	509	771	842	2,224
Net cash (outflow)/inflow	(600)	(173)	159	396	492	274
Discount factor 12%	1	0.893	0.797	0.712	0.636	
NPV	(600)	(154)	127	282	313	**(32)**

Low cost, low revenue scenario

	Year 0 Z$m	Year 1 Z$m	Year 2 Z$m	Year 3 Z$m	Year 4 Z$m	Total Z$m
Project costs	0	(130)	(160)	(340)	(380)	(1,010)
Loan (at start – Year 0)	(600)					(600)
Cash inflows	0	102	509	771	842	2,224
Net cash (outflow)/inflow	(600)	(28)	349	431	462	614
Discount factor 12%	1	0.893	0.797	0.712	0.636	
NPV	(600)	(25)	278	307	294	254

Under these scenarios, the worst-case scenario (ie low revenue; high cost) could mean that the project generates a negative NPV of ($32) million, although we could still earn a significant positive NPV (+ $254 million) under the low-cost scenario.

The rugged nature of the terrain may suggest that it might be prudent for us to base our cost estimates on the higher cost figures. However, it is possible that even these cost figures may not be high enough, depending on what problems are encountered during the construction process.

Potential significance of contract – Despite the obvious concerns about the uncertainty surrounding the cost figures, if this project delivered the best-case scenario results (high revenue; low cost), its NPV of $414 million would be higher than the profits we are expecting to generate from the other five major construction projects which we currently have in progress.

The fact this is also a government-backed contract in our home country of Zeeland adds a further potential issue. If we decide not to accept this contract, and another company delivers it successfully for the government, the government may give that company first refusal on any subsequent contracts.

As such, we may need to consider the project as part of a wider portfolio, rather than as a stand-alone project. Equally, the fact that it offers work for all three of our subsidiaries is beneficial (given the reduced demand for office building and house building in Zeeland in recent years).

(b)   **CSR issues**

Corporate social responsibility (CSR) is a business's responsibility to be accountable to all its stakeholders (including investors, employees, communities and suppliers) and to society as a whole.

CSR demands that businesses manage the economic, social and environmental impacts of their operations to maximise the benefits and minimise the downsides. Key CSR issues include governance, environmental management, responsible sourcing of materials, labour standards and community relations.

In this case, Domusco needs to consider its responsibilities to its shareholders, employees, the community and the environment before reaching a decision.

Minimising environmental damage – The proposed site for the development is home to several rare plant species and also contains a number of sites of archaeological interest and, as the environmental groups have highlighted, these will be destroyed by the development.

From an environmental sustainability perspective, there could be an argument against the development. In addition, if there are protests on the site this could lead to health and safety issues and negative publicity if Domusco becomes involved with demonstrations on the site.

However, the work can only go ahead if the development is officially approved, and permission is granted by the authorities for the land to be built on. In which case, we will be legally entitled to do the work.

Ensure safety and working conditions of employees – There are already concerns about contractors taking on inexperienced staff and breaching health and safety guidelines.

Taking on this new project will add further to the demand for labour, and so could mean that additional, inexperienced staff will be used. If there was an accident at the site, this could generate significant adverse publicity for Domusco. Therefore, we need to be satisfied that enough suitably qualified staff are available before accepting the work.

Economic interests – Alongside the potential social and environmental issues, however, Domusco has to consider its economic obligations to its investors.

Domusco is a listed company, and so it has a duty to its owners to maximise their wealth. If our analysis indicates that the project will be profitable and economically viable, then this is a valid argument for accepting the project.

However, the level of uncertainty in the figures which are available at the moment means that we should not accept the contract without carrying out a more detailed assessment of potential costs and revenues. This again highlights Domusco's responsibilities to its owners (shareholders).

Acting in best interests of society as a whole – CSR also requires businesses to act in a way that provides benefits to society as a whole. The Zeeland government has stated that the Metsa development is required to help Zeeland sustain its economic growth. This economic growth is a benefit to society. So again, there is a conflict between the economic benefits and the environmental costs of the project.

Domusco might also consider the extent to which the development will provide a **sustainable community**, for example one which combines houses, office and work spaces and leisure facilities for residents, such that residents' travel requirements are reduced.

Overall, if we do accept the project, we need to balance the aims of profitability and economic development with those of environmental sustainability and preservation.

This might involve trying to work with the environmental groups to minimise the impact of the development. Although the environmental groups oppose the development, we may be able to work with them to look at ways in which the development could be modified to reduce its negative environmental impact. For example, it might be possible to showcase some of the archaeological sites as features within the new development.

(c)   Slide:

Integrated reporting

- Simplifies accounting information, and focuses on key links between strategy, governance and performance
- Conveys information about wider aspects of performance, not just profit and financial position
- Highlights how Domusco's activities create value
- Illustrates the range of different resources and relationships which underpin Domusco's performance ('Six capitals')
- Six capitals: financial; manufactured; intellecutal; human; natural; and social. (International Integrated Reporting Council, 2018)

> **Tutorial note:** Please note that the amount of detail included in the solution here is more indepth than you would be expected to produce under timed exam conditions. It is intended to serve as learning tool.

Notes: Integrated reporting (<IR>) per the International Integrated Reporting Council (2018) aims to provide a more concise communication of an organisation's strategy, governance and performance, instead of looking in detail at accounting information (which is the primary focus of traditional financial reporting). <IR> dispenses with unnecessary levels of detail, and focuses on key information only.

The primary objective of <IR> is to demonstrate the clear link between a firm's competitive strategy, governance system and financial performance, and its wider social, environmental and economic context.

It also aims to highlight how a company's activities interact to create value in the short, medium and long term, in the context of its overall environment and the opportunities and risks it faces.

Six capitals:

Organisations depend on different forms of 'capital' for their success, not just financial capital. These 'capitals' are the inputs into the company's business, and they will increase, decrease or be transformed thorugh the company's activities.

The 'value' an organisation creates is assessed in relation to the increases or decreases in all six capitals; rather than just focusing on financial performance. The International Integrated Reporting Council (2018) note that there are six capitals:

- Financial – funds available to the group
- Manufactured – machinery and equipment
- Intellectual – organisational know-how
- Human – employees' competencies and experience
- Natural – land; water
- Social – relationships with key stakeholder groups

Aspects of natural capital could be particularly important for Domusco, in terms of reporting on our 'environmental footprint' and the carrying out of our projects in a way which limits the environmental damage as far as possible. Similarly, social capital – in relation to brand and reputation – could be important for Domusco in helping us win new contracts in future.

It is important to recognise the interaction between the capitals, and an increase in one may lead to a decrease in another. For example, a decision to invest in new equipment will increase Domusco's manufactured capital but decrease its financial capital.

<IR> doesn't try to attach monetary value to every aspect of performance, and a wide range of qualitative and quantitative performance measures can be used to assess how well the group is creating value.

However, monitoring information on the range of different capitals should help to make better resource allocation decisions, identify opportunities and manage risk.

2   **Briefing notes**

Shortcomings in risk analysis

Failure to assess riskiness of project – Domusco's board appears to have underestimated the problems involved in operating in such difficult terrain. The terrain appears to have contributed to the problems with the foundations.

Failure of scenario planning – Domusco does not appear to have planned for the possible scenario of adverse weather affecting its plans. If it had done so, it might have been able to negotiate a change in the budget with the government of Wye.

Lack of consideration of different outcomes – From my discussion with Peter, it appears the board only considered the expected value of the profitability. As such, the board does not appear to have taken into account the probability that the contract may make a loss, or the maximum foreseeable loss that the contract might make. In general terms, it is debatable whether using expected values is an appropriate method for evaluating one-off projects.

Risk appetite – The board should only approve projects where the level of risk is consistent with the company's overall risk appetite (and shareholders' appetite for risk). If Bill consistently over-rules Martyn, then Domusco may end up accepting projects where the risks involved are not justified by the potential returns from them.

Failure to map different risks – As the board is still arguing about what to do about the contract, there appears to have been a failure to consider properly the relative importance of the different risks of:

- Having to bear all of any loss on the contract, versus
- Annoying the government in Wye and jeopardising the chance to obtain future contracts

Shortcomings in risk management

Failure to reduce risks – The fact that the foundations were totally washed away and are having to be replaced by new, stronger, foundations seems to indicate that the stronger foundations should have been laid in the first place. It would be better to reduce the risk of expensive remedial work being needed by building to the required quality first time.

Failure to transfer risks – The risk of problems may have been viewed as low likelihood, but the consequences have been severe. This suggests that Domusco should have ensured that at least some of the risk was transferred. There is no mention of insurance, suggesting that the project may not have not been properly insured (or even insured at all).

Failure to share risks – Equally there seems to have been no satisfactory agreement to share risks with Wye's government. Despite the fact that Wye government inspectors approved the foundations, this does not appear to have transferred any enforceable responsibility to bear the losses to Wye's government.

3   **Briefing paper**

FAO: Board of Directors

Issues to consider re use of sub-contracted staff vs in-house staff

Quality of work – Domusco has established a good reputation as a high-quality builder, but if the sub-contractors are using inexperienced staff, there is a danger that the quality of the work they produce will not meet these standards.

There are two possible consequences of this:

If defects in the work are not spotted by Domusco's project management inspectors, then the number of customer complaints is likely to increase, and Domusco's reputation could be adversely affected.

When defects are spotted by the inspectors, the increase in the number of defects could lead to delays in completing the project while the defects are made good. Again, if a number of projects are delayed this could damage Domusco's reputation.

Impact on staff motivation – Domusco's own staff are clearly unhappy about the perceived lack of experience in the staff which sub-contractors are using, and also the fact that they know some sub-contractors are paid more than them. There is a danger that if this situation is allowed to continue, the motivation of the in-house staff (and the quality of their work) may fall. In the worst-case scenario, there will be a continued risk that in-house staff will refuse to work alongside the sub-contracted workers, as this has happened already.

Setting standards – If the directors do decide to continue using sub-contractors they will need to impose some minimum experience standards (that is, to require that sub-contracted workers must have a certain level of experience before they can work on a job). This will help deal with current issues of staff motivation.

Health and safety – Domusco has highlighted health and safety as one of its four key areas of social responsibility, yet the employee survey appears to highlight a lack of safety awareness in the workplace. The directors need to investigate these claims, in order to improve safety levels as necessary so that their own workers are not put at risk of an accident in the work place.

Basis of pay – The sub-contractors are currently paid a fixed fee for a contract, so the quicker they finish it, the quicker they can move on to the next one. In this way, the structure of the reward scheme may be contributing to the decline in quality.

If Domusco employed in-house staff they would be less likely to rush jobs simply to move on to the next one. However, this issue could also be addressed with contract staff if the terms of the contracts were renegotiated, for example, such that there is a retention clause in the contract giving Domusco the right to withhold some of the payment if the work does not meet agreed quality standards.

Availability of staff – The boom in the construction industry has led to a number of inexperienced people seeking work in the construction industry. We do not know if the contractors are using these inexperienced staff because they are cheaper than more experienced staff, or because the high levels of demand means that there are no more experienced staff available.

If the problem is being caused by the high levels of demand, then Domusco will have a similar problem as the contractors if they try to recruit more staff. They will either have to recruit inexperienced staff and train them up themselves, or try to attract experienced workers away from their existing jobs.

The idea of recruiting relatively inexperienced staff and training them up may prove more attractive. These staff will be cheaper to recruit, and if Domusco administers the training then the staff will follow the practices and procedures that Domusco want them to.

Core versus peripheral skills – Another issue which Domusco should consider is whether it brings some jobs back in-house, and leaves others to be done by contractors.

Domusco's management have previously identified that they do not wish to employ large numbers of staff who may be located in the wrong area or have the wrong skills for the jobs that need doing at any particular time. In-house labour is, in effect, a fixed cost whereas contract costs are variable. Domusco will only need to use a contractor when there are projects which need doing.

In this respect, Domusco may want to continue to use contract labour for very specialist skills (which may only be needed intermittently), but increase the number of less specialist skilled workers in-house. There is likely to be a more regular demand for labourers with less specialist skills.

Project management or construction – One final issue which Domusco needs to consider is where it sees its core competences and skills. Historically, Domusco has seen itself as a construction company. However, it is possible it could decide its core competences are now in project management and building quality management (because it always uses its own staff for these roles) rather than construction itself.

If Domusco sees these more managerial functions as its core competences, then it is more likely to keep construction workers as contractors rather than increasing the numbers of them employed in-house.

Domusco – Mini-Mock Exam 4

Tutorial notes to help you improve your exam success skills performance

Skill	Examples of the skills
Case scenario: Managing information	Exhibit 1 identifies that sustainability and corporate social responsibility (CSR) are very important factors which Domusco considers when evaluating a potential project.
	Task requirement 1(b) builds on this idea, and asks you to analyse the potential CSR issues arising from a specific contract.
	The newspaper article in Exhibit 3 clearly highlights the potential environmental issues with the project. However, CSR doesn't only mean considering environmental issues.
	The last sentence in the newspaper article presents a different perspective: that the project is vital in promoting economic growth.
	However, in addition to the material in Exhibit 3, did you also consider the key areas highlighted in Exhibit 1. (You have been told that Domusco acknowledges these as important, which therefore suggests Domusco should consider them when deciding whether or not to bid for the contract.) For example:
	Communities – will the project help to establish a thriving and sustainable community?
	Health and safety – will the project raise any health and safety concerns?
Correct interpretation of requirements	Task requirement 1(a) asks you to prepare a briefing paper which **analyses** the financial attractiveness of the potential development at Metsa.
	Two important points to note here:
	First, you are asked to 'analyse' rather than, for example, simply to 'calculate the profitability' of the contract. Analysis involves discussion and examination of the facts; so once you have done the necessary calculations, you then need to examine what they tell you about the attractiveness of the potential development. Do the figures suggest the project will be financially beneficial for Domusco?
	Second, you are asked specifically about the financial attractiveness of the development, so make sure you only focus on financial considerations in your answer. (Task requirement 1(b) then goes on to analyse some of the wider issues to consider in relation to the project, which should be another clue that you should not be discussing them in your answer to 1(a).)
Answer planning: Priorities, structure and logic	Task requirement 2 asks you to discuss how shortcomings (or weaknesses) in Domusco's risk analysis and risk management processes could have contributed to its failure to treat the risks associated with a project adequately.
	A sensible way to structure your answer here would be to distinguish between risk analysis (risk assessment) and risk management, to ensure you identify the shortcomings in each. For example:
	Risk assessment:
	Has Domusco considered the risks associated with the project (eg due to the location of the project?
	Has the board considered the significance of different risks?
	Does the project (and the level of risk associated) fit with the board's risk appetite?

Skill	Examples of the skills
	Risk management: (Has Domusco taken any steps to manage the risks associated with the project?)
	Reduce risk (eg by making sure foundations are strong enough)
	Transfer risk – (eg Domusco have any insurance?)
	Share risks – is Domusco wholly responsible, or – for example – should the government also bear some of the risk?
Efficient numerical analysis	The reference to a discount rate, and to cash flow figures, immediately before task 1(a) should have been a clue that net present value calculations were necessary here. Moreover, Exhibit 2 in the scenario gives you the NPV of the projects based on Peter's revenue and cost figures.
	However, Martyn has questioned the revenue figures, so you need to produce alternative NPV calculations using the lower revenue figures, in order to assess their impact on the project.
	The figures themselves shouldn't have been difficult to calculate, but did you produce two NPV calculations: one based on the higher cost figures, and one based on the lower cost figures?
Effective writing and presentation	If we turn back to task 2, we can identify two key parts to the requirement: (i) identifying the shortcomings; (ii) discussing they could have contributed to the failure.
	Adopting this kind of approach could also be a useful way of writing your answer to this task, so that you have a series of short paragraphs, in which the opening sentence identifies the shortcoming, and then a supporting sentence identifies the impact.
	For example:
	'Domusco does not appear to have planned for the possible scenario of adverse weather affecting its plans. [Shortcoming]. If it had done so, it might have been able to negotiate a change in the budget with the government of Wye.' [Impact].
Good time management	As a guide, you should aim to spend 20 minutes reading and analysing the overall scenario, which then leaves you with 100 minutes to plan and write your answers (ie 2 minutes per mark).
	Applying the rule of 2 minutes per mark, the time available for each task requirement in this question is:
	Task requirement 1(a): 12 (10 technical + 2 professional skills): 24 minutes
	Task requirement 1(b): 10 marks: 20 minutes
	Task requirement 1(c): 8 marks:16 minutes
	Task requirement 2: 10 marks: 20 minutes
	Task requirement 3: 10 marks: 20 minutes
	Although the numbers in part 1a should have been relatively straightforward, there is a danger that you could get bogged down with them, meaning you are struggling for time for the rest of the tasks.
	By contrast, the presentation slide on integrated reporting (1(c)) requires relatively little application (compared to the rest of the task requirements) so, provided you were familiar with the principles of <IR> this should have been an opportunity to pick up some relatively easy marks.

ANSWERS

Diagnostic

Did you apply these skills when reading, planning and writing up your answer? Identity the exam success skills where you think you need to improve and capture your thoughts here of what you want to achieve when attempting questions in future.

Section 4 – Mock Exams

ACCA

Strategic Business Leader

Mock Exam 1

Questions	
Time allowed	**3 hours 15 minutes**
This question paper is an integrated case study with one section containing a total of 100 marks and ALL Tasks must be completed.	
All Tasks contain Professional Skills marks which are included in the marks shown above.	

DO NOT OPEN THIS EXAM UNTIL YOU ARE READY TO START UNDER EXAMINATION CONDITIONS

Strategic Business Leader – Mock Exam 1

The Green Transport Group (the group) is based in the country of Meeland.

The principal activities of the group are the transportation and storage of goods on behalf of large commercial customers. The group consists of three operating companies: Terry Green Road Transport (TGRT); Terry Green Warehousing (TGW); and Terry Green Rail (TGR).

The group has recently commissioned a consultancy firm to provide advice on a range of strategic issues.

The following exhibits provide information relevant to the Green Transport Group.

- Exhibit 1: A report on the Green Transport Group and its operating companies, sourced and prepared by a company researcher working as part of the consultancy project team

- Exhibit 2: Summary of group operating company performance data (20X1–20X5) prepared by a member of the consultancy project team

- Exhibit 3: An extract of financial statements for Marston airport for the year ended 31 December 20X5 provided by Derek Horsnell, the Finance Director of the Green Transport Group

- Exhibit 4: A copy of a press release from August 20X6 announcing the proposed purchase of Marston airport

- Exhibit 5: An extract from a business newspaper commenting on the proposed acquisition of Marston airport

- Exhibit 6: An email received from Gary Walsh, the Logistics Manager at Terry Green Road Transport (TGRT) concerning the issues facing the company

- Exhibit 7: A newspaper article from the Meeland Herald detailing the events surrounding the train crash involving a Terry Green Rail (TGR) train

- Exhibit 8: Extracts from the website of Action Now!

The task requirements are included in the tasks shown below:

The current date is October 20X6.

1   You are the lead management consultant overseeing the consultancy project at the Green Transport Group. You are in the process of preparing the findings for your report which will be provided to the group board of directors.

   Required

   Prepare a report which addresses the following matters:

   (a)   **Analyse the current performance and the contribution of each of the three operating companies in the Green Transport Group portfolio, and assess their relative significance in its future strategy.**   **(21 marks)**

   Professional skills marks are available for demonstrating **analysis** skills in assessing the performance of the three operating companies and their relative significance.
   (4 marks)

   (b)   **Critically evaluate the proposed acquisition of Marston airport.**   **(16 marks)**

   Professional skills marks are available for demonstrating **scepticism** skills in evaluating the proposed acquisition of Marston airport.   **(4 marks)**

   (Total = 45 marks)

2   You are business advisor to Terry Green Junior, the Managing Director of Terry Green Road Transport (TGRT). You are reviewing the email received from Gary Walsh, the Logistics Manager of TGRT. Gary's email was prompted by an earlier request for details of the major issues facing the company. This information is required as it will form part of a presentation that you have been asked to give to Terry Green Junior and the management team at TGRT concerning the future viability of the Ice World contract.

   Required

   (a)   **Prepare two presentation slides and detailed supporting notes to be presented to Terry Green Junior and the management team at TGRT. The first slide should evaluate the issues surrounding Terry Green Road Transport's performance of the Ice World contract and the second slide should evaluate the likelihood of the contract being extended.**   **(6 marks)**

   Professional skills marks are available for **communication** skills in identifying issues connected to performance of the contract and communicating the likelihood of the contract being extended.   **(2 marks)**

   Terry Green Junior is keen to explore the opportunities to offer frozen food deliveries to a wider range of customers. Having recently read an article about the increasing use of big data technologies in reporting business performance, he is particularly interested in understanding how a greater use of data could help improve TGRT's performance. He has asked that you include some detail on this matter in your presentation.

   Required

   (b)   **Prepare a presentation slide, including detailed supporting notes which illustrate how the use of big data technologies and data analytics could improve TGRT's performance of future frozen food contracts like the current one with Ice World.**
   (8 marks)

   Professional skills marks are available for demonstrating **commercial acumen** in discussing the use of big data technologies and data analytics.   **(2 marks)**

   (Total = 18 marks)

3   It is now one month later. You are an operations manager working in TGR. The Managing Director of TGR, on behalf of Green Transport Group's board, has asked for your input following the recent train crash involving TGR. In preparation you are reviewing the newspaper article from the Meeland Herald which provides details of the incident.

Required

TGR's Managing Director has requested that you provide him with a briefing paper which address the following matters:

(a)   **Analyse the relative power and interest of the following THREE stakeholder groups in the activities of TGR following the accident outlined in the newspaper article:**

- Families of employees on the train
- 'Flower Power' wildflower protection group
- Meeland Environment Agency   **(6 marks)**

Professional skills marks are available for demonstrating **analysis** skills in assessing the relative power and interest of the three groups.   **(2 marks)**

(b)   In light of your analysis, briefly recommend different strategies for managing each of the THREE stakeholder groups.   **(3 marks)**

Professional skills marks are available for demonstrating **commercial acumen** when providing recommendations for managing the specified stakeholder groups.

(2 marks)

(Total = 13 marks)

4   You are a representative from the Meeland Chamber of Commerce. Part of your role involves providing advice to organisations on a range of business and ethical issues. The group board of directors have asked for your advice in handling the planned protests as outlined by the extracts taken from the Action Now! website. Sir John Watt has informed you that he is keen to hire extra security guards from a Meeland-based security firm to patrol the TGRT depot which has been targeted by the protestors in order to minimise the disruption caused. The group board of directors are also keen to find out more about the role of corporate social responsibility (CSR) in business. One of the director's has suggested that a good starting point would be to compare the Action Now! group's approach to CSR to that of a commercial entity.

Required

Prepare a briefing paper which:

(a)   **Assesses the decision to hire extra security guards when dealing with the planned protests.**   **(10 marks)**

Professional skills marks are available for demonstrating **evaluation** skills when assessing the decision to hire extra security staff.   **(2 marks)**

(b)   **Explains the term CSR and discusses the ways in which CSR and ethical stance might differ between the Action Now! group and a commercial 'for profit' business.**

(10 marks)

Professional skills marks are available for demonstrating **communication** skills which explain the term CSR and how the ethical stances may differ.   **(2 marks)**

(Total = 24 marks)

Exhibit 1: A report on the Green Transport Group and its operating companies, sourced and prepared by a company researcher working as part of the consultancy project team

To: Management consultant

From: Company researcher

Subject: Organisational overview and operating companies

The Green Transport Group (the group) was formed five years ago, in 20X1, when the owners of Terry Green Road Transport decided to create a group structure to facilitate the acquisition of companies which complemented its existing operations. The group consists of three operating companies: Terry Green Road Transport; Terry Green Warehousing; and Terry Green Rail. The CEO of the group is Sir John Watt, a highly experienced businessman, and he is assisted by a financial director and an operations director. The managing directors of all three operating companies also sit on the board of the group. The majority of shares in the group and operating companies are owned by the Green family.

Terry Green Road Transport (TGRT)

TGRT was founded 60 years ago by Terry Green. It is the largest road freight company in Meeland, with over 2,000 trucks. It specialises in the haulage of consumer food and drink and has significant contracts with most of the large supermarket chains. TGRT's supermarket contracts require the collection and transportation of goods from the supermarkets' distribution centres (and often go via the group's own warehouse facilities) to the supermarkets' out-of-town stores, which are often situated just off major roads and motorways. Taxes for roads are levied through a fuel tax and an annual road fund licence. The managing director of TGRT is Terry Green Junior, who was originally employed by his father as a driver. He still drives a truck for one day every month, so that 'he never loses touch with the business'. TGRT's distinctive green and white trucks are seen all over the country. They have attracted a fan club, whose members spot the trucks on the road and record their movements on a dedicated internet site. 'Terry's Wanderers' have helped to make the TGRT brand a household name. TGRT replaces its trucks every three years to ensure reliability, improve efficiency and to reduce its carbon footprint. TGRT is keen to project a modern image which is attractive to customers.

Terry Green Warehousing (TGW)

The growth of consumer internet purchasing has created demand among TGRT's customers for an integrated transport and storage solution. The group acquired a number of warehouses from its customers who wished to divest these operations. In 20X1 it consolidated these and a number of small warehousing companies it had acquired, to form TGW. Nationwide, TGW owns 4 million square metres of warehousing, with its warehouses painted green and white and prominently displaying the Terry Green logo. The warehouses are efficient and highly automated. Finding development land for warehouses is becoming increasingly difficult and the cost of land is rising. The average price for warehouse development land in Meeland is now $20,000 per hectare. (A hectare is 10,000 square metres.)

Terry Green Rail (TGR)

Increasing fuel costs, road congestion and concern about the environmental consequences of road transport caused the group to look at opportunities offered by rail transport. In 20X2 the group purchased the Freight Direct Rail Company (FDRC). FDRC was formed a number of years ago, when the Meeland government privatised the country's rail freight business. FDRC had struggled to survive in an industry dominated by two large companies who share the majority of the lucrative bulk freight contracts (coal, iron ore and oil) between them. The FDRC locomotives were quickly painted green and white, and FDRC was renamed TGR. TGR's use of the rail tracks is directly charged by the state. Despite experienced managers being transferred to the company from other companies in the group, TGR (like FDRC) has struggled to make a significant impact in the rail freight sector. Most of its customers are at locations which are not directly accessible by rail. Furthermore, the lucrative bulk rail freight contracts (coal, iron ore and oil) are in products which companies within the group have limited experience in managing.

Despite this, TGR inherited a small contract to transport oil for companies in the shipping industry when it acquired FDRC. The group's senior management have struggled to understand the culture and economics of the rail freight industry and there has been a failure to recognise that train driving requires far greater skills and training than truck driving. TGR has developed an innovative mini-container system which can easily transfer goods between trucks and trains and makes more effective use of warehouse space. Most of the supermarkets in Meeland, attracted by the environmentally friendly image, are very supportive of the rail initiative and wish to be associated with it.

Exhibit 2: Summary of group operating company performance data (20X1–20X5) prepared by a member of the consultancy project team

Table 1: Financial data for operating companies in the Green Transport Group

	20X5		20X4		20X3		20X2		20X1	
	Green	Industry	Green	Industry	Green	Industry	Green	Industry	Green	Industry
Terry Green Road Transport										
Revenue	575	2,050	565	2,025	550	2,015	520	2,050	500	2,000
Operating profit	10.80%	9.98%	10.75%	9.95%	10.80%	9.93%	10.45%	9.50%	10.25%	9.57%
ROCE	12.25%	11.50%	12.15%	11.45%	12.05%	11.45%	11.95%	11.30%	11.95%	11.35%
Terry Green Warehousing										
Revenue	315	3,200	275	3,010	270	3,050	255	2,950	250	2,850
Operating profit	14.55%	14.50%	14.25%	14.15%	14.20%	14.25%	14.00%	14.25%	13.85%	14.15%
ROCE	14.50%	14.15%	14.25%	14.10%	14.15%	14.10%	13.95%	13.90%	13.95%	13.85%
Terry Green Rail										
Revenue	112	3,150	110	3,000	105	2,850	105	2,650	105	2,500
Operating profit	4.75%	12.45%	4.50%	12.35%	4.85%	12.25%	4.95%	12.75%	5.15%	12.85%
ROCE	3.50%	8.75%	3.65%	8.55%	3.75%	8.55%	3.85%	8.35%	3.85%	8.25%

The performance of each group company is shown under the columns headed Green. Industry figures (provided by Freight Line International) are shown under the columns headed Industry. Operating profit and ROCE figures are averages for the industry while revenue figures are totals. All revenue figures are in $m.

Notes:

1 Terry Green Warehousing first traded in 20X2. The 20X1 figure is compiled from companies which were consolidated into Terry Green Warehousing.

2 Terry Green Rail was formed after the takeover of FDRC. 20X3 was the first reporting period for Terry Green Rail. The 20X1 and 20X2 figures are for FDRC.

Exhibit 3: An extract of financial statements for Marston airport for the year ended 31 December 20X5 provided by Derek Horsnell, the Finance Director of the Green Transport Group

Marston airport is situated on the outskirts of Marston town where TGRT already has three transport depots and warehouses. The airport occupies a site of 450 hectares and it has two tarmac runways, four hangars and a small terminal/flying club facility. The airfield is exclusively used by private flyers and two flying clubs. The airport is adjacent to the motorway which connects North and South Meeland.

Financial information for Marston airport is below.

	$'000
Assets	
Non-current assets	
Property, plant and equipment	6,000
Goodwill	250
Total non-current assets	6,250
Current assets	
Inventory	550
Trade receivables	80
Cash	370
Total current assets	1,000
Total assets	7,250
Equity and liabilities	
Share capital	2,550
Retained earnings	250
Total equity	2,800
Non-current liabilities	
Long-term borrowings	4,050
Current liabilities	
Trade payables	120
Short-term borrowings	250
Current tax payable	30
Total current liabilities	400
Total liabilities	4,450
Total equity and liabilities	7,250

STATEMENT OF PROFIT OR LOSS	
Revenue	975
Cost of sales	(700)
Gross profit	275
Administrative expenses	(125)
Finance costs	(100)
Profit before tax	50
Tax expense	(10)
Profit for the period	40

Exhibit 4: A copy of a press release from August 20X6 announcing the proposed purchase of Marston airport

Press release from Sir John Watt announcing the proposed purchase of Marston airport

'The Green Transport Group is pleased to announce that it has signed an initial agreement in principle to purchase Marston airport from the Marston Airport Company for the sum of $7m, funded from retained profits from within the group. We see this as a natural extension of our transport capabilities. Road, rail and air have long been complementary forms of transport and we are pleased to be able to offer our customers all three, using our innovative mini-container system as an effective transhipment method between transport modes. We also hope to attract a low-cost airline to the airport, encouraged by low landing fees and a population of over 150,000 people living within 20 miles of the airport. Marston Airport Company will become an operating company within the Green Transport Group, and renamed Terry Green Air.'

Exhibit 5: Extract from a business newspaper commenting on the proposed acquisition of Marston airport

The renowned aviation consultant, Peter Brown, appears much less optimistic than Green Transport Group about the potential contribution that Marston airport can make to the Group.

Mr Brown has recently carried out an analysis of the 20X5 financial performance medium-sized light aviation airports (like Marston) in Meeland. This revealed the following performance statistics across the sector as a whole:

Operating profit margin	Return on capital employed	Current ratio	Acid test ratio	Gearing ratio
17.5%	8.5%	2.25	1.50	40%

(The standard payment terms in Meeland is payment within 30 days of the invoice date.)

Peter Brown has also cast doubt on Sir John Watt's statement about attracting a low-cost airline to Marston airport. He says that a local regional population of at least 500,000 people is required to make such a service attractive. As such, Mr Brown believes that the population of the Marston area is much too small to make passenger services from the airport economical.

Exhibit 6: Email received from Gary Walsh, the logistics manager at Terry Green Road Transport concerning the issues facing the company

To:	b.advisor@BusinessAdvice.com
From:	g.walsh@tgrt.com
Subject:	Issues affecting Terry Green Road Transport (TGRT)

Thank you for your email.

Having reflected on your request for input, I can honestly say that the biggest issue TGRT faces at the moment concerns the Ice World (IW) contract. TGRT recently won a hard fought tender process to transport deliveries for the rapidly growing supermarket chain, IW. The contract is initially only for a six-month trial period. We are already half way through the trial. At the time of signing the contract representatives from IW stressed that TGRT's performance during the trial period would be central to extending the deal. Unlike the other supermarkets which TGRT has contracts with, IW does not sell dry goods or chilled products, it only sells frozen food products. As a result this requires us to use adapted trucks which are capable of transferring frozen goods. We have had to hire 15 specialised trucks for the six-month duration of the contract from our usual truck supplier.

The contract obliges TGRT to collect deliveries from IW's central Meeland distribution centre and make deliveries to the company's 50 stores, all of which are located in town centres nationwide. IW operates by selling high volumes of a limited range of frozen food products at low prices. The limited range means that every IW delivery contains the same products regardless of which store it is going to. Although the contract represents a great the opportunity for us, it has caused some problems.

Increasing road congestion increases the likelihood that our deliveries will miss their allocated delivery slots. The contract stipulates that late deliveries require TGRT to pay a flat penalty charge of $5,000 per occurrence. Since the contract began TGRT has made $60,000 of penalty payments. Our drivers complain that the problem is made worse by the difficulty of accessing the 50 stores. Navigating through town centres is problematic due to restrictions on the roads that larger trucks (such as those used by TGRT) are permitted to use, which adds on time when making deliveries. TGRT is obliged to pay a penalty for any food which spoils while in transit, this occurs when the
on-board freezer unit fails to keep the temperature below zero degrees. This has happened twice. Interestingly, the other day I noticed that one truck appeared to have used more fuel than would have been expected given the distance covered. Upon investigating the matter I discovered that the freezer unit was operating at temperatures lower than required to keep the goods frozen!

I hope the above proves useful.

Exhibit 7: A newspaper article from the Meeland Herald detailing the events surrounding the train crash involving a Terry Green Rail (TGR) train

Meeland Herald

Two die in rail disaster

By Steve Dean, Meeland Correspondent

Yesterday saw one of the worst rail disasters in recent history when a freight train derailed shortly after leaving a railway depot near the village of Bluebell Hill, leaving two dead.

The freight train, operated by Terry Green Rail (TGR), was pulling seven tank cars full of shipping oil and was en-route to the port of Seaford when it left the tracks and crashed into a nearby field. The crash occurred near the village of Bluebell Hill which is renowned as an area of outstanding natural beauty due to the wildflowers that grow in the region. During the crash one of the tank cars ruptured causing thousands of litres of oil to leak onto the surrounding land and wildflower meadows.

Residents in the village claim to have heard a loud noise followed by an orange explosion and plumes of black smoke rising over 100 feet high. Footage taken on mobile phones of the incident by local residents has already started to surface on the internet. It is currently unclear what caused the train to derail, however, expert sources we showed the amateur footage to agreed that the incident may well have been caused by the train travelling too fast. It is believed that the two individuals that died were the train driver and assistant driver, they were the only people on-board at the time of the incident.

A spokesperson for TGR yesterday claimed that a full statement would be issued shortly. Late yesterday evening the government-funded Meeland Environment Agency (MEA) declared 'a significant ecological disaster'. Concerns have been heightened by the air pollution caused by the raging fires on the track side which took several hours to bring under control. During a television news broadcast yesterday evening, the Head of MEA hinted that TGR would suffer extensive punitive financial penalties for any wrongdoing which led to the disaster. MEA has promised to conduct a full investigation into the cause of the disaster.

The wildflower protection group 'Flower Power', which promotes the conservation of Meeland's indigenous vegetation, claims to have received reports from Bluebell Hill residents that an area of land which contains a rare type of orchid flower has been affected by the oil spill.

Action Now!

About us

Action Now! is a not-for-profit, voluntary environmental action group which emphasises the importance of taking action in tackling climate change. The effects of climate change are all around us from rising temperatures causing drought in some parts of the world, to rising sea levels causing flooding in other regions. Although it is an inconvenient truth, we all know that man-made activity and the burning of fossil fuels is the central cause of global climate change. This needs to stop before it is too late.

Politicians in Meeland and around the world have for too many years simply paid lip-service to the growing need to take the issue of climate change seriously. Therefore we urge all our supporters to get involved to help us put the issue of climate change firmly on the agenda.

Newsfeed

A recent United Nations report ranked Meeland in the Top 10 worst polluters, as measured by CO2 emissions per head of population. The report highlighted the need for global governments to promote the use of alternative environmentally friendly fuel sources in business.

Forthcoming campaign events

In recognition of Meeland's ranking in the United Nations report Action Now! is planning a series of protests aimed at some of the country's worst CO_2 polluters. We urge all Action Now! supporters to join us at the following locations next week:

- The gates of the main depot of Terry Green Road Transport, near Central City. Terry Green Road Transport is ranked the 52nd worst CO_2 Meeland polluter by Action Now!

- The entrance of the logistics firm Chestnut Road Haulage, located near Marston Town. Chestnut Road Haulage is ranked the 67th worst CO_2 Meeland polluter by Action Now!

If you can join us then please do. In order to cause maximum disruption and to highlight our campaign to lower the levels of CO_2 pollution caused by private enterprise in Meeland please bring warm clothes as we are planning on chaining ourselves to the entrance gates at both sites. Even if we can stop both firms from getting their polluting trucks onto the roads for a couple of days then it will have been worth it. Hope to see you there!

Answers

Strategic Business Leader – Mock Exam 1

Marks

Technical marks

Task 1

(a) Up to 2 marks for each relevant point up to a maximum of 7 marks for each company in the group: Terry Green Road Transport; Terry Green Warehousing; and Terry Green Rail

Marks will be awarded for the analysis of current performance and contribution, and relative significance to the group's future strategy

Up to a maximum of 21 marks for task 1(a)   21

(b) Up to 2 marks for each relevant point

Within the overall mark allocation, up to a maximum of 6 marks to be awarded for the correct calculation and interpretation of financial information:

Gross profit margin
Net profit margin
ROCE
Liquidity
Gearing
Payables
Receivables

Up to a maximum of 16 marks for task 1(b)   16

Task 2

(a) Up to 2 marks per relevant point for evaluating the issues of TGRT's performance of the Ice World contract and points concerning the likelihood of the contract extension

Up to a maximum of 6 marks for task 2(a)   6

(b) Up to 2 marks per relevant point for illustrating how the use of big data technologies and data analytics could improve TGRT's performance of frozen food contracts

Up to a maximum of 8 marks for task 2(b)   8

Task 3

(a) Up to 2 marks for analysing the relative power and interest of each of the three specified stakeholder groups

Up to a maximum of 6 marks for task 3(a)   6

(b) 1 mark per recommended strategy for managing each stakeholder group

Up to a maximum of 3 marks for task 3(b)   3

Task 4

(a) Up to 2 marks per relevant point in assessing the factors that the board should consider when handling the planned protests

Up to a maximum of 10 marks for task 4(a) **10**

(b) Up to 2 marks per relevant point for explaining the term CSR – up to 4 marks Max 4

Up to 2 marks per relevant point for discussing the differences between the CSR and ethical stance of Action Now! and a 'for profit' business – up to 6 marks Max <u>6</u>

Up to a maximum of 10 marks for task 4(b) **10**

Professional marks may be rewarded as in the following rubric:

How well has the candidate demonstrated professional skills as follows:	Not at all	Not so well	Quite well	Very well
1(a) – Analysis skills in assessing the performance of the three operating companies and their relative significance.	The candidate has failed to analyse the performance of the group companies; for example, the candidate has calculated performance indicators, but has failed to comment on what these reveal about the companies' performance or significance.	The candidate attempted some analysis of the companies' performance (using the financial information provided) and their significance to the group. The analysis was limited largely to financial analysis.	The candidate has made a reasonable attempt to analyse the financial and other information provided in the scenario. Analysis incorporated a number of factors relating to the conditions facing each operating company. The candidate considered a number of factors which influence the companies' significance to the group.	The candidate has demonstrated excellent analytical skills by presenting a wide range of relevant calculations and then commenting on these, and on the other information provided in the scenario, in a meaningful and insightful way. The candidate has considered a wide range of factors which influence the companies' significance to the group.
	0	1	2	4

ANSWERS

Professional marks may be rewarded as in the following rubric:

How well has the candidate demonstrated professional skills as follows:	Not at all	Not so well	Quite well	Very well
1(b) – Scepticism skills in evaluating the proposed acquisition of Marston airport.	The candidate has failed to display any professional scepticism in their answer, choosing instead to accept the merits of the proposal at face value. In doing so, the candidate failed to critically evaluate the proposal.	The candidate made some, limited, attempt at deploying professional scepticism when considering the proposed acquisition. The candidate identified some potential problems with the acquisition proposal, but overall focused more on its advantages, and thereby failed to provide a critical evaluation.	The candidate employed professional scepticism concerning the weaknesses and problems of the proposed acquisition. The candidate recognised a number of the weaknesses of the proposal.	The candidate employed professional scepticism to question the appropriateness of the proposed acquisition for the group. The candidate made use of all relevant information to support their arguments.
	0	1	2	4

Professional marks may be rewarded as in the following rubric:

How well has the candidate demonstrated professional skills as follows:	Not at all	Not so well	Quite well	Very well
2(a) – Communication skills in identifying issues connected to performance of the contract and communicating the likelihood of the contract being extended.	The candidate made a weak attempt at communicating the two areas specified in the task requirement. Little consideration was given to the format of the answer, ie the need for presentation slides.	The candidate made an attempt at communicating the key issues and considered whether or not the contract would be extended. The answer was set out in the required format.	The candidate's answer adequately communicated the key issues such as the existence of the penalty payments and the likelihood of the contract being extended. Presentation slides and sufficiently detailed supporting notes were provided.	The candidate's answer comprehensively communicated the main issues connected to the performance of the contract and clearly expressed a view (in light of the issues identified) as to whether the contract would be extended or not. The answer was set out in the required presentation slide format with detailed supporting notes.
	0	0.5	1	2

Professional marks may be rewarded as in the following rubric:

How well has the candidate demonstrated professional skills as follows:	Not at all	Not so well	Quite well	Very well
2(b) – Commercial acumen in discussing the use of big data technologies and data analytics.	The candidate displayed minimal knowledge of big data technologies and data analytics, and as such illustrations of their use in the delivery of frozen food were very limited.	The candidate made an attempt to display some knowledge of big data technologies and data analytics but this was of a more theoretical nature and was not really applied to TGRT or frozen food contracts. As a result any illustrations made were fairly weak.	The candidate displayed a good understanding of big data technologies and data analytics applied to TGRT and frozen food delivery contracts. Illustrations made were realistic and applied to the situation at TGRT.	The candidate displayed a thorough understanding of big data technologies and data analytics, and how it could help TGRT in the delivery of frozen food. Illustrations made were realistic and addressed the issues identified in the exhibit.
	0	0.5	1	2

Professional marks may be rewarded as in the following rubric:

How well has the candidate demonstrated professional skills as follows:	Not at all	Not so well	Quite well	Very well
3(a) – Analysis skills in assessing the relative power and interest of the three groups.	The candidate failed to provide any meaningful analysis of the relative power and interest of the stakeholder groups specified.	The candidate made some attempt at analysing each of the three specified stakeholder group's relative power and interest. The candidate's answer was, however, not as comprehensive as it might have been and lacked a clear structure.	The candidate analysed the main issues relating to each stakeholder group's relative power and interest. The candidate's answer was well structured.	The candidate fully analysed each stakeholder group's relative power and interest. The analysis included a discussion of the implications of each group's power/interest in the operations of TGR. The candidate's answer was well structured.
	0	0.5	1	2

Professional marks may be rewarded as in the following rubric:

How well has the candidate demonstrated professional skills as follows:	Not at all	Not so well	Quite well	Very well
3(b) – Commercial acumen when providing recommendations for managing the specified stakeholder groups.	The candidate failed to provide any meaningful recommendations, and the recommendations were not linked to considerations of stakeholders' power and interest.	The candidate made some attempt at providing recommendations although these were fairly weak, but were linked to the earlier analysis.	The candidate provided at least one relevant and realistic recommendation for managing each of the stakeholder groups specified, based on the earlier analysis. The answer was well structured.	The candidate provided a range of relevant and realistic recommendations for managing each of the stakeholder groups specified based on the earlier analysis. The answer was well structured.
	0	0.5	1	2

Professional marks may be rewarded as in the following rubric:

How well has the candidate demonstrated professional skills as follows:	Not at all	Not so well	Quite well	Very well
4(a) – Evaluation skills when assessing the decision to hire extra security staff.	The candidate failed to evaluate the board's decision-making process, and instead merely described the decision with no further comment.	The candidate made some attempt at evaluating the board's decision-making process. The candidate's answer was not as well-structured or comprehensive as it might have been.	The candidate made a reasonable attempt at evaluating the board's decision-making process. The candidate's answer was well structured and evaluated the main issues associated with the decision.	The candidate provided a well-structured range of relevant, balanced considerations when evaluating the issues associated with the decision. The candidate considered the views of Action Now! in addition to TGRT and other stakeholders.
	0	0.5	1	2

Professional marks may be rewarded as in the following rubric:

How well has the candidate demonstrated professional skills as follows:	Not at all	Not so well	Quite well	Very well
4(b) – Communication skills which explain the term CSR and how the ethical stances may differ.	The candidate made a very limited attempt at explaining CSR. No attempt was made at explaining the differences between the CSR and ethical stance of both organisations.	The candidate made some attempt at explaining some of the themes behind CSR. Limited explanation was provided of the differences between the CSR and ethical stance of both organisations.	The candidate provided an explanation of the main themes behind CSR. Some of the key CSR and ethical stance differences between both organisations was provided. The candidate's answer was well structured.	The candidate provided a comprehensive explanation of CSR. Full consideration was given to the differences in the CSR and ethical stance between both organisations. Consideration was given to factors such as: purpose, values and beliefs. The relevant exhibit was used. The candidate's answer was well structured.
	0	0.5	1	2

Suggested solutions

Report

To: The board of directors at the Green Transport Group

From: Lead management consultant

Date: October 20X6

1   (a)   The first section of this report analyses the current performance and contribution of three group companies which make up the Green Transport Group: TGRT; TGW; and TGR, and assesses their relative significance to the group's future strategy.

Terry Green Road Transport (TGRT)

Current performance and contribution to the group

TGRT is a key part of the group. In 20X5 TGRT generated more than half of the group's revenue and its operating profit (57.39% and 54.8% respectively). TGRT is the largest road haulage company in Meeland and it has built up extensive experience in the haulage of consumer and food and drink products. The company's success to date is characterised by the company's ability to win contracts to provide road haulage services to most of the large supermarket chains in the country. Between 20X1 and 20X5 revenues in the road haulage market only rose slowly (2.5%). However, during this period TGRT achieved revenue growth which led to its market share increasing from 25% to 28%. TGRT would therefore be classified as a 'cash cow'. The operating profits generated by TGRT are marginally higher than the industry averages. This is positive as TGRT is generating profits which it can reinvest in its own operations or those of other group companies.

Future significance

The current Managing Director of TGRT, Terry Green Junior is the son of the founder of the company and has a strong connection to the company. This is evident as he insists on driving a truck one day every month. The desire to not lose touch with the business indicates a commitment by the Managing Director to understand the operational issues facing TGRT. The management at TGRT have been effective in creating a recognisable brand image for the company. The distinctive green and white livery used on TGRT's trucks has attracted a fan base of loyal truck spotters known as 'Terry's Wanderers'. This has helped to raise the profile of the company, making TGRT a household name. TGRT's brand image is further underpinned by the company's policy to replace its trucks every three years; this helps to project a modern image which is attractive to customers. TGRT is a key part of the group. As the group was formed by the owners of TGRT in 20X1, the fit between the parent and strategic business unit is strong. TGRT's performance and significance means it should be retained in the group.

Terry Green Warehousing (TGW)

Performance and contribution to the group

During the period 20X1 to 20X5, TGW achieved a 26% increase in revenue. This is particularly promising since the warehousing market as a whole grew by 12.28% over the same period. The company's revenues make up 31.4% of the group's total revenue. TGW has achieved marginal growth in its market from 8.77% (in 20X1) to 9.84% in 20X5. The company is performing slightly better than the industry average with regards to ROCE and operating profit margin. In 20X5 TGW contributed 40.47% of the group's operating profit. Whether TGW's performance can be regarded positively or not will depend partially on whether the company's 10% market share is considered high. In order for TGW to exploit the opportunities presented by growing demand for its services the company will need to construct new warehouses. These developments will require significant capital expenditure.

Building on TGW's current position is, however, likely to be constrained by the difficulty in finding new warehouse space. Such investment is likely to be supported by profits generated elsewhere in the group, ie by TGRT.

Significance of TGW

TGW can also be regarded as a key part of the group, and there appears to be a good strategic fit between the company and the group. As the group grew from TGRT, the skills and expertise gained in road haulage fit well with the opportunity to provide customers with an integrated transport and storage solution.

The national spread of the company's warehouses, which are painted in the group colours and display its logo, help to reinforce the group's brand image. The growth in internet shopping by end consumers, coupled to demand for integrated warehousing solutions, are likely to have been key drivers in making the decision to enter this market. As demand for online shopping appears to still be growing, it is likely that TGW will also continue to represent an important part of the group's portfolio.

Terry Green Rail (TGR)

Performance and contribution to the group

Since 20X1 revenues in the rail freight market have rapidly increased year on year; and between 20X1 and 20X5 they grew by 26% ($650m). Concerns over increasing road haulage fuel costs, road congestion and the environmental consequences of continued road usage have all contributed to this growth.

However, TGR is a small player in the rail freight market in Meeland, and its market share is in decline. In 20X5 the company's market share was 3.56%, compared to 4.2% in 20X1. Despite the revenue growth experienced in the market as a whole, TGR only achieved growth of 6.6% over the period. The company's operating profits and ROCE have also been significantly lower than the annual industry averages. Since the group's acquisition of TGR in 20X2 the company's performance has steadily worsened, with both operating profit and ROCE declining.

It could be argued that the group's involvement in the rail industry is having a detrimental impact on the company's performance. The company's failure to increase its market share in a growing industry is worrying and requires further investigation. The company is small in comparison to the two market leaders, which makes it difficult for TGR to achieve economies of scale. The situation is compounded further as the group has limited experience and expertise in operating bulk rail freight contracts for coal, iron ore and oil. This is evident as TGR only has one small contract to transport oil by rail, thereby increasing the difficulty for TGR in winning larger contracts from established players in the market.

Furthermore, the decision to distribute consumer food and drink products to supermarkets by rail may not be entirely appropriate if the retailers' warehouses are not accessible by rail. Finally, senior management at the group do not appear to fully understand the culture and economics of the rail freight sector (for example in relation to the levels of skill and training required by the drivers), and this is likely to be detrimental to the company's prospects within the group.

Significance of TGR

TGR initially appeared attractive to the group as it offered the opportunity to enter a new sector in the transport industry. In practice it has not been as successful as the group had hoped. This is due, in part, to the differences in the skills and competencies needed to operate a rail freight company, and TGR's relatively weak competitive position compared to the two market leaders.

Ventures such as TGR should only be retained if the group can develop or acquire the skills and resources to better exploit the opportunities offered by rail transport. On a positive note, the company has developed an innovative mini-container system which can easily transfer goods between trucks and trains and helps to use warehouse space effectively. This potentially represents an opportunity for TGR as a number of supermarkets are keen to support the new system due to its environmentally friendly credentials. This increases the scope for TGR to implement a new approach to distribution if deliveries can be made to regional railway stations with goods being immediately transferred onto haulage trucks for the final leg of their journey to supermarkets.

(b) The second section of this report evaluates the proposal to acquire Marston airport. We have structured our evaluation around three key areas: suitability; acceptability; and feasibility.

Suitability

The group needs to consider whether the acquisition makes sense given its current strategic position.

Synergies

The proposed acquisition may potentially offer the group the scope to realise synergies in its operations. This is backed up by the comments made by Sir John Watt, who considers road, rail and air to be complementary to one another. Whether such synergies can be achieved seems dubious though, given that the anticipated synergies between road haulage and rail have not been fully realised.

Wide spread of locations

Transporting consumer food and drink products via road and rail on behalf of major supermarkets is unlikely to lend itself to air freighting goods to supermarket stores. The wide dispersion of airport locations makes it unlikely that these would be close enough to the end destination, eg out-of-town supermarket stores. The suitability of the proposal would partially rest on the ability of the mini-container system to be integrated for use with aircraft.

Environmentally friendly

The supermarkets' support for more environmentally friendly modes of transport make it unlikely that they would be interested in using an airfreight service.

Experience and expertise

The current proposal is to purchase an airport and not an airline. Sir John Watt's press statement implies the future establishment of an airline at some point but fails to go any further than this. This raises considerations about the suitability of the proposal, namely that the group does not have any experience in operating an airport.

Demand for 'low cost'

Sir John Watt's proposal highlights an intention to attract a 'low-cost airline to the airport'; at the current time it is unknown whether such an airline would be interested. The report by the aviation consultant raises doubts over the proposal as Marston airport is surrounded by a relatively small local population. Arguably, if there was sufficient demand it is likely that a low-cost airline would already be operating from the airport.

Acceptability

The acceptability of a strategy depends on whether it is acceptable to stakeholders.

Financial performance

Determining Marston airport's financial performance in any detail is difficult, as no comparative financial information has been obtained, however the national performance statistics supplied by the aviation consultant provide a useful starting point for measuring relative performance. In 20X5 the airport site was valued at $6m. This valuation suggests that the $7m to be paid by the group represents a reasonable price. One of the issues facing TGW concerns the increasing lack of land available to be used for warehousing. Marston airport occupies a site of 450 hectares; based on the market rate the land alone is worth $9m ($20,000 × 450 hectares). As the airport is located near the motorway, purchasing the site for warehousing is likely to be highly acceptable to the group given the price.

Profitability

Marston airport is a profitable entity; it generated a profit after tax of $40,000 in 20X5. The airport achieved a gross profit margin of 28.21% and an operating profit margin of 15.38% in the year (compared to the industry average of 17.5%). Interestingly, Marston airport achieved a higher operating profit margin than all of the group companies in 20X5. By contrast Marston airport's ROCE of 2.19% is far lower than the industry average of 8.5%. This indicates that the airport has required a significant level of investment to generate very low returns.

Liquidity and gearing

Marston airport has a positive liquidity position with a current ratio of 2.50 compared to the industry average of 2.25. However, it appears to have a very high inventory balance. When this is stripped out from current assets, Marston airport's acid test ratio of 1.125 is lower than the national average of 1.50. The airport is more highly geared (59.12%) than the industry average (40%), and this reflects the airport's level of long-term borrowings, of just over $4m.

Receivables and payables

The standard payment terms in Meeland require payment within 30 days of the invoice date. In 20X5, Marston airport was receiving payment from trade receivables in 30 days; however, it was only paying its own suppliers after 60 days on average. This is likely to raise some concern over the airport's cash flow.

Marston airport's performance is mixed. Although it is profitable, the company is hindered by a significant long-term debt which has resulted in a relatively low ROCE.

Financial risk

From the group's perspective the initial purchase cost of acquiring the airport is likely to represent a small investment. Despite this, consideration needs to be given to the potential impact that funding the acquisition would have on other group entities. The process of improving the performance of the TGR and TGW business units is likely to require significant levels of investment. Acquiring Marston airport will lead to a reduction in funds available to support these business units.

Shareholders

The Green family have a strong interest in road haulage particularly given the family's close connection with TGRT. As the majority shareholders they may regard the acquisition as straying too far from the group's original direction.

Feasibility

Feasibility asks whether a proposed strategy can be implemented in light of the organisation's strategic capabilities and competencies. The group clearly has built up a high level of expertise in the provision of road haulage services through the operation of TGRT and has extended its operations into warehousing. However, it has been unable to deploy these competencies as effectively at TGR. There is a danger that the acquisition of Marston airport could lead to a similar situation – as the competencies required to run an airport do not exist within the group.

Conclusion – The proposed acquisition

As the analysis indicates, the purchase of Marston airport represents a poor investment for the group at the current time. Even though the group could fund the acquisition, it does not possess the necessary competencies needed to undertake the proposed strategy. The impact that such a move would have on shareholders and the other group companies increases the undesirability of the proposal. Despite these reservations the acquisition would provide the group with much needed land at a price below the market rate, which could potentially be developed into sites for TGW's warehousing operations. Regardless of this potential, the viability of obtaining the required planning permissions and the associated costs for such a development would need to be fully considered before this scheme could progress.

I hope that this report has addressed the issues requested. If I can be of any further help then please do not hesitate to get in contact with me.

LEAD MANAGEMENT CONSULTANT

2   (a)   **Presentation slides**

Slide 1: Issues affecting TGRT's performance of the Ice World contract

- Increasing road congestion in Meeland
- Town centre location of Ice World stores
- Road restrictions for larger trucks
- Freezer unit temperatures
- Failure to fully consider contractual obligations during tender process

Notes. TGRT's ability to win a longer-term contract with Ice World (IW) when the current trial ends will largely depend on its ability to overcome the issues currently being experienced. TGRT's performance of the IW contract has been affected by increasing road congestion and the difficulty of navigating around town centres. Fulfilling this aspect of the contract is evidently outside of TGRT's experience. TGRT's existing supermarket contracts require the transportation of goods to out-of-town store locations which are located just off major roads and motorways.

This perhaps implies that the full requirements of delivering the contract were not sufficiently thought through prior to bidding. The lack of time between winning the contract and its commencement meant that specialised trucks with freezer units had to be hired. The fact that these trucks exceed the size restrictions for use on town centre roads has exacerbated the issue of making deliveries on time and is compounded by the obligation to pay penalties.

Slide 2: The likelihood of extension

- Significance of late deliveries
- Penalty payments
- IW's interpretation of performance
- Doubts about whether contract will be extended

Notes. Ultimately, the decision to extend the current contract will depend on whether or not the 12 late deliveries and two occurrences of failing freezer units are considered acceptable to the management at IW. The fact that IW has received penalty payments in excess of $60,000 is likely to be insufficient to appease IW's management as the intention of the contract is that deliveries are made on time. As a result it is likely that IW's management may feel let down by the performance of the contract especially as TGRT has historically prided itself on the reliability of its service.

Based on this analysis it would appear doubtful that TGRT will be offered an extension on the current contract.

(b) **Slide: Big data and performance improvement**

- Install sensor technology
- 'Real time' data
- Saves staff time
- Helps deal with problems of traffic congestion
- Improved customer service
- Deliveries made on time
- Improved route management and planning
- Reduce costs and scope for penalty payments

Notes. There are a number of ways in which the use of big data technologies and data analytics could improve TGRT's performance in delivering contracts similar to the current one with Ice World (IW).

TGRT could ensure the on-board freezer units are operating at the correct temperature by installing sensors in the trucks. Sensors could measure and monitor the temperature of the freezer units, and could highlight feedback temperature variances in 'real time' via the use of an information system. This would remove the need for regular truck inspections and would therefore save staff time and would allow TGRT to identify those units which require fixing. This would ensure that vehicles are not used for deliveries until they are fixed. Advanced sensors could be used which automatically adjust the freezer unit settings to the required temperature. This should help to reduce vehicle running costs, and improve the profitability of contracts for frozen food deliveries.

TGRT could use data analytics software to relay up-to-date travel information from the trucks back to the depot to help ensure that all delivery slots are met. The installation of tracking devices which feedback 'real time' data about the driver's delivery progress should allow the logistics team at the depot to plot alternative routes while drivers are still out on their rounds.

In the event that a driver is unable to meet the required time slot, relaying the driver's progress will allow the customer service team to contact the customer (for example the individual IW store) and inform them of the delay. Whether this would have any impact on any penalty payments would depend on the terms of the contract. However, such an approach may help to improve customer relations.

The use of such data should allow the logistics team to redesign the drivers' routes to make them more realistic by taking into account road congestion and restrictions in particular town centres. This could prove particularly beneficial when planning the daily deliveries as more drivers could be assigned to make deliveries during busy times.

3   (a)   **Briefing paper**

FAO: Managing Director of TGR

Analysis of stakeholder power and interest and recommendations

> **Tutorial note:** The solution provided here makes use of Mendelow's matrix. It would have been acceptable to have considered the power and interest of the stakeholder groups specified without using a model provided you made relevant, well-explained points.

The following analysis makes use of Mendelow's matrix. The results of this analysis can then be used to determine appropriate strategies for managing each group.

Level of power and interest:

Families of employees on the train

The families of the two employees working on the train clearly would have had a **high level of interest** in the activities of TGR. This is due to fact that they were connected to the company prior to the accident as a result of their relationships to TGR employees. This interest is likely to have related to the job security of their family members and the working environment provided to them. After the train crash this interest will have inevitably increased. This is especially true if TGR is found to have acted negligently in following the correct health and safety procedures. These stakeholders are likely to be interested in pursuing claims for damages against TGR for the loss of loved ones.

The press attention and the suffering of the bereaved families is likely to increase this group's **level of power** over TGR to demand compensation. This group would be classified as **key players** (because of their high levels of interest and power).

'Flower Power' wildflower protection group

The Flower Power group have a **high level of interest** in the TGR accident given the nature of its activities. The group's interest is focused on the protection and promotion of Meeland's indigenous vegetation. This is evident as the group was quick to highlight concerns that the oil spill had affected an area of land containing a rare type of orchid.

The level of power that the group have may fluctuate as the disaster unfolds. On the face of it, the group is unlikely to be in a position to exert much influence over TGR, however, they are ideally positioned to highlight the impact of the accident on the wildlife they wish to protect, which may attract more powerful stakeholder groups, ie the national government. The group's **high level of interest** and **low level of power** mean they would be classified as **keep informed** stakeholders.

Meeland Environment Agency (MEA)

The government-funded MEA would have a **high level of interest and power** over TGR. It is evident that the MEA has some delegated powers to intervene in cases concerning ecological disasters. The MEA's primary interest is likely to focus on protecting citizens and the natural habitat from environmental damage.

As TGR has endangered both of these areas of concern the MEA is now highly interested in the company's activities. This is evident by the Head of the MEA choosing to publicly mention TGR by name during the television news broadcast. The MEA's power is illustrated by the suggestion of 'extensive punitive financial penalties for any wrongdoing'. The MEA can be regarded as being a **key player**.

(b)   **Recommended strategies**

Families of employees on the train

As key players, TGR will need to ensure that the treatment this group receives is **acceptable** to them. The nature of the incident means that supporting the group with access to a counsellor would be an appropriate initial step. Following the MEA's investigation, if TGR is found to have operated the train negligently, then making any compensation payments as soon as possible to this group would be highly appropriate. Offering an apology to this group and providing details of the steps TGR will take to prevent similar incidents in the future would also be highly appropriate.

'Flower Power' wildflower protection group

As a group with high interest but low power, TGR's strategy for dealing with 'Flower Power' should be one of keeping them informed of any developments concerning the disaster. The group will be interested to hear first-hand from TGR's management of any developments concerning any subsequent clean-up operation, and the actions that TGR is taking to try to control the detrimental impact the accident has had on the wildlife around the scene.

Meeland Environment Agency (MEA)

TGR's board should ensure that any action the company takes in respect of the disaster is considered **acceptable** to the MEA. Appropriate strategies are likely to involve openly and willingly assisting MEA's investigative team in determining the cause of the incident. Paying any financial penalties imposed and assisting with the clean-up operation are likely to be deemed acceptable.

4   (a)   **Briefing paper**

FAO: Managing Director of TGR

Decision to hire extra security guards and CSR

Decision to hire extra security guards

Cost of security guards

The costs of combating the protestors will include:

- The **costs of hiring additional security guards**

- The **costs of taking action** to deter Action Now! from proceeding with the protests, and to counter the bad publicity that may arise should the protests go ahead

The other issue, however, is whether there is any alternative to **incurring these costs**. If the protestors are determined to protest, the alternative may be disruption to TGRT's business which would damage existing customer relations if trucks are unable to get out of the depot. The potential damage to these relationships could be much more significant to TGRT than the cost of hiring the security guards.

Legality of the decision

TGRT would be within its legal right to hire additional security guards. However, careful consideration needs to be given to balancing the **rights of individuals to protest, as well as the right to protect property and the use of reasonable force** in doing so. TGRT needs to consider whether it will be held responsible for the actions of its agent, the security firm, especially if any of the protestors are hurt by the actions of the security guards. Care needs to be taken by TGRT to ensure that any poor publicity generated by the protests is not made worse, should the security firm appear to be using excessive force to remove the chained protestors.

Fair treatment of stakeholders

The Action Now! group may claim that they have a **legitimate right to protest**. Their case may be weakened by the fact that they have only selectively targeted two companies (being TGRT and Chestnut Road Haulage) which according to their own ranking of CO_2 polluters are considered to be the 52nd and 67th worst polluters in Meeland as opposed to being, for example one of the top five polluters in the country. Furthermore, the extract from the group's website provides no suggestion of how the rankings were determined. While TGRT does use polluting trucks, it is consciously trying to reduce the impact of these emissions by replacing older trucks every three years. Such actions indicate that TRGT does take sustainability seriously and calls into question the fairness of the Action Now! group's protest.

Even if the TGRT board accept Action Now! as a **legitimate stakeholder group**, it has a duty to treat its other key stakeholders fairly. Groups such as its supermarket customers and the consumers of goods being transported are also legitimate stakeholders whose requirements need to be considered. Therefore, to **preserve the continuity of supermarket supplies** the use of extra security guards may be regarded as fair.

Use of force

The main ethical issues are whether it is right for Action Now! to take such **extreme short-term action** in order to advance a cause such as climate change that is already well documented and has fundamental long-term consequences. From TGRT's point of view the ethical issue is whether **force** should be used against the protestors should they endanger the rights of the drivers to safely go about their work; if force can be used, **how much force would be right**; ultimately would it be legitimate to take action that might harm the protestors?

Sustainability

Fundamentally, the focus of the protests is ultimately upon the amount of CO_2 that TGRT's trucks emit. In the days before the protests commence, the TGRT board are unlikely to be able to make any long-term decisions about switching all of its 2,000 trucks from fossil fuel powered engines to anything more environmentally friendly. It could be argued that delaying such a decision is **not sustainable** as this will need to take place at some point in the future as global supplies of fossil fuels will eventually be exhausted. Furthermore, as highlighted by Action Now! there is strong evidence that emissions are having **adverse climatic effects**. Responding to these pressures will only really be possible once an environmentally sustainable alternative to fossil fuels has been fully established.

(b) **Corporate social responsibility**

Corporate social responsibility means the extent to which the organisation **goes beyond its responsibilities imposed by law**, and considers its ethical duties towards society and its members and its obligations to behave in ways that benefit society and do not harm it.

The range of measures that an organisation can take to fulfil its perceived duties is wide. It includes **equitable treatment of a range of stakeholders** whose interests the organisation's activities significantly affect, even though those stakeholders may not have significant power over the organisation. This includes the provision of good salaries and working conditions for employees and fair treatment of suppliers. It also includes **avoiding adverse impacts** such as externalities and **making positive contributions** that enhance society, for example charitable donations. It also involves **demonstrating accountability to society** by publishing more information than is required by law.

Corporate social responsibility can be seen as a **key part of strategy**. Companies may gain through attracting customers and other stakeholders to deal with it if it is perceived to be strongly ethical. Social responsibilities can be built into the company's **mission statement**, meaning that the company views acting responsibly as integral to the way it does business. The mission statement can be supported by guidance such as a code of ethics which enforces these values on employees.

Differences between Action Now! and a profit-making business

Central purpose

Acting in the best interests of society and the environment is the **prime objective of Action Now!** It was founded to heighten awareness of concerns over climate change caused by global warming. It does not charge for the campaigns that it organises as it is a voluntary organisation, as a result it does not balance services with payments made. A company's prime objective is to maximise long-term returns for its shareholders. For a company its social responsibility commitment influences how it achieves that objective.

Measurement of success

Action Now! would appear to measure the success of its activities by the amount of **disruption it causes** the operations of companies such as TGRT and Chestnut Road Haulage, and presumably the ensuing media interest that this generates in highlighting climate change.

A company is likely to measure its success in financial and market terms. Customer satisfaction may be a measure that a company uses, but that is measuring the satisfaction by customers who have an economic, rather than a charitable, relationship with the business.

Values and beliefs

Action Now! requires its volunteers to **share its ethical stance** and **accept a culture that is very different from a commercial business**. The prime quality required of volunteers is an **understanding of the need to protect the environment from the effects of climate change**. Volunteers are prepared to sacrifice their time, without remuneration, to further the cause of Action Now!

A commercial organisation would expect employees to have values that are **consistent with the commercial success of the organisation**. Directors' remuneration is likely to be **influenced by what the market rate is for their role** and directors are likely to wish to increase their income over time, rather than sacrifice income so that the company can do more to help the stakeholders with whom it deals.

Mock Exam 1

Tutorial notes to help you improve your exam success skills performance

Skill	Examples
Case scenario: Managing information	Careful reading of the case information should have provided a clear indication as to which Exhibits needed to be used when attempting specific task requirements.
	The detail provided in Exhibit 1 is important as it provides some context as to the background and history of the three operating companies in the Green Transport Group. Exhibit 2 is important as it provides performance data for the three operating companies over a number of years.
	This context is particularly important when attempting task 1(a).
	The detail contained in Exhibits 3, 4 and 5 was needed to attempt task 1(b) in respect of the proposed acquisition of Marston airport. Exhibit 5 contained useful detail relating to key performance ratios relevant to medium-sized light aviation airports similar to Marston airport. The inclusion of these ratios should have provided a clue that they needed to be used when formulating an answer to 1(b).
	The email in Exhibit 6 about the issues facing TGRT was needed when attempting tasks 2(a) and (b). In the preamble before Task 3, you were told that you needed to use the newspaper article (Exhibit 7) from the Meeland Herald which provided details of the train accident.
	In respect of Task 4, concerning the planned protests, it was important that you made use of Exhibit 8 which contained the extracts from the website of Action Now!
Correct Interpretation of requirements	In addition to thinking about the Exhibits and the scenario as a whole, it is also important to think about the specific context of the task requirements.
	For example, in respect of Task 3, it was important that consideration was given to the fact that Exhibit 7 detailed the fact that two people had died in the accident. The seriousness of the incident required you to adopt carefully chosen language when attempting both parts of the task. This was especially in true in the case of part (b) where care was needed to ensure that the strategies suggested for managing the two groups were appropriate and could realistically be implemented by the board.
Answer planning: Priorities, structure and logic	Task 4 (a) required an assessment of the decision to hire extra security guards in handling the planned protests. Better answers will consider a broad range of different perspectives. Spend time considering the views of different stakeholders, the legality of the approach and the impact on company goals (eg cost control/profitability). Use clear headings in order to create distinct discussion points and provide a logical flow to your answer. The trick to attempting tasks such as this is the ability to identify a wide range of issues using limited scenario information. To help generate ideas ensure that you practice plenty of questions as well as keeping up to date with business news, so that you become familiar with real-life business responses to complex scenarios.

Skill	Examples
Efficient numerical analysis	Task 1 (b) required a critical evaluation of the proposal to acquire Marston airport. As highlighted above, to ensure that you got the most from your answer you needed to use the key performance ratios in Exhibit 5 in conjunction with the financial statements for Marston airport set out in Exhibit 3.
	The information provided in Exhibit 3 should have made it possible to calculate key ratios relating to profitability, liquidity, gearing etc, which could then be contrasted and evaluated against the ratios in Exhibit 5.
	The trick, however, to producing a good answer when attempting tasks such as this is to ensure that you not only do the calculations but then interpret them and comment on them. In this case, it was important that you provided a critical evaluation of the proposal by, for example, highlighting the fact that the standard payment terms in Meeland require payment within 30 days of the invoice date. Whereas Marston airport was paying its own suppliers after 60 days on average. Such an observation would raise concerns over the airport's cash flow.
Effective writing and presentation	In the Strategic Business Leader exam, where task requirements ask you to 'evaluate', 'assess' or 'analyse' (for example) you need to explain why the points you make in your answer are important, rather than simply listing points. However, the time constraints of the exam also mean that you cannot afford to be writing lengthy paragraphs to explain a single point.
	This requires you to strike a balance between writing too much or failing to write enough. Look at the following extract from the solution to Task 3 (a) which asked for an analysis of the relative power and interest of the specified stakeholders:
	"The government-funded MEA would have a high level of interest and power over TGR. It is evident that the MEA has some delegated powers to intervene in cases concerning ecological disasters. The MEA's primary interest is likely to focus on protecting citizens and the natural habitat from environmental damage."
	As TGR has endangered both of these areas of concern, the MEA is now highly interested in the company's activities. This is evident by the Head of the MEA choosing to publicly mention TGR by name during the television news broadcast. The MEA's power is illustrated by the suggestion of 'extensive punitive financial penalties for any wrongdoing'. The MEA can be regarded as being a key player."
	These two short paragraphs outline the level of power and interest that the Meeland Environment Agency (MEA) have and relates this assessment back to the information provided in Exhibit 7. At the end of the second paragraph, a mention is made of the fact that (per Mendelow's matrix) the MEA should be treated as a key player,
	To ensure that you get the most from the points that you state you should aim to identify the issues, ie, in this case the relative power and interest of the specified stakeholder group, use the information in the Exhibit to justify and support your classification concerning the levels of power and interest, and then consider the implications of this for the featured entity in terms of how it should treat this stakeholder group.

Skill	Examples
Good Time Management	You had 4 hours (240 minutes) to tackle all of the task requirements worth 100 marks. Throughout the earlier sections in this Practice and Revision Kit, we have worked on the basis of 2 minutes per mark. This was used to reflect the fact that many of the questions attempted up until this point have featured considerably smaller exam scenarios using limited Exhibit information.

When attempting the Strategic Business Leader exam, ACCA recommend that candidates spend at least 40 minutes reading, planning and interpreting the exhibit information and the task requirements.

When taking the 40 minutes reading time into account, candidates should spend approximately 2.5 minutes attempting each mark. The 2.5 minutes per mark is based on the fact that the total exam is 240 minutes (4 hours) in duration which, when the 40 minutes reading/planning time is deducted, gives 200 minutes. As candidates can earn the 20 professional skills marks by the virtue of attempting the 80 technical marks in the exam, the remaining 200 minutes can be divided by the 80 technical marks to give 2.5 minutes per mark.

On the basis of 2.5 minutes per mark, the time available for attempting each task requirement was as follows:

Task 1 (a) = 21 technical marks: 53 minutes

Task 1 (b) = 16 technical marks: 40 minutes

Task 2 (a) = 6 technical marks: 15 minutes

Task 2 (b) = 8 technical marks; 20 minutes

Task 3 (a) = 6 technical marks: 15 minutes

Task 3 (b) = 3 technical marks: 7 minutes

Task 4 (a) = 10 technical marks: 25 minutes

Task 4 (b) = 10 technical marks: 25 minutes |

Diagnostic

Did you apply these skills when reading, planning, and writing up your answer? Identify the exam success skills where you think you need to improve and capture your thoughts here of what you want to achieve when attempting questions in future.

ACCA

Strategic Business Leader

Mock Exam 2
(ACCA Specimen Exam 2)

Questions	
Time allowed	4 hours
This question paper is an integrated case study with one section containing a total of 100 marks and ALL Tasks must be completed.	
All Tasks contain Professional Skills marks which are included in the marks shown above.	

DO NOT OPEN THIS EXAM UNTIL YOU ARE READY TO START UNDER EXAMINATION CONDITIONS

Strategic Business Leader – Mock Exam 2 (ACCA Specimen Exam 2)

Introduction

Rail Co is a public sector rail company responsible for delivering passenger rail services within Beeland.

Rail Co is governed by a supreme governing committee known as the Rail Co Trust Board. This board is responsible to the Ministry of Transport for ensuring that the Rail Co board of directors make the best use of public money and maintain effective and efficient services to the public. Figure 1 below shows the governance structure of Rail Co.

Figure 1

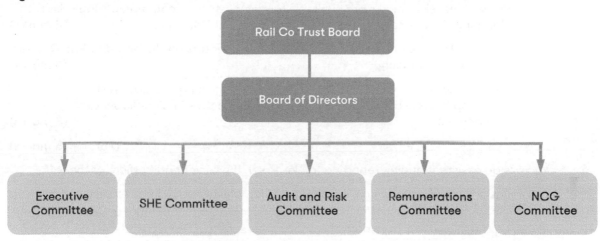

The National Audit Authority (NAA) of Beeland is a national government audit authority with responsibility for evaluating and reporting to the government of Beeland on public spending, suggesting improvements to and benchmarking against the performance of a wide range of publicly funded organisations. The NAA also has a responsibility to advise on the value for money (VFM) obtained from publicly owned enterprises and on the performance of the boards of such organisations, including the senior executives of these boards.

Rail Co has in the recent past received negative publicity in the media and from a variety of other sources relating to its poor services and performance. This has prompted the Minister for Transport of Beeland, to commission the NAA to undertake an urgent investigation of the issues facing Rail Co.

The following exhibits (1–6) provide Information relevant to Rail Co.

* Exhibit 1: Website page for Rail Co leadership and governance

* Exhibit 2: Transport report published in the Beeland Herald newspaper

* Exhibit 3: Passenger survey results and performance analysis spreadsheet for Rail Co and Its competitors (three years data)

* Exhibit 4: Rail Co board meeting minutes

* Exhibit 5: Outline person specification and summary CVs for two candidates for the new chief executive position

* Exhibit 6: Ticket sales, passenger usage data and fraud analysis at stations in towns within Region 1 – Beeland network – prepared by the financial controller of Rail Co

The task requirements are as follows and you will be told which role you are taking in each task:

1   You are a non-executive member and Chair of the nominations and corporate governance (NCG) committee.

The recently appointed Chair of the Rail Co Trust Board has requested that you provide him with information relating to the governance of Rail Co and the roles and responsibilities of the non-executive directors.

Required

You have been asked to prepare a briefing paper for the Rail Co Trust Board which:

(a)   **Identifies and explains the agency relationship of the parties involved in Rail Co and discusses the rights and responsibilities of those parties.**   **(8 marks)**

Professional skills marks are available for demonstrating **communication** skills in clarifying the agency relationships involved in Rail Co.   **(2 marks)**

(b)   **Assesses the role and value of non-executive directors on the board of Rail Co, as a public sector company.**   **(6 marks)**

Professional skills marks are available for demonstrating **evaluation** skills in assessing the role and value of non-executive directors in a public sector environment.   **(2 marks)**

(Total = 18 marks)

2   You are an assistant auditor reporting to Alex Reed, the senior audit officer of the NAA.

Alex leads a team of assistant auditors and audit analysts and will be responsible for reporting the findings of the NAA's investigations of Rail Co to a number of relevant parties, including the Minister of Transport, the board of directors of Rail Co and the Rail Co Trust Board. As part of the investigation commissioned by the Minister of Transport to be undertaken by the NAA, one of the audit analysts working on your audit team has prepared a spreadsheet supplying a variety of data following the recent passenger survey results and using other relevant performance related information.

Required

Alex Reed has asked you to prepare a report for the Rail Co Trust Board which:

(a)   **Evaluates the implications of the findings of the passenger survey results and reviews the actual and relative performance of Rail Co over the last three years.**

(12 marks)

Professional skills marks are available for demonstrating **analysis** skills used in reviewing the information presented in the spreadsheet.   **(2 marks)**

A few days later Alex Reed called you into his office to discuss Rail Co's governance and internal controls. During that meeting he referred to the transport report in the Beeland Herald newspaper (Exhibit 2) and handed you a copy of the minutes of the latest board meeting held by Rail Co (Exhibit 4).

Required

Alex has asked you to draft a letter to be sent to the Chair of the Rail Co Trust Board which:

(b) Reviews the effectiveness of the internal controls at Rail Co using evidence from the minutes of the latest Rail Co board meeting and any other suitable source and justifies that the chief executive of Rail Co is failing in his fiduciary duties to the trustees of Rail Co. (8 marks)

Professional skills marks are available for demonstrating **scepticism** skills in questioning the opinions and assertions made by the chief executive at the recent board meeting. (2 marks)

(Total = 24 marks)

It is now two months after the letter was sent by the NAA to the chairperson of the Trust Board (Task 2b).

3 You are the non-executive chairperson of an ad hoc sub-committee constituted by the NCG of the Rail Co board.

As a consequence of the NAA review and the recommendations of the Rail Co Trust Board, the Minister of Transport recommended that the chief executive of Rail Co should be removed from his position. Following the termination of the chief executive's contract, the position has now been advertised both nationally and internationally and a person specification has been uploaded to the Rail Co website. In the last two weeks, two candidates have been shortlisted for final interview and a summary of their CVs is being reviewed by the nominations and corporate governance (NCG) committee of Rail Co (Exhibit 5).

Required

Following a review of the suitability of the shortlisted candidates against the outline person specification, you have been asked by the chair of the NCG to do the following:

(a) Write a report to the chair of the NCG which evaluates the suitability of the shortlisted candidates for the position of chief executive of Rail Co and recommend with justification, which candidate you consider to be the most suitable for the position. (8 marks)

Professional skills marks are available for demonstrating **commercial acumen** in using your judgement to evaluate the relative merits of the two candidates.

(2 marks)

(b) Prepare two presentation slides, with accompanying notes, to explain to the NCG, the contribution which the chief executive should be expected to make in terms of talent management, to support the necessary change programme required at Rail Co. (6 marks)

Professional skills marks are available for demonstrating **communication** skills in conveying relevant information in an appropriate tone to the NCG committee.

(2 marks)

(Total = 18 marks)

It is now three months later. A new chief executive has been appointed and is working closely with the board of directors and the Rail Co Trust Board to improve performance.

4   You are an internal auditor working for the audit and risk committee of Rail Co.

The new chief executive asked the financial controller of Rail Co to produce a spreadsheet which analyses the ticket sales and rail usage by station within the Beeland rail network and which also analyses the estimated levels of fraud occurring across the Rail Co network.

Required

You have been asked by the chair of the audit and risk committee to review the findings of the financial controller and present a report which requires you to do the following:

(a)   **Analyse the information presented in the spreadsheet produced by the financial controller, questioning any assumptions he may have made, and explain the implications of the findings for Rail Co.**   **(8 marks)**

Professional skills marks are available for demonstrating **scepticism** skills in considering the information presented in the spreadsheet and reflecting on the impact on Rail Co's revenues.   **(2 marks)**

(b)   **Recommend to the audit and risk committee, with justifications, suitable measures or safeguards which could be implemented by Rail Co to reduce the levels of fraud occurring on the network.**   **(8 marks)**

Professional skills marks are available for demonstrating **commercial acumen** in making sound recommendations for suitable measures and safeguards to reduce fraud.

(2 marks)

(Total = 20 marks)

5   You are a project manager working for the director of Projects and Infrastructure of Rail Co.

The director of Projects and Infrastructure is putting forward a proposal to the board of directors of Rail Co for a project to invest in an online ticket sales system. The project should be fully operational within 12 months but would need to be undertaken by an external firm of developers, as Rail Co does not possess the internal expertise. However, Rail Co would manage the project.

Required

You have been asked by the director of Projects and Infrastructure to write a business case to the board, in which you will:

(a)   **Justify why the investment in online ticket sales could assist Rail Co in producing detailed and timely customer data to assist in customer relationship management.**
                                    (8 marks)

Professional skills marks are available for demonstrating **evaluation** skills in assessing the impact of online ticket sales on customer relationship management.

(2 marks)

(b)   **Produce a project initiation document (PID) which could be used by Rail Co to assist in planning the implementation of an online ticket sales system.**   **(8 marks)**

Professional skills marks are available for demonstrating **communication** skills in producing a PID to be used by Rail Co.   **(2 marks)**

(Total = 20 marks)

Exhibit 1: Rail Co 'Getting you there, on time, in comfort'

Our mission is to provide a high quality, efficient and cost-effective rail service to all our passengers.

Our vision is to become the world leader in providing reliable, profitable and safe train passenger services in a climate which embraces new technology and diversity of ideas.

Our board

The Rail Co board is responsible for the strategic direction of Rail Co. It is responsible for supervising the operational activities of the business and providing leadership and strategic direction.

Our Chief Executive reports directly to the Minister for Transport on our leadership and long-term performance and success. The board comprises:

> Henrik Kilde, non-executive chair – Appointed to the board in 2011
> John Rose, Chief Executive – Appointed to the board in 2002
> Helga Baum, Finance Director – Appointed to the board in 2006
> Milo Strauss, Director of Projects & Infrastructure – Appointed to the board in 2012
> Filip Axis, non-executive director – Appointed to the board in 2009
> Felix Erikson, non-executive director – Appointed to the board in 2014
> Harvey Flood, non-executive director – Appointed to the board in 2015
> Salma Khan, non-executive director – Appointed to the board in 2010
> Kim Lun, non-executive director – Appointed to the board in 2012
> Anders Rosburg, non-executive director – Appointed to the board in 2016

Our executive committee

Operational management is delegated to members of our executive committee. The executive committee is chaired by the Chief Executive and comprises the Finance Director, the Director of Projects and Infrastructure and five other executive managers:

> Lara Cook, Passenger services director – Appointed in 2004
> Jasper Edberg, Asset management director – Appointed in 2007
> George Fill, Director of Safety and Engineering – Appointed in 2013
> Tomas Kline, Director of IT – Appointed in 2012
> Brenda Suter, HR Director – Appointed in 2006

Our board committees

Our four board committees, made up of non-executive directors, assist the board with its responsibilities.

Safety, health and environment (SHE) committee

This committee monitors the integrity of the methods used to carry out SHE responsibilities. The committee evaluates whether policies and strategies are adequate and effective taking into account relevant legislation and standards.

Audit and risk committee

This committee monitors the integrity of the financial reporting and the audit process and reviews the internal control systems including risk management, regulation and compliance.

Remuneration committee

This committee is empowered under the articles of association of Rail Co to determine remuneration for directors. This responsibility reflects the business aim to provide independence of the decision-making process for remuneration and incentive schemes.

Nomination and corporate governance (NCG) committee

This committee reviews the size, structure and composition of the board and committees. The committee identifies and nominates candidates for appointment to the board and ensures that appropriate succession planning is in place.

Rail Co Trust Board

The Rail Co Trust Board is an independent statutory body, with powers vested by the Government of Beeland in its members. The Trust Board consists of ten members, all of whom are appointed by the Minister for Transport, for a fixed term of up to three years. Our board is accountable to the Rail Co Trust Board.

The Trust Board is our supreme governing body which holds us to account for delivering what we promise. It sets us a range of performance targets each year and holds the board to account for its effective and efficient use of the funds allocated to Rail Co by Government and by the fare paying passengers. The board is also accountable to the Rail Co Trust Board for our health and safety performance.

Our Chief Executive is personally accountable to the Government for Rail Co's stewardship of the public funding it receives.

Exhibit 2

TRANSPORT REPORT

The Beeland Herald

Beeland's most widely read Daily newspaper

Gus Smidt, Transport Editor reports on the recently published customer survey results of Rail Co

Is Rail Co going off the rails?

The latest annual customer survey results for Rail Co will not make comfortable reading for its Chief Executive John Rose, who predicted this time last year 'the future is bright for Rail Co'.

Rail Co, the company responsible for the transport of over 50% of Beeland's commuters to their daily work destinations throughout the country, appears to be losing the support of its loyal customers. This is despite an increasing population in Beeland and significant levels of government investment in its development. Although it has invested in new trains over the last five years, commuter trains are still overcrowded. Significantly, it has failed to invest in online ticket purchasing systems and commuters are increasingly unhappy that they are only able to purchase tickets from manned ticket offices within each station. Public perception of the organisation is at an all-time low and questions will now be asked by the Minister for Transport as to why revenue growth is stagnant and why customers are increasingly unhappy with its services.

Rail Co receives an annual grant from the government of Beeland, funded by general taxation of the population, to run the business efficiently and effectively. The government also sets Rail Co a number of performance targets to meet each year. These include key performance indicators on revenue growth, cost efficiency and customer satisfaction ratings.

Despite evidence of a growth in passenger numbers (platform 'footfall') of about 15% using the railway network in the last three years,

revenue has hardly increased over the same period.

In its last two annual reports, Rail Co's directors have highlighted the risk of significant numbers of passengers travelling without tickets. It has been suggested that this could be due to the fact that Rail Co does not operate ticket barriers at many of its stations. Rail Co relies on ticket inspectors operating on train services to check tickets, but evidence suggests that this can only catch a minority of those who evade paying for tickets.

As a consequence of static sales, Rail Co has repeatedly increased its ticket prices by more than inflation in the last three years and customers have complained bitterly and many are threatening to use their cars or other forms of public transport if Rail Co does not respond effectively.

A further concern for Rail Co will be that staff turnover is at an all-time high as stated in its latest annual report, which may be due to the fact that staff wages at Rail Co have not been rising with inflation and staff are coming under increased pressure from unhappy customers.

These are, indeed, worrying developments for Rail Co, as its key stakeholders seemingly become increasingly frustrated with the lack of any meaningful response by the Chief Executive, who yesterday refused to comment on the customer survey.

However, in a statement made by the Minister of Transport yesterday, he commented that although the customer survey results for Rail Co were 'disappointing', he was confident that the situation would be addressed within the coming year. He announced that the newly appointed Chairperson of the Trust Board, the supreme governing committee responsible for the performance and governance of Rail Co, 'has the full backing of the government of Beeland to undertake a thorough and effective review, and if necessary make changes to the management and organisation of Rail Co'.

Exhibit 3: Extract from Beeland's passenger survey results for the last three years

	Percentage satisfied			Trust Board target for 2016
	2016	2015	2014	Target growth on 2015
Overall satisfaction with your journey	87	90	92	+3%
Satisfaction with ticket buying facilities	60	64	65	+2%
Availability of staff	62	65	70	+5%
Helpfulness/attitude of staff	75	73	77	+2%
Punctuality/reliability of service	84	81	86	+5%
Value for money for price of the ticket	50	56	57	+2%

Examples of customer feedback comments:

'The price of the regular ticket I buy to commute to work has increased by nearly 10% since last year. I really cannot understand why, as I do not seem to be getting more for my money.'

'Why is it that when I travel on business to Ayeland, I can book my train tickets online, yet, here in Beeland I can only buy a ticket at the station? This is very frustrating and occasionally, I use my car to get to work as it is more convenient than queuing for up to half an hour to buy a train ticket.'

'I have been a loyal customer of Rail Co for over 30 years, but I am becoming increasingly frustrated with the number of passengers who I see that are clearly boarding the train without a ticket. I pay B$45 for each ticket I buy, yet some people are travelling for free. Where are the ticket inspectors?'

Competitor Performance Analysis

	ANR			Rail Co			Ceeland Rail		
	2016	2015	2014	2016	2015	2014	2016	2015	2
Revenue (B$m)	4,420	4,212	3,990	4,100	3,998	3,880	7,542	6,983	
Operating costs (B$m)	3,026	3,138	3,200	3,038	2,743	2,551	4,868	4,786	
Km travelled (millions)	890	897	889	779	762	750	1,803	1,709	
Percentage of trains on time	90%	85%	85%	82%	84%	87%	94%	92%	
Staff turnover percentage	14%	12%	15%	17%	14%	13%	8%	8%	
Average price per ticket (B$)	43	41	41	65	60	56	40	42	
Average number of employees	32,890	32,788	31,987	27,455	27,190	27,365	56,367	55,798	5
Overall customer satisfaction	90%	88%	91%	87%	90%	92%	97%	94%	
Lost time injuries to staff (days)	355	361	358	481	466	459	211	232	

Notes

1   ANR is the state-owned rail company which operates passenger services in Ayeland, a neighbouring country of Beeland. Ayeland has a population of similar size to Beeland. ANR invested in online ticket booking facilities in 2015.

2   Ceeland Rail is a state-owned rail company which operates passenger train services in Ceeland. Ceeland is not a neighbouring country of Beeland but operates on the same continent. Ceeland has a larger population than Beeland but a smaller percentage of Ceeland's commuters use the rail system to travel, due to higher concentration of the population within Ceeland's towns and cities. Ceeland invested in an online ticket booking system in 2010 and over 70% of train tickets for Cee Rail are purchased online.

Exhibit 4

Rail Co
Board meeting minutes

XX/XXXX/2016

Board members:

Present: Henrik Kilde, John Rose, Helga Baum, Milo Strauss, Filip Axis, Felix Erikson, Salma Khan, Kim Lun, Anders Rosburg, Tomas Kline, Director of IT

Apologies: None

Absent: Harvey Flood

Proceedings:

- Meeting called to order at 2:00pm by Chair, Henrik Kilde

Chair's opening statement:

Henrik Kilde opened the meeting with the announcement that he had been informed by the newly appointed Chair of the Rail Co Trust Board that it had requested the National Audit Authority (NAA) to undertake a review of the operations and performance of Rail Co. He expressed his concern with this development but that the Board was expected to give its full co-operation to this investigation.

John Rose, the Chief Executive, offered his full endorsement of the Chair's comments on supporting the NAA's investigations of Rail Co's performance. He noted that in his 14 years as Chief Executive, he has witnessed many changes and that he was confident in the current performance of Rail Co and that the NAA would not identify any problems with Rail Co.

Chief Executive's Report on customer survey results:

The Chair opened the discussion with a statement of his disappointment with the latest customer survey results and asked the Chief Executive to present an overview of the key outcomes of the latest customer survey results. The primary focus of the presentation was that Rail Co had failed to meet a number of the key performance measures set by the Trust Board for 2016. The Chief Executive did highlight that although the overall customer satisfaction target was not met, this was still at a very high level at 87%. He commented that when he took over as Chief Executive in 2002 customer satisfaction levels were at less than 65% and to have achieved such high levels of customer satisfaction is a significant achievement for Rail Co. He also highlighted that levels of punctuality had increased in the last year and this was evidence that Rail Co's investment in new trains had ensured a better service for its passengers. Rail Co's motto of 'getting you there on time, in comfort' was clearly being achieved. He stated that he believed that the target growth for punctuality set by the Trust Board for 2016 was unachievable and therefore should be ignored.

The Chair raised his concern that customers' perception of the value for money of Rail Co's tickets had declined from last year and asked the Board to consider whether this was a reflection of increasing ticket prices. The Finance Director agreed that this was a significant concern but the Chief Executive stated that he strongly believed that the majority of customers did not understand the concept of value for money and therefore this measure was flawed.

Audit and Risk Committee Report provided by Chair, Filip Axis:

Filip Axis presented a briefing to the Board on the risks of customer fraud. He noted that this has been an ongoing concern for the last few years but has not been investigated in detail. Evidence suggested that more passengers are travelling on Rail Co's network without tickets and a key factor is that approximately 40% of Rail Co's stations do not operate ticket

BPP LEARNING MEDIA

barriers. Mr Axis referred to a recent meeting he had held with Jasper Edberg, the Asset Management Director, in which they had discussed the installation of ticket barriers at more of Rail Co's stations to prevent customer fraud. The Finance Director was asked to present an analysis of the impact of potential fraud on Rail Co's revenues at the next Board meeting. The Chief Executive disagreed that this was a significant risk to Rail Co and that the cost of installation of ticket barriers would far outweigh the benefits. He also stated that most customer fraud was unpreventable and that this measure would merely create more customer dissatisfaction.

SHE Committee's Report provided by Chair, Kim Lun:

Kim Lun outlined the key issues discussed at a meeting she recently attended with Beeland's Health and Safely Office (BHSO). She reported that the Head of the BHSO had expressed his concern with the increase in the number of injuries to staff reported by Rail Co in the last year. Kim Lun stated that she had assured the BHSO that a thorough investigation would be undertaken and that this needed to be commenced immediately. Kim Lun also noted that there had been a lack of investment in the training of staff in the last three years and that this was affecting staff morale and should be investigated by the HR Director.

The Chief Executive stated that although the HR Director was not a board member, his own opinion was that training levels were satisfactory and that there was no evidence to suggest that staff morale was low. He pointed to evidence in the customer survey report which indicated an annual growth in customer satisfaction levels in relation to staff helpfulness and attitude.

- *Other business:*

    1   The IT Director made a short presentation on the use of online booking systems by other rail businesses. The presentation outlined that a number of other national train operators offered online booking facilities and evidence suggested that this had positively impacted upon revenue growth and customer satisfaction in all of these businesses. Most of the Board expressed enthusiastic interest in this potential development.

         The Chief Executive expressed his concern that investment in online booking facilities was merely a knee-jerk reaction to the current challenges to Rail Co. He suggested that improvements to training of ticket office staff would be a better investment opportunity and far less costly to Rail Co. He commented that online ticket facilities went against the traditional values of customer service focus of Rail Co.

    2   The Chair informed the Board that the HR Director was currently in a meeting with the Head of the Beeland Rail Workers Union (BRWU) to discuss its recent demands for an above inflation rate pay increase for its workers. The Chair expressed concern at this development, as any threat of strike action could have serious damaging consequences on the public perception of Rail Co.

         The Chief Executive stated that it was important for Rail Co to take a firm stand against any pressure from the unions for an increase in staff pay. He commented that the unions were merely taking advantage of the latest survey results to put the Board under pressure to increase levels of pay for its members. He stated that he had instructed the HR Director not to make any comment to the media on these developments. His opinion was that the media were responsible for stirring up the interest of the unions and that the media were not an important stakeholder.

- Meeting adjourned at 4:30pm.

- Minutes submitted by Secretary, Joanna Vonn.

Exhibit 5

Chief Executive – Rail Co

Outline person specification

Experience

1 Consistent achievement at chief executive level in an organisation of comparable size and complexity

2 A proven track record of leading and delivery of corporate vision, strategies and objectives within a complex political environment

3 A proven track record of successfully designing, leading and implementing cultural change

4 Experience of building professional credibility with boards, employees, the public and the media

Knowledge, skills and abilities

1 A comprehensive understanding of the rail industry and the political context within which it operates

2 Well-developed leadership skills which promote a positive and motivated organisational culture

3 An ability to develop relationships with all stakeholders which command respect, trust and confidence

4 Financial and commercial awareness, with strong analytical and problem solving skills

Personal qualities

1 An ability to deliver under pressure

2 Values the contributions of others and committed to employee development

3 A strong commitment to service excellence and continuous improvement

4 Results focused and performance driven

5 Leads from the front, an honest and straightforward style which gains the respect of others

Summarised CV – Candidate A	Summarised CV – Candidate B
PROFESSIONAL EXPERIENCE	**PROFESSIONAL EXPERIENCE**
• Chief executive of JPS Express, the largest passenger train service operating company in Jayland. 2009–present	• Chief executive of BV Plc, the world's third largest engine manufacturer for the aviation industry, based in Ceeland. 2007–present
• Chief executive of Beeland Oil, a multinational oil and gas company 2000–2009	• Finance director of Ceeland Rail 2004–2007
EXPERIENCE and DUTIES:	**EXPERIENCE and DUTIES:**
• Developing strategy and mission and carrying it through with confidence and vigour	• Planning strategic business objectives and implementing systems to monitor on performance against key performance indicators
• Responsible for all aspects of human performance management and development and driving enterprise human talent development	• Responsible for driving the growth of revenue and increased operational efficiency
• Working on development lifecycle projects including several complex systems infrastructure investments	• Interpreting financial data and drawing conclusions
• Close liaison with national government regulators and rail interest groups	• Identifying skills gaps and providing advice on hiring strategies
• Producing informative, well-organised presentations for senior management	• Liaising with key strategic suppliers and customers to define KPIs
• Regular liaison with external suppliers, the media and the public	• Reviewing, monitoring and authorisation of all budget expenditure
	• Motivating and providing strong leadership to all departments
KEY SKILLS and COMPETENCIES	**KEY SKILLS and COMPETENCIES**
• Ensuring that everything works to the highest possible professional standards with a focus on strong internal control	• Decisive and forward thinking, with strong vision and strategic capability
• A commitment to customer focus and driving improved performance	• Ability to network and liaise with stakeholders at every level, particularly customers and strategic suppliers
• A proven track record in change leadership – including the successful management and leadership of the privatisation of V Trains in 2013	• Experience of project management in a highly complex engineering environment
• A charismatic leader with a successful track record in managing cultural change from a public sector to private sector environment	• A proven track record of successful leadership and growth, operating within highly competitive markets
• A commitment to building and maintaining close relationships with external bodies, staff, the media, customers and the public	• Motivational and credible with highly effective interpersonal skills
• An enterprising and creative thinker, with a commercial eye, exceptional financial acumen and highly effective leadership skills	• Highly commercial and committed to quality and innovation
	• Operationally strong, financially aware and commercially astute

Exhibit 6: Initial data on stations in Region 1 – Beeland network

Analysis of fraud – information based on 2016 analysis

Ticket wn barrier	Population per town	Monthly tickets sold to town	Estimated % railway users per town	Estimated monthly ticket sales per town	Variance between tickets sold v projected ticket sales	Spend per ticket sold	Estimated fraud ($) per month	Fraud % for each town (based on total population)	Estimated fraud due to poor internal control (%) (based on total population)	Preventable annual fraud ($) (based on total population)
y	142,000	28,000	21	29,820	1,820	59	107,380	1.28%		
y	195,000	31,000	17	33,150	2,150	38	81,700	1.10%		
n	110,000	22,000	28	30,800	8,800	44	387,200	8.00%	6.72%	3,903,953
n	195,000	36,000	26	50,700	14,700	51	749,700	7.54%	6.26%	7,470,856
y	74,000	25,000	35	25,900	900	56	50,400	1.22%		
y	116,000	31,000	28	32,480	1,480	52	76,960	1.28%		
n	183,000	37,000	30	54,900	17,900	56	1,002,400	9.78%	8.50%	10,456,776
y	87,000	19,000	23	20,010	1,010	61	61,610	1.16%		
n	144,000	12,000	16	23,040	11,040	48	529,920	7.67%	6.39%	5,298,752
y	147,000	27,000	20	29,400	2,400	62	148,800	1.63%		
	1,393,000	268,000					3,196,070			

Assumed average percentage of unpreventable fraud – Region 1   1.28%

Total annual preventable fraud in Region 1: $27,130,338

Extrapolate for 20 regions $542,606,752

Note. There are 20 identifiable regions within the Beeland passenger service network. For this analysis assume that all regions are of similar size and structure.

Answers

Strategic Business Leader – Mock Exam 2 (ACCA Specimen Exam 2)

			Marks
1	(a)	Up to two marks for identifying and explaining the agency relationship of at least four parties involved in Rail Co Up a maximum of 8 marks for task requirement 1(a)	8
	(b)	One mark per relevant point for assessing the role and value of the non-executive directors on Rail Co's board The focus of the marks should be on the specific role within a public sector organisation	
		Up to a maximum of 6 in total for task requirement 1(b)	6
2	(a)	One mark for each relevant point supported by relevant calculations as appropriate Up to a maximum of 12 marks for task requirement 2(a)	12
	(b)	Up to two marks for each internal control identified and evaluated up to a maximum of six marks.	Max 6
		A further four marks for justifying, with evidence, why the CE of Rail Co should be removed.	Max 4
		Up to a maximum of 8 marks for task requirement 2(b)	8
3	(a)	Up to one mark for each relevant point which clearly evaluates each shortlisted candidate	Max 6
		Award up to two marks for a clearly justified recommendation Up to a maximum of 8 marks for task requirement 3(a)	Max 2	8
	(b)	Up to three marks per slide and notes. Up to one mark for each relevant point made relating to the impact of talent management in the change required by Rail Co. Up to a maximum of 6 marks for task requirement 3(b)	6
4	(a)	Up to one mark for each relevant point made relating to analysis in respect to the findings of the spreadsheet identifying levels of preventable fraud in Region 1, up to a maximum of six marks	Max 6
		A further two marks to be awarded for an evaluation of the impact on Rail Co's revenues	Max 2
		Up to a maximum of 8 marks for task requirement 4(a)	8
	(b)	Up to three marks for each measure recommended and clearly justified Up to a maximum of 8 marks for task requirement 4(b)	8
5	(a)	Up to one mark for each relevant point made in relation to the impact of online ticket sales on customer relationship management for Rail Co Up to a maximum of 8 marks for task requirement 5(a)	8
	(b)	Up to a maximum of 2 marks for each relevant aspect of the PID for an online ticket sales system project for Rail Co	
		Up to a maximum of 8 marks for task requirement 5(b)	8

1

Professional skills may be rewarded as in the following rubric:

How well has the candidate demonstrated professional skills as follows:	Not at all	Not so well	Quite well	Very well
1(a) – Communication skills in clarifying the agency relationships in Rail Co	The candidate has demonstrated poor communication skills. They have failed to present the required information in a clear, objective and unambiguous way. The answer is not communicated in an appropriate format (briefing paper) or tone (for review by the Rail Co Trust Board).	The candidate has demonstrated some basic communication skills in presenting an appropriate briefing paper format. Some relevant information is contained in the answer but some of the information is not relevant or unclear.	The candidate has demonstrated good communication skills in the presentation of the briefing paper to the Rail Co Trust Board. The candidate has presented most of the relevant issues and has done so concisely and, in most cases, clearly.	The candidate has demonstrated excellent communication skills. The briefing paper was correctly structured, covered all of the relevant points needed by the Trust Board in understanding the agency relationship and was set at the correct tone.
	0	0.5	1	2

BPP LEARNING MEDIA

Professional skills may be rewarded as in the following rubric:

How well has the candidate demonstrated professional skills as follows:	Not at all	Not so well	Quite well	Very well
1(b) – Evaluation skills in assessing the role and value of the non-executive directors in a public sector environment	The candidate has failed to demonstrate any evaluation of the role of the non-executive directors. The answer is merely descriptive and contains no evidence of the use of professional judgement to evaluate the non-executives' role in and value to the business.	The candidate has demonstrated some limited evaluation skills in assessing the role of non-executive directors in the business. The candidate has demonstrated limited evolution of the value of non-executive directors and there is limited focus of the public sector environment.	The candidate has demonstrated evaluation skills in assessing the role and value of the non-executive directors but the focus of the answer was not upon the public sector environment specifically.	The candidate has demonstrated sound evaluation skills in assessing the role and value of the non-executive directors and the answer is focused directly upon the public sector environment.
	0	0.5	1	2

ANSWERS

2

Professional skills may be rewarded as in the following rubric:

How well has the candidate demonstrated professional skills as follows:	Not at all	Not so well	Quite well	Very well
2(a) – Analysis skills in investigating and analysing the information presented in the spreadsheet	The candidate has demonstrated very limited analysis skills. The candidate has failed to select appropriate metrics or considered or analysed the information carefully. The candidate has demonstrated limited evaluation or reflection on any calculations presented.	The candidate has demonstrated some analysis skills in investigating and selecting appropriate calculations relating to Rail Co's customer survey results and its relative performance. However, there is only some evidence of reflection of the calculations presented.	The candidate has demonstrated analysis skills in selecting a reasonable range of relevant calculations on both the customer survey results and its relative performance. The candidate has made a reasonable attempt to comment and reflect on these calculations.	The candidate has demonstrated excellent analysis skills in presenting wide range of relevant calculations on both customer survey results of Rail Co and its relative performance. The candidate has also demonstrated sound evidence of high levels of reflection on, and consideration of, the calculations presented.
	0	0.5	1	2

Professional skills may be rewarded as in the following rubric:

How well has the candidate demonstrated professional skills as follows:	Not at all	Not so well	Quite well	Very well
2(b) – Scepticism skills in questioning the opinions and assertions made in the minutes to the board meeting	The candidate has failed to demonstrate any scepticism of the internal controls or of the opinions and assertions made by the chief executive. The candidate demonstrated no evidence of challenging or questioning the internal controls or the opinions of the CE. The candidate failed to clearly justify why the CE should be removed from his position.	The candidate has demonstrated some, but limited, scepticism of the internal controls and the opinions and assertions made by the chief executive. The candidate questioned some of the internal controls and challenged some of the assertions made by CE. However, the depth of the questioning was limited and the challenge to the CE's opinions was not presented in a professional manner.	The candidate has demonstrated scepticism of the internal controls or of the opinions and assertions made by the chief executive. The candidate recognised and challenged most of the internal controls. The challenge of the CE's opinions was reasonably sound. The challenge to the opinions of the CE could have been presented in a more professional manner.	The candidate has demonstrated deep scepticism of the internal controls or of the opinions and assertions made by the chief executive. The candidate strongly questioned, with evidence, the validity of the internal controls. The candidate challenged the opinions of the CE in a professional and justified manner.
	0	0.5	1	2

3

Professional skills may be rewarded as in the following rubric:

How well has the candidate demonstrated professional skills as follows:	Not at all	Not so well	Quite well	Very well
3(a) – Commercial acumen in evaluating the relative merits of the two candidates	The candidate has demonstrated no commercial acumen in judging the relative skills and experience presented by the two candidates. The candidate has merely restated the information presented and has showed no commercial awareness of the factors affecting the successful contribution of a new CE. No use was made of the person specification	The candidate has demonstrated some commercial acumen in judging the relative skills and experience of the two candidates. The candidate has demonstrated a limited commercial awareness of the factors impacting upon the successful contribution of a new CE. The candidate made limited reference to the person specification.	The candidate has demonstrated some sound commercial acumen in judging the relative skills and experience of the two candidates. This has been evaluated in some parts against the person specification. The candidate has demonstrated some good commercial awareness of the factors impacting on the successful contribution of the new CE.	The candidate has demonstrated excellent commercial acumen, using the person specification to form a clear judgement of the requirements of the role. The candidate has demonstrated strong awareness of the factors impacting on the successful contribution of the new CE and has made sound judgement on the choice of candidate
	0	0.5	1	2

Professional skills may be rewarded as in the following rubric:

How well has the candidate demonstrated professional skills as follows:	Not at all	Not so well	Quite well	Very well
3(b) – Communication skills in conveying relevant information in an appropriate tone to the nominations committee.	The candidate has demonstrated poor communication skills. They have failed to present the required information in a clear, objective and unambiguous way. The answer is not communicated in an appropriate format (presentation slides) or tone (for the non-executive directors of the nominations committee).	The candidate has demonstrated some basic communication skills in presenting two presentation slides. Some relevant information is contained in the answer but most of the information is not relevant or unclear and not at an appropriate tone for a non-executive director.	The candidate has demonstrated good communication skills in the presentation of the two slides to the nominations committee. The candidate has presented most of the relevant and key issues and has done so concisely and, in most cases, clearly.	The candidate has demonstrated excellent communication skills. The presentation slides and notes were correctly and effectively structured, and covered all of the key issues needed by the nominations committee to explain the contribution of talent management expected of the new CE.
	0	0.5	1	2

4

Professional skills may be rewarded as in the following rubric:

How well has the candidate demonstrated professional skills as follows:	Not at all	Not so well	Quite well	Very well
4(a) – Scepticism skills in considering the information presented in the spreadsheet and reflecting on the impact on revenues	The candidate has demonstrated no scepticism skills. They have failed to question the information contained in the spreadsheet nor has the candidate offered any evidence of any reflection on the implications of the results which were identifiable from spreadsheet information.	The candidate has demonstrated limited scepticism skills by questioning some of the information and calculations. However, there is limited evidence of the candidate's abilities in considering the information and reflecting upon the outcome of the calculations identified.	The candidate has demonstrated some sound scepticism skills in considering and questioning a number of the calculations in the information presented. The candidate has demonstrated some ability to reflect on the implications of the calculations undertaken.	The candidate has demonstrated excellent scepticism skills in effectively and accurately analysing the information presented in the spreadsheet. The candidate has also demonstrated a clear understanding of the implications of their calculations for Rail Co.
	0	0.5	1	2

Professional skills may be rewarded as in the following rubric:

How well has the candidate demonstrated professional skills as follows:	Not at all	Not so well	Quite well	Very well
4(b) – Commercial acumen in making sound recommendations for suitable measures and safeguards	The candidate has demonstrated no commercial acumen in that they have failed to demonstrate any awareness or judgement of the required safeguards and measures.	The candidate has demonstrated only limited commercial acumen in presenting only a very limited range of recommendations on appropriate safeguards and measures, some of which showed weak commercial judgement and understanding.	The candidate demonstrated some commercial acumen in that they recognised some of the measures and safeguards required, demonstrating some judgement and understanding.	The candidate demonstrated excellent commercial judgement, making recommendations for safeguards and measures which demonstrated strong commercial awareness and understanding.
	0	0.5	1	2

ANSWERS

5

Professional skills may be rewarded as in the following rubric:

How well has the candidate demonstrated professional skills as follows:	Not at all	Not so well	Quite well	Very well
5(a) – Evaluation skills in assessing the impact of online ticket sales on CRM	The candidate has demonstrated no evaluation skills. The candidate has demonstrated no professional judgement in considering the relevance of an online ticket sales system to Rail Co. The answer is largely theoretical and the candidate has demonstrated little evidence of an ability to take into consideration the impact of the decision on the stakeholders of Rail Co.	The candidate has demonstrated some evaluation skills in assessing the impact of an online ticket sales system for Rail Co. The candidate has used little professional judgement to evaluate the impact of the system on producing more timely customer information and in CRM. There is evidence of some limited evaluation of the impact of the decision on the stakeholders of Rail Co.	The candidate has demonstrated some sound evaluation skills in assessing the impact of an online ticket sales system for Rail Co. The candidate has made a reasonable attempt to evaluate the impact of the system on more timely customer data and improved CRM. The candidate has demonstrated a reasonable ability to assess the impact on the stakeholders of Rail Co.	The candidate has demonstrated excellent evaluation skills. They have clearly demonstrated excellent professional judgement in assessing the impact of the system on timely customer data and CRM. The candidate has also demonstrated a clear ability to assess the impact of the new system on the stakeholders of Rail Co.
	0	0.5	1	2

Professional skills may be rewarded as in the following rubric:

How well has the candidate demonstrated professional skills as follows:	Not at all	Not so well	Quite well	Very well
5(b) – Communication skills in producing a PID to be used by Rail Co	The candidate has demonstrated no communication skills. The document produced is not a useful PID document and could not be used to effectively communicate to the members of the Rail Co project in order to plan and implement the online ticket sales system	The candidate has demonstrated limited communication skills. The PID presented would have limited use as a communication tool for the members of the Rail Co project in order to plan and implement the online ticket sales system	The candidate has demonstrated a reasonably good level of communication skills. The PID produced has some of the required information needed to be an effective communication tool for members of the Rail Co project to plan and implement the online ticket sales system.	The candidate has demonstrated excellent communication skills. The PID produced is an excellent communication tool which could be effectively used by the members of the Rail Co project to plan and implement the online ticket sales system.
	0	0.5	1	2

ANSWERS

Suggested solutions

1   (a)   **Briefing paper**

FAO: Rail Co Trust Board

The agency relationship of the parties involved in Rail Co and their rights and responsibilities

Rail Co is what would be called a devolved government body operating within the public sector. In terms of strategic purpose, Rail Co exists to implement government policy in regard of passenger rail services. Therefore, its organisational objectives will largely be determined by the political leaders of Beeland. Ultimately it is the responsibility of the chief executive of Rail Co to report to the government of Beeland (through the Rail Co Trust Board) on Rail Co's stewardship of the public funding it receives.

The main parties involved in the agency relationship of Rail Co are the government, in the form of the Ministry for Transport of Beeland as the principal and the Rail Co Trust Board and the board of directors, comprising a mix of executive and non-executive officers, acting as the agents. As stated above, ultimately the chief executive of Rail Co is responsible to the government for Rail Co's management and stewardship of the public funding it receives. It is important to note that the way in which Rail Co is regulated and governed is focused on value for money rather than on the achievement of profits.

There is also a further agency relationship within Rail Co, in that the Rail Co board of directors is accountable to the Rail Co Trust Board. It is the responsibility of the Rail Co Trust Board to set a range of performance targets each year and to hold the Rail Co board to account for the effective and efficient use of the funds allocated by government and by the fare paying passengers.

A further aspect of the agency relationship in Rail Co is that the ultimate principal is the taxpayer and the customers, in that it is they who pay for the rail service and Rail Co exists for their benefit. It is the ultimate responsibility of the board of Rail Co to ensure that Rail Co carries out its passenger services on behalf of those who fund the activity (mainly taxpayers) and those who use and pay for the services (rail passengers). Funders (ie taxpayers) and customers are sometimes the same people (for instance, taxpayers who commute on Rail Co's trains) but sometimes they are not, and this could give rise to disagreements on how much is spent and on what particular provisions. Rail Co has a responsibility to all of its principals to deliver its services efficiently, effectively and offering good value for money. As is evidenced in the recent article in the Beeland Herald, many customers are not satisfied with the value for money offered by Rail Co.

It is the responsibility of the Rail Co Trust Board to ensure that the key outcomes of Rail Co are delivered by setting a range of performance targets, against which performance is measured periodically.

(b) **The role and value of the non-executive directors on the board of Rail Co**

Not-for-profit or public sector organisations must also be directed and controlled appropriately, as the decisions and actions of a few individuals can affect many individuals, groups and organisations which have little or no influence over them. Public sector organisations, such as Rail Co, have a duty to serve the government, but must act in a way that treats stakeholders fairly.

The non-executive directors (NEDs) are not employees of the company and are not involved in its day-to-day running. The non-executive directors usually receive a flat fee for their services, and are engaged under a contract for service.

The role of NEDs is to provide a balancing influence on the board of directors and help to minimise conflicts of interest. The Higgs Report, published in 2003, summarised their role as:

- To contribute to the strategic plan

- To scrutinise the performance of the executive directors

- To provide an external perspective on risk management

- To deal with people issues, such as the future shape of the board and resolution of conflicts

Importantly, the NEDs should have high ethical standards and act with integrity and probity. Their main role is to support the executive directors of Rail Co and monitor its conduct, demonstrating a willingness to listen, question, debate and challenge.

It is recognised as best practice that a company should have more non-executive directors than executive directors. This is the case for Rail Co, as can be seen from its structure highlighted on the Rail Co website. The NEDs of Rail Co are responsible for running the four board committees which are set up to monitor the performance of Rail Co in key areas such as health and safety and audit and risk management The NEDs are also responsible for setting and reviewing the directors' remuneration and evaluating the corporate governance structure and activities of Rail Co and ensuring that the board is adequately governed, structured and staffed. This is particularly relevant and important to a public sector company such as Rail Co, where transparency and public scrutiny are prevalent.

The Chair of Rail Co is also a non-executive director and plays a key role in the business. The Chair has the ultimate role of leading the board, whilst the chief executive leads the business. Therefore, the roles of Chair and chief executive are complementary and interlinked.

The NEDs of Rail Co can add value to the business by:

- Broadening the horizons and experience of existing executive directors, particularly if they come from a wide range of both public and private sector organisations

- Facilitating the cross-fertilisation of ideas, particularly in terms of business strategy and planning

- Playing a vital part to play in appraising and commenting on Rail Co's achievement of value for money and advising on strategies to improve this

A team of executive and non-executive directors needs to be made up of people with business acumen and hands-on experience. Non-executive directors should be able to fill the gaps in expertise not available in the executive team and provide independent and objective scrutiny to the direction of such organisations in the public interest.

2   (a)   **To:**   The Rail Co Trust Board

            From: Audit analyst, National Audit Authority

            Date: XX/XX/XXXX

A report on the customer satisfaction performance of Rail Co and the relative performance of Rail Co with its competitors over the last three years

An evaluation of the customer satisfaction survey results

	Percentage satisfied			Actual % change 2015 to 2016	Trust Board target for 2016 Target growth on 2015	Trust Board target achieved?
	2016	2015	2014			
Overall satisfaction with your journey	87	90	92	−3%	+3%	No
Satisfaction with ticket buying facilities	60	64	65	−4%	+2%	No
Availability of staff	62	65	70	−3%	+5%	No
Helpfulness/attitude of staff	75	73	77	+2%	+2%	Yes
Reliability of service	84	81	86	+3%	+5%	No
Value for money for price of the ticket	50	56	57	−6%	+2%	No

In analysing the results of the customer satisfaction survey, as indicated in the key performance measures highlighted in Appendix 3, these clearly show that overall customer satisfaction of Rail Co's services has declined in 2016. Overall satisfaction has decreased by 3% on 2015 results, and, notably, this is significantly below the target of a 3% increase for the year, as set by the Rail Co Trust Board. This is a key indicator for Rail Co as it demonstrates whether the services provided are effective in the eyes of its customers. Although 87% is still high, it does reflect a growing dissatisfaction from the point of view of the customers as a continued trend. This needs to be reversed.

Customers are also clearly not happy with the ticket purchasing facilities offered at the train stations, with a 4% decrease in satisfaction from 2015. Again, the Rail Co Trust Board target of a 2% increase on 2015 has not been met. One customer feedback comment highlights customer frustration with the lack of online facilities, 'This is very frustrating and often, I use my car instead of going by train as it is more convenient than queuing to buy a train ticket.' Other national rail operators do offer online ticket buying facilities and it would appear that its absence in Rail Co is a cause for concern, as customers are becoming increasingly unhappy with having to queue for tickets at stations.

The measure of staff helpfulness and attitude is the only performance target met by Rail Co in 2016. This is positive, as it indicates staff commitment and attitude and could be an indicator of successful staff management policies at Rail Co. The availability of staff has declined by 2% and thus clearly not achieved the target set by the Rail Co Trust Board, indicating a possible problem with adequacy of staffing levels or levels of absenteeism.

The customers' perception of the reliability of service has improved from 2015 by 3%, which is a positive outcome. This could be due to increased investment in new trains. However, if this is considered in conjunction with the results of the competitor analysis, it is evident that in fact, the punctuality of Rail Co's services is in fact decreasing year on year. These measures appear to be at odds, but it must be noted that the customers' perception of reliability could include other factors, other than trains being on time to their destination. For example, reliability could include reliability of staff on the trains or reliability of trains stopping at the correct stations.

One of the most important measures is customers' perception of value for money of the price they pay for a ticket. This has decreased significantly compared with 2015 by 6%. This is a significant negative change in customer perception and one which cannot be ignored. As stated by a customer in the annual survey, 'The price of the regular ticket I buy to commute to work has increased by nearly 10% since last year. I really can't understand why, as I do not seem to be getting more for my money.' This is important to the government because if customers do not believe that they are getting value for money and if ticket prices continue to rise, then Rail Co are in danger of losing more customers.

The above findings should also be considered in conjunction with the results of the competitor performance analysis, as discussed below.

Competitor performance analysis

	ANR			Rail Co			Ceeland Rail		
	2016	2015	2014	2016	2015	2014	2016	2015	2014
Revenue growth	4.9%	5.5%	–	2.5%	3%	–	8%	5%	–
Operating profit %	31.54%	25.5%	19.8%	25.9%	31.39%	34.3%	35.4%	31.5%	27%
Cost per km (B$)	3.40	3.50	3.60	3.90	3.63	3.40	2.62	2.8	3
Cost per employee (B$)	92,004	95,706	100,041	110,654	100,883	93,221	83,363	85,774	88,141
Ticket price increase p.a	4.9%	0.0%	–	8.3%	7.1%	–	–4.7%	–2.3%	–
Customer satisfactio improvement p.a	+2%	–3%	–	–3%	–2%	–	+3%	0%	–
Injuries per staff member	1.1%	1.1%	1.1%	1.8%	1.7%	1.7%	0.4%	0.4%	0.5%

Focusing on the key findings of this analysis, it is noticeable that revenue growth is much lower for Rail Co than its two competitors. In 2016, revenue growth for both competitors was much higher than that of Rail Co. Indeed, Ceeland Rail achieved an 8% revenue increase despite a 4.7% decrease in average ticket prices, indicating that more passengers were using the network and that there may be some price elasticity of demand. Conversely, Rail Co's revenue increased by only 2.5% with an average increase in ticket price of 8.3%, indicating a significant fall in fare paying passengers on trains in 2016, but the article in the Herald newspaper indicates that there may be a 10% increase in total passengers being carried on the service making the service increasingly overcrowded and uncomfortable. Significantly, Rail Co also failed to achieve the revenue growth target set by the Rail Co Trust Board for 2016 of 5%.

All three companies have achieved a healthy operating profit margin, but again, Rail Co is not performing as well as its competitors. Both Ceeland Rail and ANR have achieved a significant improvement since 2014 in operating profit margin, indicating an improvement in its cost control. However, Rail Co's operating profit margin has decreased by 8.4% in the same period. This should be of significant concern to the board of Rail Co as it indicates a weakness in cost control.

This point is further highlighted by considering the cost per kilometre travelled per company. Rail Co has the highest cost per kilometre, which has also risen each year since 2014. Ceeland Rail's cost per kilometre is significantly less than Rail Co and has been stable over the same period, indicating sound cost management systems. Ceeland is clearly a larger organisation than Rail Co and therefore may benefit from economies of scale, which must be taken into account, but nevertheless, both ANR and Ceeland Rail appear to be managing their costs much more efficiently than Rail Co.

Rail Co also underperforms both of its competitors in terms of trains on time and once again, it has failed to meet the target for improvement set by the Rail Co Trust Board for 2016 (a decrease of 2% on 2015 compared to a target of +3%). Obviously, it is difficult to judge this measure without further information on distances travelled per train and train type, but it does give us an indicator of how customers are likely to perceive each company. This is indeed verified by the customer satisfaction surveys for each company, which clearly shows that the customers of the two competitors are currently far more satisfied with the services they offer. Ceeland Rail is outperforming both rivals in these two key measures.

Another important measure to consider is staff turnover, as this can be a key indicator of staff satisfaction and overall well-being of staff in the company. It is clear from the analysis that staff turnover in Beeland is high compared to the other two companies. Indeed, in 2016 it was double that of Ceeland Rail. Obviously, it is difficult to make a detailed judgement without having further information relating to staff make-up in terms of full-time and part-time staff and age and length of service. However, this measure should be a clear indicator to Beeland's management that this could be symptomatic of a high level of staff dissatisfaction compared to the competitors and the reasons must be investigated and addressed if possible. If staff are poorly trained or poorly paid, or working in an unsafe environment, then this could lead to poor motivation, which will have an overall impact on customer satisfaction and staff effectiveness. Also, staff turnover will add significant costs to Rail Co's operations.

Although this review has only considered a limited number of performance indicators, it is clear that Beeland Rail is not performing as well as its competitors and that there are a number of areas which the board must address immediately.

(b)   **The Rail Co Trust Board**

Beeland

XX/XX/XXXX

Dear Chair

The following is our report on the effectiveness of internal controls of Rail Co based on the evidence I have been able to collect and analyse.

Having thoroughly reviewed the Rail Co performance data, the recent board meeting minutes of Rail Co and the transport report in the Beeland Herald, a number of internal control weaknesses can be highlighted.

First, there appears to be a serious weakness in the control of passengers accessing trains without tickets. This is referred to in the Beeland Herald transport report, where it is mentioned that this issue had already been raised in the last two annual reports. This creates a significant business risk which does not seem to have been acted upon or mitigated by the Rail Co board. It has been highlighted for over two years that Rail Co believes that significant numbers of passengers are travelling on Rail Co's network without tickets. A key internal control weakness would appear to be that approximately 40% of Rail Co's stations do not operate ticket barriers, allowing the potential for customer ticket fraud. This potentially will have seriously damaging consequences on the performance of Rail Co in that revenues are not being optimised.

Second, there appears to be a weakness in staff management and safety procedures, in that there has been an increase in the number of injuries to staff reported by Rail Co in the last year. This is evidenced in the recent performance information analysed by one of my colleagues in Exhibit 3. Although Kim Lun has assured the BHSO that a thorough investigation would be undertaken immediately, it indicates that Rail Co has potential weaknesses in safety procedures and also in staff training procedures. The performance statistics indicate that Rail Co has lower levels of training than its competitors and Kim Lun (non-executive director) has noted that there had been a lack of investment in the training of staff in the last three years, which is also a key internal control weakness and one which could seriously impede the performance of Rail Co. Staff who are not appropriately trained are more likely to have accidents and to make mistakes. Again, this will have serious repercussions on the overall performance of Rail Co and could have seriously damaging impact upon reputation if serious injuries occur.

A further internal control weakness could be seen as the lack of investment in online booking systems. Several other national train operators offer online booking facilities and evidence suggested that this had positively impacted upon revenue growth and customer satisfaction in all of these businesses (Appendix 3). Lack of focus upon IT investment and development in key strategic information systems could be seen as an internal control weakness and could hamper the long-term performance of Rail Co.

A further internal control weakness could be the current pay structure. Poorly paid staff who are dissatisfied will leave or may take strike action. HR policies on fair pay could be considered to be weak if they are not commensurate with the expected pay rate.

Throughout the board meeting, there is evidence of the chief executive's inability to react to these key internal weaknesses effectively and it would seem that in some cases, this reluctance and inactivity could have seriously damaging consequences for Rail Co. In a number of cases, there is evidence of a failure to achieve his fiduciary duty to the trustee of Rail Co.

First, his comments in relation to Rail Co's performance are inaccurate and reflect his own opinion, based on historic performance and not the actual performance in 2016. Clearly, some narrow aspects of performance have improved, but it is not in line with competitors and customer expectations in the current climate. His comment that the target for punctuality set by the Trust Board was unachievable and not relevant is highly inappropriate and shows a breach of his fiduciary duty to the trustees. It is his role as chief executive to ensure that these targets are achievable and they cannot simply be ignored. Also, his statement that customers do not understand value for money demonstrates his lack of understanding of the customers' perception of this critical measure. It is wrong for him to make such a sweeping and unjust statement and could seriously damage the reputation of Rail Co if these views were made public.

His response to the investment in ticket barriers is unfounded and demonstrates a lack of understanding of a key internal control weakness in relation to the potential level of fraud in Rail Co. He had made a significant judgement founded upon no evidence of costs outweighing the benefits and his assessment that most fraud being unpreventable is ill-judged and incorrect. Again, his lack of understanding of such an important issue is a failure of his fiduciary duty.

His comment that there is no evidence to suggest that staff morale is low is incorrect, as staff turnover is increasing, strongly indicating low morale. He pointed to evidence in the customer survey report which indicated an annual growth in customer satisfaction levels in relation to staff helpfulness and attitude but this is not linked to staff training in any way. His logic is flawed and his attitude towards staff and adequate training could be seriously damaging to Rail Co.

The CE also commented that online ticket facilities went against the traditional values of customer service focus of Rail Co. His reluctance to invest in such technology could prove to be seriously damaging to Rail Co's performance. It is clear that customers are not happy with ticket buying facilities and should this continue more will use other means of transport. To delay this decision could be damaging to Rail Co, should customers continue to choose other forms of transport to commute.

The chief executive's attitude towards the unions could be severely damaging to Rail Co, should the unions decide to take strike action. The CE commented that the unions were merely taking advantage of the latest survey results to put the board under pressure to increase levels of pay for its members. Although Rail Co must negotiate with the unions, to take an aggressive stance could be counter-productive. His comment relating to the media as an unimportant stakeholder is incorrect as adverse media reports about Rail Co are a potential reputational risk to the organisation.

In conclusion, my overall opinion is that the comments made by the chief executive demonstrate a number of serious failures and weaknesses in his fiduciary duty to the principals and trustees of Rail Co. I have grave concerns regarding his awareness of the current situation facing Rail Co and his abilities to respond effectively to the changes which will be required in the coming months.

Yours sincerely

Assistant auditor, NAA

3   (a)   **To:**   Chair of the Nominations Committee

From: Chair of sub-committee

Date: XX/XX/2016

Subject: A review of the candidates for chief executive of Rail Co

Introduction

The outline person specification sets out some very clear criteria for the role of CE in Rail Co, specifically the requirement for demonstration of experience at CE level in a similar organisation. Obviously an understanding of the rail industry is also an important factor to consider. Also, in a high profile public sector environment, an ability to operate successfully in a complex political environment and to manage the complex relationships with multiple stakeholders will be a key factor. Importantly, in this role of CE in Rail Co, it is clear that many changes need to be made in the near future to address its current failures and to achieve the targets and expectations of its key stakeholders and therefore the new CE should have the skills and abilities to manage and lead a dynamic change programme at Rail Co.

Candidate A

Candidate A clearly has a significant amount of experience as a CE, having worked at this level since 2000. As a CE of a multinational oil company, he will have significant experience of managing a highly complex business environment and multiple stakeholder influences, including government. Additionally, his recent CE experience is within the rail industry working for JPS Express in Jayland. Notably, he led the privatisation of JPS trains in 2013, therefore he has experience of working in the public sector environment prior to 2013. He has clear experience of working with the government and regulatory authorities, which will be a key skill in Rail Co in managing the relationship with the Trust Board and the Minister of Transport. His ability to build and maintain relationships with external bodies, staff and the media would appear to be a highly positive capability and one which is highly desirable in the current operating climate of Rail Co.

Notably, Candidate A demonstrates key skills in change leadership and human performance management. It is clear that a change programme will need to be carried out by the new CE in a number of key areas, including the improvement in the performance of human resources and key strategic project investments. Candidate A has a proven track record in change leadership and in managing complex projects and these will be key attributes. In addition, his focus upon strong internal control is a key competence required at this present time.

Candidate B

Candidate B also has a number of very positive attributes. Currently, he is not working within the rail industry, but does work for a very large aviation company which will clearly require many key leadership skills. Although he has not worked as a CE for quite as long as Candidate A, notably he has worked in the rail industry previously as a finance director for Ceeland Rail. Therefore he will have an excellent knowledge of the financial management requirements of Rail Co. His obvious skills and experience in financial management would be a hugely positive influence for Rail Co. His focus on KPIs and developing strategies for revenue growth and operational efficiency would be hugely positive for Rail Co. However, his experiences focus largely upon financial management which, although critically important to Rail Co, may be rather too narrow and not sufficiently focused upon the change leadership requirements of Rail Co. There is also limited evidence of managing stakeholder relationships in a complex environment such as Rail Co, particular the relationship with government and regulatory bodies. Also, there is little evidence of his abilities to lead change.

Recommendation

Both candidates have a wide range of skills and experience and both would bring very positive attributes to Rail Co. Overall, taking into consideration the current requirements of Rail Co and the likely changes which will need to be undertaken by the newly appointed CE in the near future, then my recommendation would be to appoint Candidate A. He has all of the relevant public sector experience, together with his experience of managing complex stakeholder relationships and his change leadership experience.

(b)   **Slide 1**

Talent

- Individuals who can make a difference to organisational performance through their immediate contribution or, in the longer term, by demonstrating high future potential.

Talent management

- The attraction, identification, development, engagement, retention and deployment of individuals who are of particular value to an organisation.

- It is critical for Rail Co to develop, manage and retain individuals as part of a planned talent management strategy.

Notes. The definition of talent emphasises that these are individuals who can make an impact on the performance of Rail Co. This is of utmost importance in the near future as Rail Co attempts to turn around its business performance.

Importantly, talent management should be seen as a key strategic management activity which sits alongside and indeed underpins the whole corporate strategy.

Many organisations consider the 'talents' of all their staff and work on ways to develop their strengths. Talent management programmes may include a range of activities such as formal and informal leadership coaching, networking events and board-level and client exposure. It can also include ensuring that all staff are adequately and effectively trained and motivated at all levels of the business.

Slide 2

The contribution of the chief executive in talent management

- Important that talent management strategy is led from the top

- Senior management team must assess the human talent needs of the change programme

- Driving force in attracting talent and building a high performance workplace

Notes. Ensuring that the talent management strategy is closely aligned with the corporate strategy must be a priority. The CE must lead the senior management team in understanding the main priorities of the change programme in Rail Co which should then be used to develop a human talent forecast, which can help shape Rail Co's talent management strategy.

Visible senior-level support for talent management is critical, and this is best done by the CE.

The ability to attract external talent depends upon how potential applicants view Rail Co. The creation of an attractive employer brand is an important factor in recruiting

BPP LEARNING MEDIA

external talent. Again, the CE will be a driving force in this, as the figure head and mouthpiece of the organisation he will be integral in creating the employer brand which will attract talent to Rail Co.

4   (a)   **To:**   Chair of the audit and risk Committee

From: Internal Auditor

Date: XX/XX/XXXX

Subject: Analysis of potential fraud in the Beeland network

Introduction

This report analyses the information on the ticket sales and rail usage by stations within the Beeland rail network and evaluate the potential for passenger fraud and its impact on the revenue of the Rail Co.

The analysis is based on the information in spreadsheet that was produced by the financial controller reproduced below.

Initial data on stations in Region 1 – Beeland network

Analysis of fraud – information based on 2016 analysis

Town	Ticket barrier	Population per town	Monthly tickets sold to town	Estimated % railway users per town	Estimated monthly ticket sales per town	Variance between tickets sold v projected ticket sales	Spend per ticket sold	Estimated fraud ($) per month	Fraud % for each town (based on total population)	Estimated fraud due to poor internal control (%) (based on total population)	Preventa annuc fraud ((based total populati
A	y	142,000	28,000	21	29,820	1,820	59	107,380	1.28%		
B	y	195,000	31,000	17	33,150	2,150	38	81,700	1.10%		
C	n	110,000	22,000	28	30,800	8,800	44	387,200	8.00%	6.72%	3,903,
D	n	195,000	36,000	26	50,700	14,700	51	749,700	7.54%	6.26%	7,470,
E	y	74,000	25,000	35	25,900	900	56	50,400	1.22%		
F	y	116,000	31,000	28	32,480	1,480	52	76,960	1.28%		
G	n	183,000	37,000	30	54,900	17,900	56	1,002,400	9.78%	8.50%	10,456
H	y	87,000	19,000	23	20,010	1,010	61	61,610	1.16%		
I	n	144,000	12,000	16	23,040	11,040	48	529,920	7.67%	6.39%	5,298,
J	y	147,000	27,000	20	29,400	2,400	62	148,800	1.63%		
		1,393,000	268,000					3,196,070			

Assumed average percentage of unpreventable fraud – Region 1   1.28%

Total annual preventable fraud in Region 1: $27,130,:
Extrapolate for 20 regions $542,606,:

Note. There are 20 identifiable regions within the Beeland passenger service network. For this analysis assume that all regions are of similar size and structure.

The spreadsheet prepared by the financial controller has identified the estimated fraud per month in Region 1, based upon the variance between actual tickets sold and estimated tickets sold per town (based on estimated percentage of railway users per town). This is then estimated as a percentage based on the total population of each town. It is notable that for each railway station which has a ticket barrier that the level of fraud is markedly lower than those stations without ticket barriers (stations C, D, G and I). Therefore, it can be assumed that ticket barriers are clearly having a direct impact on preventing fraud. The estimated railway users in the towns need further investigation. How was this calculated? Was this based on surveys or on demographic factors or both? This would have to be examined further.

The spreadsheet also calculates the percentage of unpreventable fraud at 1.28%, based upon an average of those stations which have ticket barriers (stations A, B, E, F, H, J). This presumes that there is an element of fraud occurring on Rail Co's network which cannot be prevented with the installation of ticket barriers. There will always be some degree of fraud occurring which is almost impossible to control. Again there is an assumption about preventable versus unpreventable fraud. Further information may be required to understand how this estimate was arrived at and whether this is the same at all stations and regions.

Therefore the spreadsheet takes this into account when calculating the percentage of fraud due to poor internal control (preventable fraud) at those stations without ticket barriers.

If we then use this information to calculate the total preventable fraud based upon the total population in each town, then it can be calculated that total annual preventable fraud is estimated to be nearly $B27 million in Region 1 alone. If we were to extrapolate this across 20 regions, it gives an estimated annual fraud of $B542 million. The assumption that this region is perfectly representative of other regions allowing such an extrapolation is a tenuous one. It is unlikely that the profile of towns, their demographics, and the proportion of rail users or preventable versus unpreventable fraud levels will be the same across regions. However, if these assumptions can reasonably be made, this is a significant amount and if we were to take this as a percentage of total revenue in 2016 it amounts to 12% of annual revenue. This is a staggeringly high figure and clearly a significant control problem for Rail Co. Even if the level of preventable fraud was assumed to be 50% of the calculated figure above (say $B270 million), this level of fraud is still unacceptable.

(b)   The first measure which Rail Co should consider is the installation of ticket barriers at those stations with a high level of preventable fraud and which currently do not have ticket barriers. Clearly, ticket barriers are a huge deterrent to fraud, as evidence by the levels encountered at stations with barriers on the network in Region 1. Obviously, Rail Co would need to undertake a thorough cost benefit analysis on such a project but from the estimated level of preventable fraud calculated above, then it is likely that such an investment would have significant benefits for Rail Co.

A further measure would be to expand ticket offices and employ more staff at ticket offices to reduce queuing time for customers. Clearly, customers are likely to become frustrated by having to queue for tickets, particularly if they may miss their train. Expansion of ticket booths or the installation of ticket machines would provide customers with more opportunity to buy a ticket.

Another measure would be to offer customers the ability to purchase tickets whilst on the trains. This is likely to mean employing more ticket inspectors on each train. Obviously, this is likely to be costly, but Rail Co could manage this by only employing more staff on peak time trains.

Rail Co should also consider the prices it charges to customers. Some customers may be motivated to travel without a ticket due to its unaffordability. In this case, these customers will inevitably take the opportunity to travel without tickets if they can do so. This could include younger customers, such as students, for example, who cannot afford a regular high-priced ticket. Rail Co should review its pricing policies and structure and consider offering a more affordable range of ticket prices to meet the needs of is customer groups, such as student concessions, off-peak travellers and frequent user discounts and passes.

Rail Co could also consider the introduction of an online train ticket booking facility. It would seem that Rail Co is indeed behind its competitors in this development and should be a serious consideration for Rail Co. Online ticket purchasing is likely to be a hugely convenient ticket buying option for its customers and is likely to encourage more customers to buy tickets in the comfort of their own home or office. Obviously, this will be a significant investment for Rail Co and a major project undertaking, but it would likely be a significant influence in reducing fraud.

Clearly, Rail Co cannot control all customer fraud and it will always encounter dishonest travellers. However, it is important to implement measures which safeguard against lost revenue which is not done with dishonest intentions.

ANSWERS

5   (a)   **Business case for the investment in an online ticket sales system for Rail Co**

Introduction

The following business case sets out how investment in online ticket sales could assist Rail Co in producing more timely customer data and assist in customer relationship management.

Current situation

Presently, Rail Co does not operate an online ticket sales facility for its customers. All tickets are purchased at ticket offices located at each station. Recent evidence suggests that as a result of inadequate ticket buying facilities at the stations combined with a lack of ticket barriers, there is a high level of fraud occurring in the network. Some of this fraud could be eliminated with the introduction of improved ticket buying facilities such as an online booking facility.

In addition, customers are used to being able to buy products and services online and as a modern organisation Rail Co should be considering offering customers such a facility. It has become an expectation of digital life that customers are provided with the flexibility to buy products and services from the comfort of their own home. Research also suggests that other national passenger rail service providers offer customers such a facility. Therefore, not to offer such facilities may be detrimental to Rail Co's competitive position.

Analysis of the benefits of an online ticket sales facility

The purpose of CRM is the building of relationships in order to affect customer acquisition, retention and loyalty, resulting in the development of 1:1 relationships with these customers. This 'customer focused' approach, which will involve building a strong relationship with Rail Co's customers as well as gathering, storing and sharing information about these customers across the organisation, will likely improve customer loyalty.

Electronic CRM, in the form of an online ticket sales system, would make it possible for Rail Co to have as much contact as possible with its customers through the internet. This internet support for Rail Co's customers would likely take the form of presales information, such as timetabling information, ticket purchasing services and after-sales support, such as online refunds or customer account queries. The internet would make it possible for Rail Co to have frequent contact with its customers, and so enable us to operate and maintain a detailed customer database, assisting us even further in developing better customer relationships. A further value of the internet for Rail Co could be seen in the quicker flow of information (real time sales data) and more consistent communications which can result from its use.

The effective use of CRM systems could assist in Rail Co's relationship-building activities while also contributing to the profitability of the business. Some of the goals which we should set would include retaining our existing passengers, improving customer satisfaction with the services we offer and increasing customer loyalty. Customers who receive excellent services remain loyal and a further advantage is that they provide free advertising by talking about the organisation's services.

Operational CRM includes customer-facing applications such as sales force automation, enterprise marketing automation and customer service and support. Rail Co may consider the implementation of a customer call centre, which is also a component of operational CRM. In this way, all interactions with the customer could be recorded, enabling Rail Co to gather even more data on the customer and thus track the customer.

Analytical CRM could also be used to analyse the data which has been created through operational CRM, to build a picture of the customer. Analytical CRM includes the capturing, storage, extraction, processing, interpretation and reporting of customer data stored in data warehouses. This will enable us to examine customer behavioural patterns in order to develop marketing and promotional strategies which can be tailored to specific customer groups, such as students, the elderly, daily commuters or leisure travellers.

Risk assessment

A detailed cost analysis must be undertaken to assess the financial viability of an investment in an online ticket sales system for Rail Co. Further risks should also be considered including the customer perception of such a system and also a stakeholder mapping exercise will need to be undertaken. The main risk is that customers will not use the system, either due to a reluctance to change purchasing habits or due to a lack of awareness of the facility. These risks can be overcome through adequate customer awareness strategies such as in-station advertising and national and regional TV and radio advertising.

(b) **Outline project initiation document**

Project objectives	To implement an online ticket sales system in Rail Co to enable customers to purchase tickets online as well as through ticket sales offices at train stations. The overall objective of the project is to increase customer satisfaction levels.
Anticipated benefits	• A reduction in numbers of passengers travelling without tickets • Improved revenues and profitability • Increased levels of customer satisfaction and loyalty • Up to the minute customer data for marketing purposes • Reduced marketing costs due to online advertising • Tailored marketing approach meaning a more targeted focus on customers' needs
Scope	An extension of the current website to include web-based ticket booking technology and customer contact facilities. A customer database to capture customer information and booking history which can be utilised for customer relationship management and marketing purposes.
Deliverables/Outcomes	A fully operational customer ticket sales site as part of the current Rail Co website within 12 months.
Constraints	Funding – to be considered as part of an overall cost benefit analysis to be completed. Resources – the project will need to be undertaken by an external systems development provider. A tender process will need to be carried out immediately. Time – the project should be completed and the booking system fully operational with 12 months of the project start date (to be confirmed).

ANSWERS

Key stakeholders	• Customers/fare paying passengers • Station and train staff of Rail Co • The board of directors • Rail Co Trust Board • The government of Beeland
Project team roles	Project manager (Rail Co projects and infrastructure staff) Development team (systems development supplier staff) Rail Co director of projects and infrastructure One NED
Risk assessment	Cost overruns Delays to project deadline Lack of customer usage or satisfaction with the system Systems security breaches
Cost estimates	To be undertaken
Performance measures	• Number of tickets sold online • Number of repeat purchase online • Reduction in levels of fraud • Number of customer accounts set up online • Impact on revenue growth

Mock Exam 2 (Specimen Exam 2)

Tutorial notes to help you improve your exam success skills performance

Skill	Examples
Case scenario: Managing information	As we have said before, it is important that you carefully read the case information as this will provide you with a clear indication as to how to use the Exhibits when answering specific task requirements.
	As the focus of Task 1 related to Rail Co's corporate governance arrangements, it was important that you made use of the information presented in Exhibit 1.
	To produce a good answer to Task 2 (a) it was essential that you made use of Exhibit 3, as this contained the passenger survey results and performance analysis for Rail Co and its competitors. Here it was also acceptable to draw upon some of the key points raised in Exhibit 2, as this contained the transport report published by the Beeland Herald.
	In respect of Task 2 (b) it was crucial that you made use of the Exhibits specified. In the preamble before the task requirement you were directed to Exhibits 2 and 4. Exhibit 4 contained the Rail Co board meeting minutes. Failure to make use of these exhibits would have made it impossible to attempt the task requirement as here you were asked to review the effectiveness of the internal controls at Rail Co.
	Task 3 which focused on the suitability of the two candidates for the role of the chief executive at Rail Co required the use of Exhibit 5, which outlined the personal specifications and summary CVs of the applicants.
	The spreadsheet in Exhibit 6 detailed the estimated levels of fraud occurring across the Rail Co network. This exhibit needed to be used when attempting Task 4. Part (a) asked for an analysis of Exhibit 6 and part (b) built upon this and required recommendations to help reduce the levels of fraud currently being experienced.
	Task 5 did not specify the use of a particular Exhibit.
Correct Interpretation of requirements	When reviewing the task requirements, it is important that you identify all of the actions that you are expected to undertake.
	For example, in respect of Task 4 (b) you were required to provide recommendations of suitable measures or safeguards which could implemented by Rail Co to reduce the levels of fraud. Although, you were required to provide recommendations, it was important that you picked up on the request to provide justification to the measures you suggested. Simply listing a number of recommendations without consideration as to how they would help Rail Co would severely limit the quality of your answer and the number of marks that you could earn.
Answer planning: Priorities, structure and logic	Task 5 (b) required the production of a project initiation document (PID) that could be used by Rail Co to assist with the implementation of an online sales system. This required you to draw upon your knowledge of project management and, in particular, the key features of a PID. A good approach to planning your answer here would have been to think about the key elements involved in most types of project, eg the need for objectives, an understanding of the risks etc, and to then use these elements by considering them in relation to the introduction of the online sales system at Rail Co.

Skill	Examples
Efficient numerical analysis	Task 2 (a) required an evaluation of the implications of the findings of the passenger survey results and a review of the actual and relative performance of Rail Co over the last three years. The information provided in Exhibit 3 should have made it possible to calculate key movements in respect of the financials relating to the performance of Rail Co and its competitors. It was important to note that there was one mark available for every relevant point made that was supported by relevant calculations. The trick to producing a meaningful analysis when provided with data such as that in Exhibit 3, is to avoid the temptation to simply repeat the figures provided with no further attempt at understanding what the data is showing.
Effective writing and presentation	To perform well in the Strategic Business Leader exam it is of critical importance that you respond to the task requirements in the format requested. Failure to do so will limit the number of marks that can be earned. In Task 3, parts (a) and (b) both required different formats to be used. Part (a) asked for a report, whereas (b) required two presentation slides with accompanying notes. In respect of part (a) it was important to make use of the To/From/Subject headings, and to break up the body of your answer using sub-headings. These are common features of business reports. In part (b), it was crucial that you prepared only two slides and accompanying notes. With the slides, it is perfectly acceptable to include headings and short bulleted lines of text as the points raised should be expanded upon in the notes.
Good time management	You had 4 hours (240 minutes) to tackle all of the task requirements worth 100 marks. Throughout the earlier sections in this Practice and Revision Kit we have worked on the basis of 2 minutes per mark. This was used to reflect the fact that many of the questions attempted up until this point have featured considerably smaller exam scenarios using limited exhibit information. When attempting the Strategic Business Leader exam, ACCA recommend that candidates spend at least 40 minutes reading, planning and interpreting the exhibit information and the task requirements. When taking the 40 minutes reading time into account, candidates should spend approximately 2.5 minutes attempting each mark. The 2.5 minutes per mark is based on the fact that the total exam is 240 minutes (4 hours) in duration which, when the 40 minutes reading/planning time is deducted, gives 200 minutes. As candidates can earn the 20 professional skills marks by the virtue of attempting the 80 technical marks in the exam, the remaining 200 minutes can be divided by the 80 technical marks to give 2.5 minutes per mark. On the basis of 2.5 minutes per mark, the time available for attempting each task requirement was as follows: Task 1 (a) = 8 technical marks: 20 minutes Task 1 (b) = 6 technical marks: 15 minutes Task 2 (a) = 12 technical marks: 30 minutes Task 2 (b) = 8 technical marks; 20 minutes Task 3 (a) = 8 technical marks: 20 minutes Task 3 (b) = 6 technical marks: 15 minutes Task 4 (a) =8 technical marks: 20 minutes Task 4 (b) = 8 technical marks: 20 minutes Task 5 (a) = 8 technical marks: 20 minutes Task 5 (b) = 8 technical marks: 20 minutes

Diagnostic

Did you apply these skills when reading, planning, and writing up your answer? Identify the exam success skills where you think you need to improve and capture your thoughts here of what you want to achieve when attempting questions in future.

ACCA

Strategic Business Leader

Mock Exam 3
(March 2020)

Questions	
Time allowed	**4 hours**
This question paper is an integrated case study with one section containing a total of 100 marks and ALL Tasks must be completed.	
All Tasks contain Professional Skills marks which are included in the marks shown above.	

DO NOT OPEN THIS EXAM UNTIL YOU ARE READY TO START UNDER EXAMINATION CONDITIONS

Strategic Business Leader – Mock Exam 3 – March 2020

Overview

Techthere4U Co (TT4U) is a firm of information technology consultants founded 20 years ago. Initially offering advice on computer efficiency and security, the company has expanded to offer a range of services, including technology support and data hosting. It currently employs 75 staff members which have grown from six since its establishment.

TT4U has based its success in the past on its good knowledge of clients' businesses and its ability to match the solutions it provides with business requirements. TT4U has had a diverse client base, operating in a wide variety of industry sectors.

The four consultants who initially founded the company remain on the board in key executive roles. The board is constituted as follows:

Board role	Comments
Chairman and non-executive director	Appointed two years ago, partner in a large law firm
Chief executive officer (CEO)	Original founder
Services director (SD)	Original founder, leads TT4U's team for smaller businesses
Marketing director (MD)	Original founder, leads TT4U's team for larger businesses
Information technology director (ITD)	Original founder, leads TT4U's public sector team
Finance director (FD)	Appointed four years ago
Non-executive director	Appointed two years ago, former partner of a large accountancy firm

Below board level, operational staff are allocated to one of the three teams serving particular types of client. Teams are led by the relevant founder-director for that team.

Two years ago, the company achieved a listing on its national stock exchange for smaller companies. TT4U is compliant with the corporate governance code enforced by this stock exchange. The founder-directors continue to own a majority of shares, but the company now also has external shareholders. Some of these external shareholders have indicated that they would like to see the company achieve a full listing on the main national stock exchange within three years.

TT4U's CEO believes that TT4U needs to undergo an internal transformation in order to be able to retain current clients and deliver the expansion required to obtain a full listing. She believes that the company's current structures are now insufficient to respond quickly enough to changes in the external environment and meet clients' evolving demands.

TT4U's board has decided to engage an external consultancy firm, Stubfield, to help in evaluating various strategic options and advising on decisions. You are the leader of the team from Stubfield, responsible for producing sections of a report and various other documents.

The following exhibits provide information relevant to the case study.

Exhibit 1: Transcript of directors' meeting about issues to be discussed with Stubfield consultants.

Exhibit 2: Summary of Mieobed client approach devised by *Business Tomorrow* magazine.

Exhibit 3: Blog on IT consultancy sector on *Business Tomorrow* magazine website.

Exhibit 4: Extract of results of client survey.

Exhibit 5: Discussion of threatening letter about TT4U's largest client, Rex Investments.

Exhibit 6: Appraisal of cloud services investment prepared by the recently appointed assistant to the finance director

The case requirements are included in the tasks below:

1   TT4U's chief executive officer is concerned about the possibility that major contracts will not be won or renewed and would like your views on what the main risks are for TT4U.

Required

(a)   **Prepare briefing notes for the board which analyse the main risks which threaten TT4U being awarded new contracts and retaining current contracts.** (8 marks)

Professional skills marks are available for demonstrating analysis skills in establishing the risks relating to TT4U. (2 marks)

At the recent directors' meeting, the information technology director proposed that TT4U should develop new services in relation to the Internet-of-things. The services director proposed that TT4U should focus on winning more government sector work. The chief executive officer wants your report to include consideration of these two strategic options.

Required

(b)   **Prepare a section of your report which evaluates the two strategic options proposed by the directors.** (12 marks)

Professional skills marks are available for demonstrating evaluation skills in using professional judgement to objectively appraise the two strategic options proposed by the directors. (4 marks)

TT4U's chief executive officer would like to have an independent external view on what was discussed at the meeting about the threatening letter. In particular, she doubts the views of the marketing director that TT4U can simply rely on its data controls. She is also uncertain whether TT4U should disclose nothing to Rex Investments, as the marketing director suggested.

Required

(c)   **Prepare a confidential email for the chief executive officer which:**

   –   **advises on the actions which TT4U can take to ensure that the controls on the confidentiality of data operate effectively; and**

   –   **discusses the risks and ethical issues relating to communicating the threat to the client, Rex Investments.** (12 marks)

(Total = 41 marks)

2   The assistant to the finance director has prepared a summary of the investment appraisal of the planned development of TT4U's cloud-based services. The chief executive officer has given you a summary of the analysis which has been prepared, as she is unsure whether it is satisfactory. She also wants you to brief the board on how the new services should be e-marketed.

Required

(a)   **Prepare a section of your report which critically evaluates the investment appraisal produced by the finance director's assistant.** (8 marks)

Professional skills marks are available for demonstrating scepticism skills in questioning the investment appraisal prepared by the finance director's assistant.

(2 marks)

(b)   **Prepare briefing notes for the next board meeting which recommend how e-marketing can be used to attract and retain clients for TT4U's new cloud-based services.** (10 marks)

Professional skills marks are available for demonstrating commercial acumen skills by showing awareness of effective methods for e-marketing the new cloud-based services. (3 marks)

(Total = 23 marks)

3   The chief executive officer believes that TT4U's current structure will have to change if TT4U is to introduce the new Mieobed approach to client relationships successfully. The chief executive officer knows that she must take ownership of the transformation. She feels, however, that she needs guidance on the transformation process and how she should lead this process, including communicating the need for change to employees.

Required

(a)   **Prepare an email for the chief executive officer which advises her on the responsibilities and activities involved in preparing for and implementing the transformation of TT4U effectively.**   **(10 marks)**

(b)   **Prepare a letter to all employees, which will be signed by the chief executive officer, explaining:**

–   **the benefits of implementing the new Mieobed approach for TT4U and its employees; and**

–   **the main changes to team structures and behaviours below board level which the new Mieobed approach will require.**   **(10 marks)**

Professional skills marks are available for demonstrating communication skills in persuading employees of the benefits of TT4U adopting the new approach in its working practices.   **(3 marks)**

The chairman wants the board to be briefed on aspects of corporate governance which need to change if the new Mieobed approach to client relationships is to be introduced successfully.

Required

(c)   **Prepare briefing notes which advise the board on the changes required to:**

–   **the membership of the board; and**
–   **the information supplied to the board**

to reflect TT4U's developing business needs and to make TT4U more responsive to its clients' needs.   **(10 marks)**

Professional skills marks are available for demonstrating commercial acumen skills in identifying changes to the membership of the board and information supplied which are realistic for TT4U and will generate better relationships with clients.   **(3 marks)**

(Total = 36 marks)

Exhibit 1: Transcript of directors' meeting about issues to be discussed with Stubfield consultants

Chief executive officer (CEO)	I've called this meeting to discuss the areas that we want Stubfield consultants to consider. I know that some of you feel that Stubfield will be looking at areas of our business where we shouldn't need advice and that they may exceed their remit.
	Nevertheless, some of our investors have communicated the view that we need external advice about our business. They feel that we're too reliant on existing business from our long-term clients. We should be providing more new services and winning new clients.
	We've advanced discussions on developing our new cloud-based services. This will enable us to extend the cloud-based services we provide. You'll recall these include provision of private clouds for specific clients and cloud integration services, enabling clients to connect their data and applications and give them more flexible access to their data resources. We have available an appraisal of our planned investment.

Finance director (FD)	As you're aware, I've been on sick leave so didn't prepare the appraisal myself. Johan, who recently joined the department to assist me, carried out the appraisal. I haven't reviewed the appraisal in detail yet. However, I see at a glance that the payback period is just outside the three-year limit that we set.
Marketing director (MD)	I had hoped to come today with some proposals for marketing the cloud-based services. However, I've been spending a lot of time dealing with Rex Investments, which, as you know, is a very difficult client. I think our launch of these services must make a big impact as a means of attracting the new business we need for expansion.
CEO	As you remember, I asked for suggestions from yourselves about areas where we can expand further. I've received two proposals, one relating to the Internet-of-things and the other to government sector work.
IT director (ITD)	We need to look beyond cloud-based services and expand in an area where we can show we can provide fresh solutions. I'd be very excited about us developing more expertise and services relating to the Internet-of-things. There is massive potential for extending internet connectivity beyond standard devices to everyday objects, such as household appliances, and making the most of the data they can generate. There are so many possible sectors – health, construction, transport, agriculture – where there are opportunities that we can explore.
Services director (SD)	I think we should focus on winning more government sector work. A lot more is available now and we already have some work on which we can build. We have the size and range of services to be looking at winning much larger contracts. I believe we are in a position to become a trusted partner for government. The government sector is less demanding of innovation than the private sector. It is therefore a lower risk option for us, as we can secure the contracts by strong service performance without the risks attached to market leadership in new services.
CEO	Now I would like us to consider the issues raised by the recent client survey. I very much regret that we haven't carried out a survey like this for some years. For me, it highlights the need to transform our business to bring our clients much closer to us.
	I intend that we should move forward by adopting the Mieobed approach to engaging with client stakeholders in our sector, which *Business Tomorrow* magazine devised. The approach is based on building open and sharing relationships with clients that help them create new sources of value for their business.
SD	I assume you'll be considering how staff should be persuaded to buy into the transformation before the new approach is implemented.
CEO	I shall, and I shall also be looking at how we operate as a board. Three directors currently combine board responsibilities with operational line management of teams. This is a model which we've had since we started, but it may not be appropriate any more. I also want to look at the way TT4U is structured as a whole. I think we ought to be much more of a matrix organisation, which should result in better communication and mutual learning.
SD	I certainly agree internal communication could be improved. I know staff are told not to sit at the same desks each day, but to sit at different desks next to different people. However, we all know the three teams sit in the same areas each day, separate from each other. We have our intranet, but the lack of contributions from staff on it is embarrassing.

MD	I think we need to go much further than having one-off client surveys. We need to be considering the current state of relationships with clients as an agenda item at every board meeting. We have to develop key performance indicators beyond clients gained and lost each period, so that we have a better idea of how we are performing in the areas that most affect client satisfaction.
	We must also consider how we are perceived in relation to our competitors. Although we do have a regular report on competitors' new product offerings, that doesn't tell us how satisfied our clients are with our services in comparison with the services our competitors offer.
CEO	Thank you for your contributions. I shall ask Stubfield for their views on the risks that we face and the strategic options that we've discussed, as well as how we can introduce the Mieobed approach successfully.

Exhibit 2: Summary of Mieobed client approach devised by *Business Tomorrow* magazine

M ission-driven	Driving strategy and attracting client stakeholders by a strong mission
I nteractive	Participation of client stakeholders enhancing our organisation and theirs
E mpowering	Enabling client stakeholders to realise personal and organisational potential
O pen	Building on the knowledge and experience of client stakeholders by sharing and collaborating
B oundaryless	Taking client stakeholders on a journey beyond existing boundaries, to transform their operations and unlock value in new areas
E thical	Founding client stakeholder relationships on responsiveness, fairness, honesty, responsibility and transparency
D ata-focused	Maintaining tight security of client stakeholder data whilst enhancing its accessibility

Exhibit 3: Blog on IT consultancy sector on *Business Tomorrow* magazine website

Business Tomorrow

Not just services, but service By Abby Urquhart

How can IT consultants stand out?

IT consultants are struggling to come to terms with what their clients take for granted. The days when they can sell themselves on the basis of being practical business advisers rather than IT experts are long over. Consultants need not bother tendering for work unless they can combine strong client and business sector knowledge with awareness of the latest applications.

Is leading innovation in cloud-based services the way forward?

Anyone who is marketing themselves as having distinctive capabilities in helping clients set up on the cloud has clearly been left well behind. Clients are now expecting the full package of cloud maximisation services.

Is the Internet-of-things an area firms can develop?

The Internet-of-things, extending connectivity and networks to traditionally non-internet connected objects such as cars and household lights, has been the next big development for some time. However, a number of sectors have clear needs for enhanced communication and monitoring. The medical sector has been eager for applications which enable remote health monitoring and notifications if emergencies arise. The building sector has been keen to develop devices which oversee electronic systems within homes and offices to detect fire risk or wasteful energy usage.

Involvement though remains risky. Development is driven more by technology than its usefulness for business transformation. There are also the security and surveillance concerns, the dislike of being watched by inanimate objects.

BPP
LEARNING
MEDIA

Is client service still important?

Business Tomorrow's recent survey suggests that client service remains a problem for many consultants. Our survey shows that the consultants who are responsive, who use business approaches of client participation and mutual development like *Business Tomorrow's* Mieobed approach, are making the largest profits.

What business is available for firms providing top-class service?

Lots of work. There are more longer-term government sector contracts available than ever before. These contracts won't be won or retained if firms don't meet government's ever-stricter service requirements. Ultimately firms cannot take for granted any of their clients' continued business. Many firms have seen long-term relationships with clients end recently. The loyal client, previously prepared to put up with less than excellent service, no longer exists.

👍 Like 85   👎 Dislike 9

Comments (2)

Ken Yardley: Firms I've dealt with often don't seem to get the basics of communication right. They don't answer their phones. They don't respond to emails within 24 hours. They don't listen to what I'm asking or telling them.

Xin Chan: The reason why Internet-of-things hasn't developed as quickly as expected is that many applications don't survive the pilot stage, since many businesses' systems are not able to cope.

Exhibit 4: Extract of results of client survey

TT4U		%	Comments
Service provision Flexibility	Excellent	17	'Service provision was exceptionally good when they first started advising us. But now we just seem to be getting the basic service.'
	Good	56	
	Average	16	
	Poor	11	
Innovation	Excellent	9	'TT4U seems good at, and comfortable with, providing the same services that it has always provided. If I wanted new services, I'd certainly go elsewhere.'
	Good	57	
	Average	22	
	Poor	12	
Information provision	Excellent	20	'For an IT consultancy, its website is really poor – it lacks detailed information about services, difficult to navigate.'
	Good	53	
	Average	20	'Its website does look old-fashioned and hasn't changed much for ages. It's noticeable that other consultants' websites are interactive and appear to evolve in response to what users want.'
	Poor	7	
			'They don't make enough use of messaging and social media.'
			'How much you're told about what they're doing seems to depend on the staff involved.'

TT4U		%	Comments
Staff			
Knowledge	Excellent	41	'They appear to know our business well and how to make best use of the technologies we have.'
	Good	38	
	Average	15	'I've marked them down because they don't appear to know about their own services. I've asked staff on various occasions about other services I know TT4U provides and they have had to ring round the office for an answer.'
	Poor	6	
Responsiveness	Excellent	20	'Emails are never answered the same day.'
	Good	30	'They often answer the question they wished you'd asked rather than the question you did ask.'
	Average	28	
	Poor	22	'You know you can always talk to the services director when you need to. I like how he's always kept in touch with us.'
Proactiveness	Excellent	16	'We call them, they never call us.'
	Good	47	'I would have liked them to have told us that we needed to invest in new systems before our old systems became too slow and unreliable.'
	Average	22	
	Poor	15	'Some staff members really make you feel you're working with them as a team. It's not consistent across the whole company, sadly.'

Exhibit 5: Discussion of threatening letter about TT4U's largest client, Rex Investments

IT director (ITD)	We've had an anonymous threat to reveal confidential data on Rex Investments unless we pay $20,000.
Marketing director (MD)	Surely we've received threats like this before and nothing has come of them?
ITD	We have, but this is a much more specific threat. It is quite detailed about the data. We do hold the data and it is confidential.
MD	We must have all the necessary controls in place – anti-virus software, passwords, etc.
ITD	I'm confident that the controls we need are there.
MD	Then we don't need to pursue this further. Whoever's making the threats didn't get the information from us. We're computer consultants. Of course we have complete and fully-functioning controls. The one thing I'd say is that we shouldn't tell Rex Investments about this. As you know, they are our largest client. Relations with them are difficult enough at the present. If we tell them, it shows we don't believe our own systems are secure. It will give them a very good reason to terminate our contract.
Chief executive officer (CEO)	I nevertheless believe that this could be a serious risk for us. I don't think we can just say that we have controls. We need to have strong assurance they are operating as they should be. If our controls haven't been working, we have to try to detect who's accessed the information. I'll ask Stubfield for views on these issues.

Exhibit 6: Appraisal of cloud services investment prepared by recently appointed assistant to the finance director

Net present value calculation

Year	Note	0	1	2	3	4
		$000	$000	$000	$000	$000
Sales	1		8,000	10,250	13,250	15,500
Contribution	2		4,400	5,638	7,288	8,525
Marketing costs	3		(600)	(769)	(994)	(994)
Other fixed costs			(900)	(900)	(900)	(900)
Pre-tax cash flows		0	2,900	3,969	5,394	6,631
Taxation paid	4		(725)	(992)	(1,349)	(1,658)
Post-tax cash flows			2,175	2,977	4,045	4,973
Investment		(10,000)				
Terminal value	5					1,500
Cash flows		(10,000)	2,175	2,977	4,045	6,473
Discount factor	6	1.000	0.943	0.890	0.840	0.792
Discounted cash flows		(10,000)	2,051	2,650	3,398	5,127
Net present value years 1–4		3,226				
Net present value years 5–10	7	23,632				

Notes:

1. Sales are based on expected increases in markets, clients served and prices.

2. Contribution is assumed to be 55% of revenue each year in line with current margins.

3. Marketing costs are assumed to increase in line with sales up to year 3.

4. Tax rate is 25% of pre-tax cash flows.

5. Terminal value represents assumed realisable value if services are no longer viable after four years.

6. Discount factor of 6% is after-tax interest rate on current long-term loans, as this project is to be financed by a long-term loan.

7. Year 5–10 figure is post-tax discounted cash flow for year 4 multiplied by six.

Payback calculation

Year	0	1	2	3	4
	$000	$000	$000	$000	$000
Cash flow	(10,000)	2,175	2,977	4,045	6,473
Cumulative	(10,000)	(7,825)	(4,848)	(803)	5,670

Payback = 3 years + (803/(803 + 5,670)) × 12 months = 3 years 1 month

Comments:

1. Project shows a positive present value after four years and a much greater present value if the services can be offered in their current form beyond four years.

2. The payback period is slightly greater than the target set by the directors, which suggests the project should be rejected.

3. Nevertheless, sensitivity analysis should be carried out to determine the probability of loss and hence whether the project should be undertaken in its current form.

Answers

Strategic Business Leader – Mock Exam 3 – March 2020

Marks

1 (a) Up to 2 marks for each risk discussed
Up to a maximum of 8 marks in total for task 1 (a)   8

(b) Up to 2 marks per relevant point discussed for each strategic
option, up to a maximum of 7 marks per option, within that
up to 4 marks for discussion of advantages of pursuing the
strategy and up to 4 marks for discussion of concerns with
the strategy.   12

Up to a maximum of 12 marks in total for task 1 (b)

(c) Up to 2 marks for each example of prevention controls
discussed - maximum of 4 marks

Up to 2 marks for each example of detection controls
discussed - maximum of 3 marks

Up to 2 marks for discussion of each risk identified relating to
communicating the threat - maximum of 3 marks

Up to 2 marks for discussion of each ethical issue identified
relating to communicating the threat - maximum of 3 marks

Up to a maximum of 12 marks in total for task 1 (c)   12

2 (a) Up to 2 marks for each calculation discussed including
revenue, contribution, payback.

Up to 1 mark each for discussion of other points such as
marketing, fixed costs, tax, working capital, investment,
terminal value, the discount factor and sensitivity analysis.   8

Up to a maximum of 8 marks for task 2 (a)

(b) 1 mark for each method recommended for attracting and
retaining clients.   10
Up to a maximum of 10 marks in total for task 2(b)

3 (a) Up to 2 marks for discussion of each suggestion relating to
the CEO and board's responsibilities - maximum of 4 marks

Up to 2 marks for discussion of each general issues relating to
the transformation process - maximum of 8 marks   10

Up to a maximum of 10 marks in total for task 3(a)

(b) Up to 2 marks for discussion of each benefit to TT4U -
maximum of 4 marks

Up to 2 marks for discussion of each benefit to employees -
maximum of 4 marks

Up to 2 marks for discussion of each change in structure and
behaviour - maximum of 5 marks
Up to a maximum of 10 marks in total for task 3 (b)   10

(c) Up to 2 marks for each suggestion relating to membership of
the board - maximum of 6 marks

Up to 2 marks for each suggestion relating to information
supplied - maximum of 6 marks

Up to a maximum of 10 marks in total for task 3 (c)   10

Suggested solutions

> **Note.** It is not always possible to publish suggested answers which comprehensively cover all the valid points which candidates might make. Credit will be given to candidates for points not included in the suggested answers, but which, nevertheless, are relevant to the requirements.
>
> In addition, in this integrated case study examination points made in one question may be re-introduced or fully developed in other question(s) as long as these are made in the specific context of the requirements of the part of the question being answered.
>
> The suggested answers presented below may give much more detail than would be expected from most candidates under examination conditions; they may also have used a particular approach or model which should not be taken as the only approach or model which could have been used. Different approaches and structuring of the answers are expected and full credit will be given for relevant and appropriate solutions to the tasks given. The answers provided here are therefore intended to support revision and tuition for future examinations.
>
> Finally, it should be noted that candidates will not get full professional skills marks in a task requirement if they have not presented their answers according to the format asked for. For example, if a task is to be completed using a report and evaluation skills are tested, even if the answer has met the specifically stated evaluation criteria, candidates will not be able to earn all the professional skills marks available if they have not used the report format.

1   (a)   **Briefing notes on risks to contracts**

These notes deal with the main risks which may affect Techthere4U Co (TT4U) winning and retaining contracts.

Strategic

The fundamental strategic risk is failure to fulfil clients' evolving demands, resulting ultimately in loss of contracts and decline in revenues. Aspects of this risk include lack of awareness of what clients want. There may also be a lack of resources to respond to client demands for new services or better provision of existing services. There is possibly a lack of high-level awareness of recent developments, as there have been no recent appointees from the IT industry to the board.

The risk is also related to competitor actions, of competitors providing new services first or having a business model which provides better awareness of client demands and standards of client care. TT4U has traditionally not differentiated itself from competitors by offering new services first, but early development of new services may be a critical factor in winning new work. The results of the survey suggest that some clients believe that there is a lack of commitment to innovation.

Operational

In the client survey, responsiveness to clients, internal knowledge, communication and flexibility are all criticised. Methods of communication with clients seem old-fashioned and the website is criticised for being poorly designed. If operations are poor, these may be hygiene factors which influence clients' contract renewal decisions.

An important selling point of cloud-based services which TT4U plans to offer is flexibility and ease of use. If the cloud is difficult to access in many places or there are frequent interruptions of service, TT4U will not be providing perhaps the most important deliverable.

Key person

Key person risk particularly applies to the founder executive directors, given their central place in TT4U throughout its history and the contacts they have built up. The departure of any of them could be seen as indicating that TT4U is undergoing a period of instability. Other staff may have particular close relations with some clients or expertise which may adversely impact TT4U if it was lost, particularly if they joined competitors.

Competition

TT4U may be less visible than other firms. Competitors may be attracting more business by better use of online tools such as search optimisation or better generation of publicity about the services which they are offering. The comments in the survey suggest that clients find TT4U's website poor and believe the company is not making enough use of other media.

Data

All the data management services provided by TT4U, not just those on the cloud, generate risks of loss to their clients. These include the risks of loss or corruption of data, whether due to accident or deliberate action by hackers. There is also the risk of confidential data being accessed by unauthorised users, and publicised or used for illicit advantage.

Reputation

Bad publicity about the services TT4U offers or the public loss of important clients can affect reputation. It may be particularly serious if TT4U is associated with a major problem, for example, a leakage of confidential data. Reputation risk can also relate to criticisms that TT4U is generally not providing a good service. The article highlights important features of service and the client survey indicates TT4U has problems in some of these areas. If these problems are publicised online by users, this can erode confidence in what TT4U offers.

Examining team's comments: Task 1(a) required candidates to analyse the main risks threatening TT4U being awarded new contracts and retaining current contracts.

The examining team noted that the task was done reasonably well with many candidates discussing enough risks to score at least 4 marks. However, 'candidates often failed to follow their discussion of problems through and show clearly how and why the problems could result in the risks of not retaining or gaining clients. In addition, some candidates discussed other risks, such as financial risks, that were not linked to relations with clients and were thus not relevant'. (ACCA 2020) Other weaknesses included problems with spending too much time on the task, discussing risk assessment in general terms, as well as providing lengthy introductions and background information which would not be useful to the board who were recipients of the information.

To earn the 2 professional skills marks, the significance of risks needed to be explained and candidates should have used exhibit data to support their discussion. The answer should have been presented in the form of briefing notes for TT4U's board.

(b) **Extract from report on the two proposed strategic**

Introduction

This section considers the two proposed strategic options put forward by the services and information technology directors.

Internet-of-things development

Advantages of strategy

Developing services in relation to the Internet-of-things has been highlighted by the recent article as a potential means of rapid growth through market development, fulfilling the desire of investors for the company to expand. Finding a niche and being able to innovate in it could enhance TT4U's wider reputation.

Some of the problems in relation to Internet-of-things development appear to be an over-concentration on technology rather than business requirements. Matching business needs with available business technology has been a core competence for

TT4U in the past. Adoption of the Mieobed approach with its focus on enhanced understanding of clients' requirements to help them transform their business would seem compatible with this new development.

Concerns with strategy

However, commitment to particular markets may be risky for TT4U. It has traditionally had a diversified client base, and commitment to particular sectors may require significant investment without necessarily guaranteeing success. If, for example, TT4U wants to provide data hosting services in connection with the data generated by the Internet-of-things, it may need enhanced capacity to process and store the data. If TT4U is to be an early mover, there may be problems with the reliability of the technology.

Whatever the sector chosen, TT4U may need to recruit staff with previous experience in work connected with the Internet-of-things. This may be costly, but may bring to TT4U valuable new expertise at a time when TT4U is looking generally to develop staff expertise by sharing knowledge and experience.

There could be problems with selling services to existing clients. The technology may be of limited application to TT4U's current client base. They may lack the system capabilities to develop effectively and problems could damage TT4U's standing with them.

Risks relating to security and also privacy have also been highlighted. Depending on which services TT4U offers, it may be more vulnerable to security breaches and also breaches of privacy regulations than for other services. These may result in legal penalties and significant threats to reputation.

Government sector development

Advantages of strategy

The policy of seeking more contracts in the government sector represents a form of market development if contracts are to be obtained from more bodies. Seeking more contracts systematically would represent a more coherent strategy in this area as contracts won previously appear to have been on a one-off basis. Winning more contracts can lead to 'success breeding success' with the target of becoming a preferred supplier to the government sector.

Many opportunities appear likely to become available soon in the government sector. Having been successful at fulfilling smaller contracts for this sector, TT4U seems well-placed to seek larger contracts as it expands.

The contracts available will represent a cash stream which should be guaranteed for a number of years. This can be set off against shorter-term private sector work which may be more vulnerable to economic downturn. Some of the contracts will be high profile, so winning them can provide good publicity for TT4U.

Concerns with strategy

Possible issues with the work include profitability. Whatever the exact priorities, government sector work will be concerned with the 3Es – economy, efficiency and effectiveness. Because of the desire to meet economy targets, the margins available on the work may be lower than on commercial contracts. Serving the government sector effectively may also require investment in staff who possess knowledge of the sector being served, for example, education.

As noted above, public sector work is high profile. If there are major problems with contracts and these are publicised and blamed on TT4U, the company's reputation could suffer seriously.

The argument that needing to provide innovative services will be less of an issue in the government sector may have some substance. However, one of the key aspects of the Mieobed approach is encouraging clients to unlock value (for themselves and

TT4U) in new fields of business development. The public sector may offer limited opportunities for that approach.

Operating the Mieobed stakeholder approach may be more complex in the government sector because of the different stakeholders with differing objectives. The priorities of the government officials with whom TT4U deals may change if there is a change of government and new conditions may be imposed.

Governments may use a number of strict indicators relating to value for money which TT4U has to fulfil. It may mean a greater demand for resources and opportunity costs in taking staff away from other work. Fulfilling government requirements will mean that TT4U has to address quickly some of the service issues identified in the client survey.

Conclusion

If the proposals are not mutually exclusive, TT4U may consider investing in both of them. They represent different types of development, so improving diversification, and have different risk-return profiles. Investing in the Internet-of-things is high risk but could generate high earnings. Investment in public sector work could provide steady cash flows to help fund investment in other areas.

Examining team's comments: Task 1(b) asked candidates to evaluate the strategic options of investing in Internet-of- things services or seeking to win more contracts from the government, providing a balanced discussion of the advantages and problems of each option.

The examining team noted that, in many instances, candidates answered this task better than any other in this exam although discussion was often more heavily weighted towards advantages rather than problems. Some candidates made good use of the Suitability, Acceptability, Feasibility framework but others merely described the framework or repeated points relating to both strategic options under the headings. To earn the 4 professional skills marks candidates needed to ensure that their answer was a balanced assessment of advantages and problems of the strategic options. It was also important to consider organisational issues and competitive positioning in the discussion. Note that the requirements asked for a section of a report so a tabular format was not appropriate.

(c)   **Email**

To: Chief executive
From: Consultant
Date: 1 March 20X0
Subject: Response to threat to reveal information

Dear CEO

You asked me as someone outside the company to give my views on the controls which are significant in relation to threats to data and also the comments made by the directors about the threat to reveal confidential information.

Control issues

You rightly believe that TT4U cannot just say it has complete confidence in its controls and not give the issue further consideration. TT4U has a fiduciary duty to take sufficient care to ensure confidential data remains secret. In addition, clients are very sensitive about the growing threat of cybercrime, indeed TT4U advises them on how to combat it. If it became public that TT4U had been the victim of cybercrime through poor data protection practices, the loss of credibility for TT4U would potentially represent a big risk to income from existing and new services.

I have no reason to doubt what the director says about the procedures already being in place. Given that TT4U is advising clients on implementation of these procedures, it would be worrying if TT4U did not have them in place itself. However, you are right that there is a distinction between having the controls in place and the

BPP
LEARNING
MEDIA

controls operating effectively. It is possible that lack of care or complacency may undermine the operation of important controls.

Even though TT4U has a system of access controls in place, this may be undermined by staff being careless with their password security. More regular changing of passwords may reduce this threat. TT4U should also review who has access to which parts of the system and restrict permissions for staff so that they have the minimum of access rights which they require to carry out their work. Access rights to the system must also be immediately terminated as soon as someone leaves TT4U.

Regular reminders to staff can help reduce complacency. This may particularly apply to having effective procedures to protect laptops taken away from the office. These should have the same level of protection as devices kept in-house, including having anti-hacking protection as well as anti-virus software. They must be updated at the same time as in-house computers. Staff should also be told to avoid poor data security practices, for example, forbidding them to copy sensitive data onto memory sticks.

As regards detection of someone obtaining information illicitly, you should start by looking at past and present staff who were able to access this data and considering whether there are any unusual or suspicious factors in relation to them. I assume the system logs failed attempts to log on, and this must be regularly reviewed in case any patterns appear to be emerging. You need also to ensure you understand what represents 'normal' use of the system, which acts as a yardstick to use to detect unusual patterns of use, for example, copying of large amounts of data.

Threat to reveal confidential information

Even if you have complete confidence in the control system, the threat cannot be brushed off, as the person contacting you has clearly illicitly obtained specific information and may be threatening other companies. You should consider contacting the authorities as they may be able to link the threats in with other cases. The authorities may insist on the client being informed. You should not pay the sum demanded, as this is unethical and could lead to further threats.

There is a risk that Rex Investments' confidence in TT4U may be undermined if it is told about this threat. I appreciate concerns have been raised about client relations and it is quite possible that the client will ask for additional assurance on the controls which you operate.

However, the risks relating to not telling Rex Investments are greater. Disclosure of the information from other sources may permanently damage the relationship and may provide Rex Investments with a reason to terminate the contract. Bad publicity relating to this disclosure may mean other clients do not wish to use the data services you provide. It is likely to threaten the success of the investment in the cloud-based services. More fundamentally, one aspect of the Mieobed approach which you are planning to introduce is data security.

Following the ethical principles of honesty and transparency would also suggest informing the client of a threat to its data. Again, I refer to Mieobed, which is underpinned by the process of open communication with clients. Failing to tell the client about this threat would suggest that TT4U is not taking the Mieobed approach seriously.

Lastly, it is possible that the person making the threats did not obtain the information from your systems but from Rex Investments. A further ethical reason for informing Rex Investments is that it may help in detecting who is making the threat and perhaps also highlight to the client shortcomings in their own procedures for keeping information confidential.

Please contact me if you want to discuss these issues further.

Regards

Stubfield

2 (a) **Extract from report on summary of investment appraisal of new cloud-based services**

Introduction

This section examines the issues connected with the summary which has been prepared and recommends improvements and areas where further detail is required.

Net present value calculation

Sales

Having a single sales revenue figure, even if this is a summary, is quite inadequate and the comment about the drivers of sale increases is unhelpful. There is no justification for the varying % of sales increases; splitting the figure down by the services offered, at a minimum distinguishing the revenue from the provision of private cloud services from cloud integration services, will give a better picture of how increasing the services offered may lead to revenue increases over time. The assumption about increased client base needs to be linked to how new services are to be marketed, and how much the focus will be on winning new clients as opposed to selling additional services to current clients. TT4U is operating in a very competitive market for cloud services, so any assumptions about being able to increase prices are doubtful.

Contribution

If different services are provided, contribution may vary on them. A figure chosen may do as a broad estimate, if it is the sort of margin which TT4U has been generating recently. However, there is no detail about variable costs. These may change over time as the service offered becomes more mature and the cost per client of providing each service falls.

Other costs

The marketing costs will depend on when new services are introduced. If they are introduced gradually over the three-year period, the estimates may be reasonable. However, if most of the services are being introduced soon, marketing is likely to peak in year 1. The fixed costs figure appears to be a general estimate. No justification is given as to why the figure is unchanged over time. In addition, the figure is sufficiently large to need breaking down into different elements and clarifying the assumptions for each element.

Tax and working capital

Using the current tax rate is a reasonable assumption if it is not expected to change much in the next few years. However, the figure does not take account of any allowances which may be available on the investment expenditure. It would also be likely that the investment would require some working capital and this needs to be brought into the calculation.

Investment

If services are likely to be developed over the next few years, then a single immediate figure for investment at the start will not be realistic. The realisable value given at year 4 lacks justification. It is difficult to see what would be realised and whether it would have any value, given the fast-changing nature of the industry.

If the net present value figure is extended to year 10, the realisable value should be excluded from the calculation as the investment is not finishing at year 4. Taking the post-tax cash flow at year 4 and using a multiple of 6 as the basis for years 5–10 has not been justified. The figure used should be discounted at the relevant discount factor for each year, not the discount factor for year 4. It is ultimately, however, questionable whether the investment should be extended to 10 years, as this seems a long period for an investment in fast-changing IT.

Discount rate

The discount rate used is incorrect. The weighted average cost of capital should be used if business and financial risk remain at the same levels. This is likely to be higher than the cost of debt, since equity has a higher cost than debt, meaning the net present value will be smaller. If either risk changes significantly, a project-specific cost of capital should be used.

Payback period calculation

The approach taken to calculate the payback period is correct, although the figures may not be reliable due to the concerns raised above. Net present value is theoretically the best method to determine whether an investment should be undertaken. However, payback can be used as an initial indication if directors are uncertain about the timeframe over which the investment will be profitable and want to ensure it is recouped quickly. The investment is only marginally outside the payback period and the uncertainties connected with the figures suggest the investment should not necessarily be rejected because it fails to meet the payback criterion.

Sensitivity analysis

The summary is incorrect in saying that sensitivity analysis will show the probability of making a loss. It will just show the amount by which figures need to change for the investment to make a loss. Sensitivity analysis also treats individual figures as independent variables, whereas there may be connections between them (for example, between revenue and marketing expenditure) or the same factors may affect more than one variable (for example, competitor response affecting income from more than one service). Scenario analysis, showing results under different optimistic/pessimistic outcomes, is likely to be more valuable.

Conclusion

The project's failure to meet the payback target period should not by itself lead to the project being rejected. The decision should be primarily based on a revised NPV calculation using the correct cost of capital and re-considering the assumptions. If the revised NPV calculation shows a positive present value for years 1–4 only, the board should consider accepting the project.

(b)   **Briefing notes for board meeting**

E-marketing cloud-computing services

The purpose of these notes is to discuss ways in which e-marketing can be used to promote the new services. The notes will be a combination of new ideas and methods which TT4U is already using, but should review and may need to enhance. The notes also show how the methods should be used within a framework of attracting and retaining clients.

(i)   **Attracting clients**

Reaching potential clients

TT4U may look at whether its search engine positioning needs to be improved. Possibly the launch of new services is the time to make use or more use of methods such as banner advertising. TT4U needs to consider the branding messages the advertising will promote, possibly separately branding the new services from TT4U's existing business.

Interesting potential clients

TT4U should look to make the most of methods such as tweeting or Facebook pages to promote interest in its new services. Social media postings could cover concerns clients have, for example, about the lack of connectivity between data holdings, which TT4U's new services will address. Social media can also promote TT4U's expertise by providing opinions or guidance from a director or employee.

The information about the new services on TT4U's website needs to indicate clearly the ways TT4U's services will provide maximisation of value for clients and the unique selling points which TT4U's services have. It needs to show clearly that it is addressing what is of interest to potential clients by, for example, providing answers to frequently asked questions about cloud services. Infrastructure issues should be regarded as a priority, as the ability to search the site easily can help keep users interested and prompt them to revisit the website.

TT4U then needs to make sure it makes maximum use of the data it has about website visitors to develop its website continuously. The pattern of clicks will help establish what particularly interests different visitors. Questionnaires about what visitors are interested in can be used to see how to develop content further, for example, in greater emphasis on data management and hosting.

Gaining potential clients

Turning users into clients needs to be focused on using the data about what they are interested in to attract them to the services offered. A personalised approach focused on opt-in emails and text messages, tailored to what is of interest to clients, is core. These messages need to encourage two-way communication. Not only will that interest clients more, but it will highlight the proactive and collaborative attitudes which the new business approach will be promoting.

TT4U can also use media releases to target particular groups, for example, clients using certain cloud services. Whilst these are less tailored, they can be used to create interest. They can be followed up by tailored communications to individual clients subsequently.

(ii) **Retaining clients**

The same emphasis on personalised communication needs to be used for current clients. The focus needs to be on continuous dialogue. More regular client surveys, focusing on what they are likely to be most concerned about, need to be undertaken. TT4U must remember this personalised approach is not just about what is delivered but how it is delivered – how proactive TT4U is with its clients.

TT4U's website should also help develop relationships with clients by getting them to register or perhaps subscribe to particular content. The website could provide a chat or messaging option.

As well as TT4U's website, other methods which could be developed include newsgroups and business blogs. Newsgroups would keep clients interested by highlighting new developments with the cloud which are linked to the services which TT4U provides.

Providing services which can only be accessed by clients, for example, extranets, can also help generate loyalty. Again it is important that these are tailored to what is important to clients and generate responses from TT4U.

TT4U needs to consider how proactive staff are in dealing with client concerns, how quickly they respond when clients contact them and also how easy it seems to be for them to answer client queries. A business offering IT expertise needs to ensure that the knowledge and awareness which all its staff have is clear to clients. TT4U should also emphasise the existing knowledge it has of existing clients' systems as a selling point for helping them develop effective cloud computing service offerings.

Examining team's comments: Task 2(b) required candidates to recommend how e-marketing could be used to attract and retain clients for TT4U's new cloud-based services.

The task was generally answered poorly. Whilst some candidates came up with creative suggestions as to how e-marketing could be used, very few answered the specific requirement as to how e-marketing could attract and strengthen relations with clients, thus failing to earn 'commercial acumen' professional marks. Many candidates used the 6Is framework and whilst such models can be helpful in providing a structured response it is important to answer the requirement set rather than simply describing the model. The examining team noted that ' E-marketing was also examined in the June 2019 exam and performance was also poor then, suggesting that this is an area where candidates need to be better prepared'. (ACCA 2020)

---

3   (a)   **Email**

To: Chief executive
From: Consultant
Date: 1 March 20X0
Subject: Transforming TT4U

Dear CEO

You asked me for my thoughts on the transformation process and how you should lead it, including communicating the need for transformation positively. Attached is the draft letter to employees for your approval which you asked me to prepare. Obviously please contact me if you would like to discuss comments and amendments.

Your responsibilities and the board's responsibilities

You are quite right in supposing that you have to lead the transformation, as the successful implementation of the Mieobed approach could be vital for TT4U's long-term success. You will need to promote the Mieobed approach as a coherent whole and sell it to staff.

However, senior management at TT4U has always operated, and been seen as operating, as a team. Your first task will therefore be to convince the rest of the board of the need for transformation, so that they become as enthusiastic about it as you are. Successful implementation will depend on their convincing staff to embrace the transformation. Before presenting the approach to staff, you need to make a clear and detailed presentation to the other directors at the next board meeting, showing how adopting the Mieobed approach will fulfil TT4U's needs and emphasising the need for all the board to provide leadership.

Preparing for transformation

Explaining the Mieobed approach will not be enough by itself. Some staff may see the way it promotes improvements, but others may have more difficultly seeing how it applies or will be sceptical about it. You will therefore need to explain what is driving the transformation and the adoption of the Mieobed approach, and create the motivation for transformation.

When introducing the Mieobed approach, you need to do it in the context of both the culture of TT4U and the practical aspects of the business. You will need to communicate changes in culture, including changes in assumptions about how communication takes place and how clients are viewed. You will also need to show how internal changes, particularly changes in organisation structure, will mean a need to change behaviour towards other members of staff.

Practical aspects of the business which you need to consider include how organisational structure changes will follow through into changes in jobs and responsibilities, and also changes in processes and rewards. These are discussed further in the attached letter. To decrease staff's uncertainties, you will need to oversee the drafting of an operational plan covering these areas.

The letter also mentions staff enhancing their skills. This is an important selling point to staff as well as an important success factor in the transformation. You will need to consider the training staff will need and draw up a training programme, maybe with the assistance of an external experienced trainer.

Lastly, the transformation may require changes in TT4U's information systems and flows of information to the board. You and the IT director will need to consider the information needs of the board, including those highlighted by the marketing director, and draw up a plan so that TT4U's systems can provide the information required.

BPP
LEARNING
MEDIA

Implementing transformation

There should be a structured process for transformation in place. Given that participation is a core element of Mieobed, adopting a consultative process through meetings and praising and rewarding good suggestions will reinforce the messages you want to put across and is most likely to motivate staff.

Participation by staff should also be part of the transformation process itself. Ideally, staff should themselves have significant involvement in creating new behaviours and working routines. However, if it appears that the transformation process is slower or not transformational in the way you wish it to be, you may need to intervene and provide direction so that the transformation programme is consistent with your future strategy.

The attached letter emphasises the need for staff to get used to working with different people in different teams. To underline the importance of this, staff should be involved in team-building exercises, in teams with other staff whom they do not work with normally. This could be combined with staff involvement in creating new routines, with teams' contributions being enhanced by having staff with a range of perspectives arising from the different work experiences they have had.

Once transformation has happened, the final stage is ensuring staff are behaving in new ways and setting new standards. You will need to obtain evidence, from senior management keeping an eye on what is happening and human resource information such as appraisal meeting feedback, that changes have been embedded throughout the organisation and staff are not going back to old ways of working. The new behaviours expected can be reinforced by changing the mission, objectives and key performance indicators of TT4U.

Examining team's comments: In Task 3(a) candidates were asked to prepare an email to TT4U's CEO, to advise on the responsibilities and activities involved in preparing for transformation to the new Mieobed approach.

There was no requirement to use a model but the examining team commented that 'Following a structured approach was the best way to generate ideas for activities. Although no marks were awarded for stating the stages of Lewin's model of organisational change, candidates could apply knowledge of the activities involved in each stage to TT4U's circumstances and generate plenty of marks'. The examining team further noted that 'performance was variable on this task. Discussion about responsibilities tended to focus on the responsibilities of the chief executive officer. Less was said about the other directors. A number of answers failed to focus on the transformation process or discussed Lewin or project management frameworks without application to TT4U.' (ACCA 2020)

(b)   **Letter**

Dear colleagues

I am writing to tell you about how we, the directors, plan to transform TT4U's business approach. A key element which we plan to introduce is participation. We will therefore need your help to make it a success.

We have decided to change our business approach because of demands for enhanced client service levels in our sector. I know we have always tried to connect with our clients and our client survey showed that some clients greatly appreciate our work. However, the survey has also shown that we need to improve in certain areas. We must therefore make this our top priority.

We are going to draw our clients closer to us by open communication and demonstrating complete empathy with their needs. We also need to understand how we can tailor our services so we can take them on a journey. We must see them as stakeholders in our work, with what we do determined by what they need and how their operations can be improved.

Benefits for our company

By knowing what is driving their business, we can develop what we offer to our clients, so that they obtain more services and generate more revenue for us. If they have a close relationship with us, it is less appealing for them to change suppliers.

We also learn by talking to clients, and developing services in conjunction with them. What we develop for one client, we can adapt for others. What we learn from clients can enhance the contribution of our most important asset – you, our staff.

Benefits for you

I am so excited to be introducing this new approach because of the value which it will provide for you. We shall be giving you the training you need to develop knowledge of all our services and your personal skills. You will also be developing your capabilities by undertaking a wider variety of stimulating work, connecting with clients so that you understand what they require, and also working with, and learning from, different colleagues on different jobs. You will be given enhanced responsibility for maintaining dialogue with clients. Helpful suggestions will be rewarded as will outstanding client service.

How your work will change

I am sure you are asking what this will mean in your day-to-day work. The structure that we are used to, of three departments, will be loosened. You will be working with different teams to service different clients or on developing particular services. Teams will contain a mixture of expertise so that we can learn from each other.

This team structure will also help enable more communication. We all have a part to play in this. When you are in the office, do not sit in the same place with the same people every day but sit with, and talk to, different colleagues. Do not just read the intranet, but make use of it. Participate in discussion forums. Pass on to your manager and colleagues ideas you have had and insights you have gained from clients.

Finally, make our clients and our stakeholders the centre of your world. It goes without saying that clients should be responded to quickly however they contact us. Make sure you respond fully to their concerns. However, if we are to take clients on a value-enhancing journey, we need to do more than react, we need to be proactive. We all have a role to play with individual clients in making suggestions to them, using our knowledge and experience and awareness of their needs to help their organisation fulfil its full potential.

This is a start of a conversation between us. We will be talking together much more about this in the weeks and months to come. I look forward to discussing it with you.

Yours sincerely

Chief executive officer

Examining team's comments: In task 3(b) candidates were asked to explain the benefits of introducing the Mieobed approach for TT4U and its employees, as well as explaining the main changes to team structures and behaviours below board level that the new Mieobed approach would require.

As with task 3(a) candidates who adopted a systematic approach and used the exhibits to identify issues performed well. However, weaker candidate responses lacked balance, focusing only on benefits to clients without linking them to the benefits for TT4U or its employees, per the requirement. Responses to the second part of the question were variable with some candidates only examining changes in structure without addressing changes in behaviour. The examining team observed that candidates may well have been under time pressure for the final question resulting in weaker responses.

To earn the 3 professional marks candidates needed to demonstrate communication skills by writing a letter to employees, using convincing arguments to persuade employees of the benefits of adopting the new approach. The examining team noted that 'professional marks reflected the poor performance for technical marks, with most candidates scoring one of the two lower grades. Marks were also limited by candidates failing to make realistic suggestions about information that would indicate the state of relationships with clients.'(ACCA 2020) When demonstrating commercial acumen it is therefore important to consider the practical application and implementation of any recommended changes.

(c) **Briefing notes on board membership and information flow**

The changes suggested to board composition and information flow reflect the need for development in TT4U's governance as it is growing and seeking to be more responsive to its clients' needs.

Executive team

The current executive team has combined operational management responsibilities with taking on board roles part time up to now. However, TT4U is now large enough to warrant full-time commitment to board roles and perhaps greater delegation to a management team immediately below board level. There is a case for the following roles being full time:

–   Operations director – an additional role to the CEO and services director, to oversee and co-ordinate the new, more complex structure.

–   Marketing director – concentrating on the effective marketing of new services and leading the winning of business from new clients.

–   Human resources director – TT4U's size, the importance of key staff to the business and the forthcoming changes in structure with impacts on staff development and motivation

Non-executive directors

The non-executive directors recruited so far help ensure TT4U complies with legal and regulatory requirements. TT4U will probably have to recruit more non-executives when it becomes fully listed. If the right non-executive directors are recruited now, they could make a strong contribution to the business at an important time for its development.

The board should consider carefully what knowledge and experience new non-executive directors should ideally have, but directors with the following backgrounds would appear to be particularly valuable:

- Experience and knowledge of the IT sector, who have worked for businesses which 'do things differently' from TT4U and businesses with a strong record of innovation in the sector.

- Experience in client service who can view this aspect of what TT4U offers critically.

Information supplied to board

The board needs to be supplied with sufficient and timely information about developments in the wider environment relating to client service. It is not enough just to know what competitors are offering. More information is needed on how services are provided and how competitors are measuring the strength of their client service. The board should also be supplied with available external information about how TT4U is ranked for client service compared with its competitors.

Findings derived from e-marketing initiatives should be summarised for every board meeting, including interest shown on the website and response to website surveys. Action taken in response to previous findings should be summarised. The board should obtain and discuss summaries of relationships with current clients. Client feedback should be sought on a continuing basis, and not just one-off surveys, if TT4U is to show itself to be serious about the Mieobed approach. The board should be particularly concerned with feedback from larger clients and clients whose contracts are coming up for renewal.

The board should also be informed immediately if there are signs of serious problems with client relationships. These can be major complaints from clients or events such as major system outages which can trigger problems with clients.

The summaries should be supported by summaries of key performance indicators which focus on client service. These include response times to client communications, meetings with clients and additional services sold to clients. Although it is more difficult to measure, there should be indicators of TT4U's flexibility in responding to client requirements. Dialogue with clients may provide the best indicators of this.

> **Examining team's comments:** The final task asked candidates to advise on the changes required to the membership of the board and the information supplied to the board, to reflect TT4U's developing business needs and to make TT4U's more responsive to its clients' needs. To perform well, candidates needed to relate their discussion of board information to the threats faced by the business and steps that the business was taking to address weaknesses. According to the examining team 'This task was generally poorly answered. The lack of content or the failure to answer the task at all suggested many candidates had run out of time, as this task was generally answered last. Answers on membership of the board were often limited to recruiting more non-executive directors to fulfil governance requirements (...) Discussion on information requirements was often limited to discussing the qualities of good information without any specific suggestions about what information should be supplied.' (ACCA 2020)
>
> Candidates could earn up to 3 professional skills marks for commercial acumen. The examining team commented that a lack of realistic suggestions about information that would indicate the state of client relationships led to many candidates not gaining these marks.

ACCA

Strategic Business Leader

Mock Exam 4 (September/December 2020)

Questions	
Time allowed	**4 hours**
This question paper is an integrated case study with one section containing a total of 100 marks and ALL Tasks must be completed.	
All Tasks contain Professional Skills marks which are included in the marks shown above.	

DO NOT OPEN THIS EXAM UNTIL YOU ARE READY TO START UNDER EXAMINATION CONDITIONS

BPP
LEARNING
MEDIA

Strategic Business Leader – Mock Exam 4 – September/December 2020

Overview

The Bloom Conservation Organisation (BCO) is a not-for-profit charitable organisation set up to protect endangered wildlife around the world. It was founded 50 years ago by Dana Bloom, a wealthy entrepreneur with a passion for wildlife protection. She set up the BCO wildlife park in her home country of Geeland and, since it was founded, the wildlife park has provided intensive hands-on management of some of the world's most threatened animals. In the wildlife park, animals breed and increase in number while the keepers and wildlife experts study them to learn more about what they need to thrive in the wild again, before releasing them. The BCO also operates 20 'in the field' animal protection programmes (that is, animal welfare and management activities occurring in the animals' natural habitats) in 15 countries worldwide. The BCO employs teams of locally-based wildlife experts and volunteers to manage and protect some of the most endangered animals in the world.

Much of the BCO's income comes from donations from the public and from corporate donors. The BCO also generates income from legacies, which are donations left when people die. Geeland, as with many other developed economies around the world, has suffered from an economic recession for several years and many charitable organisations have struggled to survive in such difficult economic times. However, the BCO has managed to maintain its position as a world-leading charity in wildlife protection by implementing programmes of cost cutting, rationalisation, and more targeted and active promotion of its activities.

The BCO has a board of trustees which oversees the management of the charity, which is undertaken on a day-to-day basis by the management board. Dana Bloom, who is now over 80 years old, has very recently stepped down from her role as chairperson and a new chairperson, Rani Jeffels, has just been appointed. Rani Jeffels has a strong commercial background, having previously been a chief executive of several of Geeland's leading corporations.

You work as a senior finance manager of the BCO.

It is currently September 20X1.

The following exhibits provide information relevant to the case study.

Exhibit 1:   Extracts from the BCO's annual report – the extracts highlight the BCO's mission, vision, aim, and objectives and its main activities in the latest financial year ending 30 April 20X1.

Exhibit 2:   'About us' page of the BCO website – the website page sets out the leadership structure and governance of the charity.

Exhibit 3:   BCO's financial activities and KPIs – a summary of the income and expenditure of the BCO for the last two financial years (20X0 and 20X1), including a summary of its KPIs.

Exhibit 4:   Charity sector research report – a recent research article detailing the main threats and opportunities facing the charity sector.

Exhibit 5:   The BCO's risk register – the latest risk register, identifying the key risks and mitigating activities identified by the risk committee.

Exhibit 6:   Article on charity leadership – a news article on the recent bad publicity surrounding leadership issues in the charity sector.

The case requirements are included in the tasks shown below:

1   The new chairperson, Rani Jeffels, has recently commenced his new role with the BCO and wants to find out as much as possible about the organisation. He has called a meeting with the management board and has asked for each board member to make a short presentation to assist him in better understanding the BCO. The chief finance officer (CFO) has been asked to present on the BCO's governance principles and activities, and its financial and non-financial performance in the latest financial year. The CFO has asked you to assist him in preparing for his presentation.

Required

Prepare a briefing note for the CFO which:

(a)   **Explains:**

(i)   **The specific nature of the principal-agent relationship of the BCO as a charitable organisation;**

(ii)   **The advantages for the BCO of having a two-tier board structure; and**

(iii)   **How the BCO's mission and strategic objectives meet its key stakeholder needs.**   **(12 marks)**

Professional skills marks are available for demonstrating *commercial acumen* skills in demonstrating understanding of organisational issues relevant to the BCO.

(2 marks)

(b)   **Analyses the financial and non-financial performance of the BCO in the latest financial year, 20X1, providing reasons for and implications of the results.**
(13 marks)

Professional skills marks are available for demonstrating *analysis skills* in considering the relevant information and evidence relating to the BCO's financial and non-financial performance.   **(3 marks)**

(Total = 30 marks)

2   In its recently published annual report, the BCO set out three strategic objectives for the next five years. The new chairperson is keen to understand in more detail how the BCO's external environment will impact on these strategic objectives and has asked the CFO to provide him with this information. The CFO has asked for your assistance in preparing his report.

Required

(a)   **Prepare a report for the CFO which evaluates the extent to which the external environment could impact on the BCO's strategic objectives.**   **(15 marks)**

Professional skills marks are available for demonstrating evaluation skills in objectively appraising the facts, opinions and findings relating to the BCO's external environment.   **(4 marks)**

In addition to the recent investment made in updating the members' database management system, the chief executive officer highlighted in the annual report that the BCO is looking for further opportunities to invest in e-business technologies. The CFO has been asked to make a presentation to the board of trustees and he has asked for your assistance in preparing his presentation.

Required

(b)   **Prepare three presentation slides (with accompanying notes) which recommend, with clear justifications, three applications of information technology that the BCO could use to enhance its e-business capabilities.**   **(15 marks)**

Professional skills marks are available for demonstrating communication skills in using compelling arguments to persuade the board of trustees of the potential of e-business technologies for the BCO.   **(4 marks)**

(Total = 38 marks)

3   The chairperson has asked to meet with the chief executive officer (CEO) to discuss the BCO's current risk management approach. The chairperson has concerns that the current risk register does not adequately evaluate the seriousness of the risks identified and that some relevant risks are not covered at all. He is also concerned that the risk mitigating activities are inadequate, in the light of recent changes and events in the external environment.

The CEO disagrees and thinks that the risk register and its risk mitigating activities are sufficient, and that the chairperson is overreacting to the BCO's latest financial results and the industry research report. She has asked for your assistance on this matter.

Required

Prepare a confidential report which evaluates the BCO's current risk register and the adequacy of each of the risk mitigating activities, clearly highlighting whether the chairperson's concerns are justified. (15 marks)

Professional skills marks are available for demonstrating *scepticism* skills in questioning appropriately the opinions expressed by the chairperson and the CEO. (4 marks)

(Total = 19 marks)

4   Soon after you completed your report on the BCO's risk register and risk mitigating activities, you attended a meeting with the CEO and the chief finance officer. At the meeting the CEO raised her concerns that the board of trustees does not have a sufficient mix of skills and diversity and that the management board had, in the recent past, not undertaken sufficient professional development. She has requested a meeting with the chairperson to discuss this issue further. The CEO has asked for your assistance in preparing for this meeting.

Required

Prepare a briefing paper for the CEO which explains:

(a)   **The importance for the BCO's board of trustees to have a sufficient mix of skills and diversity; and**

(b)   **The importance of continuing professional development for the BCO's management board members to ensure that the BCO meets its obligations to its stakeholders.** (10 marks)

Professional skills marks are available for demonstrating *commercial acumen* skills in showing awareness of organisational and wider external factors affecting the work of the BCO's board of trustees and management board. (3 marks)

(Total = 13 marks)

Exhibit 1: Extracts from the BCO's annual report highlighting the BCO's mission, vision, aim and objectives and its main activities in the latest financial year ending 30 April 20X1.

Our mission

Protecting and conserving our wildlife for future generations.

Our vision

A safer, healthier world where people respect and support our wildlife.

Our aim

To support and increase the number of healthy and thriving wildlife communities across the world and encourage everyone to be more involved in the natural environment they live in.

Our strategic objectives

We have set out three clear strategic objectives for the next five years. These are:

- Ensure that 100 threatened species are protected and returned to their natural habitat.

- Invest in 100 wildlife habitat projects across the world, through providing training and education for local staff, volunteers and communities.

- Ensure one million people are better connected with nature, through education and awareness of the natural world they live in.

Review of 20X1

Our financial position continues to be challenging. Operating a world-class wildlife park and global animal protection programmes is costly, hence our need for a range of income streams. This year, we reluctantly raised the price of admission to the wildlife park for the first time in five years. This decision was taken with a view to using the increased revenue to invest in better long-term facilities and experience for our visitors. Our wildlife park facilities continue to be popular, resulting in increased revenues from our on-site shop and café.

Income from legacies was down on 20X0, a continuing trend on the past few years, highlighting the volatile nature of reliance on legacy income. We sold one of our properties in the last year and two more will be sold next year to fund the extension of the visitor centre, which we hope will contribute to our objective of connecting people with nature. We were also successful in securing over $2 million in grant-funded donations over the next few years. This is a significant source of income for the BCO and we are grateful to those organisations which have awarded these grants.

A huge amount of work over the year went into updating our members database management system, which will be in place in 20X2 and allow us to communicate more effectively with members and permit online fee payments. Further investment in information technology is a key to our growth in the coming years, in our drive to streamline our business and to educate and communicate more effectively with our stakeholders. We will be launching a re-designed website in 20X2 and are looking for new opportunities to use e-business technologies more effectively in areas such as online education, digital marketing and social media.

It is with great sadness that we said goodbye to Dana Bloom last month. Our founder had been a tireless supporter of the BCO and her work, imagination, vision and determination has played a vital role in making the BCO the world-leading charity that it is today. She has been inspirational in creating a world where many endangered animals have been given a chance to thrive. We wish Dana a very happy and peaceful retirement.

Exhibit 2: 'About us' page of the BCO website, which sets out the leadership structure and governance of the charity.

BCO's leadership

Our two-tier board consists of the board of trustees and the management board.

Board of trustees

The governance of the BCO is vested in our board of trustees, which has overall control of the charity and is responsible for monitoring its strategic direction and ensuring it is in line with our mission and objectives. It is also responsible for monitoring the risks to which the charity is exposed, through the risk committee.

Board of trustee members

Chairperson – Rani Jeffels (61 years old) – Rani joined the board in August of this year. He has a masters' degree in economics and joins the BCO having had a successful and varied career in industry, where he held numerous senior managerial positions, including chief executive of Springvale Foods Plc.

Dr Boris Tilley (68 years old) – Dr Tilley has been a trustee of the BCO for 12 years. He has had a lifelong passion for animal protection, having worked for many overseas animal charities throughout his career. He has a doctorate in literature.

Mavis Reece-Boyd (73 years old) – Mrs Reece-Boyd has been a trustee of the BCO for 11 years and is a lifelong friend of Dana Bloom and a keen supporter of animal protection. She has a degree in fine art.

Sir Henry Ryde (75 years old) – Sir Henry has been a trustee of the BCO for 14 years and has a strong commercial background, having worked in the financial services industry before retiring and taking up his position with the BCO.

Dr Hardeep Khan (48 years old) – Dr Khan has a masters' degree in animal protection science and has worked in many of the most important animal protection sites across the world. He joined the board three years ago.

Stella Bond (58 years old) – Mrs Bond has been a trustee of the BCO for eight years and has commercial experience in retail sales.

Management board

Our highly experienced and dedicated management board is responsible for the day-to-day business of the BCO. It's main duties are to develop and propose strategies to achieve our mission and objectives and to measure and report on the BCO's performance. It takes responsibility for the management and delivery of our activities.

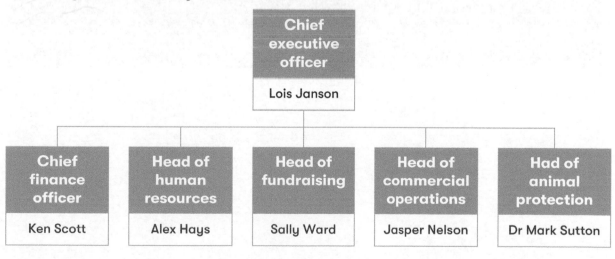

Exhibit 3: A summary of the income and expenditure of the BCO for the last two financial years (20X0 and 20X1), including a summary of its KPIs.

Summary of Financial Activities:

Year ended 30 April	20X1 $'000	20X0 $'000
Income		
Wildlife park admissions	3,103	3,005
Membership fees:		
– Individual	1,973	1,923
– Corporate	210	90
Education programmes	2,023	2,155
Wildlife park shop and café	5,675	4,923
Donations, grants and legacies	7,283	8,625
Other – sale of property	525	–
Total Income	20,792	20,721
Expenditure		
Charitable Activities		
Animal support costs: Wildlife park (staff/animal food/medical/facilities)	10,063	9,220
Animal support costs: In the field (staff/facilities/transport/medical)	4,265	4,000
Staff training	1,000	1,110
Commercial Activities		
Costs of operating wildlife park shop and café	3,533	4,163
Costs of other commercial income	1,695	1,570
Total Expenditure	20,556	20,063
Net Income	236	658

	20X1	20X0
Number of paid staff employed (wildlife park and in the field)	344	351
Number of volunteers (wildlife park and in the field)	180	154
Key Performance Indicators		
Wildlife park visitor numbers	258,583	263,595
Income per visitor from café and shop	$21.95	$18.68
Average training days per staff member	4.8	5.1
Cost per staff training day	$606	$620
Number of external education training programmes run	145	151
Number of animals returned to natural habitats	1,680	1,595

Exhibit 4: A recent charity sector research article detailing the main threats and opportunities facing the charity sector.

Why charities must change

THE GLOBAL CHARITIES INSTITUTE FOR RESEARCH

By Professor Aksel Parish

A number of events and changes have happened in the last couple of years which have given the managers of many charities some cause for concern.

Since the global recession over a decade ago, many countries are still feeling its effects and governments globally have been financially under pressure. This has impacted on the wider population, whose income has also been over-stretched.

Linked to this is the general financial position of charities. Many charities have for too long been over-reliant on a small number of funding options. If a funding source ends, the impact on a charity can be immediate and devastating. Many publicly-funded grant awarding bodies and corporate supporters of charities have reluctantly had to reduce their support for charities both financially and in terms of volunteering, as they have seen their own incomes reduced by the financial crisis.

However, public expectations of the work done by charities are still high, which places increased demands on all charities, and many have found themselves at risk of being unable to meet expectations. For example, many global nature and animal protection charities have seen demand for their support and protection increase dramatically, as habitats around the world are being increasingly destroyed by human activities. However, year-on-year these charities struggle to maintain stable funding levels.

Some of the decrease in charitable funding has been caused by 'donor fatigue', as people have become over-exposed to charitable requests and therefore stop donating. Some charities have been accused of 'hard-selling' their services, by bombarding donors with requests by post, email and on the streets. Charities have no doubt become more aggressive in trying to win donor support, resulting in some local authorities banning street donations to stop aggressive donor collection tactics. This also impacts badly on the general reputation and perception of the sector. More legislation is expected in the coming years to stop the use of 'hard-sell' marketing tactics used by some charities.

A younger generation of donors has also been brought up in a time of austerity and is less likely to donate to charitable causes. Some charities have recognised the younger generation as a potential source of donations and have used new forms of technology, such as social media platforms and mobile technologies, to effectively communicate and interact with a potential new source of supporter. However, some charities have been slow to protect and nurture the customers and donors they already have, missing the opportunity to build better relationships with them to encourage retention through the use of e-marketing and communication strategies. A failure to innovate or update organisational systems to match the needs of the society we live in may be a major downfall for many charitable organisations.

Exhibit 4: Extract of results of client survey

Potential risk	Potential impact	Risk mitigating activities
Fund-raising pressures	– Insufficient income to cover expenditure – Reputational risks of campaigns or methods used to raise funds	– Implement appropriate cost budgeting procedures – Monitor the adequacy of financial returns achieved (benchmarking comparisons) – Report fund-raising activities to stakeholders in annual report
Loss of key staff	– Experience or skills lost – Operational impact on key animal protection projects	– Succession planning – Agree notice periods and handovers – Review recruitment processes and policies
Increased competition in the sector	– Loss of income – Reduced public profile	– Monitor methods of service delivery – Monitor public awareness and profile
Operating in dangerous locations around the world	– Staff/volunteers injured or killed carrying out their responsibilities	– Monitor and review activities in recognised dangerous locations and procedures to remove staff at short notice – Closely work with local security and safety services – Regular training

The risk committee is chaired by the BCO's chairperson and has two other board of trustee members. The committee meets once a year to review the risk register and the activities being undertaken by the BCO to monitor and manage risks.

Exhibit 6: A news article on the recent bad publicity surrounding leadership issues in the charity sector.

The Geeland Times

Are charity leaders out of touch?

Charities under increasing pressure to improve sector.

By Grace Kline, Charities Analyst

Research for the Geeland Charity Commission has found that people are increasingly concerned about how charities spend their money and how they are managed and led.

The main reason given for trusting charities less, cited by over one-third of people questioned, was negative media coverage. Stories to have hit the headlines since the last survey include the collapse of two major health charities amid allegations of financial mismanagement, and the general perception that some charities are run more like clubs for old school friends, with boards of trustees being out of touch and unskilled for the modern world in which they operate.

Some of the major problems of charities in recent times have been poor strategic direction, driven largely by charities being led and managed by boards which seem to lack awareness of the changing world they now operate in. Many charities seemingly lack direction, strategy and forward planning, with issues being addressed piecemeal with limited strategic reference. Some of the blame for this has been laid firmly at the door of the trustees, those people tasked with setting the charity's strategic direction. In a modern world, where charities are facing similar commercial pressures to profit making organisations, the question is whether charities can be run effectively by trustees with no commercial background and with limited understanding of strategy formulation.

In a presentation to Geeland's charity leaders this week, the Charity Commission's chairman, Lief Morten, said that the decline of the charity sector was 'a wake-up call for everyone who runs a charity'. He said 'Poor fundraising practices, poor management and weak, out of touch leadership have all combined to reduce public confidence in the charity sector.'

Morten said: 'The public wants to see charities account better for how they spend their money and that charities are making a positive difference to their causes. However, the damage done to the sector by these examples of bad practice must be balanced by the vast amount of energy, commitment and hard work put in by most charities.'

End of Question Paper

Answers

Strategic Business Leader – Mock Exam 4 – September/December 2020

Marks

1 (a) Award 1 mark for each relevant point made in relation to the three specific areas covered.

Award up to a maximum of 4 marks for each requirement section.

Up to a maximum of 12 marks   12

Key Points

(i) **The principal agent relationship of the BCO**

- Fiduciary relationship
- Principal responsible for good governance
- Agent tasks assigned by principal
- Management board financially rewarded
- The board of trustees not financially rewarded

(ii) **The principal agent relationship of the BCO**

- Board of trustees – monitor activities of the management board

- Clear separation of duties

- Maintain trust of stakeholders

- Encourages transparency

(iii) **How our mission and objectives are driven by stakeholder needs**

- Principals acting on behalf of a wide range of stakeholders

- BCO mission – driven by needs of these stakeholders

- First objective – needs of threatened species and communities

- Second objective – needs of staff/locals

- Third objective – needs of wider communities

(b)   Up to 2 marks for each relevant point related to the financial and non-financial performance of the BCO, (1 mark for identification of a relevant issue – 1 additional mark for clearly discussing the reasons for and/or implications of each relevant issue).

1 mark for each relevant calculation up to a maximum of 4 (no marks for merely repeating numbers already presented in the exhibit).

Up to a maximum of 13 marks

13

Key Points
Financial

- Charitable activities income – driven by increased admission prices
- Visitor numbers down – concern
- Increase income from increased entry price
- If visitors drop – lose income from shop and café
- Income from shop and café increased – positive
- Corporate membership grown significantly – but small proportion of income
- Individual membership grew slightly – positive
- Income from education and training programmes decreased – impact on SO's
- Fewer external training programmes – does not meet SO's
- Donations, grants and legacies reduced – primary sources of income
- Reduced reliance on this income source – positive
- Animal support and welfare costs increased – cost control
- Inefficient cost management procedures
- Costs of commercial operations reduced – possible efficiently

Non-financial performance (KPIs)

- Staff employed decrease – impact on delivery of programmes
- Attracted more volunteers – but not use volunteers to replace skills and expertise
- Are skilled animal welfare staff being replaced by volunteers?
- Visitor number down – but each visitor spent more
- Training days per staff lower – impact on programme delivery
- External training programmes reduced – impact on SO's
- Re-wilding programmes successful – ultimate objective

2   (a)   1 mark for each relevant point made (do not penalise candidates if they have not used a PESTEL approach to structure their answer).

If PESTEL is used then award a maximum of 4 marks for each category.

Up to a maximum of 15 marks

15

Political environment impact

- Governments financially overstretched
- Increases in personal and business taxation rates
- Impact on wider population and business community
- Strategic objectives require significant financial resources

Economic environment impact

- Donations and legacies decreasing – global recession impact
- Concern for ability to achieve strategic objectives
- Economic changes globally impacting demand charities like BCO
- Strategic objectives threatened if revenues decrease
- Serious harm to our reputation and ultimately in our ability to survive

Social environment impact

- 'Donor fatigue' – over exposed to charitable requests
- Society under pressure
- Severe risk to strategic objectives
- Engage younger generation
- Austerity – less prone to donate

Technological environment impact

- Prospective positive and negative influence
- Internet allows globally reach
- Positive impact on ability to generate donations
- Opportunity to build better relationships with donors
- Use online marketing, electronically delivered training and online donations
- Failure to innovate – major consequences

Ecological environment impact

- Key external driver
- Many similar charities seen demand increase dramatically
- However – struggle to maintain stable funding levels for such organisations
- Threat to survival

Legal environmental impact

- Local authorities banned street donations
- Impacts badly on general reputation/perception of sector
- Need to retain strong legal support
- Cost of regulation (health and safety increasing costs)

BPP
LEARNING
MEDIA

ANSWERS

(b) For each slide, award 1 mark for each relevant and applied point made within the accompanying notes.

Up to a maximum of 5 marks for the notes on each per slide.

Maximum of 15 marks

Key Points

Slide 1

Social media

– Build supporters, boost donations, share success stories

– Engage with a younger generation of supporters

– Two-way communication – interactive

– Global reach – cost effective

– Make emotional connections

– Use of images, videos, comments

– Encourages supporter to interact – create online community

Slide 2

Online delivery of training and education

– Strategic objectives – invest in providing training and education

– Costly – time and money without online delivery

– Deliver anywhere in the world

– Use of mobile devices – any time of day or night

– Global access – without physical costs

– Huge cost saving and source of funds

– Allows BCO to share knowledge cost effectively

Slide 3

Digital marketing

– Cost effective – assists in reaching a wider audience

– Need well-designed website

– Requires effective Search Engine Optimisation (SEO) – easy to find

– Technology extended for non-members online donations

– Includes mobile applications, another source of e-marketing

– Apps convenient and accessible

– Tailor messages to individuals and groups

– Access potential volunteers and attracting interest of potential staff

3   Up to 2 marks for a discussion of the general issues relating to BCO's risk management activities.

1 mark for each relevant point made relating to the BCO's risk register and the associated risk mitigating activities.

Up to a maximum of 4 marks for each risk category from the risk register discussed.

Up to a total of 15 marks   15

Key Points

General issues

Environment changing significantly – should meet more than twice per year.

Reassure key stakeholders of our commitment to managing risks effectively.

Chairperson may have a relevant cause for concern in functioning of Risk committee.

Risks identified

1.   *Fund-raising*

–   Significant risk
–   Significant challenges in coming years
–   Balance drive for increased income with ethical behaviour

Adequacy of risks mitigating activities

–   Budgeting important – but not address need to increase income streams

–   Limited scope to reduce fundraising risk

–   Benchmarking – reactive approach to risk management

–   Not assist in achieving increased income streams

–   Stewardship reporting – not directly assist overcoming risks

–   Overall, Chairperson has valid point in regard to adequacy of risk management activities

2.   *Loss of key staff and employment issues*

–   Significant risk – staff key asset

–   Invest significant sums in training staff

–   Lose that expertise – risk of not attaining high standards of operation

–   Justifiable risk to focus on

Adequacy of risks mitigating activities

–   Succession planning – ensuring staff continuity and handover

–   Ensure plan in place so staff prepared to take on new roles

–   Motivate remaining staff

–   Review recruitment policies – critical in ensuring staff have correct skills

–   Risks management activities sufficient and appropriate

–   Training and retention not included – significant omission

3. *Competition*
   - Key risk – recent sector research report
   - Reduced income & loss of public awareness and profile
   - Correct to include this in risk register

   Adequacy of risks mitigating activities
   - Monitoring of service delivery and public awareness – inadequate to manage serious threat
   - Useful starting point
   - Not sufficiently proactive
   - Chairperson correct in concerns relating to the management of this risk

4. *Operating in dangerous locations around the world*
   - Significant risk
   - Need to include potential litigation – injury or death to staff or volunteers

   Adequacy of risks mitigating activities
   - Monitor/review activities in dangerous locations/procedures to remove staff – key risk management activities
   - Also ensure these tested regularly
   - Close relationship with security and safety services – key risk management activity
   - Evidence a proactive risk management approach
   - Adequate risk management activities in this risk area

   Other issues to consider and concluding comments
   - Chairperson's concerns justified
   - Significant risk from changing demographics
   - Lack of use of technology and potential threats this brings considered as key risk

4   1 mark for each relevant point made and applied to BCO.

Up to a total of 6 marks per section

Up to a maximum of 10 marks   10

(a)   **Board of trustees with a sufficient mix of skills and diversity**
- Five 55+ & only two women
- May lack knowledge/awareness of changing world
- Particularly in technology and needs and lifestyles of customers
- Only new Chairperson has recent commercial experience
- Two others have commercial background – sufficiently recent?
- Charities facing similar commercial pressures to profit making organisation

Limited understanding of strategic management
- Three trustees – on board for over 10 years
- Not represent wide spectrum of stakeholders
- Risk of losing strategic direction

(b)   **Continuing development for management board members**
- Build a strong management team
- Interact to build more cohesive team
- Up to date in areas of expertise and legal and regulatory knowledge
- Culture driven by tone from management board
- Set out a clear signal it values continual learning
- Encourage staff and volunteers
- Creating a learning organisation environment
- Motivate and retain good board members
- Encourages innovative
- Increase confident

Professional skills may be additionally rewarded as in the following rubric:

How well has the candidate demonstrated professional skills as follows:	Not at all	Not so well	Quite well	Very well
Commercial acumen skills in demonstrating an understanding of the organisational issues relevant to the BCO	The candidate has demonstrated no commercial acumen. The candidate has failed to demonstrate an understanding of how the structure and relationships within the BCO are driven by its organisational context and its objectives. The answer was purely theoretical.	The candidate has demonstrated limited commercial acumen. Some commercial awareness was demonstrated in understanding of the BCO's organisational context and activities as a charity, but the candidate has failed to consider a number of the most relevant factors.	The candidate has demonstrated good commercial acumen. Most of the discussion demonstrated good commercial awareness in recognising how the BCO's objectives and organisational context, impact on its activities and management structure. The candidate covered a good range of relevant commercially sound points.	The candidate has demonstrated excellent commercial acumen. The answer demonstrated a very high level of judgement and commercial awareness of how BCO's objectives and the impact on the BCO's board structure and activities of its organisational context. The candidate's answer was very well applied.
Briefing Note			The format of the briefing notes is appropriate and suitable for presentation to the chief finance officer.	The format of the briefing notes is appropriate and suitable for presentation to the chief finance officer.
	0	0.5	1	2

Professional skills may be additionally rewarded as in the following rubric:

How well has the candidate demonstrated professional skills as follows:	Not at all	Not so well	Quite well	Very well
Analysis skills in considering the information relating to the BCO's financial and non-financial performance.	The candidate has demonstrated poor or no analysis skills. The candidate has merely restated the information presented in the exhibit, with no consideration of the implications of this information to the BCO.	The candidate has demonstrated limited analysis skills. Some of the answer demonstrated some analytical skills but there was insufficient analysis and understanding of the relevance and impact of the key aspects of the results.	The candidate has demonstrated good analysis skills. Most of the answer was based on evidence identified from the scenario information and the candidate has made a reasonable attempt to analyse a range of key financial and non-financial issues and demonstrated reasoning and understanding.	The candidate demonstrated excellent analysis skills. All of the candidate's analysis is based on evidence identified from the scenario and there is a clear and logical analysis of the most relevant financial and non-financial factors and has presented clear and logical reasoning.
Briefing Note			The candidate has presented the answer in a briefing note format and most of the analysis is adequate for the intended audience.	The candidate has presented the answer in a briefing note format and the analysis is highly relevant for the intended audience.
	0	1	2	3

How well has the candidate demonstrated professional skills as follows:	Not at all	Not so well	Quite well	Very well
Evaluation skills in objectively appraising the facts, opinions and findings relating to the BCO's external environment.	The candidate has failed to demonstrate any evaluation skills. The candidate has not appraised the information presented and has merely re-stated information already presented. The candidate has shown poor professional judgement in failing to appraise the appropriate information in a useful and objective way.	The candidate has demonstrated weak evaluation skills. The candidate has shown limited professional judgement in appraising the information provided but has used an appropriate framework to structure the answer. However, the candidate has not adequately evaluated the information in an objective or useful way.	The candidate has demonstrated good evaluation skills. The candidate has shown good professional judgement in selecting and applying a suitable framework to evaluate the information and has made some reasonable assertions. They have demonstrated a reasonable appraisal of the information presented.	The candidate has demonstrated excellent evaluation skills. The candidate has shown excellent professional judgement in evaluating the most relevant external environmental factors impacting on the strategic objectives. The candidate has made very well justified assertions about the external environment and has demonstrated clear and objective judgement.
Report Format			The answer is presented in a suitable report format.	The answer is presented in a suitable report format.
	0	1.33	2.66	4

How well has the candidate demonstrated professional skills as follows:	Not at all	Not so well	Quite well	Very well
Communication skills in using compelling and logical arguments to persuade the Board of trustees of the potential of e-business technologies for the BCO.	The candidate demonstrated no or poor communication skills. The candidate has failed to present a logical argument for e-business technologies. The style, tone and presentation of the slides and notes would not be suitable for presentation to the Board of trustees.	The candidate demonstrated some basic communication skills. They have demonstrated some evidence of presenting relevant arguments for e-business technologies but some of it is not clear or insufficient to communicate effectively to the Board of trustees.	The candidate demonstrated good communication skills. They have presented a good range of logical and clear arguments for application of e-business technologies. However, some key points were missing and/or the arguments were not fully developed.	The candidate demonstrated excellent communication skills. They have presented a clear, balanced and logical presentation, giving clear and logical arguments for the application of e-business technologies. The answer is logical, clear and persuasive.
Slide Presentation			The candidate has presented the answer in a suitable presentation slide and note format.	The candidate has presented the answer in a suitable presentation slide and note format.
	0	1.33	2.66	4

ANSWERS

How well has the candidate demonstrated professional skills as follows:	Not at all	Not so well	Quite well	Very well
Scepticism skills in questioning appropriately the opinions expressed by the chairperson and the chief executive officer	The candidate has failed to challenge the opinions raised by the chairperson and the CEO relating to risks in the BCO's register and the adequacy of its current risk management activities. The answer is descriptive and there is no evidence of questioning the opinions in an appropriate way.	The candidate has made a limited attempt at challenging the opinions of the chairperson and the CEO in relation to the risk register and the adequacy of the current risk management activities. There is some evidence of evaluating the risk management activities but this is limited.	The candidate has made a reasonably good attempt at challenging the opinions of the chairperson and the CEO in relation the contents of the risk register and the adequacy of the current risk management activities. There is evidence of a number of challenges made to the comments made in an appropriate way.	The candidate has made an excellent attempt at challenging the opinions of the chairperson and the CEO in relation the contents of the risk register and the adequacy of the current risk management activities. There is excellent evidence of the candidate recognising and challenging most of the relevant issues in BCO's risk report in an appropriate way.
Report Format			The answer is presented in a correct report format.	The answer is presented in a correct report format.
	0	1.33	2.66	4

How well has the candidate demonstrated professional skills as follows:	Not at all	Not so well	Quite well	Very well
Commercial acumen skills in showing awareness of organisational and wider external factors affecting the work of the BCO's board of trustees and management board.	The candidate has not demonstrated commercial acumen. They have failed to link their discussion of the activities of the board of trustees and the management board to the external environment which affects them. The answer is largely descriptive, with little reference to the needs of the BCO's stakeholders.	The candidate has demonstrated limited commercial acumen. Some attempt has been made to consider relevant skills, diversity and CPD relating to the BCO, but this has not been linked adequately to the needs of the external environment and the BCO's stakeholders.	The candidate has demonstrated good commercial acumen. A reasonable amount of the answer is linked directly to the required skills, diversity and CPD requirements of the BCO, and there has been some attempt to consider the impact and needs of the external environment and the BCO's stakeholders.	The candidate has demonstrated excellent commercial acumen. Most of the answer is linked directly to the required skills, diversity and CPD requirements of the BCO, and the candidate has clearly and correctly considered the impact and needs of the external environment and the BCO's stakeholders.
Briefing Notes			The answer is presented in the correct briefing note format.	The answer is presented in the correct briefing note format.
	0	1	2	3

ANSWERS

Suggested solutions

1   (a)   **Briefing Note Section 1**

        (i)   **The principal-agent relationship of the BCO**

            Fiduciary relationship

            The BCO's board of trustees, acting as the principal, is responsible for good governance, but they rely on many different people to be able to govern well: staff, volunteers and importantly, the management board. In a principal-agent relationship, the principal engages the agent to perform a service on their behalf which involves delegation of some decision-making authority to the agent. The relationship creates a fiduciary relationship between the board of trustees and the management board, which means the management board, acting on behalf of the trustees, must carry out the assigned tasks with the principal's best interests (and therefore those of the BCO's diverse stakeholders) as a priority.

            Represent stakeholders

            The board of trustees, as the principal, represents the interests of the BCO's stakeholders, which will include not only those stakeholders and organisations which have contributed or donated funds to the charity but also the people and animals living in the wildlife communities we operate in, our staff, our wildlife park visitors and the wider community. The management board, as the agent, undertakes responsibilities assigned by the board of trustees. The management board therefore has an obligation to undertake their responsibilities assigned with a certain level of skill and care, using the particular skills and expertise each member has been employed for.

            Reward

            As agents, the management board is financially rewarded to discharge responsibilities delegated to it, without conflicting with the interests of the stakeholders which the board of trustees represent. The board of trustees is not financially rewarded for their role, as it effectively acts on behalf of the stakeholders of the BCO.

        (ii)   **The advantages of a two-tier board structure**

            –   One advantage of this governance arrangement is that there is a clear and distinct separation of duties between the monitoring function of the board of trustees and those being monitored (the management board).

            –   Additionally, the supervisory role of the board of trustees acts as an effective safeguard against management inefficiency and against fraud or irregular activities. All of this helps to maintain the trust of the stakeholders, in particular those donating funds to the BCO, who will seek reassurance that their funds are being used appropriately by the BCO.

- A further advantage is that the board of trustees, in its supervisory role, will consider the needs of all of our stakeholders, including staff and the wider community to ensure that their interests are also taken into account and the actions of the management board do not affect them adversely.

- The two-tier system also encourages transparency within the charity, between the two board levels and between the board of trustees and the stakeholders they represent. This transparency is particularly important in the charitable sector whereby the charity must be accountable for the diverse range of funds it receives.

(iii) **How our mission and objectives meet stakeholder needs**

- For most profit-seeking organisations, the mission and objectives are largely driven by the needs of the principal; that is the owners or shareholders. In particular, the objectives will be mainly focused on ensuring that the principals' returns are maximised. However, as already discussed, our principals are acting on behalf of a wide range of stakeholders and therefore our mission and objectives will have a different focus.

- Our mission is firmly focused on protecting and conserving the world's wildlife for the future. This meets the needs of a wide range of stakeholders, including the wildlife itself and the people who live and work within the communities in which they live. In addition, the wider community will also benefit from a world in which wildlife can thrive and live safely in its natural habitat.

- The first objective of protecting and returning the 100 threatened species to their natural habitats meets the needs of the threatened species themselves and the communities which they come from. Therefore, this objective meets our stakeholder needs.

- The second objective of investment in 100 wildlife habitat projects across the world through training and education for local staff and communities also meets the needs of our stakeholders, including staff and local people, who require the specific knowledge and skills to ensure that habitat projects are successfully run and managed and that donors' funds are used effectively.

- The third objective to ensure 1 million people are better connected with nature meets the needs of our wider communities and population to understand and appreciate the natural world they live in. If the wider population appreciate and understand the natural world better, this will impact directly on the wildlife species the BCO is ultimately set up to protect.

(b)   **Briefing Note Section 2**

Financial performance evaluation

The BCO maintained more or less a steady state from 20X0 to 20X1, based on levels of income and expenditure, although our surplus decreased by $422,000. Income from charitable activities increased by 5% in the year, much of which was as a result of admissions to the wildlife park. However, visitor numbers to the wildlife park were down by nearly 2% (258,583, compared to 263,595 in the financial year 20X0), meaning that the increase in revenue from wildlife park admissions came from the increased price we charged this year to visitors to enter the wildlife park. This is a concern, as visitors to the wildlife park are a key source of income. If visitors continue to fall, then this could have a knock-on impact on income from other sources, such as individual membership and income from the wildlife shop and café, if less visitors use our facilities.

However, despite the fall in visitor numbers the income from the wildlife park shop and café increased by 15%, from $4,923,000 to $5,675,000. This is encouraging and demonstrates that our shop and café are popular and a potential source for future revenue growth. This suggests that our shops and cafés are operating effectively.

Corporate membership income has grown significantly (133%) from $90,000 to $210,000 but is still a very small proportion of our income (1%) and we must look to grow this, through further work with corporate partners. Individual membership grew only slightly which we need to improve on. However, this could be looked at positively, considering that visitor numbers to the wildlife park dropped in the year and therefore our conversion rate of converting visitors to members has in fact improved. Therefore, our on-site membership marketing activities appear to be operating effectively but we still need to do more to convert visitors to members and attract more visitors overall.

Two areas of concern in relation to our revenue from commercial activities are from education and training programmes and donations and legacies. Income from running education and training programmes was 6% lower than last year. This, combined with the KPI showing that we ran fewer external education and training programmes in 20X1 compared to 20X0 (145 v 151) is concerning, when considering our long-term objective of increasing our commitment to educating and training our stakeholders. This clearly does not meet this objective. This is something we must focus on in the coming years if we are to ensure that our strategic objectives are met.

Donations, grants and legacies income reduced by nearly 16% (from $8,625,000 to $7,283,000). This is particularly concerning, as these are our primary sources of income. However, we could perceive this as a positive direction, as our total income in fact increased in 20X1, despite this decrease in this primary revenue source, meaning we are improving in other revenue sources. In 20X0 donations, grants and legacies were 42% of total income, whereas in 20X1 it was 35% of total income. This indicates that we have reduced our reliance on this income source and increased other sources to compensate, although we should note that some of this has come from the sale of property assets which is not a recurring or sustainable source of commercial income. This means we must not be complacent, as the donations, grants and legacies will continue to be important to source of income in the future and therefore we must try to maintain our active work in seeking these sources of income and looking for ways to support that donor income with sustainable commercial initiatives.

Expenditure has increased in the year by nearly 2·5%, which, although not overly concerning, must be something we monitor closely. We spent significantly more on animal support costs, which increased in the year by 8%. This is something that we must investigate further. This rise may be due to inflationary pressure on the underlying costs of resources (veterinary costs, animal feed and staff pay rises) or it could suggest we are being inefficient in our cost management procedures and are not controlling these costs effectively and making the best use of our resources. We have an obligation to obtain the optimum value for money for our stakeholders and we must manage our funds appropriately.

Costs of commercial operations reduced by 15% which is very positive. This may be due to fewer properties to manage (we sold a property in 20X1) or it could be because we have managed our shop and cafe more efficiently. We may be able to learn lessons from our cost management processes in our commercial operations and transfer these to our management of animal welfare costs.

Non-financial performance evaluation (key performance indicators)

The overall number of staff we employed decreased but we were able to attract more volunteers to work for the BCO. Although this should be seen as a positive factor, in that we are clearly attracting external support for our activities, we must be careful that we do not use volunteers to replace the skills and expertise of employed staff, some of whom will be trained experts. Obviously, we will need to monitor whether it is skilled animal welfare staff who are being replaced by volunteers, or more unskilled temporary staff in non-animal related areas (such as visitor centre staff). Loss of expert staff and a net reduction in human capital may impact detrimentally on our effectiveness.

As mentioned above, visitor numbers to the wildlife park are down but on average each visitor actually spent more money when they visited ($3·27). This is a positive factor and we should look to investigate how we can encourage visitors to spend more in the wildlife park, by increasing and continually improving the facilities and attractions we have on site and also investigate more fully where customers spend the most.

Training days were down on 20X0 as too were external training programmes run. These outcomes do not fit with our objectives of increasing education and training and we must address these if we are to achieve our stated strategic objectives.

Our programmes to re-introduce animals to the wild continue to be successful as more animals were returned to their natural habitats in 20X1 compared to 20X0. This should be a key focus of our performance measurement, as ultimately, this is the reason for our existence. All of our activities are carried out with this as our main objective.

2   (a)   **To:**   Chief finance officer

                 From: Senior finance manager

                 Date: XX/XX/20X1

                 Subject: The impact of the external environment on the BCO's strategic objectives

Introduction

When setting our strategic objectives, a key element of this process is to evaluate the external environment and its impact on those objectives. Importantly, we must continually assess our external environment to monitor its continued impact on our strategies and to identify how we should respond to these external events to ensure we maintain our strategic direction. Achievement of our strategic objectives will be affected by the current global economic climate and the pressure this places on individuals and corporations, on whom we rely for donations and for support.

Political environmental impact

As noted in a recent charity industry research article, many governments around the world have been financially overstretched by the global recession. This has had severe consequences for ourselves and the whole charity sector, as increases in austerity measures have impacted negatively on the business community and on the wider population. At the same time, demands placed on charities like ourselves have in fact increased as a result of the political and economic climate.

The recent charity sector report also noted that publicly-funded grant awarding bodies have reduced support for charities both financially and in the number of volunteers, evidence again of changing political priorities that we are vulnerable to as an organisation. However, this aspect of the political environment has not had such a significant effect on the BCO in the last year, as we were still able to secure $2 million of publicly funded grants in 20X1, evidence of effective management of this aspect of our external environment.

Economic environmental impact

All of our strategic objectives will require significant financial resources, in particular our wildlife protection activities, both within the wildlife park and in the overseas locations where we operate our programmes. In the next five years our primary objective is to protect 100 species and return them back to the wild. This will be expensive and therefore we will need to balance this with the financial resources we have available.

A large proportion of our donations come from legacies which, from our annual report, have been decreasing in recent years. This is a major concern for its impact on our ability to achieve our strategic objectives, without reducing the funding we put into these projects or reducing the number of projects we invest in. It is likely that as donors face periods of economic uncertainty, then donations to charities will likely decrease, threatening the achievement of our strategic objectives.

Compounding this is the fact that the demands placed on charities like ours are in fact increasing as a result of the current economic and political environment. As the recent research report highlighted, many global nature and animal protection charities have seen demand for their support and protection increase, as animal habitats are being destroyed by human activities, largely caused by changing economic priorities and policies. Our strategic objectives of returning 100 species to the wild and investing in 100 projects will be threatened if such economic pressures increase over the next five years.

Also, as evidenced in our recent financial results, our operational costs are also increasing, possibly as a result of inflationary pressures caused by the current economic environment. We have a duty to our stakeholders to operate economically, but this is going to be challenged and ultimately may impact on the quality of our programmes, if costs continue to rise.

Social environmental impact

Evidence from the recent charity sector report suggests that some of the decrease in charitable funding has been caused by 'donor fatigue', whereby people have become over exposed to charitable requests and therefore, have reduced or stopped donating. As competition amongst charities increases for the limited charitable donations available, it is inevitable that society will be put under pressure and may in fact turn away from charitable funding. This would be a severe risk to all of our strategic objectives, as without these donations, and the continued awareness and support from society, we simply cannot function. This is both from a financial point of view and from our staffing and volunteering perspective. Pressurised fund-raising tactics employed by some charities, such as bombarding donors with donor requests by post, email and on the streets has clearly had a negative effect on donation levels across the whole sector and we must identify strategies to minimise this impact.

Understanding the changing demographics is also an important aspect of our environmental analysis. As the research report suggested, the younger generation of donors have been brought up in a time of austerity and therefore less likely to donate spare money to charitable causes. This age group however is more accessible, through changing technology, which we could and should exploit.

Technological environmental impact

Technology could be viewed as a positive or negative influence on our strategic objectives. The internet and its global reach has allowed our message to be spread globally through the use of our website, which we intend to re-launch next year. Improved communication about all of the work and activities we undertake could have a significant positive impact on our ability to generate donations from further afield than Geeland.

However, the technological environment has advanced beyond the application of an informational website, allowing for the opportunity to build better relationships with stakeholders through the use of such technological applications of online marketing, online education and training, online donations and a wide range of interactive social media applications. A failure to innovate or update systems to match the needs of society we now operate in may be a major downside to us.

Ecological environmental impact

Fundamentally, the BCO was set up to meet a demand to protect the ecological environment, and our key external drivers have, and always will be, primarily to meet ecological needs. As the recent research report suggest, many global nature and animal protection charities have seen demand for their support and protection increase dramatically, as habitats around the world are being increasingly destroyed by man-made activities, yet year-on-year these organisations struggle to maintain stable funding levels. Therefore, the changing and growing ecological demands placed on us will present us with both opportunities and challenges in the future. It is likely that, with increasingly limited resources, we are going to have to prioritise the work we do and the areas we invest in, which may compromise the achievement of our first two strategic objectives.

Legal environmental impact

Charities have no doubt become more aggressive in trying to win donor support and some local authorities have banned street donations in their local towns to stop aggressive donor collection behaviour. This also impacts badly on the general reputation and perception of the sector. Also, more legislation is expected to reduce the use of 'hard-sell' marketing tactics used by some charities. Even if we are not involved in such tactics ourselves, this legislation will affect us and this may impact on our ability to raise funds in certain areas, such as on-street collections or postal adverts. With pressures already facing us on reduced income streams, this additional legislation could impact further on our income, thus impacting on achievement of our strategic objectives.

Summary

The current external environment is creating significant pressures on ourselves and the charity sector as a whole and these pressures will affect our ability to raise sufficient funds and awareness of our activities to achieve our strategic objectives, but there are some significant opportunities associated with some of these factors. It will be critical for us to therefore constantly monitor these external factors to assess how we can address and manage their effects on our strategic objectives, particularly in their impact on our ability to raise funds.

(b)

> **Slide 1:**
>
> **Social Media Presence**
>
> **Features:**
>
> - Two-way communication
> - Highly interactive
> - Multi-media – text, videos, audio
>
> **Benefits:**
>
> - Global 24/7 communication
> - Reach wide demographic
> - Inexpensive form of communication and marketing
> - Build emotional connection proactively

Notes

Social media is a critical component of many modern organisations' e-business strategy and is an increasingly effective strategy for charities to adopt to interact with supporters globally. Social media will allow us to enter into two-way communication and engage with a vast number of supporters one-to-one.

Social media platforms are especially relevant if we want to engage with a younger generation of supporters. Comment boards, forums, likes and tweets give us the opportunity to engage proactively with those who are interested in and support the BCO's work. This opens up lines of communication for those who want to make direct contact with us, which are currently not available.

The biggest advantage is that social media has a global reach and is inexpensive. Social media can therefore be an effective way for us to build global support, boost donations, share success stories, encourage people to sign up to campaigns or to volunteer and to demonstrate the impact of our animal protection work around the world.

Importantly, social media gives the BCO the chance to make emotional connections. Use of images, videos and human reactions are what will really bring the work of our charity to life. Potential volunteers are more likely to get involved if they can picture the animals and habitats we are trying to help. Donations will be more forthcoming if people can directly see and experience the work we do.

Social media encourages our supporter to interact through 'likes', 'comments', and writing blogs or uploading photos and videos to personalise involvement with us. Using social media could help us create our own BCO online community.

> **Slide 2:**
>
> **On-line education and training delivery**
>
> **Features:**
>
> - Web-based training modules
> - Use mobile technologies – laptops and smartphones

> – Electronic resource library
> – Continuous availability
>
> **Benefits:**
>
> – Cost savings in physical delivery
> – Globally accessible training on demand
> – Savings in time and resources
>   Source of income

Notes

One of our strategic objectives for the next five years is to provide training and education for staff, volunteers and communities, and a further strategic objective of delivering online education and awareness programmes to connect people to the natural world. Both of these objectives will be costly in terms of time and money and without online delivery may in fact be impossible to realistically achieve.

Using our website, we can offer web-based training and education programmes to our staff and volunteers anywhere in the world, accessible through a range of mobile devices and at any time of day or night. Online delivery allows global access, meaning we can offer training and education programmes globally without having to spend money on sending training staff and physical training documents and manuals. This will be a huge cost saving for us.

On-demand access also offers total flexibility, making it more likely that users will make use of our resources at a time that suits them. This means they are not having to use vital work time to attend physically delivered courses.

Similarly, online education and awareness delivery allows us to more easily spread our vision and activities globally to as many people as possible in a cost-effective manner.

We could also offer our online courses to external customers who are willing to pay for them and the materials we use. This could be an alternative form of income for us, selling our expertise globally.

> **Slide 3:**
>
> **Digital marketing**
>
> **Features:**
>
> – User friendly website and mobile applications
> – Search Engine Optimisation
> – Analytics to tailor marketing messages
>
> **Benefits:**
>
> – Marketing tailored to the individual
> – Reduces costs of traditional direct marketing activities
> – Updated instantly
> – Attract volunteers/staff

Notes

Marketing is often seen as an activity reserved for commercial organisations, undertaken to secure additional awareness and ultimately, increased sales of its products and services. However, marketing is equally important to a charitable organisation such as the BCO. Digital marketing is more cost effective and should assists in reaching a wider audience for our marketing message.

The first element of e-marketing for us, is an effective and well-designed website, something which we are planning on undertaking next year. This needs to be located easily through effective Search Engine Optimisation (SEO), and ensuring our website remains easy to use, accessible and importantly, easy to find.

ANSWERS

The potential development of mobile applications is another source of digital marketing. Apps are convenient and accessible on the go for many people, particularly the younger generation, and could be a beneficial method of marketing.

Application of digital marketing is particularly useful as it allows us to tailor messages to individuals and groups who show an interest in what we do. Again, this is a major positive in creating a strong marketing message to potential donors and customers. It is also a positive way of accessing potential volunteers and attracting interest of potential staff in a cost-efficient way.

3 To: Chief executive officer
   From: Senior finance manager
   Date: XX/XX/20X1
   Confidential: Evaluation of BCO's risk register and risk mitigating activities

Introduction

The following report will consider the BCO's current risk register, as presented in our latest annual report and assess whether the risk mitigating activities are adequate, particularly taking into consideration the current environment and challenges facing the charity sector, as outlined in the recent research report.

BCO's risk register and risk mitigating activities

Risks identified

The current risk register identifies four potential risks for the coming year which are all relevant and important risks facing the BCO at this point in time and all are correctly identified as key risks to our organisation. I will consider the adequacy of the risk mitigating activities of each in turn below.

1.   Fund-raising

The risk register identifies that we may not be able to raise the required level of funding to cover our costs. From an analysis of our latest annual report it is clear that the BCO's income is just managing to cover its expenditure and in fact, had we not sold a property in the year, then the BCO would have been in deficit. Therefore, this is a genuine and significant risk for the forthcoming years. As the charity sector has clearly come under scrutiny and much criticism recently, we will face significant challenges in the coming years to increase our income, without undertaking more promotion and awareness programmes, which inevitably will cost money. We will have to balance this drive for increased income with ensuring our activities remain ethical and do not harm our reputation.

Adequacy of risk mitigating activities

Implementing appropriate cost budgeting procedures is clearly an important aspect of managing our expenditure, but it does not actually address how to increase income streams. Therefore, this risk management activity has limited scope to improve our fundraising risk. All it does is manage the costs we incur.

Similarly, benchmarking our financial returns is a relatively reactive approach to mitigating our risks and will not assist us in achieving increased income streams. Stewardship reporting for stakeholders in our annual report is a key aspect of transparency and communication with our stakeholders, but again, it will not directly assist in overcoming the risks of our ability to raise sufficient funds.

Overall, I consider that the chairperson has a valid point in regard to whether our risk mitigating activities relating to fund raising are adequate and that he is not over-reacting. Our current risk mitigating activities are only likely to give us increased information on potential reasons of our fund-raising levels and costs and not how to address/improve them.

2.   Loss of key staff and employment issues

This is a significant risk to the BCO, as our staff are a key asset in the delivery of our animal protection activities. We invest significant sums in training staff and it could be a huge financial and potentially reputational loss when staff leave. If we lose that expertise, which we have to then either buy in or re-train we run the risk of not attaining the high standards of operation we set for ourselves. Therefore, this is a key and therefore justifiable risk to focus on as an organisation.

Adequacy of risk mitigating activities

Currently, our risk management activities include succession planning, agreement of notice periods and review of recruitment processes and policies. These would seem to be suitable risk management activities to assist in reducing and eliminating some of the risks associated with the loss of staff. Succession planning is a critical aspect of ensuring staff continuity and successful handover of responsibilities when staff leave the organisation. This should ensure that we have a definite plan in place to ensure that remaining staff are ready and prepared to take on new roles and responsibilities when required. Also, this should assist in motivating remaining staff. Review of recruitment policies and processes is also a critical aspect in ensuring that we employ staff with the correct skills and attitudes, therefore hopefully resulting in lower staff turnover. However, a key aspect of mitigation which is not considered is training programmes, which would be an effective way of motivating staff to remain committed to the organisation and thus reduce the levels of staff turnover. This may be a reason why the chairperson believes that our risk mitigating activities are insufficient. Therefore, it is recommended that our risk register should also include activities to improve retention.

Overall, our risks management activities relating to this risk are reasonably sufficient and the chairperson may be over critical of our risk management activities for this risk category. However, we must also include the implementation of appropriate and regular training programmes and skills updates for staff to enhance motivation and therefore improve retention.

3. ### Competition

Competition in the charity sector is a key risk for the BCO, as evidenced in the recent sector research report, as a result of several external environmental factors. This competition inevitably means that we face a significant risk of reduced income and subsequently, a potential loss of public awareness and profile, should potential donors and supporters choose to support alternative causes. Therefore, the Risk committee is correct to include this within our risk register.

Adequacy of risk mitigating activities

Our current risk register suggests that we should manage this risk using methods such as monitoring of service delivery and monitoring public awareness and profile. I would suggest that the chairperson may be correct in his concerns with risk management of the risk from competition, as these activities are likely to be inadequate to effectively manage such a serious threat to our position. Monitoring of public profile and service delivery are useful starting points to assess our situation in the competitive environment and they may indeed assist us in identifying areas for improvement. However, they are not sufficiently proactive to ensure we do stay ahead of our competitor and therefore the chairperson is correct in his concerns relating to the activities we undertake to mitigate this risk. We should be considering activities such as ensuring and managing key stakeholder awareness and customer/donor generation/retention strategies. Therefore, I believe that the chairperson is not over reacting to the consequences of this risk and is correct in his assessment in the adequacy of our risk management activity.

4. ### Operating in dangerous locations around the world

Because we operate our animal protection activities across the world it is inevitable that some activities will take place in dangerous locations and therefore this is a significant risk and must be considered as part of our risk register. One issue that is

BPP
LEARNING
MEDIA

not considered however, which I believe should be, is the potential litigation which may occur as a result of injury or death to any of our staff or volunteers. Therefore, the chairperson is correct in his assessment of the adequacy of our assessment of this risk and is not over reacting to the recent challenges in the sector.

Adequacy of risk mitigating activities

Activities such as monitor and review activities in recognised dangerous locations and procedures to remove staff and volunteers at short notice are key risk management activities but we must also ensure that these are carried out regularly and tested regularly. A close relationship with security and safety services is also a key risk management activity and is evidence of a proactive risk management approach. Therefore, I would in fact agree with the chief executive in this case and conclude that the BCO appears to have adequate risk management activities in this particular risk category.

Other issues to consider and concluding comments

A more general observation to make is that the BCO has a functioning risk committee, chaired by the chairperson and with two other board of trustee members, which meets once per year. In the past this may have been sufficient, at a time when the charity sector was more stable and predictable than the current environment. However, in recent times the environment has changed significantly, and it could be argued that in the light of the current rapidly changing external environment and the increasing threats this causes, the Risk committee should in fact meet more than once per year. This would reassure key stakeholders of our commitment to managing risks effectively. Therefore, in this respect, the chairperson may have a relevant cause for concern in the overall functioning of the Risk committee.

Although the risk register contains four key areas of risk facing the BCO, the chairperson is also correct in challenging the adequacy of this register, in terms of whether it covers all of the risks currently facing the BCO. The recent sector research report makes it quite clear that there are a wide range of threats and challenges currently occurring in the charity sector and many are not addressed in our current risks register. For example, there is a significant risk from the changing demographics and how we reach these in order to stay relevant as a charity. Additionally, our lack of use of technology and the potential threats this brings must be considered as a key risk. Risks such as rising operating costs, possible litigation and continued recession should also be considered.

Therefore, although our risk register has several positive attributes, the risk mitigating activities need to be reviewed and we must also update our risk register to include the current external challenges faced. Therefore, I would disagree in several cases that our risk analysis and our risk mitigation activities are sufficient and the chairperson is justified in his concerns of the adequacy of our risk management activities.

4   FAO: Chief executive officer

Briefing Notes

A recent news report highlighted the apparent weaknesses in some organisations in the charity sector and the potential implications this may have, in terms of poor strategic direction and loss of funding.

(a)   **Board of trustees' skills and diversity**

Currently, our Board of trustees does appear to lack diversity. This is evidenced in the following analysis of a board of trustee members:

(i)   Five of our six trustees are over the age of 55 and only two are women. A lack of diversity in age range of our trustees could mean that, although vastly experienced in their own areas of expertise, our trustees may lack the knowledge and awareness of the changing world we now operate in, particularly in terms of technology and the changing needs and lifestyles of our customers.

(ii) In addition, it would seem that only Rani Jeffels, our chairperson has recent commercial experience. Two other trustees do have some commercial background but it is questionable whether this is sufficiently recent to assist in the modern environment we operate in. As discussed in a recent news article, in a modern world where charities face similar commercial pressures to profit making organisation, we need to consider whether the BCO can be run effectively by trustees with such limited commercial background and with a potentially limited understanding of strategic management.

(iii) Three out of six of our trustees have been members of the board for over 10 years. Again, although vastly experienced and knowledgeable of our operations, there is also an argument that the board of trustees now requires new ideas and that our trustees could be out of touch and unskilled for the modern world in which we operate and the modern charitable environment.

These factors above should be a cause for concern for the BCO – as our trustees do not represent the wide spectrum of the BCO's stakeholders. Our board of trustees is a fundamental aspect of the success or failure of our organisation, as it is its responsibility to set out our strategic direction. If they do not have the up to date skills and mix of experience and diversity to do this successfully then we are at risk of losing our strategic direction.

(b) **Continuing development for management board members**

(i) Continuing professional development for our management board should assist members to think together from a more strategic perspective and should help to build a strong management team. Often a board has little time in board meetings to get to know each other, as everyone is focussed on the job at hand and on their own areas of responsibility. Taking time out for board development allows board members to interact in a less structured environment, helping to build a more cohesive team.

(ii) Also, importantly our management board has legal duties to use reasonable care, skill and diligence. Keeping the management board members informed and up to date in their areas of expertise and in general legal and regulatory knowledge ensures that they can effectively discharge this duty. The management board must be conversant with changes in regulation, legislation and the operating environment the BCO operates in if it is to manage its strategic direction effectively.

(iii) The culture of the BCO will largely be driven by the tone set by our management board, which permeates throughout the organisation. By investing in management board development, we can set out a clear signal to the rest of the BCO that it values continual learning. This will encourage our staff and volunteers to want to continuously learn and develop, creating a learning organisation environment, critical in these challenging competitive times we face.

(iv) Continuing professional development should help to motivate and retain good board members. They will value an organisation which invests in them, which leads to increased motivation, loyalty and retention helping to contribute positively to the achievement of our strategic objectives.

(v) As an organisation we are facing increasing challenges from our environment and we need to be innovative in the ways we operate and raise funds. Continuing professional development will assist management board members to be more innovative in their thinking as, people who have been trained well in how to do their jobs are more likely to be more confident and innovative. This in turn should helpfully assist in offering the BCO greater competitive advantage in the form of both improved processes, and also an increased likelihood of new products or services to meet our ever-changing environmental demands.

ACCA

Strategic Business Leader

Mock Exam 5

Questions	
Time allowed	**4 hours**
This question paper is an integrated case study with one section containing a total of 100 marks and ALL Tasks must be completed.	
All Tasks contain Professional Skills marks which are included in the marks shown above.	

DO NOT OPEN THIS EXAM UNTIL YOU ARE READY TO START UNDER EXAMINATION CONDITIONS

BPP
LEARNING
MEDIA

Strategic Business Leader – Mock Exam 5

The island of Oceania is a very popular tourist destination, but its importance as a business centre is also increasing, due to its relatively low tax rates.

Oceania has four main airports, and until ten years ago it had two main airlines – Oceania Air and Transport Oceania. However, ten years ago the two companies merged into one airline – Oceania National Airlines (ONA) – with the intention of exploiting the opportunities for growth in business and leisure travel to and from Oceania.

The following exhibits provide information relevant to ONA:

Exhibit 1: An introduction to the company, produced by the Finance Director

Exhibit 2: Summary of operating and financial performance

Exhibit 3: Notes about Frequent Flyer Programmes (prepared by the Sales Director)

Exhibit 4: Extracts from local newspapers

Exhibit 5: Extract from memo from the head of internal audit

Exhibit 6: Transcript from the most recent board meeting – HR and payroll systems

Exhibit 7: Notes from the Chief Executive Officer (CEO) about a potential new route, forwarded to you by the Finance Director

Exhibit 8: Extract from a voicemail message left for you by ONA's Finance Director

The task requirements are as follows.

1   You have recently joined ONA as a senior finance manager. You report to the Finance Director (who is a professional accountant) and advise on special projects and strategic matters. The board are going to discuss ONA's strategy at their next meeting, and the Finance Director has asked you to help her prepare the board report for that meeting.

Required

From the information you have been provided, write the sections of the board report which:

(a)   **Evaluates ONA's strengths and weaknesses, and their impact on the company's performance**   **(16 marks)**

Professional skills are available for demonstrating **evaluation** skills relating to ONA's strategic capability and performance   **(4 marks)**

(b)   **Analyses why moving to a 'no frills' low cost strategy would not be appropriate for ONA**   **(14 marks)**

Professional skills are available for demonstrating **scepticism** skills in questioning the appropriateness of the proposed strategy.   **(2 marks)**

(Total = 36 marks)

2   You are a project manager working at ONA.

The Sales Director and the CEO recently attended a conference about the future of the airline industry, and the opportunities and threats it faces.

Following the conference, the CEO is now very concerned about cyber risks, and the related need for ensuring that ONA has robust cyber security policies in place.

By contrast, the Sales Director's main concern after the conference is that ONA should introduce a 'Frequent Flyer Programme'. He has circulated his notes from the conference about this, and has suggested in an email to the other directors that there is no need to make a formal business case for it, because 'the Programme's justification is so self-evident that defining a business case, and undertaking benefits realisation, would just be a pointless exercise. It will slow us down at a time when we need to speed up.'

These issues are also going to be discussed at the next board meeting.

Required

The CEO has asked you to produce a briefing paper which:

(a)   **Explains why establishing a business case and undertaking benefits realisation are essential, despite the apparent 'self-evident' justification of introducing a Frequent Flyer Programme.**   **(5 marks)**

Professional skills are available for demonstrating **commercial acumen** in relation to awareness of the importance of business cases and benefits realisation.   **(2 marks)**

(b)   **Explains the increasing importance of cyber security, and identifies the key control areas which ONA needs to consider in relation to its cyber security.**   **(6 marks)**

Professional skills are available for demonstrating **communication** skills in clarifying key control areas in relation to cyber security.   **(2 marks)**

(Total = 15 marks)

3   It is now three months later. You are a business advisor that has been commissioned to provide advice to the ONA board on a range of issues.

   (a)   Recent news reports, as well as internal meetings and memos, have highlighted that ONA is facing a number of issues which could damage its reputation.

   Required

   The Finance Director has asked you to prepare sections of a report to the board which do the following:

   (i)   **Recommend the risk management procedures that ONA should adopt to deal with the risks that the recent security alerts have highlighted.**

   (5 marks)

   Professional skills marks are available for demonstrating **communication** skills for explaining clearly what the procedures are.   **(2 marks)**

   (ii)   **Identify the key stakeholders who will be interested in the disputes over maintenance procedures, and discuss the nature of their interest.**

   (12 marks)

   Professional skills marks are available for demonstrating **commercial acumen** in relation to awareness of who the most important stakeholders are.   **(2 marks)**

   (b)   The HR Director thinks that ONA needs to review a number of its HR systems, and – as the transcript shows – these systems were discussed at the last board meeting. However, the HR Director is also concerned about the other directors' approach to implementing new systems, and she has emailed you to ask for your help in trying to convince the other directors not to focus solely on the IT aspects of the project.

   Required

   Prepare a briefing paper which explains why it is important for ONA to consider people, organisation and processes when implementing business change projects.   **(6 marks)**

   Professional skills marks are available for demonstrating **analysis** skills in explaining the importance of considering people, organisation and processes when implementing projects.   **(2 marks)**

   (Total = 29 marks)

4   **New route**

   You are a financial analyst working in ONA's finance department.

   ONA has been looking to increase the number of airports it flies to, and has recently become aware of the possibility of securing prime landing slots at Hiapop airport. However, securing these slots is contingent on the payment of an initial facilitation fee to a senior official at Hiapop airport.

   The Finance Director has told you the board members are divided over whether or not ONA should agree a contract with Hiapop airport. However, she has specifically asked you for your thoughts about the potential ethical issues it raises.

   Required

   Prepare a memorandum which assesses the potential ethical issues which the board should consider when deciding whether or not to agree a contract with Hiapop airport.

   (6 marks)

   Professional skills marks are available for demonstrating **commercial acumen** in showing awareness of relevant issues and their potential impact on the decision.   **(2 marks)**

   (Total = 8 marks)

5   You are a senior finance manager reporting to the Finance Director. The Finance Director has asked for your help with a project she is working on.

ONA's annual report currently focuses primarily on its financial and operating performance in the last year. At the last board meeting, the CEO suggested ONA introduces integrated reporting but a number of the other directors weren't sure what this is.

Required

The Finance Director has asked you to prepare TWO presentation slides, with supporting notes which describe the advantages to ONA of adopting integrated reporting (<IR>), and how the information provided in an integrated report will differ from that in traditional financial reports.   **(10 marks)**

Professional skills marks are available for demonstrating **communication** skills in producing information which could be presented to the directors.   **(2 marks)**

(Total = 12 marks)

Exhibit 1: An introduction to the company, produced by the Finance Director

ONA's markets

ONA serves two main market sectors.

Regional sector – The first sector is a network of routes to the major cities of neighbouring countries. ONA's management refer to this as the regional sector. The average flight time in this sector is one and a half hours and most flights are timed to allow business people to arrive in time to attend a meeting and then to return to their homes in the evening. Twenty-five major cities are served in the regional sector with, on average, three return flights per day. There is also significant leisure travel, with many families visiting relatives in the region.

International sector – The second sector is what ONA management refer to as the international sector. This is a network of flights to continental capitals. The average flight time in this sector is four hours. These flights attract both business and leisure travellers. Twenty cities are served in this sector with, on average, one return flight per day to each city.

Most leisure travellers, in both sectors, pay standard or economy fares and travel in the standard class section of the plane. Although many business travellers also travel in standard class, some of them choose to travel business class for which they pay a price premium.

Image, service and employment

ONA is the airline of choice for most of the citizens of Oceania. A recent survey suggested that 90% of people preferred to travel ONA for regional flights and 70% preferred to travel with ONA for international flights. 85% of the respondents were proud of their airline and felt that it projected a positive image of Oceania.

The company also has an excellent safety record, with no fatal accidents recorded. ONA has placed great importance on its staff providing a high quality of service, and its service levels have been recognised by the airline industry itself. Two years ago, in 20X5, ONA was voted Regional Airline of the Year by the International Passenger Group (IPG) and one year later the IPG voted ONA as the provider of the best airline food in the world.

The courtesy and motivation of its employees (most of whom are residents of Oceania) has come to be recognised throughout the region. ONA has developed a reputation as an excellent employer. It pays above industry average salaries, offers excellent benefits (such as free healthcare) and has a generous non-contributory pension scheme. In 20X4 ONA employed 5,400 people, rising to 5,600 in 20X5 and 5,800 in 20X6.

95% of ONA employees belong to recognised trade unions.

Fleet

Fleet details are given in Table 1. Nineteen of the Boeing 737s were originally in the fleet of Oceania Air. Boeing 737s are primarily used in the international sector. Twenty-three of the Airbus A320s were originally part of the Transport Oceania fleet. Airbuses are primarily used in the regional sector. ONA also use three Embraer RJ145 jets in the regional sector.

The board has been considering taking advantage of new technology in aircraft engines by investing in new low-noise, fuel-efficient aircraft in an effort to reduce the possible complaints surrounding aircraft noise, and also to cut fuel costs.

Table 1: Fleet details

	Boeing 737	Airbus A320	Embraer RJ145
Total aircraft in service			
20X6	21	27	3
20X5	21	27	3
20X4	20	26	2
Capacity (passengers)	147	149	50
Introduced	16 years ago	19 years ago	8 years ago
Average age	12.1 years	12.9 years	6.5 years
Utilisation (hrs per day)	8.70	7.41	7.50

Performance

Since 20X4 ONA has begun to experience significant competition from 'no frills' low-cost budget airlines, particularly in the international sector. Established international operators now each offer, on average, three low-fare flights to Oceania every day.

'No frills' low-cost budget airlines are also having some impact on the regional sector. A number of very small airlines (some with only one aircraft) have been established in some regional capitals and a few of these are offering low-cost flights to Oceania.

A recent survey showed that ONA's average international fare was double that of its low-cost competitors.

(Some of ONA's key operational statistics for 20X6 are shown separately, along with summary financial information – see Exhibit 2.)

In the last three years, ONA's financial performance has not matched its operational success. Although global passenger air travel revenues increased by 12% in the period 20X4–X6 (and revenue from air travel to Oceania increased by 15% and cargo revenue by 10%), ONA only recorded a 4.6% increase in passenger revenue.

ONA's board recognise the importance of e-commerce, and the company has recently redesigned its website with a view to increasing the number of passengers who check in online and so will require less assistance from staff at the airport. The majority of ONA's competitors already require passengers to check in online.

It is also hoped the new design will increase the number of passengers who book their tickets directly through ONA's website rather than through booking agents or other intermediary websites.

Future strategy

The board are keen to develop a strategy to address the airline's financial and operational weaknesses.

One suggestion has been to re-position ONA itself as a 'no frills' low-cost, budget airline. However, the CEO has questioned whether such a move would be appropriate for the company.

Exhibit 2: Summary of operating and financial performance

(a)   **Key operational statistics for ONA in 20X6**

	Regional	International	Low-cost competitor average
Contribution to revenue ($m)			
Passenger	400	280	Not applicable
Cargo	35	15	Not applicable
Passenger load factor *			
Standard class	73%	67%	87%
Business class	90%	74%	75%
Average annual pilot salary	$106,700	$112,500	$96,500
Source of revenue			
Direct bookings (via company website)	40%	60%	84%
Third-party bookings **	60%	40%	16%
Average age of aircraft ***	12.9 years (Airbus) 6.5 years (Embraer)	12.1 years	4.5 years
Utilisation (hrs per day) ***	7.41 (Airbus) 7.50 (Embraer)	8.70	now allows 9.10

*: Passenger load factor = % of carrying capacity which is used (ie % of available seats booked)

**: Travel agents; intermediary websites

***: Data for 'International' relates to ONA's fleet of Boeing 737s; while data for 'Regional' relates to ONA's Airbus and Embraer aircraft

(b) **Summary financial information**

EXTRACTED FROM THE STATEMENT OF FINANCIAL POSITION

	20X6	20X5	20X4
Non-current assets	$m	$m	$m
Property, plant and equipment	788	785	775
Other non-current assets	60	56	64
Total	848	841	839
Current assets			
Inventories	8	7	7
Trade receivables	68	71	69
Cash and cash equivalents	289	291	299
Total	365	369	375
Total assets	**1,213**	**1,210**	**1,214**
Total shareholders' equity	250	259	264
Non-current liabilities			
Interest-bearing long-term loans	310	325	335
Employee benefit obligations	180	178	170
Other provisions	126	145	143
Total non-current liabilities	616	648	648
Current liabilities			
Trade payables	282	265	255
Current tax payable	9	12	12
Other current liabilities	56	26	35
Total current liabilities	347	303	302
Total equity and liabilities	**1,213**	**1,210**	**1,214**

EXTRACTED FROM THE STATEMENT OF PROFIT OR LOSS

	20X6	20X5	20X4
Revenue			
Passenger	680	675	650
Cargo	50	48	45
Other revenue	119	112	115
Total	849	835	810
Cost of sales			
Purchases	535	525	510
Total	535	525	510
Gross profit	**314**	**310**	**300**
Wages and salaries	215	198	187
Directors' salaries	17	16	15
Interest payable	22	21	18
Total	254	235	220
Net profit before tax	**60**	**75**	**80**
Tax expense	18	23	24
Net profit after tax	**42**	**52**	**56**

Exhibit 3: Notes about Frequent Flyer Programmes (prepared by Sales Director)

- Many airlines have developed a Frequent Flyer Programme (FFP). [Why doesn't ONA have a similar programme?]

- FFP is a loyalty programme offered to customers (members) allowing them to accumulate points for flights booked. Members can then redeem their accrued points in future (*) in exchange for free air travel (**).

- FFPs have helped airlines improve customer loyalty, operating performance and load factors.

- Passenger loyalty is critical as competition becomes more intensive on certain routes.

- FFPs can also be a valuable marketing tool (eg gather data on members' profiles, flying habits).

* Members often take up to 2–3 years to redeem their points.

** Check with Finance Department: apparently need to consider 'deferred revenue' here. (If airline sells a ticket for, say, $200 need to defer the portion of revenue corresponding to the points granted until they are redeemed or they expire.)

Oceania Daily Reporter

Turbulent times at ONA

Oceania's national airline, ONA, has always been proud of the fact its staff are dedicated to providing the highest possible quality of service to its passengers. Recently, however, the board has come under increasing pressure to cut costs. The airline's two largest costs are fuel and staff costs, and pressure to control staff costs has led to considerable unease.

The company has faced several difficult employee relations issues in the last few months. It has encountered demands for higher pay from ground staff (including maintenance staff and baggage handlers), and improved working conditions and reduced working hours from air crew (pilots; flight engineers) and cabin crew.

Negotiations resulted in some improvements in pay for baggage handlers and reduced working hours for air crew and cabin staff. However, the demands made by the trade unions were not met in full, and are on condition that productivity targets are achieved.

In addition, ONA has faced problems with its outsourced catering service (AirChef) which have been reflected in an increasing level of complaints from passengers in recent months. In turn, AirChef has complained that ONA has negotiated the price it pays for its contract down so far that it is barely profitable. Relations between ONA and AirChef have become so strained that the AirChef's CEO has threatened to withdraw from the contract altogether unless ONA agrees to renegotiate the price. In response, ONA has stated that it will only renegotiate on price when the quality of the service has improved over a sustained period.

ONA has threatened legal action for breach of contract if AirChef withdraws its service.

Oceania Times

Airline disruption and security alerts

Oceania's national airline, ONA, and its passengers, have recently experienced disruption to a number of flights as a result of security alerts at one of Oceania's airports. In every case except one, the reason for the alerts had nothing to do with ONA. The exception, however, was when a member of AirChef's staff, who was delivering meals to an ONA aircraft, failed to comply with airport security procedures. The delay was prolonged when checks by airport security staff revealed that the individual had not received security clearance to work in restricted areas of the airport.

ONA has been holding talks with the local airport authority over plans to prevent the delays and long queues which followed the security alerts recurring in future. (As well as the inconvenience caused to passengers, delays result in significant costs for ONA, due to additional staff costs – for cabin crew and ground staff – plus additional fuel costs if planes are kept waiting to take off.)

However, the relationship between ONA and the airport authority has become strained after ONA's Operations Director is alleged to have said that 'much of the recent disruption and the delays could have been avoided if the authority had reacted more effectively.'

Exhibit 5: Extract from memo from the head of internal audit

Safety is a critical issue at ONA, and we carry out regular audit reviews on safety and maintenance procedures at ONA.

In our latest audit, we observed that some maintenance procedures on the aircraft had not been carried out correctly, which meant that a number of aircraft did not fully comply with safety checks.

This matter was raised with the Engineering Director who advised that the safety procedures were being improperly applied by three technicians, who had now been dismissed. The Director stated that he believed the maintenance procedures being applied were now all perfectly safe.

Given the potential importance of these issues, we commissioned an independent engineering consultant to carry out a review of maintenance procedures.

The consultant's report identified that there were serious faults in ONA's maintenance procedures as a whole, and the Engineering Director should have known about these.

The consultant also raised concerns that the maintenance budget needs to be reviewed, because it is currently inadequate for carrying out the maintenance procedures which ONA should be doing. The faults in our procedures mean that it is simply a result of good luck that there have been no serious incidents with ONA's planes.

The trade unions are now arguing that the three technicians who were dismissed have been used by management as scapegoats to cover up failings at a more senior level.

These maintenance issues have further strained relationships between management and staff at ONA. The trade unions have now called for the three technicians to be reinstated, but also to have the pay and working conditions for all the maintenance staff reviewed.

The trade unions have not ruled out strike action if their discussions prove unsuccessful. Strike action by the maintenance staff would mean that all of ONA's flights would have to be suspended.

Exhibit 6: Transcript from the most recent board meeting – HR and payroll systems

HR Director: As I have been suggesting for a while, I believe it is time to upgrade the payroll system. We have worked with the current system for a number of years now, but it is becoming increasingly inadequate for our needs. It does not support payment increments for non-standard working, such as overtime rates. To allow this, payroll staff currently have to change an employee's standard hourly rate for the time period in question and then change it back again. This is time-consuming and payment errors have been made when payroll staff have forgotten to change the rate back again.

The human resource management system is also becoming increasingly inadequate – with the result that we are facing increasing difficulties in getting the right numbers and types of staff (both ground crew and cabin crew) in the right place at the right time.

CEO: I agree we need to upgrade our systems. However, we have to be conscious of budget limitations here. We do not have the funds – or sufficient IT system developers – to build our own bespoke system, so I suggest that we select and implement a commercial off-the-shelf solution, as there should be one which can fulfil our requirements.

IT Director: I think the point about internal IT resources is important. We have previously purchased commercial, off-the-shelf packages in other areas of the business, and members of the IT support team then had to find workarounds when users found problems with the functionality of the system.

Can I suggest we adopt a four-stage process for evaluating and implementing any new systems:

- First, evaluate whether a commercial, off-the-shelf solution is an appropriate approach
- Second, define the requirements for the new software
- Third, evaluate competing packages
- Finally, implement the selected package

HR Director: It is important that we don't focus only on IT though. Our business is large and complex, and we need to consider people, organisation and processes as well as the IT itself. If we ignore the first three areas, and focus purely on the IT, we could find ourselves faced with another failed software project.

Exhibit 7: Notes from the Chief Executive Officer (CEO) about a potential new route, forwarded to you by the Finance Director

- We need to look at opportunities for growth, and flying to new airports is one potential source of growth.

- We don't fly to Hiapop airport, but it is becoming an increasingly popular destination.

- Several established international operators already fly to Hiapop.

- In order to secure landing slots at Hiapop, ONA will have to pay an initial, one-off fee, of about $1 million, to a senior local official.

- Once the fee is paid, ONA will be guaranteed landing slots for at least 10 years.

- Forecast figures suggest that these slots could generate $50 million in additional gross profits for ONA over 10 years.

- Hiapop would be the first airport ONA serves in its country, so securing the slots could be instrumental in delivering additional growth for the airline.

- Concerns about the idea of paying the initial 'facilitation fee'? Apparently, such fees are perceived as normal business practice in Hiapop's country, but I'm a bit uneasy about this.

Can we discuss please? I'd be keen to get your thoughts on this.

Exhibit 8: Extract from a voicemail message left for you by ONA's Finance Director

'At the last board meeting, I raised the idea that ONA should consider introducing Integrated Reporting (<IR>).

'I explained that the company has only ever disclosed the minimum information it is required to by law, but that an increasing number of companies are now broadening the amount of corporate information they publish.

'In my opinion, the primary objective of <IR> is to demonstrate the link between a firm's competitive strategy, governance system and financial performance, alongside the social, environmental and economic context within which it operates.

'I believe that by integrating these different areas, our board will be in a much better position to allocate its valuable resources more effectively and thereby make more environmental and socially sustainable decisions, which should be good for ONA's overall reputation.

'The Chair seemed supportive of the proposal, and suggested that it will demonstrate that ONA takes its corporate social responsibility seriously by being more accountable to stakeholders' interests. In addition, he said that simplifying the financial information we report should show people more clearly how the company is really performing.

'The CEO also commented that encouraging shareholders to think more about our long-term strategy should help to strengthen ONA's competitive position, and move away from their current, apparent focus on cutting costs.

'However, most of the other directors said they weren't really sure what <IR> is all about, so this will need to be discussed further at the next board meeting.'

Answers

Strategic Business Leader – Mock Exam 5

				Marks

Technical marks

1 (a) Up to 2 marks per relevant strength and its impact on ONA's performance – up to a maximum of 8 marks   Max 8

Up to 2 marks per relevant weakness and its impact on ONA's performance – up to a maximum of 8 marks   Max 8

Up to a maximum of 16 marks for task requirement 1(a)   **16**

(b) Up to 2 marks per relevant point for identifying the differences between ONA's current strategy and a 'no frills' strategy – up to a maximum of 4 marks   Max 4

Up to 2 marks for analysing why these differences mean that the proposed strategy is not appropriate – up to a maximum of 10 marks   Max 10

Up to a maximum of 14 marks for task requirement 1(b)   **14**

2 (a) Up to 2 marks per relevant point explaining the importance of establishing a business case and undertaking benefits realisation

Up to a maximum of 5 marks for task requirement 2(a)   **5**

(b) Up to 2 marks for explaining the increasing importance of cyber security   Max 2

Up to 5 marks for identifying key control areas to consider in relation to cyber security   Max 5

Up to a maximum of 6 marks for task requirement 2(b)   **6**

3 (a) (i) Up to 2 marks per relevant point for ways of managing risks – up to a maximum of 5 marks

Up to a maximum of 5 marks for task requirement   **5**

(ii) Up to 3 marks for each relevant stakeholder and the nature of their interests.

Up to a maximum of 12 marks for task requirement 3a(ii)   **12**

(b) Up to 2 marks per relevant point, up to a maximum of 2 marks for any single element (people; organisation; processes)

Up to a maximum of 6 marks for task requirement 3(b)   **6**

4 Up to 2 marks per relevant point for assessing potential ethical issues   Max <u>6</u>

Up to a maximum of 6 marks for task requirement 4   **6**

5 Up to 2 marks per relevant advantage – up to a maximum of 6 marks   Max <u>6</u>

One mark per relevant point about the differences in <IR> information compared to traditional financial statements – up to a maximum of 6 marks. [Note. There is a maximum of 2 marks for simply discussing the 'Six capitals'.]   Max 6

Up to a maximum of 10 marks for task requirement 5   **10**

Professional marks may be awarded as in the following rubric:

How well has the candidate demonstrated professional skills as follows:	Not at all	Not so well	Quite well	Very well
1(a) – Evaluation skills relating to ONA's strategic capability and performance.	The candidate failed to identify internal factors (strengths, weaknesses) which will shape ONA's strategic performance.	The candidate identified some strengths and weaknesses, but has failed to properly assess their impact on ONA's performance.	The candidate has identified a good range of strengths and weaknesses, and has evaluated their impact on ONA's performance.	The candidate has comprehensively identified – and prioritised – ONA's main strengths and weaknesses, and evaluated the impact they have on ONA's performance.
	0	1	2	4

Professional marks may be rewarded as in the following rubric:

How well has the candidate demonstrated professional skills as follows:	Not at all	Not so well	Quite well	Very well
1(b) – Scepticism skills in questioning the appropriateness of the proposed strategy.	The candidate failed to identify the key differences between the two strategies and therefore why the new strategy will be inappropriate.	The candidate identified some of the key differences between the two strategies, but failed to properly explain why this means the proposed strategy will not be appropriate for ONA.	The candidate clearly identified the key differences between the two strategies, and used these to identify a good range of reasons why the proposed strategy will not be appropriate for ONA.	The candidate has clearly identified the key differences between the two strategies and then provided a comprehensive demonstration of why the proposed strategy is not appropriate for ONA.
	0	0.5	1	2

ANSWERS

BPP
LEARNING
MEDIA

Professional marks may be rewarded as in the following rubric:

How well has the candidate demonstrated professional skills as follows:	Not at all	Not so well	Quite well	Very well
2(a) – Commercial acumen in relation to awareness of the importance of business cases and benefits realisation.	The candidate has failed to demonstrate an understanding of the importance of business cases or benefits realisation; and has, for example, discussed why the FFP will be advantageous to ONA and why it should be introduced as quickly as possible.	The candidate identified some of the ways in which establishing a business case and undertaking benefits realisation contribute to effective project management, but has missed some of the most important ones.	The candidate has identified the main reasons why establishing a business case and undertaking benefits realisation are important, but has failed to consider the potential implications of not doing so.	The candidate has identified the main reasons why establishing a business case and undertaking benefits realisation are important, and has clearly explained the potential implications of not doing so.
	0	0.5	1	2

Professional marks may be rewarded as in the following rubric:

How well has the candidate demonstrated professional skills as follows:	Not at all	Not so well	Quite well	Very well
2(b) – Communication skills in clarifying key control areas in relation to cyber security.	The candidate has failed to identify any control areas relating to cyber security.	The candidate has identified some control areas relating to cyber security, but not primarily key, strategic ones.	The candidate has identified some of the key control areas relating to cyber security.	The candidate has clearly identified a range of key control areas relating to cyber security.
	0	0.5	1	2

ANSWERS

Professional marks may be rewarded as in the following rubric:

How well has the candidate demonstrated professional skills as follows:	Not at all	Not so well	Quite well	Very well
3(a)(i) – Communication skills for explaining clearly what the procedures are.	The candidate has failed to recommend procedures that should be adopted.	The candidate has recommended procedures, but not explained how they address the risks which the problems have highlighted.	The candidate has made clear recommendations, and given some indication as to how the procedures will help to address the recent problems.	The candidate has made clear recommendations, and explained clearly how the procedures recommended will help to address the recent problems.
	0	0.5	1	2

Professional marks may be rewarded as in the following rubric:

How well has the candidate demonstrated professional skills as follows:	Not at all	Not so well	Quite well	Very well
3(a)(ii) – Commercial acumen skills in relation to awareness of who the most important stakeholders are.	The candidate has failed to identify the key stakeholders in the specific context given.	The candidate has identified some of the key stakeholders, but has done so in general terms, rather than on the basis of their commercial influence in the given situation.	The candidate has identified some of the key stakeholders, in terms of their commercial influence in the given situation, and with reference to their interests in the situation.	The candidate has identified all of the key stakeholders, and has clearly identified their interests in the situation.
	0	0.5	1	2

Professional marks may be rewarded as in the following rubric:

How well has the candidate demonstrated professional skills as follows:	Not at all	Not so well	Quite well	Very well
3(b) – Analysis skills in explaining the importance of considering people, organisation and processes when implementing projects.	The candidate has failed to consider people, organisation and processes in the context of implementing projects.	The candidate has demonstrated some limited understanding of people, organisation and processes in the context of implementing projects, but has failed to explain the significance of the elements.	The candidate has demonstrated an understanding of people, organisation and processes in the context of implementing projects, and made some sensible suggestions to support the HR Director's argument.	The candidate has demonstrated a good understanding of people, organisation and processes in the context of implementing projects, and applied it to support the HR Director's argument.
	0	0.5	1	2

Professional marks may be rewarded as in the following rubric:

How well has the candidate demonstrated professional skills as follows:	Not at all	Not so well	Quite well	Very well
4 – Commercial acumen skills in showing awareness of relevant issues and their potential impact on the decision.	The candidate has failed to identify the potential ethical threats relevant to the scenario.	The candidate demonstrated that they were aware of the ethical principles which could be at stake, but failed to assess how these should influence the board's decision making.	The candidate has correctly identified the ethical principles and the board's response to them, but hasn't considered the wider commercial implications of accepting/rejecting the contract.	The candidate has used their understanding of the ethical principles, and of directors' responsibilities to a company's shareholders, to highlight a range of key issues for the board to consider when making their decision about the contract.
	0	0.5	1	2

Professional marks may be rewarded as in the following rubric:

How well has the candidate demonstrated professional skills as follows:	Not at all	Not so well	Quite well	Very well
5 – Communication skills in producing information which could be presented to the directors.	The candidate has failed to use a slide format to communicate the advantages of <IR> and how the information in an integrated report may differ from traditional annual reports (eg six capitals).	The candidate has only loosely used a slide presentation format, but has either too many or too few points, or failed to provide both elements requested (ie advantages of adopting <IR>; differences between <IR> and traditional financial reports). The candidate has produced some notes, but they are either too long, or fail to adequately explain the slides.	The candidate has used a slide format and bullet points, and has addressed both parts of the task requirement, but there may be too many points on the slides, or they may not have been expressed succinctly enough. There are slide notes but they are either too long or fail to adequately explain the bullet points selected.	The candidate has used a slide format and bullet points, and addressed both parts of the task requirement. The candidate has prioritised the key issues to ensure there are an appropriate number of points on each slide. The candidate has produced clear supporting notes which relate closely to the points selected.
	0	0.5	1	2

Suggested solutions

Note. It is not always possible to publish suggested answers which comprehensively cover all the valid points which candidates might make. Credit will be given to candidates for points not included in the suggested answers, but which, nevertheless, are relevant to the task requirements.

In addition, in this integrated case study examination points made in one question may be re-introduced or fully developed in other question(s) as long as these are made in the specific context of the task requirements of the part of the question being answered.

The suggested answers presented below may give much more detail than would be expected from most candidates under examination conditions; they may also have used a particular approach or model which should not be taken as the only approach or model which could have been used. Different approaches and structuring of the answers are expected and full credit will be given for relevant and appropriate solutions to the tasks given. The answers provided here are intended to support revision and tuition for future examinations.

Finally, it should be noted that candidates will not get full professional skills marks in a task requirement if they have not presented their answers according to the format asked for. For example, if a task is to be completed using a report and evaluation skills are tested, even if the answer has met the specifically stated evaluation criteria, candidates will not be able to earn all the professional skills marks available if they have not used the report format.

1 **To:**   The board of ONA
   From: Senior Finance Manager
   Date: [Today's date]
   Subject: ONA's strategy

Introduction

This report assesses ONA's current strengths and weaknesses, and the impact they are having on the company's performance.

The report then considers the proposal that ONA should move to a 'no frills' low cost strategy, and analyses why such a move would not be appropriate for ONA.

(a)   **ONA's strengths and weaknesses**

      Strengths

      Brand. ONA has a strong brand identity, particularly with the citizens of Oceania. The recent survey results indicate that ONA was the airline of choice for the country's residents, for both regional flights and international flights. This brand strength should help create customer loyalty, and in turn sustain customer demand.

      Regional presence. The citizens of Oceania are proud of their airline and feel that it projects a positive image of Oceania. This again should help promote customer loyalty and sustain sales.

      Customer service. ONA provides excellent customer service, and has won industry awards for both its customer service and its in-flight meals. This excellence helps ONA differentiate itself from some of its competitors, and may allow it to charge premium pricing.

      Employees. ONA is perceived as an excellent employer in Oceania. As a result, its employees have, traditionally, been highly motivated and courteous. This helps maintain the high levels of customer service it offers, and the level of service customers experience could again be a factor which helps to differentiate ONA from its competitors.

      Safety record. ONA has an excellent safety record, and has had no fatal accidents. Although the safety record is unlikely to increase sales in its own right, it is a feature which ONA can use to highlight the quality of its product.

      Flight scheduling. ONA's flight schedules in the regional sector are convenient for business travel. Convenient scheduling will increase ONA's attractiveness for business people, so will increase demand in the lucrative business market.

      Passenger occupancy in business class. ONA has a very high passenger load factor for business class customers in the regional sector. This is likely to reflect the convenient flight scheduling noted above.

      In both the regional and international sectors, ONA's business class load factors are higher than its standard class. This suggests ONA is strong in the business market, and this should be good for revenues. Although we do not know the detail of the relative pricing structures of the two classes, business fares include a premium over standard class, which suggests ONA is likely to earn a higher margin on these fares.

      Gross profit margin. ONS's gross profit margin has remained relatively constant from 20X4 to 20X6 (20X4: 37.04%; 20X6: 36.98%). This suggests ONA is maintaining its business mix between premium and standard class fares, and also maintaining its load factors. If load factors fall it is likely that cost of sales (for example, fuel costs) will increase as a percentage of revenue, thereby reducing the gross margin.

BPP
LEARNING
MEDIA

Long term liquidity. The company's gearing ratio (debt/debt + equity) has remained relatively constant, about 29%, from 20X4 to 20X6, which suggests that the company has not needed to borrow any additional money from lenders, and that its long-term liquidity is relatively solid. This is also illustrated by the fact that ONA has been able to reduce the value of interest-bearing long-term loans by more than the reduction in its cash and cash equivalents over the period.

Weaknesses

High cost base. ONA pays above industry average salaries, offers excellent benefits and has a very generous pension scheme. Whilst these features help sustain employee motivation, they are likely to make ONA's cost base less competitive than its rivals. For example, on the one hand, ONA pilots' salaries are more than 10% higher than the average in the low-cost airline sector (see Exhibit 2 (a)), while, on the other hand, the recent negotiations (Exhibit 4) will also lead to a reduction in air crew's working hours.

Declining wage productivity. Although revenue has only increased 4.8% from 20X4 to 20X6, wages and salaries have increased 15% over the same period. Consequently, the ratio of revenue to wages and salaries costs has fallen from 4.33:1 to 3.95:1. This again suggests that ONA's costs are less competitive than they could be.

(It is not clear the extent to which ONA employs all of its staff in-house, or whether some services (eg cleaning, catering etc) are provided by outsourcing partners. If other firms outsource services, while ONA provides them in-house, this could be another factor which leads to cost differentials between ONA and its competitors.)

Ageing fleet. The average age of ONA's fleet is much older than that of its low-cost rivals. The older fleet is likely to require more maintenance – again suggesting that ONA's costs are likely to be higher than their rivals.

Fleet utilisation. ONA uses its planes for less hours per day than the low-cost airlines. This may be due its scheduling arrangements, or because ONA's planes need more maintenance time. However, either way, lower asset utilisation rates are another indication that ONA's cost base is likely to be less competitive than its rivals.

Low frequency of flights in the international sector. ONA only makes one flight per day on average to each destination. This low volume makes it very difficult for the company to gain any operational economies of scale in the international sector, and so will be another cause of costs being higher than they could be.

Composition of fleet. ONA's fleet comprises planes made by three different manufacturers. This is a legacy of the fleets which the two separate companies – Transport Oceanic and Oceania Air – used before the merger. However, the Airbus 320 and Boeing 737 are both short- to-medium-range commercial aircraft, with very similar passenger capacity (see Table 1 in Exhibit 1). So, in effect, they are competitors to each other. Having two aircraft types instead of one is likely to mean that ONA's servicing and maintenance costs are greater than they would be if they standardised the planes used. Again, ONA will not be able to benefit from any economies of scale.

Slow growth rate. Between 20X4 and 20X6 worldwide passenger air travel revenue increased by 12%, and revenue from air travel to Oceania increased by 15%. Over the same period, ONA's passenger revenue only increased 4.6%.

Sources of revenue. ONA's low-cost competitors generated 84% of their sales revenue through direct, online sales, and only 16% through third-party sales. ONA generates approximately 50% of its sales revenue through each channel. Because third parties retain part of the sales price as their commission, ONA will increase the revenue it retains if it increases the proportion of sales it makes directly through its own website rather than via third parties. (The board have already recognised this, however, and this mix may change following the redesign of ONA's website.)

Passenger occupancy in standard class. ONA's average passenger load factors in standard class are much lower than its low-cost competitors, **especially in the**

international sector. If load factors decline, ONA's margins will also decline, because it will still incur the costs of the flight (fuel, flight crew etc) but will not be earning revenue from the empty seats.

As noted in the 'strengths' above, ONA's load factors in standard class are lower than in business class. This suggests there may be a weakness in capacity planning; and that for some flights it may be beneficial to re-assign standard class seats to business class.

Declining net profitability. ONA's net profit before tax fell 25% over the period 20X4–20X6 (20X4: 80; 20X6: 60), despite revenue increasing slightly.

Over the three-year period 20X4–20X6, profit before interest and tax fell from 12.1% to 9.7%, and the net profit before tax fell from 9.9% to 7.1%. These figures highlight the problem that high and increasing costs are damaging the profitability of the business.

Declining ROCE. ONA's return on capital employed (ROCE) has also fallen from 10.7% (20X4) to 9.4% (20X6). This again reflects declining net profitability due to costs increasing more quickly than revenue. ONA's asset turnover (sales/capital employed) has actually increased over the three-year period, meaning that costs are a key problem area behind the business' declining financial performance.

Current ratio. ONA's current ratio has fallen from 1.24 (20X4) to 1.05 (20X6). A falling current ratio may indicate that the company will struggle to meet its debts when they fall due.

(b) **No frills, low-cost strategy**

A no frills, low-cost strategy **combines low price with low perceived value added**, and **focuses on price-sensitive market segments**. Price is the key element of competitive strategy.

A no frills strategy is a **cost leadership approach,** and this is the case in the airline industry where no frills airlines such as EasyJet or Ryanair (in the UK) or SouthWest (in the USA) adopt a low-cost pricing strategy. The characteristic features of these airlines are low fares and basic service levels, coupled with high load factors.

A no frills strategy also requires **very tight management**; efficiency levels must be kept high so that the cost base remains low.

No frills strategies usually exist in markets where buyers have high bargaining power and/or low switching costs, because in these markets it is **difficult to build customer loyalty**. A no frills strategy does not attempt to build significant customer loyalty.

A no frills strategy may also provide a means for **new entrants to enter a market segment.** If the major providers are competing on quality of service (or other non-price factors), the low-price segment will provide an opportunity for small, new players to avoid the major competitors initially. The new players can achieve market entry through a no-frills strategy, and use it to build volume (market share) before moving on to other strategies and challenging the established players.

In order for a no-frills strategy to be appropriate for ONA it must be suitable, acceptable and feasible.

Suitability of cost structure

ONA's cost structure is not suited to a no-frills strategy. Many of the airline companies which have used the no frills strategy have been **new entrants to the market**. They have **very low overheads** and have used the no frills low-cost approach to **gain market share** before moving on to alternative strategies to consolidate their position in the industry.

A key element in their strategy is achieving a **low-cost base to sustain their low-cost strategy**.

In our evaluation of ONA's strengths and weaknesses (in part (a) of this report), we have identified that **ONA does not have a low-cost base**. It pays wages above the industry average, because its focus is on **quality of service**, rather than low cost.

Similarly, ONA's aircraft utilisation rates are lower than its competitors, its fleet is older than its competitors and it uses aircraft made by three different manufacturers. These factors all suggest that its **costs are relatively higher than its competitors**.

ONA creates its **competitive advantage through the quality of service** it offers customers, rather than through low costs.

In this respect, a no-frills strategy will not be suitable for ONA.

Changes to business model, culture and operations

Similarly, it seems highly unlikely that ONA can achieve the required changes to its cost base for it to become a low-cost, budget airline without significant changes to its business model, culture and operations.

Suitability of reducing customer service levels

Low-cost airlines usually do not offer customer services such as free in-flight meals and drinks, and they do not allocate passengers to specific seats.

ONA **prides itself on its in-flight customer service**, and has gained prestige and public relations exposure from it, winning the Regional Airline of the Year award.

If ONA moved to a no-frills strategy, it would need to abandon its tradition of excellent customer service. This is **unlikely to be a suitable strategy** for ONA because it damages one of its core competencies.

Risk to load factors. There is also a danger that ONA's existing customers may object to the decline in customer service levels in which case load factors could fall. A strategy which leads to a fall in load factors would **not be acceptable for ONA**.

Cultural change. Moving to a no-frills strategy would not only require a major cultural change at ONA, sacrificing the strengths of the organisation and the competencies of its employees, but it would also **lead to redundancies**. There would be significant redundancies in the catering department, and there may also be redundancies in the numbers of cabin crew employed.

These redundancies could prove difficult and time-consuming to implement in a **heavily unionised organisation**, and would also **damage its reputation** on the island, since most of its **employees are residents of Oceania**.

In this respect, moving to a no-frills strategy will **not be feasible** nor will it be **acceptable for ONA and its key stakeholders**.

Feasibility of revising flight schedules

ONA currently only has, on average, one flight per day to each city in the international sector. In order to benefit from economies of scale and become a volume carrier in this sector, ONA would have to **extend its flight network, flight frequency and fleet size significantly**. We do not know whether ONA has sufficient funding available to achieve this, which means the **feasibility of such a strategy** would need to be investigated.

Moreover, ONA has only expanded gradually since its formation, and only added three aircraft to its fleet between 20X4 and 20X6. Therefore, a significant, rapid fleet expansion may be **unacceptable to the culture of the organisation** which prefers gradual change to rapid transformation.

Acceptability of changing selling channels

On average, low-cost airlines achieve 84% of their sales through their own websites. However, ONA only achieved 40% of its regional sales and 60% of its international sales as direct sales.

If ONA is to become a no-frills airline, it will need a **major change in the mix of its sales channels** (to avoid losing margin as commission to third party intermediaries).

It is difficult to know whether this change will be an acceptable strategy. The low percentage of regional online sales may suggest that the **citizens of Oceania may be more comfortable buying through third parties** such as the travel agents rather than buying directly online.

Acceptability of using regional airports to reduce costs

Many low-cost airlines fly into airports that offer cheaper take-off and landing fees. However, these are often **relatively remote from the cities** they serve. This remoteness may be acceptable to leisure travellers, but not to **business travellers** – and business travellers are ONA's key customers in the regional sector.

Given that one of ONA's strengths is the high passenger load factors it achieves for regional business travel, a strategy which involves moving to airports which are less convenient for business travellers is **unlikely to be suitable or acceptable**.

Conclusion

Re-positioning ONA as a no-frills airline does not appear to be an appropriate strategy for the company.

It would require major changes in the structure, cost and culture of the company which would be difficult to justify, and which do not appear suitable, acceptable or feasible for ONA.

The extent of the changes required would represent a **revolution** rather than an **evolution** of existing processes. However, a revolution is normally only required when a company is facing a crisis and needs to change direction quickly.

There is no evidence to support the need for such a radical transformation. Although net profit has declined over the three years 20X4–20X6, the company's **financial position is still relatively healthy**, and there is no evidence that the company is a takeover target for any predators.

It can be argued that a more **incremental approach to change will be more beneficial**, building on the strengths of the organisation, its existing brand and the competencies of its employees.

If ONA really wants to move into the no frills sector it would be better advised to set up a new low-cost brand to do this – rather than trying to restructure its existing business model.

2   (a)   **Briefing paper**

FAO: CEO at ONA

Business case and cyber security

Importance of business case

Basis for decision making – Even though the case in favour of the FFP may appear to be 'self-evident', to proceed with a project without first evaluating it properly is never advisable. As far as possible, the board should make decisions on the basis of facts and data, rather than instinct.

Whilst the Sales Director's point about speed is important (in relation to allowing ONA to respond to the increasing competition it faces) this should not be used as a justification for taking decisions without evaluating them properly first.

The danger to ONA of making decisions without first preparing a business case is that enthusiasm for an initiative may mean it is adopted without sufficient consideration of its costs and benefits. As such, it could potentially end up damaging the airline's financial performance rather than improving it.

Costs and benefits – If a formal business case is developed, the costs and benefits of the proposal will have to be identified and defined at the outset. Having this information will be important for subsequently assessing whether the programme has delivered the level of benefits which were initially expected from it.

Although other airlines' experience suggests that introducing an FFP has the potential to deliver significant benefits (for example, through increased customer loyalty leading to increased passenger numbers, and in turn increased revenue), this is not a justification for simply introducing a programme without properly evaluating its implications. For example, as well as the 'cost' of the free flights offered, there will also be costs associated with administering the programme. (There will also be an impact on the accounting information systems, to ensure we can account for the deferred revenue element correctly.)

If a formal business case is developed, the costs and benefits of the proposal will have to be identified and defined at the outset. However, having this information will also be important for subsequently assessing whether the programme has delivered the level of benefits which were initially expected from it.

The business case may well support the decision to proceed with the programme, but this will be on the basis of the board making a considered choice. The process of preparing the business case could also help to identify any additional resources which will be required to make the programme successful (for example, a marketing campaign so that customers are made aware of it).

Benefits realisation – In order to be able to carry out a benefits realisation exercise, the nature of the benefits (eg increase in loyalty; passenger numbers) need to have been defined in the business case to provide a basis to measure against. (This is another reason why a business case is required.) The FFP will ultimately only be valuable to ONA if it increases customer loyalty and/or passenger numbers.

If the programme is introduced, a benefits realisation review can be carried out to assess whether the benefits anticipated in the business case have actually been delivered. For example, how many customers are actually using the FFP, and what impact is it having on the number of flights being booked?

(b) **Cyber security**

Importance of cyber security

Cyber security relates to the protection of systems, networks and data in cyberspace.

As businesses increasingly use digital technology to transform their business operations, the way they engage with customers and suppliers, and take advantage of new opportunities (for example, through big data analytics), means that cyber security becomes an increasingly important issue.

Security failures relating to information systems can cause significant damage to a business – either business disruption (eg an outage of an e-commerce platform preventing online sales), or reputational damage (eg public relations; and lack of customer engagement in the event of a security breach). The level of reputational damage for ONA could be particularly severe if a breach relates to financial data about customers who have booked flights through the company's website.

Control areas

Systems security could be assessed in relation to five key control areas:

Service configuration – Ensure that systems are configured in the most secure way for the company's needs.

Boundary firewalls and internet gateways – their purpose is to prevent unauthorised access to or from private networks, but the hardware and software used in them needs to be well set up in order for them to be effective.

Access control – Ensure that only those people who should have (or need) access to systems have access to them, and have access at an appropriate level (for example, through using passwords to restrict and control access).

Malware protection – Ensure that virus and malware protection is installed and is kept up to date.

Software management – Ensure that the latest supported version of software is used, and if any patches are supplied by a vendor that these are applied.

3   (a)   **Sections of a report for the Finance Director:**

(i)   **Risk management**

The following procedures need to be followed to reduce the risk of security alerts:

Staff follow guidelines – ONA needs to ensure that all of its staff follow all the regulations imposed by the airport authority, with disciplinary action being taken against staff who fail to comply.

Suppliers and contractors subject to same regulation as in-house staff – The fact that a delay was caused by one of AirChef's sub-contracted members of staff highlights that ONA should insist that all suppliers and contractors' staff who work in airport buildings are subject to the same regulations and level of security checks as ONA's staff are.

Passenger reminders – ONA can influence the actions of its own passengers in order to limit the risk of security alerts. Passengers should be reminded of their responsibilities on booking confirmation and at check-in desks.

Transfer of risk – ONA should review its insurance arrangements to assess whether it is adequately covered for disruption caused by security alerts.

ONA should also examine the terms of its agreement with the airport authority to see whether there are grounds for insisting that the authority bears some of the liability for disruption caused by security alerts, arising from the checks it has introduced. (This is particularly relevant here because, despite being affected by a number of delays, ONA was only responsible for one of them.)

(ii)   **Stakeholder management**

Four key stakeholder groups to consider in relation to the disputes are: trade unions; maintenance staff; ONA's senior management; and ONA's customers.

Trade unions

The trade unions have two different objectives:

Get technicians reinstated – The first is to get the three technicians who have been dismissed reinstated.

The unions feel the three technicians have been made scapegoats for the Engineering Director's failings.

They want ONA to accept that, as the independent engineering consultant's report identified, there were serious faults in the company's maintenance procedures as a whole, not just in the work of these three technicians.

Improve pay and working conditions – The unions' second objective is to negotiate improved pay and working conditions for **all** the technicians.

The unions appear to have quite a strong bargaining position here, because of the potential impact (disruption) that a strike could have.

Maintenance staff

Maintenance staff as a whole – The maintenance staff want to secure higher pay and better conditions.

Because relationships between management and staff have become strained, it is likely that there is now less goodwill towards management than would otherwise have been (given ONA's previous history of being an excellent employer). Therefore, where previously staff might have accepted whatever deal management offered, now the staff are less amenable to management's terms.

Technicians dismissed – Although the three technicians themselves do not have much power in any negotiations with ONA, the backing they have received from the unions increases their power. Their primary concern is to prove they should not have been dismissed, and so should get their jobs back.

ONA's senior management

Corporate social responsibility – The directors have a corporate social responsibility to ensure the safety of their passengers. Therefore they need to ensure that the faults which have been identified in the maintenance procedures are corrected.

Of all the directors, the **Engineering Director** has the most direct responsibility for ensuring the quality of the maintenance procedures. The critical nature of the independent consultant's report means that the Engineering Director's position must be under threat.

The other directors may feel his position is untenable, particularly after the sacking of the three technicians. So the other directors may feel one way to help ease the tensions with the maintenance staff is if the Engineering Director resigns.

Responsibility to investors – As well as ensuring the safety of the airlines' passengers, the directors also have a fiduciary responsibility to manage the profitability of ONA.

In this way, they have to be relatively robust in dealing with the unions to ensure that any pay deal which is agreed does not lead to ONA's **costs increasing** too much. (Equally, however, they have to consider the potential impact which strike action could have on the company's financial performance.)

Bad publicity – The senior management also have an additional interest here, which is to try to minimise the level of bad publicity which might be caused by the dispute. Strike action will not only lead to a direct loss of revenue on the days when ONA's planes cannot fly, but it may also damage the company's reputation with its customers, and prompt them to fly with other carriers.

Equally, if the findings of the independent report become public then this will also damage ONA's reputation for safety and could lead to a fall in passenger bookings. Management need to take action to **correct the faults which were identified in the report.**

Customers

Although customers do not have as much direct power to influence the outcome of the dispute as the unions, the staff and ONA's management, they could still have a strong interest in the outcome.

Passenger safety – Passengers will want to know that ONA's planes are safe before they board them. If the concerns about the quality of ONA's maintenance procedures become widely known, this is likely to prevent some potential customers from using ONA.

Disruption to timetable – Passengers who have already booked with ONA will also want to know that the maintenance checks on their planes have been carried out properly before they fly. But, perhaps more importantly, this stakeholder group has a strong interest in the strikes being averted. If the disputes cannot be resolved, and strike action goes ahead this will lead to the cancellation of a number of flights. This could cause severe disruption for passengers who were supposed to be on the flights, and could be a particular problem for business travellers if the disruption results in them missing important meetings.

(b)   **Briefing paper**

FAO: HR Director at ONA

People, organisation and processes in business change projects

The importance of people, organisational structure and processes in a business change project

You have raised concerns that ONA's approach to undertaking business projects tends to focus on the information technology aspects rather than the people, processes and organisational structure. The four view (or 'POPIT') model recognises the equal importance of each of the four elements (people; organisational structure; processes; and IT) when enhancing a business process. The model has been developed to take a more holistic view of process change, considering those elements which could affect the success of the project.

Processes

The processes aspect of the POPIT model looks at the level of IT support in an organisation and the level of manual processes and system workarounds. Again, these seem to be issues for concern, particularly where payroll staff are having to make manual changes to payroll records to process overtime claims. (In turn, this may reflect a lack of IT support available to make any changes to the current system.)

The project needs to identify where manual processes are currently required in order to determine whether there is scope to eliminate these. It would appear that this has already been done to an extent by considering the need for new systems which can provide greater flexibility. However, ONA could also take this opportunity to consider whether there are other further changes which could be made to its staffing and scheduling model – for example, whether there are any changes which could be made to the scheduling roster in order to reduce the amount of overtime staff have to work (and which, in turn, requires adjustments in the payroll system).

Organisational structure

The 'O' aspect of the POPIT model considers elements of structure, management configuration and support and roles and responsibilities.

Roles and responsibilities should be considered within the change process itself. Who will be involved in a change project and how will this affect their day-to-day role? They will need to be given clear guidance of what is expected as well as the resources needed. For example, although there are tight budget constraints for the payroll systems project (as the CEO has inferred), the budget allocated to a project need to be realistic and sufficient in order for it to succeed.

The 'O' aspect of the POPIT model also highlights the need to consider the way in which the payroll project can add value for ONA as a whole. It is becoming increasingly difficult for ONA to get the right numbers and types of staff in the right place at the right time but failing to do this could delay or disrupt flights. Therefore, it is important not to think of this purely as an HR system, but to think how it fits into ONA's business.

ANSWERS

People

People can be a key reason for failure of a project. If there is resistance, then this may impede the progress of the project, affect the end result or even halt a project completely. Staff morale and motivation should be taken into consideration, and ONA should try to ensure that any possible negative impacts of the change are mitigated.

The necessary skills also need to be considered. For example, ONA's payroll staff are likely to need training on the new system. If staff do not feel they have sufficent skills to use a system this can be a cause of resistance.

Although payroll staff may not be IT experts, they should be skilled in their individual area of work. For this reason, they should be encouraged to participate in the design of the new system. Had this happened in the past, the systems might have been designed to fully meet departmental needs, rather than finding workarounds.

4 Memorandum

To: Finance Director at ONA

From: Financial analyst

Ethical issues and new route

Although not all members of the board are professional accountants, as company executives they should uphold similar fundamental principles to those we would expect professional accountants to uphold. Any members of the board who are professional accountants – such as the FD – also have a specific duty to uphold the principles of their supervisory body's Code of Ethics.

The principles of professional behaviour and integrity both appear to be particularly signficant here.

Professional behaviour – This ethical principle highlights the importance of complying with relevant laws and regulations, and avoiding any action which could be a source of discredit.

Although the 'facilitation fee' is reported to be normal business practice in Hiapop's country, the alternative interpretation is that the fee is effectively a bribe to secure the landing rights. Bribery is not only unethical, it is also illegal in most countries around the world.

Integrity – The requirement to pay a 'facilitation fee' also threatens the principle of integrity – and the need to act straighforwardly and honestly in all business dealings. Making, and receiving, bribes is almost the opposite of acting straightforwardly and honestly.

As such, the need to pay the initial fee appears to present an ethical threat to ONA.

However, before rejecting the potential route completely it would be worth investigating the details of the proposed fee. For example, we are assuming that it is effectively a bribe, but it is possible the initial payment could be normal practice in Hiapop's country, and, in effect, may be more like a deposit. We know that several other established international operators already fly to Hiapop, so we could possibly enquire whether they paid a similar fee.

Although it is important that ONA behaves ethically, the directors also have a responsibility to act in the best interests of the company's shareholders. As such, we should not be too quick to rule out a contract which has the potential to generate significant additional profits, particularly given ONA's relatively disappointing performance in recent years.

Nonetheless, we need to consider this alongside any potential consequences that making the payment could have on ONA's reputation. If the payment is perceived to be a bribe, and knowledge of this becomes public, this could be very damaging to ONA's brand and reputation. If this damage leads to a loss of consumer trust, or investor confidence in ONA, the potential negative impact of this could outweigh the additional revenues or profits that ONA would gain from expanding its network.

5   **Integrated reporting**

Slide 1 – Advantages of introducing integrated reporting (<IR>)

- Balance short-term performance with longer-term performance (business sustainability)

- Improved decision making on the basis of value creation

- Report on organisation's performance as a whole ('connectivity')

- Accountability

Asdf|

Connectivity

Integrated reporting will allow us to convey a wider message about ONA's performance, not just financial performance. For example, as an airline, the environmental impact of our performance (eg in relation to carbon emissions) is very important. Reporting on our environmental performance will provide increased incentive to improve performance in this respect (eg environmental performance might become a factor which differentiates us from our competitors).

Improved fuel efficiency – which will improve environmental performance – could also improve financial performance (because fuel costs will be reduced). [This is a good example of the links between different capitals, which we'll look at on the next slide.]

Accountability

The broader perspective required by <IR> (longer time frame; different capitals considered) will make us more accountable as stewards of society's common resources – as illustrated by human, natural and social capitals in <IR>. In turn, this should also help to improve ONA's repuation (eg for social responsibility).

Slide 2 – Differences between <IR> and traditional annual reports

- Simplified financial information
- Six types of capital
- Increased focus on stakeholder relationships
- Strategic focus and future orientation

Supporting notes:

Simplified information

One of the key principles of <IR> is conciseness. Instead of producing large amounts of detailed financial information, <IR> focuses attention on the key points. As reports are shorter, and with less detail, this should make it easier for shareholders – and other stakeholders – to understand how the company is performing.

Types of capital

<IR> will highlight the different 'capitals', resources and relationships which ONA depends on to be successful.

- Financial capital – funds available to sustain ONA's service; debt; equity, or retained earnings

- Manufactured capital – assets used to provide service – eg aircraft; terminals

- Human capital – knowledge, skills and experience of employees and managers (staff are crucial in a service business)

- Natural capital – environmental resources which the organisation relies on (eg fuel)

- Social and relationship capital – key stakeholder relationships (with external stakeholders); underpins brand and reputation

- Intellectual capital – R&D; innovation; but also includes 'organisational capital': systems and procedures

This means that ONA's performance will be reported in relation to each of these different capitals, in contrast to traditional financial reporting which focuses primarily on financial performance.

Stakeholder relationships – <IR> highlights the importance of an organisation's relationships with its stakeholders, and how an organisation interacts with its key stakeholder groups. Therefore an integrated report will need to include information to demonstrate that we understand the interests of different groups, and how we are responding to them.

Strategic focus – An integrated report needs to help readers understand our strategy, and how we are looking to create value in the future. To accompany this, the report should set out the significant risks we face and the opportunities available to us, and how we respond to them. Many of these risks will be non-financial, which marks a difference in emphasis from our current report which focuses primarily on financial performance.

Mock Exam 5

Tutorial notes to help you improve your exam success skills performance

Skill	Examples
Case scenario: Managing information	You need to take the time to read carefully the case information, as this will provide you with a clear indication as to how to use the Exhibits when answering specific task requirements. In this exam the Tasks and the Exhibits could broadly be linked as follows: Task 1 required the use of Exhibits 1 and 2. Task 2 required the use of Exhibit 3. Task 3 required the use of Exhibits 4, 5 and 6. Task 4 required the use of Exhibit 7. Task 5 required the use of Exhibit 8.
Correct Interpretation of requirements	When reviewing the task requirements, it is important that you identify all of the actions that you are expected to undertake, especially when you are expected to give consideration to more than one issue. For example, in respect of Task 2 (b) you were required to not only explain the increasing importance of cyber security but also to identify the key control areas that ONA needed to consider in relation to its cyber security.
Answer planning: Priorities, structure and logic	Task 3 (b) required the preparation of a briefing paper which explained the importance for ONA of considering people, organisation and processes when implementing business change projects. A good approach to adopt when planning your answer would have been to use the headings of people, organisation and processes, as this provided a structure around which you could build your answer. These elements form part of the four view (or 'POPIT') model.
Efficient numerical analysis	Task 1 (a) required an evaluation of ONA's strengths and weaknesses, and their impact on the company's performance. As such, it was appropriate to use the financials set out in Exhibit 2 to prepare some key profitability and liquidity ratio calculations to support the strengths that you could discuss in your narrative answer. For example, ONS's gross profit margin had remained relatively constant over the period and could therefore be viewed as a strength.
Effective writing and presentation	To perform well in the Strategic Business Leader exam it is of critical importance that you respond to the task requirements in the format requested. Failure to do so will limit the number of marks that can be earned. Task 4 required the preparation of a memorandum. As such, it was important that you set out your work with the 'To/From/Subject' section at the beginning of your answer.

ANSWERS

Skill	Examples
Good Time Management	You had 4 hours (240 minutes) to tackle all of the task requirements worth 100 marks. Throughout the earlier sections in this Practice and Revision Kit we have worked on the basis of 2 minutes per mark. This was used to reflect the fact that many of the questions attempted up until this point have featured considerably smaller exam scenarios using limited Exhibit information.
	When attempting the Strategic Business Leader exam, ACCA recommend that candidates spend at least 40 minutes reading, planning and interpreting the exhibit information and the task requirements.
	When taking the 40 minutes reading time into account, candidates should spend approximately 2.5 minutes attempting each mark. The 2.5 minutes per mark is based on the fact that the total exam is 240 minutes (4 hours) in duration which, when the 40 minutes reading/planning time is deducted, gives 200 minutes. As candidates can earn the 20 professional skills marks by the virtue of attempting the 80 technical marks in the exam, the remaining 200 minutes can be divided by the 80 technical marks to give 2.5 minutes per mark.
	On the basis of 2.5 minutes per mark, the time available for attempting each task requirement was as follows:
	Task 1 (a) = 16 technical marks: 40 minutes
	Task 1 (b) = 14 technical marks: 35 minutes
	Task 2 (a) = 5 technical marks: 13 minutes
	Task 2 (b) = 6 technical marks; 15 minutes
	Task 3 (a)(i) = 5 technical marks; 12 minutes
	Task 3 (a)(ii) = 12 technical marks: 30 minutes
	Task 3 (b) = 6 technical marks: 15 minutes
	Task 4 = 6 technical marks: 15 minutes
	Task 5 = 10 technical marks: 25 minutes

Diagnostic

Did you apply these skills when reading, planning, and writing up your answer? Identify the exam success skills where you think you need to improve and capture your thoughts here of what you want to achieve when attempting questions in future.

Notes

Notes

Notes

Notes

Notes

Notes